OLD SOUTHERN BIBLE RECORDS

Transcriptions of Births, Deaths,
and Marriages from Family Bibles,
Chiefly of the 18th and 19th
Centuries

Compiled by
MEMORY ALDRIDGE LESTER

CLEARFIELD

Reprinted for
Clearfield Company, Inc. by
Genealogical Publishing Co., Inc.
Baltimore, Maryland
1990, 1996, 2002

Library of Congress Catalogue Card Number 75-136456
International Standard Book Number: 0-8063-0617-3

Made in the United States of America

NOTE

This work is a transcription of genealogical records found in 581 southern family Bibles. It comprises records of an almost entirely private nature—indispensable in locating missing family links—and is both a corrective and supplement to public courthouse records. The data was originally compiled from family and archival sources and assembled in seven volumes of typescripts during the 1950s. The Genealogical Publishing Company has reassembled the data in the various volumes and integrated the family Bibles in a single alphabet. The reconstituted work lists the Bibles in alphabetical order under the names of the principal families, indexing all associated names in the rear of the text. For added convenience family Bibles are listed in the index in capital letters under the names of the principal families.

The Publisher

CHARLES ABERCROMBIE

Charles Abercrombie and Dicey Booth m. 1769
    Their children
Abner b. 10 Jan 1771 m. Miss Patterson
Edward b. 12 Jan 1773 m. Miss Brewer
Sallie b. 29 Jan 1775 m. Thos. Raines [or Banes]
Wiley b. 17 Feb 1779 m. Miss Simmons
Leonard b. 1779 m. Miss Sarah Comer
    [Am sure that Wiley & Leonard above were twins. It appears
    that the copier forgot to put ditto marks under birth date of
    Leonard]
Jane b. 1781 m. Bolling Hall
John b. 1785 m. Miss Martin
Anderson b. 1786 m. Miss Grimes
Nancy b. 1786 m. Wm. Barnes
Charles b. 1790 m. Mrs. Martin nee Grimes
James b. 1792 m. Evelina Ross

[This Bible record sent to compiler by Mrs. Flossie Lamb Crouch,
Edgefield, S.C.]

JOHN ABNEY

John & wife Martha m. 6 Mar 1800
Jas Barnes and wife Jane Abney m. 24 Jan 1796
Wm. Griffith & wife Polly m. 25 June 1820
Danl. Clary & wife Fanny m. 15 Jan 1809
John Chapman & wife Sophia m. 30 Nov 1817
John Abney & wife Agatha m. 25 Jan 1819
Wm. Bladen & wife Eleanor m. 1 July 1827
Ira Cromley & wife Martha Chapman m. 2 June 1842
John A. Chapman & wife Mary m. 1 May 1845
Chas. Carson & wife Caroline Cromley m. 4 Dec 1865

John Abney, son of Paul & Eleanor Hamilton Abney, b. 20 May 1776
Martha, his wife, b. 12 Feb 1785
Wm. Abney b. 4 Dec 1811
Matthew W. Abney b. 12 Feb 1814
Danl. C. Abney b. 24 Sep 1817
Jos. G. R. Abney b. 2 Dec 1817
Sophia Abney b. 24 June 1801
Polly Abney b. 27 Feb 1805
Nancy Abney b. 22 May 1807
Ellen Abney b. 12 Oct 1809
Agatha Abney, wife of John Abney, b. 4 Sep 1801
Martha Ann Griffith b. 31 Aug 1821
Wm. Abney, son of John & Agatha, b. 10 Dec 1821
John B. Abney b. 11 Dec 1822
John A. Griffith, son of Wm. & Polly, b. 31 Dec 1822
Nancy Griffith b. 15 Jan 1825

Henry Griffith b. 25 July 1827
Andrew B. Griffith b. 7 July 1829
Anne Griffith b. 8 Sep 1831
Jos. Marion Griffith b. 13 Oct 1833
Sophia Isabella Griffith b. 27 Oct 1835
Amanda Griffith b. 24 Dec 1837
Matthew Wills Griffith b. 25 July 1840

Wm. Abney, son of John, d. 12 Sep 1821
Wm. Abney, son of John & Agatha Abney, d. 7 Jan 1822
Martha Abney, wife of John Abney, d. 20 Oct 1817
Eleanor Abney, wife of Paul Abney, d. 17 Sep 1819, ae 70 yrs.
Paul Abney d. 27 Dec 1820, ae 76
John Abney, Jr. d. 2 Oct 1823, ae 48
Mary Abney, wife of Wm. Griffith, d. 15 May 1855
Nancy, wife of Andrew Coleman, d. 16 Nov 1854
Jos., son of Wm. & Mary Griffith, d. Jan 1852

[Second owner, John Abney Chapman, S.C. Historian. Present owner,
Frank W. Chapman, 704 North St., Greenwood, S.C.]

                        PAUL ABNEY

Paul Abney b. 1744, d. 27 Dec 1820, m. Eleanor Hamilton b. 1740, d.
  17 Sep 1819. [She was the sister of British General Sir John
  Hamilton and a Russian princess.]
Their son, John Abney, b. 20 Mar 1776, m. Martha Wills 6 Mar 1800
  [She was the dau. of Matthew Wills & wife, Martha Abney Wills.
  Martha Abney was dau. of Nathaniel Abney.]
Nathaniel Abney b. 4 Apr 1734, d. 29 July 1806, m. 15 Apr 1758 to
  Isabella Madison b. 17 Sep 1740
        Children of Nathaniel Abney & wife Isabella Madison
Sarah b. 18 Mar 1759 on Sunday morning
John b. 7 Feb 1761
Martha b. 14 June 1763, m. Matthew Wills 1780
Eliz. b. 1765, m. John Long
Nannie b. 10 Sep 1767; Nancy Spraggins d. 16 Oct 1793
Lydia b. 24 May 1770
Joel b. 15 Oct 1774 [note less than 9 mo. before birth of sibling]
Azariah, son, b. 8 Apr 1775
Jas. b. 27 July 1777
Anna, Sr. b. 28 Sep 1778
Anna, Jr. b. 24 May 1783
Isabella b. 14 Jan 1788

[Isabella Madison was the dau. of John Madison & wife Isabella Todd
Madison, half-sister of Jas. Madison, 1st native born bishop of Va.
She and Nathaniel were married by Rev. Patrick Henry.]

                        JASPER S. ACUFF

Jasper S. Acuff b. 19 Aug 1841, d. 13 Oct 1893

Nancy J. Billingsley, his wife, b. 6 July 1846, d. 18 Jan 1898
    Children
James D. b. 10 May 1866, d. 26 Oct 1937
William L. b. 12 Sep 1868
Errett F. b. 17 Apr 1871, d. 3 Nov 1941
M. M. A. b. 24 Aug 1873, d. 6 July 1926
Cora E. b. 18 Jan 1877
John E. b. 6 May 1880
Edward E. b. 9 Mar 1889, d. 22 Mar 1889

Jasper S. Acuff & Nancy J. Billingsley m. 17 Aug 1865
James D. Acuff & Rose Terry m. 30 June 1897
Errett F. Acuff & Ellen Bobo m. Mar 1899
Nettye A. Acuff & J. A. Safley m. 16 Sep 1900
Wm. L. Acuff & Lee Blackburn m. 5 Dec 1901
Cora Ethel Acuff & T. B. Sellers m. 22 Nov 1908

[Sent by Mr. Edward B. Acuff, Moultrie, Ga. The Bible is owned by
Cora Ethel (Acuff) Sellers, 4024 King St., Portsmouth, Va.]

JOHN H. ACUFF

John H. Acuff b. 4 May 1811, d. 24 Aug 1876
Matilda E. Billingsley, [his wife], b. 6 Dec 1812, d. 4 Mar 1847
    Children
Saml. J. b. 7 Oct 1836
William L. b. 2 Mar 1838, d. 22 Dec 1839
Robert D. b. 31 Oct 1839, d. 10 Sep 1863
Jasper S. b. 19 Aug 1841, d. 1893
Darius M. b. 22 Jan 1844
Nancy Ann M. b. 3 Mar 1847, d. 30 Apr 1928
Mary Jane (Owings) Acuff b. 30 May 1823, d. Jan 1893
Sarah b. 16 Oct 1851, d. 19 Apr 1894
Wm. D. b. 19 Jan 1854

John H. Acuff & Matilda E. Billingsley m. 24 May 1835
John H. Acuff m. Mary J. Owings 17 Nov 1850

[This Bible is owned by Edward Blackburn Acuff, Moultrie, Ga. who
is the great grandson of John H. Acuff.]

NATHAN ALDREDGE

Nathan Aldredge, soldier in the Creek Indian Wars in Ga., b. 12 Oct
1789, d. 6 May 1865 Salem, Ala., m. 1st to Alizannah (Alsy) Hanson,
b. 20 Nov 1784, d. 22 Sep 1854
    Issue
Saml. Pierce b. 11 Sep 1812, d. 8 July 1888
Mary Ann b. 31 July 1814, d. 9 Feb 1897
Alizannah b. 30 Aug 1816, d. 30 Oct 1829
Dr. Jas. Fletcher b. 9 Sep 1818, d. 8 June 1877
Wm. Kendrick b. 28 May 1819, d. 1900

3

Harriette b. 28 Nov 1822, d. 4 Dec 1845
Nathan Hanson b. 28 Apr 1825, d. 30 June 1836
Margaret Jane b. 8 Apr 1828, d. 26 Sep 1892, m. Lewis Gardner Davis

Nathan Aldredge m. 2nd to Eleanor J. Crowder, widow of Robt. Crowder, on 29 July 1856
    [Issue: One child, listed in census as "M. W. Aldredge" b.
    1857. Later identified as Mrs. B. Floyd, though any descs. un-
    known and place of residence or burial unknown.]

[Bible record furnished by Mrs. Dallas Scarborough, Abilene, Texas,
a desc. of Nathan Aldredge & 1st wife.]

JOHN P. ALDRIDGE

John P. Aldridge m. Mary Gill
    Their children
Elizabeth b. 23 Dec 1802
William Owsley b. 2 Sep 1804
Maria b. 11 Apr
Emily b. 6 Sep 1814
Alexandra b. June 1817
Maria b. 26 Apr 1820
Robert M. b. 12 Mar 1823
    [John P. Aldridge was son of John Aldridge of Montgomery Co.,
    Md. Most of John's children went to Ky. and from there one
    branch now - 1955 - lives in Miss. It is from them that this
    Bible record comes. See Samuel Gill Bible Record.]
Dr. Wm. Owsley Aldridge m. Rebecca Robinson in May 1832
    Their children
Mary b. 16 Jan 1834
John Robinson b. 23 May 1836
Wm. Owsley b. 30 Oct 1837
Annie b. 12 Dec 1842
James b. 4 Nov 1844
Thos. Robinson b. 19 May 1846
Frank Saunders b. 17 July 1848
Andrew Jackson b. 21 Mar 1851, d. 10 Aug 1911
Robert Newton b. 22 Sep 1853
Jennie Ruth b. 17 Apr 1856
Alfred Downs b. 16 May 1840

JOHN SIMPSON ALDRIDGE

John Simpson Aldridge b. 9 Feb 1761, d. 17 Nov 1842, m. 18 Nov 1783
in Evangelical Reformed Church in Frederick Co., Md. to Mary Lakin
b. 20 June 1760, d. 27 Nov 1843
    Children
Joseph Lakin b. 27 Sep 1784
Rachel Plummer b. 21 Mar 1786
Raizy b. 20 Sep 1789
Elizabeth bl. 10 Mar 1791

Mary b. 15 Feb 1793
Sarah b. 10 May 1795
John b. 27 Feb 1798
Delilah b. 23 Dec 1799 [She was wife of John listed just above her.
    She was born a Layton]
Nathan b. 3 Aug 1803

[John Simpson Aldridge died in Rush Co., Ind. & was a Rev. Soldier]

[Record sent by Mr. F. R. Aldridge, Nashville, Tenn.]

JOSEPH ALDRIDGE

Joseph Aldridge, son of James & Alsey Aldridge, b. 30 Nov 1792, d.
2 Feb 1877, m. 25 Dec 1816 to Martha Graves
        Children
Artelia b. Jan 1818
Martha b. 1821
William J. b. 24 Mar 1824
Hannah b. 26 Dec 1826
Rufus Graves b. 1828
Susan b. 17 Mar 1830
Eliza E. b. 1832
Nancy J. b. 1834
James Richard b. 15 Apr 1839

[Bible record furnished by Mr. Daniel T. Aldridge, Idaho Falls,
Idaho]

[Marriages, not in Bible, copied by compiler in Caswell Co., N.C.,
records:
    Artelia m. 20 Oct 1840 to Wm. B. Stadler
    Martha m. 16 Jan 1866 to Geo. Herndon
    Wm. J. m. 6 Feb 1856 to Betty Donaho
    Hannah m. 17 Nov 1845 to Brantley Allred
    Rufus Graves m. to Annie Wyatt
    Susan m. 30 Oct 1851 to Wm. Vaughan
    Nancy J. m. 8 Nov 1843 to Rufus W. Chandler
James Aldridge, father of Joseph, was born in 1742, died 7 Dec
1807, Caswell Co., N.C. He is buried in Bush Arbor Baptist Church
in Caswell Co., N.C. This is a Primitive Baptist Church.
Children of James and Alsey Aldridge as found in settlement of his
estate are: Joseph; Susan (m. David Melton); James, Jr.; John;
Sarah; Richard Simpson (m. Lucy Pleasant on 21 Jan 1822, bondsman-
Micajah Pleasant, Jr.) March 1808 court appointed Solomon De Bow,
guardian of Sarah, Joseph, James, Susannah, Richard Simpson, or-
phans of Jas. Aldridge, deceased.
This James Aldridge was a Regulator in 1768 in the list of Orange
Co., N.C. Regulators. From data in the hands of the compiler, it
appears that the following are brothers of Jas.: Nathan (also a
Regulator), b. 1739, d. 1826 Knox Co., Tenn. and William, b. 1729,
d. Randolph Co., N.C., bur. McMasters Cemetery in Randolph.

Nicholas (also a Regulator 1768, Orange Co.) have no dates on him,
but during the Rev. War, he was in Rowan Co., N.C., died in Ga.
1794 (will). He had a son, Wm., who fought in the Rev. and died in
Ga., b. 1754 in Rowan Co.
Nathaniel may have been another brother. In the early records of
this family, Nathan and Nathaniel are not the same name and are
used in the same family. Nathaniel was in Tryon Co., N.C. His
wife was named Rosamond. He left N.C. and appears to have gone to
S.C. The 1790 census of S.C. gives a Nathaniel, Sr. & Jr.]

ANDREW ALLDREDGE

Andrew Alldredge b. 11 Oct 1782, d. 6 Nov 1848, m. 1806 to Leah
Chaney, b. 10 Mar 1784, d. 4 Feb 1854.

Enoch Alldredge b. 16 May 1807, d. 22 Nov 1879
William Alldredge b. 7 Mar 1809, d. 30 Jan 1880
Jacob Chaney b. 5 May 1813, d. 1863
Elizabeth Alldredge b. 27 Apr 1816, d. 14 Oct 1888
Mary Frances b. 2 June 1818, d. 1884
Nathan Alldredge b. 4 Sep 1820, d. 1875
Andrew J. Alldredge b. 1822

[This old Bible was left to Mary Frances, the youngest child, and
when her mother died, she moved to the home of her sister Eliz.
Alldredge Smith (wife of Garlin Smith). When the attic was being
cleared out after the death of both sisters, the Bible was found
in bad condition and was thrown out and burned. This record was
taken by one of the Smith children as best it could be made out.]

[Andrew Alldredge was the son of Nathan Alldredge and his wife Hannah. Nathan left a will in Knox Co., Tenn. 1818. He was in Orange
Co., which later was Randolph Co., N.C. before the Rev. War. Tradition indicates that he had a war record, but proof cannot be
found in N.C. records.]

EDMUND ALLDREDGE

Edmund Alldredge, son of Elijah and Mary, b. 2 Apr 1784 at Wilkes
Court House, N.C., d. 30 Mar 1858 m. 4 Oct 1810 to Jane, dau. of
David and Hannah Mulford, b. 11 Apr 1790, d. 30 Dec 1833.
    Children
Francis Bertram b. 4 July 1811
Elijah b. 11 Dec 1812
Hiram b. 26 May 1815
William b. 26 June 1817
Isaac b. 10 Apr 1819
Keziah b. 30 Aug 1821
Mary b. 4 Apr 1824
John b. 26 May 1827
Elizabeth b. 9 Jan 1830
Edmund b. 29 Nov 1833

[This Bible is owned by John Sherman Alldredge, 1225 Home Ave.,
Anderson, Ind. Record sent to compiler Feb 1942.]

["Edmund and young wife Jane went to Cambridge City, Ind. Edmund
fought in the War of 1812. John, 8th child of Ed. & Jane was born
in Ind. and married Susanna Baxla. Their son, John Sherman, served
in the state legislature of Ind. for many years." Letter from John
S. Alldredge to compiler]

ENOCH ALLDREDGE

Enoch Alldredge b. 16 May 1807, d. 22 Nov 1879, m. 12 Nov 1826 to
Amelia (Pace) Alldredge b. 24 June 1811, d. 18 Mar 1864.
    Children
John Pace b. 5 Dec 1827
Andrew Jackson b. 28 Feb 1829
Jesse J. b. 16 Aug 1831
Wm. M. b. 1 Mar 1833
Hiram W. b. 24 Apr 1835
Garlin Smith b. 17 Nov 1836
Missouri Alabama b. 20 Dec 1841
Elizabeth b. 4 May 1843
James P. b. 6 July 1845
Taylor W. b. 6 Aug 1847
Clemens C. b. 5 May 1849
David Leonard b. 16 Jan 1854

[This Bible is owned by Bennett Alldredge, Oneonta, Ala., copied
by compiler in May 1935]

[Enoch Alldredge, oldest son of Andrew and Leah (Chaney) Alldredge,
was born in Bledsoe Co., Tenn. He served in the Ala. legislature
for many years. He and all his sons and a son-in-law served in the
48th Ala. Regiment in the Civil War. Enoch was 1st Col. After he
was wounded and came home, his son Jesse J., became the Col. and
served till he too was wounded. Amelia Pace Alldredge was the dau.
of John Pace and wife Ziffory who were living in Ky. when Amelia or
Permelia was born. John Pace was from Va.]

OLIVER PERRY ALLDREDGE

Perry Alldredge b. 28 Jan 1830, d. 15 Dec 1864 at Pine Bluff, Ark.,
bur. in National Cemetery, Little Rock, Ark., m. 11 Feb 1851 to
Elizabeth M. Fowler Alldredge b. 25 Jan 1833, d. 25 Dec 1869, bur.
Fairfield Cemetery, Port Byron, Ill.

Wm. Hylander b. 14 Mar 1854, d. 21 Mar 1931, bur. Port Byron, Ill.
Chas. Leonard b. 19 Dec 1855, d. 3 Oct 1857
Isabell b. 9 May 1858, d. 4 Aug 1925
James F. b. 9 Nov 1860
Oliver Perry b. 25 Jan 1863, d. 20 Aug 1936

[This Bible record is owned by James Alldredge of Webster, S.D. This copy was sent the compiler in 1939. Mr. James Alldredge has since passed away and the Bible is possibly in the hands of his daughter, Mrs. Garner J. Waddel of Webster, S.D.]

DR. WILLIAM ALLDREDGE

William Alldredge b. 9 Mar 1809, d. 30 Jan 1880 m. 24 Jan 1828 to Nancy Brooks b. 6 May 1813, d. 19 Apr 1899.
    Children
Louisa Jane b. 16 Jan 1829, d. 5 Aug 1857
Enoch LaFayette b. 2 Oct 1832
Henry Washington b. 13 Jan 1834, d. 20 Jan 1857
Warren Houston b. 7 Nov 1836, d. 27 Aug 1864
Andrew Perry b. 5 Feb 1842, d. Jan 1863
Mary Ann Eliz. b. 13 Nov 1845, d. Jan 1864
Wm. Valient b. 4 June 1839, d. 16 Aug 1937

[Enoch Lafayette m. 1858 to Artemissa Wormack
Warren Houston m. to Eliz. Daniel
Wm. Valient m. 1st to Molly McNorton, m. 2nd on 13 Dec 1868 to Martha Matilda (Bracken) Tuttle, widow of Jones Tuttle of Miss. who d. just before the Civil War, born 18 Mar 1840, died 1 July 1907. Wm. V. & Martha Alldredge are the grandparents of the compiler. Wm. V. Alldredge and his sons changed the spelling of the name about 1890 to the simpler Aldridge.]

[This family Bible was owned by Mrs. Jesse Thrasher of Trinity, Ala., R.F.D. in 1917. It was copied by the compiler in company of her grandfather Wm. V. Alldredge that summer.]

WILLIAM ALLDREDGE (ALDRIDGE)

Wm. Alldredge b. 12 Sep 1808 [in N.C.], d. 7 Jan 1865 in Putnam Co., Ind., m. 8 Oct 1829 to Mary Ann Moore b. 28 Aug 1811 in Ky., d. 26 July 1874 in Putman Co., Ind.
    Children
Oliver Perry b. 7 Oct 1830, d. 18 Jan 1859, m. 31 May 1854 to Helen Higgins
Eleanor b. May 1833, d. 11 Nov 1833
Amanda b. 11 Nov 1834, d. 11 June 1856, m. 2 Sep 1852 to Robert Glover in Putman Co., Ind.
Louiza b. 24 Apr 1837, m. 1855 to Jacob Pickett
Hannah b. 27 Sep 1839, d. 20 Sep 1858, m. 12 Feb 1857 to John W. Williams
Rebecca b. 15 July 1842, d. 10 Jan 1844
William, Jr. b. 20 Aug 1844, d. 19 Dec 1903 in Oso, Wash., m. 25 Dec 1867 at Carpenterville, Ind. to Maria Eliz. Robinson b. 6 Apr 1852, d. 8 Sep 1832 in Everett, Wash.
Mary A. b. 1846
Lucinda b. 1849

[From F. R. Aldridge, Nashville, Tenn.]

[This family was from Randolph Co., N.C.]

JONATHAN ALLRED

Jonathan Allred b. 16 Nov 1772
Nancy (Walker) Allred b. 22 Mar 1785
    Children
Robert Allred b. 26 Oct 1803
Bailey Allred b. 15 Jan 1806
Chas. M. Allred b. 19 Feb 1809
John Allred b. 9 Mar 1814
Jonathan Allred b. 5 July 1816

Margaret Stillwell b. 16 Nov 1784
Rachel Stillwell b. 1 Mar 1786
Rebecca Walker b. 10 Apr 1821
William Walker b. 15 Apr 1823
John Walker b. 19 Aug 1825
Sarah (Copeland) Allred, [wife of Bailey Allred] b. 10 Jan 1810
Ann (Moredec?) Allred, [wife of Robert Allred] b. 13 Feb 1813
Anna (Speck) Allred, [wife of Chas. M. Allred] b. 13 Feb 1814
Epsey (Ramsay) Allred, [2nd wife of Chas. M. Allred] b. 29 Mar 1831
Emily Jane Walker b. 13 Aug 1824
Evander Walker b. 1 Jan 1832
Isaac Walker b. 10 Aug 1834
Susan Walker b. 4 Mar 1837
Emma R. Walker b. 1832

[No relationship shown with the Stillwells nor who the latter All-
reds & Walkers are.]

[This record was sent the compiler in Dec 1955 by Mr. C. E. Allred,
440 W. Hillvale, Knoxville, Tenn.]

WILLIAM BRANTLY ALLRED

William Brantly Allred b. 24 Dec 1811, d. 31 Oct 1909, m. 1st on
8 Dec 1840 to Nancy A. Stadler, b. Oct 1819, d. 22 Dec 1843, m. 2nd
on 20 Nov 1845 to Hannah Aldridge.
    Children by 1st wife
Louisa Elizabeth Allred b. 2 Feb 1842, [m. Thomas Henry Rudd]
John Brantley Allred b. 20 Sep 1843, [m. Mittie Covington]

[Notes from family: Nancy A. Stadler was the daughter of Elder
John and Nancy (Arnold) Stadler. Wm. Brantly Allred was born in
Randolph Co., N.C. He was the son of Thomas Allred and his wife
who was a sister of Brantly York, founder of York's Institute which
later became Trinity College and was moved to Durham, N.C. It is
now Duke University. This Bible is now in the possession of Eliza
beth Allred Kimbro, wife of S.E. Kimbro, Rt. 1, Yanceyville, N.C.]

9

EDMOND ANDERSON

Edmond Anderson b. 15 Mar 1813, m. 20 Feb 1834 to Nancy Turrentine
b. July 1813
    Their children
Permelia b. 17 Feb 1835
John P. b. 12 Apr 1836
James A. b. 11 Mar 1838
Rochale b. 20 Aug 1839
Warner P. b. 23 July 1842
Clayborne W. b. 12 Nov 1848
Robert S. b. 9 Feb 1853

Warner P. Anderson m. 25 Oct 1874 to Louis Sandusky.
    Their children
Louisa b. 15 July 1852
Chester b. 7 Aug 1875
Molly b. 7 or 9 Aug 1875 [must be twin of Chester, above]
Nora b. 20 Apr 1881

[Nancy Turrentine, above, was the dau. of John & Nancy Wilson Turrentine who were married in Orange Co., N.C. in 1803. John was
killed in the War of 1812. Nancy, his wife, had moved to Lincoln
Co., Tenn. when he went in the army. After his death, she moved
with her brothers-in-law and some Wilsons to Morgan Co., Ala. where
she died leaving a will in 1826. Nancy, who married Edmond Anderson was the youngest of five children.]

JOHN ANDERSON

John Anderson b. 20 Feb 1747, d. 19 Apr 1805, m. 1st on 2 Mar 1767
Elizabeth Conyers b. 26 Dec 1750, d. 25 Jan 1791.
    Children
David b. 23 Feb 1768, d. 21 Sep 1774
James b. 30 Nov 1769
Susanna Wilson b. 27 Oct 1771, d. 11 July 1814 - single
Mary b. 2 Oct 1773, d. 11 Nov 1790
Effe b. 25 May 1776, m. 11 July 1799 Jos. May - his 2nd wife
Sarah b. 11 Aug 1778 [Sarah Whilden on her tombstone]
Elizabeth b. 27 Feb 1781, d. 16 Jan 1793
John, Jr. b. 11 May 1783 [m. Sarah Way]
Wm. David b. 3 Oct 1785, d. 12 Oct 1804
Louise b. 17 July 1787, d. 6 July 1867 [m. 1st to Jacob W. Mills,
  m. 2nd to Capt. Wm. Harris]
Martha b. 29 Jan 1790 [m. Wm. McCutcheon]

John Anderson, Sr. m. 2nd to Mrs. Frances Moore McBride, widow of
John McBride, [Frances b. 17 Oct 1763, d. 5 Mar 1843]
    Children
Eliz. Penelope b. 25 Mar 1794, d. 23 Oct 1798
Frances Moore b. 14 Mar 1796, d. 7 Oct 1803
Sophronia b. 17 July 1798

Harriet Cooper b. 13 Oct 1800, d. 29 Sep 1804
Phillip Marshall b. 2 Oct 1803, d. 1 Aug 1808

[Bible owned by Miss Ella McCutcheon, Rt. 3, Bishopville, S.C.
Data in square brackets found by the late John Coit Wilson, Darlington, S.C.]

SHADRACK ATKINSON

Shadrack Atkinson b. Dec 1790, d. Sep 1867 m. to Elizabeth Bryan,
dau. of John Hill Bryan, m. to Mary Ann Elizabeth Atkinson [b. 3
Mar 1806], d. 7 Dec 1862.
      Children [no wives given as mothers of these]
John Hill Milton b. 22 Aug 1814
Wm. Harrison b. 15 Dec 1815, d. 8 Oct 1816
James Dudley b. 21 Feb 1818, d. 2 Aug 1853 in New Orleans
Sarah Dewilda b. 16 Oct 1819
Shadrack Littleton Hiram Henry b. 20 Dec 1822
Eliz. Ann b. 28 Feb 1825
Henry Dewilda b. 5 May 1827
Christopher Columbus b. 10 Feb 1829, d. 23 Oct 1906
Bryan b. 15 Dec 1831, d. 14 Sep 1843
Edward b. 18 Mar 1833, d. 10 May 1894 in New York City
J. L. M. Atkinson b. 29 May 1837 [no indication of sex]

Rob b. 26 Apr 1852 [no indication as to whose child he is]

Chris. Columbus Atkinson m. 28 July 1869 to Sarah F. Barwick, who
died 21 May 1881, m. 30 Mar 1882 to Eliz. Julia Victoria Vann.
      Children
Henry Dewilda b. 21 July 1870 [should be De Wilda]
Sarah Dewilda b. 6 Sep 1872
Mary Ann Eliz. b. 26 Aug 1875
Wm. King b. 9 Oct 1883

Henry De Wilda Atkinson d. 15 Apr 1843
Henry De Wilda Atkinson d. 16 Nov 1844

RICHARD AVERY

Richard Avery b. 1 Feb 1778, d. 15 Mar 1844, m. 1st to Mary Ryalls
d. 26 Sep 1819 in the 40th year of her life, m. 2nd on 1 Dec 1822
to Charlotte, d. 21 Aug 1836, m. 3rd on 11 Mar 1840 to Civil Ann
Gulley
      Children
Allen b. 4 Oct 1800
Bryant b. 29 Dec 1802
Calvin b. 19 Mar 1805
Elizabeth b. 17 Oct 1807
Winifred b. 9 Apr 1810
David b. 4 June 1813
Mary b. 14 Aug 1817

Charlotte b. 28 Oct 1824
Richard b. 10 Aug 1828

Elizabeth Avery m. 3 Apr 1828 to James Adams b. 23 Jan 1805
    Son
James Columbus Adams b. 16 Nov 1829

JAMES BAKER

James Baker formerly of Bristol Parish, England and Martha Hosier
formerly of Oxfordshire, England were joined in marriage by Matthew
Jones, Esq. at John Williams Esq. in Chatham Co., N.C. 11 May 1791.
    Children
James b. 15 Mar 1792 in Orange Co., N.C.
Joseph b. 24 May 1793 in Orange Co., N.C.
Laura b. 16 Oct 1794 in Orange Co., N.C.
John Williams b. 12 Sep 1796 in Pittsborough, Chatham Co., N.C.
Godina Carolina Williams b. 12 Dec 1796 in Pittsborough, Chatham
    Co., N.C.
Louisa b. 11 Nov 1800 in Pittsborough, Chatham Co., N.C., died
Sophia Louisa b. 7 Dec 1803 in Fayetteville, N.C.

JAMES BAKER, JR.

James Baker, Jr. & May Catherine Broadfoot m. 12 Mar 1818 at the
home of John R. Adam, Esq. in Fayetteville, N.C. by Rev. B. Judd.
    Children
Laura Ann b. 13 Dec 1818, d. 12 Aug 1822
James [III] b. 10 Dec 1821
Chas. Broadfoot b. 13 Mar 1823
May Catherine b. 19 Apr 1827
Joseph b. 14 Oct 1828
John Williams b. 25 Mar 1831
Wm. Broadfoot b. 3 Nov 1832
Martha Hosier b. 9 Oct 1834
Geo. Broadfoot b. 26 Aug 1836
Thomas Wilson b. 8 Dec 1839

May Catherine Baker & Wm. Huske m. 11 Oct 1849 by Rev. J. B. Huske
    at Holly Springs
Wm. Baker & Marian Buie m. 1 Jan 1861 at the residence of her fa-
    ther
Geo. B. Baker & Kate Miller m. 15 Apr 1862 at Christ Church,
    Raleigh by Rev. Dr. Mason
Joseph Baker & Laura Ann Williams m. 21 July 1857 by Rev. J. C.
    Huske
Martha H. Baker & Wm. Huske m. Dec 1873 by Rev. Jos C. Huske

Mrs. May C. Baker, wife of James Baker d. 23 Apr 1868 at the resi-
    dence of her son, John W. Baker, Jr.
May C. Huske, wife of Wm. Huske, dau of Jas. & May C. Baker d. 17
    Aug 1870 in 43rd year of her age.

Geo. B. Baker d. in Raleigh at the residence of Mrs. H. W. Moller
of consumption 17 Nov 1872 aged 36 yrs.
John W. Baker d. at the residence of Wm. Huske on Harrington Hill
1 Jan 1873 after a confinement of 12 mos.
Martha Hoosier [sic] wife of Wm. Huske, d. 25 Mar 1881 in 47th year
of her age
Louisa Baker d. 11 Feb 1801 in Chatham Co., N.C.
James Baker d. 10 Mar 1809 the day preceding his 49th birthday in
Fayetteville, N.C. [Jas. Baker, Sr.]
Martha Baker d. 3 June 1823 in Fayetteville, N.C.
Sophia Louisa Williams Baker d. 30 May 1835 in Fayetteville, N.C.
Mrs. Godina C. W. Williams d. 23 May 1846 in Fayetteville, N.C.
Jas. Baker, son of Jas. Baker & Martha, d. 17 Nov 1853
Laura Baker, eldest dau. of Jas. & Martha Hosier Baker, d. Nov 1857
aged 63 yrs.
John W. Baker, youngest son of Jas. Baker & Martha Hoosier, d. 11
Nov 1882, aged 87 yrs.
Dr. Jas. Baker, eldest son of Jas. & May Catherine Baker, d. 26 Mar
1890 in Wilmington, N.C.
Wm. Broadfoot Baker, 5th son of Jas. & May C. Baker, d. 17 Dec 1894
aged 62 yrs at his home in Cumberland Co., N.C.
Chas. Broadfoot Baker d. 5 Oct 1855 aged 32 yrs., 6 mos. & 22 days
in Bladen Co., N.C. [His death is supposed to have been caused
by a fall from his sulky 5 miles below Elizabethtown and is buried in Fayetteville, N.C.]
Dr. C. B. Baker d. aged 32 yrs. and is buried in family burying
ground in Fayetteville, N.C.

[Baker Bibles owned by Misses Frances & Margaret Broadfoot, 116
Oakridge Ave., Fayetteville, N.C. (1959)]

MOSES BALL

Moses Ball b. 2 May 1717, son of John and Winifred Ball, d. 3 Sep
1792, m. 23 June 1745 to Nancy Brashear.
Ann (Nancy) Ball b. 26 Sep 1729, d. 30 Nov 1816
Asa Brashear, son of Robert Brashear & Charity, his wife, b. 1745
William Allen, son of John Allen & Elizabeth (Brashear), b. 12 Aug
1778
Townsend Ball m. Sarah Ann Hodgkins 20 Jan 1803
Prissylla Lawrence, dau of Benjamin Lawrence & Winfret, b. 27 Dec
1728, d. 11 Nov 1810
George Ball, son of James & Cassandra, b. 30 Oct 1786, d. Apr 1807
        Children of Bazil and Lindy
Moses Ball b. 12 Aug 1796, d. 25 Aug 1812. He was a prop to his
father, a comfort to his mother, and a delight to his sister.
Siby Ball b. 6 Dec 1790
Mary Ball b. 10 Nov 1787
Elizabeth Ball b. 28 Aug 1789
Ann Ball b. 4 Feb 1792
Lindy Ball b. 8 Mar 1794
        Children of Townsend and Sarah

Cassandra Ball b. 15 Oct 1803
James Henry Ball b. 2 Mar 1806
Harriet Ball b. 8 June 1808
George Ball b. 29 Apr 1810
Robert Ball b. 25 Oct 1812
    Children of Moses and Ann
Robert Ball b. 10 Apr 1750, d. 12 Oct 1776
Ann Ball b. 26 Oct 1757, d. July 1812
Siby Ball b. 1762 [?], d. 4 Jan 1817

[From the family Bible in the possession of Miss Ida Marcey of
Clarendon, Virginia]

MARK BARBEE

Mark Barbee of Chatham Co., N.C. b. 17 Jan 1781
    Children
Abimelech Barbee b. 28 June 1802,[m. Elizabeth Beavers]
Polly Barbee b. 27 Dec 1804
Joseph D. Barbee b. 26 Nov 1806
Winnifred Barbee b. 2 Jan 1808
Dorcas Barbee b. 21 Mar 1810
Lesley Barbee b. 16 Jan 1812
Sindy Barbee b. 29 Aug 1816
Gilly Barbee b. 8 Mar 1818
Ady Barbee b. 7 Mar 1821
Simeon Barbee b. 22 Oct 1822
Eliza Barbee b. 6 Mar 1824
Ruffin Barbee b. 29 May 1825
Temperance Barbee b. 15 July 1827
Sidney Barbee b. 5 Mar 1829
William S. Barbee b. 20 Dec 1833
Wesley B. Barbee b. 1 July 1834

[The descendants of Abimelech Barbee are given in The Descendants
of William and Sarah (Poe) Herndon of Caroline Co., Va. and Chatham
Co., N.C. by Ruth Herndon Shields (Mrs. C. W.), Chapel Hill, N.C.]

WILKINS BASS

Mr. Wilkins Bass m. to Miss E. A. Saulsbury 8 Aug 1837 by Rev. Jos-
    eph Tally. [This couple was from Bibb Co., Ga.]
Mr. John S. [?] F. Freeman m. to Mrs. E. A. Bass 23 Dec 1852 by
    Rev. A. Kindred
Dr. B. F. Hanley m. to Miss Lizzie Bass on 5 Feb 1862 by Rev. Nash
    Andrews [Hanley should be Stanley?]
[Immediately below the above entry are the two death entries:]
    Died in Opeleka, Ala. Feb 1861
    Died in Atlanta, Ga. 1893
Eaton Wilkins Bass m. to Miss Tacie Oden of Virginia 1872
Dr. J. B. Duggan m. to Mary Emma Bass 11 Apr 1894
Wm. G. Freeman m. to Mrs. Susie M. Smith on 9 Mar 1891 by Rev.

Brantley

Edwin Saulbury Bass b. 8 Aug 1838
Ann Elizabeth Bass b. 1 Apr 1840
John Thomas Bass b. 17 Mar 1845
Eaton Wilkins Bass b. 24 Mar 1846
Mary Emma Bass b. 27 Mar 1849
William Gove [?] Freeman b. 24 July 1856

Edwin Saulsbury Bass was killed at the battle of Sharpsburg, 17
    Sep 1862
Ann Elizabeth Bass d. 19 June 1919 at J. H. Duggan's in Wilkinson
    Co., Ga.
John Thomas Bass d. in Richmond, 15 May 1863 of wound received at
    the battle of Chancellorsville
Eaton Wilkins Bass d. 23 Nov 1918 in Montana
Mary Emma Bass d. 21 Dec 1935 at R. M. Stanley's in Laurens Co.,
    Ga.
William Gove Freeman d. 24 Oct 1908 in Burke Co.

[A. E. Stanley had five children:
    Eva B. m. T. J. Blackshear, all of Laurens Co., Ga.
    Edda m. J. H. Duggan of Wilkinson Co., Ga.
    One child died in infancy
    Maury Stanley m. Maxa Hull of Wilkinson Co., Ga.
    Lucy Stanley m. Sam McArthur of Wilkinson Co., Ga.

Eaton Wilkins Bass and Tacie Oden had six children:
    Frances, Edwin, John, Emma, Margaret and Tacie Bass]

[This Bible is a New Testament published 1852 by Alden Beardsley &
Co. and is now in the possession of Miss Elizabeth Stanley, Lone
Oak Dr., Shirley Hills, Macon, Georgia]

JOHN BAUGHMAN

John Baughman b. 24 Oct 1774 d. 23 Jan 1860, m. 26 Aug 1800 in
Orangeburg Dist., S.C. to Mary Catherine Barbara Benecke [also
spelled Binnicker] b. 4 Aug 1778 in Orangeburg Dist., S.C., d. 21
Aug 1821.
    Children
Maria b. 1 Aug 1801, d. 4 Aug 1863, m. 17 July 1817 to John Atkin-
    son
Ulrich b. 22 Sep 1802, d. 30 Sep 1802
Henry b. 9 Jan 1804, d. 6 Sep 1892, m. 1st on 19 Feb 1829 to Sarah
    Cargill, m. 2nd in Ga. to Elizabeth Towers
Charles b. 11 Jan 1806, d. 26 July 1850, m. 22 Sep 1837 to Nancy
    Ann Peters
Catherine b. 22 Feb 1808, d. 7 Jan 1828
Mary Ann b. 11 May 1812, d. 3 Oct 1888, m. Sherwood Young Reams
Nancy b. 6 Mar 1814, d. 16 July 1856, m.22 Mar 1838 to Isaac Dulan-
    ia [probably Dulaney-Andrea]

15

Harriet b. 16 Oct 1815, d. 26 Mar 1881, m. 10 Dec 1833 to Frederick
   Jourdan
Elizabeth b. 17 July 1818, d. 11 Sep 1901, m. 25 Jan 1838 to Hiram
   Riley
John Bennecke b. 30 May 1820, d. 7 May 1906, m. 5 Sep 1844 to Eliz-
   abeth Ritchie
Wm. Gordon b. 20 Sep 1822, d. 5 Dec 1882, m. Caroline Green

Notation in Bible: John Baughman lived 2 yrs. in Charleston, S.C.
and moved to Abbeville, S.C. Sometime between 1840 & 1850 he moved
to Texas - Mrs. Hiram Riley. [Lexington Co., S.C. to Lubbock, Tex.]

John Baughman m.2nd on 29 Dec 1829 to Rachel Carraway - no children
Rachel Carraway m. 1 Aug 1837 to Jackson Brown [This Rachel
   thought to be dau. of John Baughman's 2nd wife, Rachel Carraway]

[Present owner of this Bible is Mrs. Raymond P. Swofford, 2010 33rd
St., Lubbock, Texas.]

JONAS BEARD

Catherine Kerkner m. 5 July 1761 to George Singler "and lived with
him seven weeks and he died"
Mrs. Catherine Singler m. 30 June 1762 to Jonas Beard of Saxe-Gotha
Township [Lexington Co., S.C.]
      Children
John Beard b. 25 May 1763
Geo. Frederick Beard b. 10 July 1764
Ann Catherine b. 23 Sep 1765
Frederick Beard b. 19 June 1769
Mary Beard b. 1 Mar 1772
Elizabeth Beard b. 17 Jan 1774
William Beard b. 26 Feb 1777
Dorothy Beard b. 19 June 1780

[The above record from a page of Jonas Beard's Bible owned by the
late Percy Geiger of Sandy Run, Calhoun Co., S.C. He did not have
the other pages. This copy was made by Leonard Andrea, 4204 DeVine
St., Columbia, S.C.]

NOEL BEASLEY

Noel Beasley b. 13 May 1809, d. 31 July 1892 m. 1828 to Nancy
Rhodes b. 24 Jan 1816, d. in Little Rock, Ark., bur. Cato Cemetery,
Cato, Ark.
      Children
Mary b. 1829
Jasper b. 1831
Mahala b. 24 Mar 1832
Leonard b. 1835
Theresa Ann b. 1840
Sally Jane b. 1847

Ira Thompson b. 1853
Frances b. 1855
Ellen b. 9 Mar 1857

[This record given by Eugene Rhodes, Florence, S.C. 1958.]

BENJAMIN BELL

Benjamin Bell, the father of Sarah, George, James, Lemuel [Samuel?]
  Henry, George, Elias & Joseph Bell, b. 2 Dec 1790
Barclay Arney [Arnery?], son of Daniel Arney & Sarah, b. 19 Sep
  1847 [1841?]
Charlotte Ava Arney, dau. of Daniel Arney & Sarah, b. 12 Aug 1845
Sarah Elizabeth Arney, dau. of Daniel Arney & Sarah, b. 14 Feb 1848
Lydia Tucker b. 19 Feb 1795
Barclay Arney Hamlin, son of F. M. Hamlin & Sarah E.., b. 5 Oct 1867
  Saturday night
J. Larner Hamlin b. 13 Mar 1869
Francis Mallory Hamlin b. 15 Sep 1870
Sallie Bell Hamlin b. 17 Apr 1872
Martha Reamy Hamlin b. 23 Aug 1874 Sunday Morning, 9 o'c.
George Vance Hamlin b. 9 Sep 1876 Thursday night
F. M. Hamlin b. 3 May 1847
    Children of Benjamin Bell & Lydia, his wife
Sarah b. 19 Oct 1818, d. 21 Mar 1872, ae 53 yrs, 5 mos., & 2 days
George b. 11 Feb 1820, d. 30 Aug 1823
James Montgomery b. 21 Nov 1821
Samuel [Lemuel?] b. 7 Oct 1823
Henry b. 9 May 1825
George b. 23 Feb 1827
Elias b. 25 Sep 1828
Joseph Benjamin b. 18 July 1833

Benjamin Bell & Lydia Tucker m. 15 Jan 1818
Dannel Arney & Sarah Ann Bell m. 19 Jan 1837
Joseph B. Bell & Jeffie Crutchfield m. 12 Dec 1868 [or 1865 ?]
Francis M. Hamlin & Sarah E. Arney m. 25 Sep 1866
Barclay A. Hamlin & Mary Pace Talbot m. 22 Nov 1892
James Turner Hamlin & Mary W. Brown m. 14 Feb 1894 at Richmond
Charles W. Hughes & Sallie Bell Hamlin m. 5 Aug 1895
F. M. Hamlin, Jr. & Daisy White Hamlin m. [last line illegible]

George Bell, son of Benj'n Bell & Lydia, d. 30 Aug 1823
Lydia Bell, wife of Benj'n Bell, d. 10 Aug 1834
Benjamin Bell d. 5 Aug 1839, being in the 50th yr. of his age
George Bell, son of Benjamin Bell & Lydia, d. 22 Apr 1845
Elias Bell, son of Benjamin Bell & Lydia, d. 30 June 1858 [?]
Charlotte Ann Arney, dau. of Daniel Arney & Sarah, d. 26 May 1848 ?
Barclay Arney, son of Daniel Arney & Sarah, d. 8 Dec 1854
Daniel Arney d. 22 Oct 1856, aged 49 yrs., 6 mos., & 9 days
Henry Bell, son of Benjamin Bell & Lydia, d. 15 Oct 1859
James Bell, son of Benjamin Bell & Lydia, d. 12 June 1860

Samuel Bell d. 21 Aug 1869

[Bible now in the possession of Miss Reamey Hamlin, Greensboro Rd.,
Danville, Va. Four photostats sent in by Mrs. Sam Duggan, Moultrie
Ga. Benjamin Bell of Pitt Co., N.C.]

LAUNCELOT BELL

Launcelot Bell, son of John Bell of Cumberland Co., England, ar-
rived in N.C. 7 Sep 1758, m. 14 Mar 1759 to Miriam Nicholson, dau.
of Thos. Nicholson, b. 12 Mar 1738, d. 24 Jan 1774.
     Children
Mary b. 27 Dec 1759, m. 28 June 1780 to Nathan Morris
Thomas b. 15 Oct 1761, d. 4 Feb 1780
Sarah b. 30 Sep 1763, m. 23 Oct 1785 to Benjamin Bundy
Margaret b. 11 Nov 1765, m. 24 Nov 1782 to John Winslow
John b. 6 Feb 1768, m. 30 Dec 1789 to Sarah Bundy b. 9 Jan 1759, d.
  11 June 1806
Caroline b. 8 May 1770, m. 19 Nov 1796 to Francis Albertson
Miriam b. 23 May 1773, m. 16 Sep 1797 to Benjamin Albertson
     Children of John Bell & Sarah Bundy
Launcelot b. 3 Nov 1790
Mary b. 3 Mar 1792
Miriam b. 5 Aug 1795
Josiah b. 11 Jan 1798
Sarah b. 16 Jan 1800
Thomas b. 17 Apr 1802
Rebecca b. 27 Apr 1804

[Launcelot Bell d. 24 Jan 1781, lived in Perquimans, Pasquotank
Cos., N.C., from Cumberland Co., England. Some of these later sets
of children went to Kershaw Co., S.C., Ohio & other states.]

DANIEL BELLUNE

Daniel Bellune b. 30 Mar 1760, m. Mary Boissier b. 14 Apr 1763
     Children
Mary b. 2 Feb 1783
William b. 24 Aug 1784
Michael b. 20 Feb 1786
Sarah b. 22 Dec 1787
Elizabeth b. 14 Apr 1790
Martha b. 16 July 1792

Inscription in the front of the Bible:
     Daniel Bellune His Book, Given him by his father, 5 Nov 1786

[This record was furnished by a descendant, Mrs. Elise E. Hamilton,
Chapel Hill, N.C., who is the great-great-grand daughter of Elizabeth Bellune who married Samuel Frink.]

HUDSON BERRY, SR.

Henry Berry Sr. b. 10 Sep 1752, d. 13 Jan 1840, m. 27 June 1775 to
Sarah Anthony b. 3 Nov 1756, d. 26 Apr 1842, dau. of John Anthony
of Caswell Co., N.C., son of John Anthony, of Hanover Co., Va.
Children
Nancy b. 17 Aug 1777, d. 1811 in Greenville, S.C.
William b. 17 Aug 1780, d. 14 June 1857 in Tippah Co., Miss.
Elizabeth b. 14 Mar 1784 in N.C., d. 18 Apr 1839 in Greenville Co.,
   S. C.
Micajah b. 3 Aug 1786, d. 8 Jan 1859 in Greenville Co., S.C.
David b. 30 Aug 1789, d. 29 Aug 1843 in Pontotoc Co., Miss.
Nathan b. 3 Nov 1791, d. 25 Feb 1840 in Greenville, S.C.
Hudson, Jr. b. 5 June 1796, d. 27 July 1853 in Tippah Co., Miss.
Sarah b. 8 Mar 1801, d. 1855, m. Tully Francis Sullivan, III

[Record from someone in S.C.]

MOODY BETTIS

Moody Bettis b. 19 July 1793, d. 1866, m. 23 Feb 1815 to Sophia
Swearingen b. 27 Aug 1793, d. 31 Dec 1861
Children
Zacharias Laurence Bettis b. 12 June 1816, d. 4 Sep 1879
Alfred Bettis b. 13 Oct 1817, d. 8 Jan 1823
John Moody Bettis b. 19 Aug 1821, d. 19 Dec 1822
Frederick Francis Bettis b. 23 Nov 1825, d. 24 July 1836
Marshall A. Bettis b. 12 July, d. 17 Mar 1864 C.S.A.
Jesse Richard Bettis b. 15 Aug 1835

[Moody Bettis was the son of Stephen Bettis by his first wife (her
name unknown). Moody Bettis m. in Edgefield Co., S.C. to his first
cousin, Sophia Swearingen, a dau. of Sarah Bettis & Frederick
Swearingen.]

[This Bible is owned by Mrs. Adele Bettis Kerrigan of 3830 Arbor
St., Houston 4, Texas. It was taken from Edgefield Co., S.C. to
Clark Co., Ala.]

JOHN NEVILLE BIRCH

John Neville Birch b. 6 June 1795 in Prince Edward Co., Va., d. 12
Mar 1835 in Talbotton Co., Ga., m. 27 Feb 1817 to Ann Dilworth b.
*Feb 1802 in Petersburg, Va., d. 28 Aug 1897 in Talbotton, Ga.
Children
Martha Ann b. 11 Sep 1819, m. 1 Jan 1835 to John T. Howard
James Alexander b. 11 Sep 1819, d. 1 Aug 1824 aged 4 yrs.
John Neville, Jr. b. 20 Jan 1822, d. 24 July 1825 aged 3 yrs.
Eliza Green b. 22 Mar 1824
Mary Clay b. 10 Nov 1826, d. 8 May 1877 [This is the mother of
   Chancellor Walter B. Hill.]
Susan Angelina b. 22 Apr 1828

Sara Isabella b. 5 May 1833
John Neville, Jr. b. 4 Jan 1835, d. 18 Sep 1863 [He was a Confeder-
     ate officer & died in service.], m. 1856 to M. S. Snider [Lived
     in Columbus, Ga.]

Sarah Birch Douglas d. 13 Oct 1904

[This Bible is in the possession of Mrs. Ann Douglas Alford, Worth
Co., Ga., granddaughter of Sarah Birch Douglas. The Bible was
given to Mrs. Alford by her great grandmother for whom she was
named.]

GEORGE BISHOP

George Bishop m. Elizabeth
     Children
George Bishop, Jr. d. about 1743
Elizabeth Bishop m. Mr. Dudley
Stoakley Bishop m. Elizabeth Morris
     Child of Stokley & Elizabeth
Thomas Bishop [b. 1764, d. 5 Mar 1829, aged 65 yrs.], m. Ruth, d.
     1846
     Children of Thomas & Ruth
Thomas Bishop, Jr. d. 20 Dec 1836
Ruth Bishop d. June 1837, m. T. W. Bloodworth
Morris Bishop b. 1795, d. 29 Mar 1851
Ann Bishop d. 1852, m. George Bell
George M. Bishop b. 1801, d. 6 Aug 1865, m. 1st in 1820 to Eliza
     Buford, m. 2nd in 1832 to Elizabeth Henderson, m. 3rd on 18 Jan
     1842 to Mary Ann Westbrook.

Abstract of the will of George Bishop, New Hanover Co., record Book
C, p. 35, dated 20 Dec 1743, no probate date:
     Brothers: Stoakley Bishop, James, Moses, and Woodrow Stoakley
          Sidbury
     Sister: Elizabeth Bishop
     Mother: Elizabeth Bishop [Evidently widow Sidbury m. G. Bishop]
     Father: George Bishop
     Cousin: Moses Sidbury, Jane Morgan & Morgan Morgan, Jr.

Abstract of the will of William Morris, New Hanover Co., Will Book
C, p. 247, dated 14 Feb 1767, proved Mar 1767
     Grandsons: James, son of Thomas Morris, deceased; William Morris,
          son of dau., Margaret Morris; Thomas Bishop, son of dau. Eliz-
          abeth Bishop; Maurice or Morris Ward; Morris Bishop; William
          Earl
     Daughters: Ann McClammy, Rachel Earle, Margaret Morris, Elizabeth
          Bishop
     Exrs. sons-in-law: Stokley Bishop & Oney McClammy & fr George
          Merrick
     Other Legatees: Lewis Hicks, son of Benjamin & Esther Hicks, de-
          ceased; Miss Ann Sutton

Abstract, Will Book C, p. 91:
Rachel Earle was wife of Richard Earle, d. 1777

JAMES BLACK

James Black b. 17 Mar 1740 in Scotland, came to America ca. 1760, landing in Pa., d. 20 Aug 1780 in Beaufort, S.C., m. 13 Nov 1762 to Rachel Adams b. 8 Sep 1743 in Philadelphia, d. 8 Aug 1787 in Beaufort, S.C.
    Children
Elizabeth b. 13 Aug 1766, m. 24 Oct 1784 to John Loacraft, Rev. Soldier
Charles b. 10 Aug 1777, m. Rebecca Dupont
Mary b. 6 July 1799, m. Jos. Luther Grayson
William b. 1 Aug 1774, m. Sarah Hanson Reid
James b. 13 Aug 1770, m. Eliz. Clark Salters
Ann b. 16 Dec 1768, m. 1st to Thos. Bowan Back, m. 2nd to John Blythewood
Sarah b. 29 Mar 1772, m. Wm. Baynard

[Jas. Black moved from Pa. to Augusta Co., Va. where he was a Colonial soldier in 1766. He fought in the Rev. War in S.C., was wounded 11 times and died while fighting in that war.]

[Wm. Black, son of Jas. & Rachel Black m. 2 June 1802 to Sarah Hanson Reid, dau. of Robt. Reid. Children: Jonnana Reid, Wm. Reid, Edward Junius, Sarah Hanson, Rachel, Joseph Longworth, Eliz. Rosella, Clementine Johanna. This info seems to have been taken from a will. Data from Jack Ladson, Jr., Moultrie, Ga.]

JOSEPH BLACK

Joseph W. Black b. 27 Aug 1849, d. 20 Dec 1921, m. 7 July 1873 to Florence J. Loyd b. 12 Mar 1854 [Loyd rec. says 22 Mar]
    Children
Robt. Russell b. 13 Aug 1874
Hampton Rodgers b. 21 May 1877
Lorena A. b. 29 June 1879
Wm. Ernest b. 15 July 1882
Franklin Webb b. 20 Oct 1884
Nellie Belle b. 31 May 1889
Carrie Florence b. 8 Feb 1893
Wm. Burk b. 14 Aug 1903

Joseph Marion Garrison b. 24 June 1904
Maude Black b. 19 Apr 1904
Helen Black b. 31 Dec 1905
Pinkney Jefferson Garrison, Jr. b. 2 Dec 1906
Florence Carolyn McDonald b. 5 Nov 1908
Harmon Brice McDonald b. 8 Apr 1912
Sara Eliz. Black b. 17 June 1913
Webb Black Garrison & Wm. Ernest Garrison b. 19 July 1919

EDWARD ALEXANDER BLACKBURN

Edward A. Blackburn b. 16 July 1840, m. 5 Dec 1872 to Annie Cren-
shaw b. 22 May 1851
    Children
John Nelson b. 14 July 1875, m. 1 Dec 1914 to Stella Daft Horner
Lizzie Glenn b. 17 Feb 1878, m. 5 Dec 1901 to Wm. Acuff
Edward Morrow b. 14 Dec 1879, m. 26 Nov 1913 to Mave Sullivan Cal-
vin
Annie Letitia b. 14 Feb 1881, m. 10 Oct 1905 to John W. Woolfolk
    Grandchild
Edward A. Blackburn m. 4 June 1950 to Dorothy Jane Story

Father & Mother of Annie C. Crenshaw were:
    W. M. Crenshaw b. 10 Sep 1810, d. 8 Nov 1882
    Elva Ann (Turberville) Crenshaw b. 7 May 1818, d. 15 Nov 1895

[Records furnished by Mr. Edward Blackburn Acuff, Sr. on 22 Apr 1960. He states, " Bible given by John Nelson Blackburn (b. 1809, d. 1886) to his son, Edward Alex. Blackburn (b. 1840, d. 1899) on 25 Dec 1876. This Bible is now in possession of Edward Alex. Blackburn. (b. 1920) of Decatur, Ala. This latter being the great grandson of John Nelson Blackburn ..." He further says that there is a notation in the Bible that begins, "Eliz. Martin". He feels sure that Annie Crenshaw Blackburn started to give data on her grandmother Crenshaw, who was Eliz. Terrell Martin, wife of Freeman Crenshaw, and never finished.]

JOEL BLACKBURN

Joel Blackburn b. 12 Dec 1794
Anna (Fry) Blackburn b. 25 Dec 1796
    Children
William B. b. 5 Apr 1815
Margaret b. 26 Dec 1817
Robert b. 2 Apr 1820
Elizabeth b. 5 Feb 1822
Joel J. b. 1 Mar 1824
Chloe Anna b. 2 June 1829
Vienna b. 27 Feb 1832
Paschal Jackson b. 10 Aug 1834
James b. 1 Mar 1839
Mary Jane b. 31 Jan 1840
Elizira b. 21 Jan 1842

[Joel Blackburn d. in Jefferson Co., Ala. in the home of his son-
in-law, W. L. Wilson, husband of his daughter, Elizabeth Blackburn.
"Mrs. Anna Blackburn b. 25 Dec 1796 in Anderson Co., Tenn, m. Joel
Blackburn 16 Aug 1814. Moved to Blount Co., Ala. in Nov. 1816.

She and her family were members of the Methodist Church." This
Bible is owned by Mrs. O. J. Smith, 1014 Jefferson Blvd., Tarrant
City, Birmingham, Ala. It was copied by Beasly (or Beasy) Hendrix,
Jr. on 23 July 1958.]

JOHN BLACKMAN

John Blackman, son of Col. Wm. & Eliz. (Bryan) Sasser Blackman, b.
24 Mar 1787, d. 26 Apr 1852, m. 1st to Margaret McAuley, m. 2nd to
Candis Gunter.
    Children by 1st wife
Barbara b. 1 Jan 1817
Mary b. 14 Feb 1818
Elizabeth C. b. 14 Jan 1821
Delitha Ann b. 15 Aug 1819
Margaret b. 13 Feb 1822

[Record from Ida Brooks Kellam, Wilmington, N.C.]

DAVID KING BLACKWOOD

David King Blackwood b. 19 Oct 1804, d. 4 July 1859, m. 7 Apr 1829
to Tabitha Minor b. 30 Jan 1802 in Granville Co., d. 8 Mar 1886.
    Children
John Marshall b. 19 Sep 1832, d. 22 Mar 1917, m. to Virginia Fuller
Harriet J. b. 27 Jan 1834, d. 5 Mar 1877, m. to Jas. M. Ward
Samuel David b. 6 July 1836, d. 26 Apr 1894, m. 12 Dec 1861 to Mar-
    tha Jane Craig d. 11 Aug 1912
Mary E. b. 20 Mar 1838, d. 22 Sep 1916, m. 28 May 1863 to William
    J. Blackwood
Julia Ann b. 17 Mar 1842, d. 12 Aug 1883, m. 27 Dec 1860 to Joseph
    Kirkland

JOHN BLACKWOOD

John Blackwood b. 12 Aug 1779, m. 1st to Eleanor Craig.
    Children
Isabella b. 22 May 1800
Mary D. b. 4 Nov 1802, d. 18 May 1856, m. to Jas. Strayborn
David King b. 19 Oct 1804, d. 4 July 1859, m. to Tabetha Minor
William C. b. 17 Oct 1806, d. 6 Sep 1870, m. to Martha Minor
Margaret b. 10 Sep 1808, d. 13 Aug 1885, m. to John McCauley
John J. b. 10 Apr 1810, d. 4 Dec 1881, m. to Laura Springs
Samuel P. b. 21 Jan 1812, d. 8 Nov 1851, unmarried
Nathaniel H. b. 28 Dec 1813, d. 17 Oct 1868, m. to Mary E. Jones
James Jackson b. 7 Jan 1816, d. 8 June 1869, unmarried
Eleanor E. b. 30 Dec 1817, d. 11 Aug 1838, unmarried
Alex. D. b. 10 Jan 1820, d. 2 Mar 1885, m. to Helen Horton
Robert N. b. 1 Aug 1822, d. 6 June 1902, m. to Susan Stanley
George b. b. 10 Mar 1825

[John Blackwood's second marriage was to Mary McCauley. There were

23

several children, but their names were not recorded in the Blackwood family Bible.]

SAMUEL DAVID BLACKWOOD

Samuel David Blackwood b. 6 July 1836, d. 26 Apr 1894, m. 12 Dec
1861 to Martha Jane Craig b. 23 Sep 1838, d. 11 Aug 1912
    Children
Samuel David, Jr. b. 31 Oct 1862, d. in infancy
Robert Phillips b. 29 Jan 1866, d. 22 July 1944, m. 12 Sep 1888 to
    Alice Moore Craig, d. July 1926
John Hampton b. 25 Feb 1868, d. 5 July 1916, m. May 1908 to Lizzie
    Ann Weaver
Nannie Moore b. 26 Aug 1870, m. 30 Oct 1901 to James M. Lloyd
Malcolm Craig b. 9 May 1872, d. 3 July 1937, m. 21 Sep 1898 to Min-
    nie Celia Turrentine
Mary Eleanor b. 8 May 1874, d. 3 June 1897, m. 15 Jan 1896 to Wil-
    liam Craig
Herbert Nettleton b. 29 Aug 1876, m. 21 June 1905 to Alice Moore
    Kirkland
Melissa Dudley b. 3 June 1878, m. 21 Dec 1920 to John A. McCauley
William Alexander b. 9 Oct 1882

WILLIAM BLACKWOOD, II

William Blackwood, II [of New Hope] m. Margaret King
    Children
Elizabeth (twin) b. 29 Oct 1777, m. Nehemiah White
Hannah (twin) b. 29 Oct 1777, m. M. W. Self
Mary b. 21 Dec 1778, m. John Craig
John b. 12 Aug 1779, m. 1st to Eleanor Craig, d. 16 Nov 1843, m.
    2nd to Mary McCauley
Martha b. 10 Aug 1781, m. Chas. Johnston
Janette b. 12 Mar 1783, m. M. John McCauley
Ann b. 7 Feb 1785, m. Jacob Potts
Peggy b. 27 Feb 1787, m. William Long of Tenn.
Isabel b. 5 Feb 1789
Sarah b. 18 Mar 1791, m. John Gattis of Georgia
Nancy b. 23 Nov 1792, m. James & Silas Davis
William b. 27 Sep 1794, moved away
James b. 27 Nov 1796, moved away
Katurah b. 7 June 1798, died unmarried
Johnston b. 7 Sep 1800, settled the G. S. Freeland place and moved
    away
Frances b. 1 Dec 1802, m. Anderson Long

[Copied from Dr. D. I. Craig's Historical Sketch of New Hope:
William Blackwood m. Betsey in Ireland and they were among the
early sttlers of New Hope. Children:
  James - located some miles below Chapel Hill
  John, moved away
  William, II m. Margaret King & settled on the old homestead

24

Martha m. Chas. Johnston
Mary m. John Craig
Peggy m. Joseph Kirkland
Annie m. a Mr. Morrow of Hawfields
Jennie m. a Mr. Allen of Hawfields]

ROBERT BOLTON

Robert Bolton b. 25 Jan 1775, d. 25 Jan 1824 aged 51 yrs., m. 6 Aug
1806 to Rebeckah Bolton b. 2 Dec 1788, d. 16 Aug 1840 aged 51 yrs.,
8 mos., 14 days. Rebeckah Bolton m. 29 Nov 1829 to Wm. D. Sneed.
    Children of Robert & Rebeckah Bolton
Saml b. 25 Oct 1806
Mary C. b. 19 Sep 1808 d. 5 Dec 1874, m.26 Nov 1829 to David Thos.
    Davis b. 8 Aug 1806, d. 9 Aug 1861
James C. b. 18 Aug 1810
Robert R. b. 14 Apr 1812
Danile b. 16 Feb 1814, d. 18 Dec 1833
John b. 20 Jan 1816, d. 9 May 1853
Eliz. J. B. b. 12 Feb 1818, d. 22 Mar 1830 aged 12 yrs, 1 mo., & 10
    days
Martha A. b. 14 Feb 1820, m. 22 Sep 1835 to Arthur Davis
Sarah R. b. 5 Mar 1822
Wm. D. b. 2 Apr 1824
    Children of Arthur & Martha A. (Bolton) Davis and David Thos.
        & Mary C. (Bolton) Davis
An infant b. & d. 21 Jan 1831
Martha A. E. Davis b. 1 Sep 1832
Susanna C. S. Davis b. 2 Dec 1834
David B. Davis b. 18 Dec 1836
Sarah R. Davis b. 14 Nov 1838
A. S. F. Davis b. 8 Nov 1840
Mary A. Davis b. 26 Nov 1843
James D. Davis b. 31 July 1849

T. S. Davis m. 2 Nov 1865 to Mary B. Martin
David R. Davis d. 18 July 1864 from wounds at Petersburg, Va.
Wm. T. McGill d. 6 Apr 1862 [son-in-law]
Charity Davis d. 3 Dec 1829
Robert Rowan d. 12 Jan 1841 [assumed he is a son-in-law]
Frances A. Davis d. 14 May 1916
Derrick T. Thomas d. 12 Aug 1922
Mary Ann Davis Thomas d. 11 Sep 1928
Sarah A. Davis b. 16 Nov 1836
Rebeckah F. S. Davis b. 3 Nov 1838
David T. Davis b. 3 May 1841
Robert A. Davis b. 24 July 1843
John H. Davis b. 4 Nov 1858
D. F. D. D. Thomas b. 16 Feb 1871

[This Bible was pub. in 1822 and is owned by Mr. Derrick Shade
Davis, Lykesland, Richland Co., S.C. It was given to him by his

25

aunt, Mrs. Mary Ann Davis Thomas.]

DUDLEY BOND(S)

Dudley Bonds & Mary Van Bibber m. 23 Apr 1815
Flavius Augusta Bond m. 13 Jan 1859 to Martha Maria Crawford
Dudley Bond d. 19 Nov 1857
Martha Jane Crawford Bond d. 23 Feb 1858
Mrs. Ann Mary Van Bibber Bond d. 25 Jan 1878
Henry Bond d. 25 Apr 1906
Flavius A. Bond d. 29 Nov 1912
Martha C. Bond d. 13 Mar 1914
Dudley Bonds b. 27 Nov 1792, son of Wm. Dudley Bond & wife Frances
  Meredith [note spelling with and without final s]
William Bond b. 18 Oct 1830
Hillary Bond b. 15 Mar 1832
Martha Jane b. 5 Dec 1834
Flavius A. b. 22 Sep 1836
Henry V. Bonds b. 23 July 1817
Caroline Bonds b. 23 Sep 1820
Mary Eliz. b. 15 Feb 1823
Zemily b. 18 July 1826
Thomas M. b. 23 Mar 1828
Ann Mary Van Bibber b. 3 Feb 1800
Martha Maria Crawford Bond d. 13 Mar 1918
    Children of Flavius Augusta Bond & Martha Maria Crawford
Carry Deluta b. 9 May 1860
John Anderson b. 10 Dec 1861
Jessie Lourine b. 3 Apr 1866
Charlie LaFayette b. 20 May 1868
Essie Meredith b. 22 Feb 1871
Mae Foster b. 14 Apr 1873
William Wallace b. 18 May 1875
Henry Clifford b. 27 Sep 1877
Herman b. 3 Oct 1879, d. 1887
Tandy Dudley b. 26 May 1882
    In the front of the book: "Dudley Bond, His Book, 31 Dec 1853

"Ann Mary Van Bibber, our grandmother was born in Berkshire, England, moved to Va., later to Charleston, S.C. She married Wm. Dudley Bond and they moved to Lawrenceville, Gwinnett Co., Ga." "Your
great grandmother Bonds name before she married was Frances Meredith, a native of Va. She was reared on the Yadkin River and your
grandfather (great?) Bonds was reared at the same place. He fought
through the Revolutionary War. Your own grandmother's name was Ann
Evans and she was reared in or near Savannah, Ga."
[The compiler does not know who the narrator is above.]

[This Bible was published by the American Bible Society in 1851.
This copy was sent by Mrs. S. C. Moon, Gainesville, Ga. in 1954.]

26

JOHN J. BOOTH

John J. Booth b. 20 Apr 1813, d. 11 Dec 1867 m. 13 Nov 1834 to
Olive Holmes b. 16 Jan 1812
     Children
Mary Ann b. 24 Nov 1835
James Thomas b. 15 May 1837, d. 10 July 1818
Charlotte b. 21 Dec 1838
John A. b. 19 Sep 1840, d. 6 June 1863
Samantha b. 28 July 1842, d. 2 Nov 1845 [written in later as Seman-
     tha Cartwright Booth Hux]
Martha Ursiller b. 6 July 1844
Lewis Scarbrough b. 19 June 1846
Keneth T. b. 29 June 1850
Molcey A. b. 30 Oct 1853
     Grandchild - Child of Keneth T. & Molcey A. Booth
Abigill b. 1 Nov 1871, d. 1 Dec 1871

[John J. Booth of this Bible was of Horry Co., S.C. Bible now
owned by K. R. Mishoe, Wilmington, N.C.

JOHN PATTERSON BOYD

Johm Patterson Boyd b. 10 Apr 1824 in Chester Co., S.C., d. 24 Dec
1892 in Newton Co., Ga., m. 2 July 1846 to Sarah P. Robinson, b. 17
Aug 1821 in Chester Co., S.C., d. 6 Sep 1901 in Newton Co., Ga.
     Children
Robert Patterson Boyd b. 29 Aug 1847, d. Oct 1920,[m. 1st to Sarah
     Frances Ragsdale, m. 2nd to Mary Cowan]
William Boyd b. 25 Dec 1851, d. 4 Feb 1927, m. 8 June 1875 to Fran-
     ces Crofford McCord b. 9 July 1854, d. 3 May 1940
Sarah Boyd b. 24 Sep 1853, d. 4 Apr 1918, m. 17 Dec 1876 to Benja-
     min Hill Woodruff, son of Margaret Ann McCord & James Monroe
     Woodruff
Angie N. Boyd b. 5 Sep 1856, d. 23 Jan 1901, m. to William Madison
     Hollingsworth b. 4 Apr 1856, d. 17 July 1887
Talulah Lucinda Boyd b. 14 Oct 1858, d. 6 Dec 1926, m. 2 Dec 1877
     to William Stewart Starr, son of Martha Lee & William Steele
     Starr
John Deavers Boyd b. 16 July 1860, d. Sep 1947, m. 1st on 22 May
     1883 to Emma Hill b. 1860, d. 1933, m. 2nd to Mrs. Alice Sher-
     wood, nee Robinson. No children by either wife
     Children of William Boyd & Frances C. McCord Boyd
Martha Violet Boyd b. 21 Mar 1876, m. 23 Oct 1900 to William Smith
     Elliott
John Stuart Boyd b. 18 July 1877, d. 27 July 1877
William Robert Boyd (twin) b. 18 July 1877, d. 28 July 1877
Elizabeth Paul Boyd b. 9 Jan 1879, m. 22 Dec 1901 to Lear Ruskin
     Almand
William Emmett Boyd b. 3 Dec 1881, d. 20 Aug 1904, single
Sara Clem Boyd b. 27 Apr 1884   [Teacher, now retired]
Angie Ann Boyd b. 15 Nov 1886, m. 18 May 1935 in Spartanburg, S.C.

to Joseph B. Hansen

Talulah Alma Boyd b. 5 Dec 1888, d. 30 July 1889

John Donald Boyd b. 2 Nov 1890, m. 19 May 1914 to Ysabel Lamar Middlebrook

Grover Cleveland Boyd b. 20 Dec 1892, d. 6 Mar 1897

Bonnie Prophett Boyd b. 1 May 1895, d. 7 Mar 1897

[This Bible is owned by the family of Mrs. Angie Boyd Hensen of Covington Ga. John Patterson Boyd was the son of Mary Wylie & Robert Patterson Boyd of Near old Hopewell A.R.P. Church in Chester Co., S.C.]

ROBERT PATTERSON BOYD

Robert Patterson Boyd m. 10 Aug 1820 to Mary Wylie in Chester Co., S.C.

Children

Infant child b. & d. 31 May 1821, bur. at Hopewell Church in Chester Co., S.C.

Margaret Boyd b. 18 Apr 1822, d. 1 Apr 1823, bur. at Hopewell Church in Chester Co., S.C.

John Patterson Boyd b. 10 Apr 1824 in Chester Co., S.C., m. 2 July 1846 to Sarah Paul Robinson

Martha Jane Boyd b. 16 Jan 1827, in Newton Co., Ga., d. Sep 1892 at Athens, Ga.

William Perry Boyd b. 16 Jan 1827, bapt. at Hopewell Church on 2nd Sunday in Jan 1829, d. single in 1865 while serving in CSA Army

Robert Watson Boyd b. 1 Dec 1830 in Newton Co., Ga., bapt. at Hopewell on 4th Sunday in June 1831, d. in Prison Camp in Va. in 1865, m. 18 Sep 1849 to Mary Anne Robinson by the Rev. Willis C. Norris, d. 6 June 1909 at her home in Newsite, Ala.

John Thomas Boyd b. 6 Dec 1832, d. 26 Apr 1905, m. 1st on 20 Dec 1859 to Susannah E. Thompson, dau. of Nancy Aiken & Samuel E. Thompson, m. 2nd to Zippora A. Thompson

Mary Susannah Boyd b. 2 Nov 1835, bapt. at Hopewell Church on 1st Sunday in May 1836

Eliza Matilda Boyd b. 22 Feb 1837, bapt. at Hopewell Church on 1st Sunday in May 1837, m. 22 Dec 1859 to James S. Gardner

Margaret Rosannah Boyd b. 2 Sep 1839, m. to William G. Lowery, M.D. of Athens, Ga.

Thomas Alexander Boyd b. 25 July 1841, m. 26 Sep 1865 to Mary Isabel Christian, dau. of Elizabeth Sappington & Presley F. Christian

[Several years ago the old tombstones of Robert Patterson Boyd and his wife, Mary Wylie Boyd were taken down (nobody thought to copy the dates on these old stones) and replaced by modern markers in the old Hopewell A.R.P. Church yard in Newton Co., Ga. New markers: Robert Patterson Boyd 1790-1849; Mary Wylie Boyd 1800-1880]

[This Bible is owned by the family of Mrs. Angie Boyd Hansen of Covington, Ga. It was brought from near old Hopewell Presbyterian

Church in Chester Co., S.C. to Newton Co., Ga. about 1825. One page is lost from the Bible, which was the page of the births and marriage of Robert Patterson Boyd to his wife, Mary Wylie. The marriage recorded above is on a separate page of the Bible.]

EDWARD BRACKEN

Edward Bracken b. 28 Jan 1812, m. 12 Feb 1835 to Sarah Rhodes b. 25 Dec 1813
    Children
Edward Jones Bracken b. 30 Nov 1835
Marcella Jane Bracken b. 22 Oct 1837
Martha Matilda Bracken b. 18 Mar 1840
Colorado Missouri b. 13 May 1842
America Louisa b. 10 July 1844
Henry Tomas Bracken b. 9 Sep 1846
Washington LaFayette b. 1848
Martin Luther b. 1851

[The name was spelled with an e and then an i for a while but settled down to the e finally. Edward is said to have assumed the Augustus as a middle name after he was grown. He was the son of James and Sarah (Jeffreys) Bracken who were married in Rowan Co., N.C. in 1794, moved about 1800 to East Tenn. and about 1820 to north Ala. The Brackens moved from New Castle Co., Del. to Orange Co., N.C. ca. 1754. The compiler is a grand-daughter of Martha Matilda Bracken above who m. Wm. V. Aldridge. Sarah Rhodes Bracken d. about 1854. Ed. m. 2nd to Catherine Rainwater and had: Jas., Aurora, David Hubbard, Persia Lee, John Allen b. 20 Dec 1868. The Bible is now owned by the compiler.]

SAMUEL BRACKEN

Samuel Bracken b. 1742, d. 1812, m. Martha Ector and Rebecca
    Children by Martha Ector
Jane b. 11 Aug 1767
Margaret b. 7 Mar 1769
Joseph b. 16 Sep 1771, m. 1st on 1 Jan 1795 to Lenny or Sina Womack
  m. 2nd on 10 June 1802 to Jenny Dixon, m. 3rd on 5 Jan 1841 to
  Nancy Hooper
John, Sr. b. 28 July 1773
John, Jr. b. 1 Aug 1775
Hannah b. 28 Aug 1777
Isabel b. 5 Aug 1779
Martha b. 30 Sep 1781
    Children by Rebecca
Sina b. 13 Jan 1801
Vasta [looks like U Yorky?] b. 12 Oct 1802
Agrippina b. 7 Sep 1804

[Saml. Bracken was a Rev. War soldier in N.C., having served under Capt. Williams in Col. Thos. Polk's regiment, the 4th N.C. Saml.

Bracken was possibly a son of John Bracken of Newcastle Co., Del. who migrated to Orange Co. ca. 1763. No will left but Thomas, Saml., Wm. & Isaac seem to have been sons. This Bible record belonged to Mrs. Wilson Bracken Robins of Lexington, N.C. and on her death went to her dau., Mrs. Pancake of Staunton, Va.]

W. C. BRACKEN

W. C. Bracken, son of Henry & Minerva Bracken, the children of James & Sally Bracken and Stephen & Patsy Daniel, respectively.

James Bracken, d. about aged 80 yrs., m. Sally Jeffrey, d. about aged 90 yrs.
Stephen Daniel, bur. at Ball Nob, m. Patsy Reaves Daniel, bur. at Ball Nob
Henry Bracken b. Dec 1799 in N.C., d. 11 Apr 1846 of Dispepsia, bur. at Ball Nob (Head Stone), m. to Minerva [Daniel] Bracken d. 26 Oct 1857 of Congestive Chill, bur. at Ball Nob. Both were Methodist. Henry was a school teacher & member of M.E.S. Church. Their children
John D. B. Bracken b. 25 Sep 1830, d. 1851, of Consumption, bur. at Ball Nob (Head Stone LC)
W. C. Bracken b. 1831 in Oakville, Methodist, m. 1st in 1854 to F. E. Bracken, d. 1862, m. 2nd to Sally Ann Landeres, Baptist.
Tons E. Bracken b. 1833, d. 1861 of Consumption, bur. at Ball Nob (Head Stone LC)
Stev I. Bracken (S. J.) b. 1835, d. 1882 of Congestion, bur. at Waco, Texas
L. D. Bracken b. 1836, d. 1904
Henry (Henri) Etta Bracken b. 1840 at Town Creek, d. 1861 of Congestion, bur. at Ball Nob (Head Stone LC), m. J. D. Kerr
Joe B. Bracken b. 1838, d. same day

    Children of W. C. & F. E. Bracken (four)
Eveleen O. Bracken b. 11 Aug 1855
Henry Etta Bracken b. 8 Nov 1857, Baptist
Flora V. Bracken b. 19 Sep 1860, d. 1862
    Children of W. C. & Sally Ann Bracken
Mary R. E. Bracken b. 2 June 1872, Baptist [less than 9 mos. before birth of sibling]
Leannah Bracken b. 26 Feb 1873, Baptist
Ned Bracken b. 1 Apr 1874
Solin G. Bracken b. 19 Sep 1875

[Copied from Bible in possession of Anna Ethridge, Town Creek, Ala.]

JAMES BRACKIN

James Brackin b. 7 Feb 1781, d. 19 Dec 1850, m. 20 Nov 1806 to Jane Clark b. 2 Feb 1788, d. 25 Feb 1850
    Children

Melinda b. 17 Aug 1807, d. 3 July 1837, m. 6 July 1826 to Joseph G.
   Meador
Betsy Sevier b. 25 Mar 1810, m. Samuel Wallace
Louisa C. b. 19 May 1813, d. 4 Feb 1851, m. F. M. Gaines
Granville b. 10 May 1816, m. 3 Feb 1842 to Lucy Ann Coakley b. 17
   June 1826
        Grandchildren
James B. [Brackin?] Meador b. 6 June 1827, d. Dec 1853
Thomas G. Meador b. 23 Jan 1832
Granville P. Gaines b. 4 June 1834
Mary Jane Brackin b. 21 June 1843
Melinda Sevier Brackin b. 25 July 1845
John Lardner Brackin b. 1 Sep 1847
Granville Benjamin Brackin b. 31 Dec 1853

[This record was copied from the Bible of Granville Brackin above
who passed it on to his son, Detcher Brackin, Gallatin, Tenn., sent
to the compiler by Mrs. H. B. Brackin, Nashville, Tenn. in 1957.]

                        OWEN BRADSHAW

Owen Bradshaw b. 29 Sep 1808
Ephraim b. 9 July 1810
John b. 18 June 1812
Mary b. 18 Aug 1817
William b. 15 Feb 1814

[These names were given as part of a Bible record by John Bradshaw
and sworn to Sep 1850]

Sarah E. Bradshaw b. 29 Mar 1837
Mary A. Bradshaw b. 24 Jan 1840
Elizabeth J. Bradshaw b. 5 Feb 1842
Rebecca C. Bradshaw b. 9 May 1844
Thomas J. Bradshaw b. 28 Sep 1846
John A. Bradshaw b. 18 July 1849
George Wm. Bradshaw b. 26 Mar 1852

[Photostats of above record are owned by W. D. Herring, Wilmington,
N.C.]

                        MOSES BRADSHER

Moses Bradsher m. Martha
        Children
Abner b. 2 Sep 1778
Betty b. 10 Oct 1780
Jesse b. 3 Oct 1782
John b. 30 June 1784
Nancy b. 9 Apr 1786
James Oliver b. 16 Feb 1788
Richard J. b. 17 Dec 1789

Mary b. 5 Dec 1791
Eunice b. 30 Oct 1793
Vincent b. 23 Oct 1795
Patsy [b. prob. 1797]
Hamaah b. 17 Sep 1799
Frances b. 27 Oct 1801
Moses, Jr. b. 14 Jan 1804

"Father deceased. Moses d. 9 Sep 1820
Mother d. 12 June 1840"

[Moses Bradsher came from England according to Mrs. Martha (Taylor)
Thomas, Semora, N.C. Bible owned by Mr. Arch Thomas, Semora, N.C.
Had this copy Aug 1962]

JOSIAH BRANDON

Josiah Brandon m. 10 Oct 1817 to Martha Sample
Sarah A. Brandon m. 16 Jan 1838 to R. D. Roy
Henry Sample m. Sep 1852 to Martha Hawkins
Hugh Sample m. 1 Apr 1852 to Fanny Westmoreland

Jas. S. Brandon b. 10 Aug 1818
Rachel G. Brandon b. 20 Aug 1820
Sarah A. Brandon b. 29 June 1822
Martha B. Roy b. 29 Mar 1840, dau. of Sarah & Richard Roy
Jas. Sample, Sr. b. 27 Feb 1775
Mary Sample b. 20 Apr 1775
Jas. Sample b. 5 Oct 1794 [ch. of Jas. & Mary Sample]
Ann Sample b. 22 Feb 1796 [ch. of Jas. & Mary Sample]
Martha Sample b. 23 Sep 1797 [ch. of Jas. & Mary Sample]

Rachel Brandon d. 7 Oct 1821
Josiah H. Brandon d. 7 Aug 1822
Jas. S. Brandon d. 11 Aug 1824
Richard D. Roy d. 19 Aug 1840
Mary Sample died fall of 1799
Jas. Sample, Sr. d. 3 Apr 1816
Ann Carroll, formerly Ann Sample, d. Oct 1823
Richard D. Roy d. 1 Aug 1840
Sarah Ann Elisha Roy d. 26 Jan 1843, consort of R. D. Roy & dau.
  of Josiah H. & Martha Brandon
Fannie Caroline Sample, wife of Hugh McVay Sample, d. 21 Nov 1910

[This Bible owned by Jesse W. Sample, son of Hugh, Tupelo, Miss.
Copied by Mrs. E. S. Gragory, Tuscumbia, Ala.]

JOSEPH BRASHEAR

Joseph Brashear, son of William, b. 26 Sep 1770, m. 1st to Elizabeth Cummings d. 7 Oct 1819, m. 2nd to Charlotte (Wheeler) Brashear
b. 9 May 1787, d. 22 Nov 1855

Children by Elizabeth Cummings
Nacy b. 25 Nov 1787
Peter C. b. 9 June 1801
Samuel b. 21 Sep 1808
Richard b. 12 Mar 1811
William b. 25 Dec 1813
James b. 9 Aug 1817
Joseph b. 12 Sep 1819, d. July 1854 in Indiana aged 36 yrs.
    Children by Charlotte Wheeler
Thomas b. 23 Nov 1820, d. 18 June 1895
Jabez b. 1 July 1822
Charlotte b. 19 Nov 1824, d. 21 May 1875 [m. James R. Dowell. The
    Dowells were from Md., moved south & west with the Brashears.]
Horace, (Jr.) b. 20 July 1827, d. 30 July 1854 in Ind. aged 27 yrs.
Sally Ann b. 6 July 1829, d. 2 Jan 1842

James H. L. d. in Tex. in 1842 on an expedition to Santa Fe, N.M.
    [May be James above, b. 1817.]

[Joseph Brashear was a native of Brownsville, Pa. His father, william, moved to Ky. when Joseph was 10 yrs. old. The Breckenridge,
(Ky.) News had his obituary in the issue of 26 July 1856. He died
in the home of his son-in-law, James R. Dowell. This old family
Bible belonged to Mrs. William Frymire, Ekron, Ky.]

[All the Brashears in this work descend from a common ancestor,
Benoit Brassieur and Mary, his wife, who went to Va. in 1636, Nan-
semond Co. Finding Va. unfriendly to non-Church of England settlers, they moved to Prince Georges Co., Md. in 1653. Here Benoit
got his denization papers and anglicized his name to Benjamin Brashear. Benjamin Brashear was a Commissioner of Pr. Geo. Co. and
died in 1658. Mary remarried to Thos. Sterling. Benjamin's old
home is still standing in Md. and is located on what is called The
Cliffts. It is undoubtedly one of the oldest homes in America.]

WILLIAM G. BRASHEAR

William G. Brashear b. 13 Jan 1807 in Spartenburg Dist., S.C.
Rosa Brashear b. 22 Sep 1809 in Spartenburg Dist., S.C.

Millicent Brashear b. 15 Sep 1826 in Spartenburg Dist., S.C.
Coleman Brashear b. 18 Mar 1829 in Ralls Co., Mo.
Mary Jane Brashear b. Sep 1831
Nancy C. Brashear b. 13 Jan 1832 in Ralls Co., Mo., d. in infancy
James W. Brashear b. in Adams Co., Ill.
Thomas A. Brashear b. 30 Mar 1840 in Adams Co., Ill.
Susan A. Brashear b. 18 May 1843 in Adair Co., Mo.
Richard M. Brashear b. 13 Jan 1846 in Adair Co., Mo.
Cynthia A. Brashear b. 11 Sep 1848 in Adair Co., Mo.
Twins, John W. & Martha E. Brashear b. 26 July 1851 in Adair Co.,
    Mo.
George B. Brashear b. 26 July 1855 in Adair Co., Mo.

[Taken from Bible belonging to Cynthia Bosley]

NACY BRASHEARS

Nacy Brashears b. 17 Apr 1734, [d. 1807 in Ky.], m. Pamelia Bra-
shears [probably an Edmonston]
    Children
Mary b. 1 Mar 1760
Elizabeth b. 12 July 1761
Ann b. 23 Mar 1763
Thomas C. b. 10 Nov 1764, [m. Frances Berry]
Samuel b. 12 Oct 1766
Ignatius b. 28 Mar 1768, [m. Sylvia Orme]
Robert b. 31 Aug 1769
Archibald Edmonston b. 2 Nov 1771
Levi b. 14 Nov 1773
Walter b. 11 Feb 1776 [He was a doctor, d. 1860 in La.]
Joseph b. 9 Dec 1778
Dennis b. 13 Aug 1780
Ruth b. 13 Sep 1782

[Nacy Brashears was a native of Prince Georges Co., Md. He moved
to Ky. in 1784 and settled on Salt River near the town of Shepards-
ville. He was a farmer. His son, Walter, became a famous doctor.]

ROBT. SAML. BRASHEARS

Robt. Saml. Brashears b. 20 Aug 1731
Phoebe Brashears b. 8 June 1738
    Children
Philip Brashears b. 17 Dec 1755
Margaret Brashears b. 27 May 1758
Isaac Brashears b. 23 Oct 1760
Samuel Brashears b. 6 Aug 1763
Pagay [Peggy?] Brashears b. 8 July 1769
Phoebe Brashears b. 8 July 1769
Rebeccah Brashears b. 9 Jan 1771
Nancy Brashears b. 11 May 1773
Mamey [Mary?] Brashears b. 13 Mar 1776
Basil Brashears b. 8 May 1781

[This Bible is owned by Willie Brashears, Holly Springs, Tenn., a
descendant of Basil Brashears and Robt. Saml. Brashears. A copy of
this Bible was sent to the compiler in 1937 by Mrs. Frances Hood
Smith, then regent of the D.A.R. chapter in Kingston, Tenn. A number of the descendants of Robt. Saml. Brashears in Roane Co., Tenn.
have copies of this Bible Record. There is a family cemetery on
Robt. Saml. Brashears' old property and Robt. Saml. & wife, Phoebe,
are buried there. His tombstone is standing with dates but none
can be deciphered for Phoebe. There are many old stones that have
fallen down and are broken and the data on them lost.]

SAMPSON BRASHEARS

Sampson Brashears b. 21 Dec 1788, [son of Samuel Brashears], m. in
1817 in Blountsville, Tenn. to Margaret Bright
    Children
Isaac b. 1818
John b. 1819
James b. 1821
Sarah b. 1822
Elizabeth b. 1823
Ezekial b. 1825
Sampson, Jr. b. 1826
Robert b. 1830, never married
Louisa b. 1832
Harvey G. b. 1835
Hezekiah b. 1842
Jesse C. b. 1837 [lived in Lowell, Ark.]
William R. b. 1839

[Sampson Brashears was the son of Samuel Brashears. This record
was sent by a descendant of Sampson, from Ark. some years ago.]

SAMUEL BRASHEARS

Samuel Brashears b. 6 Aug 1763, d. 25 Dec 1829, m. 25 Feb 1786 to
Margaret Eakin b. 18 Aug 1762
    Children
Margaret b. 9 Dec 1786
Sampson b. 21 Dec 1788
Robert S. b. 13 Apr 1793 [prob. named Robert Samuel Brashears after
  his grandfather]
Isaac b. 1 Jan 1796
Joseph b. 25 May 1800
Phoebe b. 8 Mar 1803
John b. 3 Mar 1805
Ezekiel b. 21 June 1807

[Samuel was a lieutenant in the Rev. War under Capt. Thos. Vin-
cens (?). After his death in Sullivan Co., Tenn., his widow and
most of his children moved to Ky. from where his widow applied for
a pension on the strength of her husband's service.]

BASIL BREASHEARS [BRASHEARS]

Basil Breashears b. 8 May 1781, d. 10 Aug 1826, m. 3 Aug 1800 to
Pagey Horton b. 16 Sep 1776
    Children
Robert b. 1 June 1801
Polly b. 29 Dec 1802
Basil b. 16 Dec 1804
Joseph b. 29 Dec 1806
George W. Camonel b. 27 Dec 1807

Phebe b. 25 Nov 1809
Polly b. 5 Nov 1811
Lorenzo Dow b. Sep 1813
Pagy [Margaret] b. 29 Apr 1816, d. 29 Sep 1856

Joseph d. 28 May 1863 near Lebanon, Ky. [compiler's grandfather]
Margaret Riggs d. 11 Aug 1863
Sarah Jane d. 5 July 1869

CHARLES BROADFOOT

Chas. Broadfoot b. 17 Aug 1774, son of Andrew & May (Conning)
Broadfoot of Wightonshire, Gallway, North Bitian, emigrated to
Petersburg, Va. in early life, moved to Rawleigh Parish, Amelia
Co., Va. and thence to Fayetteville, N.C. in 1811, d. in Fayette-
ville on 3 June 1833.
Purefee Barrett Booker, dau. of Major Tom B. Wilson, Amelia Co.,
Va. b. 24 Aug 1779, d. 26 Sep 1807, bur. at her father's
    Children
Andrew b. 30 Nov 1796, d. Ky., at Tom B. W. Broadfoot's
Tom B. W. b. 24 Oct 1798
May Catherine b. 1 Sep 1799, m. 12 Mar 1818 to J. Baker
M. Chas. b. 1 Dec 1800, d. 1 Dec 1800
Geo. L. b. 1 Dec 1801
Martha P. b. 2 Feb 1804, d. 5 Oct 1808, bur. with her mother
Wm. Gillies b. 5 Mar 1806, m. 3 Feb 1842 in Fayetteville, N.C. to
    Frances Rebecca Wetmore
Jas. Freeland b. 5 Mar 1806
    Children of Wm. G. & Frances Rebecca
Chas. Wetmore b. 13 Nov 1842, bapt. by Rev. J. B. Buxton at St.
    John's Church 5 or 6 Sundays afterwards, m. 18 Dec 1877 at St.
    John's Church to Kate Huske, dau. of Wm. & May C. Huske
Geo. Badger b. 2 Oct 1844
Wm. Willson b. 15 Mar 1847
Thos. Wetmore b. 3 Apr 1850
Jas. Baker b. 18 Jan 1853
Andrew b. 9 Apr 1855
Francis Hinsdale b. 28 Apr 1857
John Barrett b. 31 Aug 1859
May Catherine b. 10 Dec 1861
Eliz. Hinsdale b. 10 July 1866, d. 24 Sep 1866

ALLEN BROOKS

Allen Brooks, son of Joab & Catherine Campbell Brooks, b. 14 July
1793, d. 19 Oct 1866, m. 11 Feb 1817 to Narcissa Carter b. 16 Nov
1804, d. 9 Oct 1860
    Children
Phoebe C. b. 19 July 1819
Charity b. 27 Aug 1821
Catherine b. 25 Apr 1823
Joab Martin b. 15 July 1826
Elizabeth b. 22 Apr 1828

Eleanor b. 14 Oct 1830
Allison Perry b. 29 May 1835
Mary Alice b. 29 May 1835
John Micajah b. 24 July 1837
Margaret Ann b. 15 Dec 1839
Medarena b. 15 Dec 1844
Georgianna

[This record from Mabel White, Starkville, Miss., a descendant.]

ELISHA BROOKS

Elisha Brooks b. 16 Apr 1761, d. 3 Nov 1804 in Edgefield, S.C., m.
12 Jan 1786 to Nancy Butler b. 27 Sep 1765 [See Capt. James Butler
Bible record below]
        Children
Obediah b. Mar 1788, d. young
Matilda b. 15 Jan 1792 [m. John Robinson]
Frances b. 21 Nov 1793, d. young
Lavinia b. 13 Aug 1796
Elizabeth b. 17 Jan 1798
Edna b. 18 Jan 1800
Stanmore Butler b. 17 Dec 1802
Mary Simpson b. 15 Jan 1804
William Butler b. 14 May 1806

[Elisha Brooks had a first name William as shown in Rev. War records for him.]

FRANCIS MARION BROOKS

Father: Francis Marion Brooks, 1844-1891
Mother: Egeria Lorena (Willis) Brooks
Uncles: Oran Dewey Brooks, 1845-1925; Winfield Scott Brooks
Grandfather: Eri Morley Brooks, 1824-1874
Grandmother: Eleanor Grain Brooks, 1822-1857
Great Grandfather: Benjamin Franklin Brooks, 1796-1842
Great Grandmother: Mary Smith Brooks, 1800-1896

William D. Brooks, 1835-1852
Joseph C. Brooks, 1839-1854
Lodosca, wife of B. F., 1804-1882
Harry N., 1853-1858
Rebecca, 1843-1859
Oliver, 1830-1853
Mary, 1824-1850
Phoeian d. 1835

[From Family Bible of Miss Alma Egeria Brooks, Baton Rouge, La.]

JACOB REED BROOKS

Jacob Reed Brooks, son of Stephen & Rachel (Martin) Brooks, b. 10
May 1787, d. 22 Mar 1872, m. 4 Nov 1819 to Sarah Connally Gaddis b.
9 June 1800
    Children
Lawrence Mannering b. 1820
Emily Gaddis b. 22 May 1822
Levi Wellborn b. 3 Sep 1823
Cincinnatus Ney b. 16 Apr 1825
Sarah Jane b. 7 June 1827
Geo. McIntosh Troupe b. 1 June 1829
Louisa Black b. 11 Mar 1831
Atlanta Georgianna b. 16 Oct 1835
DeWitt Clinton b. 20 Oct 1834
Kosciusco Byron b. 20 Dec 1836
Aeneas Leonidas b. 19 Sep 1838
Roxanna [prob. Rosanna] b. 6 May 1841
Tamerlane Xenophen b. 9 Nov 1844

[Jacob Reed Brooks lived in Cobb Co., Ga. He was the 1st repre-
sentative of Cobb Co. in the state legislature. He had many other
honors. See THE FIRST HUNDRED YEARS OF COBB CO., GA. By Temple.
Jacob Reed Brooks, son of Stephen Brooks, was a grandson of John
Brooks who d. in Wilkes Co., Ga. 1782 with will and his 2nd wife,
Lydia. John Brooks was a son of Jacob Brooks, Sr. The latter was
the son of Wm. Brooks & wife, Sara, and was baptised in Christ
Church, Middlesex Co., Va. 1702. Jacob Brooks, Sr. d. in S.C.
1770-74 with will. His wife was Rosanna Sheppard prior to their
marriage. Mrs. Groves says that Rosanna was a widow. The Bible
record was sent by a desc., Mrs. Nina Brooks Groves, Hillsboro,
Texas.]

JAMES BROOKS

James Brooks b. 1772, d. 1838, m. 8 Mar 1804 to Nancy Brooks b.
1786, d. 1835
    Children
Godfrey I. b. 24 Dec 1804
Thomas R. b. 25 Feb 1807, m. 20 Oct 1835 to Sirena Shannon
Hannah I. b. 24 Apr 1809
Margaret C. b. 20 Dec 1811
James Irvin b. 29 Nov 1813, d. 2 Nov 1878, m. 1st to Mary Jane
   Lindsey, dau. of Dennis & Jane Lindsey, b. 10 Nov 1826, m. 2nd
   on 22 Mar 1853 to Mary Minerva Tuttle d. 19 Feb 1854, m. 3rd on
   2 Dec 1866 to Sarah A. Hightower d. 7 Nov 1878.
Johnson H. b. 13 Aug 1815
Clarissa E. b. 25 Aug 1818
Alpha C. b. 5 Aug 1821 (twin)
Samuel F. b. 5 Aug 1821 (twin)
John W. S. b. 28 Jan 1822
Margaret C. 15 Dec 1826 [may be death date or second child of same

name]
Hannah I. 6 Mar 1828 [same confusion]
Charles W. Brooks b. 13 Dec 1829
Mary A. Brooks b. 22 Apr 1832
        Children of James Irvin & Mary Jane (Lindsey) Brooks
John Fletcher b. 11 Apr 1843
James Dennis b. 14 July 1845
        Children of James Irvin & Mary Minerva (Tuttle) Brooks
Clarissa I. b. 9 Feb 1854
Thomas W. I. b. 4 Mar 1855
Susan C. b. 10 Sep 1857
Mary Frances b. 24 Feb 1860
        Children of James Irvin & Sarah A. (Hightower) Brooks
Charles W. d. 20 May 1875
Jackson S. Brooks d. 23 July 1897
        Son of Thomas R. & Sirena (Shannon) Brooks
Alex. Johnson Brooks b. 20 Dec 182_ [not legible]

James Milton Byars & Mollie F. Brooks m. 11 Nov 1885
Thomas W. Brooks & Ettie Hamilton m. 18 Dec 1888
Charles Abner Young & Nettie Raymond Brooks m. 18 May 1898
        Children of Charles Abner & Nettie Raymond (Brooks) Young
Lena Young b. 14 Aug 1899
John Earle & James Irvin b. 29 Aug 1901
Alfred Leroy Young b. 10 Sep 1903
Beulah & Buford Young b. 23 Feb 1906
Price Jackson Young b. 27 Sep 1908
Charles Elmer & Velma Raymond Young b. 12 Oct 1911
        Children of James M. & Mollie F. (Brooks) Byars
Zola Byars b. 13 Jan 1887
Minnie Louise Byars b. 8 Sep 1889
Wilbur Irby Byars b. 11 Feb 1892

[This Bible now belongs to Mrs. C. A. Young (Nettie Raymond Brooks
above). Mollie F. Brooks & Thos. W. Brooks above may be brother
and sister of Mrs. Young, Rt. 2, Moulton, Ala.]

                    JOHN BROOKS

John Brooks b. 18 Jan 1750, d. 22 June 1835, m. Nancy Stuart b. 15
Jan 1751, d. 27 July 1826
        Children
Martha b. 1 Jan 1778
Mary b. 22 Oct 1779
William b. 30 Sep 1781
John b. 30 Sep 1783
Elizabeth b. 2 May 1785
Nancy b. 20 July 1788
Sarah b. 22 Nov 1790
Saml. Clifford b. 1 Jan 1794, d. 16 Nov 1861, m. Bessie Beaufort
        Children of Saml. Clifford & Bessie (Beaufort) Brooks
Eliz. Letitia b. 12 Nov 1820

Nancy Caperton b. 6 Dec 1822
John Cameron b. 15 June 1825
Saml. Houston b. 1 Jan 1829
Wm. Haley b. 9 June 1831
Redding LaFayette
Madison Somerville b. 23 Nov 1835
Madison DeKalb b. 29 Oct 1838
Andrew Jackson b. 8 Nov 1844
Sina Gentry b. 2 Oct 1847

[This record came originally from Mrs. Peoples, Dallas, Tex. It
was sent to Mrs. Ida Brooks Kellam, Wilmington, N.C. and by her, to
the compiler. This family of Brooks was from Augusta Co., Va.]

JOHN H. BROOKS

John H. Brooks, son of Nancy & Wm. Brooks, b. 2 July 1801, d. 21
Nov 1892, m. 13 May 1830 to Caroline Williams, dau. of Godfrey &
Sarah Williams, b. 26 July 18--, d.26 Nov 1892.
   Children
Sarah Ann b. 24 Apr 1831, m. 9 May 1848 to Geo. E. Knox
Jas. H. b. 29 Jan 1833, d. 12 Oct 1838
Jos. C. b. 12 Dec 1835, m. 1st on 29 Apr 1855 to Sarah Piggott, m.
   2nd on 20 Mar 1867 to Sophia B. Conekin
Wm. F. b. 16 Mar 1838, m. 11 Dec 1859 to Mary A. Gore
John S. b. 20 Oct 1840
Sophia S. Conekin b. 9 Dec 1848
   Children of Wm. F. & Mary A. (Gore) Brooks
Eliza C. b. 22 Sep 1861
Marietta b. 28 June 1864, d. 3 Sep 1868
Sarah E. Brooks b. 8 Dec 1868

Benj. G. Brooks d. 3 Sep 1849

[Bible owned by Miss Sally Betts Knox, Wilmington, N.C., sent by
Ida Brooks Kellam, Wilmington, N.C.]

JOSEPH DANIEL BROOKS

Dr. Joseph Daniel Brooks, son of Isham & Lezina Brooks, b. 21 May
1814, d. 25 Dec 1868, m. to Teresa Maria Sikes, dau. of John &
Elizabeth Sikes, b. 12 Oct 1811
   Children
Robert Augustus Brooks b. 26 Sep 1842, d. 23 Dec 1862
James Henry Brooks b. 27 Sep 1844
Joseph Wiley Brooks b. 23 Apr 1847, d. 5 Sep 1866
Captain James Henry Brooks b. 12 Jan 1850, m. 7 Jan 1873 to Anna M.
   Moore, dau. of L.M. & M.G. Moore, b. 15 Sep 1854
William Sidney Brooks b. 11 June 1852
   Children of Capt. James Henry & Anna M. (Moore) Brooks
Edgar Roland Brooks b. 11 P.M. 14 Feb 1874
Rosa Clifford Brooks b. 5:30 A.M. 5 Sep 1876

Preston Brooks b. 23 July 1881 [Dr. Robert Preston Brooks of University of Georgia]
Roland Edgar Brooks and Rosa Clifford Brooks were christened by
Rev. W. R. Foote on 30 June 1877.

[Bible records from the sheets sent by Dr. R. P. Brooks of Athens,
Ga.]

JOSIAH BROOKS

Josiah Brooks b. 6 Apr 1796, d. 4 Oct 1895, m. 20 May 1819 in
Chatham Co., N.C. to Ruth Terrell Hunter b. 22 Sep 1803 in Chatham
Co., N.C., d. 20 Feb 1895
    Children
Cornelia Brooks b. 19 Jan 1820
Jas. Hunter Brooks b. 19 Jan 1822
Wm. T. Brooks b. 26 Nov 1826
Lucius A. Brooks b. 25 May 1828
Isaac N. Brooks b. 28 Oct 1830
Philip A. Brooks b. 4 Feb 1832
Jos. J. Brooks b. 8 Sep 1841
Benj. F. Brooks b. 6 May 1838
Thos. A. J. Brooks b. 7 Mar 1844
Carolyn Z. Brooks b. 21 Oct 1847

[Ruth Terrell Hunter was the dau. of Jas. Hunter & Sarah Eliz.
Brooks & a 1st cousin of her husband, Josiah Brooks. Record sent
by Ida Brooks Kellam, Wilmington, N.C. Bible owned by Mrs. J. A.
Beall, Atlanta, Ga.]

MICAJAH BROOKS

Micajah Brooks, 1787-1851 & Charity Brooks, 1789-1864
    Children
Madison Micajah Brooks, b. 17 Sep 1813, d. 5 Sep 1890, m. 19 Mar
    1834 to Nancy Barry (Barrie) d. near Forney on 19 Dec 1878 aged
    60 yrs., 9 mos., & 3 days. [b. 16 Mar 1818]
Thomas B. Brooks
William C. Brooks
Matthew Brooks
Jane C. Brooks [Mrs. Roby]
    Children of Madison Micajah & Nancy Barry Brooks
Mary Eliza Brooks b. 1 Jan 1833, d. 13 Oct 1855
Shadie Brooks b. 22 Mar 1837, d. 1 Aug 1861, m. 1 Nov 1855 to William B. Augustus
Samuel Barry Brooks b. 24 Mar 1839, d. 29 June 1862, a confederate
    soldier
Charles O. Brooks b. 9 May 1841 [Lived in Greenville, Tex. & has
    descendants there now]
John (Jack) Benjamin Brooks b. 28 Mar 1843, d. 8 May 1864 in the
    War Between the States
James Knox Brooks b. 2 June 1845, d. at Forney 4 June 1917.

Petre Brooks b. 19 Sep 1849, d. 9 Jan 1894, m. 1880 to Mary West
Sallie Clarissa Brooks b. 30 Apr 1852, d. 9 Jan 1929
Micajah Madison Brooks b. 30 Mar 1856, d. 10 Jan 1934 in Dallas,
    Tex., m. Matty Jenkins. [Judge Brooks lived at 5533 Swiss Ave.,
    Dallas, Texas.]
William Armstead Brooks b. 17 Jan 1859, d. 16 Aug 1932, m. 18 Oct
    1897 to Blanch C. Lane

[Record of Mrs. H. L. Peoples, Dallas, Texas]

MRS. RICHARD PLEASANTON BROOKS

Dosie Head Brooks, dau. of William Henry & Nancy (Johnson) Head.
Her father was b. in S.C., moving to Ga. at an early age.

[Early in girlhood she married Richard Pleasonton Brooks, at the
time, a partner in banking business with Mrs. Brooks' father. Mr.
and Mrs. Brooks reside at Brooklyn, one of the finest types of
stately Southern mansions of ante-bellum days. This home, during
the war, was used as a hospital and as headquarters for doctors and
officers. Mrs. Brooks organized the James Monroe Chapter, D.A.R.
of Forsyth, Ga.]

SIMON BROOKS

Simon Brooks d. 19 Feb 1843, m. Phoebe Buffinton in S.C.
    Children
Maxey b. 18 Aug 1796
Ivy b. 8 Nov 1798
Candace b. 22 Dec 1800
Hiram b. 2 Dec 1802
Terrell b. 20 Feb 1806
Eliza b. 21 Jan 1810
Simeon b. 27 Mar 1830 [copying error? grandchild?]

[This record from Mrs. Ida B. Kellam, Wilmington, N.C.]

URI BROOKS

Uri Brooks b. 1757, m. Hannah
    Issue
Sophia Brooks b. 1784
Zaphua Brooks b. 1786
Delphus Brooks b. 1788
Clarice Brooks b. 1792
Phoenian Brooks b. 1794
Franklin Brooks b. 1796
Sophronius Brooks b. 1798
Hannah Brooks b. 1799
Valney Brooks b. 1802
Godwin Brooks b. 1806
Lodoiske Brooks b. 1807

Morley records in Uri Brooks' Bible
  Eri Morley b. 1787
  Betsey Morley b. 1779
  Matilda Morley b. 1781
  Miriam Morley b. 1785
  Roenzy Morley b. 1788
  Miriam Sprague b. 1732 [last name Sprague]

[This record is owned by Miss Alma E. Brooks, Baton Rouge, La. The
record was given her by her uncle, Oran Dewey Brooks. Sent to Mrs.
Ida Brooks Kellam, Wilmington, N.C.]

WILLIAM BROOKS, II

Wm. Brooks b. 1779, d. 13 July 1846, m. Mary Burleyson (Burleson),
dau. of David of Stanley Co., N.C.
      Children
John b. 2 Mar 1802, Mecklenburg Co., N.C.
Sarah b. 10 Sep 1805
Bedie Ann b. 26 Nov 1807
Wm., III b. 5 Feb 1812
Davidson b. 28 May 1818
Cullen b. 28 May 1818
Lucy
Lydia
Calvin b. 19 Dec 1825

WILLIAM JOHNSON BROOKS

Wm. Johnson Brooks b. 5 Feb 1861, m. 27 Aug 1879 in Blount Co.,
Ala. by S. C. Allgood to Florence Brooks nee Underwood b. 25 Mar
1863
      Children
Telula Frances b. 20 May 1880, d. 29 July 1882
Clinton Randolph b. 29 Sep 1881, d.
Edie Forest b. 29 Aug 1883
Laurence Austin b. 12 Jan 1886
Ernest Troy b. Dec 1887, d. 25 Aug 1888
Willie Ross b. 26 July 1889
Flossie Lee b. 21 Aug 1891
Gussie Homer b. 10 Nov 1893, d. 11 Oct 1918
Lillace Minerva b. 14 Sep 1895, d. 2 Feb 1934
Nellie May b. 20 Aug 1897
Albie Lena b. 26 June 1899, d. 14 Jan 1900
Paul Turner b. 6 Apr 1901
Florence d. 11 Dec 1934 [This may be the wife]

[Wm. Johnson Brooks was the son of William Bluford or Buford Brooks.
Wm. Buford was the son of Jacob Warren Brooks, Sr. who was b. in
Abbeville, S.C. in 1786 & moved to Ala. in 1816. Jacob Warren
Brooks was the youngest son of Jacob Brooks, Jr. & Mary, his wife.
Jacob Brooks, Jr. was a Refugee Soldier in Ga. during the Rev. War.

He died in S.C. in 1787 and his estate settlement is in Edgefield, S.C. Jacob Brooks, Jr. was son of Jacob Brooks, Sr., bapt. in Christ Church parish, Middlesex Co., Va. 1702, son of William Brooks and his wife Sara. The compiler descends from Jacob Warren et al.]

WM. TERRELL BROOKS

Wm. Terrell Brooks b. 9 Oct 1767, d. 24 Aug 1824, m. 5 Apr 1792 in Chatham Co., N.C. to Susannah Warren b. 11 Dec 1772 in Charles Co., Md., dau. of Edward Warren, d. Oct 1858
    Children
Sarah A. b. 20 Jan 1793
Ruth Terrell b. 6 Sep 1794
Josiah b. 6 Apr 1796, d. 4 Oct 1895
Lydia Briscoe b. 1 Mar 1798, d. 3 Sep 1833 in Madison Co., Tenn.
Rev. Warren b. 7 Jan 1800, d. 1841
Mary Ann b. 24 Feb 1802
Timothy Terrell b. 23 Feb 1804
Rebecca B. b. 11 Nov 1805
Martha B. b. 19 Jan 1808
Dr. Wm. Tell b. 6 Dec 1809
Susannah Warren b. 25 Jan 1812
Rev. Terrell b. 19 Jan 1815
Edward Warren b. 4 Dec 1816

[From Mrs. Ida Brooks Kellam, Wilmington, N.C.]

WYATT BROOKS

Wyatt Brooks b. 30 Sep 1805, d. 16 Oct 1878, m. 16 Apr 1829 to Margaret b. 7 Mar 1807, d. 19 Aug 1888
    Children
Mary Jane Brooks b. 6 Feb 1830, d. 25 June 1885, m. 2 Nov 1848 to Edwin R. Nelson d. Nov 1885
Lazina Catherine Brooks b. 2 Oct 1831, m. 30 Aug 1859 to M. C. Williford
Julia(n) Frances, dau., b. 24 Oct 1833, d. Nov 1893, m. 27 Mar 1851 to William R. Matthis
Martha Caroline Brooks b. 22 Jan 1843, m. 4 July 1865 to Robert Martin
Benjamin C. Brooks b. 21 Oct 185-, d. 10 Nov 1851 aged 20 days

Jourdain Williamson Slater, son of Jas. or Joel Slater & Elizabeth, his wife, b. 11 Oct 1829
Sarah Elisebeth Brooks b. 5 Mar 1838, d. 12 Feb 1911, m. 11 May 1858 to W. G. Bateman d. 1 July 1891
Thomas Sanford Brooks b. 1 Jam 1840, m. 11 Oct 1871 to Lizzie Battle
Robert Augustus Patrick Brooks, son of Joseph D. Brooks & T. M. Brooks, his wife, b. 26 Sep 1842
Mr. T. C. Williford d. 15 May 1875

Children of W. Y. (G.) & S. E. Bateman
William Clyde Bateman d. Sep 1917
Beulah Bateman Moulton d. 22 Dec 1937
Lena Bateman Pool d. 17 Dec 1940

ZACHARIAH SMITH BROOKS

Zachariah Smith Brooks was b. 18 May 1765, d. Apr 1848, m. 1st on
17 Dec 1776 to Elizabeth Butler [See the Bible record of Capt.
James Butler, this volume. That record states that Elizabeth was
b. 1766, making the above marriage date highly questionable.]
    Children
Whitfield b. 3 Feb 1790
Lucinda b. 3 Oct 1791
Betheland b. 20 Feb 1793
Nancy b. 30 Jan 1798

[Probably living in this home in 1846, was Betheland Foote, wife of
Capt. Wm. Butler and it is stated that she was b. 28 Dec 1764. Wm.
Elisha and Zach. Smith Brooks were brothers and both served in the
Rev. War. They married sisters, daughters of Capt. Wm. Butler.]

ABSALOM RHODES BROWN

Absalom Rhodes Brown b. 22 Dec 1816, d. 14 Dec 1892, m. Caroline A.
(Vaughan) b. 24 May 1824, d. 9 Jan 1898
    Children
Wm. H. b. 17 Feb 1843
Josephine A. b. 17 Dec 1844
Martha L. b. 7 Jan 1847
Sarah J. b. 7 May 1850
John Absalom b. 15 Apr 1852
Edward E. b. 11 Feb 1854
Coleman Isaac b. 16 Feb 1856
Agnes P. b. 10 Apr 1858
Julia B. b. 30 Oct 1863
Adni b. b. 16 Feb 1867 [could be Adam, according to Mr. Ladson]

[This Bible is owned by a Mr. Brown of Augusta, Ga. and was copied
by Jack Ladson, Jr., Moultrie, Ga.]

BENJAMIN BROWN

Benjamin Brown b. 16 Sep 1786, d. 18 Aug 1863, m. Eliz. Brown b. 12
Nov 1790. [questionable phrase may say "first wife"]
    Children
Wm. b. 25 Aug 1809
Joseph b. 19 Sep 1811
John b. Dec 1813
Mary Ann b. 19 Dec 1813, twin of John above
Jesse b. 14 ... 1816
Levney b. 11 Mar 1819

Davis b. 9 Apr 1821
Daniel C. b. 5 Apr 1824
Benj. R. b. 11 May 1826
Jas. Swift b. 10 Aug 1828

[Benj. Brown was a resident of Guilford Co., N.C. Eliz., wife of
Benj. Brown was the dau. of Josiah & Eliz. Loftin Lambeth. This
data given by owner of Bible, Wisdom Brown Aydelette, 1202 Spring
Garden St., Greensboro, N.C.]

JETHRO BROWN

Jethro Brown b. 23 Oct 1766, m. 28 May 1788 to Lucy W. Williamson
b. 18 Mar 1767
    Children
James b. 28 Mar 1789
Martha b. 1 May 1791
Bedford b. 6 June 1795
Mary b. 5 Sep 1797
William b. 17 Aug 1799
John Edmunds b. 26 Sep 1801
Thomas Jefferson b. 19 Dec 1803
Elizabeth Adkins b. 31 Aug 1806

Frederick W. b. 12 Sep 1874, d. 1943, Danville, Va.
Mary Wilson Brown b. 1 Oct 1883 at Rose Hill

Jethro Brown d. 10 Nov 1828
Lucy W. Brown d. 17 Sep 1834
Martha Foulks d. 4 Aug 1843
John Edmunds Brown d. 21 Sep 1846
Elizabeth Bethell d. Aug 1863
William Brown d. 4 Oct 1863
James Williamson Brown d. 1866
Col. John E. Brown d. 29 Jan 1896
Livingston Brown d. 13 Jan 1896 at "Rose Hill", N.C.
Dr. Bedford Brown d. 12 Sep 1897 in Alexandria, Va.

[Mr. Blalock, Probate Judge of Caswell Co., N.C., had this record.
It is a connection of the Williamson Family whose Bible appears
later in this work. Copied by compiler in Aug 1962]

JOSEPH BROWN

Joseph Brown b. 1 Jan 1731, d. 15 Oct 1815 on his home place near
Belton, S.C., m. 3 Aug 1756 to Mary Porter b. 26 July 1737, d. 12
Feb 1824 at her dau., Mary Duff's, home in Pendleton, S.C. They
are buried in the Sally Reed burying ground about 2 1/2 miles east
of Belton.
    Children
William b. 5 May 1757, m. Violet Dunlap at Dahlonega, Ga.
Hugh b. 23 Oct 1758, d. 8 May 1814, m. Anna Broyles b. Culpeper Co.

Joseph b. 28 Oct 1760, d. 28 Oct 1800, m. 1782 to Jemima Broyles b.
  Culpeper Co., Va. 16 June 1754
James b. 25 Nov 1763, d. 18 Jan 1830 in Pendleton, S.C., m. Nancy
  Burdine of Culpeper, Va., b. 1770, d. 10 Feb 1849
Margaret b. 29 Oct 1766, m. Benjamin Starrett, member of Lee's
  Legion
Violet b. 4 June 1768, d. May 1858 in Hall Co., Ga., m. 4 July 1789
  to William Reid b. 1763, d. 1843
Elizabeth b. 15 June 1770, m. 1789 on Broadmouth Creek, S.C. to
  James Reese b. 14 Oct 1747, d. 1840
David b. 17 Mar 1772, d. in Tallahatchie Co., Miss., m. Mary Ander-
  son
Mary b. 6 Apr 1774, d. 7 Sep 1822, m. James Duff [dau.: Mareb Duff
  see Telford-Duff-George Lineage]
Jane b. Sep 1776, m. John Hall
George B. 31 May 1779, d. Milledgeville, Ga., m. Mary Bell.
Frances b. 26 July 1781, d. 24 Jan 1836 in Alabama, m. Moses Leste

JOSHUA BROWN

Jushua Brown b. 29 Aug 1798, d. 30 Jan 1840 in Crawford Co., Ark.,
m. 14 July 1819 in Warren Co., Ky. to Elizabeth Hudspeth, dau. of
Aggie Hutchins & ... Hudspeth, b. 12 Jan 1793, d. 3 Mar 1848.
    Children
Ellender Louisa b. 20 Apr 1820 in Crawford Co., Ark., d. at Paris,
  Texas, m. 2 July 1840 to Thos. N. Aaron
Julia Ann b. 24 Nov 1821 in Lawrence Co., Ark., m. 20 Mar 1842 to
  Frederick Bryan Ragsdale
Elizabeth b. 4 Nov 1823 in Crawford Co., Ark., d. 22 June 1851 in
  Memphis, Tenn. of cholera, m. 16 Sep 1839 to Rufus M. Farrington
  who also d. 22 June 1851 in Memphis, Tenn. of cholera
James b. 26 Jan 1825, d. 20 Aug 1849
John b. 27 Jan 1827
Joseph b. 2 Feb 1830, d. after 1850
George Hudspeth b. 22 Jan 1832, d. 16 Dec 1893, Van Buren, Ark., m.
  1st on 22 Mar 1852 to Susan Tichenall, m. 2nd on 25 Dec 1866 to
  Emeline Wood
Mary Ann b. 23 Feb 1836, d. 8 Apr 1852

[Frederick Bryan Ragsdale was the son of Frederick Bryan Ragsdale
of Prince Geo. Co., Va. and his wife, Frances Louisa Wilkins, dau.
of William Wilkens of Pr. Geo. Co., Va. Fred. B. Ragsdale, Sr. was
the son of Capt. William Ragsdale & his wife, Mary Bryan, of Pr.
Geo. Co., Va. Capt. William was the son of Godfrey & Mary Ragsdale.
Godfreay Ragsdale was the son of Godfrey Ragsdale & his wife, a
widow, Mrs. Elizabeth (Baxter) Martin. Godfrey Ragsdale was the
son of Godfrey Ragsdale & wife, Rachel, of Va., and died in 1703.
The earliest Godfrey Ragsdale was the son of the immigrant, Godfrey
Ragsdale & his wife who came to Va., and settled at Jamestown.
Both were killed by Indians about 1644 and left an only child, God-
frey. This data came from a lady in N.C., probably, and are in
longhand.]

ROBERT EMERY BROWN

Robert Emery Brown b. 2 Mar 1852, d. 4 June 1904, m. 17 May 1891 in
Wayne Co., Ky. to Margaret (Maggie) Leaowner Weaver b. 30 Sep 1864,
d. 9 Aug 1934, dau. of Cornelius Ambrose Weaver b. 13 Nov 1842, d.
28 Aug 1910 and Julia Stevens Weaver b. 22 Sep 1845, d. 23 Mar 1915
    Children
Cornelius Edward Brown b. 17 June 1892, m. 3 Mar 1913 in Wayne Co.,
    Ky. to Mattie L. Hutchinson
Robert Clarence Brown b. 19 Sep 1893, m. 14 May 1916 in Wayne Co.,
    Ky. to Alta L. East
Louis Estal Brown b. 9 Mar 1896
Eula May Brown b. 16 Dec 1898, m. 12 Dec 1915 in Wayne Co., Ky. to
    Dr. John L. Hart
    Grandchildren
Homer Lee Brown b. 7 May 1915
Robert Estal Brown b. 22 Nov 1917, d. 2 June 1919
Dorotha Virginia Brown b. 9 May 1920
Margaret Brown b. 13 Sep 1922
James Edward Brown b. 29 Dec 1924
Shirley Jeanette Brown b. 8 Oct 1935

[Copied in 1956 by Mildred Dulaney from Bible owned by Ed Brown,
Mill Springs, Ky.]

W. H. BROWN

W. H. Brown b. 6 July 1809, m. 16 Sep 1830 in Halifax Co. to Mary
L. Vasseur b. 27 July 1813
    Children
Henry N. b. 16 Aug 1831
Ferdinand b. 6 Mar 1833
Mary Jane b. 22 Nov 1834
Wm. P. b. 27 July 1836
Charlotte A. b. 26 Sep 1838
Laura H. b. 6 Sep 1840
Julia F. b. 21 July 1842
Lucy R. b. 24 June 1844
Olivia B. b. lo Mar 1846
Edwin L. b. 21 May 1850
Leigh Olin b. 12 Feb 1856

Ferdinand d. 2 Aug 1836 in Halifax Co., N.C.
Wm. P. d. in Hillsboro, N.C. 14 Sep 1837
John Jones d. 27 May 1854 aged 62 yrs., 1 mo., & 5 days
Mary Ann Hopkins d. 12 Oct 1854
David F. Jones d. 25 May 1862 aged 24 yrs.
Jackson Jones d. 5 July 1865
Martha Beaty Jones d. 4 Jan 1872
Mary Beaty Jones d. 4 Mar 1872
Martha Jones d. 1873
Evalina Kerr Jones d. 3 July 1856 aged 1 yr.

Lizzie Jones Bobbitt d. 1 May 1873 aged 20 yrs.
Mary Martin Jones d. 1o May 1877 aged 56 yrs.
Anna Herron Jones d. 14 Feb 1875 aged 82 yrs.
Mrs. Charlotte Ann Vasseur d. 8 Sep 1856 in Hillsboro, N.C.
Wm. H. Brown d. 27 Mar 1866
Mary L. Brown d. 6 July 1868

[This Wm. H. Brown Bible owned by Miss Estelle Brown, Durham, N.C.]

DAVID BRUNSON

David Brunson d. 24 Oct 1784 aged 55 yrs., m. Elizabeth Brunson,
Sr. d. 24 Feb 17-- [not legible] aged 51 yrs, 4 mos. & 5 days.
    Children
William b. 29 Dec 1756
David, Jr. b. 1 Dec 1758, d. 24 Feb 17-- aged 20 yrs, 2 mos. & 24
  days
Daniel b. 27 Jan 1761
Jesse b. 16 Feb 1764, d. 16 Sep 1767, bur. Isaac Nelson Cemetery
Margaret b. 22 Aug 1766
Susanna b. 27 Sep 1768
George b. 6 Jan 1773
Elizabeth Cantey b. 19 Jan 1777

ROBERT D. BRUNSON

Robert D. Brunson b. 11 Dec 1841, (son of Randolph Platt Brunson,
d. 13 Jan 1852 in his 39th year and Susan Margaret Lanier b. 23 Mar
1824, d. 14 Aug 1911) m. Margaret Cornwell Hollingsworth b. 18--,
d. 13 Mar 1906, m. 2nd on 25 Jan 1881 to Artemas Lowe Brunson b.
28 Jan 1848, d. 15 Aug 1923, (son of Daniel D. Brunson, b. 30 Oct
1806, d. 11 Sep 1877, a Baptist minister, and Lucretia Lowe, his
second wife, b. 6 Oct 1811, d. 10 June 1883).
    Children [Robert D. & Margaret C. H. Brunson]
Randolph Platt Brunson, son, b. 10 Dec 1867, d. 19 Sep 1882
Susan Margaret Brunson, dau., b. 2 Feb 1869, d. 18 Nov 1943, m. 4
  Nov 1896 to J. Waller Hill, M.D.
Margaret Cornelia Brunson, dau., b. 6 June 1870, d. 31 July 1920,
  m. 20 Apr 1892 to Wade S. Cothran
    Children [Artemus L. & Margaret C. H. Brunson]
Cleora Thompson Brunson, dau., b. 17 Jan 1882, m. 25 Nov 1909 to
  Wallace Caldwell Tompkins
Lucretia Lowe Brunson, dau., b. 4 Sep 1883, d. 19 Oct 1905
Artemus Lowe Brunson, Jr., son, b. 28 Oct 1886, d. 7 June 1948, m.
  Aug 1916 to Virginia Louise Thomason

Artemus Lowe Brunson, III d. 15 Aug 1923
James S. Cothran b. 30 Oct 1895
Margaret Cornelia Cothran b. 25 Dec 1899

[Bible Record of Robert D. Brunson of Edgefield Co., S.C. owned by
the late Mrs. Susan Brunson Hill, Edgefield, S.C.]

WILLIAM BRUNSON

Wm. Brunson, [eldest son of David Brunson, above] d. 11 May 1803,
bur. Bradford Cemetery, m. 25 Jan 1785 to Elizabeth Powell who m.
2nd on 26 Dec 1803 to Hartwell Macon.
        Children [Wm. & Elizabeth Brunson]
Charlotte b. 23 Apr 1786
Elizabeth b. 23 Oct 1787
Wm. Leonard b. 6 Oct 1789, m. 1st on 20 Feb 1812 to Dorothy L.
    Pearce, d. 22 Jan 1816 aged 24 yrs., m. 2nd to Elia. Ann Bradford
    [had issue by second marriage also, names not listed in Bible]
James b. 5 Dec 1793, d. 27 Dec 1793
Sarah Ann b. 13 Jan 1801
Jane Hartwell b. 30 Oct 1802

        Children [Wm. L. & Dorothy L. Brunson]
Caroline Macon Brunson b. 27 Mar 1813
Wm. Hartwell Brunson b. 8 Sep 1814
Joseph R. Brunson b. and d. 20 Jan 1816

[This Bible is owned by Mrs. Walter T. Jones, 862 N. Waterman St.,
Jacksonville, Fla. David Brunson, Sr. d. 1784 and is buried in
Bradford Cemetery, Sumter Co., S.C. according to L. Andrea.]

WILLIAM BRUNSON

William Brunson of Edgefield, S.C. was a son of Daniel and Charity
Brunson from Sumter Co., S.C. b. 1 May 1800, d. 6 Mar 1846, m. 24
Feb 1820 to Sarah Thomas, dau. of James Thomas, b. 4 Mar 1804, d.
15 May 1855
        Children
James Thomas Brunson, son, b. 25 Dec 1821, d. 28 Apr 1822
Daniel Brunson, son, b. 5 Dec 1822, m. 21 Mar 1850 to Sarah Eliza-
    beth Moss
Samuel Thomas Brunson, [variation: Samuel A. Brunson, M.D.], son,
    b. 5 Nov 1825, m. 24 Jan 1855 to Nancy F. Morgan
Mary Ann Mercy Brunson, [variation: Mercey], dau., b. 29 Dec 1827,
    m. 2 Feb 1847 to John H. Moss
William Wallace Brunson, son, b. 7 Dec 1829, m. 23 Dec 1851 to Mar-
    tha E. Robinson
Elizabeth Helen Brunson, dau., b. 29 Dec 1831, m. 24 Apr 1851 to
    Elihu K. Branch
Sarah Brunson, dau., b. 8 Oct 1833, m. 28 May 1856 to Henry W.
    Griffin
Charles Augustus Brunson, son, b. 29 June 1837, m. 24 Jan 1861 to
    Mary E. Webber
        Grandchildren
William Malichi Moss, grandson, b. 29 Dec 1847
Matthew Edgar Moss, grandson, b. 18 Sep 1849
John Henry Moss, grandson, b. 3 July 1851
Sarah Elizabeth Moss, granddaughter, b. 18 Jan 1853
Mary Virginia Moss, granddaughter, b. 4 Dec 1854

WILLIAM HARTWELL BRUNSON

William Hartwell Brunson, Methodist Minister, b. 8 Sep 1814, d. 23
June 1869, m. 7 July 1841 to Emily Henrietta Anderson b. 22 Feb
1823, d. 27 Apr 1912
       Children
William Edward Anderson, son, b. 15 Apr 1842, d. 13 Oct 1864 from
   wounds received in Va. while in the Confederate Army
Elizabeth Ervin Brunson, dau., b. 2 May 1844
Mary Eloise Brunson, dau., b. 5 Apr 1846, m. 26 Feb 1863 to Henry
   Harvey Kinder
Caroline Dorothy Brunson, dau., b. 6 Apr 1848, m. 1st on 16 Apr
   1862 to Samuel Edward McIntosh, m. 2nd on 4 Dec 1884 to W. D.
   Nelson
Henry Bascombe Brunson, son, b. 19 Apr 1850, m. 26 Dec 1871 to Mar-
   garet L. Reardon who d. 8 Mar 1889
Robert Soule Brunson, son, b. 24 June 1852, m. 31 Jan 1878 to Mary
   McCauley
Susan Jane Carter Brunson, dau., b. 17 May 1854
Wesley Bradford Brunson, son, b. 15 June 1861, m. 22 Mar 18-- to
   Maggie Sandifer
Emma Lorena Brunson, dau., b. 1 Oct 1863, d. 11 Feb 1889 in China,
   m. M. Utsey, Methodist Missionary
Margaret Willie Brunson, dau., b. 10 May 1866, d. 25 Aug 1866

[This record was made from a copy of the original and seems to have
left out a child: Ervin E. Brunson who m. Marie Hepborn/Hepburn.

The graves of the Rev. W. H. Brunson and his wife, along with many
members of the family, are at the Bethel Methodist Church. No estate settlement for him is found in Sumter, S.C. and very likely,
since he died in the Bethel Church Parsonage, he had no estate save
a personal one. He had owned some slaves, but these had been set
free by the Confederate War surrender. See the estate of William
Leonard Brunson, will signed 14 Sep 1866. Before this estate was
settled, William Hartwell Brunson died. The names of his children,
above, are shown as receiving a share of the estate of their grandfather, William Leonard Brunson.]

WILLIAM BUFORD

John S. Buford b. 17 Oct 1783, m. 15 Sep 1807 to Sarah
     Children
Ashford b. 11 June 1808
Mariah b. 4 Oct 1810

Sarah Buford d. 3 Oct 1814
Mary Buford, dau. of William & Martha Buford, b. Feb 1804

[Mrs. B. B. Lane of Chapel Hill, N.C. (1958) is a descendant and
gives the following: Mary Buford m. Jesse A. Cooper 29 July 1825.
She d. 26 Mar 1882. Mary Buford was the dau. of Wm. Buford of S.C.
a Major in the Rev. War in S.C. In addition to the two children
given above, William Buford had a son named Simeon.]

HAWKINS BULLOCK, SR.

Hawkins Bullock, Sr. d. 1 Nov 1833, m. 12 Mar 1789 in Union Co.,
S. C. to Frances Roy Gordon, d. 17 July 1837.
    Children
John Gordon b. 3 Jan 1790, d. 4 Apr 1835
Mary Wyatt b. 10 Nov 1791, m. 5 Oct 1813 to Richard R. Sims
Alexander Gordon b. 13 Feb 1797, m. 1 Feb 1818 to Milly Sorrells
Nathaniel H. b. 10 Dec 1798, m. 3 Jan 1820 to Letty Colbert
Wm. Gordon b. 27 Sep 1802, m. 6 Nov 1823 to Eleanor Sorrells
Louisa Nance b. 31 Dec 1804
Frances Roy b. 12 Dec 1806, m. 28 Dec 1826 to Hiram Hampton
Richard Henley b. 21 Oct 1810, m. 21 Jan 1836 to Mary H. R. Griffin
Harlow H. Bullock [not called son] b. 3 Jan 1812
Thos. Gordon Bullock [not called son] b. 16 May 1812
Hawkins Sherman Bullock [not called son] b. 23 Dec 1812
    [L. Andrea comments, "I know one is a son & it is possible
    that the original copyist got the yrs. incorrect."]

Thos. Gordon m. 25 May 1795 to Lydia Prestage
Wyatt Bullock m. 6 June 1803 to Eliz. Allen
Hardy Bullock m. 16 June 1808 to Mary Doherty
Susannah Bullock m. 11 Apr 1811 to Geo. A. Gordon
Nathan N. Bullock m. 3 Nov 1821 to Selasty Colbert
Thos. B. Bullock m. 19 Dec 1837 to Nancy Jackson
Alfred Bullock m. 2 Apr 1839 to Sarah E. Jackson

[Bible owned in 1930 by N. C. Bullock, Danielsville, Ga. Hawkins
Bullock, Sr. went from Union Co., S.C. to Oglethorpe Co., Ga.]

THOMAS BURCH

Thomas Burch, son of Benj. Burch & Jane, his wife, b. 20 Jan 1757,
m. 18 Oct 1785 by William Cook Esqr. to Sarah, dau. of James Jones
& Eliz'th, his wife, b. 5 Jan 1766.
    Children
Elizabeth Burch b. 1 Aug 1786
Eunice Burch b. 16 Mar 1788
Jane Burch b. 18 May 1790
Ruth Burch b. 11 July 1792
Keziah Burch b. 18 May 1795
Benjamin Burch b. 24 Nov 1801
James J. Burch b. 24 May 1804

Wm. Stapleton Burch [not called son] b. 14 June 1809

[Thomas Burch and his wife Sarah Jones of Surry & Wilkes Cos., N.C. This Bible is now in the National Archives, Washington, D.C. A photostat was sent to the compiler by Mrs. Sam Duggan, "Sandy Run", Rt. 4, Moultrie, Ga.]

BENJAMIN BURCH

Banjamin Burch m. 20 Feb 1756 to Jane
Wm. S. Burch m. 6 Mar 1789 to Elizabeth Cook [b. 27 Apr 1770]
Joel Hardeman m. 11 Aug 1825 to Elizabeth Upshaw
Benjamin Burch m. 20 Mar 1828 to Mary Ann Cook

Thomas Burch b. 20 Jan 1757
Sarah Burch b. 4 Oct 1758
William S. Burch b. 4 Mar 1761
Betty Burch b. --st Jan 1763 [blotted]
Benjamin Burch b. 21 Feb 1765
Maza Burch b. 9 Jan 1768
John Burch b. 9 Jan 1770
Mary Burch b. 10 Feb 1772
Jane Burch b. 27 Feb 1774
Chedle Burch b. 4 Mar 1776
Hannah Chedle Burch b. 4 Oct 1778
    [Two pages of b. dates of slaves, omited]
Benjamin Burch, son of Thomas & Jane Burch b. 24 Nov 1801
Mary Ann Cook b. 4 Feb 1803
Joel Hardeman b. 1 Feb 1804
Elizabeth B. Upshaw b. 19 Jan 1811
    [One entry under births is so dim it cannot be read.]

Benjamin Burch, husband of Jane Burch d. 24 Feb 1794
Benjamin Cook d. 12 Jan 1800
Effey Cook, his wife, d. 5 July 1808 [?]
Wm. T. Cook d. 18 Mar 1814
Wm. S. Burch d. 12 Jan 1822, aged 60 yrs, 10 mos. & 6 days
Thos. Burch d. 24 Jan 1828, aged 71 yrs & 4 days

[Benjamin and Jane Burch were of Surry Co., N.C. & Lincoln Co., Ky. This Bible is now in the possession of Mrs. Louise Carlton Stakely, 1368 Emory Rd., N.E., Atlanta 6, Ga. Photostats sent by Mrs. Sam Duggan, "Sandy Run", Rt. 4, Moultrie, Ga. On fly-leaf: "This Bible is the property of William S. Burch."]

JONATHAN A. BURLESON

Jonathan Adair Burleson b. 6 Oct 1789 m. 1st on 17 Sep 1813 in Madison Co., Ala. to Elizabeth Byrd b. 4 Sep 1796, d. 12 July 1839, m. 2nd on 23 Apr 1843 to Ann Humphrey.
    Children [Jonathan A. & Elizabeth Byrd Burleson]
Jane b. 25 Feb 1815, d. 24 Sep 1866
Aaron Adair b. 1 Aug 1816
Wm. Byrd b. 27 Feb 1818, d. 16 Dec 1865

Eliza Hodges b. 22 Apr 1820
Richard Byrd b. 1 Jan 1822, d. 9 Oct 1838
Rufus Columbus b. 7 Aug 1823
Elizabeth b. 30 Dec 1825, d. 2 Sep 1827
Emily b. 15 Nov 1827
Edna b. 22 Dec 1829, d. 4 Aug 1867, m. 10 July 1845 to Wm. Turney
Isabella b. 5 July 1831, m. 1 Jan 1857 to S. S. Humphrey
Dabney Adair b. 15 Feb 1835, d. 24 July 1922, m. 11 Feb 1857 to
    Sallie Orr
Mary Ann b. 15 Feb 1835, m. 5 Feb 1857 to W. Maxwell
Martha Hellen b. 22 Sep 1837

Roby Adair Burleson b. 22 July 1845, d. 5 Jan 1870 [son of Jona-
    than A. & Ann Humphrey Burleson ?]

[Jonathan Adair Burleson was the son of John & Abigail (Adair) Burleson. He was born near Lexington, Ky. His mother was a sister of
Gov. John Adair of Ky. Eliz. Byrd was the dau. of Rev. Wm. Byrd &
Lydia Adair. Rev. Wm. Byrd was a Baptist preacher in Ala. He was
born in 1775 in Va. and his wife, Lydia Adair was b. 1770, d. 1838.
The Burlesons descend from one Aaron I who came to America in 1726
from Wales, was killed in 1776 crossing the Clinch River with Danl.
Boon's party in what is now Tenn. This Bible of Jonathan A. Burleson is now owned (1960) by Miss Bettie Burleson and her sister,
Mrs. Ella Byrd Davis, Decatur Ala. It should be stated that the
marriage of John Burleson to Abigail Adair is in the above Bible.
Abigail died after she had only three children & Jonathan Adair was
7 yrs. old. John Burleson then m. Mary Hodges. All additional
data from Howard Burleson and Mrs. Pierce Pattillo, both of Hartselle, Ala. who have done great research on this family and collat-
eral lines of Orr, Glenn, Byrd, et al.]

H.H. BURKE

H. H. Burke, son of John & Rachel Burke, b. 28 Mar 1817, d. 21 Aug
1876, m. 16 May 1841 to Louisana Knight, dau. of Joshua Lawrence,
b. 25 July 1809, d. 26 Apr 1865.

Wm. Franklin Foushee, son of Wm. & Annie Foushee, b. 14 Feb 1826,
m. 27 Apr 1859 to Joanna E. Burke, dau. of H. H. & Louisana Burke,
b. 4 Apr 1842, d. 25 May 1880.

John B. Foushee, son of Wm. Frank. & Joanna Foushee, b. 1 Feb 1860
Emma L. Foushee, dau. of Wm. F. & Joanna Foushee, b. 14 Mar 1862
Annie M. Foushee, dau. of Wm. F. & Joanna Foushee, b. 19 June 1864,
    m. 20 Dec 1882 to H. T. Chapin
Susie J. Foushee, dau. of Wm. F. & Joanna Foushee, b. 21 Jan 1867,
    m. 30 Apr 1889 to Geo. A. Matton
Loula Lawrence Foushee, dau. of Wm. F. & Joanna Foushee, b. 27 Jan
    1869, m. 29 June 1892 to Robt. W. Bland [also spelled Lula]
Eliza Foushee b. 30 Jan 1871
Mattie G. Foushee, dau. of Wm. F. & Joanna Foushee, b. 28 June

1873, m. 26 Dec 1895 to James A. Thompson
Cornelia H. Foushee b. 17 June 1876
Wm. G. Foushee b. 29 Aug 1878

[This Bible owned by Mrs. Edwin B. Hatch, Pittsboro, N.C. She was
Eliz. Chapin.]

DAVID MITCHELL BURNS

David Mitchell Burns b. 30 Aug 1790, d. 11 Dec 1864 in Jackson Co.,
Ga., m. 22 Jan 1818 in Jackson Co., Ga. to Sarah Hay b. 7 Oct 1801,
d. 27 Sep 1877 [Grave stone] They are buried at Thyatira Presbyter-
ian Church in Jackson Co.
    Children
William Brantley Burns b. 7 Nov 1818, d. 6 July 1867 Banks Co., Ga.
Samuel Hay Burns b. 6 Feb 1821, d. 2 May 1857, no issue
James Harvey Burns b. 5 May 1823, m. 1 July 1847 in Franklin Co.,
    Ga. to Louisa Harriet Neal
David Mitchell Burns b. 21 Oct 1825, d. 12 May 1857, m. 26 Apr 1855
    to Sarah Randolph of Jefferson
Esther Eveline Burns b. 9 Mar 1828, m. J. M. Potts
Andrew Jackson Burns b. 24 Dec 1830, d. 6 Mar 1852
John Milton Burns b. 12 Dec 1833, d. 21 Nov 1908, m. 1st to Sarah
    Harriet Long, a cousin of Dr. Crawford Long, m. 2nd to Julia Car-
    oline Telford. [See Telford sketch] [Dr. John Milton Burns]
Margaret Elizabeth Burns b. 28 Dec 1837, m. 12 Mar 1857 to John
    Carithers
Sarah Priscilla b. 15 Oct 1841, m. John B. Davis [lived at Newnan,
    Ga. according to Egbert Burns]
Alonzo Waddle Burns b. 27 Aug 1846, d. 24 Oct 1863 at Camp Morton,
    Ind.

WILLIAM BURNS

William Burns b. 12 Feb 1752 in Ireland, d. 22 July 1827, aged 75
yrs., m. in N.C. to Margaret Mitchell b. 30 Jan 1752 in Md., d. 10
Jan 1836, aged 84 yrs. [The couple lived in Orange Co., N.C. for
several years till the winter of 1781-82 when they moved to Ga.,
settling where Maysville now stands. They are buried at Maysville,
Jackson Co., Ga. in an old cemetery.]
    Children
Andrew Burns b. 6 Feb 1775
James Burns b. 30 Apr 1777
William Burns b. 19 Oct 1779
Sally Burns b. 9 Jan 1782
Mary Burns b. 30 May 1784
John Burns b. 11 Oct 1788
David Mitchell Burns b. 30 Aug 1790 [General Burns]
Samuel Burns b. 1 Sep 1795

[Family Bible in hands of Mrs. Tom Boone (Clara Mayes), Maysville,
Ga. Printed in England, 1756.]

JEREMIAH BUSH

Jeremiah Bush b. 20 Jan 1789 in Clarke Co., Ky., d. 23 or 25 Dec 1842, m. 19 Dec 1811 to Nancy H. Gentry b. 3 Oct 1795 in Madison Co., Ky., d. 2 July 1863
    Children
Richard Gentry b. 4 Nov 1812
Felix Glenroy b. 19 May 1814, d. 8 Nov 1855
Glovennox W. b. 17 May 1816
Jas. H. Gentry b. 12 July 1818
Rhodes Gentry b. 20 Nov 1820, d. 23 Feb 1840
Ambrose G. b. 18 Jan 1823
Oliver Edward b. 7 Feb 1825
Wm. Martin b. 20 June 1827
Jane Frances b. 21 July 1829
Valentine W. b. 12 Nov 1831
James Porter b. 2 Nov 1834

John G. Bush b. 1771
Lucy Bush, wife of Ambrose Bush b. 15 Feb 1746 [Ambrose, son of Philip & Mary Bush, see below]
Ambrose Bush, Sr. d. Friday 10 Feb 1815
Lucy Bush, wife of Ambrose Bush d. 25 July 1814
Jane F. Robinson, wife of Jeremiah Robinson d. 5 July 1858
Nancy Julia Bush m. 29 Dec 1806 to Lindon Comstort

[Bible owned by C. G. Bush, Winchester, Ky., sent by Mrs. E. C. Gregory, Tuscumbia, Ala.]

PHILIP BUSH

Philip & Mary Bush
    Children
Josiah b. 5 July 1733
Sarah b. 4 Feb 1734
Philip b. 19 ... 1736 [Tombstone gives dates: b. 26 or 29 June 1737, d. 21 June 1819.]
Mary b. 5 Ju... 1738 [d. 1814, m. Robt. Richards]
Elizabeth b. 14 Jan 1740
Joseph b. 5 Apr 1741
Joshua b. 5 Apr 1741
John b. 2 Feb 1742
Fanny
William [Tombstone in Clarke Co., Ky gives: Capt. Wm. b. 26 June 1746, d. 25 July 1815]
Ambrose b. 8 Apr 1748
Frances b. 20 Feb 1749/50 all b. in Va.

CAPTAIN JAMES BUTLER

Capt. James Butler b. 1723 in Prince William Co., Va., d. 7 Nov 1781 in Edgefield Co., S.C., m. in Va. to Miss Mary Simpson.

        Children
William b. 17 Dec 1758, m. Betheland Foote Moore
James b. 2 Mar 1761, d. 7 Nov 1781, killed with his father at
   Cloud's Creek, S.C.
Thomas b. 4 Nov 1763, m. Miss Grigsby
Nancy b. 27 Sep 1765 [m. Wm. Elisha Brooks]
Elizabeth b. 17 Dec 1766 [m. Zach. Smith Brooks]
Sampson b. 6 Feb 1769 [Could this be Simpson?]
Mason

[General William Butler, oldest child above, was b. in Prince William Co., Va., d. 15 Nov 1821 in Saluda Co., S.C., m. 3 June 1784
in Edgefield, S.C. Betheland Foote Moore, dau. of Capt. Francis
Moore & Frances Foote, was b. 28 Dec 1764, d. 2 Dec 1853.]

                    DANIEL S. BYRD

Daniel S. Byrd, son of Andrew J. & M. C. Byrd, b. 9 Jan 1847, d. 20
Feb 1886, m. 23 Feb 1871 at the residence of J. C. Dollar by Rev.
D. D. McBryde to M. A. Dollar b. 22 Apr 1845.
        Children
James Robert b. 7 Nov 1872
Mary Bunn b. 15 May 1875, d. 7 Oct 1878
Caroline (Carrie) Shaw b. 4 Mar 1878, d. 17 Oct 1878
Charles Pegram b. 9 Jan 1880, d. 1 Nov [Year not clear, looks like
   1810]
Katie Lee b. 28 Dec 1883, d. 22 July 1902

J. C. Dollar m. Mar 1844 to Mary J. Bunn
James Robbie Byrd m. 20 Dec 1923 to Nora Etta Woods
Margaret J. Dollar d. 12 July 1893

[Bible owned by Mr. Thomas, Mebane, N.C.]

                    JOHN CABE

John & Mary Cabe m. 16 Feb 1786
        Children
Elizabeth b. 22 Feb 1787 [m. 26 Oct 1805 to Benj. Rhodes]
Ann b. 1 May 1788 [m. 1st on 8 Dec 1812 to John Latta, m. 2nd to
   Maj. Robt. Donnell]
Sarah b. 14 Aug 1789 [m. 22 Jan 1812 to Jos. Latta]
Mary b. 15 May 1791 [m. 23 Feb 1819 to Mann Patterson]
Rachel b. 24 Aug 1792 [m. 1st to Moses McCown, m. 2nd to Herbert
   Simms]
Catharine b. 15 Nov 1795 [m. 21 June 1819 to Benj. Rhodes]
Lydia b. 4 Sep 1797 [m. 11 Sep 1819 to Chas. W. Johnston]
Margaret b. 13 Feb 1799 [m. 1 Oct 1822 to John W. Caldwell]
Jane b. 9 Sep 1801 [m. 4 Dec 1821 to Wm. Thos. Shields]

[This record is from the Mann Patterson Bible. Mary Cabe, above,
was the 2nd wife of Mann Patterson. This Bible is owned by David

Patterson, Hillsboro, N.C., a descendant. The fact that Mary Cabe
was born Mary Strayhorn is proven by court records. The name was
originally McCabe, but the "Mc" was dropped by John. The marriages
given above are from the marriage records of Orange Co., N.C. and
were furnished by Mrs. Chas. W. Shields, Chapel Hill, N.C.]

ROBERT CALDWELL

Robt. Caldwell, Sr. b. 9 July 1732, m. 1 Jan 1755 to Mary Logan b.
11 Dec 1734.
    Children
Margaret b. 29 Oct 1755
John b. 22 Sep 1758 [Became Lt. Gov. of Ky., d. 1804]
David b. 7 June 1760
William T. b. 13 May 1762
Robert b. 23 May 1764
Phillips b. 25 Jan 1767
Jane b. 31 Mar 1770
Samuel b. 9 Dec 1771
Mary b. 23 Aug 1773
Elizabeth b. 2 July 1776
James b. 8 Jan 1778
Richard b. 1 Oct 1781

[This Bible record is from Davis L. McWhorter, Bethel, N.C. Mr.
McWhorter adds this data, "Samuel Caldwell, above, was for many
years Register of Deeds in Logan Co., Ky., was an officer in the
War of 1812, married Anne Balch, step-daughter of Prof. Geo. Marlin McWhirter, who married Martha (McCandless) Balch, widow of Rev.
Hezekiah James Balch, one of the authors of Mecklenburg (N.C.) Declaration of Independence." This Robert Caldwell was a son of Capt.
John Caldwell who married Margaret Phillips in Ireland and led a
large group of Scotch Presbyterians to America, landing in Pa. in
1727. Later Capt. John went to Va. and secured a large grant for
his colony and most of the group moved to what was later called
"Southside, Va." Several of Capt. John's sisters and their hus-
bands came with him as did some of his wife's family - the Phillips. Among the kin, was a sister of Capt. John Caldwell, Jeane or
Jane, who had been married in Ireland to Alex. Richey (Sr.) The
Richeys and Caldwells intermarried many times and many went to S.C.
during and after the Rev. War. The compiler is a desc. of Jeane
Caldwell & Alex. Richey. This Bible record was sent to Mr. Mc
Whorter by Mrs. Morton, Farmville, Va.]

WILLIAM ALEXANDER CALDWELL

"I arrived in New York City the 12th of June 1799 aged 12 yrs. with
my brother John Caldwell, my 4 sisters and my 2 cousins. We joined
our great aunt Catherine Ball and my brother Andrew I. Caldwell in
Baltimore, Maryland... Here we were joined by my father and my brother Richard Caldwell... We then went to our brother John Caldwell's in Orange County, N.Y... Later I went to Charleston, S.C.

to see kin people."

John Caldwell, my father, d. 1 Apr 1803 in Salisbury, Orange Co.,
N.Y.
Elizabeth Calderwood Caldwell d. 27 Dec 1796 in Ballymoney, Ire-
land, leaving her husband, John, 4 sons & 5 daughters.
Catherine Ball, my great aunt, d. 24 Sep 1805
Capt. Richard Caldwell, my brother, d. 22 Nov 1812 at Lake Champ-
lain, N.Y. of the 25th U.S. Regt. He left a widow, nee Mariah M.
Chandler and a son, John Caldwell & a dau., Mary Caldwell.
John Parks, my brother in law, d. 24 Apr 1813 at Newburgh, N.Y.
Flora Parks, my sister, d. 25 Jan 1814 at Newburgh, N.Y. at the
home of my brother, John Caldwell.
My sister in law, wife of my brother, John Caldwell, d. 28 Dec 1818
at Salisbury, N.Y.
Mary, my sister, d. 3 Oct 1822 at Salisbury, N.Y.
Ann Caldwell, my sister, m. Dr. James Smith in Baltimore, Md.

William Alexander Caldwell b. 16 Feb 1787 at Ballymoney, Ireland,
d. 1 Oct 1846, m.15 Jan 1811 on Lamboll St. in Charleston, S.C. to
Dinah Williamson d. 15 Dec 1858 aged 70 yrs., 11 mos. & no days.
    Children - all b. in Charleston, S.C.
John Williamson Caldwell, son, b. 16 Mar 1812, d. 1 Aug 1867 in New
York City, bur. in St. Andrew Church yard in Charleston, S.C., m.
10 Feb 1836 to Martha C. Coates
William Smith Caldwell, son, b. 6 Nov 1813
Richard Caldwell, son, b. 28 July 1815, d. 30 Oct 1879, bur. in
Magnolia Cemetery in Charleston, S.C., m. 17 Oct 1878 to Jeannie
Davis Tupper, second dau. of S. Y. Tupper, d. 7 Feb 1889, bur.
in Scotch Presbyterian Church Yard, Charleston, S.C.
Flora Caldwell, dau., b. 6 Aug 1817, d. 25 Oct 1818
Andrew Caldwell, son, b. 26 Oct 1819
Joseph Triskham Caldwell, son, b. 20 June 1823
    Children (John Williamson & Martha C. Coates Caldwell)
William Alexander Caldwell, son b. 5 Sep 1837
Mary Coates Caldwell, dau., b. 15 Dec 1839, d. 15 Mar 1925
John Williamson Caldwell, Jr., son, b. 31 Jan 1842
James Shapter Caldwell, son, b. 18 July 1843, d. 20 June 1866
George Stewart Caldwell, son, b. 24 Aug 1845, d. 26 May 1864
Richard Caldwell, son, b. 14 Oct 1850, d. 29 Dec 1918
Ina Catherine Caldwell, dau., b. 16 June 1856, d. 5 Sep 1923

    Children (Richard & Jeannie Davis Tupper Caldwell)
James Shafter [Shapter?] Caldwell, son, b. 7 Oct 1879
Samuel Tupper Caldwell, son, b. 28 Nov 1882, d. 3 Aug 1829 in Co-
lumbia, S.C., bur. in Charleston, S.C.
Virginia Godin Caldwell, dau., b. 29 May 1888

[This Bible in S.C. Archives Building, Columbia, S.C.]

WILLIAM CALHOUN

William Calhoun, son of Patrick & Martha (Caldwell) Calhoun, b. 19
Sep 1776, d. 10 Dec 1840, m. 30 Jan 1805 to Catherine Jenner De
Graffenreid, dau. of Tscharner & Lucretia (Towns) De Graffenreid,
b. 19 June 1786, d. 3 Feb 1829.

Geo. McDuffie Calhoun b. 14 Dec 1828 in Abbeville, S.C., d. 15 June
1916 in Austin, Tex., m. 17 Jan 1850 to Harriet Julia Goodwyn b. 7
Jan 1832 in S.C., d. 28 Apr 1892 in Austin, Tex. [No indication
that this is son of Wm. Calhoun]
    Children
Armistead Burt b. 12 Oct 1852 in Columbia, S.C., d. 1858 in Augus-
    ta, Ga.
Robt. Goodwyn b. 28 Aug 1854, d. 1857
John Thos. b. lo May 1856, d. 1858
Mary Eugenia b. 3 Mar 1860, d. 16 Feb 1861 in Shreveport, La.
George b. 26 Oct 1863, d. 1948 in Austin, Tex., m. 1st on 5 Mar
    1889 in Austin, Tex. to Kaye [Kate?] C. Francis, m. 2nd on 29 Nov
    1911 to Martha Alton

[Martha Caldwell, above, was the dau. of Capt. Wm. Caldwell & Rebecca Parks Caldwell. They lived in Lunenburg Co., Va. He d. 1751 &
she and all her children moved to S.C. where she died. Capt. Wm.
Caldwell was the son of Capt. John Caldwell & Margaret Phillips who
migrated to Pa. in 1727. About 1834 Capt. John went to Va. and got
a grant for his Presbyterian colony and most of the family connection moved to what later became known as Southside, Va. The compiler is a descendant of Jeane Caldwell, sister of Capt. John who m.
Alex. Richey, Sr., in Ire.]

WILLIAM DOWNS CALHOUN

William Downs Calhoun b. 5 Oct 1827, d. 30 Apr 1901, m. 1st on 17
May 1849 to Ellen Jones b. 18 May 1833, d. 14 July 1852, m. 2nd on
24 Dec 1857 to Betty J. McGowan b. 7 Sep 1835, d. 11 Dec 1910 at
2:30 P.M., bur. at Cross Hill, S.C.

Edwin Broyles Calhoun b. 9 June 1850, d. 18 Dec 1914
Lucy Lavinia Calhoun b. 26 Dec 1851, d. 14 July 1852, dau. of Wm.
William Alexander Calhoun b. 11 Apr 1866, at sun-up, d. 25 Mar
    1918, m.15 Sep 1886 to Sara Eudora Davitte d. 15 Dec 1947
Jane Elizabeth Calhoun b. 16 Feb 1870, 12 o'clock morning, m. 7 Oct
    1888 to George B. Locke
John C. Calhoun b. 19 July 1872, d. 15 July 1915

William Calhoun Locke b. 9 o'clock Friday night, 9 Aug 1889
Lois Locke b. 24 Nov 1890
Frank Locke b. 15 Dec 1892

Downs Calhoun, my father, d. 29 June 1850
Lavina Calhoun d. 27 May 1830...[a sister of W. D. Calhoun]

Lorenia E. Larey, my sister, d. 20 Sep 1885
Lavinda Young, my sister, d. 10 Jan 1877
Willis B. Calhoun d. 1 Feb 1873
Lavina Anderson, my sister, d. 7 June 1890, aged 60 yrs.

[William Downs Calhoun of Ninety Six, S.C., was the son of Downs Calhoun by his first wife, Mary Puckett. This Bible is owned by the family of Mrs. Thelma Calhoun Bidez of 602 East 50th St., Savannah, Ga.]

JAMES CAMPBELL

James Campbell b. 30 Dec 1782, d. 27 Oct 1816, m. 13 Apr 1809 to Winifred Turner b. 13 Apr 1783 (dau. of James Turner b. 7 Dec 1750, d. 9 July 1804 and Sarah Hunter, his wife, b. 11 July 1753, d. 11 Feb. 1815), d. 14 Apr 1852 m. 2nd on 16 Feb 1819 to John Hodges b. 7 Mar 1787, d. 14 Jan 1832.
    Children
Elizabeth b. 16 June 1810
Farquard b. 12 Jan 1812
Sarah b. 17 Mar 1814
Mary b. 17 Mar 1814 - half hour between their births
Catherine Winifred [Hodges] b. 6 Jan 1820
Jas. Philemon [Hodges] b. 11 Nov 1821
John W. [Hodges] b. 23 Dec 1823
Jane Penelope [Hodges] b. 9 Sep 1826

[Records sent by Mrs. Ida Kellam, Wilmington, N.C., sent her by John Murchison Hodges, Jr., Linden, N.C. John Hodges of this record, lived in Old Averasboro, N.C. Clipped in this Bible ar the following Hodges family data:]

"William Hodges came to N.C. from Va., m. Patience Hawkins of Warren or Franklin Co., N.C. Their son, Philemon Hodges, b. 25 Oct 1760, d. 1839, m. Winifred Kittrell b. 7 Oct 1763, dau. of Saml. & Catherine Kittrell of Granville Co., N.C. Their children: Nancy, Polly, John, Catherine, William, Penelope, Joseph, George, Winifred & Philemon. The underlined John is the John of this Bible.
"James Campbell of this Bible, (b. 1782) was the son of Farquard & Isabella McAlister Campbell.
"Jas. Philemon Hodges, son of John & Winifred (Turner) Campbell Hodges, was b. 11 Nov. 1821, d. 23 Aug 1899, m. 11 Nov 1847 to Glora E. Murchison b. 9 Mar 1827, d. 23 Mar 1896. She was a dau. of John Murchison, son of Kenneth Murchison of "Holly Hill," Cumberland Co., N.C., & Janet Ann McLean. Janet Ann McLean m. 1st to John Murchison, m. 2nd to John McNeill, son of Archibald & Jennei 'Bahn' Smith McNeill. John McNeill m. 1st to Luovisa Roberson, m. 2nd to Janet Ann McLean Murchison."

JOSEPH CANTEY

Joseph Cantey b. 27 Nov 1765, d. 6 Sep 1834, m. 1st on 5 Feb 1784

in St. Mark's Church to Ann Connor b. 17--, d. 13 Apr 1794, m. 2nd
on 14 May 1795 to Mrs. Adam Connor, Sr., nee Susannah McDonald b.
3 Oct 1768, d. 16 May 1843
     Children
Samuel b. 4 Nov 1784, d. 2 Sep 1855, never married
John b. 27 Sep 1786, d. 14 Oct 1812, no record of marriage
Christianna Hannah b. 22 Nov 1788, d. 26 Sep 1792
Joseph Francis b. 8 Sep 1790, d. 30 Aug 1818, m. Martha Singleton
Archibald b. 14 May 1792, d. 23 Nov .1824, never married
Isaac b. 16 Mar 1794, d. 19 Oct 1794
Thomas Sumter b. 2 Apr 1796, d. 15 May 1819, never married
Mary Evelinah b. 17 Apr 1798, d. 17 Sep 1798
Wm. James Ransom b. 11 Jan 1805, d. 30 Nov 1845, m. 3 Feb 1825 to
   Mary Ann Eliza Bennett

Adam Connor, Jr. m. Dorothy Sutton [step-son]
Samuel Cantey, father, b. 7 June 1731, d. 16 Dec 1776, m. 1st on
   12 Feb 1756 to Ann b. 4 Aug 1738, d. 15 Mar 1759, m. 2nd on 18
   May 1760 to Martha Brown, mother, b. 21 Feb 1737

[Joseph Cantey was from Clarendon Co., S.C. This Bible was owned
by the late James M. Burgess, M.D. of Greeleyville, S.C.]

THOMAS CARLTON, II

Thomas Carlton b. 25 Jan 1790, m. 1st on 25 Mar 1813 to Jane Carl-
ton b. 28 Feb 1796, d. 10 Apr 1821, m. 2nd on 12 Aug 1821 to Ruth
Burch b. 11 July 1792, d. 29 Oct 1862, m. 3rd on 18 Oct 1863 to
Ellenor.
     Children
Evelina (Eveline) Carlton, dau. b. 3 Oct 1815, d. 3 June 1847
Allin Burton Carlton, son, b. 5 Mar 1818
John Carlton, son, b. 23 Aug 1822, d. 12 Oct 1822
Jannill [?] Milton Carlton, son, b. 28 Sep 1823
Henry Carlton, son, b. 28 Oct 1825, d. 17 June 1826
Joel Anderson, son, b. 16 Oct 1827, d. 24 Jan 1865
Marthy Eads, dau., b. 15 Aug 1830
Mary Ann, dau., b. 15 Aug 1830, m. 24 Oct 1849 to James Eller
Thomas Carlton, son, b. 31 Oct 1833, d. 7 July 1860, m. 16 Sep 1856
   to Susan M. Triplit

     Children of Thomas C. & Susan M. Carlton
Sally Leenorah Carlton, dau., b. 25 May 1857
Rebecca Girtrude Carlton, dau., b. 23 Aug 1859

Thomas Burch b. 20 Jan 1757
Sarah Burch b. 5 Jan 1766, d. 6 Mar 1854

[Family Bible of Thomas Carlton, II & his wife Ruth Burch, of
Wilkes Co., N.C., now in the possession of Mrs. Mary Carlton German, Boomer, N.C. Photostats contributed by Mrs. Sam Guggan, Moultrie, Ga. Bible pub. 1826 by Kimber & Sharpless, 93 Market St.,

Philadelphia, Pa.]

NATHAN CARPENTER

Children of Benjamin Rasin & Rachel, his wife
Philip Rasin, son, b. 27 Feb 1774, bapt. by Rev. McGoy
Polly Rasin, dau., b. 27 Sep 1775, bapt. by Rev. Thorn
George Rasin, son, b. 7 Nov 1777, bapt. by Rev. Thorn
Joseph Rasin, son, b. 25 Dec 1779, bapt. by Rev. Neall
James Rasin, son, b. 14 Mar 1782, bapt. by Rev. Thorn, d. 11 Nov
1784

Children of William Burrows & Rachel, his wife
Boaz Burrows, son, b. 12 June 1783, d. 21 June 1824
Benjamin Burrows, son, b. 19 May 1785
Jonathan Burrows, son, b. 1 Oct 1787
Nancy Burrows, dau., b. 22 Mar 1789, d. 2 Dec 1791
John Burrows, son, b. 5 July 1791
Manlove Burrows, son, d. 24 July 1793
Sally Burrows, dau., b. 24 Jan 1795

James Rasin, son of Philip Rasin & Sarah, his wife, b. 22 Dec 1798
George Rasin, son of Philip Raisin & Nancy, his wife, b. 12 Aug
1805
Mary Ann Rasin, dau. of Philip Rasin & Joycey, his wife, b. Apr
1813, d. 19 Apr 1813
Joseph Rasin, son of Philip Rasin & Joycey, his wife, b. 27 Nov
1814 [date 24 Dec 1822 follows, probably death date]

[The above Bible was printed & published by T. Kinnersley, 148
Cherry St., New York, 1822.]

NATHAN S. CARPENTER

Nathan Spencer Carpenter, son of Nathan Carpenter d. at Milford,
Delaware 24 Mar 1819 and Ann Know, b. 26 Feb 1819 at Milford, Del-
aware, d. 25 Feb 1895 at Richmond, Va., m. 25 Feb 1841 at Peters-
burg, Va. to Maria Antoinette Jarvis b. 23 Dec 1819 at Richmond,
Va., d. 4 Oct 1904 at St. Albans, W.Va., bur. at Hollywood Ceme-
tery, Richmond, Va.
    Children
Philip R. Carpenter, son, b. 26 Dec 1841 at Petersburg, Va., d. 25
    Mar 1886, m. 3 Apr 1869 at Baltimore, Md. to Sallie A. Sink, dau.
    of William & S. Sink, d. 28 Jan 1881 at Newberry, S.C.
Ann Maria Carpenter b. 16 Oct 1843 at Petersburg, Va. m. 30 Apr
    1867 at St. John Parish, Wilmington, N.C. to Matthew Laspeyre
Susan Joycey Carpenter b. 7 Nov 1845 at 12:30 A.M. at Richmond, Va.
Thomas Ruth Carpenter b. 10 Mar 1848 at 7:00 A.M., Friday, at Rich-
    mond, Va., d. 19 July 1855
Nathan Carpenter b. 12 July 1850, Friday, at 2:30 A.M. at Richmond,
    m. at St. Albans, W. Va. to Bettie Snell
Mary Christianna Carpenter b. 1 Feb 1853 at 9:10 A.M. at Richmond,

Va., m. 2 Dec 1873 at St. Albans, W. Va. to Oliver T. Wilson
William Carpenter b. Saturday, 10 Oct 1855 at 4:15 P.M.
Gertrude Carpenter b. 1 Jan 1858 at Richmond, Va., d. same day
Andrew Talcott Carpenter b. at Richmond, Va., d. 8 June 1860 at
    Richmond, Va.
Virginia Guion Carpenter b. 24 Aug 1862 at Brown Marsh, Bladen Co.,
    N.C.

William Ward Carpenter, son of PHilip R. & Sarah Ann Carpenter, b.
    13 Jan 1881 at Newberry, S.C., d. 18 Sep 1881 [?] at Seneca City,
    S.C.

Thomas C. Ruth and Ann, his wife, m. 20 Sep 1821
    Children
James Monroe Ruth, son, b. 20 Sep 1822, d. 1 Nov 1823
Charles Ruth, son, d. 26 Aug 1826
Thomas J. Ruth, son, b. 28 Aug 1827, d. 19 May 1945

[New Testament published 1813 by Bennett & Walton, #31 Market St.,
Philadelphia, printer J. Bouvier. It has the following inscrip-
tions: "Year of 1817 Nathan S. Carpenter his book bought of William
Walton in the year of 1817." "Nathan S. Carpenter, April the 29th,
1817" "Nathan Carpenter, son of Nathan Carpenter and Ann, his
wife, was born February 26 day 1819" Nathan Carpenter, Sr. d. only
a month after the birth of Nathan Carpenter, Jr. and from the foregoing, it appears that his widow, Ann Knox Carpenter m. Thomas C.
Ruth 20 Sep 1821 and had several children, who were half-brothers
of Nathan Carpenter, Jr.]

JAMES CARRELL

James Carrell b. 31 Mar 1765, d. 17 Apr 1841, m. 24 Dec 1802 to
Sally Parks b. 28 Apr 1771, d. 17 Aug 1838.
    Children
Mirah b. 25 Apr 1807, d. 28 Jan 1813
William b. 14 Oct 1808 m. 1 Mar 1831 to Eleanor Selby, b. 5 Dec
    1802
Elizabeth b. 21 Sep 1810, d. 19 Apr 1818
John Parks b. 30 Apr 1813, d. 31 Jan 1838

    Children of William & Eleanor (Selby) Carrell
John Parks b. 24 June 1833
Sally Martha Ann b. 14 July 1835
Naomi Louise b. 19 June 1838
James Meredith b. 28 July 1840
William Grayson b. 24 Apr 1843
Mary Elizabeth b. 21 July 1845

[These records sent by Mrs. May Shearer Stringfield, Thomasville,
N.C. 1960. She says this Bible is owned by Mrs. Wilma Williams,
Three Mile, N.C. near Newland or Linville Falls, N.C. Mrs. Wil-
liams is the great grand daughter of Wm. Carrell of Burke Co., N.C.

through his dau., Naomi. This is presumedly Naomi Louisa. Mrs.
Stringfield adds these notes:
In Bedford Co., Va. is William Carrell with wife Mary, who in 1777
made an indenture between himself & Jos. Hardy, Wits: Robt. Ewing;
Jos. Dickson; Thos. Campbell; Sephen Dooley & Thos. Martin. 90
acres or more sold to Hardy.
No marriage bond is found there for Wm. Carrell & wife Mary. "Wm.
Carrell & wife Mary of Burke Co., N.C. had 2 sons: Wm. Jr. & James"
"1790 census of N.C. of Wilkes Co., N.C. gives Wm. Carrol with 3
males over 16.--Wm. Carrell & his sons Wm. Jr. & Jas; 4 females --
wife Mary & daus. Rachel b. 1771, dau., Mary who m. Thos. Willard;
dau. Naomi who never mar." "Brothers of Wm. Carrell - Daniel who
lived with Wm. in 1810 and Jas. of Burke Co. with wife Sarah Parks"
Mrs. Stringfield says this James with Bible record is the brother
of Wm. with wife Mary. Wm. Carrell in Va. Militia, Rev. War #39187
993 in Capt. Jonathan Hanby's Co. This also from Mrs. Stringfield.
Pension from General Services Administration, National Archives.
Wilkes Co., N.C. Book A-1, page 95 - land grant to Wm. Carrell ca.
1778-1779, from Mrs. Stringfield.]

JOSEPH CARROLL (JR.)

Joseph Carroll, son of Joseph Carroll, Sr. who d. during the War of
1776, b. 17 Mar 1746, d. 17 Feb 1803, m. 28 Feb 1771 to Martha
Swansey b. 6 Jan 1752, d. 13 July 1849.
       Children
Samuel b. 6 Jan 1772
Elizabeth b. 4 Oct 1774
Jennet b. 6 Nov 1776
Sarah b. 20 Mar 1778
John b. 19 June 1784
Henry b. 1 (rest not legible)

[Joseph Carroll was of York Co., S.C. This record sent by Leonard
Andrea, Columbia, S.C. who states that this Joseph Carroll, Jr. was
a Rev. War soldier. Wife applied for pension on his service. Pension # W-9778.]

ROBERT W. CARTER

Robert Willis Carter b. Aug 1793, d. 9 Nov 1838, m. 7 Mar 1820 to
Mary W. L. Franklin b. 1 July 1798, d. 7 Sep 1860.

Charles W. L. Carter b. 27 Dec 1820, d. 1897 in Colbert Co., Ala.,
   m. 19 Dec 1855 to Mary D. Royston
Mary Roberts R. Carter b. 8 Oct 1822, d. 6 Oct 1877
Susannah I. Carter b. 21 Sep 1823
Lucy Champe Carter b. 20 Apr 1827, d. 26 June 1827
Geo. McGuire Carter b. 29 June 1830, d. 25 Feb 1872
Eliza C. E. (E. C.) Carter b. 29 Mar 1831, d. 22 Mar 1896, m. 13
   Oct 1852 to Wm. M. Turner b. 4 June 1826, d. 4 Apr 1881
Robert Willis Carter, Jr. b. 3 Feb 1833, d. 6 Sep 1842

John H. B. C. Carter b. 27 Mar 1835, m. 13 Oct 1858 to Lucy A.
  Weaver
Mary Margaret Carter b. 11 Aug 1838, d. 16 Aug 1838

Henry Richard Carter, son of Chas. & Demaris Carter, b. 14 Nov 1858
Eliza Turner Craig, dau. of S. P. & M. E. Craig, b. 29 Aug 1873, d.
  18 Oct 1875
Jesse Allen b. 24 Dec 1815
Susan Jane F. Carter b. 21 Sep 1824, d. 30 Apr 1848, m. 9 Jan 1844
  to Jesse Allen
Jas. Robt. Allen b. 13 Nov 1847
Lena M. Craig b. 21 Aug 1876

Mary Ellen Turner, dau. of Wm. M. & Eliza Turner, b. 31 July 1853,
  d. 14 Nov 1878, m. 17 Jan 1871 to S. P. Craig d. 6 Feb 1878
Wm. Henry Turner b. 17 Oct 1855, d. 4 Mar 1909 in Jones Co., Tex.,
  m.18 Dec 1878 to Willie M. Gibbs
Chas. Fletcher (E.) Turner b. 17 Apr 1857, m. 19 Dec 1878 to Alice
  Williams
Edward Greenfield Turner b. 11 Apr 1859
Annah (Anna) Eliza Turner b. 28 Mar 1863, m. 14 Jan 1884 to R. M.
  Weaver
John Lewis Turner b. 6 Jan 1866, d. 3 Jan 1884
Robt. Saml. Turner b. 3 May 1868, m. 27 Dec 1893 to Margaret B.
  Rutland, dau. of Wells Rutland, d. 21 Mar 1934
Oliver Perry Turner b. 3 Oct 1870, d. 16 Jan 1913

Robt. W. Carter,[1st] son of John & Lucy Carter, b. 27 June 1859
Anna Lizzie Carter b. 8 Feb 1862, d. 26 Mar 1863
Mary L. Carter b. 16 June 1864, d. 11 Oct 1864
Eliza F. Carter b. 8 Apr 1866
Lucie F. Carter b. 3 June 1839 [1869?]

Lucy A. Carter 22 Aug 1867 [listed with deaths]

[Bible owned by Mrs. Alice Williams Turner, widow of Chas. Fletcher
Turner, of Cherokee, Colbert Co., Ala., copied by Mrs. E. S. Greg-
ory, 29 June 1933, of Tuscumbia, Ala. Inside cover of Bible is:
"Presented to Mary W. L. Carter by her husband, Robt. W. Carter,
M.D. 1824"]

THOMAS CASON, SR.

Thos. Cason, Sr. b. 15 Nov 1747, d. 19 Mar 1825 in Edgefield, S.C.,
m. 4 Mar 1766 to Ann Lewis b. 27 Mar 1745, d. 6 Nov 1814 in Edge-
field, S.C.
    Children
Triplet b. 15 Dec 1766
Frances b. 18 Sep 1768
Thomas, Jr. b. 28 Sep 1770
Martha b. 9 Oct 1772
Elizabeth b. 15 Apr 1775

Nancy b. 13 June 1777
Sarah b. 13 June 1777
Jemimah b. 9 Oct 1780
Joanna b. 16 Oct 1782
Lewis b. 7 Feb 1785

[From Owen Roberts, Brookhaven, Miss. He descends from Sarah Cason who mar. John Canfield, Jr. 9 May 1793, Edgefield, S.C.]

PETER CASPER

Peter Casper b. 12 Sep 1781 in N.C., m. Ester b. 23 June 1784 in N.C. They went to Union Co., Ill., City of Anna, in 1815.
    Children
Alexander b. 8 July 1806 in N.C.
Eliza b. 13 Aug 1808 in N.C.
Stephen b. 10 Sep 1810 in N.C.
Caleb b. 6 Dec 1812 in N.C.
Henry b. 6 Mar 1814 in N.C.
Eleanor b. 24 June 1817 in N.C. [note above, parents to Ill.,1815]
Catherine b. 22 Apr 1820 in Ill.
Esther b. 25 Aug 1822 in Ill.
Peter b. 25 Aug 1822 in Ill.
Anna b. 24 Feb 1825 in Ill.

[This Bible record was sent by Mrs. C. W. Carnes, Okemah, Okla. in 1962.]

ELIZABETH CASWELL

Elizabeth Caswell b. 12 Jan 1757, d. 23 Nov 1807 about 11:00 P.M., aged 50 yrs., 10 mos., 11 days, funeral was 13 Dec 1807 preached by Elijah Brazen (signed Benjamin Chapman), m. 14 Mar 1776 to Benjamin Chapman b. 13 Feb 1752.

Ann Broaddus Chapman b. 18 Sep 1777, bapt. 23 Nov 1777
John Chapman b. 7 Nov 1779, bapt. 5 Mar 1780
Thomas Chapman b. 28 Nov 1781, bapt. 7 Apr 1782
Elizabeth Male Chapman b. 20 Jan 1784, bapt. 8 Aug 1784
Mary Roane Chapman b. 20 Jan 1784, bapt. 8 Aug 1784
Frankey Chapman b. 9 May 1786, bapt. 9 Nov 1786
Benjamin Chapman, Jr. b. 5 Sep 1788, bapt. 5 July 1789
William Chapman b. 26 Aug 1792
Sarah Chapman b. 4 June 1796
James Chapman b. 9 July 1799

[Copied 12 Feb 1952 by Mrs. Andrew L. Hall from Prayer Book owned by Edward O. Hunter, Jr. of Columbia, S.C. Printed by Alexander Kincaid, His Majesty's Printer, Edinburgh. MDCCLXXII (1772) Bought 19 May 1775, price 9/6 by Elizabeth Caswell. "Elizabeth Chapman, North Carolina State, Rowan County, 7 Nov 1799. Benjamin Chapman got here that day."]

THOMAS CATER

Thomas Cater b. 17 Dec 1751, d. 20 Apr 1803, m. 18 Feb 1773 to
Rachel Miles b. 22 Dec 1755, d. 30 Jan 1802.

    Children

Rachel b. 4 Aug 1774
Mary C. b. 25 June 1776, d. 2 Mar 1823
Elizabeth b. 2 Mar 1778, d. June 1803
Susanna Baker b. 9 Aug 1780
Carolina b. 14 Oct 1782, d. 23 Mar 1809
Ann Miles b. 3 Apr 1784, d. 25 Oct 1789
Thos. Miles b. 24 Apr 1786, d. 30 Jan 1819, m. 1st on 21 Jan 1805
    to Sarah McPherson Postell, dau. of Andrew & Sarah Postell, b.
    23 Mar 1786, d. 8 Feb 1815, aged 28 yrs., m. 2nd on 14 Sep 1815
    to Catherine Johnson, dau. of Richard & Sarah Johnson of S.C.,
    b. 23 Sep 1794, d. 6 Oct 1836. Catherine Johnson Cater m. 2nd
    on 2 Nov 1826 in Barnwell Co., S.C. by Rev. Duncan to Thos. W.
    Anderson.
Silas McPherson Cater b. 2 Apr 1789
Richard Bohun b. 14 Dec 1791
William Maine b. 19 Mar 1795, d. 4 Sep 1796
McPherson b. 6 Dec 1796, d. 18 Oct 1798

    Children of Thos. Miles Cater
James McPherson b. 3 Nov 1805, d. 24 July 1806
Thomas b. 24 Oct 1806, d. aged 9 yrs. 15 days, killed by a fall
    from a horse
Eliza b. 7 Mar 1808, d. 12 Mar 1808
John Jas. b. 29 May 1809
Richard Bahun [Bohun?] b. 5 Jan 1811
Andrew Postell b. 8 June 1812
Edwina 1 Nov 1813
Sarah b. 8 Feb 1815 [same as mother's death date]
Thos. Johnson b. 26 Oct 1816 in Barnwell Dist., S.C.
James McPherson b. 6 Apr 1818 [oldest child by 1st wife had this
    name but he died as an infant, this one d. 5 Nov 1824]
Thos Miles (Jr.) b. 12 Apr 1819, d. 10 Oct 1824 posthumous child

[Catherine (Johnson) Cater m. 2nd Thos. W. Anderson & they moved
to Ga. Thos. Johnson Cater went with his mother and later m. Amelia E. Wimberly 22 Dec 1842 in Macon, Ga. by Rev. Wm. H. Ellison.
Amelia Eliz. Wimberly b. 1 June 1824, Jones Co., Ga. Bible owned
by C. F. Cater, Quitman, Ga. "John James & Thos. Johnson Cater
were half brothers" - notation in Bible is supposed to have been
written by Catherine Cater.]

LITTLETON CHAMBLESS

Littleton Chambless b. 9 Feb 1764
Cynthia, his wife, b. 3 Aug 1764

John, their first, b. 23 Jan 1785
Obedience Chambless b. 27 [?] Oct 1788
Mary (Masy?], dau. of John Chambless & wife, b. 30 July 1810
T. Zachariah L. Chambless b. 31 July 1812
William H. Chambless b. 13 Sep 1814
Thomas G. Chambless b. 13 Dec 1816
Littleton C. Chambless b. 2 July 1820
Nancy M. Chambless b. 13 Sep 1823
John T. Chambless b. 21 Aug 1826
Henry B. Chambless b. 20 Feb 1829
      [Following page torn]
. . . .   Mary [?] Chambless b. 7 Apr 184-
. . . .[Jam]es [?] Taylor Chambless b. 18 Apr 1847
. . . . Elizabeth Chambless b. 27 Mar 1849
. . . . rietta Strowd Chambless b. 21 July 1854
. . . . . nry Jackson Chambless b. 21 July 1854
James Graves Chambless b. 26 Apr 1859
. . .mer Davis b. 11 July

Mary Chambless, widow, d. 15 Sep 1813
Littleton Chambless d. 17 Jan 1822
Sary Chambless d. 15 Sep 1812
Elizabeth Ledbetter, widow, d. 1823
Cynthia Chambless, widow, d. 27 Apr 1829
William H. Chambless d. 29 Aug 1836
Obedience Chambless d. 5 Jan 1857
John D. Chambless d. 20 Mar 1857
Sarah Jane Chambless, wife of Z. L. Chambless, d. 21 Aug 1836
John W. Chambless, d. 1 July 1836
William D. Chambless d. 12 Aug 1839
Thomas Taylor Chamness d. 12 Jan [torn]
Marietta Strowd C..[torn] d. 11 Aug [torn]
Henry Littleton Cham..[torn] d. 6 Oct 1858 [?]
Sarah Elizabeth C..[torn] d. Jan 1860

Z. T. Chamness m. 4 Dec 1839 to Sarah Jane Chambless
Z. L. Chamness m. 6 Jan 1842 to Smithy Skinner [?]
John Chambless m. 10 Aug 1809 to Obedience

[Photostats made in Columbus, Ga., May 1957.]

NATHANIEL CHAMBLISS

Nathaniel Chambliss b. 4 Feb 1762, m. Mary b. 16 Apr 1764, d. 15
Jan 1811 aged 46 yrs.
      Children
Henry b. 6 Oct 1784, m. 22 Dec 1808
James C. (twin) b. 6 Oct 1784, m. 19 Dec 1805
Eliza b. 8 Oct 1786
Patsy b. 16 July 1788
Susan b. 13 Mar 1790
Henrietta b. 21 Oct

Sarah b. 16 Sep 1791
Polly b. 27 May 1793
Nathaniel b. 4 Feb 1795
William b. 7 Dec 1796

Nathaniel, son of William & Elizabeth Champion Chambliss b. 10
    July 1805
Wm. Chas., son of Wm. & Elizabeth Champion b. 16 Mar 1808

Evelina B. Chambliss, dau. of James & Lucy, b. 31 Jan 1819, m. 2
    Dec 1834
Amanda, dau. of Jas. & Lucy Chambliss, b. 22 Sep 1825
Sally Louiza M., dau. of Jas. & Lucy Chambliss, b. 2 Oct 1806
John Randolph, son of Jas. & Lucy Chambliss, b. 5 Mar 1809, m. 25
    Dec 1830
Wm. David, son of Jas. & Lucy Chambliss, b. 3 Sep 1811

William Burrell Malone, son of Geo. & Martha, b. 16 Oct 1808
Mary Green Malone, dau. of Geo. & Martha Malone, b. 6 June 1810

Jack Stith, son of Henry & Sally Chambliss, b. 9 Oct 1809
Nathaniel, son of Henry & Sally Chambliss, b. 31 Oct 1811
Martha Ann, dau. of Henry & Sally Chambliss

Laura Mason Doreman [?] b. 22 Sep 1836, d. 20 Oct 1886 [?]

Mary Sprigg, wife of Burrell Gregg, d. 26 Nov 1812
Martha Malone, wife of George, d. 12 Sep 1814
William, son of Nathaniel Chambliss, d. 19 July 1819
Sary Wrenn, wife of Boram Wrenn, d. 26 Sep 1820
Martha, wife of Nathaniel Chambliss, d. 10 or 11 Jan 1821 aged 53
Nathaniel Chambliss, d. 4 Dec 1827 aged 65 yrs., b. 22 Aug 1810
Elizabeth Chambless, mother of above Nathaniel, d. 21 Jan 1821 in
    her 91st year.
S. L. Mason, dau. of Jas. & Lucy Chambliss, d. 19 June 1831 in the
    25th yr. of her life
Henrietta J. or I. Chambliss b. [?] 21 Oct 1822

Martha, dau. of Nathaniel & Mary Chambliss, m. 23 Dec 1807
Elizabeth Chambliss, dau. of Nathaniel & Mary, m. 10 May 1804
Mary, dau. of Nathaniel & Mary, m. 6 Sep 1809
Sally, dau. of Nathaniel & Mary Chambliss, m. 21 Dec 1814

Clippings from newspapers pasted in Bible:

Married on Thursday last by Rev. J. B. King, Mr. Thos. W. Walker,
    merchant of this town, to Miss Henrietta J. Chambliss, dau. of
    Jas. Chambliss, Esq. of Pleasant Valley.
Married at the residence of Col. John R. Chambliss in Hicksford,
    Va. 29 Dec 1847 by Rev. Mr. Sprigg, Mr. Wm. H. Day of Smithfield,
    Va. to Miss Amanda M. F. Chambliss, dau. of Capt. James Chamb-
    liss of Dallas Co., Ala.

[This record given by Mrs. Jas. Thornton Nuckols, Columbus, Ga. Pleasant Valley mentioned above seems to be in Ala. James Chambliss was a Capt. in the War of 1812. His widow made application for a pension based on his service from Dallas Co., Ala. From those papers comes the following data: Lucy Chambliss was a Newsom before her marriage. She was 72 when she applied for the pension but the year that she applied is not stated. Jas. Chambliss was in the Va. Militia. He died in 1848. They were married in Southampton Co., Va. 19 Dec 1805. Inscription in Bible: "This Bible is the property of Nathaniel Chambliss since his death the property of James Chambliss."]

JOEL CHANDLER

Children of Joel and Jane Chandler

Robert Chandler b. 19 Nov 1758
Nancy Chandler b. 22 Apr 1761
David Chandler b. 22 Nov 1763
Daniel Chandler b. 1 Feb 1765
William Chandler b. 15 Dec 1768
Jane Chandler b. 25 July 1767 [?]
Robert Chandler b. 5 July 1773
John Chandler b. 25 Oct 1775
Parthenia Chandler b. 25 Dec 1777
Matthew Chandler b. 10 Oct 1782
Thomas Chandler b. 3 Feb 1785
Tabitha Chandler b. 10 Dec 1779

"Entry - William Neal, His account book, 12 July 1817."

[William Neal above was grandfather of Ella Neal Mize, 2nd wife of W. S. Mize. William Neal's father was Robert Neal who m. Tabitha Chandler.]

JOSIAH CHANDLER

Josiah Chandler b. 17 Jan 1808, d. 20 Oct 1881, m. Eliz Brownen b. 4 Aug 1812, d. 4 Feb 1888.

Henry Chandler b. 10 May 1830
Sophronia Chandler b. 5 Jan 1832, m. 27 Sep 1866 to Hampton Halliday
John T. Chandler b. 27 Oct 1833
Mary E. Chandler b. 27 Oct 1835
Frances Emeline Chandler b. 13 July 1838, d. 19 Nov 1879
Sarah J. Chandler b. 9 Apr 1841
Josiah J. Chandler b. 15 May 1843, d. 25 Feb 1863
King Sol. Chandler b. 30 Aug 1845, m. 22 Oct 1866 to Nancy E. Chandler b. 14 Feb 1847
Jas. Robt. Chandler b. 25 Mar 1848
Sandford V. Chandler b. 22 Dec 1850

Thomas R. Chandler b. 13 June 1853
George F. Chandler b. 13 June 1855

Dr. Decatur Halliday b. 6 Aug 1867
Robt. Seymore Halliday b. 20 May 1869
Francis Leurany Halliday b. 21 Oct 1870

Josephus Woodson b. 11 Nov 1886
Chas. Woodson b. 8 July 1888, d. 21 Aug 1888
Etta Woodson b. 16 June 1889
Dendy Woodson b. 23 Feb 1891
Luceal Woodson b. 4 Sep 1893
Mary Caddie Woodson b. 4 Mar 1896

Reiner A. Chandler b. 1 Oct 1867
Seller T. Chandler b. 22 July 1870
Josiah W. Chandler b. 4 Oct 1872
James R. Chandler b. 23 June 1875
Wm. E. Chandler b. 8 Mar 1878
Geo. Moses Chandler b. 23 June 1880
Ed. L. Chandler b. 26 Sep 1885

Sol. S. Chapman b. 23 Aug 1861
Grady Chandler b. 5 Jan 1903
S. A. Halliday d. 22 July 1886
Moses Chandler d. 26 Dec 1908
E. R. Woodson d. 13 Apr 1896, m. Rena Chandler 8 Oct 1885

[Written in Bible, "Eddie Woodson Brooks." Bible owned by Mrs. Sam
Taylor, Greenville, S.C. (1945) Copied in the Greenville Court
House by compiler.]

BENJAMIN CHAPMAN

Benj. Chapman b. 13 Feb 1752, m. 14 Mar 1776 to Elizabeth Caswell
b. 12 Jan 1757 in Rowan Co., N.C., d. 23 Nov 1807, funeral preached
by Rev. Elijah Brazen
        Children
Ann Broadus b. 18 Sep 1777
John b. 7 Nov 1779
Thomas b. 28 Nov 1781
Elizabeth Male [sic] b. 20 Jan 1784 (twin)
Mary Roane b. 20 Jan 1784 (twin)
Frances b. 9 May 1786
Benjamin, Jr. b. 5 Sep 1788
William b. 26 Aug 1792
Sarah b. 4 June 1796
James b. 9 July 1799

[An Episcopal Prayer Book has this record. It is owned by Mrs.
Edward O. Hunter, Columbia, S.C. It was brought from Caswell Co.,
N.C. to Richland Co., S.C. when Benj. Chapman, Sr. moved to Colum-

bia, S.C. Mr. Andrea states that this Bible record is owned by
Mrs. Andrew L. Hall, Columbia, S.C. Benj. Chapman, Sr. lived in
Caswell & Rowan Cos., N.C. & Richland Co., S.C. Date of Prayer
Book - 1772.]

GERSHAM CHAPMAN

Gersham Chapman m. 29 Oct 1788 to Mary Carew d. 23 Jan 1844.
   Children
Mary Ann Chapman b. Thursday, 22 Oct 1789, m. 1st on 6 Oct 1808 to
   John Hooker, Esq. d. 28 July 1815 [bur. in Presbyterian Church
   yard, Columbia, S.C.; leaving no children], m. 2nd on 29 Oct 1818
   to Dr. George W. Glenn, Sr. of Newberry, S.C. as his 2nd wife
Joseph Chapman b. 14 July 1791 on Thursday, d. when 5 weeks old
Catherine Chapman b. 19 Sep 1792, d. the following 12 May
Sophie (Sophia) Chapman b. 12 Mar 1794 on Wednesday evening, d. 23
   Jan 1844
Harriet Chapman b. 17 Dec 1796 on Thursday at 12:00, m. Thursday,
   28 Jan 1813 to Samuel Ried
Sarah Chapman b. Monday evening, 26 June 1797, d. 20 Jan 1798
John Chapman b. Wednesday morning, 10 July 1799, d. 27 Oct 1822
   [Bur. in Columbia by his father]
Sarah B. Chapman b. 24 Jan 1801 [Second dau. by the name], d. 9
   Dec 1843, m. James P. Caldwell
Rebecca Chapman b. 8 Oct 1802, m. Dr. John Logan
Eleanor D. Chapman b. 7 July 1804, d. 19 Jan 1844
Anne Chapman b. 4 Feb 1807, m. Thomas Jefferson Brown, children:
   Thomas, Sarah, Mary, & Jeffie
Joseph Chapman b. 25 July 1809 on Tuesday [M.D. moved to Ala.]

[Gersham Chapman bur. in 1st Presbyterian Church yard, Columbia,
S.C.. His wife, Mary, is bur. in Kings Creek (or Kennerly) grave-
yard, Newberry, S.C. She was dau. of Sir Thomas Carew, Welch-
Irish. Mother & three daughters d. of Tyler Grippe pneumonia. All
bur. in Kings Creek graveyard. From Episcopal Prayer Book owned by
Mary Carew Chapman, now in possession of Hugh Aiken of Greenville,
S.C.]

GILES CHAPMAN

Giles Chapman b. 27 June, d. 10 Apr 1819, m. 14 Sep 1775 to Mary
   Summer
John Chapman m. 30 Nov 1817 to Sophia
Ira Cromley m. 2 June 1842 to Martha
John A. Chapman m. 1 May 1845 to Mary
A. M. Chapman m. 26 Dec 1845 to Ernestine
Wm. Chapman m. 16 Dec 1851 to Frances
W. S. Peterson m. 27 May 1852 to Amanda
C. J. S. Bacon m. 27 Dec 1853 to Mary
S. B. Chappelle m. 11 Dec 1860 to Ellen
B. F. Lovelace m. 16 May 1867 to Susan
Charles Carson m. 4 Dec 1865 to Caroline Cromley

Giles Chapman, son of John Chapman b. 29 Dec 1818
John Abney Chapman ... b. 9 Mar 1821
Patsy Chapman ... b. 24 Dec 1822
Andrew Mills Chapman b. 11 Jan 1825
Thos. E. Chapman ... b. 5 Sep 1827
Wm. Chapman b. 27 May 1830
Mary Eliz. Chapman b. 31 Oct 1832
Nancy Amanda Chapman b. 8 June 1835
Minerva Susan Ann b. 7 Feb 1838
Eleanor Chapman b. 15 Mar 1841

Thos. Bladen, son of Wm. & Eleanor Bladen, b. 22 Dec 1827
Eliz. Bladen b. 25 Mar 1829

Sophia Cromley, dau. of Ira & Martha Cromley, b. 17 May 1843
Caroline Cromley b. 24 Aug 1845
John Cromley, son of Ira & Martha Cromley, b. 14 Nov 1847

Mary Emily Bacon b. 23 Nov 1861
Sophie Estelle Bacon b. 8 Dec 1863

John Watts Chapman Chappell b. 2 Mar 1862
Mary Eliz. Chappell b. 27 Aug 1863
Sophie Mathilde Fannie Chappell b. 18 Mar 1866

Sophie May Lovelace b. 15 May 1868

Giles Chapman d. in defense of his country at the battle of Buena
   Vista, Mexico 22 or 23 Feb 1847, son of John & Sophia Chapman
Patsy Cromley, dau. of John & Sophia Chapman, d. 21 Apr 1853
John Chapman, son of John & Sophia Chapman, d. 12 July 1853
Thos. E. Chapman, son of John Chapman, d. 27 Aug 1864 in conse-
   quence of a wound received in the Battle of Atlanta 28 July 1864
Sophia Chapman, wife of John Chapman, d. 8 June 1877
John Chapman d. 24 June 1854

Sophia Cromley, dau. of Ira & Martha Cromley, d. 6 Aug 1843
Edwin Cromley, son of Ira & Martha Cromley, d. 27 Mar 1857

Eleanor, wife of Wm. Bladen, d. 25 Apr 1829
Daniel C. Abney, son of John & Patsy Abney, d. 2 Feb 1845
Frances Chapman, wife of Wm. Chapman, d. 26 July 1853
Wm. Spencer Peterson d. in Battle of Atlanta, 28 July 1864
Stanmore B. Chappell was killed 18 Jan 1867

CHARLES A. CHEATHAM

Charles A. Cheatham b. 29 Apr 1842, d. 22 Mar 1874
Charles Augustus Cheatham b. 16 Feb 1871, d. 12 Aug 1905
John Oscar Cheatham b. 24 Apr 1873, d. 21 Aug 1940
Charles Oswald Cheatham b. 26 July 1902
Jack Irviox Cheatham b. 5 Feb 1922

MICHAEL W. CHRISTMAN

Michael W. Christman b. 4 Feb 1795, d. 25 Mar 1853, bur. at Fellowship Ch., Miss., m. 26 Apr 1825 to Keturah M. Young b. 23 Dec 1806, d. 18 Jan 1836, bur. at Miccoukee, Fla.
    Children
Jas. M. Christman b. 3 Feb 1826, d. 23 Dec 1851 in Mobile, Ala.
Rhoda E. Christman b. 16 Aug 1828 ["m. John Drish"]
Richard Furman Christman b. 10 Aug 1830 ["d. single in Webb, Miss."]
Jesse Mercer Christman b. 16 May 1832
Ann Christman b. 22 Sep 1834 ["d. single in 1875 in Miss."]

Phoebe, wife of John D. Williams, d. 27 July 1852
Susan Clove, wife of Wm. D. Watts, d. in 1836

[Capt. Washington Williams, our cousin, writes that Aunt Rhoda E. C. Williams has divorced her husband, Jas. Griffin Williams. This & data in square brackets above from letter as quoted. Data in this Bible from Leonard Andrea, Columbia, S.C.]

NANCY (WRIGHT) CLARY

William Clary m. 7 Oct 1811 to Nancy
Ebenezer Frost m. 1822 to Nancy Wright (Clary)
Ebenezer Frost m. 1st in 1816 to Elizabeth Gaither
John Wright m. 16 Feb 1819 to Polly
T. W. Frost m. 23 Apr 1843 to Polly (Boone)
John E. Frost m. 6 Aug 1846 to Alcey D. Hix

Mary Ann Clary b. 14 Sep 1816
Lucy Carline Clary b. 4 Feb 1818

William Clary d. 2 Apr 1819

[From Wright Frost, Knoxville, Tenn. Oct 1958 to Mrs. B. W. Gandrud of Tuscaloosa, Ala.]

MARTIN CLAY

Martin Clay b. 24 Feb 1807
Elizabeth Eliza Walker b. 26 May 1814
    Children
Washington Harvey b. 29 Mar 1834
Sinthy Matilda b. 27 Dec 1835
Mary Jane b. 10 Mar 1838
Joseph M. b. 10 Apr 1840
Eliz. Rust b. 11 Nov 1843
Martin Walker b. 27 June 1852

John Walker b. 22 Mar 1788
Sinthy Rust b. 20 May 1797

[The Clay family first settled in Southwest Va., coming into N.C.
1775 & settled in Avery Co. Bible now owned by Mrs. C. Leroy
Shuping, Jr., Greensboro, dau. of Robt. Luther Clay. Sent by Mrs.
Olive Webster, Greensboro, N.C.]

CHESLEY CLEGG

Chesley D. Clegg b. 23 Apr 1808, d. 15 Feb 1888, m. 9 Aug 1827 in
Walton Co., Ga. to Susan Owen Clegg b. 15 Apr 1809, d. 18 Aug 1891.
     Children
William Owen Clegg b. 22 May 1828
Jacob Hardeman Clegg b. 5 Oct 1829, d. 16 Oct 1829
Susan Wynn Clegg b. 7 Sep 1830, d. 4 Aug 1880
Thomas Brackett Clegg b. Apr 1832
Mary Rebeckah Clegg b. 22 July 1834
Chesley Davis Clegg b. Feb 1836, d. 23 July 1860
Virgil Abner Clegg b. 29 Nov 1837, d. 23 May 1889
Martha Amy Clegg b. 7 Oct 1839, d. 1899
Juliana Edney Clegg b. 28 July 1841
Robantey [?] Clegg b. 15 Nov 1843, d. 3 Mar 1844
John Powell Clegg b. 20 Dec 1844 went to Tex.
Perry Colley Clegg b. 6 Dec 1846
Elizabeth Echolg [?] Clegg b. 13 Apr 1851

The census of 1830, Walton Co., Ga. shows the following:

Chesley D. Clegg - one child under five & wife
Thomas Clegg - 30 & under 40 and wife under 40, three girls under
  10 & one boy under 5
Jonathon Clegg - under 60 & wife under 60, one girl under 15 [This
  Jonathon is thought to be the father of Thomas & Chesley D.
  Clegg, & brother of Thomas Clegg in N.C.]

[Chesley David or Davis Clegg had a brother, Thomas Clegg, who
went to Ga., Walton Co., about 1820, from Edgefield, S.C. They
both moved to Ga.]

THOMAS CLEGG

Peter & Ann Clegg

Isaac Clegg b. in Wales 1713

Thomas Clegg b. 1767, m. 1788 at Accomac, Va. to Bridget Polk,
moved to N.C. in 1789
     Children
William b. 15 Apr 1789, left no children
Esther Watts b. 1791, m. in 1810 to an Arent
John b. 17 Oct 1792, m. in Ga., visited N.C. in 1848, had 21 child-

ren by one wife
Isaac b. 9 Nov 1794
David b. 26 Sep 1796, m. Eliza Bynum, had a son, Carney Clegg
Elizabeth b. 19 Oct 1798
Nathaniel b. 1 Apr 1801
Thomas b. 19 May 1803
Margaret b. 2 May 1805, m. Mark Bynum
Nancy b. 22 Sep 1807, m. James Guthrie
Luther b. 15 Nov 1809
Baxter b. 15 Nov 1811, Methodist minister & teacher
Mary b. 1814

[This record was copied by G. W. Clegg, son of Nathaniel, from a small book found among his grandmother's papers after her death. This George Washington Clegg was the oldest member of the Clegg family known living in Statesville, N.C. Some desc. of this Thomas Clegg live in Greensboro, N.C. Joseph, son of John, lived in Siloam Springs, Arkansas, some in Little Rock, Arkansas, many are at Chatham, N.C., the old home of the Clegg family after leaving Va. or Md. A son of David & Eliza Clegg was John B. Clegg who lived in Moncure, N.C., was b. 1850, d. 29 Feb 1936.]

WILLIAM CLELAND

William Cleland b. 20 Sep 1783, d. 15 Apr 1835, m. 14 Feb 1808 to Hannah Plunkett b. 7 July 1791, d. 16 May 1827
    Children
Phoebe Cleland, dau., b. 6 Apr 1809, d. 9 Nov 1816
Elizabeth Cleland, dau., b. 21 Nov 1810, d. 14 Dec 1884, m. 27 July 1837
Nancy Cleland, dau., b. 20 Dec 1812, d. 18 Dec 1885
James H. Cleland, son, b. 21 Aug 1815, d. 10 May 1892 [The last member of his family to die]
Charles Cleland, son, b. 7 Oct 1817, d. 14 June 1887 [Day of month for death not fully legible]
William Cleland, Jr., son, b. 2 Feb 1820, d. 10 Feb 1841
Jane Cleland, dau., b. 24 Mar 1822, d. 10 May 1864, m. Thomas Craig Milford
David Cleland, son, b. 26 Jan 1825, d. 25 May 1864 [In Va. from wounds of Battle]

[This Bible owned by Mrs. Charles M. Darracott, 1 Poplar St., Abbeville, S.C. Bible continues as the Bible of John Mitchell Milford, see below. From File 23-518 of Abbeville Co. Estates: "Hannah, wife of William Cleland, Sr. was a dau. of William Plunkett of Newberry Co., S.C."]

REUBEN PYLES CLINKSCALES

Reuben Pyles Clinkscales b. 26 Jan 1846, d. 25 June 1908, m. 29 Oct 1872 to Mary Cornelia Hall b. 23 Jan 1856

Jas. Lawson Clinkscales 5 Apr 1875
Reuben Pringle Clinkscales b. 19 Oct 1876, d. 3 Mar 1952, m. 2 Feb
  1916 to Alice Phillips, d. 19 June 1879 [should be b. date?]
Rebecca Eliz. Clinkscales b. 9 Mar 1878
Edgar Hall Clinkscales b. 6 Aug 1881, m. 1st on 31 May 1903 to
  Kathleen McGregor, m. 2nd to Lillian Morquist
Essie Ophelia Clinkscales b. 2 Feb 1883, m. 8 June 1910 to Guy Ham-
  mond Norris d. 30 Sep 1887 [should be b. date?]
Jos. Frederick Clinkscales b. 3 Apr 1885
Milton Baxter Clinkscales b. 15 Apr 1887, m. 15 Feb 1919 to Karon
  Traynham d. 5 Aug 1942
Sallie Magdalina Clinkscales b. 28 May 1889
Lillian Alkana Clinkscales b. 9 Dec 1891, m. 28 June 1922 to Dr.
  Jas. B. Green
Wm. Augustus Clinkscales b. 1 Mar 1895, m. Rosella Gleen [Glenn?]
Laura Mabel Clinkscales b. 31 Oct 1898, m. 22 Oct 1919 to Harold
  Tracy Bolt

Mary Cornelia Clinkscales m. 22 Sep 1909 to Robt. Abney Abrams d.
  22 Sep 1954
Mary Cornelia Hall Clinkscales d. 19 June 1921
Mary C. Clinkscales Abrams d. 1 Jan 1941

[Bible owned by Mrs. Ophelia C. Norris, Hartwell, Ga.]

JESSE COBB

Jesse Cobb b. 1729 in Goochland Co., Va., d. 3 Sep 1807 in Dobbs
Co., N.C., m. 17 Oct 1771 in Newbern, N.C. to Elizabeth (Heritage).
  Children
Ann b. 3 Sep 1772
Susannah b. 3 Feb 1774
John b. 3 May 1776
Jesse Heritage b. 6 Mar 1778
Elizabeth b. 27 Apr 1780

[This Bible record was given to the compiler in Jan. 1956 by Mary
Louisa Cobb, a descendant of John Cobb above.]

ROBERT COCHRAN

Robert Cochran b. 13 Aug 1805 in N.C. m. Betsy Smith b. 1817 in
  N.C.
Wm. Stegall b. 1811 in Anson Co., N.C., m. Miss Trull b. Anson Co.,
  N.C.

John Wm. Cochran, son of Robert Cochran, b. 13 Apr 1835 in Anson
  Co., N.C., d. 7 Nov 1916 in Thomasville, Ga., m. Hester Ann Ste-
  gall, dau. of Wm. Stegall, b. 2 June 1842 in Anson Co., N.C., d.
  6 June 1901 in Thomasville, Ga.
  Children
Chas. A. b. 13 Oct 1859 in Dougherty Co., Ga., d. 31 Mar 1926 in

m. 1884 to Katherine E. Fudge b. 18 Nov 1865
Wm. Berry b. 4 Feb 1872 in Thomas Co., Ga., d. 4 Nov 1946 in Thomasville, Ga., m. 23 Jan 1896 to Mary Martha Doss b. 16 Feb 1873 in Thomas Co., Ga.,[living in Sep 1950]

[From Bible of Mrs. Wm. Berry Cochran, Sr. 412 N. Broad St., Thomasville, Ga. Her grandfather was James Thweatt Hayes b. 25 Mar 1811 in Clark Co., Ga., d. 29 Jan 1878 in Thomas Co., Ga., m. 7 Aug 1832 in Thomas Co., Ga. to Julia Hadley b. 18 Sep 1802, d. 3 Feb 1863. Father of Mrs. Wm. Berry Cochran, Sr., Reddick Parker Doss, was b. 12 Aug 1836 in Fayette Co., Tenn., d. 10 Sep 1921, m. 1 Feb 1865 to Martha Hamilton Hayes b. 30 Aug 1837, d. 24 Feb 1913. Great grand father of Mrs. Wm. Berry Cochran, Sr., George White Hayes, b. 24 Nov 1783 in Charlotte Co., Va., d. 14 Sep 1840 in Thomas Co., Ga., m. 15 Nov 1804 to Mary Hamilton b. 17 Jan 1788 in Hancock Co., Ga., d. 23 Mar 1870 in Thomas Co., Ga. Great great grand father of Mrs. Wm. Berry Cochran, Sr., John Hamilton d. 1818, left a will, m. Tabitha Thweatt, both of Hancock Co., Ga. The last information is from court records. The information for Geo. White Hayes & wife, Mary Hamilton Hayes, is from their tombstones but Mrs. Cochran says this is also in the Bible in her possession.]

JOHN M. COKER

John M. Coker d. 18 May 1866, m. 1st on4 July 1827 to Sarah Ann Garner d. 15 Oct 1838 [error?, note date of 2nd m.], m. 2nd on 11 Feb 1838 to Sarah Dalrymple d. 2 Nov 1879.
    Children
Robt. Henry Coker b. 24 Mar 1829
Ann Elizabeth b. 17 Sep 1831
William Thomas b. 11 June 1833
Sarah Margaret b. 24 June 1836 [m. William Huggins]
Mary Jane b. 29 Mar 1840, d. 13 Aug 1846
Catharine (Catherine C.) b. 11 June 1841, d. Nov 1927 [m. Charles DeWitt Chapman]
Hannah b. 11 Sep 1842
Franky (Francis) b. 15 Sep 1844, d. 14 Aug 1846
Emila b. 3 May 1846, d. 15 Jan 1915
Isabelah b. 10 Feb 1848
Rachel A. b. 20 May 1849
[Alice, not listed]

[This Bible record was recorded in an old Ledger owned by Saml. DeWitt Chapman and now owned by Charlie Chapman of near Hartsville, S.C. John Hartwell Chapman, son of Chas. Dewitt & Catherine Coker Chapman m. Claudia Augusta Huggins, dau. of William Huggins & Sarah Margaret Coker. They were the parents of Mrs. K. R. Mishoe, Wilmington, N.C. who gave this record. John Mark Coker & his 1st wife Sarah Ann Garner went to Miss. She d. & he returned to S.C. (that may be N.C.) with four small children. John Mark Coker's mother was Nancy McClendon Coker.]

WHITLEY COKER

Whitley Coker b. 25 Nov 1783, d. 1 Jan 1833, m. Ann
    Children

Irwin Wayne b. 17 Dec 1814, d. 1815
John S. b. 8 Sep 1817, d. in Yankee prison
Rebecca B. S. b. 27 Jan 1819, m. W. H. Price
Mary Gill b. 10 July 1820
Wm. David b. 6 Nov 1821
Magdalene b. 3 Apr 1824
Jas. Myers 25 Aug 1827
Lenorah Ann b. 4 Apr 1830

[Family from S.C.]

REUBEN COLLINS

Reuben Collins d. 8 Oct 1830 [left will], lived in Kershaw Co.,
S.C., m. Monaca Collins
    Children
Elizabeth b. 27 July 1783
Susanner b. 7 Apr 1785
Jesse b. 16 Dec 1790
Lewis b. 18 Jan 1793
Bartlett b. 3 Jan 1795
Jonathan b. 8 July 1797
Thomas D. b. 22 June 1802

[From the Diary of a French Roman Catholic priest who travelled
during the Revolution in upper Camden Dist., S.C. as a missionary
to the Catawba Indians: "Married Reuben Collins to Monica Durand on
the Feast Day of the Precious Blood 1782." L. Andrea says it is
known that the wife of Reuben Collins was Monica Duren. This Bible
data were copied from a photostat owned by Mrs. Dudley Winston Conner, Hattiesburg, Miss. Photostat made from the original Bible
page owned by Newton E. Collins, Monterey, Calif.]

WILLIAM COLLINS

Wm. Collins b. 1 Jan 1772 in S.C., d. 22 Feb 1842 in Ind., m. Nancy Drake b. 20 Nov 1776, d. 25 Feb 1865 in Ind.
    Children
John Collins b. 1 May 1799 in S.C., d. 8 Sep 1864 in Ind., m. 1st
   to Eliz. Seawright, m. 2nd to Clarissa Evans,(dau. of Jas. Evans
   & his wife, Eliz. Wirt) b. 1811 near Knoxville, Tenn., d. 28 Jan
   1889 in Hancock, Ind.
Nancy m. James Hodges
Mary m. Isaac Snider
Wm. Collins, Jr. m. Eliz. Snider

Children of John Collins & Eliz. Seawright
Wm. Franklin b. S.C.
Margaret Rebecca b. S.C.
Children of John Collins & Clarissa Evans
Eliz. b. 18 July 1838, d. 6 Feb 1889, m. Thos. Ferguson
Martin Van Buren b. 24 Mar 1840, d. 12 Sep 1920, m. 21 ... 1867 to
Celia Wright (dau. of Joseph Wright b. 27 Dec 1810 in Pa., d. 15
Nov 1891 in Ind., m. Eliz. Stephens b. 31 May 1811 in N.C., d. 14
Jan 1901 in Ind.) b. 4 Mar 1843 in Ind., d. 1877 in Ind., m. in
Hancock Co., Ind. [Their children are listed in this Bible, but
are so late that they are not reproduced here.]
Jas. Evans b. 14 Jan 1842, d. 3 Jan 1935, m. 21 Nov 1867 to Henri-
etta Snider
Ebenezer Erskine b. 28 May 1843, d. 1898, m. Hannah Wilson
Chris. Columbus b. 9 Jan 1847, d. 21 Jan 1929, m. 1869 to Mary Cot-
ton
Nancy Bethany b. 25 Jan 1851, d. 1932, m. 12 July 1876 to Moses
Bates

[Leonard Andrea, Columbia, S.C. states, "From estate file of Andrew
Seawright in Abbeville Co., S.C. it shows that the parents of John
Collins' 1st wife, Eliz. Seawright were Andrew Seawright & his wife
Margaret (Richey)...Eliz. d. in S.C. & is buried in old Greenville
Presbyterian Church, Donalds, S.C. After her death, her husband,
John Collins, moved to near Knoxville, Tenn. & from there to Han-
cock Co., Ind."]

DUNCAN COLQUHOUN

Duncan Colquhoun b. 18 Dec 1796, d. 17 Nov 1851, m. 12 Nov 1818 to
Sarah McNeal b. 19 Aug 1800, d. 9 May 1863
Children
Archibald Colquhoun b. 19 Aug 1819, m. Sarah Jane McMurray
Mary Colquhoun b. 13 Apr 1821, m. 1st to Mr. Whatley, m. 2nd to Mr.
Phillips, m. 3rd to Mr. Moore
Margaret Ann Colquhoun b. 26 Feb 1823, m. 1844 to Robt. M. Patter-
son
Isabel Colquhoun b. 13 Dec 1824, d. 16 Nov 1828
Malcolm Colquhoun b. 16 July 1826, m. Catherine McKee
Rachel Colquhoun b. 29 Mar 1828, m. Jas. Turner Phillips
Calvin Colquhoun b. 29 Aug 1830, m. 1st to Mrs. Fatima Snelgrove,
nee Fatima Buckner, m. 2nd to Ann Miller
John C. Colquhoun b. 2 Sep 1832, m. Ebiline Watts
Ann Eliz. Colquhoun b. 9 Nov 1834, m. Nathan Baugh
Jas. Gamble Colquhoun b. 19 Aug 1836, m. 1st to Alice Miller, m.
2nd to Rebecca Roberts
Wm. Colquhoun b. 17 July 1838, m. Sarah Phillips
Richard Marks Colquhoun b. 31 May 1841, m. Manah Wesley Snelgrove

[This Bible is owned by the family of the Rev. Edwin C. Calhoun,
Methodist minister, 229 Alex. Hamilton Dr., San Antonio 1, Tex.
This family moved from along the N.C. state line into Cheraw Dist.,

S.C., then to Henry Co., Ga. & finally to Talbot Co., Ga. where the
parents and several of the children died. Archibald Colquhoun, Sr.
d. 15 Sep 1839. Archibald Colquhoun d. 9 Sep 1855 in Bienville
Parish, La.]

WILSON CONNER

Wilson Conner b. 7 July 1768 in Craven Co., S.C. m. 8 Oct 1789 in
Marlboro Co., S.C. to Mary Cook b. 1 Aug 1774 in Cheraw Dist., S.C.
    Births [children & grandchildren mixed]
James Gassaway Conner 20 Aug 1790
Nancy Conner 20 Apr 1792
Harriott Elizabeth Conner Sep 1793
Lucy Ann Conner [date not legible]
Mary J. Conner [date not legible]
Thomas Benton Conner 21 Oct 1798
Betsy Conner 9 Mar 1801
Polly Godwin Conner 25 Jan 1804
Eliza Tarpley Conner 29 July 1807
Mariah McDonald Conner 13 June 1810
Wilson Conner Cooper 16 Sep 1812, son of George Cooper
Wilson Walker Conner 19 Apr 1813
Mary Ann Elizabeth Cooper 4 Dec 1813
Samuel Conner Griffin 23 Sep 1814, son of John Griffin
Penelope Luvaney Cooper 14 June 1815
Elizabeth Griffin 19 Oct 1815
William DeWitt Clinton Conner 23 Sep 1819
George Washington Cooper 21 Apr 1821
Thomas Benton Conner 29 Aug 1821, son of James Conner
Thomas B. C. Cooper 26 Dec 1824
Louisa Ann Conner 25 Oct 1815
Eleanor Cook Cooper 10 Feb 1817
Martha Lucy Conner 30 Mar 1818
James Conner Griffin 18 Feb 1818
Penelope Ryals 11 Sep 1798
Luvany Cooper 16 Feb 1819
Mary Ann Sullivant 10 Nov 1825
    Marriages
Nancy Conner m. 20 Dec 1810 to George Cooper
Harriott Conner m. 25 May 1813 to John Griffin
James Gassaway Conner m. 1 Oct 1818 to Penelope Rials
Lucy Ann Conner m. 31 Mar 1822 to Joseph Ryals
Mary J. Conner m. 2 Jan 1824 to Thomas C. Sullivant
    Deaths
Thomas Conner, Sr. d. 4 Aug 1768, aged 90 yrs.
Margaret, wife of Thomas Conner, d. 17--, aged 60 yrs.
John Beverly d. 1786, aged 80 yrs.
Ann, wife of John Beverly, d. 1787, aged 81 yrs.
Eleanor Cook d. 15 Sep 1793, aged 50 yrs.
Ann Conner d. Sep 1791, aged 60 yrs. [nee Ann Beverley, mother of
  Wilson Conner]
Lewis Conner d. 30 Aug 1793, aged 37 yrs.

William Conner d. July 1797, aged 32 yrs.
Bethe Conner d. 1820, aged 27 yrs.
James Conner d. 1805 by a fall from a horse
Thomas Conner Jr. Jr. [sic] d. 12 Sep 1802, aged 75 yrs.
Samuel C. Griffin d. 21 Oct 1814, aged 27 Days
Annias Lang d. 21 July 1807
Betsy Conner d. 4 Feb 1809 in her 8th year
Elizabeth, widow of Annias Land, d. 10 May 1809

[Bible owned in 1920 by Mrs. W. C. McAllister, Hawkinsville, Ga.]

JOHN CONRAD

John Conrad, Sr. b. 26 Jan 1747 in Heidelberg Township in Pa., son
of Jacob & Maria Catharine late Reger, m. Catherine late Romig.
    Children
John b. 11 July 1778
Anna Elizabeth b. 4 Sep 1780
Jacob b. 15 Aug 1782
Abraham b. 13 Apr 1784
Isaac b. 26 Jan 1791

John Conrad, son of John & Caty, b. 11 July 1778 eleven miles from
the town of Reading in Berks Co., Pa. on the Tutpehocken Creek, water of the Schuykill River, d. 26 Nov 1850, aged 72 yrs, 4 mos. &
15 days, m. 27 Dec 1803 by Edward William Harbin, Esq. at the
Plantation of his bride's father (on which she was born) to Elizabeth Miller, dau. of Frederick & Sarah Miller, b. 9 Feb 1781 on
Stewart's Creek, Stokes Co., N.C., d. 27 Dec 1837, aged 55 yrs., 10
mos., & 18 days. Their children were all born near where their
parents were married on the Yadkin River, upper or western part of
Stokes Co., N.C.
    Children
John Joseph b. 13 Oct 1805 about the fourth hour P.M., about 15
    minutes before his twin brother Frederick Thomas, m. 1 Mar 1827
Frederick Thomas b. 13 Oct 1805, twin of John Joseph
Isaac b. 8 Jan 1807, d. 17 July 1850, aged 43 yrs., 6 mos. & 19
    days

[This record is in the possession of Mrs. Hale Houts, 230 W. 61st
St., Kansas City, Mo. This is not a Bible record but a family rec-
ord copied in a little booklet consisting of eight pages written by
a scribe who went through the country and is captioned as GENEALOG-
ICAL ACCOUNT OF BIRTHS, MARRIAGES AND BURIALS of Mr. John Conrad,
His Family written 1810.]

WILLIAM JEFFERSON COOK

William Jefferson Cook b. 16 Nov 1808
Sarah E. Crossland b. 25 July 1810
Mary Ann Cook b. 5 Nov 1830
Henriatta M. Cook b. 5 Nov 1832

James O. A. Cook b. 28 July 1834
Olivia J. Cook b. 1 May 1836
Laura E. W Cook b. 15 Oct 1837
John R. Cook b. 24 Apr 1839
Thomas A. M. Cook b. 27 Mar 1841
Josephine M. Cook b. 4 Jan 1843
Fannie G. Cook b. 7 Nov 1844
Sallie W. Cook b. 28 May 1846
Ann Margaret Cook b. 16 May 1851
Sarah Josephine Breeden b. 8 Sep 1853
Annie E. Breeden b. 28 July 1855
J. Lindsey Breeden b. 7 Oct 1857
W. Cook Breeden b. 9 Oct 1859
Clarence E. Breeden b. June 1862
Josie O. Breeden b. 4 Feb 1865
Henriatta E. Breeden b. 22 Feb 1868
M. A. A. Moore b. 10 Nov 1860
Laura S. Moore b. 15 Mar 1877
Daisy Cook b. 12 May 1871
Annie Cook b. 23 July 1873
T. A. M. Cook b. 3 May 1876
Laura M. Cook b. 11 Dec 1878
Sadie Belle Cook b. Aug 1885
Rosa O. Dantzler b. 14 June 1877
Lewis M. Dantzler b. 14 Jan 1879
Sarah C. Dantzler b. 28 Nov 1880
W. Zimmerman Dantzler b. 5 Aug 1882
H. E. Carlisle b. 26 Sep 1877
A. L. Carlisle b. 24 Feb 1880
W. C. Carlisle b. 27 May 1882
Sallie C. Carlisle b. 26 Nov 1884
J. B. Carlisle b. 19 July 1887
J. M. Carlisle b. 10 Feb 1890
M. Ray Carlisle b. Mar 1892
Gladys Carlisle b. 21 May 1894
Baby Carlisle b. 9 June 1896
Carlisle Breeden b. Jan 1881
Louise Breeden b. Jan 1883
Mattie Cook Breeden b. 22 Feb 1885
James Johnson Cook b. 5 Jan 1872
A. M. Willcox b. 18 Dec 1887
Genevieve Willcox b. 20 May 1890
Laurie Willcox b. 7 Nov 1892
Clark A. Willcox b. 10 Feb 1895
William Cook Willcox b. 27 Aug 1898
Olivia Willcox
Edith Hodges b. 18 May 1892
Joe B. Hodges b. 4 Jan 1894
Charlie P. Hodges b. Jan 1896
Wilbur Hodges b. June 1899 (twin)
Henrietta Mildred Hodges b. June 1899 (twin)
Mildred Hodges

Percy Hodges
Marguerite Crossland b. 2 Nov 1893
Lillian Crossland
Mary Louise Crossland
Laura Henriatta Crossland b. 13 Sep
Laura Collins b. 10 Dec 1899
Minnie Moore Collins b. 27 Oct 1902
Mildred Moore Collins b. 10 Feb 1906
Frances Dantzler Lander b. 13 Mar 1903
May Carlisle Moore b. 7 Nov 1909
Edward C. Breeden
Jessie P. Breeden
Gwendolin Breeden
W. C. Breeden
Hilda Breeden b. 28 May 1906

William Jefferson Cook m. 12 Jan 1830 to Sarah Elizabeth Crossland
Henriatta M. Cook m. 25 Nov 1852 to Joseph L. Breeden
Laura A. F. Cook m. 5 Jan 1860 to John S. Moore
John R. Cook m. 5 May 1869 to Lucy E. Spigner
Thomas A. M. Cook m. 1 Feb 1871 to Laura Johnson
D. Zimmerman Dantzler m. 1 Feb 1876 to Fannie G. Cook
Edwin S. Carlisle m. 30 Nov 1876 to Annie A. Breeden
Lindsey J. Breeden m. 15 Jan 1880 to May Carlisle
Clark A. Willcox m. 9 Mar 1887 to Minnie A. Moore
Clifford Crosland m. 12 Dec 1889 to Hennie E. Breeden
Malcolm W. Collins m. 4 Jan 1899 to Lollie S. Moore
Laura Cook m. 25 Dec 1899 to Marion Kramer
Daisy Cook m. 6 June 1899 to Wilber Gaskin
Charles P. Hodges m. 3 Apr 1890 to Josie O. Breeden
Cook Breeden m. 15 Aug 1891 to Annie Powers

William J. Cook d. 25 Dec 1881
Sarah E. Cook d. 15 Feb 1885
Mary A. Cook d. 23 Oct 1831
Josephine Cook d. 23 Nov 1845
Ann M. Cook d. 18 May 1851
James O. A. Cook d. 29 Mar 187-
Thomas A. M. Cook d. 25 Mar 1876
Laura Johnson Cook d. 28 Nov 1872
James J. Cook d. 12 Sep 1872
S. Josephine Breeden d. Oct 1854
Annie A. Cook d. 17 July 1875
Joe B. Carlisle d. 28 Apr 1889
John R. Cook d. 15 May 1895
Joseph B. Hodges d. 9 June 1895
Mattie Cook Breeden d. 1 June 1896
Henriatta M. Breeden d. 1 Nov 1898
Baby Carlisle d. 8 Aug 1896
William Cook Willcox d. 5 Jan 1900
The Rev. D. L. Dantzler d. 30 Aug 1899
Laura Collins d. 21 Oct 1902

Olivia Willcox
Joseph L. Breeden d. 21 Nov 1905
John S. Moore d. 29 Mar 1907
Sarah C. Dantzler d. 19 Aug 1908
Laura Moore d. 29 Apr 1910
May Carlisle Breeden d. 17 June 1910
Lucy E. Cook d. 21 May 1911, bur. at St. Matthews, S.C.
Olivia Cook d. 4 Apr. 1918 [in different handwriting]
W. C. Carlisle d. 1 Dec 1924 [in different handwriting]
E. S. Carlisle d. 29 Nov 1926 [in different handwriting]
Annie Breeden Carlisle d. 14 Feb 1953

[Bible of Olivia J. Cook, Marlboro Co., S.C.]

J. A. COOPER

J. A. Cooper, Jr., son of J. A. Cooper & his wife, Charity, b. 23
Sep 1797 in N.C., m. 29 July 1825 to Mary Buford b. in S.C.
    Daughter
Caroline b. 11 May 1826

[Mrs. B. B. Lane, a descendant reports that J. A. Cooper d. 11 Aug
1866 in Mobile, Ala. Mary Buford Cooper d. 26 Mar 1882 in Santa
Rosa Co., Fla. Their dau., Caroline Cooper Curry Waters d. 5 Apr
1906 in Mobile, Ala. J. A. Cooper & Mary Buford m. in Baldwin Co.,
Ala.]

CORBIN

"Our ancestors set sail from Ireland in 1762 and on the 23rd day of
November. A number of families."

James Seawright d. 12 Dec 1762, bur. in the sea
Samuel P. Corbin m. 15 Mar 1827
Mary Susannah, dau. of Samuel P. & Caroline Corbin, b. 1 Apr 1825
Charles & Margaret Rucker m. 12th ... .
Elizabeth Corbin b. 27 Dec 1770
Sarah Corbin b. 16 Feb 1774
Ellender Corbin b. 4 Sep 1777
Margaret Rucker b. 5 Mar 1804
Hannar Susannah Corbin d. 18 June 1829
Mary C., wife of Rev. E. H. Graves, d. 22 Feb 1898 in her 69th year
Samuel Corbin b. 14 Feb 1822 "and the River was in a big freshet
    and the waters came up to the barn and crib doors."
John Seawright d. 5 Nov 1807
Jane Ellison d. 20 Mar 1817
Elizabeth Chambley d. 6 June 1798
Susannah Corbin d. 9 Oct 1814
Samuel Corbin d. 27 Dec 1822
Margaret Stivender d. 23 Apr 1885
Samuel Senn Corbin b. 1 Mar 1825, d. 22 Aug 18--, son of Samuel &
    Hanna Corbin

David Rucker b. 8 Mar 1801, d. 19 June 1858
Wesley Asbury Rucker b. 18 Sep 18--, d. 13 Sep 18-4
Lew.....4 ... 18-8
............12 ...1820
Mrs. ....ain d. 22 Mar 1820
.... Lucioas ... d. 31 Jan 1820

[This Bible is owned by the Calhoun Co. Historical Soc., St. Matthews, S.C. The Bible was found in an abandoned house on Beaver Creek and was brought to the Society. The Bible came from Ireland to Beaver Creek in old Orangebury Co. in 1762. The entries cover four pages & each page has double rows. The pages have so deteriorated that but little can be read, and all the outside rows are gone. Blanks indicate not legible.]

WILLIAM CORNELIUS

William Cornelius b. 1754 (son of Ann Phillips b. 1729, d. 4 Oct 1807), bapt. 3 June 1825, d. 27 July 1842, m. 5 June 1774 to Lettice b. 1756, bapt. 6 Jan 1825, d. 19 May 1834
    Children
Ann b. 12 July 1776
Ilsie [Jesse?] b. 20 Nov 1778
Betsy b. 12 Oct 1781
Moses b. 20 Nov 1784
Amos (Aaron) b. 12 Aug 1786
William b. 21 Aug 1789
Champion b. 31 Mar 1792
Beveraly b. 12 July 1794
Lettice b. 3 Apr 1797
Tabitha b. 30 Dec 1800

[This record copied by Mr. O. B. Cornelius, Birmingham, Ala. It was sent to Mrs. Warren P. Williamson, Mill Creek Rd., Youngstown, Ohio in June 1930. Mr. Cornelius said that the family came from England and S.C. and was Primitive Baptist.]

THOMAS COWAN, SR.

Thomas Cowan, Sr. b. 22 Sep 1767 in Delaware, son of John & Priscilla Haughey Cowan, d. 5 Apr 1831, m. 1st in Mar 1787 in Onslow Co., N.C. to Elizabeth Sage, dau. of Robert & Sarah Sage, b. Oct 1765, d. 30 Sep 1796, m. 2nd on 22 Jan 1798 in Onslow Co., N.C. to Sarah Sage, dau. of Robert & Sarah Sage, b. 14 Oct 1774 in Onslow Co., N.C., d. 14 Oct 1866.
    Children
John Cowan b. 9 Feb 1789 in New Hanover Co., N.C.
Thos. Cowan, Jr. b. 3 Nov 1798 in Wilmington, N.C., d. 3 Dec 1799
Robt. Cowan b. 27 Apr 1801 in Wilmington, N.C.
Thos. Cowan, Jr. b. 11 Oct 1803 in Wilmington, N.C. d. 26 May 1883
   in Pittsboro, N.C., m. 1st on 11 May 1831 to Margaret Matilda
   McIlhenny, dau. of James & Ann, b. 2 Feb 1912, d. 8 Aug 1833, m.

2nd on 17 Dec 1834 to Mary Ashe London
Sarah Eliza Cowan b. 27 June 1808 in Wilmington, N.C., m. 12 June
    1873 to Rev. A. P. Repiton
Priscilla Ann Cowan b. 10 Sep 1810 in Wilmington, N.C., d. 5 Oct
    1814
Caroline L. Cowan b. 5 Apr 1812, d. 4 Sep 1815
James M. Cowan b. 18 Mar 1816, d. 8 Nov 1826
James McIlhenny Cowan b. 8 Apr 1833, d. 4 Dec 1878

Sarah Sage Cowan, Jr. & Mary Ashe Cowan, great grand daughters of
    Robert Sage (b. 7 Mar 1730) & his wife Sarah (b. 25 Nov 1740), b.
    2 Nov 1852 in Wilmington, N.C., d. 3 Apr 1939 [both?]

[This record is from the Bible of Rev. John Brown, printed by Hopkins & Seymour, N.Y. Apr 1806. This copy sent to Mrs. Ida Brooks
Kellam of Wilmington, N.C. in Apr 1940 by Geo. P. James, Washington, D.C. The last item is not clear to the compiler.]

WILLIAM COX

Wm. Cox b. 6 Mar 1786, m. 16 June 1808 to Fannie Grey b. 1 June
    1785
    Children
Polly b. 25 Aug 1809 m. 12 Mar 1833 to Mason Kay
Elizabeth b. 20 Sep 1811, m. 1 Nov 1832
Reuben B. b. 12 Dec 1813
Hulda b. 2 Mar 1816
Sally b. 24 Feb 1818
Thomas b. 14 Dec 1819
Hepsi b. 18 Apr 18.. [not legible]
Lucinda b. 13 Aug 18.. [not legible]
Wm. D. b. 10 July 1828

[Leonard Andrea, professional genealogist, Columbia, S.C. says,
"From my files, I know that this Wm. is the son of Reuben Cox & his
wife, Eliz. Davis, who came to Anderson Co., S.C. from Va. soon
after the Rev. War."]

JOHN COZBY

John Cozby b. 16 Dec 1739, d. 27 June 1818, m. Elizabeth Paxton

Robert Cozby, son of John & Elizabeth Paxton Cozby, b. 22 July
1770, d. 11 June 1846, m. to Temperance Langdon Crawford (dau. of
William Crawford b. 6 Nov 1739 at Amherst, Va., d. 24 Nov 1814), b.
2 Sep 1776, d. 17 Mar 1832.
    Children
John Reid Cozby b. 9 Mar 1797, d. 13 Mar 1877, m. 31 Dec 1816 to
    Jane Oliver
Elizabeth Paxton Cozby b. 10 June 1799, d. 19 June 1821, m. 31 Dec
    1819 to Robert Oliver
Prudence Ann Cozby b. 6 Feb 1801, d. 27 May 1880, m. 22 Dec 1825 to

Samuel Y. Carlisle
Mary Campbell Cozby b. & d. in 1803
William Crawford Cozby b. 12 Aug 1804, d. 18 Dec 1886, m. 1st to
    Margaret D. Davis, m. 2nd on 2 July 1839 to Martha Elvira Persell
    [2nd wife was mother of Thomas Langdon Cozby & Lou Ella Cozby
    Latimer.]
Jane Foster Cozby b. 24 May 1806, d. 3 Dec 1882
Isabelle Trumball Cozby b. 3 June 1808, d. 3 Nov 1838
James Cooper Cozby b. 3 June 1809 [He was the father of Rev. James
    Cozby, noted Presbyterian Minister.]
Sara Brown Cozby b. 22 Dec 1811, d. 7 Nov 1833, m. Buckner G.
    Christopher
Margaret Baskin Cozby b. 2 Feb 1814, m. 24 Jan 1833 to Robert E.
    Carlisle
Esther Steele Cozby b. 21 Apr 1816, d. 6 Jan 1888, m. in 1835 to
    William B. Porter [Mother of Gilderoy Porter, famous writer &
    preacher in Miss.]
Martha Agness Cozby b. 12 May 1821, d. 1890

[The Cozbys came from Stradberry Hall, Queens Co., Ireland, origin-
ally Hermaston, Lincoln Co., England. Established in Ireland by
Francis Cozby, celebrated General of Kern (contemporary of Queen
Mary).]

DAVID CRAIG

(Captain) David Craig b. 2 Nov 1733 or 1743 in Scotland, d. 2 Nov
1785 in N.C., as in the Rev. War & had land grant in Tenn., m. in
1788 to Eleanor Johnston(e) b. 1743, d. 1831 in Mt. Pleasant, Tenn.
    Children
Margaret b. 15 Aug 1769, m. 4 Mar 1788 to Jas. Johnston
Patty b. 9 Mar 1771, m. Jas. Mitchell
William b. 18 Nov 1773, m. Mary Blackwood
Johnston b. 19 Nov 1774 m. Martha Blackwood
Isabella (Isabel) b. 6 Dec 1776, m. John Johnston 30 May 1795
John James b. 13 Nov 1779 in Orange Co., N.C.
Eleanor b. 2 or 25 Mar 1781, m. John Blackwood
David b. 15 Aug 1783, m. Delphia Gordon
Samuel Wilson b. 25 Dec 1785, m. Mary Johnston

[Mr. Henry P. Johnston, Box 7661, Birmingham 13, Ala. says, "Saml.
is buried in New Hope Presbyterian Church Cemetery, near Chapel
Hill, N.C. Mary, his wife, was the dau. of Chas. W. Johnston &
Martha Blackwood. Their wills are on file in Orange Co., N.C." He
had this Bible record from Miss Annie Hughes, Cedar Grove, N.C.
The Craigs, Blackwoods, Wilsons, Turrentines, Johnstons, Patter-
sons et al. came from Pa. to Orange Co., N.C. shortly after it was
opened up in 1752.]

JOHN CRIBB

John Cribb b. 29 Dec 1761

Samuel Cribb b. 22 Apr 1789
Noah Cribb b. 24 Dec 1791
Manuel Cribb b. 4 July 1794
Stephen Cribb b. 15 Oct 1796
Henry Cribb b. 10 Sep 1799

[This is but a fragment of a Bible. Mr. Andrea of Columbia, S.C.
copied all that was legible. It is in Georgetown, S.C.]

Baptism records from Prince Frederick Episcopal Church, Georgetown,
S.C.:
    John Cribb & wife Sarah has children baptised
Elie, a son, b. 20 Apr 1789 [Saml. above?]
Noah b. 23 Dec 1790 [note discrepancy]
Manuel b. 3 July 1794 [note discrepancy]
    John Cribb & wife Ann Cribb had bapt.
Anthony b. 5 June 1785

[L. Andrea says, "In Georgetown, S.C. is an old family graveyard of
John Cribb. When I was teaching in Georgetown Co. right after
World War I, I visited this cemetery but did not copy the inscrip-
tions. I do recall tombstones of Eli & Emanuel Cribb. Recently I
visited this cemetery in the company of Troy H. Cribb. We found
that forest fires had burned over the cemetery & not a stone was
legible. There had been, when first I saw the cemetery, a cypress
headboard to Anthony Cribb."]

                        ISAAC CRINER

Isaac Criner b. 22 Apr 1783
Granville Criner b. 18 July 1804 [bro. of Isaac]
Lucinda Criner b. 22 Aug 1816
Alfred Criner b. 2 Feb 1818
Rebecca Jane Criner b. 22 Nov 1819
Mahala Criner b. 15 Jan 1821
Polly Ann Criner b. 18 Nov 1823
Almyra Criner b. 16 May 1825
Isaac McClure [Criner] b. 25 Nov 1827
Nancy McCaine b. 15 July 1791 [wife of Isaac Criner, Sr.]
Nancy Criner b. 21 Apr 1829
Elizabeth Elena Criner b. 29 Apr 1831
Louisa Criner b. 11 Mar 1833
Martha W[oodson] Criner b. 6 Feb 1836
Rebecca Jane Criner b. 4 Sep 1828 [dau. of Granville]
James C. Criner b. 22 Nov 1838 [child of Alfred]
Samuel G. Criner b. 15 Feb 1841 [Child of Alfred]
Nancy A. Criner b. 22 June 1843 [child of Alfred]
Alfred Criner b. 6 July 1846 [child of Alfred]

Lucinda Scott m. 27 Nov 1834
Alfred Criner m. 2 Feb 1837
James F. Scurlock m. 31 1844 to Rebecca Criner

Charles E. Whiting m. 7 Sep 1848 to Nancy Criner
Newel A. Whiting m. 9 Apr 1851 to Louisa Criner
S. Robinson m. 23 Jan 1856 to Mary A. Criner
Isaac Mc. Criner m. 30 Mar 1858 to Lucy J. Strong
William C. Criner m. 29 Mar 1856 to Henrietta [Rigney]
William H. Moore m. 5 Oct 1865 to Woodson Criner [grandparents of
   Howard C. Jones]

Rebeca Criner d. 8 June 1826 [mother of Isaac Criner]
Nancy Criner d. 23 [?] July 1842 [wife of Isaac Criner]
Alfred Criner d. 22 Sep 1847, aged 29
Louisa Whiting d. 5 Mar 1863
Isaac Mc. [McClure] Criner d. 22 Sep 1863
William C. Criner d. 25 Nov 1864
Martha Woodson Moore d. 24 Aug 1875
Isaac Criner d. 15 Dec 1876
Mahala Criner d. 17 Mar 1885
Nannie Ena Latham d. 25 Apr 1900 [dau. of Martha Woodson Moore]
Almira Criner d. 31 Jan 1904
Pollie Robinson d. 24 Apr 1908 [Mary Ann Criner, wife of Seaborn
   Robinson]
Elizabeth E. Flippen d. Apr 1910

[Isaac Criner b. in East Tenn. & was supposedly the first white
settler of Madison Co., Ala. His home place has been continuously
in his family from 1804 to the present, at which time it is owned
by Howard C. Jones, a great grandson of Isaac Criner. The farm is
3 miles north of New Market, near Plevna. This Bible is now (1956)
in the possession of a great granddaughter, a sister of Howard C.
Jones.]

JOSEPH CRINER

Joseph Criner m. Elener Ingram
     Children
Nancy b. 11 Oct 180w, m. 3 Nov 1820 to Richard Bowhannon
Hili b. 13 Jan 1805
Susannah b. 20 Aug 1807
John Anthony b. 1 Sep 1809, d. 17 July 1840
Wm. Ingram b. 2 Dec 1811
Joseph L. b. 3 Mar 1814, d. 11 Oct 1843
Geo. W. b. 23 Mar 1816, d. 8 Oct 1836
Thomas D. b. 7 May 1819
Ellener (Elener) b. 8 May 1823, d. 5 Sep 1842
Sarah A. b. 14 Mar 1825
     Grandchildren
Ackerall Bowhannon b. 6 Oct 1821
Ellener A. b. 10 July 1823
Elizer [Eliza?] b. 27 Nov 1825

[Bible copied in 1926 by Mrs. B. W. Gandrud, Tuscaloosa, Ala. It
was then owned by Mrs. Matilda Walker, Gurley, Ala.]

C. M. CRONIC

Charles Miselto Cronic [known as Carlo] b. 12 Aug 1824, d. 27 Apr 1902, united with Methodist Church on 10 July 1861, enlisted in Co. A, 3rd Reg't Georgia Reserves as a private, in Upson Co., Ga., under Capt. E. A. Spivey, m. 23 May 1845 in Swifton, Crawford Co., Ga. to Louisa Sawyer, dau. of Patrick Sawyer b. 1794 & Barbara Sawyer b. 1794.

    Mary Elizabeth Cronic b. 7 Oct 1847, d. 10 July 1857
    Charles Miselto Cronic, Jr. b. 8 May 1849, d. 11 Apr 1851

Lewis Cronic b. 26 Jan 1827, d. 28 Dec 1904, enlisted as a private in Co. I, 16th Ga. Cav. Bat., trans. to Co. I, 13th Reg't. Ga. Cav., paroled 20 May 1865 (Col. S. J. Winn, Jackson Co.), m. 23 Nov 1854 to Martha Ann Sawyer, dau. of Patrick & Barbara Sawyer.

    Margaret Caroline Cronic b. 16 Oct 1855, d. 26 Dec 1914, m. 2 Oct 1876 to William J. Duck
    Mary Jane Cronic b. 26 Mar 1857, d. 18 Mar 1939, m. 14 Nov 1883 to George Felton Bowman, son of Julius T. & Sarah Caroline Pirkle Bowman. [Rev. J. H. Cronic]
    Charles Jewett Cronic b. 23 Nov 1860, d. 22 May 1917, m. 1 Oct 1880 to Sarah Jane Smith, dau. of James & Nancy Twitty Smith. [Rev. J. W. Davis]
    Lewis Hayle Cronic b. 27 Sep 1863, d. 7 Sep 1899, m. 17 Nov 1887 to Mariah Buell [Rev. J. C. Forrester]
    Barbara Elizabeth Cronic b. 28 May 1866, d. 1950, m. 26 July 1886 to William J. Smith, son of Jas. & Nancy Twitty Smith [Rev. D. C. Sampson]
    Savannah Cronic b. 3 June 1870, d. 13 May 1917, m. 13 Jan 1889 to Harrison H. Duncan [Rev. C. M. Cronic]
    William Thomas Cronic b. 14 Apr 1873, m. 17 Oct 1896 to Augusta M. Massengill [Rev. W. J. Duck]

Elizabeth Brown Cronic, wife of Hayle Cronic died of a spider bite when 30 years old, leaving a son, John, aged one month.

Rev. Charles M., Lewis, and Rev. John H. Cronic were Masons. Their remains lie in Zion Baptist church near their father, Hayle [Hazel] Cronic, and Clarisa Pike, b. 9 Sep 1815, d. 27 June 1901

Jane, Harrison & Wilson Sawyer are brothers and sister of Martha & Louise Sawyer.

[This Bible now in the possession of William Thomas Cronic, nephew of Rev. C. M. Cronic]

J. H. CRONIC

John Hayle Cronic b. 9 Feb 1830, d. 28 June 1908, m. 28 Mar 1858 to Mary Ann Kennedy, dau. of Ambrose & Martha Gideon Kennedy, b. 13 Apr 1840, d. 30 Oct 1899

Washington Ambrose Cronic b. 15 Feb 1859, d. 19 Jan 1941, m. 27 Dec
1883 to Alice Lee Johnson, dau. of Wm. Franklin & Mary Elizabeth
Smith Johnson [Rev. F. V. Cheek]
William Bartow Cronic b. 9 Jan 1862, d. 5 Sep 1909, m. 23 Dec 1886
to Mary Josephine Smith, dau. of Abraham Neelin & Antine Titshaw
Smith [Rev. J. C. Forrester]
John Henry Cronic b. 4 July 1864, d. 28 Jan 1930, m. 10 Nov 1869 to
Elizabeth Anna Tanner, dau. of Thomas & Elizabeth McNeal Tanner
[S. J. Matthews]
LaVinia Isabella Cronic b. 8 Dec 1866, d. 6 Apr 1906, m. 11 Feb
1886 to Anderson Elias Smith, son of Abraham Neelin & Antine Tit-
shaw Smith [Rev. D. C. Simpson]
Harrison Taylor Cronic b. 15 Mar 1869, d. 10 Jan 1941, m. 16 July
1893 to Mrs. M. Elizabeth J. Titshaw, dau. of Alexander & Martha
Ann Smith Johnson [Rev. W. J. Duck]
Lewis Valentine Cronic b. 13 Oct 1871, m. 25 Dec 1902 to Minnie Lee
Hulsey, dau. of Jefferson Ivan & Ida Virginia Brady Hulsey [Rev.
W. J. Duck]
Mary Elizabeth Cronic b. 24 Apr 1874, m. 21 Dec 1894 to William
Smith [Rev. W. J. Duck]
Nancy Orleavy Cronic b. 14 May 1877, d. of Rheumatic Fever 12 Apr
1885
Jasper Preston Cronic b. 27 Oct 1879, m. 26 Nov 1927 to Ada McDon-
ald, dau. of Ed & Sally Anderson McDonald [Rev. Thos. Tate]
Emma Caroline Cronic b. 18 May 1882, m. 5 Jan 1905 to George Cand-
ler Hanes, son of Thomas & Laura Simpson Hanes [Rev. J. C. Duck]

Hayle Cronic b. 7 May 1801, d. 11 Feb 1879, m. 1st on 28 ... 1822
to Elizabeth Brown b. 29 Dec 1800, d. 12 Mar 1830, m. 2nd on 20 Mar
1838 to Clarisa Pike.

Ezekiel Pike b. 1785, d. 1 May 1835 m. 14 Feb 1856 to Margaret Pike

Rachel Cronic d. 26 July 1836
Matilda Pike m. 11 Aug 1828 to George Duncan

[This Bible in the possession of Rev. J. H. Cronic's dau., Mrs. G.
C. Hanes. Bible published 1870 by J. R. Jones]

SIMEON HARRISON CRONIC

Simeon H. Cronic b. 2 Sep 1833, d. 10 Dec 1901, m. 18 Dec 1854 to
Sarah Jane Smith b. 21 Dec 1834, d. 9 July 1898.

Martha Cronic b. 1 Feb 1856, d. 22 Apr 1944, m. 4 Dec 1873 to Jas.
A. McDaniel
John A. Cronic b. 10 Apr 1859, d. 21 Nov 1882, never married
Mary Frances Cronic b. 30 Apr 1861, d. 22 Jan 1927, m. 23 Jan 1879
to U. C. Roberts
Russell Valentine Cronic b. 8 Dec 1863, d. 7 Sep 1864
William Warren Cronic b. 6 Feb 1866, d. 20 May 1936, m. 8 Mar 1890
to Elvira Williams

Margaret Lula Cronic b. 29 July 1868, d. 2 Jan 1933, m. 1 Sep 1889
   to Lonzo Elijah Wood
David Eli Cronic b. 14 Apr 1872, d. 1 June 1948, never married
Annah May Cronic b. 1 Mar 1876, d. 28 Oct 1894, m. 18 Feb 1894 to
   W. G. Tuggle

Rachel Cronic d. 26 July 1836
John Cronic d. 19 Feb 1844
Jane Cronic d. 11 Feb 1863

James Smith of N.C. was father of Job Smith who wed ... Camp and of
James Smith, Jr. who wed Sarah Ragsdale.

          Children of James Smith & Sarah Ragsdale
David Smith m. Patsy Whaley, dau. of Eli & Aline Thompson Whaley.
   Eli Whaley was son of James Whaley
Arnold Smith m. 1st to Elizabeth Thompson, dau. of David Thompson,
   m. 2nd to Frances Johnson
James Smith, Jr., m. Nancy Twitty
Edward Smith m. Mary Millsaps
Charity Smith m. Starling Clack
Betsy Smith m. Allen Ridgeway
Fanny Smith m. John Pharr

          Children of David Smith & Patsy Whaley
John T. Smith m. Saphira Bell Smith [widow of Eli Smith]
Elizabeth Smith b. 2 Jan 1833, m. Nathaniel Maynard
Jane Smith m. S. H. Cronic [see above]
Russ Smith b. 3 July 1839, d. 12 Sep 1920, was a member of Cobb's
   Legion, m. 6 Nov 1870 to Carrie Pierce [b. 21 Aug 1839, d. 4 Jan
   1921]
Mary A. Smith m. John Curbow
Crawford Smith m. Hattie Trembel
Eli Dave Smith [Minister in Methodist Church], m. Tiny Duke
William M. Smith m. Martha Thompson, dau. of Rev. Adams Thompson,
   Jr. & Nancy Neighbors; g-dau. of Harthoa Thompson; gg-dau. of
   Adam Thompson, one of the first settlers of Hall Co., Ga.; g-dau.
   of John Neighbors who was lost to his family in the Gold Rush of
   California in 1849

          Children of Arnold & Elizabeth Thompson Smith
John Smith m. Elizabeth Hosch
Fletch Smith d. in C.S.A.
Joseph Smith m. Sarah Cooper
William Smith went to Texas, m. Vinie Curbow
Jane Faithy Smith m. Pinkney Princeton Pirkle
Caroline Smith m. Jasper N. Flanagan
Adeline Smith m. Rev. George L. Bagwell, a Baptist Minister
Drucilla Smith m. Marion Peters
          Children of Arnold & Frances Johnson Smith
Russ Smith m. Fanny Elder
Georgia Smith

James Smith b. 3 Mar 1828, d. 14 Mar 1902, m. Nancy Twitty b. 27
Oct, d. 3 Aug 1873
        Children
John T. Smith m. Sarah Ridgeway
Narcissus Smith m. William Harrison
Reuben Smith m. Mary Sims
William J. Smith [b. 11 Dec 1855 d. 24 Mar 1943], m. 1st to Mary
    Clack, m. 2nd on 26 July 1896 to Barbara Elizabeth Cronic, dau.
    of Lewis & Martha Sawyer Cronic
David Smith m. Martha Holloway
Sarah Jane Smith m. 1 Oct 1880 to Charles Jewett Cronic [Rev. J. W.
    Davis officiating]
Joseph Smith m. Melissa Flanagan, dau. of George Flanagan
Nancy Smith m. George Herdon
Asbury Smith m. Tishie Holloway
Arvill Smith m. Leila Partin

[This record is from a Testament published in 1866, now in possession of J. H. Cronic, grandson of S. H. Cronic]

[David Smith b. 18 Feb 1808, d. 18 Nov 1896. Fifteenth Oct, the
Sunbury Chapter NSDAR of Winder, Ga. unveiled a marker to D. Smith
in Smith's Cemetery on Hog Mountain Rd. In his extreme old age,
David Smith came from S.C. to the home of his son, Job Smith, where
he died. Martha (Patsy) Smith b. 5 June 1812, d. 11 Aug 1900]

John Cronic m. 20 Dec 1808 to Jane (Jennie) Pirkle (dau. of Mary
Pirkle d. 9 July 1836), b. 1782, d. 6 May 1864.
        Children
Valentine Cronic b. 16 Mar 1810, d. 1863, m. 10 Jan 1832 to Mrs.
    Peggy Reynolds
William Truman Cronic b. 12 Feb 1812, d. 1857, m. 12 Sep 1848 to
    Mrs. Louise Needham who m. 2nd on 25 Dec 1858 to Andrew R. Smith
John Cronic, Jr. b. 13 Feb 1814, d. 1847 or 1848, never married
Peter Tillman Cronic b. 25 Dec 1816, d. 1886, m. Annis Johnson
Milbrey Cronic b. 16 Apr 1819, d. 5 July 1840, never married
Mary Ann Cronic b. 26 Apr 1823, d. 12 Jan 1883, m. 20 Oct 1846 to
    Anderson H. Titshaw
Margaret Cronic b. 2 Mar 1826, d. 14 Nov 1904, m. 3 Aug 1845 to Wm.
    Simpson Pike b. 12 Feb 1824, d. 7 Jan 1894
Simeon H. Cronic m. Sarah Jane Smith [see above]

[This record is from a Bible published in 1842 by Jasper Harding,
now in possession of Jesse Harrison Cronic, grandson of S. H. Cron-
ic]

PHILIP CRUME

Philip Crume, son of Daniel & Elizabeth (Brook) Crume, b. 9 Aug
1724, d. 20 Apr 1801, m. 1st on 23 Dec 1749 to Sarah Withers who
d. 9 Feb 1787, aged 57 yrs., 16 days, m. 2nd on 9 Sep 1788 to Anna
Barat.

Children
Ralph b. 12 Dec 1750
Susanna b. 10 July 1754
Mary b. 15 Mar 1756
Daniel b. 6 Jan 1758
Jesse b. 16 Jan 1760
Elizabeth b. 19 Apr 1762
William b. 2 Apr 1764
Moses b. 27 Feb 1766
Isaac b. 17 Mar 1768, d. 7 Feb 1791, aged 21 yrs. [note discrepancy, should by 22 yrs.?]
Sarah b. 11 Mar 1771
Eunice b. 7 Dec 1776
John b. 26 ... 1789
Pagga [Peggy?] b. June 1791
Nansee [Nancy?] b. 20 Dec 1792
Kezia b. 7 Feb 1795
Squire b. 17 July 1798
Anna Barret (Barrett) [Barat?] b. 17 Dec 1769, d., m. 2nd to Jacob
  Marks b. 14 Feb 1781, d. 14 Aug 1814, m. 3rd to William Morris

    Marks children
Thomas b. 5 Mar 1807
James b. 19 Oct 1808
Elizabeth b. 17 Aug 1810, d. 14 Oct 1827
William b. 21 Mar 1812

d. 25 Dec 1786 [No name here. Mrs. Gandrud who copied this Bible
said she took it down as the owner called it to her]

[This Bible is owned by Mr. W. E. Crume, Tuscaloosa, Ala., copied
26 May 1962 by Pauline (Jones) Gandrud. Mrs. Gandrud states that
this Bible was printed in 1759 and is larger than most she has
seen. It was printed by Thos. Baskett, London, England by assigns
of Robert Baskett. Price 1 pound, 5 shillings. Between the Old &
New Testaments is, "Philip Crume, Sr. was born the 9th of Aug 1724
and now it is Jan 20th 1799." 1799 is scratched out and 1800 written.
One page has "Jacob Marks his hand and pen." Mr. W. E. Crume
states, "Philip Crume was born in Frederick Co., Va. & moved to
Nelson Co., Ky. where he continued to live. W. E. Crume was born
there. Philip Crume m. 1st Sarah Margaret Weathers or Withers, m.
2nd Hannah (Anna or Ann) Barrett." Mr. W. E. Crume's great grand
father was Philip's son, John, b. 1789.]

                        JOHN P. CULLUM

John P. Cullum b. 23 Mar 1793, d. 7:00 P.M., Monday, 7 Oct 1867,
aged 74 yrs., 6 mos. & 15 days, m. 27 Jan 1812 to Mary d. Wednesday, 3 Aug 1876, aged 83.

Clarrett Cullum b. 21 Nov 1813
Barzilley Cullum b. 15 Dec 1815, d. of congestive chill 1865 near

Averysboro, N.C, m. 4 May 1837 to Sarrahan (Sarah Ann) Cullum d.
4 Oct 1881, aged 59
William Eldredge Cullum b. 17 Aug 1818, d. 7 Feb 1865, killed at
Combee Ferry, S.C., m. 16 Sep 1838 to Frances (Francis) Merritt
d. 30 May 1870
Amanda Cullum b. 1 Mar 1821, d. 4 J.. 1889 [Jan or June, prob.
June], m. 14 ... 1840 to William West d. 7 J.. 1889 [only letter
J is still preserved]
Marryan Cullum b. 15 Jan 1824
Lucyan Cullum b. 12 June 1826, "consort" [term used as wife through-
out this record] of John G. Able, d. 7 Jan 1862
Lura Cullum b. 15 June 1828
John Irvan Cullum b. 10 Oct 1830, d. 28 Feb 1907, m. 19 Nov 1871 to
Alma Elouise Sawyer
Minerva Cullum b. 21 May 1833

William Early Sawyer d. 18 June 1888
Fannie D. Sawyer d. 5 Mar 1892
John Vardell Sawyer d. 9 Apr 1884
Clarriett Cullum Sawyer d. 4 Mar 1886
J. George Sally d. May 1888
Mary Jones Cullum b. 1797

        Children of J. I. & A. E. Cullum
Mary Elouise Cullum b. 29 June 1873
Lorena Gelina Cullum b. 30 Dec 1875
John Early Cullum b. 14 Feb 1878
Jessie Irving Cullum, dau., b. 1 Dec 1879
Laurens Eldredge Cullum b. 6 Oct 1881
Minerva Blanch Cullum b. 30 Oct 1883
Claude Tolulah Cullum b. 6 Oct 1887
Searon Calhoun Cullum b. 26 Feb 1890

                        ASA DARBY

Asa Darby b. 13 Apr 1756 in Ann Arundel Co., Md., d. 30 Dec 1833 in
Chester Co., S.C., m. 30 Nov 1779 in Craven Co., S.C. to Dorcas
Goore b. 3 May 1759 in Craven Co., S.C.
        Children
Nancy b. 15 Sep 1780 [m. Edward Sealy]
George b. 11 Apr 1783 [From Clark File she was a Clark but no first
name]
Anne b. 5 Apr 1785 [m. Thos. Sanders]
Lydia b. 9 July 1788 [m. John Sanders]
John b. 28 Feb 1792 [m. 1st Mary Ann Smith, m. and Leonora Foote,
m. 3rd Mary Kidd]
Elizabeth b. 3 July 1796 [m. Thos. Estes]
James b. 29 Jan 1799 [m. Eliz. Estes as per Estes-Lockhart File]
Mary b. 9 Aug 1801 [called Mary Humphries in Asa's est. file]
Wm. Jefferson b. 22 Sep 1804 [never married, shown by will 1830]
Thomas b. date blotched with water stain [had 2 minor ch. who were
heir to his part of Asa's est.]

                        97

[The marriages above are from the estate settlement of Asa Darby.
L. Andrea of Columbia, S.C. says, "Asa Darby was a Rev. War soldier
in 6th Bat. of Upper Md. Troop. He was the son of George & Anne
Darby of Md." This Bible was owned by Mr. Aden Darby of Cobb Co.,
Ga. in 1900. Wills, etc. in Chester Co., S.C.]

JOHN DARWIN

John Darwin b. 19 Mar 1755 in Md., d. 13 July 1837 in York Co., S.
C., m. 11 Mar 1783 to Jane Bland b. 2 Jan 1762, d. 10 Mar 1827
    Children
Nancy b. 4 Feb 1784, d. 22 Mar 1847, m. 17 Jan 1800 to Jeptha Har-
    rington, Union Co., S.C.
Mary b. 16 May 1785, d. 1856, m. 28 Jan 1803 to John Kendrick
William b. 8 Nov 1786, d. 1863, m. 17 Jan 1819 to Elizabeth Powell
Rebecca b. 7 Sep 1788, d. 14 Dec 1828
Rachel b. 10 Apr 1790, d. 7 Nov 1831, m. 17 Jan 1819 to John Powell
John Bland b. 12 Dec 1791, d. 5 Feb 1854, m. 15 Nov 1819 to Gilly
    Sandlin
Jane b. 25 Jan 1794, d. 5 Feb 1857, m. 27 Jan 1825 to John Smarr
Robert b. 4 July 1795, d. 1868
Matilda b. 8 July 1797, d. 23 May 1848, m. 17 Jan 1819 to William
    Berry
Sarah b. 19 Jan 1801, d. 28 Nov 1802
Pamela b. 14 Aug 1803, d. 12 Jan 1880, m. 27 Jan 1822 to Isaac Sum-
    merford
Peyton Bland b. 18 Apr 1805, d. 28 Dec 1883, m. 27 Jan 1825 to Mary
    Wilkinson d. 13 May 1855, m. 2nd to Jerusha James [dates not leg-
    ible]

James Asbury b. 10 Apr 1827 d. 11 May 1845 [prob. grandson]
Mollie b. 27 Dec 1856, m. 1 Nov 1877 to H. Washington Hope

[Bible owned by the family of the late May Darwin Hope, Atlanta,
Ga. John Darwin went from Md. to York Co., S.C.]

ABIGAIL HOLLINGSWORTH DAVIS

James Davis d. 18 June 1878, m. Tuesday 20 Jan 1829 by the Rev. Mr.
Joseph Babb to Abigail d. 16 Dec 1870.
    Children
Mary Ann Davis b. 2 Feb 1830 on Little River, Laurens, S.C., d. at
    the family residence in Laurens, S.C. 1 Jan 1832
Jane Hamilton Davis b. 6 May 1832 on Little River, Laurens Dist.,
    S.C., d. 19 Dec 1886 at Gatesville, Coryell Co., Tex., m. 11 Feb
    1874 to Ludy P. Davenport by the Rev. Mr. John R. Riley
John Jefferson Davis b. 7 Oct 1833 on Little River, Laurens Dist.,
    S.C., d. 24 Dec 1871
James Franklin Davis b. 5 May 1836 on Little River, Laurens Dist.,
    S.C., 3 Nov 1909 near Clinton, S.C. (Dr. James Franklin Davis),
    m. 22 Aug 1872 to Mrs. Julia Robard
Mary Susanna (Susan) Davis b. 20 Apr 1838 on Little River, Laurens

Dist., S.C., d. 5 Apr 1844
George Byrd Davis b. 6 Feb 1840 on Little River, Laurens Dist.,
    S.C., d. 29 Mar 1844
Susan Elizabeth Byrd Davis b. 30 July 1846 near Little River, Lau-
    rens Dist., S.C., m. 5 Mar 1874 by the Rev. Mr. John R. Riley to
    John J. Pluss

George Hollingsworth b. 3 Oct 1763
Joseph Hollingsworth b. 22 Sep 1765
Robert Hollingsworth b. 22 Nov 1767
Levy Hollingsworth b. 16 July 1771
Jemius Hollingsworth b. 26 Sep 1773
Hanah Hollingsworth b. 10 Nov 1776
Richard Hollingsworth b. 12 July 1778
Abram Hollingsworth b. 20 Nov 1792
Elizabeth Hollingsworth b. 20 Dec 1794
Maryann Hollingsworth b. 19 June 1797
Isaiah Hollingsworth b. 28 Sep 1799
Abigail Hollingsworth b. 7 June 1802
Jane Hollingsworth b. 1 June 1805
Robert Hollingsworth b. 10 Nov 1807
Susana Hollingsworth b. 15 Mar 1810
Eunice Hollingsworth b. 14 Mar 1813
Robert Caldwell b. 18 Nov 1819

Mary Ann Caldwell d. 30 Mar 1821
Elizabeth Hollingsworth d. 11 Sep 1826
Jane Hollingsworth d. 20 Sep 1826
Robert Hollingsworth d. 23 Sep 1826
Henry Hollingsworth d. 23 Sep 1826
Jane Austin d. 8 Nov 1826
Eunice Martin d. 10 June 1839, aged 26 yrs. & 28 days
Edward Martin d. the morning of 30 Oct 1845
Robert Jefferson, son of Edward & Eunice Martin, d. 8 July 1846,
    aged 10 yrs. & 3 days
Abram Hollingsworth d. the night of 9 Jan 1873

[Bible printed & published by M. Carey, No. 121 Chesnut St., Philadelphia 1816. It is now in the possession of Thomas Wier Davis,
Clinton, S.C.]

EDWARD DAVIS

Edward Davis m. 22 Dec 1801 to Anna Knupp in N.C., went to Union
Co., Ill. in 1818.
    Children
Caty b. 29 Apr 1802 in N.C.
Susana b. 23 Dec 1804 in N.C.
Jacob b. 12 May 1806 in N.C.
John b. 22 Feb 1808 in N.C.
Solomen b. 14 Nov 1810 in N.C.
David b. 22 Nov 1812 in N.C.

Philipena b. 12 June 1814 in N.C.
Wiley b. 11 July 1816 in N.C.
George b. 11 June 1818 in N.C.
Levi b. 10 June 1820 in Union Co., Ill. [see his Bible below]
Caleb b. 14 Apr 1823 in Union Co., Ill.

[This record sent by Mrs. C. W. Carnes, Okemah, Okla. in Aug 1962]

JAMES DAVIS

James Davis m. 1777 to Susannah Reed
      Children
John b. 28 Oct 1778
Priscilla b. 1781
William b. 16 May 1783
Sarah Epperson b. 1786
Rhoda b. 1788
James B. b. 1791
Nancy b. 1793
Martha Jordan b. 1796

[From the Pension File of James Davis from Charlotte Co., Va.]

JONATHAN DAVIS

Jonathan Davis b. 1734, d. 1785, m. Margaret Bond
      Children
Ann Davis m. Elijah Ayars
Samuel Davis & David Davis b. 1760 (twins)
Ammie Davis b. 1762
Susannah
Sarah d. 1789
Richard Davis d. 1833
John Davis b. 1775

[This Jonathan Davis succeeded Elder Jonathan Davis who died 1769
as pastor of the Church of Shiloh, Cumberland Co., N.J. where the
above Jonathan Davis remained until he died.]

Susannah Bond b. 1735 in Cecil Co., Md., d. 1810 in Shiloh, N.J.,
m. 1757 to Elnathan Davis b. 13 Dec 1735, d. Dec 1802, son of Jona-
than & Esther Davis of Hopewell, Cumberland Co., N.J.
      Children
Rachel Davis b. 1758, d. 1782
Jonathan Davis b. 1759, d. 1819
Jacob Davis b. 1761, d. 1822
Ebenezer Davis b. 1762, d. 1827
Susannah Davis b. 1767, d. 1770
Samuel Davis b. 1770, d. 1836
Jeremiah Davis b. 1771, d. 1799
Elnathan Davis b. 1774, d. 1842, m. Esther, dau. of Isaac Ayers,
   they had six children

100

Susannah Davis b. 1777, d. 1837
Margaret Davis b. 178-, d. 1837

[In or about 1662 there were three brothers: John, Jonathan, & William Davis who came to New England in a Welsh Baptist company under Rev. John Miles. Some of this Davis family moved to Long Island whence Jonathan & Elnathan Davis, supposed to be sons of one of the three above brothers, came to Trenton, N.J. Elnathan Davis was a noted surveyor. He was deputy Surveyor of Cumberland Co., N.J. and Surveyor General of N.J.]

Jarman Davis b. 1732
Jonathan Davis b. 1734, m. Margaret Bond
Elnathan Davis b. 1735, m. Susannah Bond
Isaac Davis b. 1737
Edith Davis b. 1739
Naomi Davis b. 1737, m. Caleb Ayers

LEVI DAVIS

Levi Davis b. 10 June 1820, m. 12 Aug 1841 in Union Co., Ill. to Esther Casper b. 25 Aug 1822
    Children
Stephen Monroe b. Aug 1842
Eliza Jane b. 26 Sep 1844
Anna Lucinda b. 9 Nov 1846
Jacob b. 21 Apr 1849
William Marshall b. 25 Dec 1851
Isaac Newton b. 21 May 1854
James Calvert b. 29 Dec 1856
Matilda Palestine b. 31 Aug 1859
Mary Isabelle b. 27 Apr 1862
George Adolphous b. 7 June 1865

[This record sent by Mrs. C. W. Carnes, Okemah, Okla., Aug 1962]

SOLOMON DAVIS

Solomon Davis of Worcester Co., Md., said to be of Welsh descent, d. 13 Mar 1784, aged upwards of 50 yrs., m. Mary d. 29 Jan 1779 in the 48th year of her age

John Davis, son of Solomon Davis & Mary, his wife, b. 2 Mar 1752, d. on the morning of 17 Oct 1831 at the family residence, m. 9 Jan 1787 by the Rev. McKerr to Anne, dau. of Benj. & Mary Byrd of Md., said to be English, b. 29 Nov 1764, d. on the night of 23 Nov 1826 at the family residence in Laurens, S.C.
Leze Davis b. 19 Aug 1755
Jesse Davis b. 21 Jan 1758, was taken prisoner by the English, carried to New York 25 May 1782, and died the same year in August
Eli Davis b. 27 July 1760
William Davis b. 22 Sep 1763

Dr. James Davis b. 8 Dec 1774, res. of Columbia, S.C., d. 4 Aug
1838 at Edward G. Palmer's, Fairfield Dist., S.C.
Rodah Davis d. 12 Apr 1775 being the sixth yr. of her age

Children of John & Anne Davis
Geo. Davis, son, b. 8 Dec 1787, d. 30 Oct 1810 aged 22 yrs.
John Davis, son, b. 21 Nov 1789, d. 17 Nov 1790
Mary Davis, dau., b. 24 Sep 1791, d. 24 Apr 1861, aged near 70 yrs.
at the residence of Robert Creswell, Esq., her husband
Dr. John H. Davis, son, b. 14 Jan 1795, d. 8 Feb 1877 at his family
residence, Laurens, S.C.
Eliz. Davis, dau., b. 4 Oct 1797, d. on the night of 14 Nov 1843 at
the family summer residence in Laurens Dist.
Jas. Davis, son, b. 5 Jan 1801 on Little River in Laurens Dist.,
S.C., m. 20 Jan 1829 by Rev. Mr. Jos. Babb to Abigail Hollings-
worth, dau. of Robt. & Jane Hollingsworth, b. 7 June 1802 near
Cross Hill, Laurens Dist., S.C., d. 16 Dec 1870 in Laurens, S.C.

Children of Jas. & A. H. Davis (all b. on Little River)
Mary Anne Davis, dau., b. 2 Feb 1830, d. on the morning of 1 Jan
1832 at the family residence in Laurens, S.C.
Jane Hamilton, dau., b. 6 May 1832
John Jefferson, son, b. 7 Oct 1833, d. 24 Dec 1871 in Laurens, S.C.
Jas. Franklin, son, b. 5 May 1836
Mary Susanna, dau., b. 6 Feb 1840, d. 5 Apr 1844
George Byrd, son, d. 29 Mar 1844
Susan Eliz. Byrad Davis, dau., b. 30 July 1846

Edward Wm. Davis, son of Jas. Davis d. in Fairfield, S.C. 30 Sep
1870

"My grandmother Mary Davis was Mary Smock or Smack before her marriage." [author unknown]
"Mrs. Mary Moore was my Byrd grandmother's maiden name." [This was
written by Jas. Davis, son of John & Anna Byrd Davis.]

[The births etc. of slaves are also listed in this Bible but not
copied here. This Bible now in the hands of Mr. Tom Wier Davis,
Columbia, S.C.]

JULIUS DAY

Julius Day b. 25 Oct 1815, m. 25 Mar 1841 to Elizabeth Hatcher b.
4 Jan 1822
Children
James L. b. 10 Jan 1842
John B. b. 6 Dec 1843, m. 20 Nov 1867 to Cornelia Renfroe
Emma F. b. 21 Nov 1845, m. 25 Feb 1868 to Charlie A. Mathis
Pierce B. b. 5 Dec 1848, m. 22 Jan 1880 to Annie G. Duriose
Catherine R. b. 29 Oct 1851
Lizzie P. b. 5 Sep 1853
A. H. S. b. 28 June 1856, m. Winona Gray

Mary Ida b. 11 Nov 1858, m. 21 Jan 1891 to Willie M. Vann
Lucy Clara, twin of Mary Ida
Julius Beauregard b. 5 July 1861, m. 22 Jan 1891 to Eliza Hughes

Daniel Roper Duriose m. Julia A. L. Harrison b. 27 Apr 1835
Annie Gertrude Duriose b. 29 Aug 1853
Julia Elizabeth Day b. 20 Jan 1882
Daniel Roper Day b. 6 Sep 1884
Julius Francis Day b. 15 June 1887
P. B. Day, Jr. b. 19 Feb 1891

[There are dates down to the present generation which are not reproduced here. This Bible is the property of Mrs. James Thornton
Nuckols of Columbus, Ga. who was born Elizabeth Day.]

JOHN DENSON

John Denson b. 13 May 1800, d. 6 Jan 1852, m. 1st to Rebecca M.
Denson b. 15 Jan 1805, d. 17 Sep 1833, m. 2nd to Katharine Denson
b. 13 Feb 1807, d. 23 Dec 1843
    Children
Eliza H. b. 9 Feb 1826
James E. b. 11 Feb 1830, d. 4 Jan 1848
Sarah C. b. 31 Jan 1832
Lucretia Y. b. 21 Nov 1836
Martha E. b. 5 July 1839
Mary A. b. 5 Oct 1842

REV. PAUL DERRICK

Paul Derrick b. 29 Aug 1829 in Lexington Dist., S.C., m. 25 Nov
1858 to Amanda B. Hiller b. 15 Oct 1835
    Children
Samuel Joseph Houck Derrick b. 22 Sep 1859
Sidney Bartow Derrick b. 12 Sep 1861
Henry David Derrick b. 10 Oct 1863
John Edwin Derrick b. 30 Jan 1866

[From Bible in St. Matthew Lutheran Church at Cameron, S.C. See
Rast Bible below]

DAVID DICKSON

David Dickson, son of Eilliam Dickson, grandson of Michael Dickson,
b. 23 July 1750 (Old Style), m. 1st to Sarah Dickson b. 14 Feb 1750
(Old Style), d. 17 Sep 1785, aged 35 yrs., 7 mos. & 3 days, m. 2nd
to Martha Dickson b. 22 Mar 1764, d. 9 Sep 1796, aged 32 yrs., 5
mos. & 18 days, m. 3rd to Anne Allen Dickson b. 21 Mar 1772, d. Jan
1840, aged 67 yrs., 10 mos. & 8 days. David Dickson d. 23 May 1830

Wm. Hugh Dickson b. 14 Sep 1785
Michael Dickson b. 9 Dec 1788

103

William Dickson b. 20 Mar 1790
Elizabeth Dickson, dau. of David Dickson b. 16 Feb 1791, d. 16 Nov 1792, aged 1 yr. & 9 mos.
David Dickson b. 22 Mar 1792
James Dickson b. 10 July 1794
Thornton Smith Dickson b. 21 Aug 1801, d. 25 Oct 1867
Nancy Campbell Dickson b. 2 Dec 1802
Charles Allen Dickson b. 22 Mar 1804, d. Sep 1873
Patsey Ealse Dickson b. 30 Nov 1805
John Orr Dickson b. last day of June 1808, d. 23 ... 1883, m. 23 June 1833 to Mary Glass b. 12 ... 1818, d. 8 May 1847, aged 28 yrs., .. mos. & 26 days
Robert David Dickson b. 2 Jan 1810, d. 25 Mar 1889, m. Matheny Glass b. 14 Aug 1813, d. 30 Aug 1891

Thomas Hyde Dickson, son of David Dickson, Jr., b. 1 Feb 1812
Nancy Eliza Dickson, 1st dau. of David Dickson, Jr., b. 28 Mar 1813, d. 14 Sep 1814
Martha Letitia Dickson b. 10 Sep 1814
David Harris Dickson b. Oct 1816
Julia Maria Dickson b. Mar 1818
Zebulon Montgomery Pike Dickson b. July 1819

David Dickson Smith, son of Jepthey Smith & Nancy Smith, b. 6 Mar 1825 about 10:50 A.M.
William Hugh Smith b. 9 Apr 1826
Martha Dixon Smith b. 8 Dec 1827 [1817?]

James Otteres Dickson b. 10 Aug 1811
Elizabeth Caroline Dickson b. 18 Nov 1813
David Monro Dickson b. 15 Sep 1815
Loriann O. Dickson b. 14 Oct 1818
Elizabeth Ann Digby b. 14 Oct 1820
Wm. Hugh Crawford Dickson b. 26 Nov 1822
    [these listed below John Orr Dickson, son of David]

Manson Dickson b. 15 Aug 1833, d. 26 Sep 1833
Mary Ann Dickson b. 14 Feb 1835, d. 10 Oct 1835
Elizabeth C. Dickson Guice b. 27 Sep 1836, d. 6 Nov 1912
Annie Ellen Dickson b. 31 Dec 1838, d. 22 Mar 1847
David Sumpter Dickson b. 15 Apr 1841, d. 14 May 1847
William Wyatt Dickson b. 25 June 1843, d. Mar 1925
Sherman Glass Dickson b. 8 Sep 1845, d. 25 Feb 1865
John Marshall Dickson b. 31 May 1848, d. 15 Aug 1891
Martha Louisa Dickson Edwards b. 25 Jan 1851, d. 10 Jan 1915
Charles Robert Dickson b. 4 June 1853, d. 5 May 1896
Emer Saphroma Dickson b. 17 Mar 1856
    [these listed below Robert & Matheny Dickson]

David Manson Dickson b. 19 Aug 1835
Elizabeth Posey Dickson b. 10 Mar 1814
Christopher Columbus Dickson b. 17 Oct 1825

John Landers Dickson b. 13 May 1828
Martha Jane Dickson b. [not legible]
Jonathan H. Glass b. 5 May 1779
Elizabeth Echols d. 21 Sep 1828, aged 5 yrs., 7 mos. & 6 days
Elsey Orr d. 23 day of 1828, aged 2 mos.

[This is an Old Testament published 19 Aug 1803 in Philadelphia]

WILLIAM DINKINS

Wm. Dinkins b. 18 May 1746 in Craven Co., S.C., son of Wm. Dinkins,
Sr. & Sarah Dinkins, m. 1st on 14 June 1768 to Sarah Wright, dau.
of Wm. Wright, Sr. & Sarah Wright, b. 21 Aug 1750 in Craven Co.,
S.C., d. 4 Apr 1750, m. 2nd on 25 Mar 1792 to Nancy Smart. Wm.
"moved away from Sumter Co., [S.C.] after 1812."
        Children
Saml. Dinkins b. 17 Mar 1769, d. 12 Sep 1825, never married
Asa Dinkins b. 1 Aug 1771, d. 15 Nov 1819
Wm. Dinkins b. 3 Jan 1774, d. 20 Apr 1774
Wright P. Dinkins b. 12 May 1777, d. 20 Mar 1778
Sarah Dinkins b. 6 Nov 1780, d. 9 Sep 1800, never married

Wm. Wright m. 26 Dec 1745 to Sarah Paterson
Wm. Dinkins m. 12 Feb 1738 to Sarah Tompkins

[This data was copied from a family Bible by Langdon Jennings Dinkins, grand son of Wm. Dinkins, Jr. This Wm. Dinkins, Jr. was a
Rev. War Soldier.]

JAMES WILLIAM DOGGETT

James W. Doggett b. 7 Oct 1813, m. 17 Mar 1842 to Mary Lambeth b.
18 Sep 1822.

Mary Ann Mildred Doggett, 1st born of James & Mary Doggett, b. 29
    Aug 1843
Amanda Levina Doggett b. 28 June 1845
William Taylor Doggett b. 3 June 1847
Charles Russell Doggett b. 4 Sep 1849
Wesley Osborne Doggett b. 29 Jan 1852
Virginia Elizabeth Doggett b. 12 Oct 1854
John Andrew Thomas Doggett b. 16 Jan 1857

Mildred Doggett [mother of James W. Doggett] d. 3 July 1860

[Family Bible of James William Doggett, Guilford Co., N.C. in possession of James Anderson Doggett, 3608 Starmount Dr., Greensboro,
N.C.]

JAMES LEONARD DONNELLY

James Leonard Donnelly b. 4 Sep 1808, m. Elizabeth Murphy b. 22 Aug

1808
Peter Christian b. 11 Aug 1822, d. 25 Dec 1879, m. Elizabeth Don-
    nelly b. 14 Mar 1831
Juanita Christian, dau. of Peter & Elizabeth Christian, b. 17 Sep
    1861
Sarah Caroline Donnelly b. 21 June 1821, d. 16 Sep 1833
Emma Anamariah Donnelly b. 10 Oct 1836
Isaac & Rebecca Donnelly b. 10 Jan 1840
Sarah Murphy b. 6 Dec 1812
Mary Murphy, dau. of Roger & Mary Murphy, b. 23 Jan 1801, d. 18 Oct
    1806
Samuel Murphy b. 13 Oct 1803, d. 12 Nov 1827
Peter Murphy b. 15 Dec 1805
John F. LeGwin b. 8 Feb 1818, m. Mary LeGwin b. 31 Jan 1821
Paul Gerard LeGwin, son of F. B. & Ravola LeGwin, b. 5 Jan 1897
Varina Aery Yopp, dau. of Walter E. Yopp & Emma D. Yopp, b. 3 Jan
    1897
Emma Donnelly Yopp, dau. of Walter E. & Emma D. Yopp, b. 8 Mar 1897

R. W. Smith m. 4 July 1863 to Mary C. Smith
W. H. Jarmon m. 19 May 1874 to Henrietta G. LeGwin
John J. LeGwin m. Lizzie Hardy

Roger Murphy d. 26 Dec 1812
Mary Murphy d. 8 June 1834
Sarah Donnelly d. 4 Dec 1833
Henry M. Donnelly d. 3 July 1842
Jane Donnelly d. 7 Aug 1843
John Donnelly d. 10 Oct 1865

[Bible record of James Leonard Donnelly of Charleston, S.C., copied
into the Bible of his son, Samuel James Donnelly of Wilmington,
N.C. Bible owned by Mrs. George T. Musselman of Wilmington, N.C.]

SAMUEL JAMES DONNELLY

Samuel James Donnelly b. 22 Aug 1841 in Charleston, S.C., d. 5 Nov
1909 in Wilmington, N.C., m. 10 Apr 1864 at Wilmington, N.C. to
Hester Ann LeGwin b. 9 Oct 1841, d. 6 Dec 1914 at Wilmington, N.C.

Etta Edith Donnelly, dau. of Samuel James & Hester Ann Donnelly, b.
    5 Apr 1865, d. 19 Apr 1865
Ella Varina Donnelly b. 5 July 1866, d. June 1945 from falling down
    stairs
Lila Ravola Donnelly b. 3 Dec 1868 [m. 26 Feb 1896 Fronnie LeGwin]
Mary Elizabeth Donnelly b. 18 June 1870 [m. 22 Nov 1898 to Elisha
    Davis Warren]
Emma Henrietta Donnelly b. 3 Aug 1872 [m. 29 Apr 1891 to W. E.
    Yopp]
James LeGwin Donnelly b. 18 Mar 1880 [m. in Augusta, Ga. to Annie
    Schevalle of Augusta], d. 24 June 1942 in Wilmington, N.C.

Elisha Davis Warren, Mamie's husband, d. 20 Aug 1926 in Tampa, Fla.
Walter Edward Yopp, Emma H. Donnelly's husband, d. 27 Sep 1933 in
   Wilmington at his home, aged 73 yrs.
James Leonard Donnelly, father of Samuel James Donnelly b. 4 Sep
   1808, d. 6 Jan 1848
Elizabeth Murphy [wife of James Leonard Donnelly] b. 22 Aug 1808
Elizabeth Donnelly, wife of James Leonard Donnelly d. 6 Mar 1849
Peter Christian m. 31 Jan 1850 in Charleston, S.C. to Elizabeth
   Constantia Donnelly d. 24 May 1898
S. W. Lynes m. 24 May 1855 to Emma Annamariah Donnelly
John F. LeGwin, father of Hester Ann Donnelly, d. 2 Oct 1884

[This family Bible is now owned by Mrs. Emma D. Musselman of Wilmington, N.C.]

JOHN CRAWFORD DOSS

John Crawford Doss b. 17 Apr 1815, m. 7 Feb 1839 to Catherine Caro-
   line Bain b. 12 Oct 1823
Infant son b. dead 7 Mar 1840
John Joe Doss b. 29 Apr 1841, m. 15 June 1862 to Sallie E. Bailey
James Mitchell Doss b. 9 Sep 1846, m. 9 Sep 1869 to Sallie A. Pon-
   der
Infant son b. dead 17 July 1848
Essie Ann Doss b. 14 Sep 1852, d. 8 Aug 1879, m. 22 July 1866 to
   Thos. J. Patrick
Mary Eliz. Doss b. 6 May 1855, d. 23 Nov 1863
Clanton Moody Doss b. 12 Oct 1857
Dallas Van Buren Doss b. 30 May 1868
Frances Margret Doss b. 5 Feb 1865
Ellen Thos. Doss b. 31 July 1872 [wife of Chas. Crow Doss]
Tempy E. Doss d. 14 Dec 1855
Chas. Crow Doss d. 2 Nov 1950
Corrinne Catherine Doss b. 20 Mar 1892 [dau. of Chas. Crow Doss]
Irene J. Doss b. 1 Mar 1894 [dau. of Chas. Crow Doss]

[The above does not include all the children of Chas. Crow Doss.
This Bible is owned by Miss Corinne Doss, Hartselle, Ala. as of
June 1952]

JONATHAN DOWNS

Jonathan Downs d. 18 Oct 1818 in Laurens Co., S.C., m. 8 July 1772
   in Laurens Dist., S.C. to Sarah Gary
      Children
Jane b. 6 July 1774
Frances b. 10 Apr 1784
Phoebe b. 7 Apr 1791
Milley b. 5 Apr 1776
William b. 10 Jan 1787
Louisa b. 15 May 1798

[This record is from the pension record of Jonathan, granted to his widow, Sarah Downs. Sarah Gary was the dau. of Wm. Gary & his wife Milly (Brooks) Gary, who is mentioned in the will of her father, Jacob Brooks, Sr. 1774 found in Charleston, S.C. Milly Gary's dau. Sarah is mentioned also in her grandfather's will. Jacob Brooks, Sr. is an ancestor of the compiler.]

LEONARD DOZIER

Leonard the Third b. 1710 in Lunenburg Co., Va., m. 30 Jan 1733 to Anna Gayle who d. in 1785 in the same county.
    Children
James b. 2 Sep 1737, d. 1807
Susannah b. 16 Nov 1739
John b. 2 Dec 1741, d. 1807 in S.C.
William b. 16 Mar 1743
Jemima b. 22 May 1746
Keziah b. 26 May 1749
Leonard b. 7 May 1751
Thomas b. 29 June 1753
Ann b. 1755
Richard b. 15 Aug 1760

[Mrs. James T. Nuckols, Columbus, Ga., says, "Leonard Dozier I of France was the immigrant. He died in Westmoreland Co., Va. in 1693. His wife was Elizabeth ...?"]

JAMES DRAKE

Jas. Drake b. 1 Jan 1784, d. 7 Dec 1854, m. 26 Sep 1804 by Rev. Hugh Dickson of the Greenville Presbyterian Ch. to Nancy Breckenridge b. 30 Oct 1786, d. 2 Nov 1857.
    Children
Nancy b. 11 Sep 1807, d. 20 Aug 1872
Mary b. 2 Sep 1809
Thomas b. 5 Dec 1811, d. 12 Oct 1832
Jane b. 5 Dec 1813, m. 21 Dec 1837 to Thos. Pennell
John b. 10 Mar 1816
Agnes b. 25 July 1818
Robert H. b. 5 Oct 1820
Enoch b. 30 Mar 1823
Eliz. Ann b. 13 June 1825

[This Bible also contains the children of Thos. Pennell & Jane Drake, not reproduced here. The Bible record reports, "Adam Breckenridge came to Abbeville Dist., S.C. in 1750." It is owned by Mrs. Carl Austin, Belton, S.C.]

JOHN JAMES DREW

John J. Drew d. 16 Dec 1862, aged 54 yrs., 4 mos. & 5 days, m. 3 Apr 1834 to Mary E. Durant.

Amanda Fitzalen Drew b. 7 Jan 1835, bapt. 1849, d. 6 Nov 1868, aged
32 yrs., m. 2 Apr 1857 to Henry H. Goodman
Martha Caroline Drew b. 16 Nov 1836, bapt. 1849, m. 1st on 26 July
1855 to George W. Jarman d. 11 Oct 1855, m. 2nd on 19 July 1864
to W. H. Marsh
John Thomas Drew b. 1 Jan 1839, bapt. 1850, m. 8 Nov 1865 to Mary
G. Gates
William Watts Drew b. 6 Jan 1841, bapt. 1850, m. 5 Feb 1862 to
Laura H. Goodman
Amelia Elizabeth Drew b. 19 Dec 1842, bapt. 1850, m. 7 Mar 1867 to
W. J. Westcott
Mary Ann Drew b. 11 Oct 1844, bapt. 1850
Sarah Rebecca Drew b. 25 Dec 1846, bapt. 1850, m. 5 Dec 1867 to
John Westcott
Charles Bingly Drew b. 4 Dec, bapt. 1850
Jesse James Drew b. 22 Jan 1851, bapt. 1851
George Fulton Drew b. 3 Mar 1853, bapt. 3 Aug 1855
Herbert Lee Drew b. 9 Sep 1864
Minnie O... Drew b. 7 Nov 1867
Mary Virginia Drew b. 19 Apr 1869
Lillie Betts Drew b. 2 Sep 1870

Daniel Russell Goodman, son of Henry H. & Amanda F. Goodman b. 4
Feb 1858
Annie Elizabeth Goodman b. 12 Oct 1860
Mattie F. Goodman d. 9 Nov 1865

Mary A. Smith, dau. of Thomas & Jane Smith, b. 13 Nov 1792, d. 1
Mar 1866, aged 74 yrs., 9 mos., m. 18 Nov 1809 to Thomas Durant d.
12 Nov 1829

Martha Jane Durant b. 17 Oct 1810, d. 14 Dec 1854, aged 44 yrs., 11
mos. (Martha Jane Burbage)
Mary Elizabeth Durant b. 1 Mar 1812
Rebecca Waunet Durant b. 15 Dec 1814
Mary Ann Durant b. 1 May 1816, d. 17 Nov 1868, aged 52 yrs.
Thomas Aken Durant b. 19 Feb 1818
Jacob A. Durant b. 2 Feb 1823

[The Bible of John James Drew of Brunswick Co., N.C. published by
John B. Perry, Philadelphia, 1852 is now owned by Miss Sallie Betts
Knox of Wilmington, N.C.]

ADAM FREDERICK DuBARD

Adam F. DuBard b. 20 Apr 1787 & his sponsors in Baptism were Adad
F. Hamiter & Barbara Hamiter, m. 22 Dec 1825 to Katherine Turnipseed b. 10 Jan 1792.

Jesse Alcibiades DuBard b. 7 Oct 1826, bapt. by Rev. Robert Adams,
d. 30 Nov 1849 [Back of Bible states he graduated from South
Carolina College]

Martha Sybil DuBard b. 25 Mar 1828, bapt. by Rev. R. Pierce, d. 31
Oct 1854, m. 12 Nov 1845 to Julius A. Turnipseed d. 30 Mar 1858
of consumption in Ocala, Fla.
Mary Elizabeth DuBard b. 19 Sep 1829, bapt. by Rev. J. Holmes, d.
20 Sep 1853 of consumption, aged 24 yrs. & 1 Month, m. 21 Mar
1850 to George McCants, M.D. b. 1 Jan 1817 who m. 2nd on 16 Jan
1855 to Sarah Robertson
John Adam Fletcher DuBard b. 8 Dec 1830, bapt. by Rev. Samuel Dun-
woody, d. 13 Mar 1849 at Cokesbury College, aged 18 yrs., 3 mos.
& 5 days
Nathan Jacob DuBard b. 31 Mar 1832, bapt., m. 1st on 27 Nov 1856
to Mary Elizabeth Ruff, m. 2nd to Mrs. Judith Weston Ruff Kennedy
Laveniz Katherine DuBard b. 11 Mar 1838, bapt. by Rev. A. M. For-
ster, d. 25 Dec 1839, aged 1 yr., 9 mos. & 14 days

Children of Julius A. & Martha S. Turnipseed
Adam Felix Augustus Turnipseed b. 22 Jan 1847, bapt. by Rev. Paul
A. M. Williams, d. 21 May 1857 of typhoid
Edward Fletcher Turnipseed b. 21 July 1848, bapt. by Rev. Paul A.
M. Williams, d. 6 June 1849
Mary Katherine Turnipseed b. 3 Feb 1850, bapt. by Rev. Samuel
Leard, d. 23 May 1857 of typhoid, aged 7 yrs., 3mos. & 2 days
Barnwell Rhett Turnipseed b. 29 Nov 1851, bapt. by Rev. William
Martin

Anna Eudora McCants b. 20 Jan 1850
John William DuBard McCants b. 23 Jan 1832

William DuBard d. 8 May 1839, aged near 74 yrs., m. Elizabeth Ham-
iter DuBard d. 9 Sep 1849 in her 8th yr. [copying error?]
Children
Katherine Eve DuBard b. 12 Dec 1793, d. 26 Apr 1849, aged 55 yrs.,
4 mos. & 14 days. [single] Her last words were, "Weep not."
Phillip DuBard b. 14 June 1795, d. Oct 1870 in Mississippi
Adam F. DuBard b. 20 Apr 1797, was robbed and murdered 5 Jan 1871,
aged 73 yrs., 8 mos. & 15 days
Nancy DuBard b. 28 Mar 1799 [m. James Kelly]
William DuBard b. 17 Mar 1801,
Jacob DuBard b. 24 June 1803, d. 27 Feb 1821
Elizabeth DuBard b. 24 June 1803, his twin [m. John Bernhard]
Frances DuBard b. 1 July 1805, d. 10 Dec 1838 in childbirth [m.
David Turnipseed
Mary F. DuBard b. 12 Oct 1808 [m. Henry Turnipseed]

Jesse Turnipseed d. 13 Nov 1827, aged 33 yrs., 10 mos. & 3 days
Mrs. Katherine Turnipseed, relict of Jacob Turnipseed, d. 31 Dec
1827
Mary Katherine McCants, dau. of Dr. George & Mary E. McCants, d.
1r Jan 1854, aged 9 mos. & 10 days of consumption
John M. Waring b. 20 Oct 1794, d. 24 Aug

[This Bible is owned by Mrs. Furman Cooper of Greensboro, N.C. On
the fly leaf of the Bible, it states, "Miss Katherine Turnipseed,
her Bible 11th of June 1822" Adam Frederick DuBard was of Richland Co., S.C. The Bible was printed in Philadelphia, Pa. in 1819.
L. Andrea of Columbia, S.C. states that the marriages in square
brackets above are not in the Bible, but are taken from the will of
William DuBard. He also says, "Each birth and death is usually
listed by the day of the week, the hour of the day and often whether morning or night. The deaths are usually as caused by which
disease such as fever or consumption or such like... In back of
Bible is often listed other data such as the dying words... College
graduated from and so on... " I have copies of the Bibles of William DuBard, Jr. taken to Miss., m. Nancy Nipper; Phillip DuBard
taken to Miss., m. Mary Henriatta Bernhard; Nathan J. DuBard in
Richland Co., S.C. John Frederick DuBard from Switzerland was father of William DuBard, Sr. John Frederick Duberd was a minister
and was at one time pastor of Appii Forum (Cedar Creek) German Reformed Church and later went to Charleston as pastor of the German Church there and died of small pox during the Revolution. Cedar Creek Church organized in 1743, became Methodist in 1791.]

PHILLIP DuBARD

Phillip DuBard, son of William, Sr. & Elizabeth Hamiter DuBard of
Cedar Creek in Richland Co., S.C., b. 14 June 1795, d. 17 Oct 1870,
aged 75 yrs., 5 mos. & 3 days, [m.] Mary Henriatta Bernhard DuBard
d. 21 Oct 1872, aged 75 yrs., 9 mos. & 9 days.
    Children
Louisa Frances DuBard b. 20 Nov 1820, d. 27 Jan 1821, aged 2 mos. &
    7 days
William Christopher DuBard b. 5 Jan 1822
John James DuBard b. 29 Sep 1823
Allen Turner DuBard b. 5 Apr 1825
Sarah Ann Elizabeth DuBard b. 8 Apr 1827, d. 10 Nov 1859, aged 32
    yrs., 7 mos. & 9 days
Solomon Fletcher DuBard b. 1 May 1829, d. 29 Feb 1844, aged 13
    yrs., 10 mos. & 1 day
Louisa Margaret DuBard b. 20 Mar 1831
George Wesley DuBard b. 29 Jan 1833
Henry David DuBard b. 19 Oct 1834, d. 27 Jan 1838
Mary Sybil DuBard b. 10 Apr 1837
Philip Capers DuBard b. 20 Apr 1839 in Miss., d. 1 Apr 1865, aged
    24 yrs., 11 mos. & 10 days

WILLIAM DuBARD, JR.

William DuBard, Jr., son of William DuBard, Sr. of Richland Co.,
S.C., moved to Grenada, Miss. in 1837, b. 17 Mar 1801 in Richland
Co., S.C., d. 13 Aug 1866 in Grenada, Miss., m. 1st to Nancy Nipper b. 22 Aug 1802 in Richland Co., S.C., d. 1 June 1841 in Grenada, Miss., m. 2nd to Cynthis Walker.
    Children

Jacob F. DuBard b. 10 Nov 1822
John T. DuBard b. 5 July 1824
Zachariah R. DuBard b. 9 Feb 1856, d. 3 Oct 1859 [b. 1826?]
Charlotte E. DuBard b. 20 Jan 1828
Daniel W. DuBard b. 1829
Sarah Ann DuBard b. 5 Dec 1831, d. 11 Nov 1860
Harriet F. DuBard b. 5 Sep 1833, d. 28 Feb 1923
William C. DuBard b. 29 Aug 1835, d. 6 Aug 1836
Adam Frederick DuBard b. 11 July 1837, killed in action at Corinth,
    Miss. 26 Apr 1862
Harmon W. DuBard b. 1 Jan 1839, killed in action at Battle of
    Shiloh 27 July 1861
Landon C. DuBard b. 1 June 1841, d. 25 Sep 1910
        Children by second wife
Asbury G. DuBard b. 16 May 1844, d. 22 Aug 1896
William M. DuBard b. 8 Nov 1847, d. 21 Mar 1944
Marcellus G. DuBard b. 1 June 1850, d. 9 Mar 1918
Anna DuBard [no date legible]
Molly DuBard b. 1860, d. 1880

[some dates not legible]

                    ARCHELAUS CONE DUGGAN

A. C. Duggan, son of John Duggan & Mary, his wife, b. 29 Apr 1808,
d. 10:20 P.M. 27 Aug 1877, aged 69 yrs., 2 mos. lacking 2 days, m.
1st on 17 Mar 1829 to E. A. Walker, dau. of John Walker & Rebecca,
his wife, b. 8 Aug 1808, d. 5:15 P.M. 10 Aug 1861, m. 2nd on 27 Nov
1862 to N. R. Maddux d. Feb 1879.
        Children
R. K. Duggan, dau., b. 4 Jan 1830, m. 17 Dec 1846 to E. F. Jordan
I. W. Duggan, son, b. 22 Dec 1831, d. 6 Sep 1917
James Barnes Duggan, son, b. 1 Nov 1833, d. 29 Sep 1915
M. E. Duggan, dau., b. 7 Sep 1835
Chloann Duggan, dau., b. 22 July 1838
Joseph Franklin, son b. 10 Oct 1840, d. 3:00 P.M. 7 Apr 1865
Thomas Green Duggan, son, b. 28 Oct 1843, d. 3:00 P.M. 24 Aug 1880
Clarissa Ann, dau., b. 1:30 A.M. 25 June 1847
Benjamin R., son, b. 7:00 A.M. 9 Jan 1850, d. 4:30 P.M. 18 May 1865
Lizzie A. Duggan b. 5:25 P.M. Wednesday, 7 Oct 1863
Georgia M. Duggan, dau., b. 1:00 A.M. 19 Apr 1865
Archelaus M. Duggan, son, b. 7:30 A.M. Thursday, 30 May 1867
Susan F. Duggan, dau., b. 7:12 P.M. Saturday, 24 July 1869, d. 1:10
    P.M. Sunday 5 Sep 1869
Mary N. Duggan b. 1:00 A.M. Saturday, 9 July 1870
David Edmund Duggan, son, b. 1:00 A.M. Thursday, 10 Oct 1872

Amanda b. 16 May 1833
        Children
Lu [Su?] July [?] b. 2 Aug 1849
Isaac b. 5 May 1851

Celia b. 5 Nov 1847
    Children of Celia
Mary, dau., b. 7 June 1849
Loucinda, dau., b. 26 Mar 1848
Seburn, son, b. 10 May 1850

Chloe Ann Archer d. 27 Aug 1864
Elizabeth Nancy Duggan d. 6:00 A.M. Saturday, 22 Oct 1864

[The family Bible of Archelaus Cone Duggan & his wife, Elizabeth
Ann Walker of Washington Co., Ga. is now in possession of Mr. &
Mrs. Sam Duggan, "Sandy Run", Rt. 4, Moultrie, Ga. Bible (New
Testament) published 1831 by Langdon Coffin, 31 Washington St.,
Boston.]

JAMES M. DULANY

James M. Dulany b. 10 May 1832, d. 17 Sep 1898, m. 19 July 1855 to
M. E. Senter b. 10 Oct 1836, d. 18 Sep 1906
    Children
Thomas Dulany b. 1 July 1856
William N. Dulany b. 3 Nov 1858, d. 9 Jan 1863
John A. Dulany b. 3 Apr 1862
M. E. Dulany b. 9 Nov 1865
Avretta Dulany b. 5 Aug 1867 [?]
J. R. Dulany b. 3 Oct 1869
R. D. Dulany b. 9 Aug 1872
R. A. Dulany b. 3 Nov 1875
D. D. Dulany b. 14 Dec 1877

[J. R. was James Robert Dulany, m. Ophelia Brown, d. 22 Feb 1958,
bur. at Coolidge, Texas. R. A. was Rhoda Anne Dulany, m. 1st James
Hale, 2nd Sell Brown. D. D. was Daniel Dove Dulany, m. Sula Brown
(sister of Ophelia, above) 27 Oct 1901, d. 16 Jan 1957, bur. Mt.
Pleasant Cemetery near Fulton, Miss. This Bible record is copied
by Mildred Dulaney in 1956. It was then owned by Daniel Dove Dulany, Rt. 2, Fulton, Miss.]

JOE DULANY

Joe Dulany b. 25 Dec 1850, d. 11 Apr 1926. Martha Ann Johnson b.
29 June 1857, d. 5 Feb 1935.
    Children
Opha Dulany b. 27 June 1875
Rachel Dulany b. 2 Apr 1878
Leona Dulany b. 8 Jan 1880
Willie Jane Dulany b. 15 Oct 1882
George Dulany b. 11 Sep 1884
Joe Abb Dulany b. 5 Mar 1887
Florence Dulany b. 29 May 1889
Belle Dulany b. 18 Mar 1891
Charlie Dulany b. 12 Sep 1894, m. Zora Hood b. 11 Oct 1895

Children of Charlie & Zora Dulany
Vastle Dulany b. 6 Nov 1913
Clastle Dulany b. 17 Nov 1915
Vecil Dulany b. 12 July 1918
Clothel Dulany b. 21 Oct 1921
Dorothy Lynette Dulany b. 26 Mar 1936

[Joe Dulany & Martha Ann Johnson Dulany are both buried at Mt.
Pleasant Cemetery near Fulton, Miss. This information was copied
in 1956 by Mildred Dulaney from Bible owned by Charlie Dulany, RFD,
Fulton, Miss.]

DAVID DUNLAP

David Dunlap b. 17 Aug 1750, d. 14 May 1835, m. Mary b. 1758, d. 12
Nov 1828
    Children
Joseph b. ..., d. 12 July 1858, m. 11 Dec 1811 in Chipley, Ga. to
    Mary Carnes
Elizabeth b. ..., d. 12 Nov 1821

Mary Carnes Dunlap, dau. of Jos. & Mary Carnes Dunlap, m. 12 Dec
    1832 in Chipley, Ga. to Elisha Trammell

SAMUEL DUNN

Samuel Dunn, son of James & Agnes Dunn, b. May 1775, d. 20 Jan
1846, m. Mary [d. 30 Aug 1840, aged 52 yrs., 2 mos., & 13 days from
gravestones]
    Children
Sarah Dunn b. 26 Apr 1807 in S.C.
James Dunn b. 7 Apr 1809 in S.C.
Michael Dunn b. 12 June 1811 in S.C.
Nancy Dunn b. 4 Oct 1813 in S.C., m. Joshua Shelby, children: Sam-
    uel Shelby, Frank Shelby and Lydia S. Rany
William Abner Dunn b. 20 Aug 1816 in S.C.
John M. Dunn b. 20 Apr 1818 in S.C. [Walter Dunn's father]
Robert M. Dunn b. 7 Sep 1822 in S.C. [father of Wm. A. Dunn, Billy]
James A. Dunn b. 17 Dec 1824 in S.C., m. Evelyn Sargent, Pana, Ill.
Burrell M. Dunn b. 30 Oct 1827 in Ind. [prob. S.C.]

GEORGE DURANT, THE ELDER

George Durant b. 1 Oct 1632, m. 4 Jan 1658 in Northumberland Co.,
Va. to Ann Marwood d. 22 Jan 1694
    Children
George, Jr. b. 24 Dec 1659, d. 13 Sep 1671
Elizabeth b. 15 Feb 1660 [d. before her father made his will 9 Oct
    1688 according to Andrea]
John b. 26 Dec 1662, d. 15 Jan 1699, m. 9 Apr 1684 to Sarah Jooke
Mary b. 11 Feb 1665, d. 6 May 1698
Thomas b. 28 Aug 1668, m. Elizabeth Gaskill

Sarah b. 16 Jan 1670, m. 14 Aug 1690 to Elias Rowden
Martha b. 28 Aug 1673
Parthenia b. 1 Aug 1675, m. 18 June 1695 to Joseph Sutton
Ann b. 1 Apr 1681, m. 6 Oct 1698 to Wm. Thos. Barclift

Children of Thomas & Elizabeth (Gaskill) Durant
George b. 25 Nov 1696
Ann b. 16 Feb 1702

Ann Durant b. 10 Jan 1689
Elizabeth [Durant] b. 28 Jan 1692
Sarah [Durant] b. 29 Mar 1695
Mary Durant b. 19 May 1698
John Barclift b. 9 Aug 1711
Sarah Durant d. 29 Mar 1695

[L. Andrea comments, "Geo. Durant the Elder is supposed to have been born in England, London, & came to Va. and later to N.C. He held many high offices in Colonial North Carolina." This Bible was printed in 1599 and is owned by the Univ. of N.C. Library. George Durant, Sr. lived at Durant's Neck, Perquimans Co., N.C.]

WILLIAM DUSKIN

Wm. Duskin b. 1 June 1790
Ann Duskin b. 18 Feb 1800 [note similar b. date to Ann below]
Mary Johnston Duskin b. 25 Nov 1803
Mary A. Duskin b. in the year 1818
Ann Duskin, wife of Wm., b. 22 Feb 1800, d. 12 Nov 1822
Wm. Thos. Duskin d. 22 June 1823
Ruthey Jane Duskin d. 17 July 1823
Mary Ann Duskin b. 29 May 1818
Ruthey Jane Duskin b. 30 Oct 1820
Wm. Thos. Duskin b. 26 Nov 1822
Martha Thomas Duskin b. 20 Dec 1824
Sarah Jane Duskin b. 29 July 1826
Susan Wait Duskin b. 27 Aug 1830
Geo. Michael Duskin b. 24 Aug 1835
Wm. Duskin Latta b. 2 Aug 1845
Elisha D. Hendon m. 3 Mar 1859 to Sue Wait Duskin
Mary D. Hendon b. 15 Dec 1859
Wm. Dawson Hendon b. 29 July 1863
Wm. Duskin Latta m. 8 Mar 1876 to Annie B. Tapp
Woody Martin m. 7 June 1796 to Sarah [Duskin according to Johnston]
Eliz. Duskin m. 7 Nov 1797 to Isaac Penn
Polly Duskin m. 16 Oct 1804 to Counsel Moore
Wm. Duskin m. 12 Mar 1824 to Mary Jane Johnston
Geo. Michael Duskin m. 22 Dec 1868 to Harriet E. Glenn
Woodson Clements m. 24 Jan 1805 to Keziah Duskin
Michael Duskin m. 17 Dec 1818 to Eliz. Atkin
Kedar Parker m. 29 Sep 1814 to Anny Duskin
Panthey Duskin m. 20 Mar 1817 to Andrew .....

Wm. Duskin m. 7 Aug 1817 to Ann Parish
Wm. Glenn Duskin, son of Geo. M. & Harriet Glenn Duskin, b. 6 June
  1873 in Greensboro, Ala.
Mary Dasie Latta, dau. of Wm. Duskin Latta & Annie Tapp Latta, b.
  8 Dec 1878 in Orange Co., N.C.
James Duskin d. 23 Sep 1797
John Duskin d. 15 Mar 1816 in Augusta, Ga.
Michael Duskin, Sr. d. 15 Jan 1816
Sarah Martin d. Sep 1818
Mary Moore d. 29 Nov 1820
Mary Duskin d. 8 Dec 1820
Mary Jane (Johnston) Duskin d. 24 Feb 1870
Harriet Glenn Duskin, wife of Geo. M. Duskin, d. 21 July 1877
Geo. M. Duskin d. 14 Aug 1890
Martha Thomas Duskin, dau. of Wm. Duskin, d. 1 Nov 1832
Sarah Jane Latta d. 2 Oct 1845
Susan Duskin Hendon d. 23 Dec 1873

Michael Duskin b. 27 Oct 1752, m. Mary b. 6 Aug 1755
    [Children]
Sarah Duskin b. 4 Jan 1775
Eliz. Duskin b. 31 Jan 1777
John Duskin b. 14 Aug 1779
Michael Duskin b. 17 Jan 1782
Mary Duskin b. 17 Mar 1784
Keziah Duskin, dau., b. 4 Nov 1787, d. 3 June 1862
William Duskin, son, b. 5 June 1790, d. 16 Oct 1869
Anna Duskin b. 23 June 1793
James Duskin b. 13 Apr 1796
Ruthey Duskin b. 8 Jan 1799

[This record was sent to the compiler by Mr. Henry P. Johnston, Box
7661, Birmingham 13, Ala. The Lattas were from Orange Co., N.C. &
came very early into it from Pa., settled around St. Mary's & these
are buried in St. Mary's Episcopal Church Cemetery: John Latta, Sr.
b. 1 May 1734, d. 13 July 1824; John Latta, Jr. b. 21 May 1779, d.
20 June 1818; Joseph Latta b. 29 Dec 1784, d. 13 May 1884; and
Suzanna Latta d. 5 July 1792.]

CALEB EARP

Caleb Earp b. 7 Feb 1768, m. Margaret Earp b. 7 Feb 1771.
    Children
David D. b. 9 July 1795
Matthew b. 12 July 1797
Daniel b. 2 May 1799
Llewellen b. 25 Oct 1801
Caty b. 19 Aug 1803 [Catherine]
James M. b. 2 Dec 1805
Caswell b. 6 Jan 1808
Statira b. 31 Jan 1810
Matty b. 22 Apr 1812 [likely Martha]

Lavonia b. 18 June 1814
Caleb Asbury b. 1 May 1816

James McLevi Ellis Earp b. 2 Sep 1803 [could be 1823, not distinct]
John Cox b. 25 May 1821 [likely a grandson]

[This Bible owned in 1925 by Mrs. J. T. Beasley, Lavonia, Ga. Mr.
Andrea states, "Caleb Earp went from 96 Dist., S.C. to Franklin
Co., Ga."]

JOHN DICK ECCLES

John Dick Eccles b. 28 Mar 1792, m. 24 Dec 1820 to Elizabeth Jones
     Children
John b. 6 Nov 1821 in Fayetteville, N.C.
Mary Jones b. 27 Oct 1822 in Fayetteville, N.C.
Francis Hooper b. 13 Aug 1825 in Fayetteville, N.C.   .

Jannet Douglas Eccles b. 5 Oct 1801

[This old Bible is in the Historical Room of the First Presbyterian
Fayetteville, N.C.]

JOHN EDWARDS, SR.

John Edwards, Sr. & wife, Henrietta
     Children
Betty b. 25 Mar 1752
Joseph b. 1 Feb 1754
John, Jr. b. 5 July 1757
Mary b. 1 Apr 1760
Thomas b. 10 Apr 1762 [d. young, it seems]
Sarah b. 14 Mar 1765 [d. young, it seems]
William b. 10 Feb 1769

[John Edwards, Sr. came from Wales & settled in Fauquier Co., Va.
His eldest, Betty m. Bridwell]

JOSEPH EDWARDS

Joseph & wife, Mary
     Children
John b. 27 Dec 1776
Sarah b. 17 ... 1777 [month not legible]
Joseph b. 1 Jan 1781
Sanford b. 17 Feb 1783
Thomas b. 20 May 1791
William b. 12 June 1786
James b. 20 Sep 1794

[L. Andrea, Columbia, S.C. says, "Jos. Edwards served in the War
of 1776." The Bible states, "The Edwards & Bridwells came from Va.

to Greenville, S.C. about 1790. Joseph Edwards, III." At bottom of
Bible, "Jos., III & wife Betsy had ch. Hiram, Jesse, Nancy, Sarah,
Lennial, Betsy Ann & Joseph." Bible pub. 1787 in Edinboro, Scot-
land, owned by W. M. Edwards, Taylors, S.C.]

JAMES EIDSON

James Eidson, Jr. b. 15 Aug 1808, m. 10 July 1830 to Mahaly McCarty
b. 15 Oct 1813, d. 29 May 1875.

Matilda A. Eidson b. 23 Nov 1832, m. 8 Dec 1850 to Hiram Lecroy
Rowland H. Eidson b. 3 Oct 1833, killed 25 June 1864 [in Rifle
  Pitts] Atlanta, Ga., m. 15 Feb 1861 to Margret Denny
Lucretia Eidson b. 8 Feb 1836, d. [no date], m. 12 Jan 1850 to T.N.
  Clark
Jeter Eidson b. 1 June 1838
Milledge Eidson b. 9 Nov 1840
Wm. Martin Eidson b. 1 Nov 1843, killed 30 June 1862 at Richmond,
  Va.
Jas. Henry Eidson b. 9 Sep 1845, m. 18 Nov 1873 to Sallie A. Lott
Eliz. Lane Eidson b. 9 July 1848, m. 15 Nov 1968 to L. G. Asbill
Georgia Annah Eidson b. 22 Jan 1851, d. [no date], m. 16 Nov 1871
  to G. B. Asbill
John R. Eidson b. 12 Mar 1854 (twin), m. 5 Jan 1874 to Nannie
  Crouch
Mary Haseltine Eidson b. 12 Mar 1854 (twin), d. 12 Nov 1854
Simpson R. Eidson b. 6 Nov 1856, d. 17 Apr 1879

W. H. Eidson [son of Jas. Henry above] b. 18 Oct 1874
A. L. Eidson [son of Jas. Henry above] b. 13 Apr 1877
M. B. Eidson killed 1 June 1862 at Seven Pines, Va. [Milledge?]
Jas. H. Eidson d. 27 Dec 1866 [sheriff]
Capt. T. H. Clark d. [no date] [T. N. above?]
Mrs. Eliz. McCarty d. 1 Mar 1858
Jas. Henry Eidson d. 30 June 1925 [Jas., Jr.?]
Walter Hill Eidson d. 15 Apr 1929
Alonzo Lee Eidson d. 1952, m. 18 Nov 1900 to Ida Sally Corley
Harold Lee Eidson, son of Alonzo Lee & Ida Sally Eidson, b. 18 Aug
  1902, m. 1934 to Eunice Salley b. 14 Apr 1913, child: Jo. Ann
  b. 6 Nov 1946

[This Bible is owned by Alonzo Lee Eidson of Salley, S.C., copied
by Mrs. Jeanette Eidson Cantrevas, Augusta, Ga.]

WILEY EIDSON

Wiley Eidson b. 27 June 1809, d. 1 June 1862, m. 18 Sep 1834 to
Mary (Abercrombie) Eidson b. 8 Sep 1816, d. 1 July 1867.
    Children
James A. Eidson b. 21 Aug 1835
Martha Ann Eidson b. 31 Oct 1837, d. 15 May 1854
John Russell Eidson b. 7 Nov 1839

Mahlon Augustus Eidson b. 25 July 1842, d. 7 Dec 1862 with pneumonia, left for the War 22 Apr 1862
Allen Eidson b. 11 Nov 1848, d. 12 Jan 1871
Theresa Catharine b. 29 Jan 1850, d. 11 Oct 1851
Mary Catharine b. 23 May 1853
Willie Montgomery Eidson b. 10 Apr 1856
Chas. Hurt Eidson b. 14 June 1860, d. 9 Feb 1926

[This Bible is owned by Rev. James W. May of Emory University, Ga. This copy sent to the compiler by Mrs. Flossie Lamb Crouch, Edgefield, S.C.]

RICHARD ELLETT

Richard Ellett b. 30 May 1777 in Va., m. Keturah Winn b. 23 May 1783 in Va.
    Children
Edmund b. 23 May 1803
William b. 5 Dec 1804
Sarah b. 13 Mar 1806
John b. 1807
Robert Bartlett b. 1809, d. 1813
Permelia b. 22 Feb 1811
Elizabeth b. 25 Jan 1813, Madison Co., Ala.
Mary b. 15 Dec 1814, Madison Co., Ala.
Frances b. 1 Jan 1816, Madison Co., Ala., d. young
Richard b. 1818, Madison Co., Ala., d. young
Henrietta Maria b. 16 Jan 1820, Madison Co., Ala.
Keturah (Kitty) b. 1 Dec 1821, Madison Co., Ala.
Narcissa b. Mar 1822, Madison Co., Ala.
Joseph Winn b. 1823, d. young

AMOS ELLIOTT, SR.

Amos Elliott, Sr. b. 1760-1770 in Edgefield, S.C., d. 1844 in Shelby Co., Ala., m. 1st in S.C. [no name given for her] d. in Madison Co., Ala., m. 2nd on 12 Sep 1812 in Madison Co., Ala. to Nancy Hale dau. of Lindsey & Eliz. Hale of Talladega Co., Ala., b. 8 Mar 1794, in Tenn., d. 30 May 1872.
    Children
Willis b. 1787, m. 3 May 1819 to Patsy Carter b. in Jamestown, Va.
William b. 1789, d. 9 Dec 1864, m. 20 July 1813 to Mary Hale (Hail) of Tenn., dau. of Jos. Hail & Mary Eliz. Lindsey
Amos M., Jr. b. 1791, d. 1842, m. Sarah Hale or Hail, sister of Mary, dau. of Jos. & Mary Eliz. Lindsey Hail
Charles b. 1793, d. 1812
Allen b. 1805 in Tenn., m. 6 Feb 1843 to Caroline Nunnally
Jennie m. ... Rodgers
Polly m. ... Haney
Mahala b. 1818, m. 23 Nov 1833 to Jonathan Clower
Green b. 1821, m. Stasafia [Stacy Sophia] Kierdon
Elizabeth b. 1822, m. 18 May 1834 to Amos Merrill

Paralee b. 21 Dec 1823, d. 6 Nov 1908, m. 18 Jan 1843 to Francis
Nelson
Nancy b. 12 July 1827 in Tenn., d. 15 Feb 1900, m. 6 July 1843 to
Simpson Nelson b. 18 June 1822, d. 19 Sep 1889
Sarah Ann b. 21 Mar 1829, d. 1 Aug 1907, m. 17 Sep 1846 to Hardy
Nelson
John m. 27 Aug 1851 to Jane Ann Lewis
George Madison m. 1st before 1840, m. 2nd on 26 June 1844 to Mary
Dilbane
Jefferson B. b. 17 Feb 1831, d. 8 Oct 1913, m. 12 Jan 1855 to Eliz-
abeth Brasher b. 2 Oct 1836, d. 8 Feb 1906
Wylie b. 1834
James died early

[After Amos Elliott's death Nancy Hale Elliott married W. G. Bowden, St. Clair Co., Ala. This record came with some Bible records
from Mrs. E. C. Aiken, Fort Smith, Ark. It surely is not a Bible
record, but it is a fair record of a prominent family in Shelby &
Talladega Cos., Ala.]

SOLOMON EPPERLY

Solomon Epperly b. 18 Dec 1802, d. 23 Jan 1888 near Pozo, San Luis
Obispo Co., California, bur. at Lingo Ranch, m. Oct 1830 to Phoebe
Gibson, b. 22 Nov 1809, d. 29 July 1876, bur. Gilroy Cemetery, San-
ta Clara Co., Calif.
    Children
Hawkins Epperly b. 26 Aug 1831
Patience Epperly b. 9 Sep 1833
Francis M. Epperly b. 1 Aug 1835
Zerelda Epperly b. 18 Mar 1837 in Linn Co., Mo.
Zerelda A. Epperly b. 8 Oct 1838
Eleaner E. Epperly b. 10 Jan 1841
Lizzie L. Epperly b. 7 July 1843
Julia B. Epperly b. 3 Nov 1845
Isabella P. Epperly b. 15 Apr 1848
Rebecca S. Epperly b. 14 Oct 1850

[From 1880 census: Solomon Epperly, aged 77, b. Ky., father b. S.C.
mother b. S.C.
A great grandau. writes that Solomon Epperly & Phoebe Gibson were
married in Macon Co., Mo. and that the mother of Phoebe Gibson was
Patience Burk, a dau. of Thomas Burk, likely from Ky.
Family tradition says that the Epperly family were originally from
Holland. This information is from Mrs. Scott Rountree, 1148 Oak-
land Ave., Piedmont 11, Calif.]

COOPER BENNETT ESTES

Cooper Bennett Estes b. 5 Oct 1813, d. 20 Feb 1894, m. Eliz. Burton Ayers Estes b. 13 Oct 1822, d. 21 Apr 1880.
    Children

Laura Jane Estes Lindsey b. 28 Aug 1840, d. 6 Feb 1883
Nathaniel Monroe b. 5 Oct 1842
John McCagie b. 23 Nov 1844
Elias Cooper b. 13 June 1847, d. 5 Oct 1912
Perthenia Eliz. b. 21 Jan 1849, d. 15 Sep 1911
T̟hos. Jediah [no dates given, father of Mrs. J. E. Martin, 409 12th
    N.W., Ardmore, Okla.]
Jas. Albert Hulliar [Hilliar?] b. 14 Oct 1860, d. 14 May 1947
Ellen Alley McCay
Harriet Maxwell b. 13 Aug 1852
Eliza Ann Webb Estes b. 23 Apr 1855
Sarah Frances Kennedy [nee S. F. K. Estes b. 23 Jan 1866, d. 4 Mar
    1949]

[This Bible record was given to the compiler by Mrs. Jos. E. Kiger,
Chapel Hill, N.C., a desc. of Cooper Bennett Estes. The following
is from History of Ala. & Her People, Ala. Biography, vol. 2, p.
777, under biography of Jas. Albert Estes, Sr.: "His father, Cooper Bennett Estes, a native of S.C. when a mere boy moved along with
his father, Nathaniel Estes to Hart Co., Ga. where he grew to manhood & married Eliz. Burton Ayers, a daughter of Jedediah Ayers, of
Hart Co., Ga. In 1856 he moved to Fayette Co., Ala...." Legend
has it that Cooper Bennett Estes came from Edgefield Dist., S.C.]

THOS. HARRELL EVANS

Thos. Harrell Evans b. 30 May 1777 in Va., m. 2nd on 27 Oct 1815 to
Sarah Hill b. in Johnston Co., N.C.
        Children
Elizabeth Ann b. 27 Oct 1816 in Johnston Co., N.C.
Seth Thomas b. 13 Mar 1818 in Johnston Co., N.C.
Iona b. 20 Dec 1821 in Johnston Co., N.C.
Josiah b. 23 June 1823 in Johnston Co., N.C., m. 17 Sep 1846 in
    Wake Co., N.C. to Caroline Flewellin b. 12 Nov 1827 in Wake Co.,
    N.C.
Charlotte b. 14 Aug 1826
Jas. Henderson b. 8 June 1829 in Johnston Co., N.C.
Wm. Green b. 8 June 1831 in Johnston Co., N.C.
John Evans b. 23 Dec 1833

        Children of Josiah & Caroline Flewellin Evans
Sylvanus b. 29 Sep 1848 in Johnston Co., N.C.
Geo. Harrell b. 2 Oct 1850 in Johnston Co., N.C.
Jas. W. b. 10 June 1852 in Johnston Co., N.C.
Mahala Martha b. 11 July 1854 in Tuscaloosa, Ala.
Mary Jane b. 12 Aug 1856 in Tuscaloosa, Ala.
Maria Caroline b. 15 May 1859 in Tuscaloosa, Ala.
Joseph W. b. 22 Sep 1862 in Tuscaloosa, Ala., m. 5 Jan 1883 in Tus-
    caloosa, Ala. to Rebecca Mangum Patton b. 14 Oct 1867 in Bibb
    Co., Ala., child: Wm. Elbert Evans
Harriet Lavanda b. 27 Nov 1867 in Tuscaloosa, Ala.
Missouri Frances b. 22 Aug 1869 in Tuscaloosa, Ala.

Wm. Elbert Evans, son of Joseph W. & Rebecca Mangum Patton Evans, b. 22 Nov 1895 in Vaughn, Hill Co., Texas, m. 2 Oct 1920 in Tuscaloosa, Ala. to Rebecca Elizabeth Johnston b. 15 Nov 1904 in West Blocton, Bibb Co., Ala.
    Children
Wm. Elbert b. 17 Oct 1921 in Tuscaloosa, Ala.
John Robert b. 17 Nov 1921 in Tuscaloosa, Ala.
Elizabeth Ann b. 30 Apr 1923

[This Bible record may have come from Mrs. B. W. Gandrud, Tuscaloosa, Ala, who has furnished some other records.]

SAMUEL HILL FARNSWORTH

Saml. Hill Farnsworth b. 26 Jan 1806, m. 1st to Mary Jane Allen, m. 2nd on 14 Feb 1833 to Nancy Gordon Branden b. 7 Sep 1807.
    Children
Andrew Hamilton b. 11 Mar 1828
Henry Allen b. 20 Nov 1829
Mary Jane b. 2 Mar 1832
Margaret Frances b. 7 Feb 1834
Eliza Terissia b. 22 July 1835
Robert Alexander b. 6 Mar 1837
Samuel Gordon b. 18 Mar 1839
William Terry b. 26 Mar 1841
George Washington b. 10 Jan 1843, m. 1st on 22 Sep 1870 in Hickman Co., Ky. to Mary Ann Aldridge b. 25 May 1851 in Hickman Co., Ky., d. 9 July 1887 in Tehuacana, Texas, m. 2nd on 11 Sep 1888 to Martha (Mattie) Brown b. 18 May 1848 in Mercer Co., Ky., d. 1 Mar 1911 in Harrodsburg, Ky., m. 3rd on 28 May 1912 in Hale Co., Texas to Mrs. Susan Emily Whitmire b. 20 Jan 1850, d. 15 Mar 1937, bur. in Hillsboro, Texas

[Original records copied from the Bible of Geo. Farnsworth by his dau., Mrs. Nannie Ramsey and added to by her dau., Mrs. Henry Bollman (Mary Lou Hammonds), Lockney, Tex, Rt. M.]

REASON FERGUSON

Reason Ferguson b. 15 July 1809 in Bedford, Va., m. in 1826 to Susan Harvey b. 1808 in Monroe Co., Va.
    Children
Eliza Ann b. 15 Mar 1827 in Ky., m. James Morrison
Willis Haden b. 15 Sep 1829 in Ky., m. 1st in 1867 to Mrs. Eliza Brook Burnett, m. 2nd on 23 May 1872 to Mrs. Susan Moon Driskill
Martha Jane b. 17 Jan 1821 in Ill., m. Green Edwards
John Harvey b. 17 Apr 1833 in Ky., m. 1st to Nancy, m. 2nd to America Hughs
Henry Clay b. 23 Dec 1835 in Ky., m. Nancy Williams
Berthinia Thurman (or Buthenia I.) b. 23 July 1837 in Ky., m. 1st to Pleasant Gilbert, m. 2nd to Jas. Robertson
Sarah Margaret b. 22 Feb 1840 in Ky., m. George Wingler

Joseph Wilson b. 18 Mar 1842 in Ky., m. Catherine
Mary Elizabeth b. 27 Mar 1844 in Ky., m. Frank Courtney
Reason Turner b. 27 Mar 1846 in Ky., m. Mollie Flemming
Susan Frances b. 6 Jan 1849 in Texas, m. Rance Brooks
Lucy Emily b. 3 Apr 1851 in Texas, m. John Petitt

Joseph Ferguson m. 1 May 1801 in Franklin Co., Va. to Sarah Hughes.
Children: Archibald, John H., Reason b. 15 July 1809 m. Susan Harvey [above], Mary, and Margaret.

[Records from Mrs. Susan Ferguson Brooks.]

BENJAMIN F. FEW

Benj. F. Few b. 11 May 1830, m. 23 Apr 1863 to Rachel M. Kendrick
b. 2 Feb 1840
     Children
Robert Alston b. 6 Jan 1865, d. 8 Aug 1897, m. 10 Apr 1897 to Mary
    T. Davis
William Preston Few b. 29 Dec 1867, m. 17 Aug 1911 to Mary Reamy
    Thomas
Sallie Leona Few b. 24 May 1870, d. 23 Apr 1897, m. 23 May 1894 to
    Marion Luther Marchant
Ignatius Pierce Few b. 28 Mar 1872, m. 8 Mar 1894 to Fannie Maude
    Cannon
Ellie Few b. 17 Jan 1875

Benj. Ferguson, son of Ignatius F. Few, m. 19 June 1920 to Caroline
    Weston

[Notes by Leonard Andrea, Columbia, S.C.: Dr. Wm. Preston Few was
president of Duke University, Durham, N.C. The parents of Dr.
Benj. Ferguson of this Bible record were Sarah Ferguson & William
Few, Jr. This Bible is owned by Miss Ellie Few, Greer, S.C.]

JOHN FOSTER

John Foster b. 23 Dec 1770
Margaret Furlow b. 7 May 1775
John Foster m. 12 Mar 1795 to Margaret Furlow
Mary Foster b. 27 Sep 1796
William Foster b. 27 Dec 1798
Malina Foster b. 14 May 1801
John Furlow Foster b. 20 Jan 1804
Nancy Foster b. 5 Nov 1806
James H. Foster b. 18 Aug 1809
Samuel M. Foster b. 15 Jan 1812
Robert H. Foster b. 2 [not legible] 1815 (twin)
Margaret F. Foster b. 2 [not legible] 1815 (twin)
George Washington Foster b. 24 Feb 1818
Mary Beal, my dau., d. 8 Oct 1815
James H. Foster, my son, d. 10 Apr 1822

[in handwriting of John Foster]

John Foster d. 6 Aug 1826
Margaret F., wife of John Foster, d. 14 Mar 1829
Samuel M. Foster d. 30 July 1836
Margaret F. Tillman d. 8 Sep 1841
John Furlow Foster d. 1 June 1877 [added in vacant space]
Jane D. Foster d. 17 Sep 1869
Mattie Foster, infant dau. of G. W. & J. D. Foster, d. 15 June 1869
    [in handwriting which is unidentified]

[L.Andrea says a page is missing from this Bible here, likely a
further death list and a marriage list]

Jane Diademima Fielding b. 2 July 1824
George W. Foster m. 2 Feb 1843 to Jane D. Fielding
Margaret Elizabeth Foster b. 23 Nov 1843
Mary Lillian Foster b. 19 Oct 184- [last number not legible]
Nancy Reynolds Foster b. 7 May 1848
John Fletcher Foster b. 25 Jan 1851
Samuel Green Foster b. 4 Oct 1853 [added "He died 23 Nov 1940"]
Fannie Myrtus Foster b. 12 Apr 1856 [added "She died 23 July 1939"]
Anna Estelle Foster b. 10 Dec 1858
George Washington Foster, Jr. b. 30 May 1861 [added "He died 30 Aug
    1933"]
William Edward Foster b. 30 Jan 1864
James Fielding Foster b. 7 Aug 1866
Mattie Foster b. & d. 15 June 1869
Jane D. Foster, my wife, d. 17 Sep 1869
Myrtus E. Preston, my grand child, b. 20 Nov 1877
George W. Foster, Sr., d. 5 Dec 1903 [writing of Mrs. Margaret F.
    Harper]
Maggie E. Foster m. 8 Feb 1872 to George W. Harper
John Fletcher Foster m. 1 Dec 1875 to Sallie E. Marshall
Fannie M. Foster m. 6 Oct 1876 to Richard Archibald Preston
Mamie Reynolds Foster m. 2 Dec 1881 to Joseph C. Williams
Nannie R. Williams d. 17 Nov 1892 [later addition "Mr. Williams
    later married Susie Snow" [The two entries re Nancy R. Foster
    Williams, had been added at the bottom on a page, and evidently
    when she died, says L. Andrea]
Anna Estelle Foster m. 18 June 1878 to Joseph Thaddeus LaBoon, son
    of Emily Mullikin & Mason Canada LaBoon
Joseph T. LaBoon b. 4 Dec 1852 [added "He died 30 Apr 1932"]
Nannie Reynolds Foster Williams d. 17 Nov 1892 [duplicate entry]
Mary Farnell Foster d. 5 Aug 1894
S. E. M. A. Foster d. 9 July 1896
James A. Aycock d. 23 Jan 1901
Mollie Foster Aycock d. 17 Oct 1901
George W. Foster, Sr. d. 5 Dec 1903 [duplicate entry]
Joe G. Foster d. 18 Jan 1915
Edward F. Michael d. 26 Jan 1920
    [in handwriting of George W. Foster, Sr.]

Samuel Green Foster m. Sarah Emily Margaret Abia McGaughey, a dau.
of Mr. Holmes McGaughey
George W. Foster, Jr. m. 1st to Mary Farnell, m. 2nd to Sophronia
Betty Nickels, m. 3rd to Maria Johnson
Aunt Betty Nickels Foster b. 9 Sep 1852, d. 24 July 1919
W. Ed. Foster m. Mary Smith
James Fielding Foster m. Uvah Smith
Mary Lillian Foster m. James A. Aycock
        [in handwriting of Winton Travis Harper, no dates]

[At the bottom of this page is an entry in pencil, made by David F.
Michael, son of Rachel Marianne LaBoon & Anderson Green Michael.]

"Ma gave me the dates of her parents on a piece of paper and for
fear I lose the paper, I am copying it here.
"Her father Joseph LaBoon, was born on Brushy Creek in Pendleton
Dist., S.C. 12 Jan 1808, d. 1 Oct 1871 in Anderson Co., S.C. He
was the son of Pierre called Peter LeBon and his wife, Rachel Jar-
ves and the grandson of Pierre LeBon and his wife Anne, who came
from Rochefort in France to Maryland and later to S.C.
"Her mother was Elizabeth Tripp and she died in Anderson Co., S.C.
27 May 1872. She was the dau. of John & Dorcas Tripp.
"Ma's uncle Mace Laboon who married Aunt Emily Mullikin Laboon,
settled in Walton Co., Ga. and they are buried on his plantation."

[In the Bible is a certified copy of the Final Settlement of the
Estate of Mrs. Elizabeth LaBoon, dated 7 Mar 1873 at Anderson C.H.,
S.C. by John Harrison LaBoon, Administrator...Heirs listed as the
children of the late Mrs. Elizabeth LaBoon, listed as: Vann Law-
horn LaBoon; Joseph Allen LaBoon; John Harrison LaBoon; Peter La-
Boon; Peter LaBoon, deceased; Rachel Marianne LaBoon, the wife of
Anderson Green Michael; Dorcas Sara Anne LaBoon, the wife of William Franklin Wyatt. Also paid to Dr. John M. Fields, for Medical
service. This is the copy sent to Ga. in order to obtain receipt
from Mrs. Michael.]

George W. Harper, son of Lucinda Melton & Ansel Harper, b. 3 July
1826 in Oconee Co., Ga.
George W. Harper m. 8 Feb 1872 to Margaret E. Foster
John Foster Harper b. 30 Dec 1872
Ada Jane Harper b. 7 Dec 1875
Winton Travis Harper b. 5 Aug 1879 [added "He died 3 Dec 1942"]
George W. Harper, my husband, d. 13 Apr 1883
Georgia Ann Harper b. 25 Jan 1883 [Evidently, Mrs. Harper had not
entered the birth of her last child until after her husband died]
Ada Jane Harper m. 29 Dec 1901 to David Franklin Michael
David Franklin Michael, son of Rachel M. LaBoon & A. G. Michael, b.
13 Apr 1875
        [in handwriting of Mrs. Margaret (Maggie) Foster Harper]

Margaret Estelle (Elizabeth) Harper, my mother, d. 24 Apr 1920
Mary Georgia Ann Harper, my sister, m. 21 Jan 1913 to William A.

Stepp [no children]
John Foster Harper, my brother, m. Mrs. Ophelia Hale nee Hunt, the
    widow of John F. Hale on November [no day or year] [no children]
George Washington Foster, my grandfather, son of John & Margaret
    Furlow Foster, b. at Salem in Oconee Co., Ga.
        [Children of his sister, Mrs. Ada J. Harper Michael]
Fairrie Belle Michael b. 31 Oct 1902
George Harper Michael b. 1 Mar 1905
Edward Franklin Michael, my nephew, b. 11 June 1907, d. 26 Jan
    1926, from an accidental discharge of a shotgun while he was
    hunting rabbits
Ralph Leonardo Michael b. 13 Apr 1910
Elder Foster Michael b. 12 Jan 1913
Henry David Michael b. 14 May 1915
Margaret Rachel Michael, my niece, b. 8 Sep 1919, d. 30 June 1920,
    bur in the LaBoon Plantation Graveyard beside her great grand-
    father, George W. Foster
        "The brothers & sisters of my father, George W. Harper"
Uncle Ansel Harper, Aunt Sarah Ridgeway, Aunt Hallie Cross, Uncle
John Harper, Aunt Martha Felker, Aunt Elizabeth Malcolm
        "The brothers & sisters of my mother, Margaret E. Foster Harper
Uncle Fletcher Foster, Uncle George Foster, Uncle James Foster,
Aunt Mollie Aycock, Aunt Fannie Preston, Uncle Sam Foster, Uncle Ed
Foster, Aunt Anna LaBoon, Aunt Nan Williams
"Mother told me that she had heard father say that his grandfather
Harper was a yankee and was a hatter and came from somewhere in New
England and settled at Laurens, S.C. and married a daughter of a
man named Ansel Dollar. He then came to Manchester, Georgia and
ran a shop where he made hats. His son, Ansel Harper, moved to
Salem in Oconee Co., Georgia where my father, George W. Harper, was
born 3 July 1826."
"My father died when I was so small, that I never knew much about
the older Harpers, except his brothers & sisters."
Fairriebel Michael, my niece, m. 5 Apr 1931 to Henry Hudson Robison
    son of Lizzie Frances Peters & George Nicholas Robison
Henry Hudson Robison, Jr. b. & d. 22 July 1932
George Nicholas Robison b. & d. 29 Aug 1935
David Michael Robison b. & d. 4 Sep 1937
George Harper Michael, my nephew, m. 16 Dec 1928 to Sara Estelle
    Mobley, dau. of Lizzie Hammond & Sanders Mobley
Sara Patricia Michael b. 20 Jan 1931
Mary Joan Michael b. 19 Sep 1934
Ralph Leonardo Michael, my nephew, m. 18 June 1932 to Elsie Raw-
    lings, dau. of Ellen & William Oscar Rawlings
James Leonardo Michael b. 19 May 1933
William Franklin Michael b. 17 Mar 1935
Douglas Clyde Michael b. 7 Nov 1940
Elder Foster Michael, my nephew, m. 9 Nov 1935 to Thelma Louise
    Shepherd, dau. of Sadie Hensley & Matthew Shepherd
Bettie Jane Michael b. 12 Oct 1936
Frances Yvonne Michael b. 20 Sep 1938
Larry Holmes Michael b. 12 Apr 1941

James Marvin Michael b. 19 Jan 1943 [not in hand of W. T. Harper]
Henry David Michael, my nephew, m. 19 Dec 1936 to Lois Virginia
  Harrison, dau. of Ruth Barton & Marcus Paul Harrison
      [in handwriting of Winton Travis Harper who lived as an old
      bachelor at the old Harper Home in Walton Co., Ga. He gave
      this old home to his sister, Mrs. Ada Jane Harper Michael &
      during much of his life, his sister resided with him or near
      him. He was devoted to his Michael nephews & niece. He con-
      tinued to make entries up to his death.]

Marcus David Michael was b. 12 Apr 1938
Winton Travis Harper d. 3 Dec 1942 [added by George LaBoon]

[These records were edited and copied by Leonardo Andrea, Columbia
55, S.C. on 5 July 1948. On front fly leaf is written, "John Foster, His Bible" "I was born in South Carolina near the Savannah River. My parents were Irish." The old Bible has so come apart that
Winton T. Harper took all the pages with any entries on them,
placed them in an envelope with the LaBoon Estate paper, which had
been placed in the Bible for safe keeping by David F. Michael, a
brother-in-law of Winton F. Harper. The Bible pages are owned by
Mr. George LaBoon of Good Hope, Walton Co., Ga. These pages were
given to him by his first cousin, the late Mr. Winton Travis Harper
before he died in 1942. The portion of the Bible containing the
date of printing is missing along with many other pages. In fact,
the Bible has fallen to pieces. Mr. W. T. Harper told his cousin,
George LaBoon that one page of entries had been lost. Some of the
record pages are torn and bits lost. Most of the writing is legible.]

WILLIAM L. FOSTER

Wm. L. Foster b. 18 Feb 1811, d. 16 Nov 1853, m. Lucinda (Taylor)
Foster b. 4 Apr 1817, d. 22 Nov 1894
      Children
John A. b. 28 Feb 1840
Ann Eliza b. 2 Mar 1842
Joseph A. b. 13 May 1847
Richard M. b. 22 Oct 1848, d. 15 Jan 1883
Geneva C. b. 18 Dec 1849
William R. b. 16 Oct 1851
Missourri b. 11 Jan 1854

[This Bible is owned by Mr. John Pointer, Semora, N.C. (Caswell
Co.) Sent 1952]

JESSE FOX

Jesse Fox, son of Thomas Fox, Sr. (b. 1725, d. 16 Nov 1822, aged 96
yrs.) & Elizabeth Fox, b. 3 Jan 1774, d. 26 Mar 1850, aged 76 yrs.,
m. 17 Mar 1805 to Farba Ward, dau. of John & Winney Ward, b. 11 Dec
1788, d. 17 Jan 1853, aged 64 yrs., bur. at the homestead on Chin-

quepin Creek beside her husband, on land reserved by his heirs for a grave yard.
Children
John Fox b. 14 Dec 1805
Mary Fox b. 7 Sep 1807
Rachel Fox b. 15 Sep 1809
Daniel Jesse Fox b. 4 Dec 1811
Lucretia Fox b. 11 Jan 1814
Elizabeth Fox b. 24 Dec 1815
Elouisa W. Fox b. 2 Dec 1817
Henry Washington Fox b. 23 Oct 1819
Sophia Fox b. 3 Sep 1821
Susannah Fox b. 27 Sep 1823
Felix S. Fox b. 29 Aug 1825
Emiline Fox b. 15 Feb 1828
Joseph H. Fox b. 3 July 1830

JOHN FOX

John Fox d. 1 July 1884, m. 1st on 29 Mar 1827 to Anna Magdalena Mathias, dau. of John Eva Mathias, d. 18 Nov 1830, m. 2nd on 1 Nov 1832 to Eliza Ann Poindexter, dau. of Thomas K. & Mary Poindexter, b. 28 Dec 1812, d. 9 Nov 1899.
Children
Sarah Ann Fox d. 18 Oct 1830
Joseph Ward Fox d. 17 Nov 1830
Amanda Maria Fox b. 14 Aug 1833, m. 1st on 6 Sep 1850 to Jacob
  Wolfe, m. 2nd on 20 Feb 1868 to Henry J. Seibles
Thomas Shelton Fox b. 1 Sep 1836
Mary Jane Elizabeth Fox b. 5 July 1839, m. 8 Feb 1863 to Alfred J.
  Norris, son of Milton & Mary Norris
James Poindexter Fox b. 6 June 1842, d. 16 July 1878
John Jesse Fox b. 25 Apr 1845

Wm. E. Sawyer m. 22 Aug 1841 to Louise Fox
Daniel Willis m. 29 June 1846 to Emeline Fox

ENOCH FOY

Enoch Foy b. 17 May 1777, m. 1st on 3 Sep 1799 to Lucy Foy b. 8 Dec 1783, d. 19 Jan 1805, m. 2nd in April 1805 to Applis Sanderson, b. 15 Jan 1787, d. 27 Feb 1812.
Children
Morris Foy, son, b. 14 Oct 1800
Polly Foy, dau., b. 22 Mar 1802
Nancy Foy b. 28 Jan 1806
James Foy b. 29 Sep 1807
Joseph S. b. 17 Sep 1809
Miles Foy b. 21 May 1811

[Records from the Bible of Enoch Foy. Purchased & dated 1803, copied by Mary B. Jacobs of Wilmington.]

Joel Franklin b. 23 Sep 1757, d. 23 Sep 1807, m. 9 Jan 1794 to Susannah (Susan) Lewis b. 11 Apr 1770, d. 10 Jan 1855, aged 84 yrs. &
10 mos.

Mary E. C. Franklin b. 4 Jan 1795
Ann M. H. Franklin b. 31 July 1796, m. 14 May 1812 to John Wesley
    Lightfoot b. 24 Jan 1792, d. 6 Jan 1822
Mary W. L. Franklin b. 1 ... 1798, m. 7 Mar 1820 to Robert W. Cart-
    er b. 11 Aug 1793, d. 9 Nov 1838
Chas. W. L. Franklin b. 12 May 1800, d. 15 Aug 1801
Susannah H. (W.) L. Franklin b. 3 June 1802, d. 4 Nov 1823, aged 21
Sarah (Susan or Sally) W. B. Franklin b. 20 May 1805, d. 25 Sep
    1859, aged 54 yrs, m. 19 Nov 1822 to Hector Atkisson, d. 11 Oct
    1871
Jane M. L. Franklin b. 10 Jan 1807

Susan M. M. Lightfoot b. 6 Apr 1813
Joel F. Lightfoot b. 16 Oct 1814
John Wesley Lightfoot b. 8 Jan 18--, d. 26 Aug 1818
Mary M. C. Lightfoot b. 7 Apr ----
Caroline E. B. Lightfoot b. 7 Apr ----

Chas. W. L. Carter, Jr. b. 27 Dec 1820
Mary Roberta Randolph Carter b. 8 Oct 1822
Susannah Jane Franklin Carter b. 20 Sep ---- [erased]
Lucy Campe Carter b. 20 Apr 1821, d. 26 Jan 1827
Georgiana Maguire Carter b. 27 June 1828
Eliza C. E. Carter b. 29 Mar 1831
Robert W. C. Carter, son of Robt. & Mary W. L. Carter, b. 3 Feb
    1833, d. 6 Sep 1842
John H. B. Carter b. 27 Mar 1835
Mary M. Carter b. 11 Aug 1838, d. 19 Aug 1838

Caroline Horatia Atkisson b. 20 Nov 1823, dau. of Hector & Susan W.
    B. Atkisson
Joel Anne Atkisson b. 20 Oct 1825
Sarah Margaret Eliz. Willis Atkisson b. 17 Nov 1827
Arthur Merriweather Atkisson b. 26 Nov 1830
Martha Jane Atkisson b. 18 Feb 1833

Robt. P. Moore m. 29 Dec 1871
Saml. P. Craig m. 18 Jan 1871 to Mary E. Turner
Jane M. L. Olde d. 6 Nov 1851 - youngest child of Joel & Susannah
    Franklin
Susan J. Allen d. 4 May 1848
Caroline E. Royeston d. Feb 1852
Henry B. Old d. 22 Apr 1854
Fanny J. Anderson, dau. of Henry & Jane Old, d. July 1854
Lucy Champe d. 2 June 1828

[This Bible was published in 1815. It is owned by Mary & Sallie (Misses?) Garner, Barton, Ala.]

REV. JOHN PHILIP FRANKLOW

Rev. John Philip Franklow b. 17 July 1758, came from London, England, after Revolution, m. 6 June 1785 to Sarah b. 1 Nov 1759
    Children
Rachel Ann Franklow b. 14 Mar 1786, d. 26 May 1792
John Hepworth Franklow b. 14 Jan 1788, m. 6 June 1811 to Mary Smith
Sarah Frances Franklow b. 25 Feb 1790
Deborah Leah Franklow b. 23 Jan 1794

[From Bible in St. Matthew Lutheran Church at Cameron, S.C. See Rast Bible below.]

JOHN FRAZER

John Frazer b. 5 Nov 1782, m. Milly Bond
    Children
Pamelia b. 5 Nov 1802
Cynthia b. 27 Apr 1804
Margaret b. 15 Dec 1805
Edna b. 1 Dec 1807
Wm. Baxter b. 8 Mar 1810
Henry Livingston b. 28 Jan 1812
Elizabeth b. 12 Oct 1813
Alexander b. 22 Sep 1815
Mary Sewell b. 11 Feb 1818, m. Thos. J. Florence b. 17 July 1814
Nancy b. 21 Oct 1820

    Children of Thos. J. & Mary Sewell (Frazer) Florence
Jane b. 11 Oct 1838
Ann Eliza b. 8 Feb 1843
Elizabeth b. 10 Sep 1846
Henry Baxter b. 31 Aug 1849
Ella b. 1 Oct 1853

Arthur Frazer d. 12 Dec 1829 in the 68th year of his life
Mary Goodrum Frazer, his wife, d. 20 May 1840 in her 58th yr.

[Information from the Frazer Bible & family records, sent to L. F. Driver, Thomasville, Ga. 20 Apr 1927 by his aunt, Mrs. Mary Florence Frazer Johnson (H.C.), Opelika, Ala.

Great grandfather Frazer was of Scotch descent (I think named Sewell) landed in Charleston, S.C.

Grandfather, Arthur Frazer m. twice, m. 2nd to Mary Goodrum whose mother was a Knott of S.C., 4 children by first wife, 12 by 2nd, the following are known: Mrs. Anna Boring , John & Fairwick by 1st wife (a dau. of Fairwick m. Joseph Bettick of Louisville, Ky.);

Wm., John Haywood, John Anderson, Alan, Addison, Martha, Amelia, Lucinda, Eliza & Irene by 2nd wife. Arthur Frazer & Cousin Alexander Frazer came to Ga., lst settled near Lincolnton, county seat of Lincoln Co., then to Harris Co. Buried on plantation with other relatives - place still known by his name. Their desc. went to Ala.

John Haywood Frazer m. Kittie Glaze in Columbus, Ga.
John Anderson Frazer b. 18 Aug 1800, d. 9 Dec 1861, bur. in LaFayette, Chambers Co., Ala., m. Louisa Graves of S.C.
Addison Frazer b. 30 Sep 1809, m. 5 Feb 1835 in Lincoln Co., Ga. by G. W. Gibson to Mary Ann Florence, dau. of Thos. Florence, b. 25 Apr 1818
Martha bur. in Auburn, Ala., m. Hilary Bostick
Amelia bur. in Auburn, Ala., m. brothers: Isaac McElhany & Dr. Frank McElhany
Lucinda m. Morgan Guice
Eliza m. Meredith Wright, Pike & Montgomery Cos., Ala.

Children of Addison & Mary Ann Florence Frazer
Thomas LaFayette b. 21 Dec 1835, m. Ella Narcissa Ross b. 4 Sep 1844, d. 7 June 1905
Frances Olivia b. 28 Feb 1839, m. Prof. Oscar F. Casey
Lucy b. 28 Jan 1843
Wm. Addison b. 19 Oct 1852
Mary Florence b. 20 July 1855, m. 12 June 1877 to Henry Clay Johnson
Mattie Irene b. 7 Sep 1857, m. 4 Feb 1879 to Lewis Sanders Driver

Children of Thos. LaFayette & Ella Narcissa Ross Frazer
Mary Ella b. 11 June 1877, m. Albert W. Ware, had dau., Pauline who m. Bernard Neeson Neal
Thos. Ross b. 4 Mar 1879, m. Gussie Siler
John Addison m. Marie Jefferson - no children

Children of Oscar F. & Frances Olivia Frazer Casey
Florence Olivia
Julia m. J. B. Green, Opelika, Ala.
Laura Lee m. John Gary Sims, Montgomery, Ala.
Addison Duchel
Frances m. Walter Ross Glenn, Auburn, Ala.
Mary Wadsworth m. Lilburn Chandler, Wilmington, Del.

Children of Henry Clay & Mary Florence Frazer Johnson
Mary Lou b. 3 Apr 1878
Florence Olivia b. 28 June 1879
Henry Clay b. 22 Nov 1885
Thos. Frazer b. 2 July 1894

Children of Lewis Sanders & Mattie Irene Frazer Driver
Lewis Frazer b. 24 Sep 1880
Chas. Addison b. 12 Dec 1882
Geo. Herbert b. 30 Dec 1884

Edward Leigh b. 11 Dec 1886
Frank b. 16 Apr 1888

Great grandmother Florence was Jane Lashbrook

Grandfather, Thomas Florence, b. 5 Mar 1789, d. 3 June 1863, m. 1st
to Lucy Blalock b. 5 May 1789, d. 14 Mar 1829, m. 2nd to Ann Bla-
lock b. 4 Oct 1801, d. 12 May 1862
    Children
John b. 24 July 1807
Obadiah b. 19 Dec 1809
William b. 23 Feb 1811
George b. 15 Nov 1812
Thomas b. 7 July 1814 [note discrepency with date above, 17 July]
Nancy b. 8 Apr 1816
Mary Ann b. 25 Apr 1818 [m. Addison Frazer above]
Jane b. 3 June 1820
Gibson b. 11 Oct 1822
Lucy b. 23 Oct 1824
Toliver b. 9 Jan 1827
Stern b. 26 July 1832
Ann b. 18 Jan 1834
Frances b. 8 Dec 1835
La Fayette b. 29 Aug 1837
Ezekiel b. 24 May 1839
Josephine b. 17 July 1842

CHARLES CALHOUN FULLER

Charles Calhoun Fuller of Longmire, S.C. b. 11 Oct 1850, d. Satur-
day, 4 Apr 1925, m. 3 Apr 1872 at Edgefield Co. Ho. by Rev. Luther
Broadus, Pastor of Edgefield Baptist Church to Lillie E. Adams of
Edgefield, S.C., b. 17 Aug 1851, d. Monday, 7 Apr 1919.
    Children
William Walton Fuller, son, b. Monday, 24 Feb 1873, m. 17 May 1909
  by Rev. G. H. Burton to Kate Reynolds
Mary Louise Fuller, dau., b. Wednesday, 12 Aug 1874, d. 30 Oct
  1940, m. 22 Mar 1893 to J. N. Robinson
Dr. Ralsa Marshall Fuller, son, b. Saturday, 1 Apr 1876, d. 29 Sep
  1944, aged 68, m. 1st on 22 Jan 1902 by Rev. G. H. Burton to Lura
  Beatrice Reynolds who d. Saturday, 20 Feb 1904, m. 2nd on 28 Oct
  1908 by Rev. Rankin to Sudie Britt who d. Wednesday, 11 Nov 1916
  [11 Nov was a Saturday in 1916, however, it was a Wednesday in
  1908, 1914, 1925, 1931, 1936, etc.]
Suvannah Irene Fuller, dau., b. Tuesday, 5 Mar 1878, d. Feb 1943
Edgar Adams Fuller, son, b. 8 Nov 1879, d. in hospital, Sunday, 19
  June 1910, accidentally shot, m. 25 June 1903 by Rev. G. H. Burton to Alice Henderson
Mary Ann Fuller, dau., b. 4 Mar 1881, d. 16 Sep 1944, m. 3 Dec 1903
  by Rev. G. H. Burton to William A. Byrd
Ruth Fuller, dau., b. 15 Nov 1882, m. 8 June 1905 by Rev. L. Stokes
  to Felix Appleby Moorer

Jasper O'Neal Fuller d. Monday, 2 Mar 1892
Thomas Earl Fuller d. 11 Nov 1938, aged 54
Louise Britt Fuller d. 25 Dec 1946
Walter R. Hilton m. 15 Nov 1912 by Rev. J. S. Harris to Minnie
    Fuller
Charles Calhoun Fuller, Jr. m. 1 Nov 1911 to Lillie Mae Bailey
Dr. Luther Hogan m. 6 June 1919 by Rev. A. M. Hogan to Lila Shep-
    pard Fuller

[Bible of Charles Calhoun Fuller of Liberty Hill, Edgefield Co.,
S. C. owned by W. W. Fuller of Edgefiled, S. C.]

RICHARD FURMAN

Richard Furman, a minister, res. of High Hills & Charleston, S.C.,
b. 1755, d. 1825, bur. in Charleston, m. 1st to Elizabeth Hayns-
worth b. 1755, d. 1787, m. 2nd to Maria Burn.
    Children
Son, unnamed, b. 1775, d. 1775
Rachel, res. of High Hills, m. Capt. Thomas Baker
Wood, a teacher & writer, res of various places in S.C. & Tenn.,
    b. 1779, d. 1840, bur. in Elizabethton, Tenn., m. 1st to Hannah
    Bowers, m. 2nd to Laura Lyon
Richard b. 1783, d. 1784
Richard B., res. of Daniel's Island, near Charleston, a physician,
    b. 1790, d. 1846, bur. in Charleston, m. Susan Boleyn Keith
Samuel, a minister, res. mostly of Sumter, S.C., b. 1792, d. 1877,
    bur. in Bethel Cemetery, near Sumter, m. Eliza Scrimzeour
John Gano b. 1793, d. 1795
Josiah Brodhead, a minister, res. of Darlington Dist., S.C., b.
    1795, d. 1842, bur. in Darlington Dist., S.C., m. Henrietta Dar-
    gan, no children
Chas. Manning, a banker, res. of Charleston, S.C., b. 1797, d. 1872
    bur. in Charleston, S.C., m. Jessica Perpall
Maria Dorothea b. 1799, d. 1870
Henry Hart, a cotton buyer, res. of Charleston, La., b. 1801, d.
    1841, bur. in Charleston, La.
Sarah Susannah, a writer, res. of Charleston, S.C., b. 1804, d.
    1835, bur. at Long Town near Winns, S.C.
John Gano, II, a soldier & writer, res. of Charleston, S.C., St.
    Louis, West Point, Chicago, b. 1806, d. 1830, bur. near Chicago,
    never married
Thomas Fuller, a physician, res. of Fairfield, S.C., b. 1807, d.
    1866, bur. at Little River Ch. near Winns, S.C., m. Nancy Arm-
    strong, no children
James Clement, a minister & educator, res. of Society Hill, Winns-
    boro, Greenville, S.C., b. 1809, d. 1891, bur. at Greenville, m.
    1st to Harriet Eloise Davis, m. 2nd to Mary Glenn Davis
Anne Eliza b. 1812, d. 1897
William Brantley b. 1817, d. 1818

[This old Bible is in the library of Furman University, Greenville, S.C., copied by the librarian in March 1962 for the compiler.]

JOHN FURNAS

John Furnas b. 5 Mar 1736, d. 5 Aug 1777
Mary Furnas b. 10 Sep 1742, d. 6 Sep 1782
    Children
Joseph b. 1763
Rebecca b. 19 Apr 1764
Thomas F. b. 23 Mar 1768
Esther b. 4 July 1770
Robert b. 27 June 1772
William b. 29 May 1775

JOHN FUTCH, SR.

John Futch, Sr. m. Hester
    Children
John Futch b. 4 Sep 1790
Henrietta Futch b. 5 June 1793
Comfort Futch b. 8 Feb 1795
Elizabeth Futch b. 16 Oct 1798
David Kendrick Futch b. 13 June 1801
Chas. Bishop Futch b. 20 Dec 1804

    [parents not given]
Esther LeGwin b. 24 Sep 1814, m. 6 May 1830 to Thos. J. Johnson
    who was b. 12 Sep 1805 and m. 2nd on 6 May 1858 to Emma Hargroves
Eliz. LeGwin b. 6 Feb 1816
John LeGwin b. 8 Feb 1818, m. Mary Garrison
Wm. LeGwin b. 4 Mar 1820
Henrietta LeGwin b. 14 Mar 1822
David Kendrick LeGwin b. 4 Oct 1824
Lot LeGwin b. 8 Apr 1827
Nancy LeGwin b. 26 Mar 1832

    Children of Thos. J. & Esther (LeGwin) & Emma H. Johnson
Thos. Hanes Johnson b. 23 Feb 1831, m. 13 Sep 1854 to Julia Frances
    Bishop b. 12 Nov 1834
Andrew Jackson Johnson b. 13 May 1836, m. Marietta B. Bishop b. 2
    July 1843
John Wm. Johnson b. 27 Aug 1841, m. Sarah Frances Martin b. 29 Dec
    1845
Margaret Christian Johnson b. 26 Mar 1860
Jas. C. Johnson b. 21 Jan 1863

    Children of Thos. Hanes & Julia Frances (Bishop) Johnson
Wm. Murphy Johnson b. 4 July 1855, d. 7 July 1855
Mary Fanny Johnson b. 5 July 1856
Hester Isabella Johnson b. 5 May 1858, d. 6 Feb 1860

Children of Andrew Jackson & Marietta B. (Bishop) Johnson
Geo. H. Johnson b. 10 Aug 1866
Sallie B. Johnson b. 5 May
Helen K. Johnson b. 7 Mar

Children of John Wm. & Sarah Frances (Martin) Johnson
Frances LeGwin Johnson, Sarah Burwell Johnson, Hester Dolly Johnson, & Edna Wilmington Johnson

[This record was sent to the compiler by Mrs. Ida Kellam, Wilmington, N.C. 1956.]

GULBRAND PEDERSON GANDRUD

Gulbrand Pederson Gandrud b. 8 Mar 1844 in Norway, d. 10 Aug 1916
in Pope Co., Minn., m. Marthe Andersdatter Hov b. 24 June 1848 in
Norway, d. 1 Sep 1900 in Pope Co., Minn.
    Children all b. in Pope Co., Minn.
Karaline Gulbrands datter b. 10 Aug 1867
Anners Gulbranson b. 27 Sep 1869
Peder Gulbranson b. 8 Dec 1871
Christofor Gulbranson b. 12 Mar 1874
Matilda Gulbrans datter b. 13 May 1876
Alfred Gulbranson b. 16 July 1878
Ida Louise Gulbrans datter b. 8 Oct 1880
Laura Rosine Gulbrans datter b. 14 Apr 1883
Gustav Martinus Gulbranson b. 10 Dec 1885
Oluf Gulbranson b. 10 Aug 1888
Elvin Anton Gulbranson b. 3 Feb 1881
Bernet Wilhelm Gulbranson, [now Anglicized to Bennie William Gan-
    drud] b. 7 May 1894

[Contributed by Mrs. B. W. Gandrud, Tuscaloosa, Ala.]

MILTON A. L. GARRETT

Milton A. L. [Alphonzo Lumpkin] Garrett b. 6 Oct 1855, d. 27 Mar
1928, m. 1st on 20 Dec 1883 in Lasater, Texas to Sarah Anna Cleo-
patra Garrett b. 8 May 1857, d. 10 Mar 1924, m. 2nd on 15 Aug 1925
to Lenora Harrell Myers.
    Children
Anna Garrett b. 15 Oct 1884, d. 15 Oct 1884
Sallie Lou Garrett b. 31 Aug 1885, m. 11 Mar 1908 to Clifford Lee
    Batson
Dora Alberta Garrett b. 4 Aug 1887, m. 29 Dec 1910 to Allen Kyle
    Sims
Eugenia Culberson Garrett b. 7 Aug 1889
James Milton Garrett b. 6 Mar 1892, d. 1 Mar 1937
Lizzie Lee Garrett b. 27 Feb 1894, d. 30 June 1897
Charles Allen Garrett b. 1 Feb 1897

[Milton A. L. Garrett & his wife Sarah Anna Cleopatra Garrett were
cousins. His parents were Wilson Lumpkin Garrett b. 27 Sep 1832,
d. 21 Nov 1854 (1857 written over 1854), m. 11 Oct 1854 to Nancy L.
(Lois) Fitzpatrick b. 15 July 1833, d. 6 Dec 1888. These records
were copied by Mildred Dulaney from photostat of a Bible owned by
Dr. Charles Garrett, Hillsboro, Texas. The Bible was published by
A. J. Holman & Co., Philadelphia, 1882.]

ARCHIE G. GARY

Archie G. Gary (son of Absalom Gary b. 8 [?] 1788 and Hetty Rabb b.
5 Feb 1792, d. 27 June 1861, aged 69 yrs., 4 mos., 22 days) b. 24
Feb 1809, d. 1 Apr 1863, aged 54 yrs., m. Rebecca Gary b. 22 Jan
1814, d. 24 Mar 1871, aged 57 yrs.
      Children
Frances E. Gary b. 7 Aug 1831
Mary A. Gary b. 5 June 1833
Andrew A. Gary b. 16 Apr 1835, d. 5 Mar 1905, aged 69 yrs., m. 1st
   on 3 Apr 1859 to Nancy E. Johnson b. 25 Dec 1839, d. 27 Jan 1883,
   m. 2nd on 17 Feb 1884 in Cussita, Cass Co., Texas to Lilla Etta
   Moore b. 17 Nov 1856
Hetty C. Gary b. 12 Apr 1837
Wm. B. Gary b. 13 Mar 1840, d. 5 July 1862, aged 22 yrs of typhoid
   fever in Miss. during the War
Rebecca E. Gary b. 3 Dec 1841
Archey G. Gary b. 31 Oct 1843, killed 20 Sep 1862 in Battle of
   Chickamaga, aged 19 yrs., 10 mos.
Nancy K. Gary b. 30 Dec 1845, d. 19 May 1847, aged 1 yr.
Sarah L. Gary b. 29 Oct 1847
Martha E. Gary b. 17 Jan 1849
Augustus J. Gary b. 1 June 1850, d. 2 Nov 1867, aged 17 yrs., 5 mos
Lucy A. Gary b. 8 Dec 1851

      Children of Andrew A. Gary
Eliz. E. b. 4 July 1861, d. 9 Oct 1865, aged 4 yrs., 3 mos.
Wm. A. b. 26 Jan 1863, d. 5 May 1912, aged 49 yrs. at Mineral
   Wells, Texas, m. 28 Dec 1884 to S. B. Bass
Augustus Mitchell b. 22 Apr 1874 in Cass Co., Texas, d. 20 June
   1921 at Sulphur Springs, Texas, m. 9 Oct 1898 to Mattie Eliz.
   Elder b. 9 Oct 1879 in Grayson Co., Texas
Mary Rebecca b. 10 June 1886
Carrie Leila b. 18 Apr 1889

Carroll Andrew b. 21 Aug 1899 in Greenville, Texas
Augustus Mitchell Gary, Jr., son of A. M. & M. E. Gary, b. 22 Apr
   1907, m. 26 Oct 1929 in McAlester, Okla. to Mary E. Inge

[Copied by the compiler on 5 June 1945 from a record loaned by
Mrs. Clem Wilson, Rt. 6, Box 459, Little Rock, Arkansas.]

CHRISTIAN GATES

Christian Gates b. 1762, m. 3 Jan 1795 to Elizabeth b. 7 Feb 1775.
    Children
William b. 23 Nov 1797
George b. 22 Nov 1799
Samuel b. 30 Jan 1802
Mary b. 26 Oct 1804
Catherine b. 20 Apr 1807
Elizabeth Margaret b. 8 Jan 1811
John Christian b. 2 Jan 1813

[From Bible in St. Matthew Lutheran Church at Cameron, S.C.]

CONRAD GATES

Conrad Gates b. 30 Apr 1774, m. Elizabeth
    Children
Lewis Gates b. 26 Nov 1799
Joseph Gates b. 24 Dec 1801
Harriot Gates b. 11 Mar 1806
John M. Gates b. 19 Jan 1810
Ann M. Gates, his twin, b. 19 Jan 1810
James Russell Gates b. 10 Apr 1813

[On fly leaf of Bible: "John Anthony Menicken b. 15 May 1785 at
Cologne on the River Rhein ... and was married to Elizabeth Gates
2 Mar 1809." From Bible in St. Matthew Lutheran Church at Cameron,
S.C.]

REV. JOHN GIBSON

 Rev. John Gibson b. 20 Nov 1759 in Calvert Co., Md., d. 9 Feb 1859
in Greene Co., Va., m. 1st to Nancy Gibson [first cousin] b. 1757,
m. 2nd on 3 Aug 1798 to Eliz. Harvey, m. 3rd on 4 Dec 1826 to Mrs.
Eliz. (Bush) Smith, widow of Downing Smith who d. 1811
    Children by first marriage
Marie or Mary b. 5 Jan 1782
William b. 31 Mar 1783, m. a Morris
Peter b. 29 July 1784, m. 24 Dec 1809 to Francis Estes [Frances?]
Elizabeth b. 2 Aug 1786
John b. 5 Dec 1787, m. 28 Jan 1822 to Eliz. Collins
Nancy b. 2 Feb 1790, m. 9 May 1849 to Harry Marshall (as his 2nd
    wife)
Nelly b. 4 Oct 1791, m. James Gentry
Samuel b. 24 July 1793, m. 6 Nov 1820 to Eliz. Lankford
Peggy b. 11 Nov 1795, m. Wm. E. Harris
Thos. b. 21 Oct 1797, m. 5 Sep 1827 to Frances Gentry
    Children by second marriage
Joshua b. 4 June 1797 [? step son?], m. 20 Dec 1821 to Eliz. Stone
Franky b. 1 Feb 1800, m. [2nd] on 3 Aug 1825 to Eppa Marshall
Henry b. 27 Oct 1802, m. 5 Sep 1825 to Polly Maupin
Sarah Powers b. 8 Feb 1804, m. 25 Nov 1828 to Dowing Smith 1811-
    1891

Susan b. 17 Feb 1806, m. 12 Dec 1825 to Thos. Maupin
[No children by third marriage]

PHILIP PHILIPS GILCHRIST, SR.

Philip P. Gilchrist b. 9 Nov 1825, m. 22 Aug 1860 at Brentwood [or
Birdwood], Albermarle Co., Va. by Rev. Mr. Brown to Alice A. Garth
b. 5 Oct 1840
    Children
Philip P. b. 3 ... 1861
Ellen b. 19 Jan 1863
George M. b. 5 Mar 1866
Frank Malcolm b. 1867
Alice Armene b. 1 Apr 1870
Wm. Garth b. 12 Sep 1873
Dan b. 4 Apr 1875
Celestine b. 8 May 1879

[Bible owned by Miss Katie Frank Gilchrist, Courtland, Ala. Copied
by the compiler in May 1958.]

SAMUEL GILL

Saml. Gill m. Ruth Van Meter
    Children
Cassandra b. Dec 1779
Mary b. 30 Mar 1782
Saml. b. 17 July 1785
Elizabeth b. 1 Aug 1787
William b. 1 Dec 1789
Erasmus b. 27 June 1792
Joseph b. 30 Nov 1795
Martha b. 10 Mar 1798
Emily b. 1 Dec 1799

[Cassandra above m. James Aldridge, brother of John P. Aldridge who
married Mary Gill. These people all went to Ky. from Md. These
family records were sent by Mrs. Frank N. Robertshaw of Greenville,
Miss. to the compiler in 1939.]

JAMES HENRY GILLAM

James Henry Gillam b. 9 Mar 1846, d. 22 Dec 1923, m. 1st on 14 Sep
1865 to Susan Rachel Fitzpatrick b. 24 Feb 1842, d. 27 Nov 1888, m.
2nd on 16 Dec 1890 at Battle, Texas to Maria Catharine Fergusson d.
12 Oct 1930.
    Children
Robert Fitzpatrick Gillam b. 1 Dec 1866, d. 18 Sep 1898
Kate Gillam b. 31 Aug 1869, d. 2 Jan 1871
Harry Riddle Gillam b. 15 Aug 1870 [1871?], d. 18 Oct 1896, m. 2
  Jun 1895 in Ovilla, Ellis, Texas to Bertie Powers
Unnamed child b. 8 Mar 1873, d. 8 Mar 1873

Jesse Warren Gillam b. 25 Sep 1875, d. 10 Mar 1876
Annie Lewis Jones Gillam b. 29 Sep 1878
James Walden Gillam b. 19 Feb 1881, m. 17 Nov 1906 to Mary Louise
    Hammer
Callie Elizabeth Georgia Gillam b. 9 Apr 1883
Carrie Rachel Gillam b. 2 Dec 1893
Ruble K. Gillam b. 23 June 1897, d. 7 June 1951, m. 24 Jan 1922 in
    Abilene, Texas to Virginia E. Cameron [Their son, James Cameron
    Gillam, b. 30 May 1934, d. 30 May 1934 - from telephone conver-
    sation with James W. Gillam]

[Copied by Mildred Dulaney from photostat of Bible owned by Jim
Gillam, Mart, Texas.]

ALFRED GILREATH

Alfred Gilreath b. 29 Oct 1801, m. 1st to Elvadetia Gilreath b. 18
Sep 1803, m. 2nd to Mariah Shockly b. 29 July 1810, d. 16 Mar 1888,
wife of Henry Darby and second wife of Alfred Gilreath.
    Children
Abimahlech Martial Gilreath b. 17 June 1832
Mary Evaline Gilreath b. 20 July 1833
Nancy Elizabeth Gilreath b. 23 Apr 1835
Julia Benna Gilreath b. 8 Sep 1836
Amelia Melvina Gilreath b. 4 Mar 1838, d. 30 Sep 1861 "the death of
    the Righteous"
Lawrence Perry Gilreath b. 25 Sep 1840
Eliza Lascitee Gilreath b. 11 Dec 1842
Benjamin Jabez Gilreath b. 11 Oct 1848
Emmy (Emma) Caroline Gilreath b. 4 June 1850, d. 28 Apr 1902, m.
    James H. Thompson
Andrew Nolen Gilreath b. 28 Nov 1852, d. 10 Nov 1912, m. 1st on 4
    Jan 1883 by the Rev. Samuel M. Green to Miss Nancy K. Bradley d.
    30 Sep 1903, aged 52, m. 2nd time

    Children of Andrew Nolen Gilreath
Mariah Gilreath, dau., b. & d. 1 Dec 1883
Annie Bradley Gilreath b. 28 Aug 1886, d. 1 Aug 1887
Mamie Lee Gilreath b. 1 Mar 1889, m. 1st to John Brockman, m. 2nd
    to Paul Trammell
Dorothy Gilreath, by second wife, m. Morris Reeves of Atlanta, Ga.

[Marriage page is missing and part of the death page. Mrs. Trammell has a record of whom each child of Alfred Gilreath married,
but this is not in the Bible. Copy of the Bible of Alfred Gilreath of Greenville Co., S.C., which is now owned by Mrs. Paul
Trammell of Greenville, S.C.]

JAMES GLASCOW

James Glascow m. 27 Feb 1810 to Margaret Morrow

James M. Glascow m. 17 Dec 1832 to Maria Bradford [in margin "Moved to Ala."]
Mariann Glascow m. 11 Dec 1833 to John P. McClellan [in margin "Moved to Miss."]
Jane E. C. Glascow m. 31 Mar 1836 to Giles Burditt [in margin "Moved to Ala."]
Nancy C. Glascow m. 27 June 1839 to William Hunter

James M. Glascow b. 30 June 1814
Maria Ann Glascow b. 11 June 1816
Jane E. C. Glascow b. 11 June 1818
Nancy C. Glascow b. 21 July 1824
Loueser Catherine Glascow b. 16 Oct 1824
Sarah E. Glascow b. 7 Dec 1831
James N. Glascow b. 1 May 1835
Susannah S. Glascow b. 4 Oct 1837
James N. Glascow b. 10 Jan 1839
Elizabeth Frances Glascow b. 27 Nov 1841
Nancy Clementine Burditt b. 28 Apr 1837
Mary Gentry Burditt b. 10 May 1838
Sarah Elizabeth Burditt b. 17 Aug 1841
William H. A. Burditt b. 23 Mar 1844
James S. McClellan b. 13 Nov 1834
Jane Margaret McClellan b. 13 Sep 1836
David P. McClellan b. 15 Nov 1838

WILLIAM T. GLAUZIER

William T. Glauzier b. 19 July 1826, m. to Caroline S. Glauzier b. 27 Mar 1829
    Children
Emma C. b. 29 Dec 1849
Elizabeth Agnes b. 18 Apr 1851
James W. b. 13 May 1853
Ervin D. b. 24 Aug 1855
Frances Katharine b. 12 May 1858
John T. b. 21 July 1860
Anna Maria b. 24 July 1862

JAMES GLENN

James Glenn, Revolutionary soldier from Lincoln Co., N.C., b. 22 July 1759 in Berkeley Co., Va., d. 24 July 1843 in York Co., S.C., m. 26 Mar 1789 to Martha Craig Boyd, widow, b. 8 Sep 1769, d. 8 Jan 1839.
    Children
Jane McClain Glenn, dau., b. 20 Mar 1790, [d. unmarried]
John Glenn, son, b. 8 Mar 1792, d. 27 Nov 1854, [m. Sarah Johnson]
James Erwin Glenn, son, b. 11 Dec 1793 [no m. data given]
William Glenn, son, b. 8 July 1795, [m. Elizabeth Boyd]
Henry Glenn, son, b. 17 June 1797, [m. Jane Brown]
Robert Glenn, son, b. 9 Apr 1799, [m. Pamela B. McGill]

140

Mary Glenn, dau., b. 2 May 1801, [m. David Johnson]
Samuel Glenn, son, b. 2 Jan 1803, [m. widow Reid/Reed]
Franklin Glenn, son, b. 10 Mar 1806, [m. Mary Craig]
Eliza Adeline Glenn, dau., b. 6 Apr 1808, [m. White Stowe]
Milton Glenn, son, b. 24 Dec 1810, [m. Mary Kendrick]
Martha Glenn, dau., b. 9 July 1813, [m. Warren Kendrick]

[Bible data owned by Robert B. Paslay, 202 Andrews Bldg., Spartanburg, S.C. The marriage information was added by Mr. Paslay from a
D.A.R. Membership paper. This family is buried at Bethel Presbyterian Church along the York Co., S.C. & Mecklenburg Co., N.C.
line. He has a will in York Co., S.C. James Glenn is a son of
John Glenn by the first of his three wives, Jane Elizabeth Spratt
from Pa. to Va. to Gaston Co., N.C.]

GEORGE WASHINGTON GOING

George Washington Going b. 16 May 1862, d. 2 Aug 1934
Mrs. Martha (Mary) Jane Vaughan Going b. 26 May 1871, d.24 Nov 1899
Mrs. Annie Jeter Going b. 12 Dec 1868, d. 30 Dec 1914
    Children of George W. Going
Bernice Going b. 2 Dec 1887, m. 6 Oct 1909 to William Hagood, Jr.
Walter Franklin Going b. 26 July 1889, m. 12 June 1912 to Jacquelin
    Almeda Mack
Paul Going b. 7 Oct 1893, d. 29 Oct 1899
Henri Rochelle Going b. 18 Nov 1895, m. 20 June 1923 to Edith Pur-
    vis
James Clyde Going b. 5 July 1905, m. 28 Nov 1928 to Sarah Elizabeth
    Bell
George Washington Going, Jr. b. 1 Apr 1909, d. 1937, m. 29 Nov 1933
    at Rock Hill, S.C. to Eloise Barfield
        Grandchildren & great grandchildren
Elizabeth Hagood b. 20 Dec 1910, m. 10 Sep 1931 to David Ralph
    Spearman
George Cleveland Hagood b. 18 June 1916
Jacquelin Almedia Going b. 26 July 1926
Ethel Bernice Going b. 25 Apr 1926
Walter Franklin Going, Jr. b. 25 Dec 1919
David Hagood Spearman b. 16 Nov 1932
William Benjamin Spearman b. 17 Aug 1937
Infant son of Clyde & Sara Going d. 16 July 1934

[Bible is owned by Mrs. Walter F. Going of Columbia, S.C. Printed
in Chicago, Ill. in 1885. Some later entries were eliminated. G.
W. Going was of Kelton, Union Co., S.C.]

WILLIAM GEE WASHINGTON GOING

William Gee Washington Going b, 17 July 1824, d. 7 Oct 1815, aged
91 yrs., bur. at Mt. Joy Church, m. 16 Sep 1847 to Nancy Manerva
Jane Dupree b. 3 June 1827, d. 13 Nov 1903, bur. at Mt. Joy Baptist
Church. She joined the Baptist Church at Pacolet Shoals in 1845 &

was baptized in the Pacolet River.
    Children
Nancy Ann Rebecca Everlener Going b. 25 Oct 1848
William Mack Isaac Going b. 7 Feb 1850, m. 26 Oct 1873 to Dealey
    Cole
John Thomas Richard Going b. 16 Aug 1851, m. 15 Nov 1874 to Izora
    Cole in Ga.
Elijah Vinson (Vonson) Going b. 25 Mar 1853, m. 1 Mar 1877 to Mar-
    garet Farr
Silvia Ann Francis (es?) Jane Going b. 26 Dec 1855, d. 8 Mar 1855
Butler Brooks Going b. 25 Feb 1856, d. 9 Sep 1931, bur. in Rosemont
    Cemetary in Union, S.C., m. 7 Sep 1879 to Sariah Smith
David Anderson Going b. 30 May 1856, m. 26 Nov 1882 to Josephine
    Lulear Stewart
James Daniel Fenard (Lenard) Going b. 5 May 1860, d. 1 July 1898,
    m. 14 Feb 1894 to Emma Blalock, Ga.
George Washington Going b. 16 May 1862, m. 1st on 9 Jan 1887 to
    Martha Jane Vaughan, m. 2nd on 29 Jan 1904 to Mrs. Annie Jeter
    Smith
Robert Lee Going b. 26 Dec 1864, d. 5 Jan 1865
Robert Right Gary Going b. 10 Apr 1866
Rhoda Cerdela Alice Sarah Elizabeth Going b. 12 Sep 1868, d. 4 Mar
    1928, bur. at the Phillipi Baptist Church in Union Co., S.C., m.
    17 Oct 1886 to William Vaughn (Vaughan)
Oliver Francis Marion Going b. 16 June 1870, m. 10 Feb 1897 to El-
    len McPherson in Greenville, S.C.

Elijah Vinson, son of Willis & Sarah Vinson, d. 3 May 1887 in Ga.
    where he had lived several years
Judy (Julia Ann) Fields d. 17 Sep 1884, bur. at New Hope Baptist
    Church, Barto Co., Ga., m. 1st in S.C. to John Shaw who died, two
    children: Thompson Shaw & Mary Ann Shaw, m. 2nd to Griffin DuPree
    who d. in Ga., 19 children, the eldest of whom was Nancy Manerva
    J. DuPree
William Isaac Going, son of Elijah V. Going, b. 29 Dec 1877
Mace Going, son of Elijah V. Going, b. 16 Mar 1881
Bernice Going m. 6 Oct 1909 to William Hagood, Jr. of Easley, S.C.

[W. G. W. Going was a res. of Kelton, Union Co., S.C. The pages
only from this Bible are owned by Mrs. Walter F. Going of Columbia,
S.C. Printing date is not known. This Bible is very interesting;
it names the day of the week, usually the hour of the day & the
place where each person was born or died. The day & place of bur-
ial is usually stated. The date of adult (Baptist) baptisms are
usually noted.]

ANTHONY FOSTER GOLDING

Dr. Anthony F. Golding (son of Anthony Golding by his second wife,
Isabella Reid d. 21 June 1822) b. 10 Aug 1791, d. 18 Feb 1858, m.
4 Sep 1816 to Caroline Matilda Brown (dau. of Jacob Roberts Brown &
Christini Neely of Newberry Co.) b. 11 Dec 1793, d. 23 Oct 1883.

Children

Marquis LaFayette Golding b. 17 July 1817, d. 4 Nov 1826
Clemenlina Brown Golding b. 25 Dec 1818
Sallie Morgan Golding b. 1 Feb 1821, d. 14 Sep 1824
Christina Neely Golding b. 3 Mar 1823, d. 22 Aug 1846 "Our Little
  Kitty"
John Reid Golding b. 30 Dec 1824, d. 10 Sep 1830
Henry Laurens Golding b. 11 Feb 1827, d. 3 Feb 1850
Thomas Willis Golding b. 20 Dec 1829, d. 18 Jan 1835
Nancy Campbell Golding b. 14 Aug 1831, d. 4 Nov 1833
John Brown Golding b. 2 Nov 1833, d. 28 Aug 1860
Robert Cunningham Golding b. 11 Nov 1835
Caroline Matilda Elizabeth Golding b. 18 Nov 1837; Caroline M. E.
  Smith Colton d. 18 Nov 1900
Pamela Cunningham Golding b. 16 Nov 1839; Pamela C. Fogarty d. 2
  June 1914

Thomas Wadsworth Golding, my brother, d. 1 Feb 1822 [By A. F. G.]
John Reid Golding, my brother, d. 16 July 1824 [By A. F. G.]
Rachel, my sister, wife of Samuel Caldwell, d. 18 July 1826 [By A.
  F. G.]
David Golding, my twin brother, b. 10 Aug 1791 [By A. F. G.]
Pamela Nancy Golding, our aunt & widow of David Griffin, d. 6 Jan
  1858, aged 72 at Houston, Chicasaw Co., Miss. [By one of children]

[The marriage page is missing from this Bible, owned by Mrs. Charles H. Duke, 2411 Monroe St., Columbia, S.C., published by Sharpless of Philadelphia, Pa., date missing]

ROBERT HOWELL GOODWYN

Robt. H. Goodwyn b. 19 July 1795 in Richland Co., S.C., d. 30 May
1861 in Columbia, S.C., m. 4 Jan 1821 in St. Matthew Parish to Mrs.
Charlotte Ann Hart b. 12 Apr 1799 at Midway, d. 11 Feb 1875 at Co-
lumbia, S.C.
    Children
John Thomson b. 1 May 1822 at Midway, d. 10 July 1855, m. 1st on
  6 July 1843 to Sally C. Brown, d. Sep 1847, aged 25 yrs., m. 2nd
  on 4 Nov 1852 to Sallie Coles Taylor
Robert Hart b. 8 Feb 1824 in Amelia, S.C.
Wm. Sabb b. 11 Aug 1825 at Totness, m. 29 Oct 1846 at Totness to
  Celestina Rosa Raoul
Caroline Myddleton b. 28 June 1827 at Totness, m. 27 Oct 1846 to
  Wm. Bonneau Murray
Sarah Eliz. b. 11 Sep 1830, m. 12 Apr 1848 in Columbia, S.C. to
  Stephen L. DeVeaux
Harriet Julia b. 7 Jan 1832, d. 28 Apr 1892 in Austin, Tes., m. 17
  Jan 1850 in Columbia, S.C. to George McDuffie Calhoun
Mary Eugenia b. 12 Sep 1833 at Totness
Martha Taylor b. 27 May 1835 at Totness
Charles Howell b. 20 Nov 1837 in Columbia, d. 12 June 1838
Ellen Adella b. 26 June 1839, d. 24 Oct 1849

Rebecca Taylor b. 24 Nov 1844, d. 3 May 1845
Charlotte Thomson b. 10 Sep 1847, d. 12 Sep 1847

[Bible now owned by Mrs. Nell Peterkin Reid, Oakland Plantation, Fort Motte, S.C. See W. R. Thomson Bible, this vol.]

DURHAM GRADY

Durham Grady b. 21 Jan 1776, d. 29 Oct 1822, aged 46 yrs., 9 mos., 8 days, m. 10 Jan 1804 to Susannah b. 14 Feb 1785

Polly Slocumb Grady b. 14 Nov 1805
Sally S. Grady b. 14 Nov 1805, m. Farquard Smith b. 13 Dec 1801

[Children of Farquard & Sally S. (Grady) Smith]
Susan Smith b. 23 Dec 1825
John D. Smith b. 5 Apr 1827
Alexander Smith b. 22 June 1828
Isabella Smith b. 10 Jan 1830
Mary Smith b. 30 Mar 1831
William C. Smith b. 30 Nov 1832
James Smith b. 28 June 1834
Eliz. C. Smith b. 1 May 1836
Walter D. Smith b. 6 Sep 1837
Farquard Smith b. 8 May 1839
Henry E. Smith b. 23 Mar 1841
Edward Smith b. 17 Mar 1843
Jane b. 26 July 1846
Jesse Slocumb b. 7 Jan 1847

Ezekial Slocumb b. 18 June 1760
Sally Slocumb b. 21 Jan 1776
Jesse Slocumb b. 20 Aug 1780
Susan Slocumb b. 14 Feb 1785

[Bible sent by Mrs. Ida B. Kellam, Wilmington, N.C. Owner of Bible is Eugene Whitmel Smith, Jr., Lebanon Plantation, Dunn, N.C.]

WILLIAM WILSON GRAVES

William Wilson Graves d. 20 Mar 1862 in Clark Co., Ark. [1850 census show him b. ca. 1813 in Va.]; Sarah E. Graves, widow of Wm. H. [?] Graves, d. 11 Sep 1889 in Madison Co., Miss. [Her obituary & census show her born in York Co., S.C. 12 Jan 1822].
    Children, b. in Ark.
Margaret Catherine Graves, dau., b. 2 June 1844
Thomas Allison Graves, son, b. 27 Mar 1847, m. 9 Jan 1872 to Arte-
    mis Field
Mary Jane Graves, dau., b. 2 July 1849
Joseph Alexander Graves, son, b. 2 Oct 1851
Martha Virginia Graves, dau., b. 12 Jan 1857
Billie (William) Susan Graves, dau., b. 20 Aug 1862, m. 29 Nov 1883

T. B. Edwards

James Hearn m. 4 Jan 1899 to Sue E. Graves
James Hearn m. 3 June 1800 to Lydia Graves
Sallie O. Monroe m. 5 Feb 1873 to John L. Kerr
James W. Monroe m. 28 Mar 1866 to Elizabeth A. Atkinson
Mary J. Monroe m. 29 Mar ... to R. J. Atkinson

Thomas Charles Monroe d. 1865
Mrs. Sue E. Hearn d. 3 June 1899
Robert Allison d. 21 Jan 1862
Willie Leon Edwards d. 19 Nov 1897
Mrs. W. H. Field d. 28 Feb 1900

Robert W. Monroe b. 17 Dec 1853 in Autauga Co., Ala.
Lucia M., dau. of Mr. & Mrs. T. B. Edwards, b. 5 July 1890
Benjamin Leon, son of Mr. & Mrs. T. B. Edwards, b. 4 Feb 1885
Thomas Marvin, son of T. H. & M. S. Edwards, b. 22 Feb 1887
Joseph S. Edwards b. 9 Sep 1897
W. R., son of T. A. Graves b. 20 Feb 1873
S. F., dau. of T. A. Graves, b. 15 Sep 1876

[This Bible was printed in 1855 and is owned by the family of Mrs.
G. H. L. Dunagin, 2238 W. Beach Blvd., Biloxi, Miss.]

DANIEL GWYN

Daniel Gwyn b. 21 Mar 1751, d. 2 May 1833, m. 7 Feb 1774 to Zip-
porah Rice b. 30 Apr 1756, d. 16 Aug 1829.
        Children
James b. 20 Dec 1774
Elizabeth b. 9 June 1776
Zeri b. 10 Apr 1778, d. 10 July 1840
William b. 23 Sep 1783
Thomas b. 1 Jan 1786
Dorothy b. 6 Mar 1788, d. 25 Jan 1844
Nancy b. 26 Apr 1790
Hugh b. 21 May 1791
Daniel, Jr. b. 5 May 1793, d. 27 July 1834 in Elizabeth City, N.C.
Rice b. 9 May 1795, d. 19 Dec 1872, m. Eliz. Boyd
Richard b. 22 Apr 1796
John b. 27 Feb 1799
Littleton Ayres b. 22 Apr 1801, d. 13 July 1853, m. 21 May 1833 to
  Pamela A. Watt b. 26 May 1814

    Children of L.A. & P.A. Gwyn
Richard b. 14 Mar 1834, d. 26 Apr 1834
Littleton Ayres, Jr. b. 27 Feb 1836, d. 19 Aug 1840

[There are several marriages with no dates & they are not identi-
fiable by the compiler. One looks as though Rice Gwyn m. Elizabeth
Boyd Rice, probably Eliz. Boyd. This record was sent by Mrs. Stel-

la Gwyn Waugh, Danville, Va. Her sister, Mrs. Elizabeth Strange, Danville owns the Bible. Mrs. Waugh sent a photostatic copy, beautiful writing. She says someone tore out some pages of this Bible, leaving it incomplete.]

JOHN HAM

John Ham b. 4 Dec 1764 in Cheraw, S.C., d. in Lauderdale Co., Ala., m. Pheby in Union Co., S.C.
    Children
Moley b. 1 Jan 1786
James b. 30 Mar 1787
Jacob b. 28 Feb 1789
Blassingame b. 6 Sep 1790
Nancy b. 9 June 1792
Cloydious b. 17 June 1794
Frankey b. 3 Mar 1796
Thomas Pinckney b. 1 July 1798
Elizabeth b. 1800
Buckley b. July 1802
John Nickel b. 13 July 1804
Sally b. 13 June 1808, d. 1811

HARMAN HANCOCK

Harman Hancock b. 25 May 1771

Sarah Hancock b. 16 July 1800
Henry Hancock b. 2 Dec 1801
Penny Hancock b. 9 Mar 1804
Geo. Washington Hancock b. 13 Jan 1806
Mary Hines Hancock b. 4 Feb 1811

Elizabeth Hancock b. 31 Aug 1832

[Bible now (1959) owned by G. D. Cox, Winterville, N.C.]

JAMES HANDCOCK

James Handcock, son of Dearham Hancock, b. 5 Aug 1745, m. Elizabeth
    Children
Hardee b. 11 Oct 1769
Amey b. 25 May 1769 [? too close. Twin of Harmon]
Harmon Handcock b. 25 May 1771
Thomas b. 9 Jan 1773, d. 27 Apr 1784
James b. 29 Nov 1774
Levi b. 3 June 1776, d. 29 Oct 1780
Josiah b. 24 or 25 Nov 1777
Pipse b. 27 Dec 1779, d. 21 Apr 1784
Sarah b. 29 Aug 1781
Daniel b. 23 Mar 1784
Elizabeth b. 29 June 1785

Nancy b. 3 Apr 1787

Warren Pettit, son of Naseby & Sally, b. 31 July 1817, d. 21 July
    1819
James Pettit, son of Naseby & Sally, b. 3 Oct 1819
Nathan Pettit, son of Naseby & Sally, b. 5 Oct 1823

[A slip of paper in the Bible is a summons to Eliz. Handcock as a
witness to a suit between Geo. C. Ellis & Thos. Hardee, 17 May 1822
signed, W. Cherry, Sheriff. This Bible is now (1959) owned by Mrs.
J. T. Gaylord, Winterville, N.C. The date in it is MDCCLXIX (1769)
printed by Alex. Kincaid, His Majesty's Printer, Edinburgh.]

WM. YOUNG HANSELL

Wm. Young Hansell b. 4 Mar 1794
Susan Byne Harris, dau. of Augustin & Ann Harris, b. 1 Jan 1797

Augustin Harris Hansell, son of Wm. Young & Susan Byne Hansell, b.
6 Aug 1817 in Milledgeville, Ga., d. 10 Feb 1907 in Thomasville,
Ga., m. 20 May 1840 in Milledgeville, Ga. to Mary Ann Baillie Paine,
dau. of Charles J. & Ann J. Paine, (Charles Joshua Paine, son of
Orris & Margaret Paine, b. 15 Nov 1795 in Petersburg, Va., d. 11
Feb 1859 in Milledgeville, Ga.) b. 12 May 1823 in Milledgeville,
Ga., d. 12 Aug 1905 in Thomasville, Ga.
    Children
Chas. Paine, son, b. 14 Sep 1844 in Milledgeville, Ga., m. 14 Jan
    1869 by Rev. Saml. Benedict to Rhetta C. Charlton
Ann Davies, dau., b. 16 May 1841, Milledgeville, Ga.
Susan Valeria, 2nd dau., b. 19 June 1842 in Milledgeville, Ga.
Frances Baillie, dau., b. 28 Jan 1853 in Thomasville, Ga., m. 30
    Oct 1879 in Thomasville, Ga. by Rev. E. P. Kerr to Frances B.
    Hansell

Mary Hartridge, dau. of Chas. Paine & Rhetta Charlton Hansell, b.
    25 Dec 1869 in Thomasville, Ga.

[Augustin Harris (son of Walton Harris, a Rev. War soldier, who was
b. in Va. in 1739, d. in Greene Co., Ga. in 1809, m. Rebecca Lanier
dau. of Sampson Lanier of Va.) b. 1767, d. 1836, m. Ann Byne, dau.
of Rev. Edmund Byne of Burke Co., Ga. This information given by
Mrs. Cochran]

RENNE HARDING

Renne Harding, son of William Harding, b. 28 Aug 1774, m. 9 Sep
1803 to Rebecca Harding b. 15 Sep 1777
    Children
Nancy & Keziah, daughters, b. 29 May 1805
Elizabeth, dau., b. 6 Aug 1807, d. 31 Dec 1807 of whooping cough
William, son, b. 30 Nov 1808, m. 7 Feb 1838 to Jane E. Harding b.
    31 Mar 1815

Greenberry Patterson, son, b. 30 Oct 1810

Saml. Speer Harding b. 16 Sep 1838
Keziah Ann Harding b. 17 July 1840
Bertha Elizabeth b. 23 Oct 1841
Greenberry Patterson Harding b. 24 Nov 1842

Thomas Harding b. 28 Aug 1781 [Possiby a brother to Renne Harding]

[This Bible is owned by Mrs. Hale Houts, Kansas City, Mo., who sent this record (1958).]

BENJAMIN HARPER

Benj. Harper b. 28 Dec 1776, d. Dec 1826, m. Eliz. Blair b. 7 June 1773, d. 30 Apr 1819, aged 44 yrs.
    Children
James Blair b. 24 Mar 1799, d. 1806, aged 9 yrs.
Mary Knox Harper b. 20 Oct 1799
Martha Eliz. Harper b. 4 July 1804, d. 1805, aged 1 yr.
Benj. Harper b. 16 Mar 1806, d. 1 July 1816, aged 10 yrs.
John Harper b. 1 Nov 1809, d. 13 Sep 1814, aged 3 yrs.
Margaret Eliz. Harper b. 13 June 1813

Mary H. Stewart d. Jan 1826 [Mary Knox Harper?]
Jas. H. Stewart d. 16 Jan 1863, aged 37 yrs.

John Pinckney Stewart b. 10 June 1823, d. 9 Mar 1857 in Tulip, Ark. aged 34 yrs., m. 16 Nov 1843 to Eliz. Howard b. 14 Dec 1824, d. 20 Aug 1891

Jas. Harper Stewart b. 20 Nov 1844, m. 15 Dec 1868 to Eugenia Abby
    Johnston d. 29 July 1877
Wm. Howard Stewart b. 19 Sep 1847, m. 1 Apr 1874 to Antionette
    Adelle Cureton
John O. Stewart b. 2 Feb 1854, m. 12 Nov 1885 to Pauline Withers
    Stewart
Richard P. Stewart b. 11 Feb 1857, Tulip, Ark.

JOHN HARRIS

John Harris b. 4 Dec 1764 at Cheraw, S.C., d. Lauderdale Co., Ala.
A Revolutionary soldier.
    Children
Moley b. 1 Jan 1786
James b. 30 Mar 1787
Jacob b. 28 Feb 1789
Blasingame b. 6 Sep 1790
Nancy b. 9 June 1792
Cloydious b. 17 June 1794
Frankey b. 3 Mar 1796
Thomas Pinckney b. 1 July 1798

Elizabeth b. 1800
Buckley b. 11 July 1802
John Mickel [?] b. 13 July 1804
Sally b. 13 June 1808, d. 1811

JAMES M. HARRISON

James M. Harrison b. 17 Feb 1824, m. 18 Nov 1847 to America Moss d.
24 Oct 1911.
    Children
John Harrison, son, b. 22 Dec 1848
Sarah F. Harrison, dau., b. 15 May 1850, d. 15 June 1850
William Moss Harrison, son, b. 14 Oct 1851, m. 18 Jan 1877 to Mary
    Callaway
James Nathan Harrison, son, b. 18 Jan 1854, d. 6 Dec 1935, aged 84
May Elizabeth Harrison b. 21 May 1856, d. 29 May 1940
Wiley Stanmore Harrison b. 10 Sep 1858, m. 7 Jan 1885 to Hennie
    Spratlin
Carroline America, dau., b. 26 Nov 1861, d. 2 Jan 1953
Stewart Elbert [E. S. or Ebbie below?] b. 31 Aug 1864
Julia Reed b. 9 Sep 1866, d. 31 Aug 1896
John Hugh Harrison b. 9 May 1868
Fannie Griffin Harrison b. 16 Sep 1870

C. A. Harrison b. 26 Jan 1831
May Clio Harrison, dau. of W. M. & M. C. Harrison, b. 7 Nov 1877
Lula Gertrude b. 26 July 1880
Emily America b. 11 Jan 1888
Henry Hulin, son of Ebbie & Maosa Harrison b. 30 July 1895
Mattie Harrison, dau. of J. N. Harrison b. 16 Aug 1895
Wiley Henry Harrison, son of W. S. & H. Harrison b. 8 Oct 1885
Lina b. 17 Nov 1886
Enoch Stanmore b. 6 Oct 1888
Daisy b. Aug 1890
Ruth b. 15 June 1892
Susie Meay b. May 1894
E. S. Harrison b. Apr 1897
W. S. Harrison b. 1 June 1899

E. S. Harrison m. 25 Oct 1894 to Maosa Sutton

Col. W. H. Moss d. 27 Feb 1882 in the 82nd yr. of his age
Mrs. S. E. Moss d. Nov 1894 in the 91st yr. of her age
J. P. Moss d. Mar 1883
E. S. Harrison d. 22 Dec 1896
H. S. McLendon d. 16 Nov 1881 in the 69th yr. of her age

[This Bible is owned by Miss Martha Harrison, Trenton, S.C., published Hartford in 1848 by Sumner & Goodman.]

DERRILL HART

Derril Hart b. 11 Dec 1790 at Sandy Hill, d. 21 Sep 1815 at Hart-
land, m. 12 Apr 1814 at Midway to Charlotte Ann Thomson b. 12 Apr
1799.
      One child
Derrill Charlotte Hart b. 2 Nov 1815 at Midway, d. 20 Aug 1893, m.
   9 Nov 1845 in Columbia, S.C. to Joseph Francis Denck b. 21 Apr
   1813, d. 21 May 1889

Joseph Hart Denck b. 12 Jan 1847 in Charleston, S.C.
Charlotte Thomson Denck b. 14 Oct 1852 in Charleston, S.C.

[This Bible also has the granchildren of Robt. Howell Goodwyn &
their dates begin with 1853. Bible now owned by Mrs. Nell Peterkin Reid, Oakland Plantation, Fort Motte, S.C. See also W. R.
Thomson Bible, this vol.]

                    DR. OLIVER JAMES HART

Dr. Oliver Jas. Hart d. 4 Dec 1898, m. 26 Feb 1845 by the Rev.
Thos. John Young to Joanna Adelia Townsend (dau. of John Richard &
Mary Sealy Townsend who d. 28 Nov 1866) d. 18 Apr 1905.
      Children
Sarah Clark b. 9 May 1846, d. Oct 1847, bur. in St. John's Church-
   yard, St. John's Island, S.C.
Richardine Wilhemina b. 30 Dec 1848
Geo. Washington Seabrook b. 27 July 1851
William Thomas b. 14 Apr 1853
Oliver James b. 20 Aug 1854, d. 1 June 1892
John Townsend b. 6 June 1856
Joseph Seabrook b. 24 Apr 1858
Richard Henry Jenkins b. 29 Apr 1860
Mary Sealy b. 29 Aug 1863
William Rogers b. 22 Feb 1867
Sarah Elizabeth b. 24 Aug 1870

[Bible owned by Mrs. Joseph Everett Hart, York, S.C.]

                       JOHN HARVEY

John Harvey, son of Joseph & Lucy Harvey, b. 30 Sep 1781, d. 1824
in Barren Co., Ky., m. Patsy Chamberlain who d. 1873 as widow of
Henry Martin
      Children of John & Patsy Harvey
Betsey m. Washington Creed
Susan b. 1808, m. in 1826 in Monroe Co., Va. to Reason Ferguson b.
   15 July 1809 in Bedford Co., Va.
Polly b. 1810, m. William Cox [Twin?]
Lucinda b. 1810, m. Agrippa Clary [Twin?]
Prudence m. Robert Arms
Wilson Nicolas b. 8 May 1818, d. 14 Jan 1885, m. 22 Jan 1837 to
   Fannie Kerr b. 10 Jan 1820, d. 26 June 1878 [1898?]
Frances m. Henry Kerr

                          150

Emily

[Bible records sent to compiler by Mrs. Clarence Griffin, Rocky
Mount, N.C., owned by Mrs. Susan Ferguson Brooks.]

JOSEPH HARVEY

Joseph Harvey b. 12 Nov 1756, d. 25 Mar 1828, Barren Co., Ky., m.
12 Nov 1778 to Lucy Ballard b. 9 Nov 1761, d. 4 Oct 1851, Monroe
Co., Va.
    Children
Betsey b. 14 Oct 1779, m. John Lawrence
John b. 30 Sep 1781, m. Patsy Chamberlain
James b. 21 Feb 1784, m. Olive
Thomas b. 8 Jan 1787, m. 11 Jan 1811 to Nancy Lawrence
Wilson b. 28 Sep 1789
Martin b. 10 Feb 1792
William b. 20 Sep 1794, m. 23 Dec 1813 to Polly Bishop
Austin b. 3 Aug 1797, m. 9 Jan 1818 to Bushing [or Bushong]
Abner b. 1 Oct 1800, m. 20 Dec 1821
Patsy b. 26 Nov 1804, m. 21 Feb 1820 to William Davis

WILLIAM HARVEY

Wm. Harvey, Sr.
    Children
Wm. Harvey, son, b. Oct 1766
Sarah b. 8 June 1769, m. 1791 at Prestbury, England to Joseph
  Hughes
Edward b. 26 Mar 1771
Richard b. 7 Feb 1773
Ann b. 22 Aug 1774
Samuel b. 22 June 1778

    Hughes children
Tom b. 21 Mar 1792
William b. 29 Dec 1796
Elizabeth b. 30 June 1799
Phoebe b. 13 Jan 1802
John b. 31 July 1804
Sarah b. 15 Nov 1808
Mary b. 10 Mar 1810
Joseph b. 6 June 1812

[This is an English Bible that was sent to Kansas City, Mo. The
package had become unwrapped and there was no way for the postmaster
to either forward or return it. Perhaps some of the family is in
America.]

JOSEPH HATCH

Joseph Hatch b. 2 Dec 1762, m. 6 Feb 1787 to Ann Blackledge

Children
Lucy Louisa b. 21 Jan 1788, m. Francis Lamotte from the island of
  St. Domingo
Fanny m. Solomon E. Grant
Ann Bass m. Ivy Watson
Richard Blackledge b. 8 Oct 1797, m. 26 Dec 1820 to Rhodes Clarissa
  Rhodes b. 9 Apr 1800

        Children of Richard B. & Clarissa Hatch
Joseph Rhodes Hatch b. 17 Oct 1821 in Jones Co., N.C., m. 13 June
  1850 to Ann E. Williams b. 23 Oct 1833
James Edward Hatch b. 4 May 1824, d. 24 Aug 1827
Ann Blackledge Hatch b. 28 Aug 1827, m. 12 Oct 1847 to Benj. J.
  Griswold
Maria Louisa (or L. M.) Hatch b. 19 Oct 1829, m. 25 May 1847 to
  Daniel Smith
Richard Blackledge Hatch b. 26 Dec 1831

        Children of Joseph Rhodes & Ann E. Hatch
Ira W. b. 4 June 1851
James Rhodes b. 3 Feb 1853
Winnie W. b. 13 Feb 1855
Buckner H. b. 5 Feb 1857
Wm. B. b. 17 Nov 1858
Annie Maria b. 18 May 1860
Malvina T. b. 12 Feb 1862
Richard B. b. 28 Apr 1867
Joseph Eugene b. 9 May 1869
Cullen B. b. 16 Feb 1871
Robt. Walton b. 12 Apr 1874
Francis Marion b. 19 Aug 1876

                    JEREMIAH M. HAYMAN

Jeremiah M. Hayman b. 28 Dec 1822, son of James Hayman of S.C., m.
27 Aug 1846 to Martha Jane Carlton b. 10 July 1829, d. 21 May 1895.
        Children
Alderman Hayman, son, b. 8 Nov 1847, d. 9 Nov 1847
Martha Jane Hayman, dau., b. 29 Jan 1849, d. 19 Nov 1849
Susan Rebecca Hayman, dau., b. 15 Apr 1852, d. 16 June 1879, m. 2
  July 1868 to Felix J. Seward
Sarah J. Hayman, dau., b. 17 Apr 1854, m. 28 Dec 1876 to John C.
  Blount
Mary Ann Hayman, dau., b. 12 Feb 1856, d. 21 June 1856
Josephine Hayman, dau., b. 16 June 1857, d. 18 Nov 1858
William Cunningham Hayman, son, b. 11 Nov 1859, m. 3 Oct 1894 to
  Diane McNair
Lillie Oregon Hayman, dau., b. 16 June 1861, m. 26 May 1880 as his
  2nd wife to Felix J. Seward
Georgianna Virginia Hayman, dau., b. 2 Jan 1864, m. 9 July 1882 to
  Owen J. Frier
Ruby Susan Hayman, dau., b. 26 Apr 1879, m. 27 Sep 1899 to Magnus

T. Swift

[The death date of James Hayman & his son, Jeremiah M. Hayman can be found in the family cemetery in Bartow Co., Fla. James Hayman moved from Ga. to Bartow Co. He came to Ga. as a child from S.C.]

DAVID HENDRICKS

David Hendricks b. in Pa., came to Rowan Co., N.C., d. 1788, m. Margaret Elizabeth Pillsbury b. 1732, d. 1801
    Children
Sallie Hendricks m. Thomas Holeman
Kate Hendricks m. a Mr. Hunter
John Hendricks b. 17 Dec 1785, d. 8 Feb 1845, m. Lydia Garner d. 14 May 1864
David Hendricks b. 1761, m. Mary Hill "related to John Hill"

Mary Hendricks, dau. of David & Mary (Hill) Hendricks, b. 19 Oct 1801, d. 19 Apr 1856, m. 12 Feb 1824 to James Kinyoun b. 5 Feb 1804, d. 9 May 1857, son: John Kinyoun b. 4 Oct 1825

[This record was sent by Mrs. Hale Houts, Kansas City, Mo. She states that this Bible & other Hendricks records were in the hands of Mrs. J. H. Hendricks, East Bend, N.C. in 1937.]

David Hendricks b. 1754, d. 12 Feb 1788, m. Margaret b. 1752, d. 1801.

David Hendricks b. 2 May 1761, d. 20 Dec 1820 m. Mary b. 9 Mar 1758, d. 23 Dec 1822
John Hendricks b. 17 Dec 1785, d. 8 Feb 1845 m. Lydia b. 13 Mar 1800, d. 14 Mar 1864

    Children of John Hendricks
David Hendricks, son, b. 24 Oct 1826, d. 27 July 1849
Henry Hendricks, son, b. 3 Aug 1841, d. 9 Dec 1856
Catherine Hendricks, dau.

Eliz. Hendricks b. 11 Feb 1705, d. 1 Oct 1814
Francis Monroe Hendricks b. 27 Aug 1838, d. 28 Nov 1920, m. Martha b. 13 Feb 1839, d. 6 Aug 1916

[Sent by Miss Cora Hendricks, dau. of F. M. & Martha Hendricks. Note the discrepency in the b. date of Margaret E. P. Hendricks & the wide span between David b. 1761 & John b. 1785. Typographical error in David's date, should be 1781 or is John, David's son?]

TOBIAS HENDRICKS

Family of Tobias & Modolanah Hendricks, all b. in Rowan Co. Solomon Hendricks b. 6 Sep 1784 just after a heavy rain
Mary Hendricks b. 21 A!r 1787, about an hour before daybreak

Samuel Hendricks b. 21 Jan 1790 during a big snowstorm
Buffia Hendricks b. 2 May 1792 when the sun was about an hour high
Tobias Hendricks b. 17 Oct 1794 about 9 or 10 o'clock at night
George Hendricks b. 29 Feb 1797 a little after dark
Reuben Hendricks b. 30 Mar 1801 during a total eclipse of the sun
Sarah Hendricks b. 21 Apr 1803 during a heavy thunderstorm
Phebe Hendricks b. 21 Apr 1805 during a total eclipse of the moon
Elizabeth Hendricks b. 28 Jan 1807 during a terrible sleet storm
Martha Hendricks b. 8 June 1809 during a heavy rainstorm

[From the record of Alexander Johnson Hendricks, son of Thomas Alston Handricks & Ann Campbell Johnson, b. 19 Apr 1850 in Franklinville, N.C., d. 7 Jan 1935 in Mobile, Ala. "Mr. George G. Hendricks was an ex-sheriff of Randolph Co., N.C. & was a merchant in Asheboro, N.C. when I met him in June 1907. He showed me the following record of his great, great grandparents' children's births, which Mr. Tobias Hendricks had recorded in an old leather-bound account book instead of a family Bible. In that old account book he had entered up whiskies, brandies, etc. which he has sold to his neighbors; and he had charged tham up in shillings & pence instead of dollars and cents. And on account of the peculiar manner in which the old gentleman, Mr. Tobias Hendricks, Sr. had entered these births, I copied them off just as he had them entered. Mr. George G. Hendricks was born in Randolph Co., N.C. 25 Feb 1855. He was the son of Alston Hadly Hendricks who was b. in Randolph Co., N.C. 30 June 1827, son of Reuben Hendricks, 7th child & 5th son of Mr. Tobias Hendricks & his wife Modolanah Hendricks."]

ANDREW JACKSON HENRY

Andrew Jackson Henry b. 11 Aug 1831 in Bibb Co., Ala., d. aged 55 yrs. [d. 19 Oct 1886 from tombstone], m. Elizabeth Bird [(Spivey)] b. 6 Mar 1838 in Tippah Co., Miss., [d. in 1819 from tombstone].
    Children
Joseph Polk Henry b. 18 Aug 1856 in Bosque Co., Tes.
Patrick Julian Henry b. 2 Jan 1858 in Bosque Co., Tex.
John Walter Henry b. 11 Oct 1859 in Limestone Co., Tex.
William Jackson Henry b. 22 Sep 1861 in Johnson Co., Tex.
Emma Frances Henry b. 5 Jan 1864 in Bosque Co., Tex.
George Washington Henry b. 14 Feb 1865 in Bosque Co., Tex.
Andrew Temple Henry b. 31 Dec 1866 in Bosque Co., Tex.
Emmett Francis Henry b. 15 July 1869 in Bosque Co., Tex.
David Milton Henry b. 31 Jan 1871 in Hill Co., Tex.
Marvin Bird Henry b. 20 Mar 1873 in Hill Co., Tex.
Lucius Volney Henry b. 7 Feb 1875 in Hill Co., Tex.
Orpah Ruth Henry b. 5 Feb 1877 in Hill Co., Tex.
Olive Leona Henry b. 28 Nov 1878 in Hill Co., Tex.
Jake Henry b. 26 July 1881 in Williamson Co., Tex.

[Record sent by Mrs. Pauline Pearce (Mrs. M. C. Pearce), Kerrville, Texas, who said that Elizabeth Bird Henry's maiden name, not given in Bible, has been proven to be Spivey. Aug 1959.]

WILLIAM HERBERT, JR.

William Herbert b. 19 May 1765, d. 23 Mar 1835, m. 14 Aug 1785 to
Polly Herbert b. 9 Mar 1768, d. 18 Mar 1839
    Children
William Herbert b. 12 Jan 1789
Katherine b. 9 May 1791
Patsy b. 29 Aug 1793
Polly Humphries b. 18 Aug 1796
Betsy b. 9 Feb 1799
Elijah Humphries b. 3 Sep 1801
Daniel Sheffey b. 13 June 1805

Elizabeth Herbert & James Hawthorne m. 19 July 1821

[Copied from the Bible owned by Mrs. Joe Fields, Elk Creek, N.C.
The above William Herbert was the son of William Herbert b. 9 Mar
1733 in Bristol, England. He married Lady Sarah Humphries nee Fry,
dau. of Lord Fry. They were married on a ship coming to America in
1760. William died in Fincastle Co., Va. in 1776. His wife Sarah
died in Wythe Co., Va. in 1785 or 1786. Data obtained by Mrs. Percival Clarke Blackman nee Mary Herbert Bays, Rock Hill, S.C.]

THOMAS SEAWELL HERNDON

Thos. S. Herndon b. 19 July 1832 in Orange Co., N.C., d. 17 July
1882, m. 12 Oct 1856 to Delilah M. [Mildred] Herndon b. 3 Oct 1837.
    [Children]
W. [William] R. [Rhodes] Herndon b. 27 July 1857, m. 21 Dec 1881 to
  Louisa Poe
Sarah M. [Mildred] Herndon b. 9 Oct 1858
George A. Herndon b. 4 Nov 1860, m. 7 Dec 1882 to Phidelia A. Mark-
  ham
Thomas Bunyan Herndon b. 5 Aug 1862
Millie A. [Angeline] Herndon b. 17 May 1866
Nazor V. [Vernon] Herndon b. 23 Sep 1871, [d. aged 27 yrs.]
John Anderson Herndon b. 23 Sep 1871, [d. 23 Feb 1952 in Chapel
  Hill, N.C.]
H. [Hiram] L. [Linwood] Herndon b. 10 May 1873, [d. 16 May 1948 in
  Durham, N.C.]
M. [Manley] D. [David] Herndon b. 10 Oct 1876
    [Grandchildren]
Thomas E. Herndon b. 23 Oct 1883
Elmer S. [Stokes] Jones b. 9 Aug 1890
Ernest E. Jones b. 14 Feb 1892 [d. in his teens]
Robert H. Herndon b. 14 June 1884
Luvenia Herndon b. 23 July 1886

[This Bible is now in the possession of Mrs. E. S. Lanier (Nancy
Herndon) of Chapel Hill, N.C., dau. of J. A. Herndon. This family
is in Part Four, Herndons of the American Revolution by John Good-
win Herndon of Haverford, Pa. All b. in Orange Co., N.C.]

GABRIEL HERRING

Gabriel Herring b. 20 Oct 1767, d. 27 Nov 1845, m. 14 Feb 1792 to
Jannet Andres b. 9 Apr 1770, d. 9 Feb 1846
    Children
Benjamin Herring, son, b. 14 Dec 1792, d. 29 Sep 1833, m. 16 Dec
1824 to Susanna Jones
George, son, b. 26 June 1794, d. 20 Mar 1826
William, son, b. 3 Apr 1798, d. 5 Apr 1864
Elizabeth, dau., b. 7 Feb 1801, d. 7 May 1871
James Herring, son, b. 23 Jan 1803, d. 26 Sep 1852, m. 28 July 1825
to Jane Alderman
Mary Jane, dau., b. 7 Sep 1808, m. 22 Jan 1835 to Jacob Butler &
left for Ga. the 22 Feb 1835
Nathan, son, b. 9 Feb 1811, m. 29 Sep 1826 [1836?]

    Children of James & Jane Herring
Nancy J. Herring, dau., b. 15 Apr 1827
George A. Herring, son, b. 5 June 1830
William J. Herring, son, b. 23 Dec 1833
    Children of Benjamin & Susanna Herring
Geo. Herring, son, b. 20 Nov 1825
Mary Jane Herring, dau., b. 12 Nov 1827
Margaret Herring, dau., b. 28 June 1830

Robt. Strange Herring, son of Nathan & Sara, b. 6 Nov 1837

Richard Herring, my father, d. 4 Apr 1803, aged 77 yrs., 1 mo. & 11
days
Sarah Herring, my mother, d. 19 June 1813, aged 80 yrs., 5 mo. & 10
days
E. Herring, my brother, d. 17 July 1833
Stephen Herring, my brother, d. 26 Nov 1838, aged 65 yrs., 5 mo. &
17 days
Ann Spearman, my sister, d. 11 May 1839, aged 61 yrs., 7 mo. & 4
days
John Herring, my brother, d. 3 Mar 1814

[This Bible was printed in 1802, owned by M. R. Herring, Jr., Lum-
berton, N.C., son of M. R. Herring, Sr. of Sampson Co., N.C.]

JACOB HIBLER

Jacob Hibler m. 21 Feb 1794 to Miss Jensey Belcher, dau. of Robert
Belcher & Susannah, d. Jan 1824

Eliza Belcher Hibler b. 14 Apr 1795, d. 7 Dec 1800
Edmund Barns Hibler b. 16 Apr 1798
Thomas Jefferson Hibler b. 16 May 1800, d. Saturday, 15 Aug 1846
John b. 7 Jan 1802, d. 7 Apr 1803
William Henry b. 17 Jan 1804
Eldred Marshall Hibler b. 23 Feb 1806, d. 25 June 1860 in Coohoma

Co., Miss.
Twins (Both daughters, d. within one week
Robert Beazly b. 11 Mar 1809, d. Friday, 24 May 1835
John William Hibler b. 14 Jan 1811, d. in the 11th yr. of his age
James Lawrance b. 24 Nov 1812, m. 13 Feb 1838 to Mary Ann Amoson,
    dau. of Thos. Amoson & Nancy
Benjamin b. 25 Oct 1814, d. 4 Dec following

[Children of James L. Hibler]
Laura Jane Hibler b. Monday morning about 8:00, 10 Dec 1838
A son b. 6 Oct 1840, d. the same day
Thomas Hibler b. Monday morning, 15 Aug 1842
Son stillborn 10 May 1844
Robert Hibler b. Monday morning 10 Nov 1843 [1845?]
James Edmund Hibler b. Monday morning, 29 Sep 1847
Son b. 10 Dec 1849, d. the same day
Son b. 13 Feb 1851, d. same day
Mary Frances Hibler, dau., b. 11 Aug 1852, Wednesday morning

[The foregoing Bible Records were furnished by Mrs. James K. Polk,
Jr., Macon Plantation, Inverness, Miss.]

GEO. D. HOLCOMB

Geo. D. Holcomb b. 25 Dec 1769, d. 5 Mar 1845, m. Rachel b. 17 July
1779, d. 27 Sep 1829
    Children
Ruth b. 15 Dec 1798
Grimes b. 11 Oct 1802, m. 1st to Parmelia Holcomb d. 16 Jan 1834,
    m. 2nd on 21 Sep 1835 by Robt. Shaver, Esq. to Mary S. Stockboger
Louisana b. 30 June 1805
Nancy Williams b. 29 Feb 1808
Rachel Delany b. 21 June 1810
Wm. D. b. 2 Apr 1813, d. 26 Nov 1829
Jean b. 5 June 1815
Margaret b. 7 Nov 1817
Geo. W. b. 21 July 1820, d. 18 Apr 1822
Elizabeth I. b. 21 Sep 1823

Delilah, dau. of Jane Jackson Holcomb, b. 6 May 1836
Yarnett D. Patterson, son of Jas. Patterson, b. 26 July 1827
Eliz. T. Patterson, dau. of Jas. Patterson, b. 13 Apr 1829
Elicader Carter, son of Henry Carter, d. 17 June 1844

[The Holcomb family was among the early settlers of Yadkin Co.,
N.C. Mr. W. A. Collins of Winston-Salem is a desc. & is now the
owner of the Bible.]

GEORGE THOMPSON HOLMAN

Geo. T. Holman (son of James G. (Yancey) Holman b. 19 Aug 1769 in
Cumberland Co., Va., d. 3 Aug 1843 in Dade Co., Mo., aged 73 yrs.

11 mos. & 15 days and Mary Barbara Holman b. 24 Apr 1791 in Guilford Co., N.C., d. 16 Nov 1816 in Guilford Co., N.C., aged 25 yrs., 6 mos. & 22 days) b. 12 Aug 1813 in Guilford Co., N.C., m. 8 Sep 1837 at the residence of Rev. John Lambeth by the order of the Christian Church, known as Kelly Ite (The witnesses were: Lewis Apple & Edna Lambeth) to Lucinda Lambeth of Guilford Co., N.C. (dau. of Joseph Lambeth b. 29 Mar 1796, d. 20 Oct 1840 in Guilford Co., N.C., aged 44 yrs., 6 mos. & 21 days and Levina (Flack) Lambeth b. 10 Sep 1796, d. 22 Oct 1867 in LaClede Co., Mo.) b. 17 May 1817 in Guilford Co., N.C.

Children
Jas. Lambeth b. 24 Aug 1838 in Guilford Co., N.C.
Mary Levina b. 16 July 1840 in Guilford Co., N.C.
Geo. Thompson Washington b. 22 Apr 1843 in Camden Co., Mo.
John Lovick Liberty b. 11 Mar 1846 in Camden Co., Mo.
Andrew Josias b. 19 Nov 1848 in Camden Co., Mo.
Joseph Thos. Brooks b. 1 Apr 1851 in Camden Co., Mo.
Wm. Noah Webster b. 25 Apr 1861 in LaClede Co., Mo.
    [Births written by Danl. Matthews, Teacher 24 Mar 1877]

My half brothers & sisters [Geo. T. Holman]
Spencer Anderson Holman b. 22 Mar 1795 in Pr. Edward Co., Va.
Susannah Yancey Holman b. 26 Sep 1796 in Pr. Edward Co., Va.
Sarah Anderson Holman b. 27 Feb 1798 in Pr. Edward Co., Va.
Jas. Landry b. 20 Feb 1802 in Pr. Edward Co., Va., d. 16 Feb 1836
    in Davidson Co., Tenn.

My wife's brothers & sisters [Geo. T. Holman]
John Dillard Lambeth b. 6 June 1818 in Guilford Co., N.C., d. 9 Jan
    1888 in LaClede Co., Mo.
Lovick Loftin Lambeth b. 20 Feb 1820 in Guilford Co., N.C.
Andrew Flack Lambeth b. 9 Apr 1821 in Guilford Co., N.C., d. 11 Feb
    1877 in LaClede Co., Mo.
Polly Lambeth b. 18 Sep 1822 in Guilford Co., N.C.
Josiah Brooks Lambeth b. 9 June 1824 in Guilford Co., N.C., d. 5
    Feb 1875 in Lawrence Co., Mo.

[Copied by Mrs. J. A. Doggett, Greensboro, N.C.]

JOHN CONRAD HOLMAN

John Conrad Holman b. 20 Sep 1775, m. 2 July 1807 to Rachel Noble b. 26 May 1790
    Children
William Conrad b. 8 Sep 1809
Eva Mary b. 6 Apr 1811
John Russell b. 9 Apr 1813
James Thomas b. 23 Oct 1814
Jesse Knodel b. 27 Nov 1818
Elizabeth Rachel b. 8 Dec 1819
Ann Catherine b. 22 Jan 1821
John Joseph b. 9 Oct 1823

Eugenia Rebecca b. 11 Feb 1826
David Luther b. 16 June 1829

[From Bible in St. Matthew Lutheran Church at Cameron, S.C. See
Rast, this volume.]

LEWIS W. HOLMES

Lewis W. Holmes m. 13 Nov 1851 to Ann Bodie
Willis Holmes m. 20 July 1854 to Amanda Bodie
Willis Holmes m. 12 Feb 1880 to Jemima Edwards
George Willis Holmes m. 7 Nov 1897 to Georgia Jackson
Willis D. Holmes m. 7 Oct 1920 to Mary Louise Smith

George Willis Holmes b. 18 July 1874
Amanda Holmes b. 2 May 1879
Lewis Edwards b. 12 July 1889
Annie Holmes, baby, b. 7 Nov 1888
Willis D. Holmes b. 19 Aug 1898
Julia Holmes b. 22 Feb 1900
Fedder Holmes b. 30 Dec 1902
Micheal Holmes b. 26 July 1820
Lewis Watson Holmes b. 10 Apr 1822
Willis Holmes b. 21 Mar 1827
Frederich Holmes b. 21 Oct 1830
Amos Holmes b. 13 Nov 1779
George Willis Holmes b. 18 July 1874
Micheal Holmes b. 9 Aug 1855
Wm. Amos Holmes b. 10 June 1857
Mary Holmes b. 20 Feb 1859
Emmer Holmes b. 13 Feb 1864
Laura Holmes b. 3 Oct 1867
Jesse Holmes b. 11 Dec 1869
Ann Holmes b. 30 Oct 1871

Elizabeth Holmes d. 22 May 1879
Little Amanda Holmes d. 5 June 1879
Little Lewis Edwards d. 29 Aug 1880
Willis Holmes d. 3 Apr 1905
Amos Holmes d. 20 Sep 1854
Solomon Eikner d. 27 Feb 1868
Micheal Holmes d. 13 Sep 1855
Mary Holmes d. 20 Mar 1865
Emma Holmes d. 6 May 1865

[Copied from Bible owned by Willis Holmes, Edgefield, S.C. Fly
leaf: "Philadelphia, Sterotyped and published by C. Alexander &
Co., Athenion Bldg., Franklin Place and sold by All principal Book
sellers in the U.S.A., dated 1834."]

WILLIAM HOLMES

Wm. Holmes, son of Oliver & Sarah (White) Holmes, b. 20 Nov 1846 in
Wayne Co., N.C. Julia C. Peel, dau. of Robt. & Eliza Peel, b. 18
Nov 1849 in Wayne Co., N.C.
    Children
Robert b. 7 Feb 1870
Jas. O. b. 16 July 1872
Eva b. 26 June 1874
Sally Eliza b. 4 Apr 1877
Julia C. b. 19 Mar 1880
Bessie b. 25 Oct 1882
Bettie b. 16 Dec 1884

[From Cullen B. Hatch, Mt. Olive, N.C.]

LEONARD HORNSBY

Leonard Hornsby d. 12 Apr 1779 in the 80th yr. of his age ("Leon-
ard Hornsby, son of Leonard, wrote this 10 Aug 1780.") m. Elizabeth
d. 21 Jan 1801 in the 81st yr of her age ["widow" added later in
pencil.]
    Children
William Hornsby b. 25 Aug 1731 [or 1739, not clear]
Mary Hornsby b. 6 Jan 1740/1
Ann Hornsby b. 5 Feb 1742/3
Leah Hornsby b. 19 Feb 1744/5
Sharlotte Hornsby b. 25 Nov 1746
Lezze Hornsby b. 22 Feb 1748/9 [will has her as Elizabeth]
Janet Hornsby b. 30 Mar 1751
John Hornsby b. 7 June 1753
Leonard Hornsby b. 13 May 1755
James Hornsby b. 31 July 1757, d. 21 Apr 1781
Moses Hornsby b. 9 Dec 1759
    Children of John Hornsby & his wife Elizabeth
Noah Hornsby, son, b. 23 Dec 1779
John Hornsby, Jr., son, b. 19 Dec 1781
William Hornsby, son, b. 29 Mar 1784
Leonard Hornsby, son, b. 31 July 1789
Moses Hornsby, son, b. 19 July 1890
Hughston Hornsby b. 25 Dec 1792
Elizabeth Hornsby, dau., b. 4 Jan 1795
    Children of Joseph Hornsby
Margaret Hornsby, dau., b. 23 Oct 1801
Elizabeth Hornsby, dau., b. 13 Sep 1804
Cinthah Hornsby, dau., b. 2 Apr 1807
    Child of Leonard Hornsby
Marmaduke Hornsby, son, b. 15 Jan 1815
    Children of William Blake & Phamuel, his wife
Leah Blake, dau., b. 12 Jan 1775
Thomas Early Blake, son, b. 2 [?] Nov 1776
John William Blake, son, b. 16 Jan 1781
William Blake, deceased 22 Jan 1781
    Children of Jeremiah Roden and his wife Mary

Ann Roden, dau., b. 28 May 1762
Elizabeth Roden, dau., b. 20 Feb 176- [illegible]
Leonard Roden, son, b. 7 Apr 1765
Jeremiah Roden, son, b. 9 Aug 1767

[There are no marriage pages in this old Bible. This Bible came
down through several generations to the late Mrs. Claude B. Jordan
of Bascomville, Chester Co., S.C. It is now in the possession of
her husband. Printed MDCCLVI (1756) Edinburgh, Scotland.]

SAMUEL HOUSTON

Peter Houston b. 15 Dec 1765
Martha Houston b. 3 June 1767
James Houston b. 5 Apr 1769
Elizabeth Houston b. 12 Jan 1771
Prudence Houston b. 15 Oct 1774
Sarah Houston b. 14 Oct 1772
Samuel Houston b. 7 June 1776
John Houston b. 6 June 1779
Robert Houston b. 20 Aug 1781
Jane Houston b. 16 Dec 1783

[It is assumed that the above are children of Saml. Houston whose
name is at the top as being the head of this family. Bible owned
by Fred Brown, Lenoir, N.C.]

FRANCIS HOWARD

Francis Howard, son of William & Sarah Howard, b. 30 Sep 1739, d.
Jan 1785, m. 18 Apr 1762 to Anne Allenor Allen, dau. of William &
Frances Allen, b. 20 Sep 1755, d. 26 Aug 1777
        Children
Henry b. 2 Dec 1763, m. 20 Dec 1787 to Margaret
Rebecca b. 21 Apr 1765
Rhesa [?] b. 4 Feb 1769 [Should be 1767?]
Groves b. 25 Apr 1769
Patty b. 28 Mar 1771
Betty b. 24 Oct 1773
William b. 13 Mar 1775
Francis b. 7 Feb 1777

        Children of Henry & Margaret Howard
Anne, child, b. 22 Sep 1788
Hugh b. 2 July 1791
Alfred b. 2 Aug 1794
Alexis b. 17 June 1797
Cary [son] b. 1 Apr 1800
William H. b. 16 Apr 1803
Alanson b. 8 June 1806

Mary Howard d. 22 Aug 1811

[Record from Mrs. Pattie G. Gwaltney, Reidsville, N.C.]

WILLIS HOWARD, SR.

Willis Howard, Sr. d. 1 Mar 1829 [supposed to be 100 yrs. old]
Fanny Willis, his consort, d. 8 Dec 1807 in the 53rd yr of her age.

Willis Howard, Jr. b. 11 Apr 1781, d. 10 July 1859, m. 1st on 4
May 1821 to Lany (Laney) Howard b. 21 Aug 1792, d. 3 May 1822, m.
2nd to Eliz. Spring who d. 10 June 1857 in the 76th yr. of her age.

Falba Howard, dau. of Willis Howard, Jr., b. 15 Nov 1815, d. 3 Feb
1894, m. 31 Jan 1839 to John F. Rivers
Lany Howard, 2nd dau. of Willis Howard, Jr., b. 14 May 1831, m. 25
Sep 1853 to Jas. Stapleton

Nancy Emily Rivers, dau. of Falba Howard Rivers, b. 15 Dec 1839, d.
6 Mar 1918

William Howard b. 14 Apr 1811

[No data as to whose son Wm. is. Bible owned by Mrs. Amie Howard
Sorrell, Dearing, Ga.; Published 1800.]

JOHN ROLPHE HUDSON

John Wills Napier, son of Richard Claiborne Napier & Mary Wills
Napier, his wife, b. 1 Apr 1785 near Augusta, Ga., d. 31 Aug 1864
in Nashville, Tenn., m. 23 Dec 1815 to Cassandra Williams, dau. of
Daniel & Sally (Nixon) Williams, b. 18 May 1789 near Wilmington,
N.C., d. 9 Nov 1836 in Dickson Co., Tenn.

John Rolphe Hudson, son of Chas. Hudson & his wife Anna Goode, b.
13 Dec 1802 in Mecklenburg Co., N.C., m. 7 Dec 1834 to Araminta
Claiborne Napier, dau. of John Wills Napier & Cassandra Williams,
b. 20 Feb 1817 in Dickson Co., Tenn.

Amanda Eliza Hudson b. 10 Feb 1838 in Dickson Co., Tenn., m. 24
Feb 1859 to Wm. Eldred War
Susan Florence Hudson b. 20 Aug 1840 in Dickson Co., Tenn., d. 18
Jan 1846 in Dickson Co., Tenn.
Lucy Hudson b. 3 Oct 1844 in Dickson Co., Tenn., m. 20 June 1872 to
Robt. L. Morris
Mary Cassandra Hudson b. 7 Nov 1847 in Dickson Co., Tenn., m. 3 Nov
1870 to Benj. Christopher Robertson who d. 7 Feb 1872 in Talla-
hassee, Fla.
Florence Isabel Hudson b. 12 Nov 1860 [1850?] in Nashville, Tenn.,
d. 25 Sep 1872 in Nashville, Tenn., m. 13 July 1869 to Robt.
Weakley Brown
Minnie Claiborne Hudson b. 28 May 1853 in Nashville, Tenn., m. 4

Oct 1877 by Dr. Wm. E. Ward to Preston H. Miller from Savannah, Ga.
John Wills Hudson b. 8 July 1857 in Nashville, Tenn.

Jennie Hill Brown, dau. of Robt. Weakley Brown & Florence Isabel Hudson, b. 26 Aug 1870 in Nashville, Tenn., d. 8 Nov 1876 in Nashville, Tenn.
Florence Isabel Hudson, dau. of Robt. Weakley Brown & Florence Isabel Hudson, b. 8 July 1872 in Nashville, Tenn.

[This Bible is owned by Mrs. John H. DeWitt, Nashville, Tenn. This copy sent by Mrs. Estella Toll, Lawndale, Calif.]

JOSHUA HILLIARY HUDSON

Dabney Hudson b. 17 Dec 1801, d. 7 May 1836, m. 9 July 1822 to Narcissa Cook (dau. of Benjamin Cook b. 9 Mar 1778, d. Jan 1845, m. 8 May 1798 to Sarah Ward b. 1 Dec 1776, d. May 1847) b. 26 Oct 1800, d. 27 July 1875.
    Children
Mary L. Hudson b. 6 July 1823
Sarah J. Hudson b. 2 Jan 1825
John B. Hudson b. 24 Jan 1827
Eliza L. Hudson b. 2 Nov 1828
Maria L. Hudson b. 4 Feb 1830
(Judge) Joshua Hilliary (Hillary) Hudson b. 29 Jan 1832, d. 22 July
    1909, m. 4 May 1854 to Mary Miller
Dabney R. Hudson b. 24 Sep 1833
Conidia N. Hudson b. 26 July 1835

Phillip Miller b. 1 Jan 1800 in Germany, d. 1 Mar 1864 in Germany, m. 21 June 1836 to Elizabeth Harwell b. 3 Oct 1813 in Marion Co., S.C., d. 20 Nov 1899.
    Children
Mary Miller b. 11 Jan 1838, d. 2 Dec 1902, m. 4 May 1854 to Joshua
    Hilliary Hudson
Anna M. Miller b. 28 Feb 1839
Martha E. Miller b. 23 Nov 1840
John M. Miller b. 28 Aug 1842
Henry C. Miller b. 2 May 1844
Lizzie Miller b. 5 Sep 1848
Phillip Miller, Jr. b. 23 Mar 1846
Susannah Miller b. 31 July 1851
George Miller b. 5 Mar 1854

    Children of Joshua Hilliary Hudson & Mary Miller
William Preston Hudson b. 15 Feb 1855, d. 15 Jan 1857
Narcissa Elizabeth Hudson b. 1 Aug 1856; Narcissa Hudson Jordan d.
    8 Feb 1940
Anna Hudson b. 15 Dec 1857; Anna Hudson Bristow d. 2 Dec 1935
John R. (Rush) Hudson b. 11 Dec 1859, d. 17 July 1875
Willie Cook Hudson b. 6 Sep 1861; Willie Caroline Hudson Williams

d. 28 Dec 1934
Mattie Hudson b. 11 July 1864, d. 29 Sep 1865
Mary Hudson b. 29 May 1866, d. 9 Aug 1866
Henry M. Hudson b. 22 July 1868, d. 4 Mar 1869
Clara Hudson b. 4 Apr 1870, d. 14 Aug 1888
Grace Hudson b. 3 May 1872, d. 6 Oct 1876
Joshua Hillary Hudson, Jr. b. 4 Apr 1874, d. 3 June 1875
Norine Hudson b. 7 June 1876; Norine Hudson Crosland d. 24 Nov 1930
Frederick Eugene Hudson b. 5 Aug 1878, d. 2 Sep 1879

[The Family Bible of Judge J. H. Hudson of Bennettsville, S.C. is
owned by Mrs. William A. Huey, 4127 Devine St., Columbia, S.C. The
Bible has several family records.]

WILLIAM HUGGINS

Wm. H. Huggins b. 24 Feb 1830, m. 2 Sep 1857 to Sarah Margaret
Coker b. 24 Jan 1836, d. 13 July 1889.

Thos. Hartwell Huggins b. 25 Sep 1858, d. 10 Nov 1862
Ida Jane Huggins b. 27 Apr 1859, d. 16 Nov 1880, m. 14 Feb 1880 to
J. Pearsall Herring
Julia C. Huggins b. 23 Mar 1861, m. 24 Dec 1879 to Johnnie Moore
Anna Virginia Huggins b. 9 Mar 1863, d. 27 Nov 1865
Sarah Florence Huggins b. 25 Feb 1866
Lula M. Huggins b. 6 Apr 1868
Charlie C. Huggins b. 14 May 1870
Lela Stout Huggins b. 18 July 1872
Claudia Augusta Huggins b. 2 Feb 1875, d. 9 Sep 1935, m. 5 Jan 1895
    to John Hartwell Chapman, b. 8 Oct 1872 in Florence, S.C., d. 19
    Aug 1931
Nanny McLendon Huggins b. 4 Apr 1877

[Bible owned by Mrs. K. R. Mishoe, Wilmington, N.C.]

DEMPSEY HUNT

Dempsey Hunt b. 22 Jan 1793.   Grisham Thomas b. 1783
    Children
Demarys Hunt, dau., b. 20 Jan 1812
John Hunt, her [Demarys'] brother, b. 16 Aug 1815
Henry Hunt, son of Dempsey, b. 30 May 1818
Geo. F. Hunt, son, b. 7 Mar 1820
Sally Hunt [illegible]
Carney C. Hunt b. 3 Apr 1828
Dianna Hunt b. 13 Feb 1824

Cannon Lassater b. 8 May 1794 [2nd wife?]

Alex Hunt [illegible
James Moore [illegible]

[Bible of Dempsey Hunt of Moore Co., N.C. Printed by Mathew Carey 1814, No. 121 Chesnut St., Philadelphia, Pa. "This Bible is the property of Dempsey Hunt, his book - 28 Jan 1817 - Wm. Campbell" This Bible owned by Mrs. Ida Brooks Kellam, Wilmington, N.C. a great grand dau. of Dempsey Hunt.]

WM. IRBY

Edmund Irby, son of Wm. Irby b. 14 Jan 1796
Harrison Irby, son of Wm. Irby, b. 1812

Wm. Irby, son of Edmund Irby, b. 18 Nov 1819, d. 30 Nov 1857, aged
    38 yrs & 27 days, m. 10 Aug 1843 to Rosey Warren who d. 24 July
    1866
Mary Irby, dau. of Ed. Irby, b. 20 Mar 1822

Thos. H. Warren, son of Thos. Warren & Rosey, his wife, b. 27 Aug
    1826
Eliz. W. Warren b. 10 Oct 1830 [or 20, not clear]
Robt. C. Warren b. 28 Feb 1832
Andrew J. Warren b. 14 July 1836, d. 7 Nov 1864
Geo. L. Warren, son of Thos. Warren & Rosey his wife, b. 8 May 1838
Thos. A. Warren b. 12 Feb 1840, d. 12 July 1864. "Rosy Irby was his
    mother
Dr. Wm. (D. W.) Irby, son of Wm. Irby & his wife Rosey (Rosa), b.
    5 July 1844, d. 2 Aug 1865, aged 21 yrs. & 27 days
Jas. W. Irby, son of Wm. Irby & Rosey his wife, b. 4 Apr 1846, m.
    8 Jan 1868 to Marshanna W. Shearin

    Children of Jas. W. & Marshanna W. Irby
Lottis Irby, dau., b. 25 Jan 1869
Sidney Vester Irby, son, b. 2 July 1870, d. 26 Dec 1870
Phullip Burrod [?] Irby, son, b. 11 Oct 1872
Etheldra Ledman Irby, son, b. 4 Aug 1874, m. 20 Feb 1899 to Ida L.
    Journigan
Samuel Tilden Irby, son, b. 6 Dec 1876, d. 20 Oct 1877
Mary (Mamie) E. Irby, dau., b. 20 Mar 1878, d. 9 Sep 1886, aged 8
    yrs. & 5 mos.

Maggie W. Irby b. 15 June 1902
Allen Irby b. 11 Nov 1904
Addison Claude Irby b. 21 Aug 1908
Dolphine Aletha Irby b. 27 June 1911
Etheldra David Irby b. 19 Mar 1915

Wm. Frederick Irby d. 23 Oct 1888
Wm. K. Irby of Newsome Depot, Southampton Co., Va. m. 17 Oct 1886
    by Rev. S. Core to Lottie C. Irby of Enfield, Halifax Co., N.C.

[This family of Edmund Irby lived in Halifax Co., N.C. Bible owned
by Mrs. Margaret Irby Pierce, 2712 Van Buren St., Wilmington, N.C.]

Hartwell Jackson b. 5 July 1777, d. 15 July 1859, m. 1st on 13 Jan 1801 to Eliz. Bostwick b. 5 Mar 1780, d. 29 July 1818, m. 2nd on 29 Oct 1818 to Margaret Bradford b. 3 Nov 1793, d. 19 Sep 1865.
    Children
Abraham M. b. 2 Nov 1801, d. 17 Jan 1883
Wm. b. 24 Apr 1803, d. 5 Apr 1886
Joseph b. 16 Oct 1804, d. 14 Nov 1879
Hartwell, Jr. b. 16 Mar 1806, d. 5 June 1886
Mary b. 3 Aug 1807, d. 12 Oct 1853
Zachariah b. 27 Mar 1809, d. 21 Oct 1825
John B. b. 12 Dec 1810, d. 25 May 1887
Edmund b. 25 June 1812, d. 11 Oct 1829
Asa Meek b. 30 Oct 1814, d. 18 Feb 1889
Lutitia b. 14 July 1818, d. 10 Nov 1900
Andrew Bradford b. 7 Aug 1819, d. 28 Apr 1892, m. 3 Jan 1836 to
    Eliz. Ann Thomas b. 24 Mar 1818
Lovely Anne b. 14 Oct 1820, d. 29 Sep 1889
Hillman b. 1 Dec 1821, d. 5 Dec 1873
Lorena L. b. 1 Apr 1824, d. 9 June 1874
Drewry W. b. 7 July 1825, d. 24 Feb 1909
Almeda P. b. 2 Dec 1827, d. 18 Sep 1893
Zarephath b. 5 Aug 1829
Eliz. Ann b. 24 Nov 1832, d. 23 Aug 1900
Sarah Caroline b. 27 Jan 1835, d. 14 Apr 1897
Amelia D. b. 13 Nov 1837

"Our mother Nancy Jackson d. 18 Nov 1837 at the advanced age of 88 yrs. When she died she was Nancy Kennedy." [The family says this refers to Hartwell Jackson's mother.]
    Brothers & sisters of Hartwell Jackson
John m. 1st Heard, m. 2nd Edmonds
Wyche
Nancy m. Wm. Thomas
Edmond m. ... Bailey
Green [bro.]
Betsy m. ... Stocker

    Children of Andrew B. & Eliz. Ann Thomas Jackson
Sophronia Jackson b. 4 Oct 1836, d. 13 June 1837
Henry E. Jackson b. 13 June 1838, d. 29 Oct 1905
Lovely Ann Jackson b. 20 Oct 1840, d. 16 June 1915, m. Thos. House
Green B. Jackson b. 29 Oct 1843, d. 23 Mar 1862
Wm. B. Jackson b. 18 Mar 1845, d. 24 June 1903, m. 1st to Victorine
    Stroberge, m. 2nd to Mattie Griffith, m. 3rd to Mrs. Saml. Rosser
Eliz. Blanche Jackson b. 24 Sep 1848, d. 10 Apr 1925, m. Judson
    Haygood
Rebecca Beatrice Jackson b. 13 Aug 1851, d. ..., m. Wm. J. Thornton
Andrew Campbell Jackson b. 19 Sep 1854, d. 15 Apr 1919, m. Electra
    A. Fullilove

JOSEPH JACOBS

Joseph Jacobs b. 31 Mar 1775, d. 25 Sep 1830, m. 1st on 14 June 1804 to Ann Adkins b. 15 Sep 1780, d. 12 Apr 1807, aged 23 yrs., m. 2nd on 14 Dec 1810 to Jane Larkins b. 15 Sep 1788, d. 22 Feb 1854.

Susannah (Susan) b. 22 Apr 1805, d. 6 Dec 1829
Margaret Ann b. 15 Mar 1807, d. 28 Sep 1811
Hester Ann Larkins d. 26 Oct 1813
Joseph C. Hull b. 27 July 1815, d. 10 Nov 1822
Benjamin Justin b. Mar 1818
Sarah Cynthia b. 9 Nov 1820, m. 20 Dec 1838 to Jesse Bowden
Mary Jane Flournoy b. 21 Apr 1823
William Boring Jacobs b. 25 Mar 1825
Thomas Jacobs b. 29 Sep 1827, d. 12 Dec 1827
Rebecca J., dau. of Joseph & Jane Jacobs, b. 24 Dec 1829

Mary Augusta b. 24 Oct 1829
Catherine Jane Jacobs b. 13 June 1841; Catherine Jane Bowden d. 26
 Jan 1842
Joseph N. Bowden b. 30 Nov 1843
Allace Jane King b. 27 Aug 1842
Margaret Jane Bunting b. 16 Nov 1848

    Children of Amey
Handy b. 18 Aug 1807
Harriet b. 27 June 1811
Robert b. 10 June 1814. He was drowned
    Children of Harriet
George b. 6 Jan 1827, d. 18 Oct 1834
Christopher b. 20 Dec 1829
Susan Jane b. 28 Mar 1831, d. 3 Mar 1889
Peter b. 1 May 1833
Fanny b. 27 Feb 1835
Catherine b. 28 Apr 1837; Casey d. 2 Oct 1855, aged 18 yrs.
Hester Mariah b. 14 July 1839
Caroline b. 14 July 1841, d. May 1843

[Copied by Mary B. Jacobs, 1936. Slaves listed in the same Bible.
Published by His Majesty's Special Command 1799. Bought 1804.]

DANIEL JAMES

Daniel James b. 27 July 1801, d. 12 Jan 1845, son of John & Elizabeth (Sandlin) James, m. 16 Sep 1819 to Arrabellah Clement Fulton
b. 6 Feb 1802, d. 23 May 1872, dau. of James B. Fulton (b. 21 Jan
1765 in Bordenton, Burlington Co., N.J., served in the Rev. last
year in Frederick Co., Md., m. 27 May 1787 in Georgetown, Md. to
Anastatia Tuel b. 9 Oct 1763 in Montgomery Co., Md., d. in York
Co., S.C.)

Children

Amanda Fitz-Allen b. 27 June 1820, d. 1 Sep 1841, m. 24 Dec 1840 to
 Washington S. Bird
Laodicea (Dicey) b. 20 Oct 1823, m. John C. Horney
Albert Allison b. 26 Aug 1824, m. Sarah Collins
Anastasia Tuel b. 28 May 1826, m. 1st to Wm. Plexico, m. 2nd to
 McCloud
Eliz. Clement b. 30 Apr 1828, d. 6 June 1832
Rachel O. b. 12 Sep 1829
Sherrod Allen b. 6 Nov 1831, d. 21 Oct 1832
Elalia b. 23 May 1833
Jerusha b. 9 Oct 1835, d. 27 Oct 1895, m. Peyton Bland Darwin
Harriet b. 9 Jan 1838, m. 4 Mar 1856 to Wesley Crepps
Sarah Arrabellah b. 14 Apr 1840, d. 21 Dec 1910, m. 17 July 1860 to
 Jas. Alpheus Carroll
John Daniel b. 8 Feb 1843

[L. Andrea of Columbia, S.C. comments, "The Tuel-Fulton families
were said to be the first Roman Catholic Family in York Co., S. C."
Bible data owned by Mrs. Albert Rhett Heyward, nee Annabel Carroll,
Columbia, S.C., has handsome portraits of this family. One of the
best is of Jas. B. Fulton presented to him by the S.C. legislature.]

WESTWOOD WALLACE JAMES

Westwood Wallace James b. 3 Sep 1795, d. 24 Mar 1866, m. 17 May
1821 to Katharine C. Owens b. 7 Oct 1804, d. 22 Aug 1864
 Children
Frederic Augustus b. 15 Mar 1822, d. 14 Oct 1875
Hersylia Angeline b. 13 Mar 1825, d. 25 July 1878, m. 1st on 1 May
 1849 to Nathan J. Galloway who d. 18 July 1850, m. 2nd on 9 Oct
 1865 to Wm. G. Campbell b. 6 Mar 1825
Angerona Amaltha b. 24 Feb 1827; Mrs. Angerona Amaltha (James) Baker
 d. 10 Mar 1908
Martha W. b. 17 Dec 1828; Martha W. Steel d. 18 July 1854
Westwood Wallace, Jr. b. 16 Oct 1830, d. 14 Dec 1868
Robert P. b. 4 Nov 1832, d. 17 July 1850
Edward C. b. 27 Dec 1834
Katharine F. b. 26 Feb 1837
Margaret E. b. 6 Aug 1839
Virginia V. b. 31 Aug 1842

Ed. O. Campbell, son of Wm. G., b. 16 Oct 1855, d. 15 Dec 1885
N. Arthur Galloway d. 26 Nov 1869
B. B. Hawkins d. 10 Apr 1874
Joseph Curtis Baker d. 14 Mar 1876 [Miss Kate Gilchrist says he
 was born in Maine.]
W. J. Baker d. 4 July 1905
Mrs. Emma Baker Campbell d. 19 June 1916

"This Bible was presented to Mr. Wm. Campbell by his Bible Class 24
Dec 1875." inscribed in gold letters on the front cover of this

lovely big Bible. [It is now owned by Miss Kate Gilchrist.]

LITTLEBERRY JETER

Littleberry Jeter b. 1 Feb 1793, d. 19 June 1874, m. 21 Sep 1820 to
Sarah Hobson b. 27 Nov 1797, d. 11 Sep 1870
   Children
James Thos. Jeter b. 28 Nov 1821, m. 25 Apr 1848 to Miss C. E. Mob-
   ley [Mrs. Vivian Glenn Jeter says he was married twice more.]
Mary Frances Jeter b. 25 July 1823, d. 11 Sep 1829
Cicely Elvira Jeter b. 5 Oct 1825, d. 9 Feb 1866
Wm. Hobson Jeter b. 7 Aug 1827, d. at Battle of Cold Harbor 30 May
   1864
John Cotesworth Pinckney Jeter b. 6 Jan 1829, m. 21 Nov 1855 to
   Miss Mary Crayton
Sarah Jane Jeter b. 12 Jan 1832, m. 29 Apr 1857 to R. D. McJunkin
Richard Gillam Robeson Jeter b. 25 Nov 1833, d. 4 June 1900, m. 25
   Nov 1857 to Miss Harriet C. McJunkin

[This Bible is owned by Mrs. Vivian Glenn Jeter, widow of Edgar
Claude Jeter who died in Fairfield Co., S.C. Mrs. E. C. Jeter now
lives at Rt. 3, Winnsboro, S.C. Littleberry Jeter lived and died
in Union Co., S.C.]

ALEXANDER JOHNSON

   Children of Sylvester Johnson
Alexander Johnson, m. Martha Ann Smith
William Franklin Johnson d. 17 Nov 1901, m. 15 Aug 1850 to Mary
   Elizabeth Smith
Susan Johnson m. 14 Dec 1848 to John T. Pearson
Margaret Elizabeth Johnson m. 6 Jan 1844 to David Reese Milligan
James Jefferson Johnson m. 1st on 4 May 1854 to Jane Brady, enlist-
   ed in Co. B. 32rd Regt. Ga. Vol. Capt. John B. McDowell, Talbot
   Co., on his return from service (unknown to him) found his wife &
   two children had died of yellow fever, m. 2nd on 17 Dec 1865 to
   Sarah Elizabeth Brady, sister of Jane Brady, no children, both d.
   in Macon, Ga.

   Children of Alexander & Martha Ann Smith Johnson
Thomas Jefferson Johnson b. 3 Oct 1846, d. in Texas, m. 23 Feb 1870
   to Gelina Owens
Charles Franklin Johnson b. 8 Feb 1848, d. 16 Feb 1928 in Konawa,
   Okla., m. 13 Dec 1869 to Nancy J. Cronick
Louisa Antionnett Johnson b. 9 Aug 1852, d. 17 Apr 1917 in Okla.,
   m. 19 May 1871 to Wm. M. Isom
Stephen Alexander Johnson b. 16 Apr 1854, d. 29 Apr 1901, m. 6 Dec
   1874 to Savannah Isom
Sarah Frances Johnson b. 18 June 1857, d. 6 Feb 1936 in Texas, m.
   21 Aug 1879 to George T. Isom
Simeon Sylvester Johnson b. 16 Sep 1860, d. 12 Oct 1902, m. 1st on
   28 Jan 1883 to Lunie Tanner, m. 2nd on 30 Dec 1885 to Cora Tanner

Mattie Elizabeth Johnson b. 12 Mar 1864, d. 24 Aug 1940, m. 3 Oct
    1883 to J. A. D. Titshaw
William C. Johnson b. 8 Mar 1866, [living in 1951], m. 11 Oct 1885
    to Annie Cheek
Nancy Jane Johnson b. 28 Apr 1872, d. 26 June 1913, m. 22 Feb 1887
    to Jas. A. Waddell

    Children of William Franklin & Mary E. Smith Johnson
Lou Jennie Johnson b. 6 Feb 1853, m. 8 May 1895 to Wiley W. Wilson
Martha Jane Johnson b. 13 Nov 1855, d. 2 Oct 1929, m. 12 Feb 1882
    to James Tate Zorn
Emeline S. Johnson b. 27 Dec 1858
Mary Frances Johnson b. 11 July 1860
John Forest Johnson b. 23 Sep 1861, d. in Texas, m. 3 Mar 1890 to
    Nancy Ann Bagwell
Lucinda Franklin b. 16 Nov 1862, d. 14 Feb 1932, m. 29 Feb 1880 to
    Wm. Alfred Lamb
Alice Lee Johnson b. 13 Apr 1866, d. 2 Aug 1941, m. 27 Dec 1883 to
    Washington A. Cronic
Amanda Josephine Johnson b. 27 Feb 1868, d. 16 Mar 1944, m. 15 Jan
    1885 to Elisha Austin Zorn
James Wm. Johnson b. 14 June 1869
Eulalia (Bush) Johnson d. 9 Feb 1939, m. John J. Hunter

[Copied by Mrs. S. C. Moon]

ABEL GIBERSON JOHNSTON

Abel Giberson Johnston b. 17 Apr 1869 in Portsmouth, Scioto Co.,
Ohio, m. 27 May 1889 in Shelby Co., Ala. to Catherine Ann Walker b.
28 Oct 1872 in Bibb Co., Ala., d. 6 Feb 1952.
    Children
Jessie Mae Johnston b. 8 May 1890 in Shelby Co., Ala.
Samuel Johnston b. 15 Aug 1892 in Shelby Co., Ala., d. young
John Johnston b. 3 Oct 1894 in Shelby Co., Ala., d. young
Charles William Johnston b. 1 Aug 1897 in Shelby Co., Ala.
Thomas James Johnston b. 24 Sep 1900 in Shelby Co., Ala.
Rebecca Elizabeth Johnston b. 15 June 1904 in Bibb Co., Ala.
Abel Giberson Johnston, Jr. b. 20 Jan 1906 in Bibb Co., Ala.
Bertha Mae Johnston b. 16 Apr 1909 in Bibb Co., Ala.

LARKIN JOHNSTON

Larkin Johnston (oldest child of William Johnston b. 19 Dec 1697,
d. 16 Aug 1756 in Spotsylvania Co., Va., m. 12 Oct 1723 to Ann Chew
who d. 2 Nov 1742, dau. of Hannah Roy & Larkin Chew [This on a
loose leaf in the Bible]) b. 1 May 1727 in Spotsylvania Co., Va.,
d. 16 Mar 1816 in Jasper Co., Ga., m. 2 May 1745 to Mary Rogers b.
2 Jan 1727 in Stratton Parish, Va., d. Saturday, 25 Oct 1800 at
Hico, Person Co., N.C., bur. by her brother John [Rogers] "at his
place on Hico on the Tuesday after she died, being kept out of the
ground 4 days according to her request. We lived together upward

of 55 yrs. in which time she brought me 10 children & 8 of which is alive - 1802".

    Children

William b. 25 Oct 1745 or 1746, d. 29 Nov 1759
Ann b. 22 June 1749 old style or 3 July new style, m. 26 Aug 1772 to Saml. Cush [Desc. spell Cash]
Larkin b. 11 July old style, d. 9 Mar 1757
Lucy b. 15 May 1755, d. 9 Oct 1832 in DeKalb Co., Ga., m. 30 Nov 1783 to John Landers
Sarah b. 18 May 1758, m. 1st on 25 Jan 1778 to Francis Howard, m. 2nd to Henry Finlies second [sic] [could be Finlles]
Littleton b. 18 Feb 1761, d. 7 July 1842 in Jasper Co., Ga., m. 1st on 4 Jan 1781 to Lucy Childs, m. 2nd to Sarah Dirbin, widow
John b. 22 Dec 1763, d. 14 Nov 1817 in Elbert Co., Ga., m. 1st to Sarah Long [Lohg?], m. 2nd to Mary Wansen, widow
Theodorick b. 20 Aug 1766, m. Elizabeth Stuard [sic]
Sophia b. 15 Dec 1769, m. 20 Aug 1802 to Lurkin Huarndon [family says it was Larkin Herndon]
Richard b. 14 Mar 1778 in the 52nd yr. of his mother's age, d. 17 Jan 1837 in Walton Co., Ga., m. Mar 1802 to Elizabeth Humphel [His own Bible states Elizabeth Hemphill of Caswell Co., N.C.]

[Larkin Johnston lived in Spots. & Halifax Cos., Va. & Granville & Caswell Cos., N.C. Record sent by Leonard Andrea, Columbia, S.C.]

GEORGE TANNEHILL JONES

George Tannehill Jones b. 10 Oct 1790, d. 4 May 1871 of paralysis, aged 80, m. 10 Dec 1812 to Rebecca Campbell Brown b. 26 Feb 1796, d. 20 Oct 1873 of paralysis

John T. Jones b. 16 Nov 1814, d. 15 Dec 1857 with consumption, m. 5 Mar 1839 to Jane Larkin
William Brown Jones b. 12 Apr 1817, d. 5 May 1892, m. 24 Dec 1840 to Jane Erwin
Nancy Ann Jones b. 27 Sep 1819, d. 9 Dec 1866 with consumption, m. 12 Apr 1838 to George Anderson
George Washington Jones b. 1 Apr 1822, d. 11 or 10 Mar 1867 or affection of the liver and pneumonia, m. 20 Dec 1849 to Maria Gay Jones d. 20 Mar 1880 of consumption
Stephen Alexander Jones b. 20 Aug 1824, d. 14 Feb 1845 of pneumonia
Eliza Matilda Jones b. 6 Mar 1827, d. 28 Feb 1853 of pueril fever, m. 2 Apr 1846 to James R. Nance
Andrew Tannehill Jones b. 20 Jan 1830, d. 2 Aug 1852 of congestive fever, m. 2 Sep 1851 to Sarah Ann Davis
Sarah Elizabeth Jones b. 17 Mar 1832, d. 25 Aug 1859 with consumption, m. 1853 to B. B. Smith
Martha Jane Jones b. 5 May 1835, d. 11 Feb 1854 of pueril fever, m. 8 Mar 1853 to John C. Larkin

Maria Virginia Anderson b. 5 Dec 1855
Lavinia C. Jones b. 15 July 1852, d. 20 Mar 1904 of heart trouble

Infant son of G. W. & L. C. Jones b. 2 Oct 1880 [G. W. was son of
Wm. Brown Jones & Lavinia Chardavoyne was dau. of Geo. Washington
Jones; they were first cousins.]
Martha J. Jones d. 1 Aug 1896
Irene Gay Jones d. 23 Dec 1886
George W. Jones d. 16 Feb 1901 with cancer of the tongue [son of
Wm. B.]

[Bible record of George Tannehill Jones of Madison Co., Ala. copied
by his great grand daughter, Mrs. Gandrud in 1926 while in possession of her aunt's family, the Rev. Robert T. Blackwell and children of New Market, Ala. She says that George Tannehill Jones was
born Tannehill but added Jones to his name because he was reared by
his Jones grandparents. He was born in S.C. & his wife Rebecca, in
Tenn. She has oil portraits of them as well as of her Harris great
grand parents (Maria's parents).]

JACKSON JONES

Jackson Jones b. 1 Dec 1817, d. 7 July 1865, aged 47 yrs., m. 5
July 1849 by Rev. John H. Robinson to Mary F. Beaty b. 6 July 1829,
d. 4 Mar 1872, aged 42 yrs.
        Children
Edwin LaFayette b. 14 Aug 1850
Martha Ann b. 3 May 1856, d. 20 May 1858, aged 2 yrs.
Walter Jackson b. 10 June 1859
Nettie Beaty b. 18 Apr 1864

David F. Jones d. 20 May 1862, aged 24 yrs.

[Bible owned by Mrs. Thomas Lynch, Hillsboro, N.C.]

JAMES JONES

James Jones m. 17 Feb 1767 to Susan V. Jones

Dicy Jones b. 5 May 1771, d. 5 May 1848
Wila Jones b. 22 July 1772, d. 27 Aug 1831

John Jones b. 8 Sep 1797
Benjamin Jones b. 19 June 1799
Miriam Jones b. 1 Oct 1801
Sarah Jones b. 19 Aug 1803
Anna Jones b. 24 Dec 1805
Lucy Jones b. 3 July 1806
James Jones b. 15 Dec 1808
Elizabeth Jones b. 15 Aug 1812

Elenor Kersey d. 8 Mar 1798
John Kersey d. 19 Apr 1812
Drury Kersey d. 13 Feb 1813
Sarah Kersey d. 25 Dec 1815

Martha Kersey d. Sep 1822
Alex. T. Kirsey d. 1 Feb 1852
Wm. Parker d. 18 Apr ...0
Sally Jones d. 24 Jan 1845

[Bible belongs to Jesse Case, Rt. 1, Blanche, Caswell Co., N.C.]

JOHN JONES

John Jones & wife Susanna came to America from Wails [Wales?], England about 1740 & settled in Caswell Co., N.C. near Yanceyville.
Children
Col. Ezekiel Jones, a soldier in the American Rev., m. Rosanna Gill
of Hawfields, Alamance Co., N.C.
John Jones b. 25 Apr 1792, d. 27 May 1854, aged 62 yrs., m. 24 Dec
1816 to Anna Herron b. 10 Aug 1793, d. 14 Feb 1875, aged 82 yrs.,
6 mos., 4 days

Children of John & Anna Jones
Jackson b. 1 Dec 1817, d. 5 July 1865, m. 5 July 1849 to Mary Beaty
d. 4 Mar 1872
Yanc(e)y b. 9 Aug 1820, m. 21 July 1850 to Martha Miles
Ezekiel Pickard b. 6 May 1823, m. 28 Dec 1843 to Mary Ann Martin
who d. 10 May 1877, aged 56 yrs., 26 days
Rosanna(h) Jane b. 15 July 1825, m. 11 July 1844 to John Stacey
John LaFayette b. 20 July 1828, m. 3 July 1851 to Martha Beaty who
d. 4 Jan 1872
Mary Ann b. 16 July 1830, d. 12 Oct 1854, m. 1 Jan 1852 to Wm. Hop-
kins
James Penick b. 16 Oct 1832, m. 12 Jan 1858 to Isabel Caroline Mar-
tin
David Franklin b. 22 Jan 1838, d. 25 May 1862, aged 24 yrs.

Children of John LaFayette & Martha (Beaty) Jones
Mary Eliz. b. 26 June 1852; Lizzie Jones d. 1 May 1873, aged 20 yrs.
Caroline Kerr b. 28 Sep 1854; Evalina Kerr Jones d. 3 July 1856,
aged 1 yr.
Edwin LaFayette b. 14 Aug 1850 [not sure of year]
Mary Ella b. 27 Oct 1853
Martha Ann b. 3 May 1856; Martha Jones d. 1873
Walter Jackson b. 10 June 1859
Nettie Beaty b. 18 Apr 1864

Iradel [not clear] Herron b. 8 May 1796, d. 15 July 1866, aged 70
yrs. [brother of Anna?]
John L. D. H. Stacey b. 11 Dec 1845

[This Bible owned by Mrs. Thomas Lynch, Hillsboro, N.C. Note seem-
ing discrepency in dates. Immigrant came in 1740, had one son b.
early enough to be in the Rev. and another b. in 1792. Perhaps
there is a generation missing.]

173

NATHANIEL JONES

Nathaniel Jones, son of Evan Jones & Elizabeth, b. 1749, d. 8 Feb 1815, m. 1st on 20 July 1772 to Millison Blanshard, dau. of Benjamin Blanshard, b. 20 Oct 1754, d. 12 Mar 1785, m. 2nd on 2 Nov 1786 to Rachel Perry, dau. of Burwell Perry & Elizabeth, b. 28 May 1766.
   Children
Robert Jones, son, b. 19 May 1773, d. Oct 1780
Elizabeth Jones, dau., b. 24 Dec 1774
Sarah Jones, dau., b. 1 Aug 1776
Evan Jones, son, b. 15 Apr 1778, d. 13 Oct 1780
Mary Jones b. 21 Dec 1780
Nancy Jones b. 23 Jan 1783
Seth Jones b. 9 Mar 1785
Joel Jones b. 3 Nov 1787
Alfred Jones b. 11 Dec 1789
Burwell Perry Jones b. 9 Apr 1791, d. 11 Jan 1835, m. Frances who
   d. 14 May 1833
Timothy Walton Jones b. 28 Jan 1793, d. 26 Apr 182-
Wesley Jones b. 30 Nov 1794
Millison Jones b. 14 Jan 1797
Temperance Jones b. 28 July 1800
Martha Jones b. 24 May 1802
Helan Jones b. 20 Jan 1805

Nathaniel, son of B. P. Jones, d. 27 Jan 1833
Archibald Jones d. 20 Apr 1841
Alfred M. Jones d. 15 July 1846

[Millison Jones, dau. of Nathaniel & Rachel (Perry) Jones, was called Amelia, & she m. John Norman Pulliam of Granville Co., N.C., and they later moved to Fayette Co., Tenn. Both are buried in the "Family Burying Ground" on his plantation in Fayette Co. This plantation has passed out of the Pulliam Family, but the stones mark their graves, with record on them.
Evan Jones held 600 acres of Her Majesty's Land in Princess Anne Co., Va. in 1705. Ancestors are bur. in Old Bath Church.
Nathaniel Jones of White Plains removed to Wake Co., N.C. in 1750. In Wake Co., about this time, was another Nathaniel Jones, no known kin, who named his eldest son after himself. The families intermarried once or twice a few yrs. later, after the second generation had grown up. The other Nathaniel Jones came from "Crabtree." Bible Records from D.A.R. Magazine, Feb 1938.]

WILLIAM MOORE JONES

   Grandparents
Thomas Jones b. Warren Co., Ga., d. Bulloch Co., Ga.
Patsy Denmark b. Bulloch Co., Ga., d. Bulloch Co., Ga.
Charles Groover b. Thomas Co., Ga., d. Bulloch Co., Ga.
Sarah R. Reissier b. Bulloch Co., Ga., d. Bulloch Co., Ga.
   Parents

Malachi D. Jones b. Bulloch Co., Ga., d. 20 Nov 1881 in Brooks Co., Ga.; Sarah Reissier Groover b. 13 Sep 1813 in Bulloch Co., Ga., d. 20 Feb 1884 in Brooks Co., Ga.
    Brothers & sisters
Sophronia G. Jones b. in Bulloch Co., Ga., d. 17 Apr 1905, m. in 1855 to Wm. N. Jones
Nathan D. Jones b. in Thomas Co., Ga., d. 1861
Julia E. Jones b. 1836 in Thomas Co., Ga., d. 2 June 1910, m. in 1856 to Jas. E. Powell
Chas. E. Jones b. 31 Jan 1838 in Thomas Co., Ga., d. 27 Dec 1911, m. Susannah Mizzell
Martha Jones b. 1838 [twin?], d. 1839
William Moore Jones b. 13 Sep 1841 in Thomas Co., Ga., d. 2 Mar 1936 (or 1865), m. 8 Feb 1865 (or 1863) near Monticello, Fla. by Rev. S. G. Childs to Nancy Ophelia Foy b. 17 Aug 1844, d. 12 May 1905
M. Frank Jones b. 25 Dec 1843, d. Nov 1920, m. in 1866 to Cornelia Powell
Andrew Jackson Jones b. 15 Dec 1845, d. Aug 1929
Thomas T. Jones b. ..., m. Gussie Powell
Clinton R. Jones b. ...
Walter C. Jones (Rev.) b. 18 Mar 1852 in Lowndes Co., Ga., m. 20 Jan 1892 to Mollie Powell
Sarah A. D. Jones b. ..., m. 23 Dec 1883 to Henry J. Burke
    Wife's maternal grandparents
John Parramore b. 26 Aug 1775, d. 6 May 1846; Nancy Brinson b. 10 Apr 1783, d. 16 Jan 1844
    Wife's parents
Jas. M. Foy b. Mar 1817 in Rockingham Co., N.C., m. 25 Aug 1843 in Thomas Co., Ga. to Mary F. Parramore b. 25 July 1828
    Wife's brothers & sisters
Nancy O. Foy b. 17 Aug 1844 in Gadsden Co., Fla., d. 12 May 1905, m. Wm. M. Jones
Pleasant S. Foy b. 24 Oct 1846 in Thomas Co., Ga., d. 18 Nov 1906, m. Jennie H. Adams
Susan E. Foy b. 25 June 1848, d. 5 June 1887, m. 20 Nov 1880 to S. G. Culpepper
Roseann Cornelia Foy b. 9 Nov 1851, d. 1927, m. 1870 to Malcolm Mc Gregor
James M. Foy, Jr. b. 28 Jan 1856, d. 24 Aug 1874
    Children of Wm. M. Jones
Ida Brent b. 31 Dec 1865, d. 10 Apr 1925, m. 8 Dec 1897 to Jas. S. Smith
Jas. Malachi b. 20 Aug 1869 in Brooks Co., Ga., m. 10 Dec 1891 to Mattie Malette
John Wm. b. 2 Dec 1874 in Thomas Co., Ga., d. 17 July 1928, m. 25 June 1902 to Marion Linton
Redden Ales. b. 5 May 1878, d. 25 Jan 1920, m. 16 Apr 1903 to Margaret Hight
Francis Chandler b. 15 Feb 1887, m. 1st on 30 Dec 1906 to Nelle Groover, m. 2nd on 14 Aug 1926 to Jennie Yerby

[This Bible record is from Mrs. Ruth Hill, Monteagle, Tenn.]

GEORGE JULIAN, SR.

George Julian, Sr. b. 1 Mar 1752, d. 9 Sep 1822, m. Eleanor Long b. 14 Mar 1752, d. 14 Mar 1794.

John Julian, son of Geo. Julian, Sr. & his wife Eleanor, b. 22 Aug 1776, d. 2 Jan 1865, aged 88 yrs., 4 mos., 11 days, m. 9 Mar 1797 [in Knox Co., Tenn.] to Sarah Alldredge [dau. of Nathan Alldredge & wife Hannah. This record is also in the Knox Co. marriage records.] b. 7 Mar 1779, d. 10 Jan 1857, aged 77 yrs., 10 mos., 3 days
   Children
Nathan Julian b. 17 Feb 1799, m. 8 Apr 1819 to Rachel b. 9 Apr 1802, d. 29 Feb 1870
Geo. Julian b. 22 Feb 1801, d. in 1878, 12 miles south of Sacramento, Calif., bur. in Sacramento Cemetery, m. 29 Mar 1820 to Sarah Stafford b. 8 Sep 1800, d. 11 Feb 1843, aged 42 yrs., 5 mos., 3 days
Nancy Julian b. 30 Aug 1802, d. 4 Apr 1838, aged 35 yrs., 5 mos., 26 days, m. 27 July 1820 to Martin Irwin
Eleanor Julian b. 5 Nov 1808, d. 23 Apr 1830, aged 21 yrs., 5 mos., 18 days, m. 29 Jan 1824 to Joseph Stallard
Hannah Julian b. 30 Sep 1819, m. 22 Sep 1836 to Wm. Murphey

      Children of Nathan & Rachel Julian
Levicia Julian b. 18 Sep 1822
Susannah Julian b. 16 Aug 1824
Julia Ann Julian b. 11 Apr 1827
Indianna Julian b. 7 Dec 1829
Vanburen (Van Buren) Julian b. 4 Nov 1832, d. 2 June 1862
John Jay Julian b. 7 Apr 1835
Nathan Jefferson Julian b. 16 Feb 1838, d. 18 Nov 1862, 18 miles east of Nashville, Tenn. & 14 miles from Gallatin, Tenn.
Emeline Julian b. 6 Mar 1841
Martha Ann Julian b. 15 Sep 1849

      Children of Saml. & Susannah Tippett [Fippett?]
Anna Louisa Tippett b. 22 Jan 1851
Laura Alice Tippett b. 19 Sep 1852
Rachell Jemima [a word here cannot be made out] b. 24 May 1854
Ella Willie Ann Tippett b. 28 Mar 1856

John Julian Stallard b. 1 July 1825
John Alexander Irwin d. 20 Dec 1866
Rebecca Julian McCollosh d. in 1876 of consumption near Duth Flat, bur. at Dutch Flat
Nancy Julian Wiley d. 1845

"Mother's family, given me by Henry Martin when he was here on his last visit: Elijah, Enoch, David, Jesse, Amos, Mary Forsyth, Ruth Hulse, Lida Henry, Rachel Julian, Martha Williams & Rhoda Eskew.

Enoch d. in the War of 1812 at the river Raising. Amos went to Ill. The address of Nathan Eskew is Mason, Ill. Set down by J. J. Julian 31 Mar 1892." [John Jay Julian]

[Death entries of Sarah Stafford Julian, George Julian, Sr., Eleanor Julian, John Alexander Irwin, Geo. Julian, Rebecca Julian Mc Collosh, & Nancy Julian Wiley were made by J. J. Julian in 1907 & initialed by him. This Bible is owned by Ralph Waldo Julien, Jr., 4241 Park Ave., Gary, Ind.]

GEORGE W. JULIAN

Geo. W. Julian (son cf John Julian (1776-1865) m. in Knox Co., Tenn. to Sarah Aldridge Julian (1779-1857)) b. 22 Feb 1801, d. 13 Sep 1878, m. 30 [29 in Bible of George Julian, Sr.] Mar 1820 to Sarah Stafford Julian b. 8 Sep 1800, d. 11 Feb 1843
    Children
Nancy b. 24 Jan 1821, d. 5 Aug 1845
Rebecca b. 4 Jan 1823, d. 1876, m. McCulloch
John S. b. 16 Mar 1825
Sarah b. 6 Sep 1827, d. 1853
Hannah b. 26 Mar 1831, d. 30 Apr 1892
Nathan B. b. 29 Sep 1833
T. Benton b. 18 Apr 1836
Mary Ann Plumer b. 14 Mar 1839, d. 23 Dec 1917

[This Bible record sent by the late Mrs. Alfred White, Ann Arbor, Mich. She had it from Mrs. R. E. Keig, Napa, Calif. Mrs. Edward St. Clair, Oakland, Calif. is a desc. of Mary Ann Plumer Julian above who m. Luke Secord. Mrs. St. Clair found that Sarah Stafford wife of Geo. W. Julian, was the dau. of John Stafford, a Rev. War soldier of Ky.]

LEWIS JULIAN

Lewis Julian b. 27 June 1808, m. 20 Nov 1825 to Martha Frazier b. 6 Jan 1807. Died 1862 [which?]
    Children
John Calvin b. 8 Sep 1826 in Randolph Co., N.C.
James Pierce b. 6 Apr 1828 in Warren Co., Tenn.
Mary Ann b. 1830 in Clarke Co., Ala.
Isaac N. [Newton?] b. 8 Oct 1832 in Ala.
Dr. Thos. Jefferson b. 19 Apr 1835
George Washington b. 8 Aug 1837
Sarah E. b. 15 Nov 1839 in Clarke Co., Ala.
Nancy H. E. C. b. 12 Apr 1842 in Tippah Co., Miss. [Called Harriet]
Wm. Henry Harrison b. 21 Oct 1844 in Tippah Co., Miss.
Alexander H. [Hamilton?] b. 21 Nov 1846 in Tippah Co., Miss.
Henri Howgil b. 28 Nov 1849
Edgar Tobias, a minister [no dates]

[Mrs. Electa Spangler, dau. of the above Henri Howgil, gave this record. Note early age at which Lewis Julian was married. He was the son of Tobias Julian b. 26 May 1779, d. 1852, bur. at New Salem Methodist Church, Randolph Co., N.C., m. Esther Morgan, dau. of Lewis Morgan, a Welshman, b. 1779, d. 1855. This data is from the late Mrs. Rebecca White, Ann Arbor, Mich., a Julian desc., sent to the compiler by Mrs. White. Martha Frazier was the dau. of Thos. Frazier b. 1782 who migrated to Ohio from Randolph Co., N.C.]

SAML. D. JULIAN

Saml. D. Julian b. 14 July 1780 [in Rutherford Co., N.C.], a Methodist minister, moved to Union Co., Ky. in 1818, d. 10 Dec 1851 in Warrick Co., Ind., m. 17 Mar 1803 to Mary Cowdry b. 17 Mar 1786.
    Children
James B. b. 30 Nov 1804, d. 5 Mar 1805
Alice b. 4 Dec 1806
Saml. D., Jr. b. 8 July 1809, d. 6 May 1875
Whitman H. b. 6 Mar 1811, d. 7 Mar 1842
John Wright [a Methodist minister] b. 13 Oct 1814, d. 13 Apr 1900
Nancy Polly b. 9 Nov 1817, d. 11 Aug 1856
Claibourne C. b. 31 Mar 1820, d. 17 Jan 1853
Jesse R. b. 7 Jan 1825, d. 10 Jan 1853
Elizabeth A. b. 25 July 1827
Wm. Wiltshire b. 23 Dec 1829, d. 1 Oct 1894

[This Bible record was sent by Mrs. Alfred White of Ann Arbor, Mich. to the compiler in 1940. Mrs. White is a Julian desc. & has done a manuscript on the Julian family. The Julians descend from Rene St. Julien who was the immigrant to Md. & of French origin.]

JOHN KAY

John Kay b. 17 Feb 1799, d. 19 Sep 1883, m. 14 Mar 1822 to Nancy Smith Kay b. 26 Aug 1803, d. 17 Apr 1873.
    Children
Sarena Kay b. 16 Mar 1823, d. 6 Sep 1843, m. Newton Smith
Samantha Kay b. 24 Oct 1824, m. A.[?] Rainwaters
Sophronie Kay b. 19 Aug 1826, m. Joe Jolly
Salina Kay b. 19 May 1830, d. 1 June 1862, m. Robert Stevenson
Robert Smith Kay b. 20 Jan 1833, d. 6 July 1863, m. Mary Ellen Cannon
Elizabeth Kay b. 7 May 1839, m. Ben Masters
Amanda J. Kay b. 3 Aug 1840, m. Martin Green
Adaline P. Kay b. 2 Oct 1841, m. Steve Lewis
Margaret Kay b. 24 Mar 1844, m. William Wilbanks
John Wyatt Kay b. 10 July 1846, d. 4 Feb 1917, m. Martha Jane Stott, dau. of Drayton Stott & Harriet Richardson, his wife, b. 4 July 1848
Letus Kay b. 1 Sep 1835
Enly Kay b. 15 Nov 1838 [Note too close to Elizabeth]

        Children of John Wyatt & Martha Jane (Stott) Kay
Leila Kay m. William T. Mounce
Crayton Kay m. Nannie Meritt
Cornelia Kay m. William S. Hall
Lillian Kay m. John F. Smith
Eula Kay m. Manson S. Jolly
Lawrence E. Kay d. at birth

[Robert Smith Kay entered Service 20 July 1862, Private Roll of Co.
"L" Orr's Regt. Rifles, S.C.V., McGowan's Brigade, Wilcox's Divi-
sion A. P. Hill's Corps & was killed in battle at Gaines Mill. He
and his wife, Mary Ellen Cannon, had one dau., Florence Kay (Owen)
who was the grandmother of Elizabeth B. Murphy who contributed this
record. Elizabeth Kay & her husband, Ben Masters, moved to Ala.
They had a son, Clint Masters who died in Texas.]

                        GERSHAM KELLY

Gersham Kelly m. 1st to Bridgett Tatum of Greenville Dist., S.C.
        Children
Ann b. 25 Jan 1771
James b. 23 Mar 1773
Moses b. 8 Oct 1775
Mary b. 25 Jan 1779
Elizabeth b. 25 Feb 1781
Jane b. 6 Aug 1783
William b. 22 Sep 1786
Harriet b. 15 July 1789

                     ALSTON WOOD KENDRICK

Alston Wood Kendrick, son of Isham Kendrick & his wnd wife Eliz.
Duncan, from Warren Co., N.C. to Spartanburg, S.C., b. 21 Jan 1801,
d. 12 June 1853, m. 29 Oct 1827 to Sara (Susan(nah)) Few (dau.
Wm. Few, Sr. b. 9 Feb 1771 Ga., d. 12 July 1856 S.C.) b. 1 Feb 1803
        Children
Wm. Isham b. 28 Apr 1835, m. 1st on 25 Sep 1856 to Mary Ann [Bar-
    ton] b. 23 May 1837, d. 15 Oct 1857, m. 2nd on 18 Nov 1861 to
    Julia B. [Rea nee Gilreath]
Rachel M. b. 25 Feb 1840, m. 23 Apr 1863 to Dr. B. F. Few

        Children of Wm. I. Kendrick
Benj. I. Kendrick b. 12 Oct 1857, d. 9 June 1858
Wm. Alston Kendrick b. 25 July 1862, d. 1 July 1863

Robt. Alston Few b. 6 Jan 1865
Wm. Preston Few b. 29 Dec 1867

[Names of wives prior to marriage added by a desc.]

                     J. J. KENDALL

                          179

J. J. Kendall b. 15 Oct 1815, m. 1st on 12 Mar 1835 to Jane Thompson Moffitt b. 20 Feb 1816, m. 2nd on 16 June 1839 to Fanny Writty Moffitt b. 10 July 1820, m. 3rd on 12 July 1843 to Elizabeth Field (Fields) b. 14 Oct 1823, d. 31 Mar 1862.
    Children
Mary Methang [?], dau., b. 22 Dec 1835
Sarah Aneny [?] Kendall, dau., b. 14 Jan 1838
Katherine Kendall b. 28 Apr 1840
Elizabeth Jane Kendall b. 11 Dec 1841
John Wesley Kendall b. 28 Aug 1845

Marthy Johnson d. 26 July 1873
Hiram Kivett d. 4 Apr 1844
Isabell Kivett m. 17 Jan 1875 to Leonard Langley
Lorenzo D. Kivett, son of Hiram & Phebe Kivett, b. 28 Apr 1828 [or 1826], m. 16 Sep 1847 to Eliza Johnson, dau. of Sarah & Saml. Johnson, b. 4 Jan 1832.
Elizabeth L. E. Langley, dau. of Leonard & Isabel Langley, b. 12 Dec 1875
Joel Preston Langley b. 1878

[The above information was copied by Calvin Hinshaw of Staley, Randolph Co., N.C.]

AMBROSE KENNEDY

Ambrose Kennedy b. 11 Apr 1801, sheriff of Hall Co. 1850, organized Masons at Chestnut Mt. (of which all sons were members), was active in Presb. Church, represented Hall Co. at Milledgeville, Ga. (with H.W. Blake) Thurs. 5 Nov 1863-1865, d. 8 Aug 1877, m. 31 Dec 1829 to Martha Gideon b. 1 Dec 1804 in Jackson Co., d. 25 June 1871.

John Kennedy, an adopted son, b. 14 Feb 1825, was left as Home Guard in the Civil War, d. 27 Jan 1907, m. 15 Nov 1849 to Mary Louise Canning b. 22 June 1828, d. 6 June 1904
Nancy Ann Kennedy b. 3 Nov 1830, d. 21 July 1879, m. 19 Dec 1850 to Seaborn Maddox
Elizabeth Kennedy b. 14 Dec 1831, d. 9 Nov 1871, never married
Martha A. Kennedy b. 12 Jan 1833, d. 29 Apr 1900, m. 23 Dec 1853 to Lafayette Bell
Caroline Kennedy b. 31 Jan 1834, d. 20 May 1907, m. 2 Jan 1859 to Ansel R. Cooper
Sarah Jane Kennedy b. 21 Apr 1835, d. 9 Apr 1903, m. 24 Dec 1867 to Thomas Benton
Lydia R. Kennedy b. 14 July 1836, d. 1 Aug 1916, m. 1 Feb 1881 to Robert C. Young
William Kennedy b. 7 June 1838, elected First Lieutenant of Company D, 27th Ga. Inf. 10 Aug 1861, killed 15 June 1862
Mary Ann Kennedy b. 13 Apr 1840, d. 30 Oct 1899, m. 28 Mar 1858 to John Hayle Cronic
Harrison Kennedy b. 25 Oct 1842, d. 26 Dec 1906, m. 17 Oct 1866 at the home of Wiley G. Smith by Rev. D. G. Maddox (witnesses: Wil-

lie Rosch & Lydia R. Kennedy) to Sidney Bliss Smith, dau. of Rev.
Wiley Calvin Smith a noted Baptist Minister, b. 10 Mar 1848, d.
19 Sep 1904. Harrison enlisted in same Co. as Wm. on 4 Mar 1862
& was wounded in leg.
Joan Kennedy b. 29 June 1844, d. 16 Nov 1898, m. 19 June 1875 to
Mack H. Adams
Henry C. Kennedy b. 29 June 1844, enlisted in same Co. as Wm. on 16
Mar 1863, all with Col. L. B. Smith of Hall Co., Ga., d. 12 June
1864 in defense of his country at Pittsburg, Va.
Ambrose Taylor Kennedy b. 4 Oct 1848, d. 1 Sep 1875 in Utah, never
married, went West

Sarah E. Kennedy b. 5 Sep 1850, d. 3 Dec 1927, never married
Martha Jane Kennedy b. 5 Nov 1852, d. 5 July 1932, never married
Emily Sanannah Kennedy b. 16 Mar 1855, d. 23 Mar 1917, m. M. J. Orr
William Ambrose Kennedy b. 22 Mar 1857, m. 7 Aug 1877 to Chloie
Pirkle
Lydia Lavinia Kennedy b. 27 Sep 1859, d. 6 June 1916, never married
Joan A. Kennedy b. 18 July 1862, m. 18 Mar 1883 to James J. Adams
Lesly T. Kennedy b. 27 Nov 1864, d. 28 Mar 1906, never married
Henry Harrison Kennedy b. 21 Oct 1867, d. 2 Sep 1902, m. 22 Sep
1901 to Lavina Braselton
Mary Labascia Kennedy b. 16 Jan 1870, d. 6 Feb 1946, never married
John Green Kennedy b. 16 July 1873, m. 20 Nov 1909 to Luna Black-
stock

    Children of Harrison & Sidney Bliss Smith Kennedy
David Walter Kennedy b. 2 Dec 1867, d. 27 Apr 1927 in San Francisco
Calif., bur. in Holy Cross Cemetery
Wiley Calvin Kennedy b. 18 July 1872, d. 20 May 1943, m. 14 Oct
1894 to Cora Merritt
William Harrison Kennedy b. 20 Apr 1874, m. 29 Dec 1899 to Maude
Anderson
Lyman Perino Kennedy b. 20 Apr 1876, d. 8 Sep 1936
Infant son b. 6 Aug 1880, d. 18 Aug 1880
Estella C. Kennedy b. 6 Aug 1882, d. 24 Aug 1882
Annah Kennedy b. 26 June 1893, d. 16 Aug 1892

    Children of John Green & Luna Blackstock Kennedy
Annie Louise Kennedy b. 10 Sep 1910
Chestia Belle Kennedy b. 4 Oct 1912
Henry Washington Kennedy b. 22 Apr 1916

[This Bible now in the possession of John Green Kennedy. American
Bible Society, 1848.]

                        JOHN KERNODLE

John Kernodle [res. of Alamance Co., N.C.] b. 28 Mar 1793, d. 17
Mar 1866
        Children
George Kernodle b. 27 Nov 1821

Josiah Kernodle (Joseph) b. 29 Apr 1823
Hepzibah Malissa Kernodle b. 14 Nov 1824
Polly Kernodle b. 16 Apr 1826
Sample Kernodle b. 18 Mar 1828
Adam R. Kernodle b. 11 Sep 1829
Lovick L. Kernodle b. 11 Mar 1832
Edney Elizabeth Kernodle b. 14 July 1833
Lucinda Catharine Kernodle b. 26 June 1836
Minerva Jane Kernodle b. 17 May 1839
William Sanders Kernodle b. 25 Sep 1841
James Monroe Kernodle b. 8 Nov 1844
Emmaline Kernodle b. 31 Mar 1848
Nancy Ann Alisonsie Kernodle b. 30 May 1851
Sarah Rosabelle Kernodle b. 2 Oct 1853
Franklin Kernodle

[This Bible is in the possession of Ida Almeta Kernodle & her brother, Roy W. Kernodle, Altamahaw, N.C. George Kernodle m. 1st on
19 Feb 1821 to Lucretia Lambeth, m. 2nd to Nanch Lambeth (both dau.
of Josiah & Elizabeth Loftin Lambeth), m. 3rd to Eliza Flack of
Rockingham Co., N.C.]

JOHN KINCAID, SR.

Robin Kincaid m. in 1787 to Susan Avery [It is not known whether
   there were any children to this union. He was also m. to ...
   Dunn. They had four children: John, Andrew Dunn, Robert & Ibby
   (Elizabeth).]
Martha Kincaid m. in 1780 to John Avery
Victoria Kincaid m. in 1780 to James McDowell
Matilda Kincaid m. in 1780 to John Erwin
Elizabeth Kincaid m. in 1780 to Robert Erwin
Julia Kincaid m. in 1781 to Hamp Erwin
Samuel Kincaid m. in 1790 to Julia Perkins
Joseph Kincaid m. in 1790 to Margaret Erwin
Hanna Kincaid m. in 1791 to John McFalls
Helen Kincaid m. in 1797 to Thomas Erwin
John Kincaid, Jr. m. in 1783 to Margaret Erwin [They had three
   children whose names are not known. He was a Capt. in the East
   South Carolina Regulars. He served for six yrs. through the Rev.
   War. He was at battles of Saratoga, King's Mountain & Yorktown.
   He was the first man in America to build & operate a cotton gin
   by water. His brothers James, William & Robin also were in the
   Rev. They served six yrs. & were at the surrender of Cornwallis
   at Yorktown in 1781.]

[John Kincaid, Sr. moved to Burke Co., N.C. from Byron, N.C. in
1792. He bought 1400 acres of land six miles Northeast of Morganton, N.C. & died ther in 1805.]

ELISHA KING

Elisha King, son of Wm. & Nancy King, b. 1793, m. 17 Sep 1830 to
Sarah Rhodes, dau. of Jos. Edward Rhodes, b. 1813, d. 188, bur. in
Lee Co., Ga., Hebron Cem.
    Children
Israel Pinkney b. 11 Mar 1830 [Note m. date of parents]
William b. 13 Oct 1831
Hannah Henretta b. 24 Aug 1833
Elizabeth Ann b. 12 Oct 1835
Mary b. 23 July 1837
Joseph b. 31 Jan 1839
Calvin b. 23 Nov 1840
Wiley Scarborough b. 5 Oct 1842
Julius Brockington b. 25 Feb 1845
Sarah Frances b. 28 Sep 1847
James [not sure he is their child]

[This record is from Eugene Rhodes, Florence, S.C.]

JAMES KINYOUN

James Kinyoun, son of Joel & Lovey, b. 4 Feb 1804, d. 9 May 1857,
aged 53 yrs., 3 mos., 4 days, m. 12 Feb 1824 to Mary Hendricks,
dau. of David & Mary Hendricks, b. 19 Oct 1801, d. 19 Apr 1856,
aged 54 yrs., 6 mos.
    Children
John Hendricks b. 4 Oct 1825, m. 18 Dec 1856 to Bettie A. Conrad,
    dau. of John J. & Keziah Conrad, b. 22 Jan 1835, d. 27 Mar 1872
Lemuel Gregory b. 19 Dec 1827
David William b. 13 Nov 1829
Mary Mallisa b. 10 July 1832, d. 9 Sep 1843, aged 11 yrs, 1 mo., 28
    days
Sarah Catherine b. 10 Sep 1835
Lutitia Ann b. 3 Nov 1837

    Children of John & Bettie A. Kinyoun
Mary Bettie b. 20 May 1858, d. 11 Aug 1870
Joseph James b. 25 Nov 1860 in East Bend, Yadkin Co., N.C., d. Feb
    1919 in Washington, D.C., m. 27 June 1883 in Johnson Co., Mo. to
    Susan Eliz. Perry, dau. of Nathan Washington Harrison Perry & his
    1st wife Katherine Elizabeth Houx, b. 17 Feb 1860, d. 23 May 1948
    in Kansas City, Mo. Both bur. at Centerview, Mo. Daughter: Bet-
    tie Kinyoun d. 27 Mar 1888 in New York, bur. Centerview, Mo.
Lula Alice b. 30 Jan 1866
Flora Ridings b. 9 Mar 1868
Stella Keziah b. 30 Apr 1869
Nellie b. 1 July 1870
John Conrad b. 27 Sep 1871, d. 23 Sep 1872

[From Mrs. Hale Houts, 230 W. 61st St., Kansas City, Mo.]

JAMES BISCOE KIRK

Jas. B. Kirk b. 12 Mar 1812 in St. Mary's Co., Md., d. 1 Feb 1890
in the home of his son-in-law G. T. Dunlap, Georgetown, D.C., m.
1st on 1 Aug 1843 at Georgetown in the house on N St., formerly Gay
St. by Rev. L. Gassaway to Emily Wright Redin, d. 5 July 1863, m.
2nd on 17 Sep 1867 to Isabella Wright Redin who d. Dec 1876.
    Children
Emily Redin Kirk b. 3 Apr 1815 at Woodlawn, St. Mary's Co., Md.
Jas. Wm. Kirk b. 27 Feb 1847 at Woodlawn
Fanny Redin Kirk b. 26 Nov 1849 (my mother) at Woodlawn
Isabella Kirk b. 6 Nov 1852 at Woodlawn
Nancy Redin Kirk b. 1 Mar 1855 at Woodlawn
Richard Redin Kirk b. 8 May 1857 at Woodlawn
Mary Catherine Kirk b. in Culpeper Co., Va. (whither her parents
    removed in the fall of 1857)

[This Bible was bought at an antique store or second-hand book
store somewhere in Va. about 2 yrs. ago (1956) by Jack Ladson, Jr.
& sent to the compiler. If anyone should be able to establish a
lineal connection with these people, the compiler will be glad to
give the book back to the family.]

                        WILLIAM KIRKLAND

William Kirkland d. 21 June 1836 at Ayr Mount [near Hillsboro,
N.C.], m. 25 Dec 1792 to Margaret Blain (Mary B.) d. 6 July 1837.

Ann McNabb Kirkland, their dau., b. 22 May 1794, m. 7 Dec 1809 to
    Thos. Ruffin, son of Sterling & Alice Ruffin, d. 15 Nov 1842
Elizabeth Machen Kirkland, their dau., b. 31 May 1796, d. 19 Sep
    1822, m. 10 Sep 1812 to George McNeill, son of John & Anne Mc
    Neill, d. 1820
Margaret Scott Kirkland b. 22 Sep 1797, d. 1820, m. 6 Oct to John
    McRae, son of Duncan & Rhody
William Kirkland b. 10 Jan 1799, d. 3 July 1799
William Kirkland b. 5 Jan 1800 [?]
Jane Rebecca(h), their dau., b. 22 Feb 1800, d. 21 Oct 1845, m. 1
    Oct 1817 to Robert Strange, son of James & Anne Strange, d. 24
    Jan 1877 in Wilmington, N.C.
John Umstead Kirkland, their son, b. 20 Mar 1802, d. 25 Jan 1879 at
    Ayr Mount in the 77th yr. of life, m. 19 Feb 1829 in Newbern,
    N.C. to Elizabeth Adams Simpson, dau. of Samuel & Eliz. Simpson,
    b. 29 Oct 1809, d. 29 Jan 1849
Martha Shepperd Kirkland, their dau., b. 29 May 1803, m. 16 Nov
    1820 to Edwin Lewis De Grafenredt
James Kirkland b. 12 Feb 1805, d. 5 Mar 1805
Alex. McKenzie Kirkland b. 3 Dec 1807
Mary Anderson Kirkland b. 24 Aug 1809
Susannah Umstead Kirkland b. 7 Dec 1810
Phebe Bingham Kirkland, their dau., b. 26 Dec 1811, d. 15 May 1844,
    m. in 1841 to Nelson McLester of Columbus, Ga.
David Kirkland b. 3 June 1813, d. same day

Mrs. Susan M. Broadnax, dau. of Thos. & Anne Ruffin, d. 8 Sep 1851
at Cascade in Rockingham Co., N.C.

Children of George & Eliz. McNeill
Wm. K. McNeill, son
John Kirkland McNeill, son, d. Mar 1820
Thos. Ruffin McNeill, son, d. Oct 1828

Anne McRae Kirkland, dau. of John & Margaret d. ...
John McRae, son of John & Margaret Kirkland, d. ...
Wm. McRae, son of John & Mary [Marg.?], d. ...

John K. Strange, son of Robt. & Jane, d. 28 Dec 1852 in his father's home, Myrtle Hill, Fayetteville, N.C.

Samuel Simpson Kirkland b. 25 May 1831, d. 24 Dec 1904 at Edge-
field, S.C.
Wm. Kirkland, son of John & Elizabeth Kirkland, b. 13 Feb 1833
Annie Ruffin Kirkland b. 25 July 1835
John Kirkland, Jr. b. 24 Apr 1837
Thomas Ruffin Kirkland b. 14 Mar 1839
Alex. McKenzie Kirkland b. 17 June 1841
Susan Mary Kirkland b. 6 Feb 1843, d. 8 June 1914 in Raleigh, N.C.
Eliz. Simpson Kirkland b. 5 Jan 1845
Margaret Jane Kirkland b. 24 June 1847
Maria Simpson Kirkland b. 2 Nov 1850
Robert Roulhac Kirkland, son of John & Elizabeth, b. 20 July 1855,
d. 12 Jan 1862

William Kirkland b. 3 July 1836, son of Alex. & Anna
Robert Strange Kirkland b. 31 Aug 1838, son of Alex. & Anna

Maggie McLester, dau. of Phebe & Nelson McLester, b. 3 Sep 1848 in
Columbus, Ga.

Children of John N. & Hattie McLaren Kirkland
John B. b. 29 Mar 1865
James W. b. 28 Sep 1867
Hattie b. 1 June 1870
Bessie b. 25 Dec 1872
Sadie b. 6 Mar 1875

John Kirkland d. 3 Apr 1913
W. W. Kirkland d. 12 May 1915
Harriet McLester, wife of John McLester, d. 12 Apr 1908
Sadie McC. Kirkland d. 5 Apr 1918
Saml. Simpson b. 28 Feb 1883
Alex. McKenzie Kirkland d. 4 May 1843
Kenneth Wm. Kirkland, a native of Scotland, d. 28 Jan 1849
Alex. R. Strange d. 16 Jan 1851 in Glasgow, Scotland

[This Bible is owned by Mr. Saml. Kirkland who lives at the old family home Ayr Mount, Hillsboro, N.C. This beautiful old red brick home was built by Wm. Kirkland of this record. It was started in 1788 and was 12 yrs. in building. He named it Ayr Mount for the ancestral home in Scotland.]

WILLIAM KIRKMAN

William Kirkman b. 17 July 1801, d. 31 Dec 1876, m. 1st on 18 July 1822 to Mary Ward b. 5 Jan 1807, d. 28 Feb 1861, m. 2nd on 25 Sep 1864 to Nancy Lnm b. 11 Oct 1819
    Children
Lutitia (Lectitia) L. Kirkman b. 24 Nov 1823, m. 27 Feb 1840 (60) to Peter Freeman
James M. Kirkman b. 5 Mar 1826
Elizebeth W. Kirkman b. 14 July 1829
Tobitha J. Kirkman b. 2 June 1831
Thomas S. Kirkman b. 9 June 1834
John H. Kirkman b. 4 Nov 1836
Warren B. Kirkman b. 14 Oct 1839, d. 4 June 1852
Margaret M. Kirkman b. 25 May 1842
Robbert F. Kirkman b. 13 Oct 1850, d. 26 May 1851
Rebecca C. Kirkman b. 25 Apr 1844

James M. Kirkman b. 23 Nov 1858 (1857), d. 25 Feb 1941, m. 3 Mar 1892
Mary E. Kirkman b. 6 Oct 1861, d. 8 Sep 1862
Martha E. Kirkman b. 20 May 1864
Joseph I. Kirkman b. 21 May 1867
Tobitha A. Kirkman b. 11 Mar 1870
Eduary D. Kirkman b. 30 Mar 1873
William H. Kirkman b. 14 Feb 1876

Maudie I. Kirkman b. 21 Oct 1893
Gurnie Kirkman b. 18 May 1896
Annie Leaner Kirkman b. 30 Apr 1898
Author Kirkman b. 20 Dec 1899
Cecil Rosevelt Kirkman b. 10 Oct 1901

Ellen Kirkman m. 16 Feb 1891 to D. J. [F.?] York
Martha Ann Kirkman b. 23 June 1838
Rhudeemy E. Allred b. 18 Apr 1868, d. 10 Aug 1933

ISAIAH JACKSON KIRKSEY

Isaiah Jackson Kirksey b. 1816, d. 1891 at McKinley, Ala., m. 9 Jan 1839 to Mary Ann King b. 1818, d. 1861 at McKinley, Ala.
    Children
Eliza Eleanor b. 1839 in Ala., d. young
Foster King b. 1842 in Ala., d. 1842, aged 1 mo.
Jehu b. 1843, d. in Okla.
Henrietta Eleanor b. 1845 in Ala., d. 1913

Cicero Luas b. 1847 in Ala., d. 1903
Mary Cummings b. 1850 in Miss., d. 1852
Eleanor Ann b. 1852 in Miss., d. 1946
Elisha Brown b. 1854 in Miss., d. 1896

[Kirksey Bible (Greene Co., Ala.) record sent to Mrs. Pauline Jones
Gandrud, Tuscaloosa, Ala. by Mrs. Etta Palmer, Columbus, Miss.]

GEORGE E. KNOX

George E. Knox m. 9 May 1848 to Sarah A. Brooks, dau. of John H. &
Caroline (Williams) Brooks
    Children
Mary Williams b. 22 Aug 1849, d. 10 Nov, aged 2 mos. & 17 days
John Fulton b. 11 Apr 1853, d. 2 June 1861, aged 9 yrs., 1 mo. & 22
  days
Caroline Glass [?] b. 17 June 1854
James Henry b. 15 Mar 1855
Jesse Cunningham [?] b. 22 Feb 1857
Sarah Jane b. 3 Mar 1859
George Abner b. 5 Mar 1861
John J. b. 17 June 1864
William E. b. 13 Aug 1866
Charles O. b. 30 Apr 1868
Robert L. b. 21 Nov 1870

[This Bible now belongs to Miss Sally Betts Knox, Wilmington, N.C.]

JAMES CAVANAUGH KOGER

James Cavanaugh Koger, son of Joseph & Mary (Wilson) Koger, Sr., b.
27 Jan 1792 at Round-O, S.C., d. 7 Feb 1825 at Round-O, S.C., m.
Tuesday Evening, 14 June 1814 by the Rev. D. Brown to Elizabeth
Haynes Lemacks b. 12 Nov 1794
    Children
Ann Koger, dau., b. 14 May 1815
James Henry Koger, son, b. 12 Feb 1817, m. 7 Apr 18-- to Mary W.
  Lemacks
Mary Adeline Koger, dau., b. 31 Dec 18-- [not legible], d. 26 Oct
  1847, m. 3 Jan 1837 to Samuel A. Heath, son of Samuel & Rebecca
  Heath, b. 4 Mar 18-- [not legible]
Joseph H. Koger, son, b. 9 Nov 1820, d. 26 Oct 1842
Charles Evans Koger, son, b. 5 June 1822

      Children of James H. & Mary W. Koger
James Huggins Koger b. 1 May 1842
Mary Elvira Koger b. 3 Oct 1844
Annie Lemacks Koger b. 16 July 1849
James Aljinor Koger b. 3 Mar 1851

James Roger Heath b. 19 Jan 1838, d. 2 Aug 1838
Thomas Newell b. Tuesday, 25 Oct 1814

Children of Benjamin Risher, Sr. & his wife Mary Koger Risher
Benjamin Risher b. 5 Oct 1805
Joseph Koger Risher b. 31 Mar 1807
Francis Fountain Risher b. 13 Apr 18-- [not legible]

[Bible Copy owned by The Calhoun Co., S.C. Historical Society.]

CAPTAIN JOSEPH KOGER

Joseph Koger, son of Joseph Koger, Sr., b. 7 Sep 1749 in Colleton
Co., S.C., d. 11 Feb 1835 at Round-O, S.C., m. 15 Feb 1777 at Round-
O, S.C. to Mary Cook, dau. of Judith Read & Wilson Cook, b. 26 Nov
1754 in Conn., d. 23 June 1824 at Round-O, S.C.
    Children
John Koger, son, b. 25 Dec 1777, d. 4 Mar 1823 [or 1828], m. Nancy
    Gruber
Joseph Koger, Jr., son, b. 27 Oct 1779, d. 25 Aug 1866 in Miss., m.
    1st on 25 Mar 1802 to Mrs. Abigail Sligh Milhous, m. 2nd on 27
    Sep 1812 to Mary Murray
Mary Koger, dau., b. 4 July 1782, m. 4 Jan 1804 to Benjamin Risher
Rebecca Koger, dau., b. 3 Sep 1784, d. 19 Nov 1785
Elizabeth Rebecca Koger, dau., b. 22 Oct 1786, d. 22 Apr 182- [not
    legible], m. Stephen Ackerman
Henry Nelson Koger, son, b. 23 June 1789, d. 14 Feb 1813, single
James Kavanau Koger, son, b. 27 Jan 1792, d. 7 Feb 1825, m. 14 June
    1814 to Elizabeth Haynes Lemacks
Eve Maria Koger, dau., b. 8 Oct 1794
Ann Rumph Koger, dau., b. 14 Jan 1797

Charles E. Koger m. 23 Nov 1821 to Mary J. White
John Lemacks Koger, son of Charles E. Koger, b. 25 Aug 1824
Ann Rumph Gruber, dau. of J. & Mary Koger, d. 23 Aug 1818
Ann Elvira Jones Koger, dau. of J. & S. Koger, d. 20 Aug 1820
Mary Newell, dau. of J. & M. Koger, d. 25 Oct 1814

[Copy owned by the Calhoun Co., S.C. Historical Soc. This Joseph
Koger was an officer in the American Rev. His parents came to S.C.
from Va. The tombstone for his father has this inscription: Joseph
Koger 1705-1783. His wife, according to the family, was either a
Lemacks or a Fewax.]

JOSEPH KOGER, JR.

Joseph Koger, Jr. b. 27 Oct 1779 at Round-O in Colleton Co., S.C.,
d. 25 Aug 1866 in Noxobee Co., Miss., m. 1st on 25 Mar 1802 in
Charleston, S.C. by the Rev. William Jenkins to Mrs. Abigail Mil-
hous (nee Sligh) b. 15 Feb 1769, d. 17 June 1812, m. 2nd on 27 Sep
1812 by the Rev. Wm. Scott to Mary Murray b. 24 May 1790 in Dorchester Co., S.C., d. 15 June 1870 in Noxobee Co., Miss.
    Children
Alfred James Koger, son, b. 27 Dec 1802, d. 23 Jan 1804
Mary Koger, dau., b. 4 July 1804

Elizabeth Koger, dau., b. 8 Aug 1806 [m. Isaac Murray]
Maria Louise Koger, dau., b. 4 July 1813, d. 10 Jan 1850 in Miss.
   [m. William Stokes]
George Washington Koger, son, b. 20 Mar 1815, d. 27 Sep 1819 in S.C.
Thomas Jefferson Koger, son, b. 22 Mar 1817, d. 8 Oct 1862 in C.S.A.
   service [m. in Mobile, Ala. to Sarah Elder]
Martha Matilda Koger, dau., b. 25 July 1821 [m. Rev. J. T. Heard]
Margaret Ann Koger, dau., b. 10 June 1823 [m. Thomas H. Dixon]
Mary Caroline Koger, dau., b. 27 Nov 1825 [m. in Mobile, Ala. to
   Nicholas Augustus Gaines]
Marcia Alvira Koger, dau., b. 12 Mar 1829, d. 29 Sep 1831 in S.C.
Mildred Henrietta Koger, dau., b. 7 Oct 1832 [m. 1st to George
   Black, m. 2nd to Dr. D. W. Moorer]

[Info from a copy owned by Mrs. Benjamin F. Storne, Blacksville,
S.C. Marriages added from a DAR paper. Joseph, Jr., son of Joseph
Koger, Sr. & Mary Cook of Round-O, S.C.]

                           JOHN LaGRONE

John LaGrone came to Amer. from Luxomberg & settled 4 miles from
Newberry, S.C., m. in Edgefield Dist. to Agnes Hartley

Jacob, son of John & Agnes LaGrone, b. 27 Aug 1806, m. 22 Jan 1829
to Jerusha McCarty b. 10 Apr 1809
      Children
Agnes Eliz. b. 22 Dec 1829
Mary Matilda b. 22 Dec 1830
David Philp b. 22 Nov 1832
Permelia Catherine b. 12 July 1935
John Wm. b. 22 June 1838
James b. 2 Oct 1840

[This Bible record sent to the compiler by Mrs. Flossie Lam Crouch,
Edgefield, S.C. whose family it is.]

                         JAMES S. LAMB

James S. Lamb was a member of the S.C. Palmetto Regiment, killed
in Mexico during the Mexican war; Pamelia Lamb d. 12 Jan 1844
      Children
James Franklin Lamb b. 10 Aug 1835, d. 2 May 1900, m. 20 Dec 1855
   by Rev. John Trapp to Mary Adaline Riley b. 23 Jan 1837
Barrott Lamb, son, d. 13 Dec 1862 near Fredericksburg, Va. in defense of his country
John S. Lamb d. 14 Dec 1862, mortally wounded in the same battle

      Children of James F. & Mary A. Lamb
Francis Pamlia Lamb b. 3 Sep 1856
Martha Ella Lamb b. 23 July 1858
James William Lamb b. 17 June 1860
Thomas E. Lamb b. 26 Sep 1868, m. 1 July 1888 by Rev. Thomas Walk-

                              189

er in Aiken, S.C. to Hassie E. Smith b. 1 July 1869, dau.: Flossie Permelia Lamb b. 18 Sep 1889
John Stephens Lamb b. 24 June 1866
Joseph (twin) b. 27 Dec 1870, d. 4 Jan 1871
David (twin) b. 27 Dec 1870, d. 9 Jan 1871

[Bible published in 1802.]

JOHN LAWSON

John Lawson b. 8 Feb 1766, m. 25 Mar 1790 to Elizabeth Allen b. 1 Feb 1773, d. 6 Mar 1850.
    Children
Henry b. 20 Apr 1790 [Note m. date of parents]
William b. 24 Jan 1791
Robert b. 5 July 1792
Sarah b. 17 Feb 1794
John, Jr. b. 26 Jan 1796
Catherine b. 29 Mar 1802
David b. 25 Nov 1803
Francis b. 3 July 1806
Thomas b. 19 Mar 1809
Joseph Jones b. 8 Sep 1811, m. 1 Oct 1835 to Abigail L. Walker b. 10 Mar 1817
    Children of Joseph Jones & Abigail L. Walker Lawson
R. W. b. 10 Oct 1837
Catherine Lewis b. 3 July 1841
Benjamin b. 28 Oct 1843
Betty J. b. 8 Aug 1846
Eva M. b. 27 Oct 1848

THOMAS LENOIR, SR.

Thomas Lenoir, Sr. m. Mourning Crawley b. 2 May 1709 in Va.
    Children
Ann b. 28 June 1731, m. John Westmoreland
Robert b. 3 May 1733
Betty b. 19 July 1735
Leah b. 18 Dec 1737
Mary b. 30 Sep 1739
Thomas b. 11 Aug 1741
Isaac b. 15 Oct 1743
Lewis b. 25 Nov 1745
John b. 16 Nov 1747
William b. 8 May 1751

[Bible of Thomas Lenoir owned in 1930 by Mrs. Annie Lenoir Cassety of Beulah, Miss. This data from a fly leaf of the Bible of William Lenoir of Wilkes Co., N.C.: Thomas Lenoir Sr. who m. Mourning Crawley left a will in Edgecombe Co., N.C. which was probated at the July Court 1765. Book A, p. 147. The will shows the daughters' married names: Ann Westmoreland, Mary Perry, Leah Whitaker & Betty

Lattimore. Thomas Lenoir Sr. moved from Brunswick Co., Va. to Edgecombe Co., N.C.]

THOMAS LENOIR, JR.

Thomas Lenoir b. 11 Aug 1741 in Bristol Parish, Va., d. 1816, m. 1st on 20 Sep 1761 in Edgecombe Co., N.C. to Martha Atkinson b. 17 Jan 1746, d. 23 Dec 1780, m. 2nd on 3 Mar 1783 to Mrs. Mary Blanchard, a widow, d. 2 Nov 1788, m. 3rd on 30 June 1790 to Mrs. Sarah (Ransome) Gwyn, widow of Richard Gwyn of Yadkin Valley, N.C. [No issue by third wife.]
    Children
James Lenoir b. 2 July 1762 [m. & moved to Lenoir City, Tenn.]
Amelia Lenoir b. 16 Sep 1767 [m. James Gwyn of Wilkes Co., N.C.]
Thomas Lenoir b. 23 Dec 1769
Leah Lenoir b. 9 Oct 1772 [m. 1st to James Dickey, m. 2nd to Robert McFaddin of Sumter Co., S.C.]
Thadrick Lenoir b. 8 Apr 1775
Elizabeth Lenoir 12 May 1775 [?]
Lucy Lenoir b. 30 June 1779
William Lenoir b. 16 June 1785 [m. Sarah S. James & moved to Marion Co., Miss.]
Hope Lenoir [son] b. 30 Jan 1786 [m. Mary Smith & moved to Pearl River, Miss.]

[This Bible page of births is owned by Mrs. Lizzie Lenoir Meade of Waynesville, N.C., a desc., who furnished the following information about the family: "Thomas Lenoir was a soldier in the Revolution in S.C. He came to S.C. about 1767 & settled seven miles below Camden on a plantation now owned by Mr. William Boykin. He came to the Camden area with the BOYKINS, WHITAKERS & PERRYS... & with his father-in-law, Jas. Atkinson, Sr. In later years after the Rev., he & his step-son, Absalom Blanchard, owned & operated a chair factory in Camden. Absalom Blanchard later moved to Pearl River, Miss. to be with his dau. Mary Blanchard who m. William Thomas Lenoir, son of Hope Lenoir. After his 3rd m., Thomas moved to Wilkes Co., N.C." The marriages in brackets above were supplied by Mrs. Meade. Two children of Sarah (Ransome) Gwyn m. two children of Thomas Lenoir. Mrs. Meade also lists: Martha Lenoir m. Richard Ransom Gwyn of Wilkes Co., N.C. Court records of Lershaw Co., S.C. & Sumter Co., S.C. of the Estate of James Atkinson show that Martha, wife of Thos. Lenoir, Jr. was Martha Atkinson. James Atkinson's will filed in Sumter, dated 31 Oct 1785 says "... My dec'd daughter Martha Lenoir and her children..." Ruth Herndon Shields says that Dr. Felix Hickerson (108 Battle Lane) of Chapel Hill, N.C., in his wonderful book about the Yadkin River section of N.C., called Happy Valley, has a great deal of information and many interesting letters & pictures about this & other branches of the Lenoir family. But he does not have the above Bible record of births.]

THOMAS SUMTER LESESNE

Thomas Sumter Lesesne d. 26 May 1880 in his 51st year, m. 20 Oct
1852 to Sarah Camilla McClary
     Children
Frances Ann Lesesne, dau., b. 14 Oct 1853, m. 10 Oct 1880 to Wil-
     liam Welborn Brailsford
Sarah Ellen Lesesne, dau., b. 24 June1855, d. July 1918, m. 17 Nov
     1865 to William Hamilton Thompson d. 3 Nov 1933
Thomas Clarence Lesesne, son, b. 15 July 1857, d. 29 June 1903,
     single
David McClary Lesesne, son, b. 10 Sep 1859, m. Ruth Thames
William Heyward Lesesne, son, b. 2 Oct 1864
Samuel McDowell Lesesne, son, b. 2 Jan 1866, d. aged 6 yrs. & 19
     days
Emma Eugenia Lesesne, dau., b. 12 Aug 1869, m. James H. Fluitt
John Bonneau Lesesne, son, b. 20 Dec 1872, m. Ann Dixon

     Grand children
Samuel Lesesne Thompson, grand son, b. 26 Apr 1881, m. Ellen Dukes
Rosa Ellen Thompson, grand dau., b. 13 Aug 1883, m. Edwin Snipes
Jenny May Thompson, grand dau., b. 3 Sep 1884
Willie Eugene Thompson, grand son, b. 27 July 1886, m. 9 Sep 1919
     to Marion Edings Bailey
Camilla Lesesne Thompson, grand dau., b. 2 Nov 1891, m. Dwight
     Owens
James Thompson, grand son, b. 11 Feb 1894, d. single overseas in
     W.W. I
Eddie Thompson, grand son, b. 25 June 1896, m. Norma Neves
Lilla May Thompson, grand dau., b. 25 June 1896, m. Herbert Cox
Ira B. M. Thompson, grand son, b. Oct 1898
Miriam Fluitt, grand dau., b. 19 Feb 1895

[Bible owned by the family of Mrs. Andrew Lyman Hall, RFD 4, Box
245, Columbia, S.C.]

ALFRED M. LESTER

Alfred M. Lester b. 29 Jan 1805 in Newberry Co., S.C., m. 27 Oct
1831 in Lexington Co., S.C. to Mary Ann Poindexter b. 22 July 1810
in S.C.
     Children
Calvin Wilson b. 10 Apr 1833, d. 8 Sep 1864 at the Battle of Frank-
     lin, Tenn. [Capt. in the Confederate Army, never married]
Sarah Ann b. 12 Mar 1836
Reuben Patrick b. 19 Feb 1839, d. 30 Nov 1866 [while studying for
     the ministry in Birmingham, Ala., never married]
Burke Allen b. 7 Dec 1841
Mary Ann Mariah b. 4 July 1846
Martha Jane b. 22 Aug 1848
Samuel Robert b. 5 July 1852 [father of Robert McDonald Lester,
     Sr.]

[Some say the M. in Alfred's name stood for Musgrove, the maiden
name of his mother. There has always been some dispute. They
moved to Shelby Co., Ala. in 1837. Mary Ann was the dau. of Reuben Poindexter & Sarah McIver who were married in Campbell Co., Va.
This m. with date is in the Quaker Recs. of Va. by Hinshaw. Reuben
was a son of Capt. Jos. Poindexter in the Rev., son of John &
Christian Poindexter of Louisa Co., Va., & Eliz. James Kennerly.
See John's will. Alfred M. Lester was the son of Charles Lester &
Jane Musgrove of Newberry Co., S.C. See O'Neall's Newberry Annals.
Chas. was the son of James & Caterine Lester. James & Charles were
in the Rev. War. Chas. was b. ca. 1760 in Va. James d. in 1808 in
Newberry Co., S.C. Jane Musgrove's father believed to be John Mus-
grove who d. during the Rev. War, but this is not proven conclu-
sively yet. Sara McIver Poindexter went to Ala. with the Lesters &
the rest of her family, Reuben having d. earlier in S.C. Thos.
Kennerly Poindexter & his brother Reuben were the only children of
Capt. Jos. Poindexter to go to S.C. Mrs. Nannie Tillman, Edgefield,
S.C. descends from Thos. Kennerly. See Poindexter Bibles below.]

DAVID LEWIS

Isaiah Lewis b. in the morning, 3 Sep 1769
Persilla Lewis b. 4 Sep 1770
Jacob Lewis b. in the morning, 14 Mar 1772
Joab Lewis b. on the night of 23 Dec 1773
Abner Lewis b. on the night of 22 Sep 1775
Neriah Lewis b. 25 June 1778
Benjamin Lewis b. 26 May 1781
Elizabeth Lewis b. 21 Sep 1783
Cozbi Lewis b. 17 July 1785
Tarleton Lewis b. 11 Aug 1787
Hannah Lewis b. 2 Oct 1789
David Lewis b. 24 Jan 1814
Rosannah Lewis b. 26 Oct 1815

[Note from Mrs. Hale Houts, 230 W. 61st St., Kansas City, Mo.
(1958), owner of this record: "The last two children are of 2nd m.
David Lewis m. 1st in Jan 1768, New Garden Quaker Meeting, N.C. to
Ann Beeson, m. 2nd in S.C. to Penelope." This record was made by
Amos Meuron Perry, brother of Mrs. Houts' grandfather, Nathan Washington Harrison Perry, when on a visit from east Tenn. to relatives
in S.C. & Ga. This is an attested copy dated 15 Jan 1846. It is
not indicated who the owner of the Bible was.]

JOHN LEWIS

John Lewis b. ..., d. 10 June 1802, m. Priscilla Brooks b. 16 Oct
1725
    Children
David Lewis b. 21 Mar 1747
Jacob Lewis b. 24 May 1750
Rosannah Lewis b. 5 July 1752

Stephen Lewis b. 4 June 1757
Richard Lewis b. 22 July 1759
Sarah Lewis b. 15 Jan 1763
John Lewis b. 9 Mar 1765
Jean Lewis b. 15 July 1755

[This Bible record was found by Mrs. Hale Houts of Kansas City, Mo. many yrs. ago & a copy of it was sent to the compiler by Mr. Byron Lewis of Bridgeport, Ill. in 1943. One Lewis Bible on this family was owned by a Noland R. Lewis of Columbus, Ga. in 1863, says Mr. Byron Lewis. John Lewis, Sr. of this Bible record d. in Randolph Co., N.C. (will). His wife, Priscilla seems to have been the dau. of Jacob & Rosanna Brooks. While we lack final proof, the indication is so clear that it cannot be ignored. The families lived near each other in N.C. & moved to S.C. & Ga. together.]

THOMAS PLEASANT LEWIS

Thomas Pleasant Lewis b. 18 [or 13?] Sep 1817, d. 25 Feb 1877, m. 24 Oct 1849 to Caroline Mary (N.) Neal b. 1 Mar 1831 in Pickens Co., Ala., d. 4 Feb 1890.

Mary Annie Lewis b. 29 July 1850 in Tuscaloosa, Ala, d. 27 July 1884, m. 14 May 1878 to William H. Harrison
Carrie Washington Lewis b. 24 Oct 1853 in Tuscaloosa, Ala., m. A. O. Mills
Grace Neal Lewis b. 26 July 1855 in Tuscaloosa, d. 14 Sep 1860
Tamesia (Mesia or Tanesia) Pleasant Lewis b. 2 Oct 1857 in Tusca-
    loosa, Ala., d. 12 May 1945, m. 6 Apr 1898 to J. G. Praigg
Sallie Skinker Lewis b. 2 Feb 1860 in Tuscaloosa, Ala.
Lillian Lewis b. 13 July 1873 in Tuscaloosa, Ala., d. 13 July 1873

Charlie Lewis Harrison b. 20 June 1879
Kathleen Harrison b. 25 June 1881 in Tuscaloosa, Ala.

Robert Neal [father of Caroline Neal Lewis] b. 13 June 1802, m. 7
    Feb 1828 [m. recs. of Tuscaloosa Co., Ala. show license dated 6
    Feb 1830, returned 9 Feb 1830 by Nat. H. Harris] to Caroline S.
    Washington b. 6 Sep 1806, d. 30 May 1831

Mary S. Washington b. 7 Jan 1801
Mary S. Kidder d. 3 May 1882
H. C. Kidder d. 25 Oct 1870
George T. Washington d. 9 Aug 1871

[The original Bible is now in the possession of Mrs. Owen Meredith, Sr. of Tuscaloosa, Ala., a friend of the last member of the family, Mrs. Tamesia Lewis Praigg. The Bible was presented by the American Bible Society, N.Y., 3 Apr 1870. Undated newspaper clipping in Bible: "Married on 14th, Wm. H. Harrison of Chattanooga, Tenn. and Mary A. Lewis."]

TARLETON LEWIS

Hannah Lewis b. 2 Oct 1789, Friday morning
    Tarleton Lewis' children
James b. 13 Nov 1807
Ann Beeson b. 10 Jan 1810
Ruth Wells b. 7 Oct 1811
Margaret b. 27 Jan 1815
David b. 7 Oct 1818

[This came from Mrs. Hale Houts. We assume Hannah is Tarleton Lewis' wife.]

GEORGE LILLINGTON

George Lillington b. 1 Jan 1765, d. 15 Feb 1794, m. 4 June 1786 to Sarah Coit
    Children
Mary Lillington 25 Mar 1787
Sarah Lillington 25 Apr 1789, d. 20 May 1790
John Alex. Lillington 9 Sep 1790

[In the front of this book is: "John Rutherford to Col. Alex. Lillington 1772" Col. Alex. Lillington was father of George whose record is given here, according to his descs. This Book of Common Prayer, pub. in Eng. in 1731 by order of His Majesty, etc., is owned by Mrs. Wm. V. Cash, Washington, D.C., a desc. of Alex. & his son Geo. Lillington. This copy was made from a photostat by Ida B. Kellam of Wilmington, N.C., owned by Mrs. Wm. G. Head of Wilmington, N.C.]

JOHN LIVINGSTON

John Livingston b. 18 Dec 1764, d. 11 Dec 1823, son of Martin & Sarah Livingston, m. 25 Nov 1783 to Isabella Hipp b. 23 Aug 1764, d. 29 Mar 1829, dau. of John & Sarah Hipp.
    Children
Martin b. 23 May 1785, d. 27 Feb 1786
Susannah b. 14 Mar 1787, d. 31 Dec 1842, m. 2 Feb 1808 to David
    Williamson [Congressman from S.C.]
Sarah b. 25 Sep 1789, d. 1857, m. Emmanuel Hoffman
John Henry b. 31 Mar 1792, d. 21 Dec 1849, m. 1st to Ann Jones, m.
    2nd to Mary Davis
John Hipp b. 9 Dec 1794, d. 15 June 1854, m. 1st to Levithia Bus-
    bee, m. 2nd to Mary Carson
Frederick b. 3 Aug 1797, d. 11 Mar 1851, m. Martha Jeffcoat
George b. 25 Jan 1800, d. 25 May 1818
Elizabeth b. 5 Mar 1803, d. 14 Feb 1879, m. Wm. Harley
Barnett b. 22 Sep 1805, d. 29 Oct 1864, m. Eliza Rhodes

[L. Andrea of Columbia, S.C. says, "Tradition in this family is that they came down from N.Y. State to Newberry Co., S.C. & that

John Livingston, after his marriage, came to North Fork of the Ed-
isto River in Orangeburg Co., S.C. Bible owned by the Livingston
Family Assn., Livingston, S.C."]

ANDREW BAXTER LONG

Andrew B. Long b. 13 Nov 1808, d. 11 Jan 1901, m. 1st on 5 Mar 1833
to Sarah Almira Long b. 17 Mar 1811, d. 15 Aug 1843, m. 2nd on 30
Jan 1844 to Nancy A. d. 19 Mar 1901.
    Children
Mary Patton b. 23 Apt 1834; Mary P. Guffey d. 19 May 1855
Isabella Frances b. 26 Jan 1836
Louisa Narcissa b. 7 Nov 1837
John Whitfield b. 16 Oct 1839, d. 12 Oct 1861, a soldier in the
    Confederate Army
Benjamin Franklin b. 7 June 1841
Almira E. b. 29 Jan 1845
Margaret E. b. 16 Feb 1847
William Loxley b. 3 Sep 1849
Andrew Baxter b. 23 May 1854, d. 26 Nov 1862
George Washington b. 29 Apr 1856
Joseph Andrews b. 27 Aug 1858 [or 1859]
Lee Louring b. 1 Jan 1862

    Nancy Long's children [called Long]
Mary D. b. 11 Jan 1836
Sarah b. 31 Oct 1837
Susan O. b. 14 Dec 1839
Leuraney J. b. 20 Dec 1841

WILLIAM ETHELBERT LONG

William Ethelbert Long b. 1 Dec 1848, d. 26 Nov 1926, m. 7 Dec 1871
by Rev. Tillman D. Purefoy at the home of the bride's parents to
Frances Amanda Yarbrough, dau. of Gilson & Martha Griffith Yar-
brough, b. 5 Jan 1850, d. 16 Nov 1933.
    Children
William b. 1872, d. in infancy
William Walter b. 24 July 1873, d. 30 Apr 1941
John Paul b. 12 Apr 1875, d. 28 Oct 1934
Annie Florence b. 1877, d. Oct 1940
Nancy Julia b. 19 Dec 1878, d. 11 June 1953
Michael b. Oct 1882, d. Oct 1897
Ada b. 1883, d. young
James Frank b. 21 Apr 1885, d. 4 July 1934
Claud Nero b. 24 Aug 1887,
William Ethelbert b. 1889, d. in infancy
William Ethelbert b. Apr 1891, d. 18 Sep 1918

[A copy of a framed Family Record that hung in the home of William
Ethelbert Long, now owned by Claude H. Long of Saluda Co. Notarized at Edgefield, S.C., 1 May 1954.]

JOHN LOWRANCE

John Lowrance b. 16 Feb 1716 in East New Jersey, d. 23 Apr 1781 in
Rowan Co., N.C., m. 1st in 1738 to Mary Perkins b. 1729, d. 1760 in
Rowan Co., N.C., m. 2nd in 1762 to Annie Nichols.
     Children [all of Rowan Co., N.C.]
Daniel b. 28 Feb 1739
Margaret b. 28 Sep 1740 [m. M. Hunt]
Joseph b. 18 Nov 1742
John b. 14 Feb 1745
Abraham b. 18 July 1746
Andrew b. 27 Aug 1748 [m. Hannah Adams]
Mary b. 11 Nov 1750 [m. M. Woods]
Elizabeth b. 24 Jan 1753 [m. Rev. John Crawford, son of Jacob]
Catherine b. 25 Aug 1756 [m. Rev. John Newton, founder of Athens
     College, Athens, Ga.]
Jacob b. 17 ... 1759, wounded at the battle of Kings Mt., N.C.
Jane b. 28 June 1763, m. John Gracey "killed by Indians & two
     children scalped but one got well." [Jane or John killed?]
Annie b. 1765, m. James Hart
Joshua b. 1767, m. Elizabeth Baxter
Sarah b. 1769, m. David Baxter
Lydia b. 1773, m. McLean [or McLane]
Alexander b. 1778, m. Miller
Ely b. 1775

GEORGE LOYD

     Children of George & Polly Loyd
Alford b. 20 June 1806
Green b. 28 Feb 1808
Washington b. 5 Feb 1810
John Emory b. 30 July 1813
James b. 2 Aug 1815
Thomas b. 30 July 1818
Naomi b. 3 Sep 1820
Mary Ann b. 6 Nov 1822
Martha Folds b. 20 Nov 1825

George Pierce Loyd [Believed to be a grandson] b. 25 Dec 1845
William Sanders Loyd b. ...

Polly Ann Parker b. 23 Jan 1820
Martha Jane Parker b. 13 Mar 1824
Emily A. Parker b. 7 Feb 1827

[George Loyd lived in Jasper Co., Ga. All Loyds in these records
from Jasper & Newton Cos., Ga. Bible records owned by Mrs. J. W.
Black, Covington, Ga. (in 1938)]

197

WASHINGTON LOYD

Washington Loyd b. 5 Feb 1810, d. 17 Feb 1892, m. 14 May 1837 to
Phebe P. Lumsden b. 16 Mar 1819, d. 21 Dec 1867.
   Children
John W. b. 8 July 1838, d. June 1880, m. 27 July 1865 to Lucy Ann
   Woodruff
Mary E. b. 30 June 1841, d. 27 July 1913, m. 15 Jan 1864 to L. W.
   Jarman
George W. b. 11 Dec 1843, m. 11 Dec 1886 to Lean L. Livingston
Ojias A. b. 9 May 1846, d. 18 Sep 1916, m. 5 Oct 1865 to Mary L.
   Cowan
James W. D. b. 4 Jan 1849, d. 8 Dec 1921, m. 21 Nov 1872 to Elger
   L. Blanton
Susan N. (M.) b. 13 July 1851, m. 30 Nov 1871 to John Lee King
Florence J. b. 22 Mar 1854, m. 7 Aug 1873 to J. W. Black
Robert L. b. 24 Mar 1856, d. 29 Jan 1919, m. 5 Dec 1878 to Florence
   J. Roberts
Alice A. b. 10 Aug 1859, d. 1 Oct 1926, m. 29 Dec 1884 to John R.
   Roberts

ELLIOT BUTT LOYLESS

Elliot Butt Loyless b. 22 Mar 1807, m. 27 Oct 1829 in Richmond Co.,
Ga. to Nancy Barton Rhodes b. 22 Feb 1809.
   Children
Mary Caroline Matilda b. 16 Nov 1830
Sarah Lavina b. 6 Mar 1832
Ann Elizabeth b. 3 May 1833
Martha Jane b. 7 Aug 1835
Henry Melville b. 9 Nov 1837
James Elliott b. 5 Oct 1839
Lucy Hilton b. 16 Aug 1842
Thomas Wesley b. 13 Sep 1844
William Arnold b. 4 Sep 1846
Frances Cassancra b. 25 Mar 1848
Samuel Anthony b. 7 May 1851

[This furnished by Jack Ladson, Jr., Moultrie, Ga., who adds that
Nancy Barton Rhodes was dau. of Absalam Rhodes who was b. 8 Apr
1770 in Union Co., S.C. Nancy Barton's mother was Mary Barton,
dau. of Willoughby Barton, Jr. & Rebecca McCoy. Willoughby Barton,
Jr. was a famed Indian fighter & Capt. in the War of 1812.]

JEREMIAH LUMSDEN

Jeremiah Lumsden b. 13 Sep 1753, d. 18 Jan 1837, m. Elizabeth Lums-
den b. 2 Nov 1754, d. 17 Feb 1845.
   Children
Wilmoth b. 12 Aug 1779
Lucy b. 11 Dec 1780, d. 7 Mar 1802
Elizabeth b. 7 Sep 1782, d. 6 Nov 1830

Sally b. 20 Apr 1784
Anny b. 3 Aug 1783
Polly b. 6 May 1787, d. 19 Oct 1831
Susannah b. 31 Dec 1788
John b. 2 Dec 1790, d. 16 Mar 1830, m. Susannah Jones d. 30 Apr 1830
Pheba b. 7 Mar 1793
Nelly P. b. 2 Nov 1794, d. 3 Mar 1875, aged 81 yrs.
.... b. 4 Oct 1796 [not legible]
Charles W. b. 19 Nov 1798, d. 20 Jan 1815

Jesse M. Piper [Lumsden?] b. 24 June 1801
Henry M. Parrot b. 20 Aug 1808
Jesse M. Lumsden d. 26 May 1878
Elmoth Lumsden d. 6 June 1810
E. J. Lumsden d. 15 Aug 1907
R. S. Lumsden d. 17 Jan 1912
July Lumsden b. 26 Sep 1808

    "Heirs of Jesse M. Lumsden & wife July Lumsden
Elizabeth b. 16 Jan 1830
Jeremiah b. 18 Aug 1831
Larry H. b. 17 Feb 1833
William b. 7 Dec 1834
Elender b. 27 Oct 1836
Elijah b. 11 Apr 1839
Lucy b. 3 Apr 1844"

[Bible owned by Mrs. A. S. Piper, Covington, Ga. 1938. There are
some later Piper records, but they are very much later.]

DARBY M'CARTY

    Children of Darby & Hannah M'Carty
James b. 4 July 1736
Mary b. 10 Dec 1738
Isaac b. 18 Apr 1741
Sarah b. 3 July 1743
Rachel b. 28 Oct 1745
Elizabeth 18 June 1748
Hannah b. 9 Dec 1750
Enoch b. 29 Apr 1753
Jonathan 29 Apr 1756
Lydia b. 30 Apr 1756
Benjamin 22 Dec 1759

[This Bible record appeared in a copy of Genealogy & History some
yrs. ago. It was stated by PPO of Tenn., the contributor that some
of the letters to the 1st names were missing in the left margin but
enough were left to see what the name was. The Bible was found in
1948 in Hawkins Co., Tenn. according to PPO. The Bible was printed
by Alex Kincaid, His Majesty's Printer, 1762, Edinburgh, Scotland.
PPO further states that there are records of 3 more generations in

the Bible. "James' wife was killed by Indians in Hawkins Co., Tenn. in 1788."]

JOHN McCALL

John McCall b. 1 Dec 1772 at Appin, Argylshire, Scotland, d. 9 Apr 1858 at Clio, S.C., m. 1 Feb 1810 to Mary Currie (dau. of Lauchlin Currie d. 29 Nov 1827 & Catherine Currie d. 10 Oct 1813) b. 2 Nov 1775 in Richmond Co., S.C., d. 2 Dec 1852 at Clio, S.C.
    Children
Solomon b. 20 Jan 1811
John L. b. 23 May 1812, d. 25 May 1894, m. 27 Apr 1842 to Nancy Sin-
    clair
Daniel b. 29 Nov 1814, d. 23 Nov 1837
Samuel Allen b. 14 Mar 1815, d. 17 Sep 1818
Lauchlin Currie b. 31 May 1817, d. 11 Sep 1848

Catherine McCall d. 22 Sep 1816
Malcolm McCall d. 18 Oct 1819, aged 8 yrs. 3 mos.
Anna Celia Currie d. 29 Nov 1848
John Thomas Peabody 13 Oct 1867, aged 57 yrs. 11 mos. 20 days

[Comments by Leonard Andrea of Columbia, S.C. who sent this record: "John McCall came at the age of 14 yrs. & made his home in upper Marion Co., S.C. with a kinsman who had arrived earlier. Several other members of the family of John McCall came from Scotland with him & made their home with David McCall of upper Marion Co., S.C." Bible owned by Mrs. C. S. McCall, Bennettsville, Marlboro Co., S.C.]

ROBERT McCARTER

Robt. McCarter b. 6 Nov 1786, d. 27 Sep 1840, m. Cynthia Barnett b. 9 Dec 1786, d. 6 Aug 1824
    Children
Martha Barnette b. 17 Feb 1806
James Adams b. 10 Sep 1806 [too close], d. 31 Oct 1881, m. 17 Mar
    1839 in Greenville, S.C. to Martha A. Waddell b. 22 Mar 1825
Hannah M. b. 7 [?] Nov 1810, d. 20 Sep 1847 [?]
Thomas A. b. 9 July 1814, d. 12 Jan 1886
Christopher L. b. 19 Jan 1817, d. 21 June 1849 in La.
Robert C. b. 16 Apr 1819
Wm. E. T. b. 4 Nov 1821, d. 20 Aug 1847 [?]

    Children of James Adams & Martha A. (Waddell) McCarter
Benj. F. D. McCarter b. 21 Apr 1843, d. 3 July 1862
Myles E. McCarter b. 29 July 1845, d. 29 Jan 1901, m. 10 Feb 1880
    to Annice Green, child: Jas. Jackson b. 29 Jan 1881, d. 15 Oct
    1913, m. 14 Aug 1913 to Pearl P. Pool

Christopher Judge Trezvant McCarter, son of Chris. L., b. 12 Jan
    1849 in La.
Jas. Adams McCarter, grandson of Chris. McCarter, b. York Co., S.C.

[Sent by Leonard Andrea, Columbia, S.C. His comments: "At the death of Jas. J. McCarter, his mother, Mrs. Annice Green McCarter, gave the Bible to Keturah Rosamond, nee Roberts, she being the eldest great niece of Jas. Adams McCarter alive in Greenville, S.C. These McCarters are buried in McCarter Presbyterian Church in Greenville, S.C. which they founded. Bible owned by Mrs. Jas. P. Rosamond, Reid School House Road, Greenville, S.C.]

WILLIAM WADE McCARTY

Wm. Wade McCarty b. 24 Oct 1847, d. 3 July 1923, bur. Old Palestine Church Linwood Community, Cherokee Co., Tex., m. 4 Feb 1872 to Ollif C. Sowers b. 21 Oct 1854, d. 3 Oct 1895, bur. by her husband.
    Children
Mary Florine b. 23 Jan 1873 in La., d. 2 Feb 1899, m. Billy Patton
Sarah M. (W.) b. 8 Mar 1875 in La., d. 4 Dec 1903, m. Brum Lewis
Ollif A. b. 21 Feb 1877 in La.
Geo. Lafayette b. 8 Dec 1878 in Winfield, La.
Lulah H. b. 5 Apr 1881 in Winfield, La., m. Henry Haney
Cleo T. b. 17 July 1883, d. 23 May 1928, m. Hugh Foster
Florda U. b. 24 Sep 1885 in Tex., d. 5 Apr 1910, m. Jim Tucker
Lena Frances b. 3 Dec 1889 in Tex., m. Billy Harris
Wm. Ernest b. 15 May 1892 in Cherokee Co., Tex.

ANDREW McCLELLAND

Andrew McClelland b. 1 Jan 1748 in Bladen Co., N.C., d. 17 May 1827 in Scott Co., Va. m. Rebecca Robinson [or Robertson]
    Children
David b. 29 Sep 1778 in White Marsh, Bladen Co., N.C.
Elizabeth b. 12 Sep 1781
George b. 14 Jan 1783, d. 1858 in Jackson Co., Tenn., m. Margaret
    Mayrant
Josiah b. 5 Sep 1785, d. 28 Nov 1858, m. 2nd on 24 Dec 1812 in Barren Co., Ky. to Rhoda Condra
Thomas b. in Scott Co., Va., d. aged 5 yrs.
Sarah b. in Scott Co., Va., d. as small child
Rhoda b. 1791 in Scott Co., Va.
Moses b. 4 July 1793 in Scott Co., Va., m. Delilah Webb
Samuel b. 5 Sep 1795 in Scott Co., Va., m. Rebecca M. Lane

[Bible record sent by James O. Vassar, Rt. 1, Decatur, Ala.]

JOHN WALSTEIN McCORD

John W. McCord b. 13 ... 1811, d. 15 May 1894, m. Mary Cook (dau. of Thomas Cook d. 24 July 1857) b. 10 July 1816, d. 20 Feb 1889
    Children
Infant son b. 5 Oct 1835
Sarah Jane b. 21 Dec 1836, d. 17 Aug 1860
John Thos. b. 2 Feb 1840
Mary Eunice b. 2 Oct 1842, d. 17 Feb 1889

James Rufus b. 31 Oct 1845
Eliza Ellen b. 27 Sep 1847
Wm. Perkins b. 30 Oct 1849, d. 28 June 1852
Abigail Louisa b. 4 Apr 1852
Theodore Walstein b. 2 May 1854
Joseph Cook b. 4 Jan 1857, d. 29 Dec 1921
Nimrod Reynolds b. 10 Mar 1860

[Sent by Mr. E. B. Acuff, Moultrie, Ga.]

WM. G. McDONALD

Wm. G. McDonald b. 17 Apr 1796, m. 27 Nov 1817 to Thama Andrews
Thos. McDonald b. 8 Dec 1799

Eliz. Ann McDonald b. 14 Oct 1822
Narcissa McDonald b. 30 Sep 1824, m. 26 Feb 1840 to Murdock McKin-
    non
Jas. McDonald b. 18 Sep 1828
Amos J. McDonald b. 2 May 1831
Rebecca J. McDonald b. 17 Dec 1833
Sarah Cornelia McDonald b. 10 June 1836
Robt. Alex. McDonald b. 9 Aug 1838

[Bible owned by Mrs. T. E. Wyche, Salisbury, N.C., sent by Mrs.
Olive Webster, Greensboro, N.C. The McKinnon family came from
Scotland & settled in Cumberland Co., N.C. about the middle of the
18th century. The McDonald family came from Scotland about the
same time & settled in Moore Co., N.C.]

ALISON A. McDOWELL

Alison Alexander McDowell b. 10 Apr 1823, d. 2 Mar 1902, m. 13 May
1852 to Mary Ann Reaves b. 18 Feb 1832, d. 14 July 1883.
    Children
Mary Elizabeth McDowell b. 16 Feb 1853 [m. James McLeod]
Robert Archibald McDowell b. 12 June 1854 [m. Beulah Fort]
Ella Jane McDowell b. 3 Nov 1855, d. as a young girl
David Alexander McDowell b. 1 June 1857 [m. Augusta Reese]
Edward Allison McDowell b. 6 Apr 1859 [m. Eva Scott]
William Laurence McDowell b. 28 Jan 1861 [m. Elizabeth Niles]
Hattie Emma McDowell b. 28 Jan 1863 d. 8 Nov 1882 [m. John T.
    Team]
Nannie Eleanor McDowell b. 16 Dec 1864 [m. 1st to John B. Moffet,
    m. 2nd to William R. Law, Sr.]
Adelia Carolina McDowell b. 20 Mar 1867 [m. John Y. Reese]
Anna Theodosia McDowell 28 Sep 1871 [m. 1st to Robert Young McLeod,
    M.D., m. 2nd to John Wm. Clark]
Ruth Rebecca McDowell b. 14 Oct 1875, d. 30 July 1876

THE REV. ARCHIBALD McDOWELL

Archibald McDowell b. 24 Nov 1774, d. 29 Mar 1859, m. 25 Dec 1800
to Mary Drakeford b. [not legible], d. 12 Apr 1871
    Children
Margaret McDowell b. 27 Mar 1802, d. [not legible] 1802
Elizabeth McDowell b. 13 Nov 1803, m. 23 Sep 1824 to Stratford
Nancy McDowell b. 26 Feb 1806, m. 30 Sep 1833 to Johnson
William Drakeford McDowell b. 16 July 1808, d. 23 Mar 1853, m. 20
    Oct 1842 Don't know to whom
Aletha McDowell b. 31 Mar 1811, m. 19 May 1836 to William Russell
James L. McDowell b. 15 May 1815, d. 14 Dec 1876, m. Elizabeth
    Reaves
Martha McDowell b. 29 July 1815 (twin)
Mary McDowell b. 29 July 1815 (twin), d. 21 June 1816
Archibald McDowell, Jr. b. 10 Apr 1818, m. Mary Hayes Owen
Emma Leiaza McDowell b. 4 Nov 1820, d. 23 July 1855, m. 3 Feb 1853
    to Geo. Kelly 1st wife
Alison Alixander McDowell b. 25 Apr 1823, m. 13 May 1852 to Mary
    Ann Reaves
Sarah Jane McDowell b. 22 Aug 1826, m. 24 Oct 1855 to Geo. Kelly
    2nd wife

John Edward Columbus McDowell b. 26 Mar 1844
James Alexander McDowell b. 1 Apr 1846
Mary Elizabeth McDowell b. 16 Feb 1853
Archibald Robert McDowell b. 12 June 1854
Ella Jane McDowell b. 3 Nov 1855
David Alexander McDowell b. 1 June 1857
Edward Alison McDowell b. 6 Apr 1859

[This Bible, printed in 1801, is now owned by the family of Mrs.
John W. Clark, 329 Waccamaw Ave., Columbia 5, S.C. The parents of
Archibald McDowell came from Scotland & reared their son as a Presbyterian, but he, in his youth, joined the Flat Rock Baptist Church
& later became a prominent & useful minister in the Baptist Church
& served many churches in the Kershaw Co. area. He m. Mary Drakeford, dau. of Sarah Scott & Richard Drakeford, of Flat Rock, Kershaw Co., S.C.]

CHARLES T. McMANNEN

Charles T. MacMannen b. 14 Oct 1835, d. 21 June 1907
Mary Jane Turrentine b. 5 Mar 1835, d. 15 Nov 1884
    Children
Walter S. McMannen b. 3 July 1855, d. 26 Aug 1913, m. 15 Dec 1880
    to Anna E. Treadwell, son: Walter Raleigh McMannen
Fannie Estelle McMannen b. 7 July 1862, d. 10 Oct 1891
Lizzie Lee McMannen b. 27 Nov 1865, d. 25 Jan 1888
Linda Florence McMannen b. 15 Jan 1868, d. 14 Feb 1951, m. T. D.
    Delegal, no children
Alice May McMannen b. 8 Sep 1870

Grandchildren
Mary Lillian McMannen m. 2 Oct 1901 to Wm. E. Harden
Walter Raleigh McMannen m. 15 June 1910 to Ouida Powell

Great grandchildren
Ray McMannen Harden b. 23 July 1902
Wm. E. Harden b. 16 Aug 1905
Leola Lillian b. 1 Jan 1909, d. 3 Jan 1943

Great great grandchildren
Patricia Jean, dau. of Ray McM. Harden, b. 5 Jan 1925
Wm. Eldred m. 9 July 1936 to Fern Dodd, dau.: Linda b. 4 Nov 1942
Leola Lillian m. 10 Dec 1934 to Joe Sullivan, children: Diana Martha Sullivan b. 7 Nov 1935 & Thelma Lucile Sullivan b. 13 Apr 1937

Samuel Turrentine d. 24 Sep 1873
Fannie Turrentine, his mother, d. 28 May 1874

[This Bible owned by Mrs. Lillian McMannen Fitzgerald, Perry, Fla. Mary Jane Turrentine, above, b. Orange Co., N.C.]

McMASTERS

Peggy Cuper McMasters b. 22 Aug 1798
Susanah McMasters b. 4 or 11 Mar 1801
Polly McMasters b. 8 Mar 1803
David McMasters b. 12 Nov 1804
William McMasters b. 27 Jan 1806
Micager McMasters b. 25 Aug 1808
Algenun McMasters b. 3 Nov 1811

[The above record was taken from an old book published in 1823. The book belongs to Herbert Staley, Staley, N.C. This copy was given to the compiler by Mr. Calvin Hinshaw of Staley in Jan 1957.]

ANGUS McMILLAN

Angus McMillan b. 22 Oct 1801 in N.C., m 1st to Nancy Jarman b. 25 Apr 1803, m. 2nd to Jane Glass nee Stockard b. in 1812.

Parents
Sarah Gilchrist & Alexander McMillan
Grandparents
Catherine Buie & Malcolm Gilchrist of Moore Co., Fayetteville Dist. N.C.
Parents of my wife
Ann Hopkins & John Jarman
Grandparents of my wife
Rachel Hall & John Jarman, Sr.
Great-grandparents of my wife
Mary Meade & Robert Jarman

Children of Angus McMillan & Nancy Jarman
Malcolm G. McMillan d. 6 Sep 1822, aged 1 yr.
Martha J. McMillan b. 14 Apr 1823
Alexander Jarman McMillan b. 14 Oct 1825, m. Sarah Patterson
Sarah Ann McMillan b. 9 Feb 1828, m. John Freeman
Daniel Bester McMillan b. 19 Feb 1830 in Joshua, Tex. [or d. there]
    moved to Joshua, Texas
Andrew Jackson McMillan b. 15 Apr 1832
George H. McMillan b. 7 Jan 1837, d. as a youth
William A. McMillan (twin) b. 31 Jan 1839, m. Elizabeth Mims of
    Selma, Ala.
Eliza Phillips McMillan (twin) b. 31 Jan 1839, m. John McGhee of
    Durant, Miss.
        Children of Angus McMillan & Jane Glass
Angus A. McMillan b. 2 Oct 1847
William Glass, stepson

[The McMillan family Bible is now owned by the family of Mrs. Ann
Gibson (G. Truett) Phelps, P.O. Box 424, Lexington, Miss.]

                        JOHN McMURRAY

John McMurray b. Mar 1785, d. 1 Mar 1852; Mary Shffner b. Aug 1789
        Children
James b. 13 June 1808, d. 19 Oct 1850
John Wesley b. 6 Feb 1811
Eliz. b. 9 Oct 1814
Mary b. 10 June 1817
Eleanor b. 1 Mar 1819; Eleanor Wharton d. 24 Sep 1841
Jesse Addison b. 1 Oct 1821, d. 23 Aug 1843
Isabelle b. 12 Oct 1825
Nathaniel Brown b. 1 Dec 1827
Wm. b. 4 June 1830
Margaret M. b. 3 Apr 1833, d. 6 July 1858, m. 18 May 1855 to John
    D. Taylor

Theodore Wingfield Taylor m. 26 July 1853 to Alice [?] Kirkman
Jennie Taylor m. Will Glass
Mary d. 16 Aug 1813
Mary Mc [?] d. 3 Aug 1828

[James McMurray was a member of the Nottingham Colony that settled
in Rowan Co., N.C. (1753?) The present owner of the Bible is Mrs.
Mark Lewis, Old Pleasant Garden R., 6 miles from Greensboro, N.C.
Sent by Mrs. Olive Webster of Greensboro, N.C.]

                DR. ABBOTT MILTON McWHORTER

Dr. Abbott M. McWhorter b. 1828, d. in Myasville, Calif., m. Mahala
Jane Davis b. in S.C., d. in Gaylesville, Ala.

Dr. Robert Lee, son of Dr. Abbott M. McWhorter, b. 12 July 1864, d.
5 Apr 1936 in Gaylesville, Ala., m. 1st to Effie Leona McConnell b.
25 Sep 1869, d. 19 Dec 1904, m. 2nd to Gussie Wheeler b. 17 Oct
1873.
    Children
Abbott Milton b. 17 Aug 1890, d. 25 July 1892
Della Estelle b. 25 May 1892, d. 30 June 1893
Rachel Louise b. 22 Mar 1894, d. 4 Nov 1909
Horace Lawrence b. 7 Jan 1896, d. same day
Hobart Amory b. 19 Dec 1896, d. ca. 1950 in auto wreck, Birmingham,
    Ala.
Paul Kerr b. 27 Aug 1900
Haynie Margarette b. 15 Jan 1903

[From Mrs. Hobart Amory McWhorter, Birmingham, Ala.]

REV. ALLEN MARLIN McWHORTER

Alan Marlin McWhorter b. 16 May 1795 in Abbeville Dist., S.C. (son
of Moses McWhorter, son of Henry McWhorter, a native of Ireland)
brought over as a boy, m. 17 Jan 1819 in the 24th yr. of his age in
Abbeville Dist., S.C. to Eliz. Ann Baker b. 14 Feb 1798.
    Children
Elijah Harvey b. 15 Mar 1820, m. 1st to Narcissa Williamson d. 7
    Sep 1843, m. 2nd on 30 Mar 1847 to Milly Burnett
Bersheba Eliz. b. 14 May 1822, m. 2 June [or Jan] 1838 to Michael
    Aderhold, to Ga.
James Alcorn b. 8 Oct 1824, m. Charlotte Goodson [He d. young & his
    widow remarried & took her two McWhorter children to Ill., lost
    sight of.]
Egbert Beall b. 28 May 1826, m. Lydia Tanner, to Ga.
Abbott Milton b. 11 May 1828, m. 13 July 1851 to Mahala June Davis,
    to Ala.
Dionishus Wesley b. 31 Mar 1830, m. 1846 to Mary Truett, to Ark.

[From Mr. Davis L. McWhorter, Bethel, N.C. 1960. He adds, "The
will of Moses McWhorter (father of Alan M.) is dated and probated
in 1797 in Edgefield, S.C. & names 3 sons by his 1st wife (name unknown): Moses; Lowden of Cowden; John and 5 children by his 2nd
wife, Eliz. Puckett: Geo. Allen: Sarah Douglass; Danl. Puckett; Allen Marlin; Jane Allen. Bible records of son John have been given.
Those of his half brother, Allen Marlin, were sent me in 1932 by a
grandson, Valentine Burnett of Bowden, Ga. then aged 78 yrs. The
death of Allen McWhorter is not known. He was away from home &
supposedly lost his life trying to escape Yankee soldiers in 1864.
His wife died in 1863. The oldest dau. of Harvey McWhorter, Dru-
silla b. 1841, lived past 90 yrs. & gave much family data to the
writer. When her mother d. she & her sister were reared by their
grandparents. Later she married, as his 2nd wife, Michael Aderhold
who had been the husband of her Aunt Bersheba. He was b. in 1809 &
many yrs. her senior." Rev. Allen McWhorter was a Methodist
preacher, Villa Rica, Ga.]

DAVID McWHORTER

David McWhorter [m. 31 Mar 1766 from Lancaster Co., Pa. marriage records] to Mary Posten b. 11 July 1750
    Children
John b. 30 Oct 1768 [m. Eliz. Anderson]
Robert b. 22 Oct 1770 [m. Eliz. Cherry]
David b. 12 Oct 1773 [m. Eliz. C., dau. of Jeremiah McWhorter]
Saml. b.' 30 Sep 1775 [m. Margaret Cherry]
Solomon b. 2 Oct 1777
Mary b. 27 Nov 1779 [m. John, son of Moses McWhorter]
William b. 14 May 1782 [m. Susanna Sigmon of Ga.]
Isaac b. 10 Nov 1785 [moved to Ky., Ill.]
Sarah b. 5 Sep 1787

[This record sent by Davis McWhorter, Bethel, N.C., who adds that "David McWhorter or McWhirter - the Bible uses McWhirter but they all used the o later - is listed in the Chester Co., Pa. tax lists in the 1760's. The family removed to Rutherford Co., N.C. about 1770. In the Rev. War David performed patriotic service as a blacksmith & desc. claim that as a result of serious wounds received in the milita which caused his early death after the Rev. After the Rev. he removed to Abbeville, S.C. where his estate was administered in 1789 by his widow Mary. Some pages of his Bible are missing that would have had other dates. The marriages given after the children's names are from family records. The name of David McWhorter occurs on one of the pages of the Bible, indicating ownership. This was sent me by Mrs. Shelley McWhorter Wright, Chattanooga, Tenn. in 1953."]

JOHN McWHORTER

John McWhorter b. 11 July 1774, d. 4 Feb 1839, m. 16 Dec 1800 to Mary McWhorter (dau. of Mary McWhorter, Sr. b. 11 July 1750) b. 27 Nov 1779, d. 17 Feb 1863 [They were cousins].
    Children
David Washington b. 6 Nov 1801, m. Eliz. Nichols
Moses Edward b. 19 Sep 1803 [lived in Athens, Ga.], m. Hannah
  Nichols [sister of Eliz. above]
Sarah Love b. 5 Apr 1807, d. 12 Nov 1890, unmarried
John N. [for Newton] b. 28 May 1809, m. 14 June 1838 to Caroline
  Brock
Mary Matilda b. 9 Aug 1811; Mary Matilda Myers d. 27 Jan 1892; Henry Myers, her husband, d. 31 Mar 1897
Isaac A. b. 12 Oct 1815, m. Dec 1838 to Eliza Hill
Andrew P. [for Poston] b. 25 Sep 1817
Belinda Adeline b. 23 Aug 1820, d. 23 June 1848, unmarried
Eliza Ann b. 5 Feb 1823

[Record sent by Davis L. McWhorter, Bethel, N.C. He adds, "John McWhorter was a school master in Pickens Co., S.C. He is descended as follows: John McWhorter (4), Moses McWhorter (3), Henry McWhort-

er (2), Moses McWhorter (1). John is named as a son in his father's will (Moses) in 1797 in Edgefield, S.C. The family 1st located in Lancaster Co., Pa. in 1750's. Later went to Mecklenburg
Co., N.C. & thence to Abbeville Co., S.C. John married his distant
cousin, Mary McWhorter, dau. of David & Mary (Poston) McWhorter of
upper S.C. This Bible record was sent me in 1937 by the owner, &
a desc., Mrs. Lillian (Myers) Blackwell, Seneca, S.C. From John
McWhorter's will in 1839 in Pickens Co., S.C. it is learned that
Eliza Ann, dau. of John, m. Robt. M. Beaty."]

REV. LEROY McWHORTER

Leroy McWhorter [Baptist preacher, Carroll Co., Ga.] b. 1797, d. [5
Apr] 1875, m. Mary Eliz. Thompson who d. 9 Oct 1875
        Children
Moses [Allen] b. 25 Nov 1820
Sarah M. b. 11 May 1822
Mary Ann b. 11 May 1822
Johnson b. 3 Jan 1826
Laura b. 30 Nov 1827
Thos. Benson b. 27 July 1829
Elizabeth b. 5 July 1831
Newton Alex. b. 20 Apr 1833
Frank b. 4 Oct 1836

[Mr. Davis L. McWhorter gives the father of Henry McWhorter who was
the immigrant from Ireland as Moses but doesn't give the source of
this information, however he has done work for years on this family
and has much authentic data.]

HENRY MACHEN

Henry Machen b. 9 Dec 1745, d. 10 Dec 1821, m. 16 Nov 1772 to Fran-
ces Ballinger b. 9 Jan 1756, d. 10 Dec 1826.
        Children
James b. 21 Sep 1773
Thomas b. 1 May 1775
Henry b. 8 May 1776
John b. 24 Jan 1777
Judith b. 10 Nov 1778
Mary b. 12 May 1781
Elizabeth 14 May 1782
Hannah b. 15 May 1785
Francis B. 28 Feb 1787
Sarah b. 16 May 1789
Edward b. 24 Mar 1791
Frances b. 4 Mar 1793
Grace Greenwood b. 23 Jan 1796
Nancy K. b. 9 Aug 1798

[The above Bible record sent to the compiler by Miss Pauline Rice
of Little Rock, Ark. in 1954.]

JOHN W. MACK, SR.

John W. Mack, Sr. b. 12 Mar 1826 at Cordova, S.C., d. 8 Apr 1900;
Mrs. Susan Mack, his relict, d. 21 July 1912.

Mrs. Mary Knight Gibson, widow of Wylie Gibson, b. 14 Feb 1828, d.
18 Feb 1818 in Columbia, S.C., was left a widow when her husband
was killed on James Island while serving in the Confederate Army.

John W. Mack, Jr. b. 16 July 1851, d. 25 Mar 1923 at Cordova, S.C.,
m. 1st on 25 Dec 1871 to Almeda P. Gibson b. 15 Nov 1857, d. 27
July 1887, m. 2nd on 1 Sep 1887 to her sister, Ella Estelle Gibson
b. 4 Mar 1861, d. 12 Aug 1833.
    Children
Otis C. Mack b. 10 Dec 1872, d. 19 June 1873
Leila E. Mack b. 10 Dec 1874 - Mrs. Curtis L. Smoak
Iola F. Mack b. 8 Dec 1875, m. 18 Apr to Donald J. Hughes
Mary V. Mack b. o Sep 1877
Jacob A. Mack b. 13 Jan 1879
Clyde C. Mack b. 10 Feb 1881, m. Lena Mitchell Holman
Cecil W. Mack b. 10 Dec 1882
Edgar J. Mack b. 8 Oct 1884
Almeda Gibson Mack b. 15 June 1889 - Mrs. Walter F. Going
Ethel Leon Mack b. 12 July 1890
Junelle Mack b. 16 June 1892, d. 15 June 1894

[There are other marriages & deaths in this Bible. We did not have
time to copy all of them. Also in this Bible are the complete entries for the family group of Walter F. Going & his wife, Almeda G.
Going, 228 Wateree Ave., Columbia, S.C. Mrs. Going stated that
John W. Mack, Sr., Susan Mack, Wylie Gibson & Mary Knight Gibson
were her paternal & Maternal grandparents, according to L. Andrea.]

SAMUEL MACKIE

    [Children of Samuel Mackie]
Rosannah Mackie b. 28 Jan 1793, m. a Whiteside
Jane Mackie b. 5 Oct 1794
Mary Mackie b. 19 Nov 1796
William C. Mackie b. 30 Aug 1798
Rachel Mackie b. 27 July 1800
Thomas Mackie b. 10 Aug 1802
John Mackie b. 8 Sep 1804
Samuel L. Mackie b. 4 Aug 1806
Marthew Mackie b. 5 Jan 1809
Andrew H. Mackie b. 26 Aug 1813

    Children of John & Elizabeth (Scott) Mackie [Note spelling]
William C. McKie b. 9 Sep 1837, d. 18 Aug 1838
Thomas C. McKie b. 1 Oct 1838, d. 30 Sep 1863, aged 23 yrs.
Samuel J. McKie b. 3 Feb 1840, d. 21 May 1862, aged 22 yrs.
Sarah J. McKie b. 26 Apr 1842

Franklin L. McKie b. 25 Feb 1844
Mary E. McKie b. 2 June 1845
Charles D. McKie b. 25 Feb 1846
John S. McKie b. 15 Sep 1847
Louisa E. McKie b. 12 Apr 1849
Juley Ann McKie b. 31 Oct 1851, d. young

[This Bible record of the children of Samuel & Mary Clark Mackie &
of the family of their son, John Mackie & wife Elizabeth Scott
Mackie was preserved by the late Sarah Jane (Mackie) Wright, and is
now in the possession of her dau., Mrs. W. Y. Harber of Commerce,
Jackson Co., Ga.]

THOMAS MADDEN

Thomas Madden b. 13 July 1772 in Laurans Co., S.C., d. 12 Nov 1846
in Vermilion Co., Ill., m. 16 Feb 1799 in Union Co., S.C. to Ruth
Hollingsworth b. 30 Aug 1780 in Union Co., S.C., d. 6 June 1852 in
Vermilion Co., Ill. [Cain Creek Quaker Church Records of Union Co.,
S.C. show Ruth Hollingsworth wed out of unity & was dau. of Jane
Henry & George Hollingsworth.]
    Children, all b. in Laurens Co., S.C. except Caroline
Ann N. Madden, dau., b. 10 Aug 1800 [Nancy], m. 20 Apr 1825 in Boone
Co., Ky. to Barnett Weaver
Lydia P. Madden, dau., b. 25 July 1801, d. 21 Nov 1861, m. 5 Oct
1821 to Robert Williamson
Lochlin Lewis Madden, son, b. 28 Apr 1804, d. 18 Feb 1869, m. Nan-
cy Spenc-, a widow
Mary Madden, dau., b. 30 Sep 1806, m. 25 June 1828 in Boone Co.,
Ky. to Archibald McNeil
Rebecca C. Madden, dau., b. 17 Feb 1809, d. 23 Jan 1817
George J. Madden, son, b. 19 Oct 1810, d. 11 June 1815
Lina H. Madden, dau., b. 26 May 1812, d. 5 Oct 1824 in Florence,
Ky.
Lorenzo Dow Madden, son, b. 23 Jan 1815, d. 6 Aug 1817
Zephaniah H. Madden, son, b. 12 Dec 1816, d. 4 Apr 1876 in Clinton,
Ill., m. 1st on 10 Mar 1842 in Danville, Ill to Amanda Carter b.
9 Oct 1824, d. 7 Oct 1844, m. 2nd on 1 Oct 1848 in Danville, Ill.
to Angelina Downey b. 20 Dec 1822 in Augusta Co., Va., d. 27 July
1906 in Danville, Ky. [d. date shows Zephaniah as an M.D.]
America Madden, dau., b. 5 Sep 1819, d. 2 July 1841, m. 22 ... 1839
in Vermilion Co., Ill. to Green P. Garner
Caroline Madden, dau., b. 9 Aug 1821 in Boone Co., Ky.; Mrs. Caroline Madden Elliott d. 28 Jan 1891 in Clinton, Ill.

[Bible owned by Mrs. Vera J. Adams, P.O. Box 1702, Long Beach,
Miss.]

MICHAEL MAGEE (McGEE)

Michael Magee b. 17 June 1756, d. 21 June 1834, m. Anna Melvina
Sims b. 23 Mar 1763, d. 25 June 1838

Children
Jesse b. 15 Sep 1783
John b. 18 Feb 1785, m. 1st to Eliz. Agnew, m. 2nd to Harriet Cazy
   Martin, m. 3rd to Lucy Bradley Thorton, m. 4th to Anne Mattison
Jane b. 26 June 1787, m. Thos. Dodson
Mary b. 18 June 1789, m. Saml. Dunn
Eliz. Steed b. 18 May 1791, m. ... Sims
Nancy b. 18 Jan 1793, m. Wm. Barmore as one of his 3 wives
Burrell b. 18 Dec 1795, m. Sarah Hodges
(Rev.) William b. 24 Oct 1797, m. Aseneth Rice
Michael b. 11 July 1800, m. Martha Alexander
Abner Hill b. 7 Oct 1803, m. Eliza Rice

[Leonard Andrea of Columbia, S.C. who copied this from the S.C.
Traveling Library of the D.A.R. is of the opinion that some of it
was not copied correctly from the original. Michael McGee or Magee
was b. in N.C., the son of Michael Magee & his wife Mrs. Eliz.
Steed, nee Hill, dau. of Green Hill of Brunswick Co., Va. Mr. An-
drea says that some of these b. dates do not agree with those on
their tombstones at Turkey Creek Baptist Church in S.C. Abner Hill
McGee's wife listed here as Eliza, is Louisa Rice, wife of Abner H.
McGee on her tombstone. Michael Magee of this record was a Rev.
War soldier.]

TOM MALONE

Tom Malone m. 2 Oct 1789 to Jane Muzzell
   Children
Walter
Tempy m. 27 Jan 1814 [Caswell Co., N.C. m. records show this as 7
   Sep 1819] to William Smith
Polly m. 6 May 1830 to Henry Miles
Franky m. ... Boswell
Jim Blackwell Malone m. Sallie Murray
Nancy Malone m. Stephen Murphy
Judith never married
Elizabeth never married

[Sent by Mrs. A. L. Turner, Rt. 1, Mebane, N.C. in 1952 to Mr. Blalock, Yanceyville, N.C. It is a family record that Mrs. Turner had
proven.]

JAMES THOMAS MARSHALL

James Thomas Marshall b. 12 Dec 1821, d. 30 June 1897, m. 14 Dec
1844 to Jane Frances Gibson b. 2 Apr 1827, d. 20 Dec 1909
   Children
Thomas Benton Marshall b. 15 Jan 1846, d. 25 Apr 1908, m. 14 Sep
   1876 to Alice King
Montgomery Hamilton Marshall b. 1 May 1847, d. 23 Oct 1885, m. 14
   May 1873 to Anna Maria Clark
John Alex Marshall b. 15 Aug 1848, d. 13 Feb 1871

Eliza Ellen Marshall b. 10 Mar 1850, d. 13 Sep 1918, m. 20 May 1869
to James Bernard Norris
Willie Minor b. 24 May 1853, d. 6 Dec 1941, m. 22 Dec 1874 to Down-
ing Lemuel Smith b. 22 Jan 1846, d. 8 Sep 1924
Pocahontas Smith Marshall b. 2 Dec 1854, d. 28 July 1929
Martha Washington Marshall b. 18 May 1856, d. 30 May 1891, m. 24
Feb 1886 to Saml. Hinkle
Nancy Jane Nicholas Marshall b. 5 Apr 1858, d. 21 July 1870
Emily Alice Marshall b. 1 Mar 1860, d. 18 Apr 1862
Oriana Moon Marshall b. 8 May 1863, d. 22 Feb 1951, m. 10 Sep 1889
to Geo. Wm. Fuller
Robert Edward Lee Marshall b. 25 Apr 1865, d. 21 Feb 1940
    [Above lived near Milton, Albemarle Co., Va.]

    Children of Willie Minor & Downing Lemuel (Smith) Marshall
John Wm. Rosser b. 13 Sep 1875, d. ..., m. 9 Sep 1908 to Bessie T.
Oneohundret [?]
Sarah Jane b. 3 Mar 1879, d. 5 Apr 1937
Susie Pocahontas b. 1 Dec 1881
Eva Minor b. 10 July 1883, m. 7 Sep 1910 to Dr. E. S. Gregory,
Tuscumbia, Ala.
Jas. Downing b. 18 Oct 1884, d. 7 Nov 1929, m. 22 July 1911 to
Charlotte Eliz. Greene
Ruth Catherine b. 16 June 1888, m. 22 Dec 1922 to Geo. Elmer Mast-
erson
Lemuel Franklin b. 21 Apr 1890, m. 27 Oct 1916 to Grace S. Stulting
James Hamilton b. 28 Sep 1893, m. 9 Sep 1925 to Hester Jane McLar-
rin
Mary Eliz. b. 29 July 1896

[The Smiths lived at Shadwell, Albemarle Co., Va. Records from
Mrs. Gregory, Tuscumbia, Ala.]

JACOB MARTIN

Jacob Martin b. 24 Apr 1790, d. 6 Oct 1876, m. 31 Jan 1816 to Catharine Martin b. 23 Mar 1791, d. 22 Oct 1877.

Polly (Mary) Martin, dau. of Jacob & Catherine Martin, b. 14 Oct
1816, m. 22 Dec 1836 to James J. Wilson
William Garrison Martin, son of above, b. 20 Aug 1817, d. 25 Aug
1817
Frances Martin, dau. of the above, b. 22 July 1818, m. 19 Oct 1848
to Elihu Wigington
Thomas Hembre Martin, son of the above, b. 22 Dec 1820
Elizabeth Martin, dau. of the same, b. 15 Jan 1822
William Chesley Martin b. 31 Mar 1823, m. 5 Apr 1849 to Martha Har-
per
James Warren Martin b. 6 May 1825
Sanford Marion Martin b. 14 Feb 1829
Charity Martin b. 28 Feb 1831, m. William Seawright
Kiziah (Kisiah) Martin b. 28 Aug 1832, d. 12 Aug 1857, m. 8 Dec

1852 to Frances Manley Owen b. 9 Feb 1833

John T. Wigington b. 24 Aug 1849
Mary Katharine Wigington b. 10 June 1851
Matilda, the servant of them, b. 8 Dec 1847

William C. Richey [son of Elizabeth Martin Richey] b. 27 June 1845
Jacob Sanford Richey [son of Elizabeth M. Richey] b.8 Dec 1849 [My
   father L.R.M.]

Warren Preston Owen b. 15 July 1854, d. 27 June 1855
Catherine Elizabeth Owen b. 30 Apr 1857, d. 21 Aug 1857

Batis James Martin b. 24 Dec 1868
George Thomas Martin b. 25 July 1870
Jacob Marion Martin b. 10 Nov 1871

Thomas Martin, Sen. d. 6 Jan 1830, aged 63 yrs., m. Hester Martin
   d. 13 Mar 1855

[This Bible record of Jacob & Catharine Martin of Anderson Co.,
S.C. was preserved by their granddau., the late Mrs. Margaret Wilson Toney, Commerce, Ga.]

WILLIAM J. MARTIN

William J. Martin b. 14 Mar 1781, d. 1828; Betsey Kemp Macon b. 12
Sep 1784, d. 1827.

Nathaniel Martin b. 31 Aug 1802
Robert Gillespie b. 14 Mar 1804
Henry Lyne b. 12 July 1806
Nathaniel Macon b. 7 Feb 1808
William Kemp b. 9 Nov 1809
Ann Marion b. 13 Mar 1811
Hannah Plummer b. 4 Feb 1812
Susan Lyne b. 13 Oct 1814 [m. Nicholas Barbour]
Plummer Macon b. 14 Sep 1816
Gabriel Loy b. 12 June 1818
Daniel Anderson b. 14 Feb 1820
Richard b. 1821
Seynora Macon b. 30 Oct 1823
Henrietta
Robert Alton b. 5 June 1826

[Record in Prayer Book of William J. Martin, son of William Martin
of Halifax Co., N.C., grandson of Col. Nicholas Long of Halifax
Co., N.C. Col. Long was a prominent man in that county. He came
to N.C. from Va. in 1750 & bought thousands of acres of land.]

JOHN MAY

John May, clerk of the vestry of Bristol Parish, Va., m. in 1735 to
Agnes Smith.
    Children
John b. 1737
Betsy b. 1739
Richard b. 1743
Stephen b. 1745
David b. 1747
Agnes b. 1749
William b. 1752

[This is from someone in Columbus, Ga. It is in pencil & has in
red pencil, "Bible Record."]

FOSTER MAYNARD

Foster Maynard b. 1765, d. 11 Jan 1848 in the 73rd yr. of his age,
m. 1st to Elizabeth b. 1773, d. 1 July 1811 in the 38th yr. of her
age, m. 2nd to Aes(e)nath d. 8 Mar 1815, aged 22 yrs. & 5 hours, m.
3rd to Rachel d. 28 May 1847 in the 58th yr. of her life.
    Children
Margaret Maynard, dau., b. between 6 & 7 in the evening, 3 Mar 1797
    d. 23 Aug 1798, aged 17 mos. & 20 days
Nancy Maynard, dau., b. about 9 o'clock in the evening, 20 Aug 1800
    d. 5 Oct 1800, aged 1 mo. & 13 days
Foster Thomas Maynard, son, b. between 7 & 8 in the morning, 18 Nov
    1801, d. 17 Aug 1814 in the 13th yr. of his age
Elizabeth Maynard, dau., b. between 3 & 4 in the afternoon, 22 Jan
    1805
Aldren (Aldrin), son, b. at 6 A.M., 4 Dec 1806, d. 8 Mar 1808 in
    the 2nd yr. of his age
James Aldren, son, b. at 1 A.M., 17 Jan 1809
Julia Ann, dau., b. about 9 o'clock in the evening, 19 June 1811
Maria, dau., b. between 7 & 8 o'clock in the evening, 20 Mar 1813
Sary Ann, dau. of Foster & Aesnath Maynard, b. between 10 & 11 o'
    clock in the evening, 16 Mar 1815 [after d. date given for her
    mother], d. 9 June 1815, aged 4 mos. & 3 days [b. calculated: 6
    Feb 1815]
Heannery (Henry) Capper, son, b. about 10 o'clock in the evening,
    19 Aug 1816, d. 16 Sep 1830, aged 14 yrs. & 23 days

    Children of Benjamin F. & Elizabeth Butcher
Frances Wiley, dau., b. 7:30 P.M., 2 Mar 1858
Elizabeth Maynard, dau., b. at half past one noon, 6 Feb 1860
Willie (Willia) Edward, son, b. 22 July 1867, d. four & 1/2 o'clock
    24 Sep 1868, aged 1 yr., 2 mos., 2 days

William Maynard d. at quarter to six o'clock in the evening, 26 Mar
1876 in the 78th yr. of his age, knew all around him; Eliza Maynard
d. 21 Apr 1892, aged 72 yrs.

Children
George Walter, eldest son of William & Eliza (Eliz.) Maynard, b. 14
  Oct 1835, d. 8:45 A.M., 18 Mar 1912, aged 76 yrs., m. 25 Dec 1862
  at 9:45 P.M., 25 Dec 1862 to Josie (Josephine) Crawford (dau. of
  Andrew Crawford d. at 4 o'clock A.M., 30 Mar 1871, aged 68 yrs. &
  2 days and Eliza Crawford d. at 7 o'clock P.M., 9 Mar 1881 in her
  77th yr.), d. at 3 P.M., 3 Mar 1924, aged 85 yrs. & 3 mos.,
  child: Egbert Phillips Maynard d. 9 Feb 1864, aged 4 hrs.
Elizabeth R., dau., b. Feb 1838, d. 7 July 1911, aged 72 yrs., m.
  at 8:30, 14 Oct 1857 to Benjamin P. (F.) Butcher
Camilla, dau.
Alice May, dau., b. 1 May 1848
Maggie E., dau., b. 10 Feb 1852
Edward W., son, b. 1850

Laura C. Murrell Maynard b. 11 Oct 1840, d. 12 Nov 1905, m. John
  Washington Maynard b. 21 Jan 1820, d. 24 Jan 1867
Benjamin Hatcher Maynard b. 24 Jan 1857, d. 22 June 1922, m. Henri-
  etta Matthews b. 2 Feb 1859, d. 5 Mar 1901
Julia Maynard b. 17 Nov 1890, m. James Ligon Simpson b. 5 Feb 1884
Edward W. Maynard m. 24 Apr 1872 to Sarah E. Hines of Anne Arundel
  Co.
Egbert P. (Phillips) Maynard d. 2 P.M. 18 Aug 1924, aged 59 yrs., m.
  3 Mar 1885 by Rev. G. D. Smith to Thomazin Y. Town
Milton H. Maynard m. 28 Apr 1897 by Rev. Frank G. Porter to Sarah
  Heath
Walter B. Maynard m. 14 Sep 1897 by Rev. Wm. Litsinger to Ellen R.
  Christhilf
Mabel Maynard m. 25 Dec 1901 by Rev. J. L. Walsh to Isaac J. Smith
R. C. (Raymond Clayton) Maynard m. 27 Aug 1910 by Rev. F. G. Port-
  er to Josie H. Littleton who d. 5:30 P.M. 17 May 1923, aged 32 yr.
G. (George) Foster Maynard m. 22 Nov 1911 by Rev. Alford to Iola
  Brown
Frances C. Maynard m. 22 June 1930 by the Rev. F. A. Hightman to
  Charles E. Shaffer
Charles G. Maynard m. 23 Nov 1932 at LaPlata, Md. to Elsie M. Den-
  nis

James Ligon Simpson, Jr. b. 28 Nov 1914
William Maynard Simpson b. 24 June 1916
Michael Willis Simpson b. 17 Dec 1924

  Children of Egbert P. & Thomazin Y. Maynard
Elizabeth Vernon, dau., d. 17 Aug 1893, aged 6 mos., 1d days, 4 A.M.
Raymond Clayton, son, d. 10 Oct 1924, aged 35 yrs., 8:20 P.M.

  Children of Raymond Clayton & Josie H. Maynard
Richard Arthur, son, d. 4 P.M., 3 Feb 1918, aged 5 days (twin)
Foster Earle, son, d. 4 Feb 1918, aged 6 days (twin)
Joseph Herman, son, b. 3 Feb 1921 at 7:30 A.M.

Children of George Foster & Lillian I. (T.) Maynard
Hampton Howell, son, d. 12 Feb 1917, aged 1 mo.
Eurith Linthicum, dau., b. 24 Nov 1919

Charles Maynard, son of Charles & Frances Maynard Shaffer, b. at 7
   A.M., 10 June 1930

[Copied by Mrs. Julia Maynard Simpson, Williamston, S.C.]

JAMES MEDLOCK

Jas. Medlock b. 1800, d. 16 Jan 1837, m. 23 Apr 1823 to Sarah Jones
b. 12 May 1801, d. 8 Jan 1882.
   Children
Eliz. Jane m. 3 Oct 1843 to Waldemar Murff
James Travis b. 1826, d. 1885
Mary Henderson b. 24 Jan 1828, d. 4 June 1872, m. Benj. J. Johnson
   b. 20 Mar 1822, d. 20 Apr 1860
Mazie Caroline b. ..., m. Jas. A. Simmons
Martha Ann m. David Pope
Sarah Lucinda m. John Calvin Cluck

[This rather incomplete record sent by Mrs. Paul B. Murff, Floydada, Fla. This family from Ware Shoals, S.C.]

JAMES TRAVIS MEDLOCK

Jas. Travis Medlock b. 1826, d. 1885, m. 1st on 4 Sep 1848 to Cor-
nelia Narcissa LaFayette Jones b. 1828, d. 1861, m. 2nd on 11 May
1861-2 to Martha James Babb
   Children
Sarah Jane b. 16 May 1849, d. 1924, m. 5 Dec 1843 Charlie A. Moore
Martha Ann Henriette Townes b. 20 Aug 1850, m. Jas. Cork
Mary Eliz. Ludella b. 3 June 1852, m. G. B. Taylor
Kate b. 1854, d. 1943, never married
Jas. Travis, Jr. b. 18 Aug 1856, m. Kate Bullock
Mazie Ann b. 1859, d. 1876, never married
Arthur b. 1862, d. 1949
Cornelia b. 1863, d. 1952, m. ... Taylor
Clara A. d. 1922, m. ... Balentine
John A. b. 1865
Emma E. b. 1867
Joseph B. b. 1868, d. 1954
Mattie O. b. 1870, m. Thos. Downey
Nannie Eudora b. 1876, d. 1955, m. 24 Feb 1907 to W. H. Balentine
Sudie b. 1877, d. 1943, unmarried
Julia A. b. 1879, d. 1940, unmarried
Walter H.
Calvin b. 1882, d. 1883

[Sent by Mrs. Paul B. Murff, Floydada, Fla.]

MEREDITH

Ann Meredith b. 8 Nov 1764
John Meredith b. 28 May 1767
Elizabeth Meredith b. 5 Sep 1769
Hanah Meredith b. 28 Oct 1773
Nathan Meredith b. 24 Apr 1775
William H. Meredith b. 12 May 1777
James Meredith b. 10 Mar 1780
Joseph Meredith b. 25 Mar 1782
Eleanor Meredith b. 22 Feb 1784
Janet Meredith b. 16 Dec 1785
Sarah Meredith b. 16 Jan 1792
Eliza Margaret Meredith b. 3 Nov 1818
Eleanor Jane Meredith b. 26 June 1822
James H. Meredith b. 21 Apr 1826
Charles Bennerman b. 18 May 1774
James Henry Bannerman b. 6 Mar 1865
Sarah Ann Meredith b. 30 June 1830
James Washington Flinn b. 11 Nov 1844
Margaret Ann Flinn b. 2 Sep 1847
Andrew A. Flinn b. 14 Apr 1850
Sarah Eliza Flinn b. 27 Dec 1852
Sarah Elizabeth Meredith b. 15 Aug 1851
William James Meredith, son of James H. Meredith, b. 27 Dec 1853
Alista A. Meredith, wife of W. J. Meredith, b. 19 Sep 1855
Mary Stella Meredith b. 3 June 1878
Herman Spencer Meredith b. 22 Nov 1880
Rosa Vertma Meredith b. 20 Jan 1883
Cora Alberta Meredith b. 28 Aug 1885
Leslie James Meredith b. 16 Aug 1887
Custus Elizabeth Meredith b. 3 Sep 1889
Suda Eugene Bannerman b. 2 Oct 1890
Sarah Elizabeth Anders b. 29 Sep 1853
Mary Catherine Meredith b. 2 Jan 1856
John Mongomery Meredith b. 2 Oct 1858
Alice K. Meredith b. 20 May 1869
Leroysolam Brown b. 21 Sep 1892
John Collins, son of Lewis Collins, b. 22 Oct 1826
Amanda J. Collins b. 10 Mar 1857
John William Collins b. 14 Aug 1859
Charles L. Mongomery Collins b. 23 Feb 1862
Neomie L. Collins b. 2 Mar 1877
Salie Rutha Eleanor Collins b. 11 Nov 1880
John Jeremiah Collins b. 4 Dec 1882
Charles Losie M. Collins b. 22 Mar 1885
Ida May Dowlas b. 7 Mar 1897
Matty Jane Dowlas b. 2 Nov 1899
Katy Lou Meredith b. 21 May 1892
Sudai Eugene Bannerman b. 2 Oct 1890
James Flinn, Sr. b. 7 June 1794
James M. Flinn, son of James & Elizabeth Flinn, b. 23 Apr 1817

William M. Flinn b. 3 May 1820
John A. Flinn b. 16 Apr 1822
Sophia Ann Flinn b. 10 Aug 1827
Martha Jane Flinn b. 23 Nov 1829
Franklin C. Flinn b. 23 Jan 1831
Sarah E. Elizabeth Flinn b. 17 Jan 1833
D. V. Flinn b. 27 Jan 1835
George W. Flinn b. 9 Sep 1837
James W. Flinn b. 11 Jan 1844 [Note James Washington Flinn above]
M. A. Flinn b. 2 Sep 1847 [duplicate of above]
William James Meredith, Jr., son of Herman Spencer Meredith
    Children of Mary Estelle & Thomas S. Memory
Simms Edward, Ruth Meredith, Louise, Emily, & Thomas Spencer Memory
    Edward Memory m. Eva Barnes, children
Doris and twins, Billy & Bobby
    Children of Cora Alberta & Ramsey Weathersbee
Frances Meredith Weathersbee b. 27 Feb 1917
Ramsey Weathersbee, Jr. b. 12 Mar 1921
Mary Helen Weathersbee b. 20 Sep 1922
    Children of Custy Elizabeth & John H. Hightower
John Hightower, Jr. b. 25 Apr 1920
Elizabeth Meredith Hightower
    Children of Katy Louise & George Ross Douglass
George Ross Douglass, Jr. b. 1 June 1925
Doris Stringfield Douglass
Donald Douglass
Sinclair Douglass b. 14 Sep 1933
Evelyn Douglass

Ann Meredith d. 26 Aug 1795, aged 31 yrs.
Nathan Meredith d. 13 Nov 1788, aged 61 yrs.
Elizabeth Meredith d. 4 Nov 1820, aged 78 yrs.
Eleanor Meredith d. 7 Oct 1822, aged 36 yrs.
John Meredith d. 7 May 1829, aged 36 yrs.
Eliza Margaret Meredith d. 23 Sep 1833, aged 18 yrs.
James Meredith d. 17 Aug 1863, aged 83 yrs., 5 mos., 7 days
Sarah Meredith d. Feb 1871, aged 79 yrs.
Enoch Herring, my father, d. 17 July 1833, aged 71 yrs., 5 mos., 17
    days
Margaret Herring d. 18 Feb 1848, aged 82 yrs.
Amelia Flinn d. 19 Sep 1875
Sarah E. Ruthie Collins d. 19 Sep 1888, aged 2 yrs., 10 mos., 8
    days
James "H." Meredith d. 6 Mar 1890
Margaret E. Meredith d. 5 July 1897
James Flinn d. 10 Jan 1848
Sarah E. Flinn d. 9 May 1854
Andrew M. Flinn, son of James M. & E. J. Flinn, d. 25 Sep 1853
James M. Flinn d. 20 May 1851
Lewis Collins d. 26 Nov 1870, aged 73 yrs.

Enoch Herring m. 27 July 1786 to Margaret Anders
James Meredith m. 10 Nov 1812 to Sarah Herring
James M. Flinn m. 7 Mar 1843 to E. Jane Meredith
James H. Meredith m. 24 Mar 1847 to Margaret E. Anders
A. A. Cromartie m. 11 Feb 1869 to Elizabeth Meredith
J. F. Brown m. 23 Feb 1869
J. W. Flinn m. 23 Dec 1869 to Susan C. Brown
William James Meredith m. 8 Mar 1853 to Alisa Ann Stringfield
John M. Meredith m. Henrietta Robinson
Mary Catherine Meredith m. John Bowden
Alice Kelly Meredith m. Eugene Bannerman
Frances Meredith Weathersbee, dau. of Cora Alberta & Ramsey Weath-
    ersbee, m. 16 Mar 1939 to Lieut. John Lawrence Counihan
James H. Meredith m. 24 Mar 1847 to Margaret E. Anders
        Their children
Sarah Elizabeth b. 1851, m. A. A. Cromartie, children: Ralph, Irene,
    Lelia, Raymond, Lawrence, Blanche, Aaron & Eula
William James Meredith b. 27 Dec 1853, m. 8 Mar 1877 to Alista Ann
    Stringfield, children: Mary Estella, Herman Spencer, Rosa Verta,
    Cora, Alberta, Leslie James, Custis Elizabeth, & Katie Lou
Mary Catherine b. 1855, m. John Bowden, children: Willie King, Cus-
    tis Atwood, Maggie, & Willie
John Montgomery b. 1858, m. Henrietta Robinson, children: James,
    Sanford, Minnie, Lelia, May & Ray Meredith
Alice Kelly b. 22 May 1869, m. Eugene S. Bannerman, children: Sudie,
    Eugene, Kyle, & Charles Washington
        Descendants of William James Meredith & Alista Ann Stringfield
Mary Estelle Meredith m. 1905 to Thomas S. Memory
Herman Spencer Meredith m. 1911 to Mrs. Jessie Cox
Rosa Vertna Meredith m. 12 Sep 1912 to Dr. Charles F. Strosnider
Cora Alberta Meredith m. 27 Nov 1907 to Ramsey Weathersbee
Leslie James Meredith m. 14 Dec 1916 to Lucile Riley
Custy Elizabeth Meredith m. 1916 to John H. Hightower
Katy Louise Meredith m. 1922 to George Ross Douglas

                            DAVID MIKEL

David Mikel b. 20 Dec 1815, d. 12 Feb 1896, m. 1 Jan 1835 to Cath-
erine H. Mikel b. 13 Apr 1812, d. 27 Sep 1895.
        Children
John Mikel b. 24 Mar 1836; John W. Michael d. 18 Nov 1881
Martha Ann Mikel b. 25 Jan 1839, d. 7 June 1842
William Mikel b. 30 Nov 1841; William D. Michael d. 24 Nov 1887
James K. Mikel b. 23 Oct 1844, d. 22 Apr 1927
Anderson Green Mikel b. 16 Sep 1847, d. 14 May 1917
Samuel B. Mikel b. 24 Aug 1850, d. 28 June 1853
Elizabeth Fendon Mikel b. 18 Sep 1853
Mary Emer Mikel b. 12 July 1856; Mary Etta Michael Smith d. 31 Aug
    1918

Elizabeth Mikel [mother of David] d. 29 July 1853

                            219

[This Bible is owned by the Misses Mary & Annie Lowe, Good Hope, Ga. It was published in 1836 by Samuel S. & William Wood, 261 Pearl St., New York, N.Y. David Mikel was a son of Elizabeth Kelly & Jacob Michel of Oglethorpe Co., Ga. Catherine Hughes, wife of David Michael was a dau. of Elizabeth Hemphill & Richard Johnston. Marriages from public records:
Anderson Green Michael m. 5 Jan 1866 to Rachel Mary Ann LaBoon
James K. Michael m. 14 Feb 1867 to Mary D. Hale
Mary Emma Michael m. 19 Nov 1884 to William Smith
Elizabeth Fendon Michael m. 19 Jan 1871 to John Elder Lowe
John W. Michael m. 1 Oct 1868 to Nancy C. Johnston
William D. Michael m. 15 Nov 1869 to Mary C. McGaughey]

DAVID M. MILFORD

David M. Milford, son of Jane Cleland & Thomas Craig Milford, b. 29 Oct 1843, d. 3 Oct 1885, m. 1st on 21 Jan 1869 to Clara Black, dau. of ... Cobb & Ramsey Black, b. 11 Apr 1846, d. 22 Sep 1872, m. 2nd on 31 Dec 1874 to Nancy Rebecca Talitha Milford, dau. of Elizabeth Cleland & John Mitchell Milford, b. 9 Nov 1849, d. 29 Apr 1914 [called Tilly.]
    Children
Rosa Bell Milford, dau., b. 15 Feb 1870, d. 2 Sep 1887
Lilly Marie Milford, dau., b. 11 Feb 1872, d. 7 Feb 1956, m. Eugene
    J. Wilson of Darlington, S.C.
Jennie Milford, dau., b. 8 Mar 1877, d. Apr 1931, unmarried
Thomas Craig Milford, son, b. 20 May 1879, d. 21 Dec 1925, m. 1st
    on 9 Dec 1903 to Lillie Jane Purdy, m. 2nd on 12 May 1918 to Nell
    Patterson
Mary Eve Milford, dau., b. 23 June 1882, d. 17 Mar 1884

    Children of Lilly Purdy & Thomas Carl Milford
Mary Elizabeth Milford, dau., b. 28 Dec 1904, m. 10 July 1926 to
    Earle V. DePew
Martha Margaret Milford, dau., b. 13 July 1906, m. Chester J. Nichols
Willie Belle Milford, dau., b. 3 Mar 1908, m. Charles Mixon Darracott

Thomas Carl Milford, Jr., son of Nell Patterson & Thomas Carl Milford, Sr., b. 19--, m. Susie Caughman
Robert Purdy, father of Lilly Jane Milford, d. 23 May 1919

[See Bible record of William Cleland, this volume.]

GEORGE MILFORD

George Milford b. 8 Nov 1783, d. 3 Aug 1871, m. Eleanor Milford b. 26 Jan 1789, d. 7 Dec 1864.
    Children [family knows & tombstones show, no daus. married]
John Mitchell Milford, son, b. 12 Dec 1809, d. 4 Mar 1892, m. 1st
    to Elizabeth Cleland b. 21 Nov 1810, d. 14 Dec 1864, m. 2nd to

Elizabeth McWilliams b. 12 Oct 1827, d. 15 July 1876
Rebecca Phagan Milford, dau., b. 25 Mar 1812, d. 29 ... 1878 [Tomb-
stone says b. 28 Mar 1812]
Thomas Craig Milford, son, b. 30 Sep 1817, d. 13 Jan 1882 [Tomb-
stone says b. 30 Sep 1818], m. 1st to Jane Cleland b. 24 Mar 1822
d. 10 May 1864 [m. 2nd to Nancy McWilliams]
Mary Jameson Milford, dau., b. 27 Oct 1820, d. 20 Jan 1887
Isabella Eleanor Milford, dau., b. 15 May 1823, d. 26 Mar 1899
Joshua Pruett Milford, son, b. 31 Oct 1827, d. 10 Jan 1875, m. the
Widow Callahan
Margaret J. Milford, dau., b. 19 May 1831, d. 30 Aug 1915
George Watt Milford, son, b. 29 Dec 1834, d. 6 Feb 1921, m. Nancy
Alcanza Branyon b. 5 Aug 1849, d. 14 May 1910

Thomas Milford d. 14 Apr 1843 [The family thinks this entry is for
the father of George Milford.]

[This Bible record of George Milford of Abbeville Co., S.C. is
owned by Mrs. Charles M. Darracott, 1 Poplar St., Abbeville, S.C.]

JOHN MITCHELL MILFORD

John Mitchell Milford b. 12 Dec 1807, d. 4 Mar 1892, m. 1st on 27
July 1837 to Elizabeth Cleland b. 21 Nov 1810, d. 14 Dec 1864, m.
2nd on 21 Jan 1867 to Elizabeth McWilliams b. 12 Oct 1827, d. 15
July 1876. (no children by the 2nd wife).
    Children
William Thomas Milford, son, b. 13 June 1839, d. 5 Mar 1899
Mary E. Milford, dau., b. 8 July 1842 d. 2 Apr 1900, m. 11 Oct
1865 to John W. Ellison
Shady Ann Elizabeth Milford, dau., b. Aug 18--, d. 17 June 1892
John Mitchell Milford, Jr., son, b. 22 Apr 1845, d. 18--
Nancy Rebecca Talitha Milford, dau., b. 9 Nov 1849, d. 29 Apr 1914,
    m. 31 Dec 1874, as his 2nd wife, to David M. Milford

[Two brothers wed two sisters the first & second times: John
Mitchell Milford m. 1st to Elizabeth Cleland, m. 2nd to Elizabeth
McWilliams. His brother, Thomas Craig Milford, m. 1st to Jane Cleland, m. 2nd to Nancy McWilliams. The estate of T. Craig Milford
was administered 28 Oct 1882 by his eldest son, N. P. Milford, Administrator. His bond was signed by W. J. Milford & H. T. McIl-
waine. The estate was appraised by R. Thomas Gordon. File 211-
5533, Abbeville Co., S.C.]

ABRAM MILLER

Abram Miller b. 23 Aug 1802 in Jackson Co., Ga., m. 13 Apr 1834 in
Pickens Co., Ala. to Jane Gilkey, dau. of Samuel & Elizabeth Gilkey,
b. 13 Jan 1810, d. 2 June 1861.
    Children
Samuel G. Miller, son, b. 27 Feb 1835
William S. Miller, son, b. 23 Aug 1836

Elizabeth Miller, dau., b. 2 Sep 1838, d. 8 Aug 1871
Robert F. Miller, son, b. 15 Dec 1839, d. 7 June 1840
Emily Ann Miller, dau., b. 12 Nov 1841
Rebecca Jane Miller, dau., b. 29 Oct 1843, d. 7 Aug 1871
Abram Alexander Miller, son, b. 20 Jan 1846, d. 26 Sep 1849
Reuben H. Miller, son, b. 26 Sep 1849

William Miller d. 1 Feb 1849, aged 90 yrs., in the full hope of a
  happy resurrection

[Enon Cemetery near Akerman in Choctaw Co., Miss.: "Abram Miller b.
23 Aug 1802, d. 23 Oct 1870" Abram was son of William Miller b. in
1858 in Waxhaws in Anson Co., N.C., lived in Jackson Co., Ga. 30
yrs. & d. in 1848 in Noxobee Co., Miss (from his Rev. Pension) See
the will of William Miller dated 24 Feb 1842 in Winston Co., Miss.]

HENRY MINOR

Henry Minor, son of Thomas Carr Minor & Anna Redd, b. 4 Jan 1783 at
Topping Castle, Caroline Co., Va. (half mile from the Island ford
of Northanna River), m. 14 Sep 1809 at Petersburg, Va. by Rev. Mr.
Squire [?] Episcopalian clergyman to Frances Throckmorton Barbour,
dau. of Mordecai Barbour & Betsy Strode, b. 13 Apr 1788.
     Children
Henry b. 7 July 1810 in Clarksville, Tenn.
Mordecai b. 13 July 1812 in Nashville, Tenn., d. 12 June 1821
Anne Virginia b. 23 Aug 1814 in Petersburg, Va.
Elizabeth Barbour b. 12 Dec 1816 in Huntsville, Ala. [Then Miss.
  Terr.]
Frances Cosby b. 14 Jan 1819 at Shaw Place
Maria Barbour b. 23 July 1820 [probably at Shaw Place], m. Feb 1845
  in Tuskaloosa [Ala.] to Ezra Fiske Bouchelle
Louisa b. 22 Sep 1822 near Huntsville, Madison Co., Ala., d. 26
     July 1823
Mordecai LaFayette b. 22 Apr 1824 in Huntsville, Madison Co., Ala.
John Lancelot b. 3 June 1826 at Tuskaloosa [Ala.], New Town
Philip Pendleton Barbour b. 23 Jan 1828 at Tuskaloosa Old town
Lucy Landon Barbour b. 3 June 1831 at Tuskaloosa, Old town

[This Bible is owned by Mrs. Ralph Banks, Eutaw, Ala.]

DR. WILLIAM TOMPKINS MINOR

Dr. Wm. T. Minor b. Jan 1797 in Va., d. 3 July 1854, aged 57 yrs.,
m. 22 Jan 1825 to Fanny Thacker Washington who d. 2 Apr 1879, aged
76 yrs.
     Children
Lucian b. 22 May 1826
Mary Ann b. 22 Sep 1827
Elizabeth Pratt b. 1829
Wm. Vincent b. 1831
Fanny Mildred b. 1833

Henry Augustine b. 23 Feb 1835
Wm. Adams b. Dec 1837
Louisa Eliz. b. 12 Dec 1839
Frances Ricks b. 4 Feb 1841
Mildred Pratt b. 1 Aug 1843
Wm. Peter b. Nov 1845
Sally Washington b. 1848

[This Bible is the property of Mrs. Rayburn Neville, nee Mary Moseley, Trinity, Ala.]

WILLIAM MINTER

William Minter, son of John Minter & Frances his wife who came from
Wales & settled in Va. about 1780, b. 5 July 1736, m. in 1757 to
Martha Hillhouse [b. 30 Apr 1736].
    Children
John Minter b. 10 May 1769, d. 16 Dec 1846 at 11:00 A.M., aged 77
    yrs., 7 mos. & 6 days, m. 22 May 1792 to Jane Gilham [b. 21 Apr
    1773], d. 24 Sep 1834, at 7:00 P.M., aged 61 yrs., 5 mos., 3 days
William Minter b. 25 May 1770, d. 25 Jan 1820
Margaret Minter b. 17 Oct 1772, d. 1773
James Minter b. 9 Aug 1774
Josiah b. 28 May 1776
Mary Minter b. 1778
Joseph b. 1780
Jacob b. 11 Feb 1783
Sarah b. 15 Dec 1785
Johathan b. 1 June 1789

    Children of John & Jane Gilham Minter
Martha Minter b. 20 May 1793, d. 4:30 P.M. 26 Apr 1853, aged 60
    yrs. lacking 24 days, m. 23 Feb 1813 to William Sherer b. 19 Nov
    1790, d. 30 Dec 1865 at 6:00 P.M., in the 76th yr. of his age
Isaac Minter b. 15 Feb 1795
William Minter b. 13 May 1797
John Thomas b. 13 May 1800
Mary Ann b. 15 Mar 1804
Jesse Jackson (Jaeson) b. 26 May 1806, d. 16 May 1834 at 4:00 A.M.
    aged 28 yrs. lacking 10 days

    Children of Martha Minter & William Sherer
James G. b. 16 May 1814
J. Thomas b. 16 Sep 1815
Torrisa b. 8 June 1817
Absalom b. 12 Mar 1819, m. 2 Jan 1845 to Tennet A. R. Kirkpatrick
Elisha A. Sherer b. 25 Jan 1821, m. 19 Dec 1844 to Eliza Kirkpatrick
Madison b. 26 Oct 1822

Adeline Love b. 2 May 1804 [listed below John T. Minter]
Elzy D. Minter b. 4 Feb 1825
Thomas I. Minter b. 17 June 1826

Julian Minter b. 23 May 1828
Joseph Monroe Minter b. 17 Feb 1830
Clarance A. b. 2 Nov 1833
Mary Jane b. 2 Sep 1836

William T. (J.) Sherer, son of E. A. & E. Sherer, b. 27 Nov 1846,
 d. 13 Sep 1855, aged 8 yrs., 9 mos., 16 days
Samuel N. Sherer b. 12 Mar 1848
Harriet A. Sherer b. 27 Jan 1850; Harriet A. Stewart d. 14 Aug 1932
 aged 81 yrs.

John W. Sherer, son of A. & T. A. R. Sherer b. 11 Nov 1846
Wm. L. Sherer b. 28 Nov 1849
Samuel C. Sherer b. 24 Sep 1851

William C. Sherer, son of J. C. & S. C. Sherer, b. 9 Nov 1836, d.
 May 1864 in Illinois, in his 28th yr.
James A. Sherer, son of J. C. & Sarah C. Sherer, b. 2 Aug 1839 in
 S.C., moved to Ala. 1856, enlisted in the Confederate Service
 1861, & d. 26 Apr 1862
John M. Sherer b. 20 Dec 1841, m. 21 Mar 1866 to Samaria Jones
Margaret M. Sherer b. 14 Mar 1844; Margaret A. Shere d. 23 Sep 1846
Joseph T. Sherer b. 11 Dec 1846
Martha J. Sherer b. 28 July 1850
Frances Sherer b. 8 May 1853
Thomas W. Sherer b. 17 Dec 1855
Richard S. Sherer b. 29 June 1858, d. 21 Aug 1861
George H. Sherer b. 18 Jan 1860

Martha Elizabeth Sherer, dau. of N. & Harriet Sherer, d. 3 June
 1855, aged 5 yrs., 10 days
Elisha Sherer, son of J. C. Sherer & Mattie Sherer, b. 18 Aug 1912

[From the Bible, "Philadelphia published & sold by Kimber & Sharpless, at their Book Store, #93 Market St., 1824." Oscar Minter
Sherer, son of Absalon Sherer notes that the information seems to
have been recorded in this old Bible by two or more families. Elisha Sherer, his birth record above, now has possession of this
Bible. He now lives in Washington, D.C., and the compiler copied
this information 20 Sep 1950.]

LT. NIMROD MITCHELL

Lt. Nimrod Mitchell [Officer in the S.C. State Militia in the Amer.
Revolution] b. 21 Apr 1743 in Edgecombe Co., S.C., d. 14 June 1790
in Laurens Co., S.C., bur. at Warrior Creek Church, Gray Point,
S.C., m. 25 Dec 1766 in Granville Co., N.C. to Mary Elizabeth Ann
Penn b. 16 July 1746 in Caroline Co., Va., d. 2 Feb 1818 in Laurens
Co., S.C.
 Children
Wm. Mitchell b. 15 Jan 1768, d. 25 July 1821, m. Chloe Smith, had
 ten children: Sarah, Nancy, John, Ephriam, William, James, Polly,

Caleb, Benjamin, & Elizabeth [Estate settlement in Abbeville Co.,
S.C. Box 59, pkg. 1398]
Malinda Elizabeth Mitchell b. 20 May 1770, d. 26 July 1842, m. Ben-
jamin Smith, had seven children: Mary, Elizabeth Owens, Sara Jane
Atkins, Permelia Ward, Noah, Mitchell, Zadock, & William [Estate
in Laurens Co., S.C. Box 67, pkg. 1816]
John Taylor Mitchell b. 1 May 1772, d. Oct 1838, m. 2nd to Nancy,
had ten children: Penn, James, David, William, John, Permelia,
Catherine, Nancy Inman, Polly & Elizabeth Neely [Land part. deed
_ Book 0, p. 67 Laurens Co., S.C.]
George Penn Mitchell b. 8 Feb 1774, went to the west
Benjamin Mitchell b. 25 Dec 1775, m. 1st in Fairfield Co., S.C. to
Patsy, m. 2nd in 1808 to Miss ....
Mary Cook Mitchell b. 3 Mar 1777, d. 12 Sep 1838, m. 14 May 1792 to
William A. Putnam, nine children: Mitchell, Abner, Nimrod, Daniel,
William W., Elizabeth Garrett, Ruth Lavinia Thomas, Mary & Martha
[Estate in Laurens Co., S.C. Box 60, pkg. 3, 1860]
Nimrod Mitchell, Jr. b. 6 Aug 1779, living in Fairfield Co., S.C.
in 1800, seven children: Vicci Bell, John, Albert Washington,
Theodosia Lord, William, George, & Dicey Ophelia Bell [Estate in
Abbeville Co., S.C. Box 58, pkg. 1382, 1837]
Ruth Lavania Mitchell b. 1 Oct 1784, d. 15 Jan 1850, m. John Vaughan
seven children: John Jr., & Richard Harrison Vaughan (names of
two known) [Estate in Laurens Co., S.C. Box 107, pkg. 23, 1848]
James Perry Mitchell b. 2 Sep 1786, m. Gracy in Fairfield Co., S.C.,
went to Tenn. in 1823

STEPHEN MOORE

Stephen Moore b. 19 or 30 Oct 1734 in New York City, m. 25 Dec 1768
in Quebec, Canada by Rev. Mr. Montgomery, Chaplain of the King's
10th Regiment, to Grisey Phillips b. 18 Feb 1748 or 49 in Boston.
    Children
John b. Nov 1769 in Quebec
Phillips b. 16 July 1771 in New York City
Frances b. 5 Nov 1773 at Westpoint [N.Y.]
Ann b. 12 Jan 1777 in Granville Co., N.C.
Mary b. 21 Sep 1778 at Mt. Tirzah [N.C. home of Moores]
Marcus b. 27 Nov 1780 at Mt. Tirzah
Portius b. 16 Oct 1785 at Mt. Tirzah
Cadmus b. 30 Jan 1787 at Mt. Tirzah
Samuel b. 15 June 1789 at Mt. Tirzah
Sidney b. 15 Dec 1794 at Mt. Tirzah

[Lt. Col. Stephen Moore came to N.C. & built a home in Person Co.
which he called Mt. Tirzah. He died there 20 May 1799. His wife,
called Grisey in the Bible, was named Griselda. In 1779 he was
given charge of a Regiment of N.C. State Troops. He was in the 1st
Battle of Camden (S.C.). He is the ancestor of Mrs. Mary McIver
Stanford (Mrs. Chas.), Chapel Hill, N.C. who gave this record.
Mary, of this record, m. Hon. Richard Stanford who was b. 2 Mar
1767, d. 9 Apr 1816 while representing N.C. in Congress, bur. in the

Congressional Cemetery. His dates are from the Bible of his dau.,
Cornelia Adaline who m. Alexander Smith Webb.]

WILLIAM HENDERSON MOORE

William Henderson Moore d. Wed., 8 June 1904, m. 5 Oct 1865 to Martha Woodson Criner d. 24 Aug 1875.

Clara Dean Moore b. 23 Aug 1866
Elvalena Moore b. 28 Dec 1868, m. 12 Feb 1890 to Walter Jones
Nancy (Nannie) Eva Moore b. 8 Dec 1871, d. 4 A.M. Wed., 25 Apr
    1900, m. 4 Mar 1897 to John W. Lahtam (Latham)
William Woodson Moore b. 21 June 1875, d. 25 Aug 1875

[This Bible is now in the possession of Pauline Jones Gandrud, a
granddau., Tuscaloosa, Ala.]

FRANCIS CALLOWAY MORGAN

Francis Calloway Morgan b. 2 Oct 1826, m. 3 Feb 1848 to Ann Eliza
Fitzpatrick b. 5 Sep 1828, d. 23 Sep 1890
    Children
Nancy Casandra Morgan b. 24 Apr 1849 [d. 29 Oct 1881], m. E.M. West
    [m. 21 Mar 1872 to Elza Milton West according to West Bible]
William Claudius (Claude) Morgan b. 1 Nov 1850, m. 4 Feb 1875 to
    Caladonia Shead
Jesse Colbert Morgan b. 13 Mar 1853, d. 13 Jan 1863
Fannie Ida Morgan b. 7 Aug 1855, d. 11 Aug 1856
Thomas J. Morgan b. 3 July 1857
Linzy Morgan b. 8 June 1860, d. 1 Nov 1869
Georgia Virginia Morgan b. 5 Jan 1865
Charley Augustus Morgan b. 14 Jan 1867
Frank Basil Morgan b. 29 June 1872

William C. Morgan d. 17 May 1862 [father of Francis Calloway Morgan]
Jesse Fitzpatrick d. 14 Feb 1865 [father of Ann Eliza Fitzpatrick]
William O. Morgan d. 4 Feb 1871 [son of William Colbert Morgan &
    brother of Francis C. Morgan]

[Copied by Mildred Dulaney from a photostat of a Bible owned by
Claudia Morgan Thompson, Fort Worth, Texas.]

WILLIAM COLBERT MORGAN

Wm. Colbert Morgan b. 4 Mar 1794, d. 17 May 1862, m. 1 Apr 1819 to
Lucinda Morgan b. 15 Jan 1797.

W. O. (Wm. Oglesby) Morgan, son of Wm. Colbert & Lucinda (Oglesby)
Morgan, b. 22 Feb 1820, m. Susan B. Morgan b. 8 July 1836, their
son: Leonidas Morgan m. Rebecca Hambrick

[Bible owned by May Clonch, Waco, Tex. There are other records in

226

this Bible but they were not copied because no connections were
shown.]

ROBERT MORRAH

Robert Morrah b. 22 Feb 1800 in Abbeville Co., S.C., d. 19 Aug 1856
in Miss., m. Aug 1826 in S.C. to Eleanor Means [dau. of James &
Margaret (Mayes) Means who were from Union Co., S.C. to Abbeville
Co., S.C.] b. 3 Dec 1807 in S.C., d. 1 Oct 1873 in Miss.
    Children
James Means Morrah b. 8 July 1827, d. 6 Nov 1827
Hugh Alexander Morrah b. 2 Jan 1829, d. 19 July 1856, m. Adelaide
    Sinclair, one child: Robert Morrah, d. young
Margaret Ann Morrah b. 17 Apr 1831, d. 3 Aug 1834
William James Morrah b. 3 Sep 1833, d. 6 May 1856, single
John Robert Morrah b. 10 June 1836, d. 18 Mar 1863 in C.S.A., m.
    Sallie Berry, one child: Ella Morrah m. George Stapleton
Thomas Jefferson Morrah b. 22 Sep 1838, d. 26 Oct 1842
Mary Elizabeth Berry b. 13 Feb (or Apr) 1841, d. 23 May 1915, m. 11
    Feb 1863 to Pleasant Bogan Berry (b. 26 Dec 1839, d. 21 May 1926)
Eloisa Viella Jane Morrah b. 20 July 1843, m. Henry Simms Cole
Margaret Ann Morrah b. 18 Apr 1845 [alive in 1940], m. Simuel Lacey
Walter Scott Murray b. 23 Dec 1847, d. 5 Sep 1853
Ellen Jane Morrah b. 15 July 1850, d. 8 Nov 1853

    Grandchildren
Willie Eleanor Berry m. 16 Feb 1882 to Parham Blackburn Bridges b.
    15 Apr 1850, d. 21 May 1926, children:
        Pleasant Burton Bridges m. Mai Tomlinson, children: Eleanor
            Bridges m. Talbot Steel and Elizabeth Bridges m. John Steven
            Miller
        Robert Walker Bridges m. Ava Pierson, children: Ruth Bridges
            m. Earl Sparkman and Robert Walker Bridges, Jr. m. Frace
            Aasland
        Bessie Bridges m. Verne D. Calloway
        Mabel Eleanor Bridges, single
        William Parham Bridges m. Isabel Bratton
Margaret Viola Berry m. 16 Mar 1885 to Dr. Enoch Knox White, M.D.,
    children:
        Walter Henry White m. Hazel Ware, two children: Knox White &
            Neal White
        Berry White, single
Robert German (Berman) Berry m. 1st on 1 Dec 1890 to Unie Barnes,
    children: Cortex Barnes Berry, Maggie Morrah Berry, Marie Berry,
    Enoch Knox Berry, & William Pleasant Berry; m. 2nd on 15 June
    1904 to Hattie Belle Didlake, children: Phillip Hunter Berry, &
    Robert German Berry, Jr.
John Morrah Berry m. 29 Sep 1897 to Annie Bell, children: Raimund
    Berry, Curry Bernard Berry, Rodney Curtis Berry
Mary Pleasant Berry m. Benjamin Sylvanus Waller, M.D., Children:
    Mary Nell Waller who m. Irving McDonald & John William Waller who
    m. Doris

227

Children of Eloisa V. J. Morrah & Henry Sim(m)s Cole of Miss.
Mary Lillian Cole m. Robert Burns, children: Wallace Cole Burns m.
Anna Archer; Viola Burns m. W. Edward McIntyre; Robert Burns, Jr.
m. Hortense Inman
Sallie Berta Cole m. Henry S. Shields, children: Sallie Cole
Shields m. Thomas Berry Dickson; Harry B. Shields m. Marian
Baker; Albert Shields m. Ethel
Inez Viola Cole m. W. Henry Barnes, child: Inez Barnes m. George
Watson
John Simms Cole m. Eula Noble, child: James Clifton Cole m. Betty
Eastland

Children of Margaret Ann Morrah & Simuel Lacey
Bonnie Lacey m. Walter Berry, children: Lacey Berry, Clifton Berry,
Pleasant Berry, J. W. Berry
Berta Lacey m. Ernest Cox
Ernest Lacey d. single

[This family moved circa 1835 from Abbeville Co., S.C. to Ala. &
later to Miss. This data copied from the Big Bible of Robert
Morrah by great granddau., Mabel Eleanor Bridges, 810 Euclid Ave.,
Jackson, Miss. Hugh Morrah of Abbeville Co., S.C. and his second
wife, Ann Richey, widow of George Wilson, were the parents of Robert Morrah, their only mutual offspring. The Mississippi data was
given by the Cole family to their cousin, Mabel Eleanor Bridges.]

JOHN MORRIS

John Morris b. 2 Nov 1780 in S.C., m. 8 Apr 1807 in S.C. to Drucil-
la Earp b. 15 Aug 1789 in Ga.
    Children, all b. in S.C.
William Oliver Morris, son, b. 16 Jan 1808, m. Sarah Nevans "late
in life"
Clarissa Ann Morris, dau., b. 4 Dec 1809, m. 4 Oct 1844 [husband's
name not legible]
Susan Wiley Morris, dau., b. 13 Nov 1811, m. 13 Nov 1833 in S.C. to
John (B.) Thomas
Waddy Earp Morris, son, b. 12 Oct 1813, d. 25 Mar 1814
Harriet Jane Earp Morris, dau., b. 18 Sep 1815, d. 2 Nov 1815
Eliza Jane Morris, dau., b. 29 July 1817, m. in 1841 to John Germany
Robert Andrew Morris, son, b. 13 Jan 1820, m. in 1853 to Lucinda
Wedgeworth
Martha Elizabeth Morris, dau., b. 13 Feb 1823 m. James N. Germany
Margaret Lennie Morris, dau., b. 13 Feb 1829, m. in 1846 to George
Washington Park Dennis

William Morris, Esq. b. 30 June 1783 in S.C.

[Last names without dates added by Mrs. Joseph D. Lyons, 135 Wood-
land Circle, Jackson, Miss. whose family owns this Bible which was
taken from S.C. to Neshoba Co., Miss. circa 1835.]

DAVID MORROW

David Morrow m. Priscilla Dougherty, dau. of George & Priscilla Goforth Dougherty.
   Children
Rebecca Hunter b. 12 May 1801
Wm. Isaac Irvine b. 27 Nov 1802
Eliza Dougherty b. 4 May 1804
Priscilla Clemens b. 21 Jan 1806
George Dougherty b. 26 Feb 1808
Martha Jane C. b. 6 Dec 1809
Caroline M. H. b. 16 May 1811
Nancy Ann R. b. 8 Jan 1813
Rachel Emmeline R. b. 2 Dec 1814
Mary Cassandrae M. b. 26 June 1816
Penelope I. b. 1 Mar 1818
John T. B. b. 12 Apr 1820
Eglantine E. L. b. 18 Oct 1822
Augusta Letitia b. 24 Apr 1824

[Sent by Mr. E. B. Acuff, Moultrie, Ga.]

GEORGE WASHINGTON MORROW

Geo. Washington Morrow b. 26 June 1798, m. 28 Aug 1828 to Eliza Janette Graves b. 24 June 1813.

William Henry Morrow b. 23 June 1829
Selina Adelaide Morrow b. 25 Apr 1830
Elijah Graham Morrow b. 8 Nov 1832

Elijah Graves m. 5 May 1812, m. Arianna Stanford

Cornelia Mebane Graves b. 8 Aug 1814
Richard Stanford Graves b. 27 July 1816

[This record given by Mrs. Mary McIver Stanford (Mrs. Chas.), Chapel Hill, N.C.]

DRURY VAUGHAN MOSELEY

Drury V. Moseley b. 13 [18?] July 1820, d. 24 Sep 1868, m. 15 Jan 1845 to Mary Ann Minor b. 22 Sep 1827.
   Children
Fanny Temperance b. 31 Mar 1846, m. 23 Jan 1867 to Geo. G. Roop
Wm. Minor b. 9 Oct 1849
Mildred Washington b. 13 Dec 1851, d. 5 Aug 1855
Edward Drury b. 16 Mar 1854, m. 11 Dec 1883 to Helen J. Baker
Louisa Lile b. 23 June 1856, m. 19 Dec 1882 to Geo. G. Roop
Lucy Washington b. 13 Sep 1858, d. 19 Jan 1863
Lucian Minor b. 30 July 1861, m. 18 Dec 1884 to Laura Foote Bouldin
Maria Lancelot b. 1 Dec 1863, m. 12 Jan 1886 to Hampton Graham

Annie Vivian b. 9 July 1866
Drury b. 19 Dec 1868

Mary Annie Roop d. 26 Aug 1875
Lucy Margaret (Washington) Harris d. 30 July 1861

[Bible owned by Mrs. Rayburn Neville, Trinity, Morgan Co., Ala.]

WILLIAM MOSELEY

Wm. Moseley b. 3 June 1776 in Charlotte Co., Va., d. 12 Dec 1830,
m. Temperance Vaughan b. 9 Aug 1783 in Mecklenburg Co., Va., d. 11
June 1864
    Children
William b. 24 Aug 1810 in Bedford Co., Tenn.
Edward b. 19 Aug 1812 in Bedford Co., Tenn.
Hillery b. 16 Feb 1815 in Bedford Co., Tenn.
John Patrick b. 13 Oct 1816
Drury Vaughan b. 18 [13?] July 1820 near Decatur, [Morgan Co.] Ala.
Sallie b. 30 Aug 1825 near Decatur, Ala.

"Grandfather Moseley came from Va. in 1808. Stopped in Bedford
Co., Tenn. and later came to Madison Co., Ala. At the request of
Gen. Garth he came on to Morgan Co., Ala. Col. Lane who died in
Colbert Co., Ala. selected the place in which he settled [Moseley
settled] and where he died."

[This Bible is owned by Mrs. Rayburn Neville, Trinity, Ala. who was
nee Mary Moseley and a direct desc. of Wm. Moseley.]

JOHN MOYERS

John Moyers, son of James, b. 30 Jan 1792, d. 13 Nov 1875, m. Thurs-
day, 15 Oct 1812 to Mary Snoddy, dau. of Thos. Snoddy, Esq., b. 15
July 1790, d. 8 Nov 1861.
    Children
Melinda Mathews b. 23 July 1813, d. 1 July 1817
Hannah Davis b. 23 Dec 1814
Jas. Alexander b. 21 Aug 1815, d. 18 July 1819
Thos. Snoddy b. 30 May 1818
John Newton b. 12 Mar 1820, d. 26 Jan 1892
Andrew Emmous b. 1 Jan 1822
Mary Blackburn b. 25 Oct 1823
David Henry b. 12 Nov 1825
Susannah Jane b. 9 Jan 1828
Melcena Lausden b. 23 May 1830
Narcissi Ann b. 10 Feb 1834

[Sent by Mr. E. B. Acuff, Moultrie, Ga. He had it from Mrs. Irene
Myers Rogers, Murfreesboro, Tenn. John Moyers had all his children
spell their name Myers, according to Mr. Acuff. The family Bible
was given to Newton Myers by his father John when he died. At New-

ton's death, it went to his dau., Lenora Myers Hill, Mrs. Frank Hill. In 1912, when the Bible was copied, Mrs. Hill was alive & had it. Her son, Newton Myers Hill of Portland, Tenn. had it once. Mr. Hill does not have it but thinks his sister, living in Calif. does have it, according to Mr. Acuff.]

STEPHEN MULLINS

Stephen Mullins b. 31 Oct 1760, m. Apr 1792 in Laurens Co., S.C. to Dorcas b. 12 Apr 1775, d. 25 Aug 1842.
    Children
Samuel b. 22 Dec 1792
Hosea b. 19 Apr 1795
Nancy b. 17 Feb 1797
James G. b. 2 Dec 1798, d. 19 July 1829
Mary S. b. 13 Nov 1800
Dianna b. 15 Aug 1802
Mauldin b. 5 Apr 1804
Elizabeth b. 26 Nov 1806
Martha b. 1 Apr 1810
Julia F. b. 25 May 1813

[This Stephen Mullins d. in Blount Co., Ala. 17 May 1833. He had fought in the Rev. War from Charlotte Co., Va. This record was sent some years ago to the compiler.]

WALDEMAR MURFF

Waldemar Murff b. 31 Aug 1818, d. 11 Mar 1899, m. 1st on 3 Oct 1843 to Elizabeth Jane Medlock b. 3 Feb 1824, d. 27 July 1849, m. 2nd on 24 Feb 1853 to Mary Malinda Burdine b. 19 May 1832, d. 1869, m. 3rd on 13 June 1871 to Elmina Jane Watson d. 12 Aug 1900.
    Children
James Randell b. 21 Apr 1845
Connell ONeal b. 5 May 1847
Lorenzo Burdine b. 25 Dec 1853
Theodore Belton b. 27 Oct 1855
Henry Walton b. 6 Oct 1859
John Wesley b. 4 Jan 1863
Charlotte Elizabeth b. 10 Aug 1867
Martha Elvira b. 1 Apr 1872

[This Bible owned by Mrs. Velda Renfro, Rt. 2, Aberdeen, Miss.]

DANIEL MURPHREE

Daniel Murphree, son of the Rev. Soldier Solomon Murphree, b. 9 Oct 1781 in Pendleton Dist., S.C., d. 4 Mar 1851 in Blount Co., Ala., m. 16 Sep 1802 to Pheraby Bynum.
    Children
Solomon b. 28 Aug 1805
Jesse b. ... 1806

James b. 28 May 1808
Barzillia b. 13 Apr 1811
Caleb b. 16 Dec 1812
Patsy b. 9 Apr 1815
Levi b. 12 Aug 1817
William B. b. 6 Dec 1820

[This Bible is owned by Mr. Joe Murphree, Oneonta, Ala., copied by
Ernest Allen Connally, Waco, Tex. in 1948. Mr. Connally is a desc.
of the Rev. Soldier, Solomon Murphree, Sr.]

SOLOMON MURPHREE

Children of Solomon Murphree
Rebecca b. 22 Dec 1779, m. Rev. Asa Bynum
Daniel b. 9 Oct 1781, m. Pheraby Bynum
Mary b. 12 Oct 1783, m. Benj. Easley
Edith b. 8 Feb 1786, m. ... Stephens
Rhoda b. 17 Jan 1788, m. John Bynum
Marian b. 21 Nov 1789, m. Warham Easley
Hannah b. 25 Aug 1791, m. Jesse Ellis
Elizabeth b. 7 Nov 1793, d. single
Sarah b. 17 May 1796, m. William Faust

[Solomon Murphree was born in 1752, was a Rev. soldier, lived in
Pendleton Dist., S.C., moved to Tenn. & finally to Blount Co., Ala.
Murphree's Valley is named for him. He organized Mt. Moriah Baptist Church, 10 miles northeast of Oneonta, Ala. in 1822. He died
near Anniston, Ala. in 1848. The name of his first wife is unknown.
By a 2nd wife, Solomon Sr. had a son, Solomon, Jr. The Bible is
owned by Mr. Joe Murphree, Rt. 3, Oneonta, Ala. It was copied by
Ernest Allen Connally of Waco, Tex. who is a desc. of Solomon Murphree, Sr. E. A. Connally is now professor in the school of archi-
tecture at the University of Ill.]

ALEXANDER MURPHY

Alexander Murphy, son of Edmund & Nancy Rhodes Murphy, b. 18 Apr
1801, d. 24 Dec 1875, m. 1st on 23 Jan 1823 to Miss Elizabeth Allen, dau. of Robert Allen, d. 2 Sep 1825, no children, m. 2nd on
15 Nov 1827 to Miss Eliza Kinlow, d. 19 June 1843, m. 3rd on 3 Mar
1844 to Mrs. Henry Seaborn Jones [Margaret Torrance], d. 6 Nov 1867
aged 64 yrs., 3 mos., 12 days.
    Children
Sarah J. Murphey b. 11 July 1829, d. 1 Nov 1833
Frances S. Murphey b. 2 Apr 1831, d. 30 June 1866, m. Thomas Jones
Robert Allen Murphy b. 12 Mar 1833, m. 1st to Grace Jones, m. 2nd
    on 15 Oct 1856 to Henry Seaborn Jones [She was formerly named
    Henrietta but took the name of Henry upon the death of her father]
Alexander Murphey, Jr. b. 15 Aug 1835
William Rhodes Murphy b. 5 Nov 1836, m. 15 Oct 1856 to Sarah Jane
    Jones

Margaret Torrance Murphey b. 5 Feb 1845, m. 20 Dec 1877 to William
   Warnock
Caroline Eliza Murphey b. 14 Aug 1846, d. 2 Oct 1866

[This Bible was published in 1832 and is now in the possession of
Miss Murphey of Hepzibah, Ga. It was copied by Mr. Jack Ladson,
Jr. of Moultrie, Ga. The notes in square brackets are by Mr. Lad-
son. He adds that the book LOST ARCADY is in error when it says,
"Alexander Murphy wed first to Eliza Kinlow but had no children by
her. He next married Elizabeth Allen and had five children by her."
The Bible shows the book to be in error.]

MARK MURPHY

Mark Murphy, son of Simon Murphy ("Simon Murphy who married Sarah
Duke, was the son of Richard and Mary Byrd Murphy" penciled in on
a piece of paper.) and Sarah Duke Murphy, b. 8 Mar 1753 in Craven
Co., S.C. on Padgett Creek, m. 19 Mar 1786 six miles from the city
of Union to Holly Duke b. 27 Feb 1769 in N.C.
      Children
Demaris Jackson b. 8 Apr 1787
Simon P. b. 6 Jan 1790, m. 26 Sep 1811 to Rebecca Harris b. 14 Sep
   1792
Mariona b. 20 Oct 1792 "married Thomas Cooper and when she died
   Thomas Cooper married her sister Sarah Murphy" (penciled in)
John M. b. 2 Mar 1792 [?]
Joseph P. b. 3 Feb 1795
William P. b. 26 Nov 1800
Sarah b. 31 Jan 1803
Jeremiah b. 3 Mar 1805 ... Jeremiah B.
Elizabeth b. 1 June 1807
Emanuel b. 15 Sep 1809
Lemuel Majors b. 4 Oct 1812

"Mark Murphy, his Bible,/ God give me grace herein to look/ Not
only to look, but to understand,/ For learning is better than house
or land"

SAMUEL MUSGROVE

Samuel Musgrove b. 1747 in Lancaster Co., Pa., m. 10 Sep 1767 in
Pa. to Eliz. b. 1750.
      Children
Huldah b. 10 June 1768
Moses b. 8 May 1770
Mary b. 22 June 1772
Saml. Davies b. 22 Mar 1775
David b. 23 Nov 1776
Margaret McDugle b. 17 June 1780
Elizabeth b. 25 July 1781
Sarah b. 21 Nov 1783
William b. 19 May 1788

Ann b. 19 Dec 1790

[One record has a James b. 14 Mar 1779 and another child, Jane b. 9
Feb 1885. The same record indicates that wife, Eliz. was a Brand.
Saml. Musgrove was in the Rev. War. He died 2 Sep 1834. Eliz.,
widow, applied for a pension, aged 93 on 30 Jan 1843. See pension
dosier W 9211 by Dr. Gaius Brumbaugh, pp. 67-68 Natl. Gen. Soc.
Quarterly, June 1946.]

WILLIAM H. MUSGROVE

Wm. H. Musgrove, son of W. G. & Nancy Musgrove, b. 15 Jan 1796, m.
Sally, dau. of John & Lucy Fowler, b. 28 Feb 1802.
   Children
Polly Nourainhie [?] b. 23 Nov 1822, m. Jacob W. Pullen
Jan Kaphiro [?] b. 16 Dec 1823
Lucintha Margaret b. 11 Dec 1825, m. Melton or Milton B. Pullen
A. E. [dau.] b. 11 Jan 1828
Sally Selemina b. 1830, m. John Adams
Martha Maria, dau., b. 1832
Virginia LaFayette, dau., b. 2 Oct 1835
Wm. Whitaker b. Feb 1834, d. Sep 1834
John Fowler b. 16 Apr 1838
Lucy Williamina b. 1840

[This family lived in Blount Co., Ala. in 1850 census. They were
from S.C. The Musgroves were a wealthy & prominent family in S.C.
before the Rev. War. Two brothers were Tory Colonels. Robert Mc
Donald Lester, husband of the compiler, is a desc. of John Musgrove
who was a patriot, through his dau., Jane, who m. Chas. Lester.
This record is from Mrs. Inez Cline, Hot Springs, Ark.]

GEORGE MYRICK

George Myrick [of Autauga Co., Ala.] b. 15 Jan 1810, d. 14 Oct 1890
m. 21 Nov 1833 to Nancy M. Temple ([dau. of] Benjamin Temples b. 22
Mar 1777, d. Oct 1843 and Jincy Temples b. 9 Nov 1785, d. May 1833).

William W. Myrick b. 19 May 1836
Joseph B. Myrick b. 21 Jan 1839, d. 11 Jan 1901
Rebecca F. Myrick b. 7 Mar 1843
George A. Myrick b. 14 May 1845, d. 11 Mar 1907
Edward D. Myrick b. 24 Mar 1847
John H. Myrick b. 25 June 1849
Lemuel (Lemual) N. Myrick b. 14 Apr 1852, d. 23 Sep 1879
Nancy E. Myrick b. 9 Aug 1854

William H. Temples b. 9 Aug 1803
Martha Ann B. Temples b. 23 Nov 1806
Uriah A. Temples b. 8 Dec 1808
Henry A. Temples b. 4 May 1811
Nancy M. Temples b. 19 Oct 1814, d. 28 Oct 1892, m. George Myrick

Peter E. Temples b. 15 Aug 1817
Sarah K. Temples b. 6 May 1819
Mary J. Temples b. 12 Mar 1822
Armistead B. Temples b. 26 Apr 1827

Emma N. Myrick d. 14 May 1887

WILLIAM NEAL

William Neal came from Pittsylvania Co., Va. to Franklin Co., Ga. &
is buried at the old Neal place near Sims bridge on the Grove River

Robert Neal, son of William, b. 5 July 1777, d. 23 July 1818, m. 18
Dec 1796 to Tabitha Chandler, dau. of Joel & Jane Chandler, b. 10
Dec 1779, d. 18 Aug 1840.
    Children
William Neal [son] b. 5 Jan 1798, m. 16 Aug 1820 to Lavina Conally
A. Elizabeth Neal b. 1 Apr 1800, m. 26 Aug 1819 to Thomas Bush
Joel C. Neal b. 13 Jan 1802, m. 11 Nov 1829 to Louisa McCluster
Stephen (H.) Neal b. 9 Jan 1804, m. 1st on 3 Jan 1828 to Laura Ma-
    lone, m. 2nd to Polly McWhorter
Mary Hays Neal b. 16 Mar 1807, m. 22 Dec 1825 to Russell T. Allen
Robert Abacrumbie Reeves Neal b. 5 July 1810
Tabitha Caroline Neal b. 12 Feb 1812, m. 3 Mar 1830 to Alfred Smith
Virginia Newberry Neal b. 4 May 1814, m. 16 Aug 1832 to James King
Susan Clementine Neal b. 23 July 1816, m. 1 Oct 1835 to John W.
    Pruitt
Martha Elmina Neal b. 12 Nov 1818, m. 1st on 20 May 1838 to James
    D. Jones, m. 2nd on 5 Mar 1863 to Asa Harper

WILLIAM NEAL

William Neal d. 4 Apr 1835 in Franklin Co., Ga., m. 16 Aug 1821
[See above, note discrepency] to Lavina Connally b. 31 Oct 1803.
    Children
Arminda Elizabeth Neal b. 7 Nov 1822, m. W.B. Burns, Franklin Co.
Lucinda Clementine Neal b. 24 Jan 1825, m. Crawford H. Little,
    Franklin Co., Ga.
Louise Kesiah Neal b. 4 Feb 1827, m. 1 July 1847 to James H. Burns
Thomas Anderson Neal b. 18 Jan 1829, d. 9 Sep 1900, m. Margaret Ash
Tabitha Harriet Neal b. 3 July 1834, m. Wm. Jasper Key, d. 20 Apr
    1868

JOHN OATES NEILL

John O. Neill b. 6 Dec 1836 in Cleveland, N.C. m. 13 Jan 1857
[While res. of Murray Co., Ga.] at the home of John Bain by Uriah
Duncken (Wits: John & Sallie Bain) to Mary Elizabeth Neill [nee
Bain] b. 20 Feb 1837 in Gilmore Co., Ga.
    Children
Edward Newel b. 10 Nov 1858 in Morgan Co., Ala., m. 10 Nov 1880 to
    Nannie E. Johnson

Mary Jane b. 6 Apr 1861, m. 29 Jan 1879 to Chas. W. Brown
Harriet Emma (Emma Harriet) b. 12 Feb 1864, m. Oct 1885 to Elbert
    H. Peck
James Franklin b. 22 Dec 1866 in Lawrence Co., Ala., m. Matilda
    Gurley
Lewis Arthur b. 3 June 1869 in Morgan Co., Ala., m. 25 Oct 1899 at
    Shelbyville, Tenn. to Jessie Dearing
John Brawley b. 28 Feb 1873 in Morgan Co., Ala.
Caty Bascum b. 25 May 1876
Carrie Elizabeth b. 20 Dec 1878

Otie Bascum Neill m. June 1905 to Ina V. Draper

ELISHA NELSON

Elisha Nelson b. 1 Aug 1795, d. 30 Nov 1865, m. Jane Brasher b. 11
Apr 1795, d. 13 Jan 1884.
    Children
Thorisa b. 15 July 1815, d. 11 July 1905
Elizabeth b. 16 Feb 1818 in St. Clair Co., Ala.
Sylvanus b. 29 June 1820, d. 20 Aug 1820
Simpson b. 19 June 1822 in Shelby Co., Ala., d. 16 Sep 1889, m. 16
    July 1843 to Nancy Elliott
Francis A. b. 25 Dec 1824, d. 4 May 1897, m. Paralee Elliott
Hardy S. b. 13 Nov 1827, d. 28 June 1901, m. Sarah Ann Elliott
Henry B. b. 5 May 1830, killed at the siege of Vicksburg in 1863,
    m. 16 Jan 1851 to Adelia Griffin
Wm. Danl. b. 16 May 1833, d. 22 Aug 1867, m. 1 June 1851 to Albana
    Hearne
Ellender Paralee b. 13 Apr 1835, d. 18 Jan 1918, m. 23 Mar 1854 to
    D. M. Clower
Mary Jane b. 19 June 1839 in Ashley Co., Ark., d. 14 Jan 1884, m.
    Jerry Avery

ROBERT WHITAKER NELSON

Robert Whitaker Nelson b. 10 July 1857 in Columbia, S.C., d. 5 Oct
1935 in Shreveport, La., m. 15 Sep 1878 in Society Hill, S.C. to
Hannah Barton Kirven b. 1 Jan 1856 at Society Hill, S.C., d. 28 Oct
1928 at Shreveport, La.
    Children
Robert Clyde Nelson b. 29 June 1880, d. 15 June 1929 [m. Edna Dur-
    ham]
Ross Barton Nelson b. 7 Oct 1882, d. 16 June 1941 [m. Florence
    Scott]
Raymond Allison Nelson b. 25 Dec 1884, d. 4 June 1944 [m. Ethel
    Scott]
Russell Edward Nelson b. 5 Sep 1885, d. 2 June 1944 [m. Kate Custer]
Maude Winston Nelson b. 7 July 1887 [m. 13 Mar 1905 to M. Judson
    Scott]
Lucille Whitaker Nelson b. 18 Mar 1889 [m. Hayes McCray]
James Malcolm Nelson b. 10 Sep 1890, d. 13 Mar 1948 [m. Lois Curtis]

SIMPSON NELSON

Simpson Nelson. Nancy Elliott b. 12 July 1827 in Tenn., d. 15 Feb 1900.
    Children, b. in Shelby Co., Ala.
Jas. Hardy b. 14 Apr 1844
Nancy Jane b. 3 Jan 1846
Elizabeth & Wm. Danl. b. 21 Mar 1848
Amos E. b. 20 Oct 1850
Mahaly Ann b. 17 Mar 1853
Wiley Thos. b. 16 Jan 1855, d. 22 June 1935 in Union Parish, La.,
    m. 15 Dec 1899 in Union Parish, La. to Ida Henry Griffin
John M. b. 12 Jan 1856
Charles M. b. 20 Feb 1860
Francis T. b. 19 June 1863
Mary Lenora b. 28 Feb 1865
Simpson Elliott b. 12 Aug 1867

[This Bible record was sent to the compiler because of Jane Brashear who m. Elisha Nelson. We are sure that it is authentic.]

ALEXANDER NeSMITH

Alexander NeSmith b. 23 Feb 1779, m. 1st to Jennie (Martin) NeSmith b. 9 Nov 1777, m. 2nd on 11 Nov 1823 to Nancy Roberts b. 1 May 1800.
    Children
Thomas NeSmith b. 12 Dec 1802
Martha NeSmith b. 31 Mar 1804
Jennie NeSmith b. 24 Oct 1805
Robert Martin NeSmith b. 10 May 1807
William NeSmith b. 19 Mar 1809
John Brison NeSmith b. 25 Dec 1812
Elizabeth NeSmith b. 14 Oct 1814
Rachel NeSmith b. 23 June 1816
Dorcas NeSmith b. 11 July 1818
Alex. NeSmith, Jr. b. 5 Aug 1820
Isaac NeSmith b. 31 Aug 1824
Oliver Perry NeSmith b. 11 May 1826
Benton NeSmith b. 13 Feb 1828
Caroline NeSmith b. 10 Nov 1830
Francis Marion NeSmith b. 10 May 1833
Eliza NeSmith b. 22 Nov 1836
Sam Houston NeSmith b. 15 Apr 1838
Malinda Burleson NeSmith b. 5 May 1840

[This Bible record was copied by the compiler from a copy of the Bible owned by Mrs. John Henderson of Moulton, Ala. Henry Benton NeSmith of Lufkin, Tex. wrote a short family history in 1921 and has in it a copy of the same Bible record that was owned by his

father, Benton NeSmith, who moved to Ark. after the Civil War &
later to Okla. Alex. NeSmith wa the 3rd son of Thomas & Jennet
(Robeson) NeSmith who were originally from Pa. They m. in Mecklenburg Co., N.C. & settled in York Co., S.C. before the Rev. War.
Thos. fought in the Rev. War in S.C. (Dec 1955)]

JAMES NESMITH

James NeSmith b. 31 Jan 1774, d. 20 Sep 1835, m. Elizabeth b. 7 Mar
1773, d. 1 Aug 1832.
    Children
James, Jr. d. 11 May 1860
Charles R. b. 3 May 1798, d. 3 Dec 1868, m. 29 Mar 1821 to Patience
    Roberts b. 15 Dec 1802, d. 3 Apr 1876

    Children of Charles R. & Patience Roberts NeSmith
Nancy V. b. 30 June 1839
Nathaniel M. b. 7 June 1837, m. Sarah Palmer
Thomas R. b. 4 Feb 1822, m. Mary E. Carlton
John H. b. 23 Nov 1823, m. 1 June 1848 to Emily Giddings
Elias E. b. 15 Oct 1835, d. 1 Mar 1889, m. 17 Aug 1847 to Elizabeth
    Ann Humphreys
Frances H. C. b. 4 Dec 1827, m. 6 Nov 1859 to Wm. Palmer
James P. b. 26 Oct 1829, d. 12 Dec 1865, m. 8 Jan 1860 to Elizabeth
    Mattox
William D. b. 19 Nov 1831, d. 10 June 1890, m. Rocksey Davis
Chas. H. b. 16 Nov 1833
Mary E. A. b. 5 Mar 1835, m. 15 Sep 1853 to John Palmer

[This Bible is owned by Mrs. Sherrod G. McCall, Moultrie, Ga.
There is more in the Bible but it is of a later date. This James
may be desc. from a John NeSmith who was an immigrant to Charleston,
S.C. ca. 1720.]

JOHN RHEA NESMITH

John Rhea Nesmith b. 10 Oct 1828, d. 4 Aug 1911, m. Pamelia Green-
hill Leigh b. 1826 in Va., d. 1895.
    Children
John Leigh b. 23 Sep 1851, d. 1928 in Fort Worth, Tex., bur. in Mt.
    Olivet Cemetery, m. 1st to Naomi Simmons, m. 2nd to Mrs. Georgia
    Goodwin, widow from Ala.
Mary Elizabeth b. 25 Sep 1853, d. 15 Feb 1926, m. Ben Frank Brit-
    nell of Russellville, Ala., bur. in Mt. Pleasant Cemetery, New-
    burg, Ala.
Robert Henry b. 25 Oct 1855, lived in Dallas, Tex. in 1936, m. Mar-
    tha Williams
James Emmett b. 1 Sep 1857, d. 20 Mar 1919, m. 14 Dec 1880 to Mar-
    tha Counts
William Wallace b. 20 Jan 1860, lived in Bridgeport, Tex. in 1936,
    m. 16 Nov 1880 to Laura Jane Childs
Annie Thomas b. 7 Mar 1863, d. 2 July 1911, m. Pinckney Gargus

George Washington b. 2 July 1867, d. 27 June 1898, m. Evelina Ne-
Smith, his 2nd cousin

[John R. Nesmith was a Baptist minister. He served in the Civil
War under Gen. Roddy. He represented Lawrence Co., Ala. in the
state legislature many years. His son, W. W., represented Lawrence
Co. in both the house & senate of Ala. W. W. 's son, John Rhea,
was a page in the senate while his father was there. John's son,
James Emmett, represented the county after his father & brother
were there. On his 82nd birthday, the Russellville, Ala. paper
carried his picture & an account of his long & useful life. He had
46 grandchildren & 38 great grandchildren at that time. He had 4
sons who were prominent ministers in western states.]

THOMAS NeSMITH

Thomas NeSmith b. 22 Nov 1741 in York Co., Pa. (or raised there),
d. 7 Oct 1814, m. early in the yr. 1770 in Mecklenburgh Co., N.C.
to Jennet Robeson b. 17 Sep 1751 at a place called Brandywine in
Pa. 10 days after the landing of her parents from Ireland, d. 16
July 1821.
    Children, all b. in York Co., S.C.
Dorcas NeSmith b. 8 Apr 1771
William NeSmith b. 2 Dec 1772, d. 4 Mar 1822
Thomas NeSmith b. 22 Nov 1774, d. early in Jan 1785
John NeSmith b. 22 July 1777
Alexander NeSmith b. 23 Feb 1779
Isaac NeSmith b. 10 Oct 1781, d. 10 Apr 1861 in Blount Co., Ala.,
    m. 20 Feb 1806 in Blount Co., East Tenn. to Lettice Sherrell b.
    21 May 1784 in Washington Co., Va., d. 28 May 1857
Mary NeSmith b. 9 Dec 1786

    Children of Isaac & Lettice Nesmith
John Neisbit Nesmith b. Friday, 19 June 1807 in Blount Co., E. Tenn.
    m. 1st 2 Apr 1826 in Jackson Co., Ala. Selina Walker b. 15 Feb
    1810 in the Cherokee Nation, S. W. part, d. 15 Aug 1846 in Blount
    Co., Ala., m. 2nd 6 Apr 1847 Frances M. Low d. 4 Sep 1856 Blount
    Co., m. 3rd 31 Jan 1858 to Rebecca Ann Lancaster
Jennet Robeson Nesmith b. Thursday, 1 Mar 1810 in Madison Co., Ala.,
    m. 11 Sep 1825 in Jackson Co., Ala. to Lewis Copeland
Uriah Sherrell Nesmith b. Saturday, 3 Sep 1814 in Blount Co., East
    Tenn., d. 6 June 1863 in Blount Co., Ala., m. 25 Nov 1834 in
    Blount Co., Ala. to Melinda Killian
Sall(y) Duckworth Nesmith b. 19 May 1819 in Blount Co., Ala., m. 1
    Sep 1836 in Blount Co., Ala. to Daniel Murphree

    Children of John N. Nesmith & Selina Walker
Hannah Sherrell b. 18 Jan 1827 in Jackson Co., Ala., m. 10 Mar 1846
    to Jos. C. McAdams
Eliz. Jane b. 9 May 1828 in Jackson Co., Ala., d. 5 Oct 1830 in
    Jackson Co., Ala.
Lettice Evergreen b. 12 Feb 1830 in Jackson Co., Ala., m. 9 Oct

1849 to Jonathan Howell
Sarah Virginia b. 17 Feb 1834 in Blount Co., Ala., m. 8 Sep 1852 to
    Marion Berry
Martha Alabama b. 12 Dec 1831
Burton LaFayette b. 15 Dec 1836, d. 2 Jan 1839 in Blount Co., Ala.

Mary Elender Nesmith m. 28 Oct 1854 to James Horton
Uriah Washington Nesmith d. 6 Feb 1862 near Mobile, Ala.

[Originally the name was spelled NeSmith in America. In Scotland
where they were originally it was spelled Naesmyth. In the generation of Thomas' children, the spelling became Nesmith. This is one
of the very oldest clans in Scotland. In a history of the ancient
clans of Scotland, that the compiler saw some yrs. ago, this family
is listed as oldest, going back before Robert the Bruce. Once when
the Scottish clans were in one of their numerous wars, a follower
of the King, Robert the Bruce, was being chased by the enemy and
became hard pressed. He rushed into a blacksmith shop and, grab-
ing a hammer, began to hammer on some metal. He handled it so awk-
wardly that the enemy were not taken in. They remarked that he was
Nae smyth. The other version has it that he was called on to mend
the king's armor and made such a bad job that the king remarked that
he was a very brave man but nae smyth. He was knighted by the king
& part of the symbols on the coat-of-arms is a broken hammer.]

THOMAS NESMITH

Thomas Nesmith, oldest child of Alexander & Jennie Martin Nesmith,
b. 14 Dec 1802 in York Co., S.C., d. in 1856 in Lawrence Co., Ala.,
m. 29 Jan 1829 in Roane Co., Tenn. to Elizabeth Roberts [His father
m. 2nd to Nancy Roberts, making father & son, brothers-in-law.]
    Children
Robert Burns b. 10 Nov 1829, d. 29 Apr 1863, m. Elvira Ann Lucinda
    Long, dau. of Solomon Scott Long & Mary Belle Ables, b. 22 Mar
    1833 in Falkville, Ala.
Christopher Columbus b. 1835, never m.
Thomas Benton b. 1832, d. 1897
Alexander b. 1838
Isaac b. 1841
George Bryson b. 1845

    Children of Robert Burns & Elvira Nesmith
Solomon Thomas b. 16 Dec 1852
Walter Scott b. 15 Oct 1854
William Alexander b. 4 Sep 1856
Elizabeth Evelina b. 16 Jan 1859
Mary Ellen b. 16 Nov 1860
Robert Burns, Jr. b. 6 Nov 1862

[This Thomas Nesmith was the grand son of Thos. Nesmith, Rev. War
soldier whose Bible record is above.]

WILLIAM NESMITH

William Nesmith b. 2 Dec 1772, m. Jane Craig b. 20 July 1775
Children
Thomas Henry Nesmith b. 7 June 1796
Polly Erwin Nesmith b. 10 Oct 1797
Wm. Alexander Nesmith b. 14 June 1799
Jenny Robeson Nesmith b. 17 Mar 1802
Dorcas Caroline Nesmith b. 26 Aug 1804
Betsy Bryson Nesmith b. 26 Apr 1806
Isaac Campbell Nesmith b. 5 June 1811

[The above Bible Record was sent to the compiler by Mrs. Johnny
Alda Haefer of Houston, Tex. in 1936. It was taken from her fa-
ther's Bible who in turn had it from E. D. Nesmith of Town Creek,
Ala. who owned the old Wm. Nesmith Bible.]

YOUNGER NEWTON, SR.

Younger Newton, Sr. b. 30 Aug 1763 in Henrico Co., Va., son of
Giles & Eliz. Newton, d. 30 Aug 1847 in Marlboro Co., S.C., m. 178-
[not legible] to Elizabeth Cargill b. 16 Jan 1765 near Roanoke
River, Va., d. 18-- in Marlboro Co., S.C.
Children
Sarah b. 5 Oct 1785, m. 1st to Tristam Parker, moved to Newton,
Ohio, m. 2nd to Mr. Barney in Ohio
Elizabeth b. 4 Mar 1789, m. Saml. Snead & moved to Anson Co., N.C.
Younger, Jr. b. 6 June 1792, d. 20 Mar 1867, m. 1st to Nancy Smith,
m. 2nd to Harriet Covington [marriages added by a grandson of
Newton, Sr.]
Mary b. 19 July 1796, m. John P. Usher
Cornelius b. 25 Dec 1797, d. 9 July 1878 [m. 31 Dec 1818 to Dorcas
Purnell, dau. of Rev. Robt. Purnell, b. 9 Dec 1797, d. 9 Mar 1872]
Benjamin b. 19 July 1799 [went to Ind.]
Julia b. 5 Apr 1802 [d. 26 Aug 1872]
Susannah b. 20 Mar 1804
Daniel Cargill b. 6 Aug 1806 [d. 3 Nov 1857, m. Mary Covington b.
15 Oct 1809, d. 15 Sep 1879]
Giles b. 15 Oct 1815, d. 24 Dec 1890 [m. 11 Nov 1841 to Harriet
Adams b. 7 Dec 1821, d. 19 Nov 1872]

Giles Newton, father, d. 15 Oct 1807

[This Bible was owned by the late Hope Hull Newton, attorney, Bennettsville, S.C.]

JOHN NICHOLS

John Nichols b. 26 Dec 1770, d. 26 Dec 1853, m. 26 Feb 1793 to Han-
nah Starritt d. 26 June 1819.
Children
Mary b. 24 Feb 1795

William b. 7 Dec 1796
Elizabeth b. 1 Feb 1799, d. 26 Nov 1871, m. 21 Apr 1828 to David
   Washington McWhorter (son of John McWhorter who m. 16 Dec 1800 to
   Mary McWhorter) b. 6 Nov 1801, d. 6 Mar 1874
Joanna b. 19 May 1801, d. 16 Mar 1805
John B. b. 1 Aug 1805
Hannah b. 4 Jan 1806, d. 16 Jan 1856, m. Moses E. McWhorter

        Children of David W. & Eliz. Nichols McWhorter
Wm. Pat b. 5 Oct 1830, d. 22 Sep 1812
Theodore E. b. 25 Sep 1833, d. 30 Aug 1863
John Newton b. 12 May 1836, d. 15 Apr 1864
David Starritt b. 1 Sep 1838, d. 22 Dec 1908, m. 1st on 20 Dec 1860
   to Eliza Prickett d. July 1902, m. 2nd on 17 Nov 1904 to Fannie
   Willbanks, no children by either wife

Ambrose Nichols d. 4 Aug 1812
Eliz. Nichols d. 29 June 1819

[From Mr. Davis L. McWhorter, Bethel, N.C. He adds, "This Bible
may have first belonged to the Nichols family. The 1839 will of
John McWhorter is in Pickens Co., S.C.]

                        BURWELL NORWOOD

Burwell Norwood d. Nov 1839 in Trinity, Ala., m. 10 Nov 1810 in Va.
to Elizabeth Glover d. May 1866.
        Children
Julia Norwood b. 21 Sep 1811
William Norwood b. 7 Dec 1812
Benjamin G. Norwood b. 22 Dec 1813
Elizabeth Norwood b. 21 July 1815
James W. Norwood b. 21 July 1816
Burwell G. Norwood b. 12 Dec 1818
Mary Ann Frances Norwood b. 22 Apr 1820
Rebecca G. Norwood b. 12 Jan 1822
John G. Norwood b. 11 Jan 1823
Nathaniel Norwood b. 17 July 1824
Letitia Jane Norwood b. 16 Sep 1826
Henry G. Norwood b. 1 Feb 1828
Richard Weaver Norwood b. 8 Apr 1830, d. Jan 1906, m. 1st on 19 Jan
   1854 at the home of Robert M. White, Moulton, Ala. to Martha C.
   White b. 7 Mar 1833, d. 17 July 1885, m. 2nd on 29 Sep 1886 to
   Susie L. Galey d. 17 Jan 1929; Susie I. Galey b. 12 Mar 1847
Joseph L. Norwood b. 28 July 1832; Joe Lipscomb d. 1 Jan 1886
Martha Jane Norwood b. 30 Mar 1833

        [Children of Richard Weaver Norwood & Martha C. White]
Laura Emma Norwood b. 14 Sep 1855, d. 25 Sep 1857
Anna P. Norwood b. 4 Feb 1857, d. 2 May 1928, m. 14 Nov 1910 to Tho-
mas J. Holland
John Wm. Norwood b. 27 May 1859, d. 10 Sep 1859

Richard W. Norwood, Jr. b. 22 Dec 1862, d. 11 Nov 1933 in Tex., m. in 1885 to Mollie (Mallie) Alexander who d. 25 Mar 1945 in Texas
Ella T. Norwood b. 18 Feb 1865, m. 3 Dec 1886 in Moulton, Ala. to M. B. Rutherford
Thomas E. Norwood b. 13 Feb 1868, m. 22 Feb 1892 at Town Creek, Ala. to Minnie V. Bracken who d. 22 May 1944

Mary Alice Norwood m. 14 Oct 1920 at Wheeler, Ala. to Oscar W. Sherer
Mack Rutherford d. 3 Dec 1939

[Copied by Mrs. Oscar Sherer of Tuscumbia, Ala.]

STEPHEN OATES

Stephen Oates d. 14 Oct 1817; Feriby Oates
        Children
John b. 19 Aug 1784
James b. 17 Oct 1786
Salley b. 16 Jan 1789
Elizabeth b. 14 Apr 1791
Stephen b. 4 Aug 1793
Susanna b. 19 Jan 1796
Carraway b. 18 Oct [page torn]
William b. 7 Mar 1798
Nancy b. 30 Mar 1800
Polley b. 9 July 1802 [might be Talley or Toby]
Wyatt b. 9 Dec 1808

        Children of James Oates & Margaret
Zacharia John, son, b. 18 June 1811
Mary, dau., b. 5 Nov 1812
Matthew, son, b. 20 Jan 1814
Nancy, dau., b. 20 Nov 1815

        Children of James Oates
Lewisa O. b. 22 July 1819
Eliza b. 6 Jan 1821
Eliz. b. 26 Aug 1822
Wm. James b. 19 June 1826
Stephen Westley b. 28 June 1829

John William Oates, son of Stephen Westley & Sarah Oates, b. 21 Mar 1849

        Children of Jesse Hudson & wife Elizabeth
Delilah Hudson, dau., b. 27 Oct 1808 [may be 1803]
Elizer Hudson, dau., b. 20 Sep 1810
Wm. Westley, son, b. 22 Feb 1812 (1813)

        Children of Stephen Oates, Jr. & Temperance Oates
Dicey, dau., b. 4 Nov 1814

Eliz., dau., b. 4 Mar 1816 (1818)
Wm. Dawson, son, b. 27 Oct 18..

Rhoda Oates, dau. of Nancy Oates, b. 17 June 1845

Children of Wyatt Oates: Salley, James, Fanney, Polley

John Carroway b. 23 May (Feb.) 1776
Hillery Carroway b. 5 June 1778. Clary, his wife, b. ...
Lewey, dau. of Hillery & Clary b. 21 Oct ...

Children of James Oates deceased & Sarah Oates
John, son, b. 8 Dec 1753
Susaner, dau., b. 24 Mar 1756
James, son, b. 25 Dec 1757
Saml., son, b. 4 Feb 1760
Wyatt, son, b. 26 July 1762
"Stephen Oates was supposed to be born 2 years after the last date
  above - 1764"

Pherraby Carraway b. 12 Dec 1754
Delilah Carraway b. 10 Mar 1757
Mosis Carraway b. 10 Nov 1770 (?) (1740) [sic]
Maron [Marion?] b. 14 Sep 1773 [Carraway?]

[The following names appear on one page, no dates, relationships.]

John Oates	Elizabet Oates
Saml. Oates	Jesse Oates
James Oates	Jethro Oates
Wyatt Oates	Elizabeth Oates
Stephen Oates	Michael Oates
Susaner Oates	Susaner Oates

"Stephen Oates m. 9 July 1783 to Ferriby Carraway State of N.C.,
More [Moore] Co. - Know all men by these presents that I, Stephen
Oates, am held and firmly bound to Jethro Oates."

[This Bible record was sent by Mrs. Joseph C. Kiger (nee Jean Moore
of Tuscaloosa, Ala.) who is an Oates desc. The Oates family went
to Ala. at some point from N.C. Mrs. Kiger states, "James Oates d.
in Dobbs Co., N.C. in Jan 1766. James & his bros. John & Jethro
were sons of Joseph Oates & wife Elizabeth Wyatt. She was the dau.
of John Wyatt & his wife Rachel Calloway. Rachel was the dau. of
Caleb & Eliz. (Lawrence) Calloway." This Bible was willed by James
Oates to his youngest son Stephen. Photostat copy in Ala. Archives.]

NICHOLAS OVERBY

Nicholas Overby b. 20 Jan 1784 in Va., d. 18 Mar 1868 in Stewart
Co., Ga., m. 10 Jan 1812 in Abbeville Co., S.C. to Mary Hallum b.

3 Feb 1783 in Laurens Co., S.C., d. 4 Nov 1862.
    Children
Basil Hallum b. 19 Nov 1814, d. 27 Nov 1859, m. 1st on 18 May 1837
    to Asenath Thrasher, m. 2nd on 27 June 1854 to E. S. Harrolson
Ann Eliz. b. 12 Jan 1816, m. 3 June 1845 to B. Allen
Benj. Mitchell b. 18 Sep 1818, d. 17 Nov 1891, m. 18 Aug 1841 to
    Lucy C. Seay
John Bayliss Earl (Earle) b. 8 Jan 1821, d. 14 May 1854

Nicholas G. Overby b. 16 Oct 1826
Nimrod W. Overby b. 8 Oct 1827

"I raised three sons to manhood." [Maybe the last 2 are sons who d.
    as infants; they are not grandchildren.]

"I came to Abbeville, S.C. from Va. in 1789. I moved to Ga. in
    Nov. of 1863 " [On flyleaf of Bible.]

"Meshack Overby 1753-1841 lived to be past 90 yrs. ... Married Mary
    Mitchell. I am aged 84. My brother Nimrod Overby lived to be
    85. My brother Benj. Overby lived to be 84. My 1st American
    ancestor was Nicholas Overby 1622-1732 who lived to be 110 yrs.
    He came to Va. from Paris, France. Raised 3 sons: Nicholas, Obi-
    diah & Peter. Bristol Parish Recs. of Va. have some recs. of my
    family."

[This record and notes sent by Leonard Andrea, Columbia, S.C.
Nicholas Overby of this Bible moved from Abbeville, S.C. to Stewart
Co., Ga.]

OBADIAH OWEN

Obadiah Owen d. 14 Nov 1821, m. Martha Ford b. 19 Dec 1783, d. 6
Feb 1873.
    Children
Nancy Owen b. 21 Oct 1802, d. 28 Jan 1853, m. (Dr.) Micajah Estes,
    son: Balus Estes m. Fannie
Elijah Owen b. July 1804, d. 24 Oct 1864, m. Elizabeth Kelly
Jane Owen b. 15 Mar 1806, d. 26 Aug 1893, m. Jesse Martin
John Owen b. 3 Feb 1808, d. 16 July 1883, m. Catherine Owen
William Owen b. 12 Oct 1809, d. 8 July 1885 near Lavonia, Ga., m.
    Tabitha Brewer
    Gr. Children: Oscar, Leila, Coda, Estelle McDonald (Higginbotham)
Kizziah Owen b. 13 Nov 1811, d. 20 Aug 1852, m. 1st to Alanson
    Forbes, m. 2nd to Susan McDonald
Cynthia Owen b. 6 Mar 1814, d. 23 Nov 1882, m. William Brewer who
    d. 2 Mar 1884
Catherine b. 18 Mar 1815
Levisa Owen b. 31 Aug 1818, d. 5 June 1889, m. 28 Feb 1865 to
    Clackson Mize
Joshua Owen b. 18 Mar 1820, d. 24 Oct 1882, m. Drucilla Watson b.
    25 Jan 1821, d. 29 Apr 1909

Saml. Paine b. 28 Jan 1731 in Boston, Mass., d. 1791 there, m. 5
Dec 1757 to Bethiah Gray b. 5 Oct 1737, d. 1820 in Thomson, Maine.
   Children
Saml., Jr. b. 20 Oct 1858, d. 4 May 1821 in Richmond, Va.
Nathaniel b. 18 Aug 1761, d. 1795 in N.C.
John b. 29 May 1763
Joshua b. 3 Sep 1765, d. 5 Sep 1794 in New York
Hannah b. 1769, d. 4 Dec 1824 in Boston, Mass.
Orris b. 16 Aug 1771, d. 19 Oct 1834 near Milledgeville, Ga., m.
   1st to Margaret Hay of Richmond, Va., m. 2nd to E. Catherine
   Weisham
William b. 11 Feb 1773, d. 9 Oct 1777
Snow b. June 1774
Jean b. June 1776, d. 28 Sep 1777
Jean 2nd b. 28 Feb 1778

   Children of Orris Paine & Margaret Hay
Orris
Chas. Joshua, children: Margaret, Mary Anne Baillie, Georgia Vir-
   ginia, Walter Hay, and Thomas Spalding
Jean Moncúre m. Richard Orme
   Children of Orris Paine & E. Catherine Weisham
Wm. m. Nina Smetz
Maria
Lizzie

[Mrs. Cochran sent this Paine Bible record and it is included because many of this family came South & intermarried there. In the
History of Henrico Parish & Old St. John's Church, Richmond, Va.
1611-1904 by J. Stanton Moore, is recorded the marriage of Orris
Paine to E. Catherine Weisham 5 Oct 1816. Vol. XX, page 87, Va.
Magazine of History & Biography mentions that in the Richmond Gaz-
ette of 2 Oct 1805, there appears an obituary of Mrs. Paine, wife
of Orris Paine but the obit. is not given. (1st wife)]

ROBERT ELBERT PARKER

Robt. E. Parker b. 19 Sep 1844, d. 14 May 1903, m. 19 Apr 1865 to
Margaret Ann Pennell b. 19 June 1843.
   Children
Levi Alonzo b. 12 Mar 1866, d. 13 Dec 1929, m. 21 Dec 1892 to Ermie
   Stevenson
John Thomas b. 25 Nov 1870, m. 14 Dec 1893 to Mamie Nelson
Robert Luther b. 17 Feb 1873, m. 16 Oct 1902 to Ida Eliza Nickels
Claudia Keturah b. 17 Apr 1875, m. 9 Feb 1898 to Luther E. Dean
Maggie Lucia b. 31 July 1877, m. 28 Dec 1898 to Luther E. Bowie
Elbert Reese b. 15 July 1879, m. 28 Apr 1904 to Valeria Powers
Ralph Eugene b. 19 Aug 1881, m. 29 Nov 1904 to Olivia Celestia
   Pearman
Annie Larrimer b. 28 June 1887

[This Bible was taken from Anderson Co., S.C. by Robert E. Parker
to Atlanta, Ga. It was owned by his son, Ralph E. Parker, Atlanta.]

DAVID PARKS

David Parks b. 5 Feb 1797, d. 13 June 1873, m. 1st on 1 Feb 1827 by
Rev. John Williamson to Anne A. Orr b. 28 Nov 1803, d. 10 Sep 1835,
m. 2nd on 11 July 1837 by Rev. Abner I. Levenworth to Anne Chambers
Locke Byers who m. 1st on 13 Apr 1824 by Dr. Jas. McGee to Washing-
ton Byers.
    Child
Mary Adeline Emily b. 21 Feb 1835, d. 1 July 1858, m. 18 May 1852
    to Ebenezer Nye Hutchison
        Their children
David Parks Hutchison b. 6 Mar 1853
Adam Nye Hutchison b. 26 Aug 1854, d. 18 May 1858
Wm. Sylvanus Hutchison b. 27 July 1855, Wilmington, N.C.
Mary Adeline Hutchison b. 2 June 1858, died same day.

HENRY PARKS, SR.

Henry Parks, Sr. b. 16 July 1809 in Randolph Co., N.C., d. 24 Nov
1868 in Weakley Co., Tenn.; Susan Stout Parks b. 8 Mar 1818 in N.C.,
d. 9 Jan 1882 in Weakley Co., Tenn.
    Son
H. S. Parks b. 5 Jan 1852 in Tenn., d. 1 Nov 1929 in Springtown,
Tex., m. 21 Jan 1874 in Weakley Co., Tenn. to L. Frances Edwards b.
13 Dec 1855 in Ark., d. 12 July 1942 in Springtown, Tex.
    Their children
R. E. Parks b. 8 Nov 1874 in Tenn., d. 6 Oct 1875 in Tenn.
J. A. Parks b. 15 Aug 1876 in Tenn. [living in 1954]
Altona Parks b. 7 Jan 1878 in Tenn. [living in 1954]
Minnie Ada Parks b. 24 Nov 1879 in Tenn., d. 8 Mar 1880 in Tenn.
Anna May Parks b. 7 May 1881 in Tenn. [living in 1954]
William Henry Parks b. 9 Feb 1883 in Tenn., d. 5 July 1929 in Tex.
Grover Cleveland Parks b. 11 Feb 1885 in Tenn., d. 18 Sep 1911 Tex.
Mary Susan Parks b. 27 Apr 1887 in Tenn., d. 9 Feb 1922 in Okla.
Winfred D. Parks b. 15 Feb 1889 in Tenn. [living in 1954]
Florence Carvada Parks b. 30 Sep 1892 in Tex. [living in 1954]
George W. Parks b. 8 Feb 1895 in Tex., d. 20 July 1895 in Tex.
Laura Alice Parks b. 8 Feb 1895 in Texas, d. 11 June 1895 in Texas

[Copied by Winfred D. Parks, 27 Jan 1954, Ponca City, Okla. She
says that Florence Carvada Parks m. Dean and is called Vada. The
Bible was in Miss Parks' possession.]

WILLIAM C. PARKS

Wm. C. Parks b. 18 Jan 1821
Celia J. Parks b. 6 Oct 1846
Ellen Virginia b. 7 July 1849
Mary Jane b. 5 July 1847

James Thomas b. 15 Dec 1851
William Charles b. 23 July 1863
Marcus Lee b. 30 Aug 1869
America C. b. 17 June 1854
Cynthia M. b. 22 Aug 1856
Susan Adella b. 21 Apr 1866
Walter Judson Parks b. 8 May 1871
Annie Elizabeth Parks b. 7 May 1874
William Gordon b. 30 Oct 1878
Lillie B. Parks b. 16 Oct 1881
Fred Maynard Parks b. 6 Dec 1884

Wm. C. Parks m. 1 Feb 1865 to Celia J. Young
America C. Parks m. 25 Dec 1873 to Frank B. McMillan
Cynthia M. Parks m. 23 Nov 1875 to S. Marshall Grear
Annie E. Parks m. 19 Dec 1894 in Boone, N.C. to E. S. Coffey
Jas. L. Hemphill m. 4 June 1884 to Alice Ferguson
Jas. L. Hemphill m. 30 Jan 1912 in Wilkesboro, N.C. to Kate McEwen
Carl M. Spainhour m. 31 July 1928 in Green Bay, Wisc. to Emily Rob-
  ertson Palmer
Lettie Spainhour m. 30 Mar 1916 to Peter W. Hamlett
Willie Spainhour m. 10 Aug 1916 in 1st Baptist Church, Morganton,
  N.C. to I. G. Greer
Annie Spainhour m. 17 Mar 1918 to Ernest Walker
Paul Gordon Spainhour m. 6 Oct 1919 to Maud Mast
Sue Spainhour m. 21 June 1929 to Hal Taegue
Walter Spainhour m. 25 June 1930 to Mary Jennings

Marcus Lee Parks d. 2 Nov 1869
Lillie Parks d. 12 June 1885 of scarlett fever
Wm. Gordon Parks d. 24 June 1889 of scarlet fever
Wm. C. Parks d. 23 May 1892 at his home near Mouth of Wilson, Va.
Walter Judson Parks d. 3 Aug 1894 in Boone, N.C.
Mrs. Celia J. Parks d. 12 Sep 1898 at Mouth of Wilson, Va.
Mrs. America C. McMillan d. 15 Aug 1924 in Marion, Va.
Paul Gordon Spainhour d. 18 Mar 1929 in Mt. Alto Hospital, Washing-
  ton, D.C., bur. at Cove Creek, N.C.
Cynthia Greer d. 6 Feb 1939
Kate Hemphill, wife of J. L., d. 27 Nov 1937
R. L. Patton d. 8 Jan 1920
Wm. R. Spainhour d. 1 Sep 1933 in Boone, N.C.

[This Bible is owned by Mrs. Willie C. Spainhour Greer (Mrs. I. G.)
Chapel Hill, N.C. She notes that Wm. C. Parks m. 1st on 21 May
1845 to Louisa F. Porter, m. 2nd on 1 Nov 1860 to Mrs. Susan A.
Camden, m. 3rd on 1 Feb 1865 to Celia J. Young.]

MANN PATTERSON

Mann Patterson b. 29 Mar 1772, d. 28 May 1835, aged 63 yrs., m. 1st
on 20 Oct 1804 to Polly Barbee b. 20 Oct 1784, d. 11 July 1814,
aged 29 yrs., m. 2nd on 25 Feb 1819 to Polly Cabe b. 15 May 1791;

Mary Patterson, wife of Mann Patterson, d. 10 May 1854, aged 62 yrs.
   Children
Sarah b. 23 Oct 1807, m. 8 Jan 1828 to John C. Rhodes
John Tapley b. 1 Nov 1804, m. 25 Feb 1825 to Clementiner H. Barbee
James Newton b. 28 Jan 1806, d. 21 May 1865, m. 1st on 27 Jan 1831
   to Lucy H. (Hawkins) Couch d. 22 Apr 1848, m. 2nd on 27 Jan 1858
   by Rev. Levi Horn to Mary Caroline Barbee
Nancy b. 23 July 1809, m. 19 Nov 1829 in Jackson, Tenn. by Rev. Cy-
   nas Caldwell to Aaron Strayhorn
Amelia Huston b. 9 Apr 1811, d. Sep 1840, m. 29 Jan 1829 to Thomas
   T. Boroughs
Mary Roberson b. 1 Mar 1813
Jane Cabe b. 9 May 1820, d. 19 Dec 1858, m. 5 Jan 1858 by Rev. E.
   Dodson to Henry Whitted
Margaret b. 4 Aug 1822
Catharine b. 14 Aug 1823, m. 22 Sep 1864 by Rev. Geo. Purifoy to
   Nathaniel Bain
Mann Page b. 12 Dec 1824, d. 17 Aug 1875
Rachel b. 23 Jan 1826, d. 2 Mar 1828
William Norwood b. 24 Oct 1828, m. 30 Mar 1859 in Jones Co., N.C.
   by Rev. Thos. Skinner to Mary R. Jones
David Atlass b. 1 Mar 1830, d. 22 Apr 1865 in Salisbury, N.C. in
   the hospital
Robert D. b. 17 Dec 1831, m. 19 Nov 1874 to Annie O'Donnell

Martha L. Patterson m. 10 June 1841 by Rev. Wm. Jones to Benjamin
   D. Rogers
Mary Elizabeth Rogers b. 19 July 1843
Henry Whitted b. 9 Dec 1858
Sarah Yeargain d. 11 Aug 1824 after 13 mos. illness
Jas. H. Patterson d. 9 Oct 1906 [?]

"Mann Patterson His Book 30 Aug 1810"

[This Bible is owned by Mr. David Patterson, Hillsboro, N.C.,
printed 1802, 118 Market St., Philadelphia, Pa. for Matthew Cary.]

                          ISAAC PEARSON

Isaac Pearson b. 10 Nov 1778, d. 21 Dec 1857, m. Elizabeth Cald-
well b. 12 July 1777, d. 17 Aug 1855.
   Children
William Simpson b. 17 Jan 1821, d. 17 Apr 1852
John Henry b. 21 Jan 1809, d. 3 May 1871
Robert Caldwell b. 9 Dec 1807, d. 18 Nov 1867, m. Jane Sophronia
   Tate b. 27 June 1807, d. 24 July 1877
Isaac
Alfred d. in infancy

John Henry Pearson, son of Robert Caldwell & Jane Sophronia Tate
Pearson, b. 24 Aug 1852, m. Florence Louisa Walton b. 16 (11) Aug
1855, d. 18 Mar 1930.

                    Children
Jane S. b. 19 Jan 1880
Clifton b. 4 Nov 1881, d. 15 July 1939
John b. 1883
Florence W. b. 1884
Lucile b. 1886
Marie b. 1888
Eliza b. 1890
Cameron b. 1898

[This Bible record was sent to the compiler in 1952 by Miss Jane
Pearson of Morganton, N.C. She states that the first known ances-
tor is John Pearson, & his wife was Hannah Simpson. They lived in
S.C. Their son Isaac came to Burke Co., N.C. where he m. Elizabeth
Caldwell. The Pearsons & Caldwells were friends in Ireland. An
old record says that the Caldwells who first came to Pa. moved to
Burke Co., N.C. on account of their friendship for the Pearsons.]

                        JOHN PEARSON

John Pearson b. 30 May 1743, d. 25 Oct 1817, m. 21 May 1765 to
Sarah Raiford.
        Children
Martha Pearson d. 2 Nov 1756 (Day of birth)
Mary Pearson (McKamie) d. 19 Sep 1824
John Pearson
Sarah Pearson (Elkin) b. 7 Mar 1773, d. 5 July 1852
William Pearson d. 23 Sep 1795
Philip Pearson
Grace Pearson (Lakin) d. 9 Sep 1881
Judith Pearson (Smith) b. 16 Jan 1785, d. 5 Aug 1840
Nancy Pearson (Mayo) d. ...
Martha Pearson (b. 18 Mar 1778) d. 22 Mar 1807

Judith Elkin (Ruff) b. 1 Aug 1807, d. 12 Sep 1878
William H. Ruff b. 21 June 1847
Eunita Manning Ruff b. 17 Dec
Grace Smith (Stearne) b. 1822, d. Apr 1852
Annie Stearne (Ruff) b. 21 Sep 1864

[Copied from Bible of Nancy Pearson Mayo by Mrs. Mamie Tillman,
Edgefield, S.C.]

                        MOSES PEARSON

Moses Pearson b. 27 Dec 1798; Sarah Pearson b. 21 Sep 1805, d. 7
Feb 1844.
        Children
Rhoda b. 20 Nov 1824, d. 10 Feb 1845
Mahala b. 7 Dec 1827
Timothy b. 25 Oct 1829
Anna b. 2 Apr 1832

Joshua b. 7 Nov 1834
Abram b. 15 July 1837
Nathan b. 7 June 1840
Sarepta b. 30 Dec 184-, d. 1848
Orlando b. 3 July 1846
Hosea b. 24 July 1848
Zimri b. 28 Dec 1850

Eunice Pearson b. 21 Feb 1821 [listed under repitition of Moses's
  name; second wife?]

[Miss Helen Pemberton says that a son Obed Arnold is not listed.]

SAMUEL PEARSON

Saml. Pearson b. 1724, d. 8 Jan 1790, m. 1st to Martha Worthington,
m. 2nd to Christian Potts, m. 3rd to Mary Rogers, m. 4th to Mrs.
Mary Steddom (no children of 4th wife listed)
      Children
Mary b. 26 Feb 1750
Enoch b. 14 Jan 1752
William b. 1 Apr 1754
Martha b. 15 Jan 1759
Benjamin 26 Feb 1763
Hannah b. 23 Mar 1765
Samuel b. 11 Mar 1767
Eunice b. 5 Mar 1770

[From Miss Mary Helen Pemberton, West Milton, Ohio.]

THOMAS PEARSON

Thomas Pearson b. 24 Mar 1728, d. 13 Oct 1820, m. 1st to Ann Powell
b. 6 Aug 1729, d. Oct 1773, m. 2nd to Mary Inscoe Campbell b. 24
Jan 1735, d. 22 Aug 1809.
      Children
Mary b. 16 June 1753
Joseph b. 27 Mar 1755
Ann b. 28 Apr 1759
Enoch b. 27 Sep 1761
Benjamin b. 7 Oct 1766
Thomas, Jr. b. 14 Feb 1769
Samuel b. 5 May 1771
Jonas b. 14 Sep 1773
Rebekah b. 20 Sep 1776, dau. of Mary
Mary b. 23 Sep 1778

[From Miss A. Bohmer Rudd, Washington, D.C. She adds, "For other
data concerning Thos. Pearson, see History of Miami Co., Ohio by
Beers, p. 423. See Newberry Annals (S.C.) by O'Neall part 2, p.
333. Thos. Pearson is buried in Mill Creek Cemetery (Friends),
Monroe Twp., Miami Co., Ohio." In File Case on Wm. Pearson in DAR

Library: William Pearson b. 1754, d. 1800. It is not stated who he is or his connection with this Thomas.]

THOMAS PEARSON

Thos. Pearson b. 27 Mar 1792 in Pa., m. 3 Apr 1825 to Hester Ann b. 31 May 1806.
    Children
Almyra b. 1826
Gatyra Elizabeth b. 1827
Joseph Findley b. 22 Feb 1829, d. 1905, bur. in Eastern Cemetery,
   Louisville, Ky., m. 22 Dec 1850 to Martha Precious Groble, child-
   ren: Harvey, Joseph, William, Anna, Lillie, Ida Belle
"Thomas & Hester Ann had other children"

Thomas Pearson served in the Rev. War. "Served in Waxhaws" [N.C.?]

[Mrs. W. B. Henderson, 9732 Skylark, Garden Grove, Calif. says Thos. had a pension which he applied for in Pa., later went to Louisville, Ky. where he died, and there is a pension record for him in Washington, D.C. She cannot mean this Thomas.]

ROBERT PEEL

Robt. Peel m. Eliza
    Children
John b. 3 July 1840
Wm. b. 1 Nov 1841
Eliz. b. 18 Dec 1843
Rob b. 12 Sep 1845
Jas. b. 4 Oct 1847
Julia b. 18 Nov 1849
Marenda b. 6 Jan 1853
Hepzibah b. 8 May 1855
Henrietta b. 24 Sep 1857
Eliza Jane b. 6 Feb 1863

[From Cullen B. Hatch, Mt. Olive, N.C.]

THOMAS PENNELL

Thomas Pennell b. 1 July 1811, d. 22 Apr 1883, m. 21 Dec 1837 by Rev. E. Pressly to Jane Drake b. 5 Dec 1813.
    Children
Nancy Jane b. 10 Dec 1838, m. 30 Dec 1859 to Benj. F. Pruitt
Mary Elizabeth b. 24 Mar 1841, m. 19 Apr 1865 to Willis C. Pruitt
Margaret Ann b. 19 June 1843
Louise Josephine b. 17 Jan 1846
Martha Clementine b. 18 Nov 1849, m. 23 Jan 1871 to P. B. Griffin
James Robert b. 5 June 1851
Thomas Enoch b. 1854
John Weston b. 18 Oct 1857

```
           Grandchildren
Thos. W. Pruitt b. 21 Sep 1860
Wm. Franklin [Pruitt] b. 7 Dec 1861
Jane E. Pruitt b. 17 Mar 1862
Jane Paralee Pruitt b. 21 Dec 1863
Benjamin Ernest Pruitt b. 23 Dec 1865
Martha Clementine Pruitt b. 8 Mar 1868
Josephine Pruitt b. 29 Sep 1870
```

[This Bible is owned by Mrs. Carl Austin, Belton, S.C. See also the Bible of James Drake above in this vol.]

SIR EDWARD PENNINGTON

Sir Edward Pennington b. 10 Dec 1849 in Newton Co., Miss., m. 3 Feb 1870 by the Rev. Isaac L. Pennington to Sarah Jane Williamson b. 22 July 1857.

```
      Children
Georgia Ann Pennington, dau., b. 27 Mar 1872
Edna Ellas Pennington, dau., b. 18 Nov 1874
Eli Sidney Pennington, son, b. 11 Aug 1876
William Jackson Pennington, son, b. 10 Nov 1879
Martha Ann Pennington, dau., b. 23 Mar 1882
Sir Thomas Pennington, son, b. 1 Nov 1884
Love Ellree Pennington, child, b. 1 Feb 1889
Sarah Lydia Pennington, dau., b. 19 Nov 1892
Mary Lou Pennington, dau., b. 6 Mar 1896
```

[This Bible is owned by the family of Mrs. G. H. L. Dunnagin, 2338 West Beach Blvd., Biloxi, Miss. Old Pennington Private Graveyard in Newton Co., Miss:
"Father" I. L. Pennington 28 Oct 1810 / 17 Jan 1890
"Mother" Martha A. Pennington 3 July 1816 / 1 July 1887
      Children of O.A.J. & Nancy Pennington
Isaac Milford Pennington 22 Dec 1867 / 14 Oct 1876
Martha Alma Pennington (dates not decipherable)
Infant son (dates not decipherable)
      "Grandparents"
Rev. Isaac L. Pennington b. 28 Oct 1810 in Ga.
Martha Ann Humphreys, his wife, b. 3 July 1816 in La.

William C. Williamson b. in 1818 in S.C., d. in Newton Co., Miss. Laney Harris, his wife, d. Sep 1869 in Newton Co., Miss.]

JOSIAH PERRITT

Josiah L. Perritt b. 4 Aug 1825, son of Lewis Perritt; Lucretia Strickland b. 9 Mar 1831, dau. of Rubin Strickland.

```
      Their children
Mary b. 21 Apr 1853
Laura L. b. 23 Apr 1854
Amanda Jane b. 28 Jan 1856
```

Francis Marion b. 6 Sep 1858
Marthy Ann b. 10 Dec 1860
Moliscy [?] Josaphene b. 29 Mar 1863
Leeola Elizabeth b. 23 Feb 1866
John James b. 20 Apr 1868
Josiah Henry b. 4 Jan 1871

EDWARD PERRY

Edward Perry had four sons: Hugh, Edward, Thomas, and Nathan Washington. [Hugh Perry's descendants live in and near Baltimore; James & Roswell are among them. Edward remained in Me. Thomas & Nathan Washington went to Va. & thence to S.C. where Nathan Washington died in 1800.] "Edward Perry was an immigrant to the country of Maryland, St. Mary's City. His father was the only one that ever came to the United States. He had no brothers and two sisters, one of whom married a Cooksey."

Nathan Perry b. 9 Apr 1755, d. 6 Sep 1800, m. Dikander Perry b. 2 Mar 1755.
    Children
William b. 5 Mar 1780
Sarah b. 16 Oct 1781
Phebe b. 27 Feb 1783
Catherine b. 12 Dec 1784
Silas b. 9 Dec 1786
Amos b. 19 Feb 1789
James b. 10 June 1791
Edward b. 2 Apr 1797
Peggy b. 24 June 1799

Grandmother Tear b. 28 July 1729

[Mrs. Hale Houts, 230 W. 61st St., Kansas City, Mo., says that this is not a Bible record but is a record in a religious book calle The Distinguishing Character of True Believers by Mr. Thos. Boston, published in Edinburgh 1791. She also states that the last two children named are undoubtedly by a 2nd marriage. Administration papers on the estate of Nathan W. Perry show his widow to have been named Margaret.]

CAPT. JOSEPH POINDEXTER

Joseph Poindexter b. 1736, d. 26 June 1826, Rev. War Soldier from Va., m. 17 Feb 1763 in Louisa Co., Va. to Eliz. James Kennerly b. 1747, d. 1826.
    Children
Ann b. 13 Feb 1764 [m. John Shelton]
James b. 6 Nov 1765 [m. Mary Thompson]
Samuel b. 29 Dec 1767 [m. 1st to Ann Slaughter, m. 2nd to Sara Garth, m. 3rd to Martha Oley (Otely?)]
John b. 19 Mar 1770 [m. Miss Chilton]

William b. 19 Jan 1772 [m. Judith Thompson]
Joseph [Jr.] b. 19 Feb 1774 [m. Frances Harrison]
Richard b. 13 Feb 1776 [m. Miss Ford]
Thos. Kennerly b. 15 Jan 1778 [m. Mrs. Mary Kennerly, formerly Rall]
Reuben b. 13 Mar 1780 [r.. Sara McIver]
Andrew b. 23 Sep 1783
Elizabeth b. 29 Oct 1785 [m. Raleigh Chilton]
Lewis D. b. 14 May 1790 [m. 1st to Nancy Smith, m. 2nd to Mrs. Mary
   Daniel nee Mary Shelton]

[Capt. Jos. Poindexter is bur. at Naruna, Campbell Co., Va. Miss
Tommie H. Clack, Abilene, Tex. sent data in 1953. She says that
Joseph Poindexter, Jr. of above record had a son Joseph who married
Amanda Jane Blair in 1734 in Bedford Co., Tenn. This third Jos.
was b. 1807, d. 1848. Frances Harrison, wife of Jos. P., Jr. was
born 1784, d. 11 Nov 1811. Frances Harrison & Jos. Poindexter, Jr.
m. 23 Dec 1799 in Halifax Co., Va. Amanda Jane Blair b. 1815, d.
1883. Her people were from Guilford Co., N.C.]

                   REUBEN POINDEXTER

Reuben Poindexter b. 1 Jan 1780, d. 12 Mar 1816, m. 3 Aug 1806 to
Sarah McIver.
     Children
Benjamin L. b. 13 Apr 1807
Elizabeth Jane b. 8 May 1809, d. Aug 1817
Mary Ann b. 22 July 1810
Robert W. b. 18 Oct 1813
James b. 29 Oct 1815, d. Oct 1817

[This Bible record was found in an old trunk belonging to Saml.
Robt. Lester after his death. His mother was Mary Ann Poindexter,
3rd child abovd. Mary Ann m. Alfred Musgrove Lester in Lexington
Co., S.C. They moved to Shelby Co., Ala. in 1837. Robert McDonald
Lester is the son of Saml. Robert Lester & Ann Virginia Watson
Lester. Reuben Poindexter was the son of Capt. Joseph Poindexter
of the Rev. War in Va. He m. Eliz. Kennerly & the Kennerly & Poin-
dexter families of Va. have been written up by many descs.]

                 THOMAS KENNERLY POINDEXTER

Thomas Kennerly Poindexter b. 9 Oct 1785, d. 26 June 1843, m. 8 Dec
1811 to Mary Kennerly b. 13 Aug 1784, d. 23 June 1839

Eliza Ann Poindexter b. 28 Dec 1812, m. 1 Nov 1832 to John Fox
Maria(h) Wesley Poindexter b. 24 Sep 1814, m. 20 May 1844 to H. J.
   Drafts
Mary Ann Poindexter b. 9 May 1817, d. 4 May 1877, m. 24 Oct 1848 to
   Jasper Sawyer d. 12 June 1863
Martha Jane Poindexter b. 17 Apr 1819, m. 7 Nov 1846 to Jas. E. Lee

Amanda M. Fox b. 13 Aug 1833, m. Jacob G. Wolf

Thos. Shelton Fox b. 1 Sep 1836
Mary Jane Eliz. Fox b. 5 July 1839
    Children of Jasper Sawyer & Mary Ann
Amanda Martha Adelaide Sawyer, dau., b. 13 Sep 1849, m. 3 Sep 1867
    to Albert M. Boozer
Mary Eliza Sawyer, dau., b. 20 May 1851, m. 7 Dec 1876 by Rev.
    Clifton to Jacob M. Crim
Maria Josephine Sawyer, dau., b. 25 June 1857, m. 10 Oct 1878 by
    Rev. J. A. Clifton to Wade Leaphart
    Children of Albert M. Boozer & Amanda
Albert Earle Boozer, son, b. 7 Aug 1868
Lemual Thos. Boozer, 2nd son, b. 24 Nov 1870
Baylis Poindexter Boozer, 3rd son, b. 27 Feb 1873
Mary Lavinis, dau., b. 15 Nov 1874
Amanda Antoinette, 2nd dau., b. 18 July 1877
Bessie Pauline, 3rd dau., b. 20 Sep 1879

Albert M. Boozer, son of Lemual Boozer & his wife Carolina, b. 19
    Sep 1843
David Kennerly d. 12 May 1809, m. 1st on 18 May 1803 to Susanna(h)
    Lilles d. 18 June 1806, m. 2nd on 22 Mar 108 [1808?] to Mary Rall
Shearried Kennerly b. 3 Aug 1804
Susannah Kennerly b. 18 June 1806
Reuben Poindexter d. 12 Mar 1816, aged 36 yrs., 2 mos. & 12 days
Saml. Kennerly d. 15 June 1824
Thos. Geo. Sawyer d. 10 July 1863

[Bible owned by Mrs. Mamie Tillman of Edgefield, S.C. See the records of Reuben Poindexter & Capt. Joseph Poindexter, above. Thos.
K. & Reuben seem to be the only sons of Capt. Jos. Poindexter to
have gone to S.C. Reuben m. in Va. to Sara McIver. After Reuben's
death in S.C., she and all her children moved to Shelby Co., Ala.
where she died after 1850. Reuben's grandson Robert McDonald Lester, Sr. built a Methodist church which is still active and is
called Lester's Chapel in Shelby Co., Ala. Reuben's dau., Mary Ann
m. Alfred Musgrove Lester & moved to Shelby Co. where much of his
land is still in the Lester family. The first Poindexter to come
to America was George who had a grant in Glouster Co., Va. in 1653.
Most of the name, if not all, in America descend from this George.
One of his descs. was a vestryman in the famous old Bruton Parish
Church, Williamsburg, Va.]

CHARLES POLK

Charles Polk b. 9 July 1732 in Cumberland Co., Pa., d. 10 Mar 1821
in Mecklenburg Co., N.C., m. Mar 1762 to Mary (Polly) Clark b. June
1744, d. 8 Oct 1776.
    Children
Peggy b. 25 Dec 1764 [m. Wm. Freeman]
John b. 17 Nov 1766 [m. Ester Pool]
Deborah b. 10 Dec 1768 [m. Gideon Freeman]
Thomas b. 28 Feb 1771 [m. Keziah Prior]

Michael b. 20 June 1774
Mary b. 24 Sep 1776 [m. John Brooks, this marriage may be in Bible]

[Mary Polk above m. John Brooks in N.C. & they went to Henry Co., Tenn. in 1826-27. Mary d. aged over 100 yrs. in Weakly Co., Tenn. This Bible record and the added data came from a desc. of Mary (Polk) Brooks, Mrs. Walton of Beulah, Miss. who also states that the following are children of Mary Polk & John Brooks, not necessarily in order: William; Charles; James; John, Jr.; Jesse Michael b. 1802; Cully; Thomas; Naomi; Sally; and Betsy. Jesse Michael, above is the ancestor of Mrs. Walton and she says she found his Bible in Ohio.]

JOHN POMFRET

John Pomfret b. 2 Feb 1720, d. 6 May 1814

Franky Pomfret b. 7 Aug 1747
Mary Pomfret b. 31 Mar 1749
Joseph Pomfret b. 31 Mar 1751
Eliz. Pomfret b. 15 Jan 1753
John Pomfret b. 6 Jan 1757
Ann Pomfret b. 4 May 1759
Amy Pomfret b. 23 Jan 1760-61
Sarah Pomfret b. 8 Jan 1763

[The above John Pomfret was a son of another John Pomfret according to Mr. James Webb of Oxford, N.C. who compiled a book, "Our Webb Kin of Dixie" in 1940. He states that the record of the births of John Pomfret's children was found in an old book, Constitution of the Presbyterian Church, published in 1797. This John Pomfret d. in Granville Co., N.C. Mr. Webb says that John Pomfret's wife was Ann Hunt, dau. of James Hunt, b. 14 Jan 1723, d. 6 Mar 1794, Granville Co., N.C. Copied from Mr. Webb's book by the compiler.]

PHILLIP PORTER

Phillip Porter b. 1 July 1764, m. Mary Smith b. 1769.
    Children
Elizabeth b. 25 Feb 1784
Hugh b. 14 Feb 1786
Rebecca b. 25 Feb 1788
William b. 20 Feb 1790
James b. 20 Feb 1792
Martha b. 5 Apr 1794 [called Patsy]
John b. 20 Mar 1796
Joseph b. 2 June 1798
Baziel [Basil or Bazel?] Smith b. 2 Sep 1801
Job b. 8 Apr 1804
Thomas b. 2 Dec 1807
Mary Ann b. 12 Feb 1814

[This Bible page is owned by Mrs. John Brock, nee Unity Porter, of
Pickens Co., S.C. The marriage & death dates are missing from this
record. Only this page is preserved. L. Andrea notes, "From my
Clayton data, Hugh Porter above, m. Eleanor Clayton. James Porter
above m. Nancy Clayton. From James Porter's tombstone he died 16
Feb 1892, lacked 4 days of being 100 yrs. old. Bishop Francis As-
bury mentions Phillip Porter as a local Methodist minister. This
Phillip Porter founded the Porter's Chapel Methodist Church in
Pickens Co., S.C."]

JESSE HAMILTON POSEY

Jesse Hamilton Posey b. 28 Oct 1782, d. 9 July 1840, m. in 1802 to
Eleanor Brooks b. 13 Mar 1784, d. 7 Jan 1837.
    Children
[Judge] Sidney Cherry Posey b. 4 May 1803, d. 22 Dec 1868 in Flor-
    ence, Ala., m. 14 Feb 1833 in Florence, Ala. to Harriet Calista
    DePriest
Pleasant Milton Posey b. 5 Mar 1805, d. 25 July 1840, m. 11 Oct
    1827 to Caroline Porter
Phares Townsend Posey b. 8 Dec 1806, d. 2 Oct 1841, m. 20 Aug 1828
    to Elizabeth Hutchings
Jesse Hamilton [sometimes Hampton] Posey b. 9 Mar 1809, d. Oct 1878,
    m. 4 Dec 1830 to Sarah Hancock d. 17 July 1840
Madison Bruce Posey b. 6 Aug 1811, m. 11 Oct 1837 in Green Co., Ala.
    to Mary Frances Winston
Wm. Pinkney Posey b. 4 Nov 1814, m. 7 Feb 1837 to Nancy Fluker
John Walker Posey b. 10 Apr 1822, d. 10 July 1840
Albert Percival Posey b. 21 Apr 1825
Rufus Earle Posey b. 26 Feb 1827, d. 1846

    Children of Judge S.C. & Calista Posey
John C. Posey, eldest child, d. 12 Aug 1861, wounded at 1st battle
    of Bull Run
Andrew Huchings Posey, 2nd born, , served 2 1/2 yrs. in Confederate
    Army, was wounded, taken prisoner & d. June 1871 in Chattanooga,
    Tenn.
Mary L. Posey, dau., b. 10 Nov 1843, d. 10 Aug 1906 in Florence,
    Ala.
Rachel A. Posey, dau., b. 4 Oct 1845, d. 7 Aug 1906, m. 16 Dec 1869
    in Florence, Ala. to Dr. Jas. T. Morgan of Murfreesboro, Tenn.

    Children of Dr. Jas. T. Morgan & Rachel
Eugene Morgan d. in infancy
Mary Wilson Morgan b. 8 July 1877, d. 14 Feb 1916, m. June 1906 to
    George Emory Kirkland d. 11 Nov 1936 in Florence, Ala., children:
    1. Emory Morgan Kirkland b. 31 July 1909, m. 23 Dec 1933 to Sarah
    Simms Brewer; and 2. Mary Kirkland b. 11 Dec 1915
Maude Hampton b. 1878, d. Dec 1898 at the Posey plantation, Sunny-
    side, Florence, Ala.

Mary Posey Kirkland d. 11 Feb 1921

Cherry Posey, dau. of Dr. Horatio DePriest, b. 26 Mar 1814

[Mr. Emory Morgan Kirkland who owns the Bible above notes, "The De Priests were from S.C. The Morgans from Tenn. The old plantation home, Sunnyside, was 4 miles out from Florence. While Judge Sidney C. Posey and family were absent the place caught fire and though the slaves tried to extinguish the fire the house burned down and all the fine furniture, silver & books were destroyed." Eleanor Brooks, wife of Jesse H. Posey, was the oldest dau. of Wm. Brooks & Nancy (Cannon) Hudgins who removed to Blount Co., Ala. with all their family about 1818 from Abbeville, Edgefield & Newberry Cos., S.C. Eleanor Brooks & Jesse H. Posey were married in S.C.]

DAVID PRESSLY

David Pressly b. 12 Jan 1764 in Scotland, d. 11 May 1834 in Anderson, S.C., m. 16 Nov 1784 to Ann Edmondston [who was over 82 in 1845 according to pension W-24977].
    Children, all b. in 96 Dist., S.C.
David, Jr. b. 29 Jan 1786, d. 31 Aug 1786
James b. 7 Aug 1787
Mary Ann b. 26 Aug 1789
David II b. 26 Mar 1791
Alex. Edmondston b. 27 Jan 1793
Esther Brown b. 1 May 1795
Jean b. 8 Dec 1796
Jean Miller b. 15 Feb 1798
Elizabeth b. 3 Apr 1800
Agnes b. 17 Mar 1802
Rachel b. 10 Dec 1808

[David Pressly enlisted in the fall of 1776 under Capt. McCawley & served under Gen. Francis Marion & took part in the Battle of Black Mingo. L. Andrea notes, "This was copied from a copy & I do not certify it as in the pension." He adds, "In David Pressly's will he names 4 sons-in-law as: Elijah Willbanks, Lauchlin Johnson, Charles B. Porter, & Richard M. Porter."]

WILLIAM H. PRICE

William H. Price b. 14 Dec 1818, d. 21 Dec 1882; Rebecca Bradley Smith Price b. 27 Jan 1819, d. 6 Apr 1901.
    Children
Julia A. R. Price b. 28 July 1846, d. 1906, m. a Beasley
Margaret Ansedenia Price b. 2 Nov 1847, d. 1866
William Wesley Price b. 8 Oct 1849, d. 16 Dec 1928, m. 27 Apr 1930
    [error?] to Sally E. Stuckey
Lenorah Jane Price b. 18 Nov 1851, d. 19 Mar 1907, m. a Driggers
John Ervin Price b. 17 Dec 1863, d. 17 Dec 1938, m. 1 Nov 1899 to
    Alice Gertrude Stuckey b. 4 Oct 1869, d. 21 July 1938
        Children of John Ervin & Alice Gertrude Stuckey Price
Rebecca Price b. 12 May 1901, m. in 1948 to James O. Hamilton who

d. in 1952, no children
Henrietta Price b. 3 Feb 1905
J. E. Price, Jr. b. 5 July 1906, m. 20 Feb 1938 to Imogene Beasley
   b. 30 May 1916
Rosa Eugenia Price b. 14 Oct 1908
Ruby Eleanor Price b. 20 Nov 1911, m. in 1936 to Jesse H. Gardner,
   no children
       Children of J. E. Price, Jr. & Imogene Beasley
Gertrude Alice Price b. 17 Oct 1939
Ruby Jean Price b. 18 Nov 1940
Patricia Ann Price b. 25 June 1942
John Ervin Price, 3rd b. 9 Nov 1945
Jimmie Marion Price b. 15 Mar 1949

[Copied by Flossie Crouch from Bible owned by J. E. Price, Jr.,
Bishopville, S.C.]

HENRY PURDY

Henry Purdy b. 5 Oct 1751, d. 16 Aug 1816, aged 65 yrs., m. 5 Dec
1786 by the Rev. Robert Hall of Greenville Presbyterian Church in
Abbeville Dist., S.C. to Agnes (Nancy) Richey b. 1761 in Va., d. 28
Apr 1847, aged 86 yrs.

James Purdy b. 3 Sep 1787, d. 22 Dec 1849
Elizabeth Purdy b. 7 Nov 1788
Margaret Purdy b. 21 Feb 1790, d. 23 Aug 1855
Grizella Purdy b. 2 Jan 1792
Ann Purdy b. 6 Sep 1793
Henry Purdy b. 3 Oct 1795
Agnes Purdy b. 5 Jan 1798, d. 29 Sep 1929
Mary Purdy b. 12 Sep 1800
Sarah Purdy b. 7 Sep 1803. d. 14 Aug 1885, m. 1st James Boyd d. 21
   Jan 1840, m. 2nd on 6 July 1843 to Wm. Tucker "From diary of Rev.
   A. Rice."
Jane Purdy b. 11 Feb 1806, d. 3 July 1830
Allah Purdy b. 1 Nov 1808, d. 19 Mar 1812
William Norrel Purdy b. 31 May 1811, d. 16 Aug 1879, m. 21 Mar 1839
   to Mrs. Jane Spillers

[This Bible record is taken from the old Bible now owned by Miss
Hattie Jane Purdy, desc. of Wm. Norrel Purdy, of Iva, S.C. A page
of another Bible was sent to the Pension Bureau in Washington in
1843 by Agnes Purdy when she applied for pension on Henry Purdy's
Rev. War service. This has the exact information as the Bible
quoted above, but it has only the births and marriage of Henry Purdy & Agnes Richey. Agnes Richey was variously called Agnes and
Nancy. In the pension papers she is called Nancy. Henry Purdy was
almost certainly born in Md. He was the first school teacher in
Abbeville Dist. Nancy Agnes Richey was b. in Amelia Co., Va., dau.
of James Richey, Sr. & wife Margaret (Caldwell) Richey. James
Richey, Sr. also has Rev. War record in Va. The compiler is a desc.

of Henry Purdy & Jas. Richey, Sr. The same data is in the family
of Mrs. Leila Richey Mize of Athens, Ga. & Leonard Andrea of Columbia, S.C. The Bible in which this record is found was published in
Edinburgh, Scotland in 1793, printed by Mark & Charles Kerr, His
Majesty's Printers. It has the King's coat-of-arms above the place
and the printers' names. Above that, it says, "The New Testament
of our Lord and Saviour, Jesus Christ, translated from the original
Greek, and with the former translations diligently compared and re-
vised by His Majesty's Special Command. Appointed to be read in
churches."]

SIMEON S. PUTMAN

Simeon S. Putman b. 16 Dec 1815, m. E. Millie Howell b. 11 Mar 1824.
    Their children [?]
Martha L. b. 27 July 1844
Mrs. E. Y. Hollis b. 7 June 1838
David J. Hollis b. 25 May 1859
Margaret Hollis b. 20 Nov 1860
Mary Elizabeth Hollis b. 27 Apr 1862
Silas M. Putman b. 23 July 1850
Hiram A. Putman b. 3 Jan 1852
Sarah E. Putman b. 24 Dec 1855
Mary Magdelene Putman b. 3 Oct 1858

[Note those named Hollis are out of sequence; the connection is not
known to the compiler. The record was given by Mrs. O. H. Putman,
5112 1/2 First Ave., N., Birmingham, Ala. Mrs. Putman states that
this family came into Ala. from S.C.]

FREDERICK BRYAN RAGSDALE

Frederick Bryan Ragsdale [son of Fred B. Ragsdale] b. 24 Nov 1804
in Prince Geo. Co., Va., d. 19 Feb 1851 in Van Buren, Ark., m. 20
Mar 1842 to Julia Ann Brown b. 24 Nov 1821 in Lawrence Co., Ark.
    Children
Mary Elizabeth b. 18 Feb 1843 in Crawford Co., Ark., d. 11 Feb 1872
    in Hays Co., Tex., m. 24 Aug 1864 to Light Stapleton Townsend
John Charlton b. 9 Sep 1844 in Crawford Co., Ark., m. 24 Feb 1876
    to Naomi Townsend
Frances Louisa b. 17 Nov 1846 in Crawford Co., Ark., d. young in
    1855 in Van Buren, Ark.
William George b. 2 Mar 1848 in Crawford Co., Ark., d. young in
    1854 in Van Buren, Ark.
Virginia Armstead b. 4 Nov 1849 in Crawford Co., Ark., m. 13 Dec
    1882 to Henry Clay Hubbs

Frances Louisa Ragsdale, sister of Fred. B. Ragsdale, d. 30 Oct
    1860 in Miss.
Wm. Geo. Ragsdale d. 25 Apr 1849 in Miss.

[Bible copied in 1892 by John Charlton Ragsdale for his nephew, Light Sumner Townsend. The Bible was lost in 1918.]

GEORGE RAST

George Rast b. 3 Apr 1763, m. 3 Oct 1786 to Hannah Vice.
    Children
Elizabeth b. 5 Sep 1787
Magdelen b. 2 Oct 1789
Catherine b. 5 Apr 1792
Margaret b. 1 July 1794
Hannah b. 19 July 1797 ...... Cummings
Mary b. 20 July 1799
John Adam b. 22 July 1802
Christini b. 2 Apr 1805

[From Bible in St. Matthew Lutheran Church at Cameron, S.C. See Franklin, Holman, Derrick & Gates Bibles, this vol.]

JOHN REDIN

John Redin, great great grandfather, b. 7 Apr 1753, d. 5 Aug 1834
    in Fairfax Co., Va., m. Mary Mathews b. 23 Sep 1759, d. 4 Mar
    ...., aged 60 yrs. in Boston, Eng.

William Redin, great grandfather & their only son, b. 8 Dec 1791 at
    Wisbeach, Eng., m. 23 June 1817 at Boston, Eng. to Ann(e) or Nan-
    cy Wright b. 5 Nov 1789 in Norwich, Eng., removed with her par-
    ents to Wisbeach, Cambridgeshire, Eng. when she was 2 or 3 yrs.
    old and, to Boston, Lincolnshire, Eng. in 1815, d. 18 Dec 1837 at
    Georgetown, bur. 21 Dec 1837 at Rock Creek Church. Left for Amer-
    ica 8 Aug 1818
Isabella Wright Redin, brought to America aged about 3 mos.
Richard Wm. Redin, brother to Isabella Wright Redin, b. 30 Apr 1820
    at Georgetown [no state given, probably refers to Rock Creek,
    Md., i.e., Washington, D.C.]
Mary Anne Redin b. 28 Mar 1822 at Georgewown
Emily Wright Redin b. 26 Dec 1823 at Georgetown
Fanny Brown Redin b. 20 Dec 1825 at Georgetown
Catherine Foxhall Redin b. 8 Dec 1827 at Georgetown

[This record comes from the Kirk Bible given above.]

JAMES REESE

James Reese b. 14 Oct 1747, d. 1840; Elizabeth Brown Reese b. 15
    June 1770.
    Children
Joseph Brown Mackey Reese b. 22 May 1792, d. 7 Nov 1848, m. 1st
    to Melinda Duff, m. 2nd to Sophia Taswell Emerson
William Brown Reese b. 29 Nov 1793, d. 7 July 1860, m. 1st to Sarah
    Cocke, m. 2nd to Henrietta Brown

Julia Ann Reese m. Samuel Martin, children: James, Eliza, Hugh, Dr. Samuel, William, Joe, Margaret & Mary
Margaritta Reese m. Isaac Watkins, child: Albert G. Watkins, Congressman
Mary Porter Reese m. Gen. William Brazzleton, children: James, Emily & Julia
Emily Reese m. Napoleon B. Bradford, two sons: James Bradford m. Miss Oldham and William Bradford m. Mary Hodge

CALVIN RHODES

Calvin Rhodes, son of Jos. Ed. & Sarah (Polly) Beck Rhodes, b. 20 Sep 1811, d. 12 Nov 1894, bur. at Swift Creek Baptist Cemetery, m. in 1828 to Sarah Ann Pollard b. 29 Oct 1808, d. 9 Aug 1884, bur. at Swift Creek Baptist Cemetery.
 Children
Elizabeth b. 2 Feb 1829, d. 11 Nov 1913
William Edwin b. 15 Nov 1830, d. 21 Apr 1903
Joseph Bertram b. 28 June 1834, d. 5 Nov 1912
Mary Ann b. 26 May 1836, d. 25 Mar 1901
James Thomas b. 3 July 1838, d. 1 Aug 1912
Martha Ann b. 1840, d. 1903
Dorsey b. 1844
Henry Harmon b. 16 Nov 1846, d. 15 Aug 1903

[Record sent by Eugene Rhodes, Florence, S.C.]

CURTIS RHODES

Curtis Rhodes, son of Jos. Ed. & Sarah (Polly) Beck Rhodes, b. 5 Jan 1808, d. 26 Jan 1863, m. in 1830 to Queeney Goodson b. 6 Sep 1813, d. 22 Feb 1883.
 Children
Orpha b. 4 Jan 1832, d. Jan 1896
Frances b. 27 Aug 1834
Mary (Polly) b. 2 Aug 1836, d. 30 Nov 1908
John Fonville b. 17 June 1838, d. 14 May 1910
Robert Joseph b. 28 Apr 1840, d. in 1862 in Richmond, Va.
Wiley Calvin b. 31 Mar 1842, d. 7 Jan 1844
Ashley Joshua b. 16 Oct 1845
George Q. b. 10 Nov 1847, d. 6 Sep 1890
Susan Adella b. 11 Apr 1850, d. 2 Dec 1922
Thomas Pierce b. 12 July 1852, d. 3 Dec 1922
Olin M. b. 22 June 1854, d. 15 Oct 1923

[Curtis Rhodes was born in Sampson Co., N.C., died at his home, 6 miles north of Darlington Court HOuse, S.C. The shock of bringing home from Richmond, the body of his son Robert who died of measles in the Civil War and finding his son-in-law, Peter Byrd, a corpse was too great a strain and he shortly developed pneumonia which proved fatal. Curtis & his wife are buried in the old Flowers Graveyard, 1st burying ground for Swift Creek Baptist Church, Dalington Co., S.C. This record furnished by Eugene Rhodes, Florence, S.C.]

GENERAL JAMES RHODES

General James Rhodes m. 10 Apr 1793 at night to Anna Bass Rhodes.
  Children
Sally Ann b. 10 Jan 1794
Anna Maria b. 5 Sep 1797
Rhodes Clarissa b. 9 Apr 1800
Joseph Andrew b. 6 Jan 1803, d. 31 Aug 1812
James b. 5 Nov 1805
Wm. Thomas b. 20 Feb 1808

[Gen. James Rhodes & his wife are bur. in Wayne Co., N.C. This
Bible record is from a ms. on the Garber family by Dr. A. M. Garber
of Demopolis, Ala. He m. Anna Maria Rhodes, granddau. of Gen.
Rhodes. This copy sent by Mr. Cullen B. Hatch, Mt. Olive, N.C.
Edmund Hatch m. 15 Mar 1742-3 to Lucy Richard of Edenton, N.C.,
from court marriage records. The following are their children as
taken from Edmund Hatch's Bible by Dr. T. M. Whitfield in 1928.
Edmund's will in 1770 lists the additional children: Lucy, Elizabeth, Charles, & Hephzibah.]

Benjamin b. 3 Jan 1747
Edmund b. 8 Feb 1749, d. 21 Jan 1789, m. 5 Mar 1772 to Mary Bryan
Sarah b. 21 Aug 1751, d. Feb 1787
Lemuel b. 6 May 1754
Joseph b. 2 Dec 1762

JESSIE RHODES

Jessie Rhodes b. 2 Sep 1769, d. 21 Apr 1838, m. Martha S. (Perry-
man) Rhodes b. 1774, d. 17 Nov 1831.
  Children
Grace Rhodes b. 15 May 1794
Hesekiah Rhodes b. 20 Jan 1796
Clayborn H. Rhodes b. 4 Feb 1798
Cynthia Rhodes b. 21 June 1800
Silas P. Rhodes b. 19 Oct 1802
Delinda Rhodes b. 2 Jan 1805
Alemeter Rhodes b. 10 Jan 1807
Rosanna Rhodes b. 31 Mar 1809
Samuel Rhodes b. 23 Oct 1811
James W. Rhodes b. 2 Oct 1813
Margarette Rhodes b. 1 Dec 1818
Green H. Rhodes b. 16 Aug 1818 [?]

[This was copied from the old family Bible by Geo. W. Vaughn for
Mrs. Thos. C. Eiler, grand dau. of Jesse & Martha Rhodes. This
copy was sent to the compiler in 1954 by Estella Toll. She had it
from John J. Rhodes, son of James W. Rhodes . The spelling of the

264

name Jessie for a man is most unusual, but Miss Toll said that was
the way it was sent to her.]

JOSEPH RHODES

Joseph Rhodes [d. dates not clear enough to decipher] m. 12 Jan
1792 to Rachel Rhodes d. 29 Oct 1845.
    Their children
Elizabeth Rhodes b. 4 Jan 1793
Benjamin Rhodes b. 16 Feb 1796, m. 26 Nov 1815 to Temperance Rhodes
Mary Rhodes b. 10 Sep 1798
Joseph Rhodes, Jr. b. 17 July 1801
John Rhodes b. 20 Oct 1803
Rachel Rhodes b. 6 Jan 1806
Famey Rhodes b. 20 Jan 1808
Jacob Rhodes b. 13 June 1810
Sarah Rhodes b. 25 Dec 1812
Absolem Rhodes b. 7 July 1815

    Children [of Benjamin & Temperance Rhodes]
John Pool Rhodes b. 16 Jan 1817
Isaac Michel b. 16 Oct 1827
Sarah Melinda Rhodes b. 16 Apr 1829
Westley Rhodes b. 20 Oct 18.. [torn off]
Martha Rhodes b. 25 May 18.. [torn off]

Benjamin Rhodes b. 14 Dec 1612, d. 6 Mar 1700 [In back of Book]

[This record is taken from a Book of Sermons published by the Methodist Society of New York City in 1804. It was found by the compiler in the possession of her cousin, Mrs. Wanda Aldridge Turner
of Birmingham, Ala. It was once the property of Joseph Rhodes and
passed from him to Sarah Rhodes Bracken & her husband, Edward Brack-
en. Joseph Rhodes, Sr. m. Rachel Pearson in 1792 in Rockingham Co.,
N.C. The county record is pub. in a DAR magazine and is also in
the State Archives at Raleigh, N.C. That record verified the date
in the family record. Rachel Pearson was the dau. of Sullivan Pearson & his wife Elizabeth. Sullivan Pearson left a will in Rockingham Co., N.C. & among the children is Rachel. Joseph Rhodes was
the second son of John Rhodes who left a will in Guilford Co., N.C.
in 1792. Rockingham was taken from Guilford. John Rhodes went to
Orange Co., N.C. in 1755 from Orange Co., Va. and later went to Rowan Co., N.C. He was in Guilford when it was cut off from Rowan &
Orange. Many items on him are in Rowan and Guilford and some in
Rockingham. He furnished supplies in the Rev. War. The compiler
is a desc. through Sarah Rhodes who married Edward Bracken in 1835
in Lawrence Co., Ala.]

JOSEPH EDWARD RHODES

Jos. Ed. Rhodes b. 9 Jan 1775, bur. in old family burying ground in
Swift Creek Township, Arlington, S.C., m. 9 Aug 1804 in N.C. to

Sarah (Beck) Rhodes b. 5 Sep 1786, bur. at Swift Creek Township.
    Children
Curtis b. 5 Jan 1808
Elizabeth b. 24 Aug 1809
Calvin b. 20 Sep 1811
Sarah Ann b. 2 Feb 1813
Nancy b. 24 Jan 1816
Caleb b. 13 Oct 1817
Everett b. 14 June 1822
Joseph Edward, Jr. b. 2 Oct 1825
Polly b. 5 Apr 1827

[This record from Eugene Rhodes, Florence, S.C.]

WILLIAM H. RHODES

William H. Rhodes d. 10 Jan 1915, m. 27 Jan 1858 in Spartanburg Co.
to Nancy A. Redd d. 31 Jan 1900.
    Children
Mary Jane Rhodes b. 27 Mar 1859, d. 20 Jan 1925
William T. Rhodes b. 30 Mar 1861, d. 6 Sep 1926
Harvey T. Rhodes b. 6 Feb 1866, d. 20 Feb 1949, m. 26 Nov 1903 to
    Annie Farr Clifton
Charles F. Rhodes b. 26 Jan 1870, d. 11 Sep 1873
Carie Agnes Rhodes [Carie A. Bobo] b. 30 July 1873, d. 9 June 1898

[Copied by Eugene Rhodes]

JAMES RICHEY (RITCHIE) II

James Richey d. 5 June 1833 in his 82nd yr. [bur. at old Greenville
Presbyterian Church, Donalds, S.C.], m. [abt. 1785] to Elizabeth
Dunn [b. about 1760] d. 1 May 1828 [bur. at old Greenville Presby-
terian Church].
    Children
Nancy b. 17 Sep 1788 [m. Simeon Spruell]
Margaret b. 14 June 1790 [m. Posey, probably Hansford Posey]
James Washington b. 13 Sep 1792 [m. 1st to Julany Shirley, m. 2nd
    to Mrs. Margeret Ritchie Seawright, dau. of Robert Ritchie, widow
    of Andrew Seawright, m. 3rd to Nancy Martin]
Sarah b. 29 June 1794 [d. 1884, m. James Wilson]
Mary b. 7 Aug 1796 [m. William Lord, moved to Ga. & lived near Com-
    merce in Jackson Co. & were founders of the Lord family there.
    The late Hon. J. E. J. Lord, member of the Ga. Legislature from
    Jackson Co. was a desc.]
William b. 14 Oct 1800 [d. 14 Apr 1853, m. in 1822 to Mary Sea-
    wright b. 5 Feb 1803, d. 24 May 1864, dau. of Andrew Seawright
    (1777-1827) & Margaret Ritchie (1785-1857), dau. of Robert Rit-
    chie, 3rd son of James & Margaret Ritchie]
Samuel b. 6 Jan 1805 [m. Mary Strickland 31 Oct 1833 in Madison Co.,
    Ga., lived in Gwinnett Co., Ga., no children]
John b. 1 July 1807, d. 23 Jan 1879, m. 1st on 6 July 1826 to

Thirsa Kay b. 1810, d. 28 Dec 1834 in the 25th yr. of her age, m.
2nd on 9 Apr 1835 (6) to Nancy Adaline Seawright, dau. of Andrew
& Margaret Seawright, b. 10 Aug 1814, d. 7 Jan 1850 in the 37th
yr. of her age, m. 3rd on 19 Sep 1850 to Margaret Jane Dixon
Elizabeth, dau., b. 10 Nov 1810, m. 15 Sep 1829 as first wife to
Redmond G. Wyatt [He m. 2nd to Eleanor Ann Seawright. A desc. of
1st wife is Leonardo Andrea of Columbia, S.C. See also the Wyatt
Bible below]

Children of John Richey, son of James above
Elizabeth Caroline b. 26 May 1827
James Milton b. 26 Feb 1831, killed in Confederate Army
Malinda Jane b. 6 Apr 1833
Thirsa Rebecka Richey b. 15 Feb 1836
John Robert Richey b. 26 Jan 1837
Mary Ann Richey b. 26 May 1838
William Franklin Richey b. 25 Nov 1839
Louisa Terissa Richey b. 5 Aug 1841
Samuel Newton Richey b. 17 Dec 1842
Andrew Costantine b. 30 Mar 1844
Margaret Vashti Richey b. 3 Jan 1846
William B. Richey b. 12 Aug 1855
James Washington Richey b. 29 Apr 1857

[This Bible record was given to the compiler by Mrs. Leila Richey
Mize, 1729 Lumpkin St., Athens, Ga. who descends from William
above. She found the record in a Bible owned by Jas. W. Richey,
Donalds, S.C. The same record was given by Leonard Andrea, 4204 De
Vine St., Columbia, S.C. In the Bible found by Mrs. Mize were the
death dates of Jas. Richey Sr. & his wife Margaret (Caldwell) Richey. The old Bible was many yrs. ago owned by a Mrs. Brown of Elbert Co., Ga.]

JAMES WASHINGTON RICHEY

James Washington Richey [of Donalds, S.C.] b. 13 Sep 1792, m. 1st
on 9 July 1812 to Julaney Shirley b. 17 Apr 1797, d. 2 Dec 1833, m.
2nd to Margaret Richey b. 15 Aug 1785, d. 2 Jan 1857, widow of An-
drew Seawright, m. 3rd to Nancy Martin.
    Children [all by first wife]
Mary (Polly) b. 1 Apr 1813
James Nathaniel b. 28 Apr 1815
Elizabeth b. 9 Sep 1817, d. 1818
Benjamin b. 17 Nov 1819, d. 1819
Agness Luany b. 10 Aug 1822
Sarah b. 9 Mar 1825, d. 1842
Levinda b. 25 Feb 1827, d. 1842
Mastin b. 17 Sep 1829, d. 1829
William Johnston b. 6 Nov 1830, murdered 2 Aug 1855
Samuel Thompson b. 22 Nov 1833

"Grandmother Margaret Richey d. Sep 1802
Grandfather James Richey d. in Aug. 1808
James Richey d. in June 1833" [their son]

[According to Leonard Andrea of Columbia, S.C. who has done exhaus-
tive research on this family, the 2nd wife of Jas. W. Richey was
his 1st cousin. The Bible was in the possession of Hugh Martin,
Donalds, S.C. in 1926. James Washington Richey became the guardian
of Seawright children. The graves of James Washington Richey, Margaret Seawright Richey & Andrew Seawright are marked in Greenville
cemetery near Donalds, S.C.]

ROBERT C. RICHEY

Robt. C. Richey b. 13 Feb 1812 in Abbeville Dist., S.C., d. 24 Mar
1885, m. 21 [or 23] Apr 1836 in Abbeville Dist., S.C. to Nancy Hill.
    Children
Margaret E. b. 15 Apr 1837, d. 10 June 1838
Jane Frances b. 18 Oct 1838, d. 17 Apr 1840
Luther Alburtus b. 6 Dec 1840 [m. Mary Agnew]
Marion Wilson b. 12 Dec 1842 [m. Sallie Whitten]
Wm. Jefferson b. 1 Aug 1845, d. 18 Sep 1864
Robt. Saml. b. 10 May 1847, d. 27 Aug 1848
Langdon Augustus b. 20 Nov 1852, d. 22 Jan 1884
Isaac Newton b. 16 Nov 1854 [m. Anna Agnew]
Nancy Ann Emma b. 15 June 1859 [m. Jackson Smythe]

[Bible record from Mrs. Jos. Liddell (Sally Richey), New Albany,
Miss. who says, "Robt. C. Richey moved to near New Albany, Miss. &
had two sisters or half-sisters who came to Miss. with him, Aunt
Polly Hawthorne & Aunt Rilla Agnew whose husband was Wilson Agnew."
Sent by Leonard Andrea, Columbia, S.C.]

WILLIAM RICHEY

William Richey b. 1775, d. 16 Nov 1846, m. 22 Jan 1801 to Jane Stone
b. 1781, d. 9 Mar 1839, aged 58 yrs.
    Their children
James b. 21 Oct 1801
William b. 7 Nov 1803
Robert b. 5 Dec 1805
Nancy b. 22 Jan 1808
George b. 18 May 1810
Jane b. 25 Dec 1813
Nimrod b. 1 Sep 1816
Margaret b. 29 Sep 1818
Hanry Jackson b. 1822
Harvey S. b. 21 Mar [or May] 1826

[This Bible belonged to Mrs. Nesbit Burriss (Jennie Frohm) of Anderson Co., S.C. & was copied by Leonard Andrea of Columbia, S.C. a
Richey descendant, many yrs. ago. He sent it to the compiler in

1941. In the back is this: "Margaret Richey, wife of James, d. in
the month of Sept. 1802. Jas. Richey died in the month of Aug.
1808 in the 85th yr. of his life." This fits perfectly with the
story handed down that James Richey was a small child when his parents, Alex. & Jeane (Caldwell) Richey came to America in 1727.]

RITCHIE

Alexander Ritchie, senior son of Alexander Ritchie & Jane, his
   wife, b. 20 Aug 1739
Alexander Ritchie, son of Alexander Ritchie & his wife Mary, b. 29
   June 1764
Elizabeth Ritchie b. 22 Jan 1770
Susannah Ritchie b. 2 July 1772
John Ritchie b. 4 Oct 1775
James Ritchie b. 24 Nov 1778
Mary Ritchie b. 24 Feb 1782
Hugh Ritchie b. 8 Dec 1784
Alexander Jones b. 28 Dec 1794
A. D. Ritchie b. 12 Mar 1793
William Ritchie b. 26 May 1795
Mary Ritchie b. 11 Feb 1798
Harvey Ritchie b. 3 Dec 1800
John Ritchie b. 8 Dec 1804
James Ritchie b. 8 Mar 1806
Joseph Ritchie b. 17 Dec 1809
Robert Ritchie b. 14 Apr 1811
      Children of Robert Ritchie & Margaret
Taylor O. Ritchie b. 13 July 1847
Hiram K. Ritchie b. 13 July 1847
James P. Ritchie b. 10 Nov 1852
Sarah Ritchie b. 24 Feb 1854
Joseph Ritchie b. 18 Sep 1856

Mary Ritchie d. 2 Feb 1807
Susannah Ritchie d. 3 Jan 1803
Hugh Ritchie d. 9 Aug 1803, 4:12 A.M.
Mary Ritchie d. 8 May 1817, about 10 o'clock
Alex. Ritchie, Sr. d. 11 Jan 1818 at 3:30 A.M.
Alex. D. Ritchie d. 1 July 1821
Polly, his wife, d. 7 June 1820
James Ritchie, son of Ales., Sr., d. 27 Jan 1821
John Ritchie, son of Alex. Ritchie, Sr., d. 28 Sep 1845
Elizabeth Ritchie d. 22 Apr 1839
Alex. Ritchie, son of Alex. Ritchie, Sr., d. 14 Nov 1848
Sarah Ritchie d. 8 Aug 1889
Louisa Ritchie d. 11 Nov 1852
Joseph Ritchie d. 16 Oct 1856
James Ritchie d. 6 Feb 1876
Margaret Ritchie, wife of Robert Ritchie, d. 14 Jan 1893
Robert Ritchie d. 13 Jan 1899

Robert Ritchie m. 1 Apr 1846 to Margaret
Alexander Ritchie m. 18 Dec 1761 to Mary Wilson
Alexander Ritchie m. 29 May 1792 to Elizabeth Doherty
Alex. D. Ritchie m. 4 Sep 1817 to Polly Brasfield
Polly Ritchie m. 4 Feb 1818 to James Overton
William Ritchie [son of Alex. & Elizabeth] m. 2 Sep 1824 to Clarissa N. Lane
John Ritchie m. 16 Sep 1834
James Ritchie m. 14 July 1840 to Barbara Parkey
Robert Ritchie m. 1 Apr 1846 to Margaret King

[Now in the possession of Robert L. Ritchie, Ft. Worth, Tex. A copy was sent to the compiler by Mr. Ritchie about 10 yrs. ago. This family, though it spells the name differently, is the same family as the James Richey of S.C. who was a son of Alexander Richey, Sr. who d. in Prince Edward Co., Va. in 1749 leaving a will. This Alex. Ritchie is junior to the Alex. of Pr. Edward who was the immigrant from Ireland to America in 1727. Thus he is the brother of James, Sr. of Va. & Abbeville Co., S.C.]

ELI RITCHIE

Children of Eli Ritchie & Rebecca Ritchie
Lucinda Ritchie b. 20 Mar 1814, died early
Matilda Ritchie b. 16 Dec 1815, m. Noel Bottoms, moved to Ark.
Mary (Polly) Ritchie b. 14 Oct 1817, m. Thomas Crawford, lived near Clayton
Nancy Ritchie b. 11 Dec 1819, m. John Queen, Tax Collector, lived at Mt. City, Ga.
John (Jack) Ritchie b. 15 Nov 1820, m. Margaret Dickerson, moved to Colorado about 1860
Louisa Ritchie b. 25 Dec 1823, m. Thomas Hopper, lived in Tennessee Valley
James Madison Ritchie b. 6 Jan 1825, m. Elizabeth Dickerson, lived in Tennessee Valley
Sarah Ritchie b. 15 Nov 1826, unmarried
Riley Burton Ritchie b. 10 Feb 1829, m. Sarah Ann Martin [parents of A. J. Ritchie], lived in Tennessee Valley
Narcissa Ritchie b. 14 Sep 1831, unmarried
Jeptha Ritchie b. 12 Mar 1833, never married, lived in California, a gold miner
Elizabeth Ritchie b. 20 June 1836, m. 1st to Jack Bradley, m. 2nd to Barak Norton, lived on Betty's Creek in Tennessee Valley

[Bible record in pension papers. "Eli Ritchie m. 4 Mar 1813 in Pickens Dist., S.C. to Rebecca Moore. The soldier's widow, Rebecca Ritchie was allowed a pension on her application executed 15 July 1872 in Clayton, Rabun Co., Ga. She was then aged about 82 yrs. The date and place of her birth and names of parents not shown."]

THOMAS RIVERS

Wm. Thomas Rivers b. 11 Sep 1785, d. 24 July 1849, m. 15 Nov 1804
to Mary Milligan b. 31 Oct 1778, d. 9 Aug 1857.

Wm. G. Rivers b. 14 Feb 1806, d. 25 Aug 1869
Harriet Rivers b. 2 Apr 1808, d. 27 Sep 1868
Elizabeth Rivers b. 29 Oct 1809
Susanna Rivers b. 2 May 1811
Thomas J. Rivers b. 17 Oct 1812, d. 9 Apr 1853
John F. Rivers b. 31 Dec 1814, d. 3 Aug 1898
Francis M. Rivers b. 3 Mar 1816, d. 23 Sep 1849

John F. Rivers m. 31 Jan 1839 to Feraby Howard

Nancy Emily Rivers b. 15 Dec 1839
George W. Rivers b. 5 May 1841
Sol H. Rivers b. 4 Feb 1843
Elizabeth A. Rivers b. 1 Dec 1844
Mary Suvannah Rivers b. 5 Jan 1847
John Floyd Rivers b. 28 Dec 1816 [?]
Dilligence Rivers b. 25 Nov 1850
Thoms. Wm. Rivers b. 10 May 1853
Willis David Rivers b. 29 Nov 1855, d. 5 May 1899
Albert P. Rivers b. 9 Dec 1857

[This Bible of Thomas Rivers of Warren Co., Ga. is owned by Mrs.
John Leland Marrett, Maple Crest Seneca, S.C., pub. c. 1760.
Copied by Flossie L. Crouch.]

ZACCHEUS ROBARTS

Zaccheus Robarts b. 12 May 1753, d. 29 Dec 1826 about three hrs.
before day, m. 11 Dec 1788 to Nancy (Brashears) Robarts b. 11 May
1773, d. 12 July 1850.
    Their children
Edward Robarts b. 10 Sep 1789, d. 26 Dec 1789
Basil Robarts b. 17 Sep 1790 [or 91, not clear], d. 15 Apr 1795
Zerubabel Robarts b. 8 Apr 1792, d. 12 Apr 1795
Brasher Robarts b. 19 Feb 1795
Robert Zaccheus Robarts b. 28 May 1797, d. 29 Apr 1875, m. 3 Nov
    1852 to Mary Roberts d. 8 June 1886
Nancy Robarts b. 1 May 1800, m. 11 Nov 1823 to Alexander Nesmith
Elizabeth Robarts b. 4 Sep 1802
[One child b. 1805, but name is torn off page]
Zedekiah Robarts b. 29 Oct 1807
Isaac Robarts b. 3 July 1812, m. 27 Feb 1831 [not sure of yr.] to
    Elizabeth
John C. B....[not clear] Robarts b. 19 Oct 1814
David F. Robarts b. 17 July 1809

Bazzel Brasher d. 10 Aug 1826
"Zaccheus Robarts His Book."

[This Bible was owned by Mrs. H. M. Hedgecock of Kingston, Tenn., a
desc. of Zaccheus Robarts-Roberts. She gave it to the State Library in Nashville, Tenn. in 1945. This copy was made by the compiler from the Bible 29 Oct 1944. The name was spelled Robarts
early in the record and then later entries spelled the name Roberts.
Zaccheus Roberts was b. in Pa. & fought in the Rev. War in S.C. He
is bur. on his old farm on the Clinch River, Roane Co., Tenn. There
is no marker, but there is a wooden shed built over the grave and
it is known to present day descs. who live in Roane Co. Some of
the dates in this Bible are also in the Robert Samuel Brashears and
the Alexander Nesmith Bibles. An Edward Roberts was b. in Merion-
shire, Wales in 1687 & came to Pa. when he was 12 yrs. old. He d.
25 Nov 1768. This might be the father of Zaccheus & his brother
Elias. There seems to also be a brother of these two men who was
named Isaac. More research might prove this Edward the father of
the 3 mentioned men. We know that Zaccheus was b. in Pa. because
in a short biographical sketch of his grandson, Benton Nesmith in
several Ala. books of prominent men of Ala., it is stated that his
grandfather Zaccheus Roberts was b. in Pa. & fought in the Rev. War.
This Zaccheus Roberts was the 2nd great grandfather of the compiler.
His dau., Nancy Roberts m. Alexander Nesmith; their dau., Eliza, m.
John Leander Watterson; their dau., Martha Malinda Alexander Watterson m. Rev. Franklin LaFayette Aldridge; and they were the compiler's parents.]

WILLIAM ROBINSON

William Robinson b. 17 Dec 1789, m. 28 July 1816 to Anny (Annie)
Merrit b. 12 Mar 1790.
    Children
Elizabeth P. Robinson b. 27 July 1819 [m. Thomas Newton Guffin]
Sarah P. Robinson b. 17 Aug 1821 [m. John Patterson Boyd]
George M. Robinson b. 5 Jan 1824 [m. Eliza Jackson]
Mary Anne Robinson b. 26 July 1826 [m. Robert Watson Boyd]
John Robinson b. 17 Mar 1829 [m. Alice Farr]
Susannah Robinson b. 16 Feb 1832 [m. Ross McCreight]
Jane Robinson b. 13 Apr 1835 [m. William Partridge]
Louisa Lamar Robinson b. 10 Jan 1838 [m. Jesse Burnett]

[This Bible is owned by the family of Mrs. Angie Boyd Hansen of
Covington, Ga. It was taken from the old Hopewell Church area of
Chester Co., S.C. to Newton Co., Ga. sometime about 1831. The
marriages of the Robinson children are from Newton Co., Ga. Mar-
riage bonds and also from the estate of the William Robinson in Ga.
The "P" as middle initials of the first two daus. has been proved
in their Bibles as standing for Paul. Sarah Paul Robinson is by
Tradition named for her grandmother of the Robinson side. Archi-
bald Paul of Chester Co., S.C. in his will has a deceased dau.
named Sarah Robinson. Will of Archibald Paul sg. in Chester Co. 3
Sep 1802, no wife listed. Children are: Sarah Robinson, deceased;
James Paul, deceased; William Paul; John Paul; Martha Robinson;
Elizabeth Russell; Margaret Russell; & Moses Paul.]

THOS. WM. ROE

Thos. Wm. Roe b. 10 June 1819, d. 16 Mar 1874, m. 14 May 1844 in
Buncombe Co., N.C. to Sarah Stradley b. 29 Sep 1822.
  Children
Mary Ann Roe b. 27 Mar 1846, m. 27 Jan 1876 to Luther P. Hawkins
Kessiah Emma Kee Roe b. 10 Sep 1848, m. 7 Oct 1867 to Butler P.
  Watson
Sarah Boardmore Roe b. 22 Jan 1851, m. 18 Dec 1870 to Thos. Wash-
  ington Hunt
Anna Whilden Roe b. 23 Apr 1853, m. 22 Aug 1876 to Rev. Geo. H.
  Carter
Martha Lucretia Roe b. 3 Nov 1857, m. 4 Apr 1882 to Robert Kay
Susannah Mingus Roe b. 7 June 1860, m. Budd Mathis Moore
Thos. Wm. Roe, Jr. b. 5 May 1863, d. 27 Feb 1932, m. Maude Anderson

James Roe, my grandfather, b. 1765, d. 1820 in Woolwich, England,
  m. Eliz. Dash b. 1768 in Woolwich, Eng., d. 1848. They came to
  Charleston, S.C.
Wm. Wheeler, my grandfather, b. in Isle of Wight, Eng., d. 22 Feb
  1846 in Greenville, S.C., aged 81 yrs., m. Phillis Wheeler, d. 17
  Nov 1850, aged 86 yrs.
Thos. Roe, my father, b. 1791 in Woolwich, Eng., d. 1847 in Green-
  ville, S.C., m. Ann Wheeler b. 1795, d. 1846, came from Isle of
  Wight to Greenville Co., S.C.

[There are other entries in this Bible & some on the Hunt family.
The 1st entries were in old script & these were entered by Miss
Eliza Powell of Greenville, S.C. who was a cousin & member of the
Roe household. St. Jas. Episcopal Church in Greenville is built on
the home site of Eliza Powell, long a teacher in Greenville & she
willed the funds to erect St. Jas. This Bible is owned by Mrs.
Sally Hunt Thomas of Travelers Rest, S.C., copied by Leonard Andrea
of Columbia, S.C.]

GEORGE RICHARD ROSS

Geo. Richard Ross, son of John Ross, b. 31 Jan 1811, d. 24 Feb
1873, m. Elizabeth Fowler b. 26 Dec 1814, d. 4 June 1887.
  Children
Margaret Eliz. b. 7 Jan 1847, d. 9 Mar 1905
Nancy Isabella b. 27 Mar 1848, d. 4 Nov 1896
Lawrence Calhoun b. 10 July 1850, d. 14 Sep 1897
Chas. Clinton b. 18 Jan 1852, d. 29 Sep 1896
John Richard b. 11 Aug 1854, d. 18 May 1886
Mary Frances Catherine b. 5 Mar 1857, d. 26 Dec 1884

JOHN ROSS

John Ross b. 29 Oct 1784 in Laurens Co., S.C., moved to Monroe Co.,
Miss. in 1837, d. 22 May 1877 in Monroe Co., Miss., m. 1st on 15
Mar 1810 to Elizabeth Ferguson b. 5 Oct 1789, d. 18 Oct 1826, m.

2nd on 5 Jan 1830 by Rev. John B. Kennedy to Sara Rebecca Ross b.
18 Apr 1793, d. 19 Sep 1841, m. 3rd on 9 Jan 1851 to Mary Ann An-
glin d. 20 Sep 1879.
    Children
George R. b. 31 Jan 1811, d. 24 Feb 1873
Nancy I. [or J.] b. 11 Apr 1812
Eliza Caroline b. 26 Oct 1813, m. Miller, d. 2 June 1855
I. [or J.] Leland b. 21 Sep 1816
Henry Edwin b. 5 Mar 1818, d. 13 July 1818
Frances Catherine b. 24 July 1819, m. Cain d. 1 June 1843
Miles F. b. 9 Mar 1821
Cyrus Lee b. 1 Feb 1823
Franklin S. [or L.] b. 21 Dec 1824
James Montgomery b. 18 Oct 1826, d. 29 Nov 1826
Wm. Stanhope b. 16 Sep 1831, d. 4 Feb 1862
Frances Preston b. 7 Apr 1835

BENJAMIN RUSH

Benjamin Rush b. 3 Feb 1717
Cahume [Catherine or Calvin] Rush b. 3 July 1717
Annie Rush b. 1 Feb 1717 [Amie? Miss Kelly thinks copied wrong]
Elizabeth Rush b. 13 Sep 1723
Jane Rush b. 5 Feb 1725
Allen Rush b. 21 July 1727
Bathsheba Rush b. 7 July 1729
Bethlehem Rush b. 31 Aug 1731

Martin Rush b. 19 Nov 1794, m. 6 Oct 1817 to Susan Bell Rush b. 3
   Jan 1795

Nancy b. 14 Feb 1819
William H. b. 13 Feb 1820
Benjamin b. 8 Apr 1821
Grigsby T. b. 3 June 1822
Toliver b. 1 Mar 1825
Simeon b. 9 May 1829

[This record was sent prior to 1927 from Mrs. Ann Darden Cruger of
Dallas, Tex. to Miss Nellie F. Ayers of Memphis, Tenn. She says,
"I will send you the record of the Rush family as Papa has it. He
got it in N.C. several yrs. ago." The record was sent to the com-
piler by Miss Maud McClure Kelly of the Archives Dept. of Ala. She
states that Amie must have been a Harrison from Prince William Co.,
Va. Her deduction is from the fact that in 1735 in Prince William
Co., Burr Harrison leased for a nominal sum a certain place in that
county to Benjamin Rush and his wife Amie with the proviso that "at
the expiration of the before mentioned lives of said Benj. Rush &
Amie his wife" the place be returned to Burr Harrison in good order.
Miss Kelly says, "I went to see Mr. Rush, Lake, Miss. who had a
copy of this old Rush Bible that had been made by Simeon Rush in
the 1880's while on a visit to the old home in Pekin, N.C. The old

Bible belonged to Simeon's father, Martin Rush (1794-1883) who is
buried on the W. L. Cotton farm 1 mile from Pekin. This is the old
farm & homestead of William Rush (1755-1827) who m. Abigail Terrell.
The Bible descended to Simeon's half-brother, Martin Rush (1842-
1926) who is bur. near Mt. Gilead." Miss Kelly states that Simeon
must have made mistakes in copying the old Bible as he skipped a
whole generation. She says, "I am descended from Benjamin who is
given in his son William's Bible as dying 23 May 1801 on Cape Fear
River, aged 86." She says that Benjamin was m. 3 times & two of
his wives are proven. The following is her account:
William Rush m. Ann Gray, their son:
William Rush m. Elizabeth, their son:
Benjamin Rush m. Amy Harrison Elkins, their son:
Benjamin Rush m. 2nd to Alice Grigsby, had son William, m. 3rd to
  Elizabeth Perry
William Rush (1755-1827) m. Abigail Terrell, their son:
Martin Rush m. Susan Bell, their son:
Simeon Rush b. 9 May 1829, copied the Bible record.]

JOHN WESLEY RUSSELL

John Wesley Russell b. 6 Feb 1813, m. Tempest b. 23 Nov 1814 [An-
other record says that his wife was Temperance Ann Burgess, and
they spent their lives in Jackson Co., Ala.]
    Children
Robert Russell b. Aug 1834 [wounded in Civil War, d. later from
  wounds]
Isabell Russell b. Sep 1836
Elizabeth Russell b. 24 Aug 1840
Ruth Russell b. 6 Oct 1842
Wm. L. [Lorenzo] b. 1 Dec 1844
David Worth Russell b. 13 Mar 1847 [m. Minerva Scruggs]
Tempie Lavina Russell b. 29 Mar 1852 [m. 1871 to Stephen Young]

[Bible now in the possession of Mrs. Fred Lorenzo Russell (Grace
Peake), Atlanta, Ga. Record sent by Pauline Jones Gandrud.]

JAMES RUTLEDGE

James Rutledge b. 28 Aug 1786, m. Sep 1807 to Susanna Rutledge b.
Sep 1790.
    Children
John Rutledge b. 12 Mar 1809
Joseph Rutledge b. 14 Feb 1811, settled in Troup Co., Ga. 9 miles
  from LaGrange where he built a home in 1850-1852, m. Jane Rut-
  ledge b. 22 July 1815, d. 17 Mar 1861
James Rutledge b. 12 Apr 1813
Anna Rutledge b. 1 Jan 1815

    Children of Joseph & Jane Rutledge
Mary Susan Rutledge m. George W. Robertson
John Rutledge

Children of George W. & Mary S. Robertson
William Butler Robertson 1852
Tallulah Robertson 1854
Annie Jane Robertson 1856, m. Marquis LaFayette Fleming, children:
   Olin Butler Fleming, Mary George Fleming Cooper, Lucille Fleming
   Davis
John W. Robertson 1859
George E. Robertson 1862

[These pages were cut from a small sized Bible and some of the
dates were cut off. The Bible is owned by the family of Mrs. Duke
Davis, P.O. Box 327, LaGrange, Ga. "James Rutledge His Book now
who can doubt it. 29 Aug 1826."]

JOHN RUTLEDGE

John Rutledge, Jr. [Sr. in 1796] b. 17 Oct 1738, d. 8 July [?] 1803,
m. 1st on 13 Dec 1763 to Hannah b. 16 May 1746, d. 5 Aug 1792 [?],
moved from Lynches Creek 25 Feb 1768 [?], 7 miles below Camden, m.
2nd on 6 Nov 1796 to Elizabeth Rutledge b. 28 Aug 1769 [Nee Downs
added in pencil], d. 24 May 1831.
      Children
Jane Rutledge b. 22 May 1864 [?]
Edward Rutledge b. 6 June [?] 1766
Elizabeth Rutledge b. 12 Jan 1768 (twin)
Rebecca Rutledge b. 12 Jan 1768 (twin)
Richard Rutledge b. 1 May 1770
John Rutledge b. 10 [?] Apr 1772
Penelope Rutledge b. 8 Sep 1775
Abraham Rutledge b. 19 Sep 1777
Isaac Rutledge b. 23 Apr 1779
Javoub Rutledge b. 29 June 1782
Haney [may be Naney] Rutledge b. 1th Aug 1784
James Rutledge b. 24 Nov 1787
Sarah Rutledge b. 8 Dec 1791
Nancy Rutledge b. 13 Dec 1799
Mary Rutledge b. 8 Oct 1802

[The Bible is owned by the family of John Thomas Cupit, Rosepine,
La. There is a will for John Rutledge on record i- Camden, S.C.]

GRAVES SAMMONS

Graves Sammons b. 16 May 1769 in Sussex Co., Va., m. 3 Nov 1791 in
Sussex Co., Va. to Sarah Ann Sledge b. 10 Aug 1769 in Sussex Co.
      Children
Patsy Sammons b. 7 Sep 1792
Betsy Sammons b. 13 Aug 1795
Howell Sammons b. 28 Apr 1798
Sally Sammons b. 15 Aug 1805
Ferrett Sammons b. 23 Oct 1806
Isham Sammons b. 9 July 1811 in Rowan Co., N.C.

Sukay Sammons b. 24 Oct 1814 in Rowan Co., N.C.

HOWELL SAMMONS

Howell Sammons b. 28 Apr 1798 in Sussex Co., Va., d. 18 Nov 1878, m. 1st on 25 Sep 1817 in Rowan Co., N.C. to Euthama (Fama) Riggins b. 16 Jan 1801 in Rowan Co., N.C., d. 27 Mar 1839, m. 2nd on 15 May 1839 in Ga. to Mary Longley.
    Children
Mahala Sammons b. 25 Nov 1818 in Rowan Co., N.C.
Mary Sammons b. 28 Nov 1821 in Rowan Co., N.C.
Sarah Sammons b. 15 Mar 1823 in Shelby Co., Ala.
Louisa Sammons b. 16 Nov 1827 in Shelby Co., Ala.
Armenta Sammons b. 1 Aug 1831 in Shelby Co., Ala.
Angeline Sammons b. 20 July 1833 in Shelby Co., Ala.
Amanda Sammons b. 6 Nov 1835 in Shelby Co., Ala.
Matilda Victorias Sammons b. 30 Aug 1837 in Shelby Co., Ala.
William Littleton Sammons b. 26 Mar 1839 in Shelby Co., Ala., d. aged 2 yrs.
Griselda Sammons b. 3 Apr 1840
Eli Graves Sammons b. 22 Sep 1842
James W. Sammons b. 18 Oct 1844
John Wesley Sammons b. 26 Aug 1846
Memdora Jane Sammons b. 29 July 1848
Henry Hillsman Sammons b. 3 Nov 1849
Martha Sammons b. 25 Sep 1851
Albert Judson Sammons b. 2 Dec 1855
Martin Hilliard Sammons b. 5 Jan 1859

JAMES SAMPLE, SR.

Jas. Sample, Sr. b. 27 Feb 1775, d. 3 Apr 1816, m. in 1793 to Mary Bonner b. 20 Apr 1775, d. Oct 1799.
    [Children]
Jas. Sample, Jr. [Sr. at time of death] b. 5 Oct 1794, d. 18 Sep 1862, aged 68 yrs., m. 1 July 1819 to S. Parthenia McVay b. 24 Apr 1802, d. 18 Aug 1834
Ann Sample b. 22 Feb 1796, d. 18 Oct 1823, m. 8 Mar 1814 to Thos. Carroll
Martha Sample b. 23 Sep 1797, m. 10 Sep 1817 to Josiah K. Brandon
    [Children of Jas. & Parthenia, entered 20 Aug 1834 by Jas.]
Polly McVay Sample b. 15 Apr 1820, d. 3 Aug 1840, m. Eldad N. (S. W.) Newton on 16 Jan 1838 in Florence, Ala., b. 28 June 1813, d. 31 July 1840
Martha Ann (N.) Sample b. 12 Mar 1822, d. 18 Mar 1852 in Florence, Ala., m. 22 May 1838 in Florence, Ala. to B. B. Barker
.... Manly Sample b. 29 Aug 1824
Henry Wood McVay Sample b. 24 July 1826, m. 23 Sep 1852 in Florence, Ala. to M. A. Hawkins
Jas. Sample [Jr. at death] b. 25 Aug 1829, d. 20 Sep 1855, aged 26 yrs. & 26 days
Hugh McVay Sample b. 6 Aug 1831, d. 20 Oct 1917, m. 1 Apr 1852 in

Pontotoc, Miss. to Frances C. Westmoreland d. 21 Nov 1910

Jas. M. Sample m. 28 Aug 1902 to Sallie S. Phillips
Jas. Sample, son of Hugh M. & Frances Sample, b. 26 Jan 1853
Mrs. Polly McVay, consort of Maj. H. McVay, d. 20 Sep 1817
Mrs. Averiller V. Manly, dau. of Maj. Hugh McVay, d. 27 Jan 1833
Florence Alabama Sample d. 2 Jan 1844
Jas. Sample m. Dec to Susan M. Anderson [date torn]

[This Bible owned by Jas. Sample, son of Hugh, Verona, Miss. James (which?) bought the Bible in 1816. Copied by Mrs. E. S. Gragory, Tuscumbia, Ala.]

JOHN SAMPLE

John Sample b. 24 June 1770 in S.C., d. 10 Oct 1846, aged 70 yrs., 3 mos. & 7 days, m. Margaret Caldwell b. 22 June 1768, d. 10 May 1842, aged 73 yrs., 10 mos. & 18 days
        Children
Samuel Caldwell Sample b. 15 Aug 1796
Thomas Jefferson Sample b. 4 Nov 1800
(Dr.) John Sample, Jr. b. 5 Aug 1806, m. 1st to Frances Cecelia
    Reid b. in Pendleton Dist., S.C., m. 2nd to Amy Cupit Raulins
Archibalk K. Russell Sample b. 12 May 1808[or 1818?]

        Children of Dr. John & Frances C. Sample
Catherine Mary Sample b. 9 Dec 1830, bapt. by Bro. Little, Presby-
    terian
John Archibald Sample b. 19 Nov 1832, bapt. by Bro. Watson
Margaret Ellen Sample b. 9 Dec 1835, bapt. by Bro. Watson
Indiana A. Sample b. 29 July 1838, bapt. by Bro. Watson
Jacob Reid Sample b. 22 Jan 1840, bapt. by Bro. Collingsworth
William Samuel Sample b. 2 Mar 1844, bapt. by Bro. Collingsworth
Frances Cecilia Sample b. 28 Apr 1846, bapt. by Bro. Collingsworth
        Children of Dr. John & Amy C. Sample
Maderia Clementine Sample b. 21 Feb 1852, bapt. by Bro. John Lusk
Allen Rusk Sample b. 27 Mar 1854, bapt. by Bro. Allen Castle
Samuel Caldwell Sample b. 18 Oct 1856, bapt. by Bro. John G. Jones
Catherine Jane Sample b. Dec 1859, bapt. by Bro. John Lusk
Jefferson Davis Sample, dau., b. 13 May 1862, bapt. by Bro. E. A.
    Flowers
Howard Lee Sample b. 30 Sep 1865, bapt. by Bro. B. Jones
John Sample, Jr. b. 21 Aug 1869, bapt. by Bro. J. J. Clark

[Mrs. Frances Cecelia Reid Sample b. 11 Dec 1811 in Pendleton Dist. S.C., migrated with her parents to Ind. where she m. 30 Apr 1829 to Dr. John Sample. She joined the Presbyterian Church in winter of 1831-32 at Connersville, Ind. Upon her removal to Miss. in 1837 she joined the Methodist Church with her husband. She died after an illness of only 8 days of black tongue fever at her home in Cad-do Parish, La. Excerpts from a long obituary in Nashville Christ-ian Advocate & obituary written 3 July 1848 at Red River P.O., Cad-do Parish, La., by her husband, Dr. John Sample. He was b. in S.C. & when a small boy, his father removed to Phila., Pa. John Sample told his children that he well remembered the day the Declaration of Independence was signed. After the Rev., John Sample removed to Fayette, Ind. This Bible is owned by the family of Mr. James Dudley Schooler of Port Gibson, Miss., who did not send the d. or m. lists from this Bible.]

JOHN SANDERS

John Sanders b. 17 Feb 1775, d. 30 Nov 1830 in the 56th yr. of his life, m. 1st on 16 Mar 1797 to Jemima (Mimmy) Jones b. 14 Nov 1778, m. 2nd on 21 May 1807 to Elizabeth Temprance Peters b. 13 Aug 1787, d. 23 Oct 1812, m. 3rd on 23 Mar 1814 to Mary Boddie b. 7 Mar 1785, d. 21 Apr 1843 in her 58th yr.
        Children
Baldy b. 28 Dec 1797
Tranquilla b. 14 Jan 1799
Jemima (Mimmy) b. 3 May 1801
Susan Peters b. 17 June 1808, d. 8 Dec 1808
Nancy Peters b. 10 June 1810
Elizabeth Temprance Peters b. 10 Oct 1812, d. 18 Nov 1812
Elizabeth Willis b. 15 Jan 1815
John Fletcher b. 10 Feb 1817, d. 16 May 1867 in his 51st yr., m. 5
    Oct 1847 to Martha Edmundson b. 28 Apr 1828
William b. 1819 [torn off]
[One name here torn off at bottom of page.]
Willis Henry, son of John & Mary Sanders, d. 29 Jan 1823
Robert Alexander, son of John & Mary Sanders, b. 4 Feb 1825
Claudius Brock, son of John & Mary Sanders b. 17 Sep 1829

        Children of John Fletcher & Martha Edmundson Sanders
Robert b. 10 Aug 1848
John b. 27 Dec 1849, d. 25 June 1902, m. 12 Dec 1883 to Anna Bridges
    Snead
Wright b. 5 Jan 1852
Rufus b. 1 Feb 1853
Willis b. 27 May 1855
Edgar b. 24 June 1857
Sallie b. 8 Aug 1859
Emile b. 19 Jan 1861
Fletcher b. 28 June 1863
Martha E. b. 30 Mar 1865

        Children of John & Anna Bridges Snead Sanders
John Marvin b. 23 Oct 1884
Junius Pearson b. 15 July 1887, d. 26 Jan 1953
Omar D. b. 24 Aug 1886, d. Sep 1886
Bessie Agnes b. 28 Jan 1889
Thomas Snead b. 27 June 1893
Pauline b. 22 Feb 1901
Annie Clyde b. 22 Mar 1896

Sallie b. 7 Sep 1898

Ryal Edwards b. 17 Feb 1793 [no connection to Sanders family shown]
James Henry Sanders d. 2 Dec 1822
Willie Mabel Rountree Sanders, dau. of Wright & Minnie Sanders, b.
12 Nov 1876

[This Bible is owned by Mrs. Fred O. Bowman, Sr., Chapel Hill, N.C.
She is the Sallie Sanders above b. 1898. This Bible was printed in
1769 in Edinburgh, Scotland for Alexander Kincaid, His Majesty's
Printer. From a newspaper clipping in the Bible, "Mrs. Susan Edmondson, Esq. of Wilson, N.C. d. 21 Feb 1872, aged 84 yrs. She was
born 20 Jan 1789. She was a Methodist."]

JAMES W. SARGENT

James W. Sargent b. 3 Feb 1770 in Frederick Co., Md., d. 3 Apr 1847
in Felicity, Ohio, m. in 1791 to Sarah McNeal b. 24 May 1766 in
Frederick Co., Md., d. 28 Jan 1845 in Felicity, Ohio.
    Children
Anna b. 15 Dec 1792
Erasmus b. 22 Apr 1794
Nelson b. 19 Feb 1796
Catharine b. 19 Feb 1799
James T. b. 8 Sep 1802
William R. b. 19 Apr 1806 in Felicity, Ohio, d. 3 May 1864 in Fe-
    licity, Ohio, m. 15 Nov 1836 to Mary Clark Wells b. 19 Sep 1812
    in Felicity, Ohio, d. 25 Apr 1883 in Grundy Center, Iowa
John McNeal b. 12 Nov 1812

    Children of Wm. R. & Mary Clark Wells Sargent
Melancthon b. 25 Sep 1837
Elbert M. b. 8 Mar 1840
Mary Ann b. 28 Mar 1844
Sarah M. b. 23 Feb 1847
Margaret W. b. 20 May 1849
Joseph W. b. 24 June 1851
Wm. Clark b. 11 Nov 1853

[This Bible is from Miss Bertha K. Sargent, a descendant. She
found the additional data in Md. Parish records: Jas. W. Sargent,
son of Wm. Sargent & his wife Sarah Aldridge who were m. in Frederick Co., Md. Wm. Sargent d. in 1779. He was the son of James &
Eleanor Taylor Sargent who m. 9 Dec 1735.]

FREDERICK SCHUMPERT

Frederick Schumpert b. 23 Nov 1783, sponsors were Everhot Sweten-
berg & his wife Katherine Shaffer, d. 28 Jan 1846, m. 19 Mar 1805
to Mary Kinard b. 18 Dec 1787, sponsors were George Lever & his
wife Mary Chapman.

Katherine Schumpert b. 28 Jan 1806, sponsors were Frederick Schaf-
fer & wife Magdalena Eighlberger, m. 4 Jan 1827 to Bailey Conwell
Magdalena Schumpert m. 21 Oct 1830 to Jacob Long
Rhoda Schumpert m. 15 Mar 1834 to Robbert Y. Brown
Jacob K. Schumpert m. 1 Apr 1834 to Harriet Abney
Sarah Schumpert m. 2nd day A.D. 1837 to James Cureton
Amos Schumpert m. 24 Feb 1839 to Eliza Gray
J. F. Schumpert m. 20 Oct 1853 to Rachel Y. [?] Welch

Rebecca Schumpert d. 1 Nov 1823
Rhoda Brown d. 30 Apr 1835
Wm. Schumpert d. 16 Apr 1851
Elizabeth Schumpert d. 16 Apr 1854

[This Bible was printed in 1820, given to Ophelia C. Norris by the
late Elisha Cureton of Moreland, Ga. in 1925. The above Bible
record was copied by Mrs. Guy H. Norris.]

SEAWRIGHT

Jane Seawright b. 31 Jan 1771 [m. Isaac Cowan]
John Seawright b. 15 Nov 1772 [m. Jennet (Jane) Richey]
Mary Seawright b. 15 Aug 1775 [m. William Blain]
Andrew Seawright b. 5 Nov 1777 [m. Margaret Richey]
James Seawright b. 12 Aug 1779 [m. Margaret Miller]
Margaret Seawright b. 4 Mar 1782 [m. William Cowan, probably]
Eleanor Seawright b. 12 Nov 1784 [m. Leander Hopkins]

Isaac Cowan d. 25 Dec 1831
Jane Cowan, Sr. d. 11 Mar 1859

[A Loose Sheet in an old Bible in a Donald Home, contributed by
Carr Henry of Washington, DC, 1952.]

JAMES SEAWRIGHT

James Seawright b. 29 Oct 1809 [son of John], m. 1st on 15 Feb 1835
to Elizabeth Brownlee b. 10 Jan 1810, d. 31 Jan 1848, m. 2nd on 16
Mar 1852 to Sarah C. McLeese b. 2 Apr 1820, d. 8 Apr 1915 [?].
    Children
John Brownlee Seawright b. 20 Oct 1835
Sarah Jane Seawright b. 25 Feb 1838, d. 25 Sep 1855
Martha Ann Seawright b. 25 July 1839, m. 5 Feb 1861 to John B.
  Clinkscales
Mary Elizabeth Seawright b. 14 Oct 1842
Enoch Wilson Seawright b. 11 Mar 1845
James Seawright b. 15 Jan 1848
Susan Elizabeth Seawright b. 1 July 1856
Eliza Berthenie Seawright b. 5 Jan 1858
Ella Nora Seawright b. 5 Jan 1860

JOHN SEAWRIGHT

John Seawright b. 15 Nov 1772, d. 16 Mar 1850, m. Jane R. Seawright b. 12 Feb 1790, d. 13 June 1872.
    Children
James Seawright b. 29 Oct 1809, m. 15 Feb 1835 to Elizabeth Brownlee
Robert R. [Richey] Seawright b. 10 Sep 1811, d. 7 Nov 1881, m. 15 Jan 1846 to Essie Pyles
Polly Ann Seawright b. 7 Feb 1814, d. 27 June 1828
E. W. [Ebenezer Wilson] Seawright b. 24 Apr 1816, m. 17 Sep 1846 to M. [Mary] R. Rochester Pyles
John N. Seawright b. 17 Nov 1818, d. 14 July 1858, m. 23 Dec 1852 to Jane E. Cowan
William Seawright b. 2 June 1821, m. 31 Jan 1856 to Elizabeth Gaines
Elizabeth Seawright b. 30 May 1824, m. 15 Jan 1846 to Samuel Pruitt
Margaret Caroline Seawright b. 22 Jan 1827, d. y.
Andrew Thompson Seawright b. 11 Nov 1828, m. 8 Feb 1855 to Cornelia Hawthorne
Emily Caroline Seawright b. 31 Dec 1831, m. Col. Samuel Donald
Isaac Cowan Seawright b. 26 Apr 1833, m. 2 July 1857 to L. C. Hawthorne

Andrew Seawright d. 19 Aug 1827
Rebecca Seawright d. 11 Nov 1827
William L. Seawright d. 9 Sep 1856
J. C. Seawright d. 28 June 1862
Robert N. Seawright d. 8 Aug 1869
Sara Jane Seawright d. 21 Sep 1855

[From Mr. & Mrs. W. O. Brownlee, Due West, S.C.]

THOMAS SHEARER

Thomas Shearer b. 17 Nov 1782; Sarah Shearer, was Sara Brooks, dau. of William Brooks, b. 6 Mar 1788

Warren Waldo Shearer b. 17 May 1809
Oiver Vassar Shearer b. 8 Sep 1810, d. 25 July 1876, m. 11 Oct 1845 to Elvira Jane Wallis b. 14 Nov 1816, d. 23 July 1910
Joseph Berry Shearer b. 20 June 1812
Thomas Brown Shearer b. 19 Feb 1814
Nancy Ellenor Shearer b. 16 Nov 1815
William Beck Shearer b. 5 Apr 1818
Martha Beal Shearer b. 25 Oct 1819

Sarah Elizabeth Shearer b. 29 June 1836, d. 8 June 1897, m. 20 Oct 1857 to Edward Parish
Mary Catherine Shearer b. 14 Nov 1837, d. July 1920, m. 15 Sep 1859

to James Mason Kern
Oliver Brent Shearer b. 14 Aug 1845

Florence Olivia Shearer, dau. of Oliver V. Shearer, b. 2 Oct 1849
Fannie Rebecca Shearer b. 15 Mar 1851, d. 21 Sep 1852
Andrew Vassar Shearer b. 3 Nov 1853, d. 18 Oct 1912, m. 20 July
   1888 to Fannie Lawn Ligon b. 7 Nov 1863

John Ligon Shearer b. 10 July 1891
Oliver Vassar Shearer b. 31 May 1897

John Ligon Shearer, Jr. b. 12 Mar 1918
Daniel Donovan Shearer b. 5 Dec 1923

[The above Dr. Thos. Shearer & wife lived in Blount Co., Ala. till
about 1855 & moved to Chickosaw Co., Miss. Copied for Major E. E.
Skinner by Margaret Donovan Shearer from Bible in her possession.]

DANIEL SHEW

Daniel Shew b. 2 Feb 1784 in Wilks Co., N.C., m. Eve Dorothy York
b. 15 Oct 1792 in Randolph Co., N.C.

John Philip Shew b. 11 Sep 1813
Henry Shew b. 14 Nov 1815
Joel Shew b. 23 Sep 1817
Eli Shew b. 11 July 1819
Mary M. Shew b. 17 May 1821
Matilda Shew b. 11 July 1823
Leonard Merion Shew b. 4 July 1823
Geo. Washington Shew b. 8 July 1828

[This Bible record was sent to the compiler by Mrs. Verna Bergmann,
Sandy, Utah. It came from an old German Bible she found in the
home of Wm. Henry Shew, Clinton, Ind. He d. in 1942. He said that
the Bible had come to him from his father, Joel Shew.]

GEORGE HUSE SHINER

Geo. H. Shiner b. 20 June 1797 near Winchester, Frederick Co., Va.,
d. 27 Aug 1856 near Lyndon, Whiteside Co., Ill., m. 10 Dec 1820 to
Rachel Curlet Pierce, dau. of Michael Pierce, b. 1 Apr 1800, d. 5
Mar 1866 near Old Buckingham, Ia. [should be Va.?].
   Children
Tobias Riley b. 9 Jan 1822
Washington b. 9 May 1823
Stewart Baldwin b. 19 Jan 1825
Feilding b. 26 Dec 1826
Mary Ann b. 28 Oct 1829, d. 2 Aug 1831
Mary Elizabeth b. 21 Oct 1832
Geo. William b. 11 Feb 1835
Gabrilla Augusta b. 17 Mar 1837 near Dublin, Wayne Co., Ind.

Alford Pierce b. 5 June 1839 near Dublin, Wayne Co., Ind.
Sarah Jane b. 12 Jan 1841 near Dublin, Wayne Co., Ind.
Rachel Mali-s-e b. 23 Jan 1844 near Bowling Green, Clay Co., Ind.

Sarah Lester [also Lister] d. 16 Sep 1832, aged 90 yrs., 4 mos., 11
days in the home of Geo. Huse Shiner [Geo. Shiner & his younger
sister were reared by their maternal grandmother, Sarah Lester,
on a little farm on Opequin Creek, 4 miles east of Winchester.]

[This Bible owned in 1915 by Sarah Woodward.]

REUBEN SIMS

Reuben Sims b. 27 Dec 1750, d. 10 Aug 1816, m. 10 Oct 1772 to Nancy
d. 12 Oct 1834.
        Children
John b. 19 Sep 1773
Charles b. 1 Oct 1776
Priscilla b. 2 May 1779
Mary b. 19 July 1781, d. 26 Oct 1856, m. 12 Sep 1802 to John Lyles
    b. 25 Dec 1776, d. 27 Sep 1842
Elizabeth b. 19 Oct 1783
Sicila b. 12 Aug 1786
Nancy b. 8 Sep 1789
Jemima b. 16 May 1792

        Children of John & Mary S. Lyles
Benj. Saunders b. 4 Aug 1803
Eliz. Chrismus b. 8 June 1805, m. 1st on 1 Apr 1819 to Thos. T.
    Lyles, m. 2nd on 1 Apr 1828 to William Lyles who d. 13 Mar 1832
Thos. Jefferson b. 26 May 1808, m. 29 Nov 1842 to Eliz. Richards;
    Ann Eliz. Richards Lyles b. 20 July 1824, d. 14 Feb 1845
Reuben Sims b. 8 Nov 1811
John Valentine b. 19 Apr 1816

Arramanos Lyles, father of John Lyles, d. 2 Sep 1817

[Bible owned by Mrs. Wm. A. Huey, 2803 Gervais St., Columbia, S.C.
The Sims & Lyles families were of Union Co., S.C.]

SLOAN-BLAKELY

    Early in 1700, four stalwart sons of Erin, County Antrim,
Scotch Irish, landed in this country, and settled in Newberry Dist.
They were Richard (Dickie) Archibald, Robert and John. The last
was your g. g.father.
    Dickie went to Edgefield, and John to Laurens. I think Robert
& Archie went to Fairfield or Chester. Dickie married three times.
When he married his last wife he was 105 years of age, he died at
107.
    These four brothers served through the War of Independence.
Your g.g.father was wounded near Musgrove Mill in what was then

known as seige of 96'. He carried the ball with him through his
long life.

Your g.g. father was born 14th day of Sept. 1716 and died 26th
day of Dec. 1829, aged 113 y. 3 mo. 12 d. He brought his young
wife and two children with him, also a little Irish Lassie. During
a scourge of small pox, his wife and both children died and himself severly marked. After a widowhood of some years and at the
age of 58, he led this Irish Lassie (Jennet McNeere) at the age of
13, to Hymen's Altar. This proved to be a happy and fruitful marriage. They raised and educated 11 children, 6 boys and 5 girls:
Vie. Bettie, John, Robert (your g.f.), Mary, David, Mattie, Arch,
Rosa, Jennie, Thomas, and William. Now of these, Bettie, Rosa and
Archie never married. John married quite young to his cousin
(Sloan) in Newberry. And being prejudiced against our institution
of slavery, picked himself up and went to Indiana, Lincoln Co. To
diverge a little, I found some of his family when I was a prisoner
(North). They were not friends of ours in that great struggle.
One of his grand-sons, if he was at his post at the time, helped to
burn Columbia. BUT--Robert, your g. father, married Mattie Taylor
and had 3 children: William married McKelvey and had 6 children;
Isabella m. David Blakley and had 7 children, and James m. Mattie
Blakley and had 8 children.

Children of James and Mattie Blakley: Walter, Sam, Karl, Willie Blakley, Lidie & Lucy twins, Mattie married John Compton and
had 12 children, Mary married an Irishman, no kin, had 12 children,
Robert Sloan. He was a millwright and built several mills in the
country. Amongst them the Fleming Mill on Duncans Creek. Jennie
married Stoddard, had no children. David married a Sloan and
raised 6 children, all of whom passed the 3 score & ten, two of
them, James F. & John 84, and all lie in Spartanburg. Thomas married a Brown and had no children. They are buried at Clinton, S.C.
William married a Fowler had one child, John F. Sloan, Fountain
Inn, S.C.

Now your great grand mother, died in 1836 in her 75th year.
Your g.g.f. was 91y, 11m. & 10d. And your g.g.m. was 45 when their
last child William Sloan was born, yet he lived to see this boy 23
years old. Of his 11 children they lived from 70 to 97 years. I
just remark your g.g.f. was an inveterate pipe smoker and took his
toddy every morning. It is truthfully said, not one of these long
lived sons & daughters of this glorious commonwealth was ever a de-
fendant in any criminal procedure or was ever in durance vile.
They were all Seceders and genuine Scotch Irish. I am satisfied
that the president of S.C. University, Benjamin Sloan, is the grand
son of one of these 4 immigrants, either Robert or Dickie

Your g.f. was b. April 8, 1787 & d. Sept. 21, 1857.
Your g.m. was b. Oct. 4, 1796 & d. Sept. 2, 1867.
The above is taken from memory and family records.
                    J.P. Sloan

Now your great-grand-father was Robert Taylor whose father and
mother both came from north of Ireland. Scotch Irish Presbyterians,
true to the manor born. He married a Hayes of the same blood and

285

faith, they had 6 children: Mattie, Billy, Margaret, Jim, Jinnie, and Jack. They all married and tilled the ground, which brought forth for them a comfortable and wholesome living.

Now we turn to your maternal grand parents, Sam Blakley. He married a Flemming who was the mother of Mattie and Bettie Blakley, you are familiar with them. Your g.f. married again, to Sallie Franks, who is the mother of Dr. S.F.B. & Lidie Blakely. He was the father of David Blakley, William Blakley, John & Jonathan Blakley and Katharine Blakley of Greenville and Isabella Rowland and one James Blakley of Alabama. They were the children of Wm. Blakely Senr. of Revolutionary fame, who lived a great part of his life and died on his 87th birthday and was buried at Old Providence Church, a member of that church and denomination. I believe he gave the grounds for the church and grave yard. Your g.f. B. buried a child, the first interment at Providence. That old church building was bought by the colored brethren and stands on the East corner of the Pore house lands and still holds its name, Providence.

There is no better family ever raised in this county than the Blakely, they very truthfully boast of their ancestors, those that are living, and may well say our fathers were true men and our women Christian mothers. They sprang from English ancestry.

As far as I know them they are an agricultural people, a few speculators and mechanics and merchants, all very successful.

Respectfully submitted by your Father and Mother.

John Sloan d. 26 Dec 1829, aged 113 yrs., 3 mo., & 12 days., a native of Ireland, a soldier of 1776, and a sincere believer in Jesus Christ. "How lovely is thy dwelling place,/ O Lord of Hosts to me,/ The Tabernacles of thy Grace,/ How pleasant, Lord, they be."

Robert Sloan b. 8 Apr 1787, d. 21 Sep 1857, aged 70 yr., 5 mos., 13 days, m. 16 Mar 1820 to Marya Taylor, dau. of Robert & Elizabeth Taylor, b. 4 Oct 1798, d. 2 Sep 1867 in Laurens Dist., S.C., in her 72nd yr.

William Winder Sloan b. 3 Apr 1822, d. 11 Dec 1865, aged 43 yr., 8
  mos., 8 days
Isabell Katherin Sloan b. 7 Sep 1825
James Park Sloan b. 14 Oct 1828, d. 10 Apr 1911
Margaret Jane Sloan b. 23 May 1824, d. 13 June 1824, aged 20 days

Children of William Winder Sloan & Talula McKelvy Sloan
James Laurence Sloan b. 16 Feb 1854, son of Wm. & Lucy Talula Sloan
Laura Talula Sloan b. 30 Aug 1855, d. 11 Mar 1873, aged 17 yr., 6
  mos., 11 days
Wm. Preston Brooks Sloan b. 12 Feb 1857
Mary Isora Sloan b. 31 Mar 1860
Mattie Caroline Sloan b. 18 Jan 1862
Thomas Jackson Sloan b. 4 Mar 1864, d. 23 Oct 1864

Children of Isabell Katherin Sloan Blakely & David Blakely
Robert Thompson b. 8 May 1857

James Milton b. 6 Aug 1858
Augustus Byrd b. 9 Dec 1859
Mattie Jane b. 8 July 1863
Blufort Bee b. 30 Nov 1861
Elizabeth Hortense b. 5 July 1865
Laura Isabell b. Mar 1867

Children of James Park & Mattie Emiline Blakley Sloan
Margaret, first born 28 Feb, d. 15 Mar 1869
Walter Barkley b. Wednesday, 30 Nov 1870, bapt. 11 Mar 1871 at
    Providence Church by Rev. David F. Haddon
Samuel Robert b. Thursday, 7 Dec 1872, bapt. 16 Mar 1873 at Bethel
    Church Ora by Rev. D. F. Haddon
Karl Winder b. Thursday, 19 Nov 1874, bapt. 21 Mar 1875 at Bethel
    Church, Ora by Rev. D. F. Haddon
William James b. Wednesday, 23 May 1877, bapt. on the 2nd Sabbath
    in July following at Bethel by Rev. David Haddon
Eugene Blakley b. Thursday, 25 Dec 1879
Lidie Jane & Lucy Belle b. 13 Mar 1882
Mattie Elizabeth b. Wednesday, 7 Jan 1885

Wm. Winder Sloan m. 13 Jan 1853 to Lucy Talula McKelvy, dau. of
    Hugh & Mary McKelvy
Isabell Katherin Sloan m. 9 Sep 1856 to David Blakley
James Park Sloan m. 21 June 1866 to Mattie Emeline Blakley, dau. of
    Samuel Scott & Jane Fleming Blakley
Samuel Scott Blakley b. 19 Sep 1814, d. 19 Jan 1892
Sallie Franks Blakley, 2nd wife of Samuel Scott Blakley, b. 14 Nov
    1820, d. 15 Mar 1898
Elizabeth Jane Blakley d. 10 Apr 1896, aged 51 yrs., 8 mos., 17 d.

[The above information was taken from a scrapbook compiled by Capt.
James P. Sloan and his wife. He was a Capt. in the Confederate
Army. This book is now the property of his grand-son, James Sloan
of Clinton, S.C. 1953. "Some recollections and Sketches of the ancestors of J.P. & M.E. Sloan. Written by J.P. Sloan and given to
his son, Willie Sloan and wife."]

AMBROSE SMITH

    Children of Ambrose Smith
Jacob b. 12 July 1836
Manuel b. 2 May 1847
James b. 3 Aug 1849
    Children by 2nd wife: Nancy, Katie, Rudolphus

[See Jacob Smith Bible below]

DAVID SMITH

David Smith b. 7 Sep 1746, d. 14 Sep 1783, m. 31 Dec 1771 to Charity b. 6 Apr 1756, d. 21 Aug 1818.

Children
Edith b. 26 Dec 1772, d. Mar 1842
Samuel b. 29 Sep 1774, d. 17 Mar 1813
William b. 5 Aug 1776, d. 10 Oct 1833
Rachel b. 10 Jan 1778, d. 20 May 1842
Mary b. 10 Dec 1779, d. 1 Feb 1799
David, Jr. b. 18 Sep 1781, d. 11 Feb 1805
Jonathan b. 20 June 1783, d. 2 Sep 1819
Whitfield b. 7 Sep 1785, d. 25 Mar 1817
Charity b. 8 Jan 1788, d. 15 Oct 1843
Elizabeth b. 27 Jan 1790, d. 24 Nov 1790
Needham b. 25 Mar 1793, m. 20 Apr 1819 to Sarah b. 13 Dec 1794
Lewis b. 22 Oct 1795, d. 1 Sep 1796

[From Mrs. Ida B. Kellam, Wilmington, N.C. who adds, "David Smith
was the son of Samuel Smith who was the son of John Smith of Johnston Co., N.C. Owner of this Bible is Mrs. Louisa Williams Hicks,
502 W. Divine St., Dunn, N.C. Bible published 1762. Covers lost
also part of the records."]

FARQUHARD SMITH

Farquhard Smith b. 13 Dec 1801, m. 16 Dec 1824 to Sally Slocumb
Grady b. 14 Nov 1805.
     Children
Susan b. 23 Dec 1825
John Durham b. 5 Apr 1827
Alexander b. 22 June 1828
Isabella b. 10 Jan 1830
Mary b. 30 Mar 1831
Wm. Curtis b. 30 Nov 1832
James b. 28 June 1834
Elizabeth Evans b. 1 May 1836
Walter Douglass b. 6 Sep 1837
Farquhard b. 8 May 1839
Henry Elliott b. 23 Mar 1841
Edward b. 7 Mar 1845
Jane b. 26 July 1846
Slocumb b. 7 Jan 1849

[Farquhard Smith's father or grandfather was a John Smith who moved
from Va. to N.C. Smithfield, N.C. was named for Farquhard Smith.
This Bible is owned by Mrs. Samuel Kirkland, Ayr Mount, Hillsboro,
N.C. She was Emily Smith.]

JACOB SMITH

Jacob Smith b. 24 Oct 1782, m. 1st to Susan Spoon b. 28 Sep (Aug)
1789, m. 2nd to Suffie [probably Ritsel] b. 23 Feb 1800.
     Children
Ambrose b. 15 Mar 1808
Polly Ann b. 24 Feb 1811

288

Lizzie b. 20 Mar 1813
Tillie b. 14 Mar 1815
Loucian (Loricean) [called Lucy B.] b. 17 June 1820
Francis b. 11 Oct 1823

[From Elmer Smith, Rt. 5, Goshen, Ind. who states, "Jacob Smith came
to Orange Co., Ind. from Orange Co., N.C. in 1816. He has a land
grant entry in Orange Co., Ind. of that date. His will was probated in 1824 in Orange Co., Ind. See also the Ambrose Smith Bible]

JOHN CAMPBELL SMITH

John C. Smith d. 5 Dec 1875 at his home in Cumberland Co., N.C.,
aged 70 yrs., 2 mos. & 20 days, m. 1 Jan 1830 to Elizabeth Campbell
                              Children
James C. b. 22 Oct 1830, d. Dec 1888
Isabella Winifred b. 28 Sep 1832, m. 22 Dec 1852 to Edward Sanders
Sarah Eliz. b. 11 Oct 1834
John Alex. b. 30 Sep 1836
Farquherd (Farquard) b. 23 Sep 1838
Mary Catherine b. 18 Dec 1840
Wm. Robert b. 12 Nov 1842
Jane b. 2 Nov 1844

    [Children of Edward & Isabella W. Smith Sanders]
Louisa E. Sanders b. 11 May 1856
William A. Sanders b. 30 June 1858
Julia B. Sanders b. 9 July 1860
John B. Sanders b. 22 Sep 1861
Julia M. Sanders b. 17 Dec 1867
Edward A. Sanders b. 12 Apr 1869
Robt. Campbell Sanders b. 26 July 1872
Willie Hunter Sanders b. 11 Nov 1873

[There are a number of later marriages following that of John C. &
Eliz. C.]

MOSES SMITH

    Children of Moses Smith & wife Ann
Phoebe b. 6 Apr 1785 [m. Dunn & moved to Ind.]
Jane b. 12 Dec 1787 [m. Cullins & moved to Ind.]
William b. 16 Apr 1790
George b. 26 May 1794
Robert b. 1 Nov 1796
Benjamin b. 6 Sep 1799 [m. Lucinda Dodson]
Samuel b. 6 Jan 1802
Ebenezer b. 14 June 1804 [m. Mary Ann Haddon & moved to Ind.]

[The following ar tombstone records for this family in Greenville,
S.C.:
Moses Smith/ Rev. War Soldier/ d. 6 June 1837, aged 81 yrs.

Ann/ wife of/ Moses Smith/ d. 6 Dec 1830, aged 69 yrs.
Benj. Smith/ 4/ Sep 1799/ 1 Nov 1877
Lucinda, wife of Benj. Smith: 24 July 1816/ 4 Sep 1872
Saml. Smith/ 15 May 1803/ 30 Sep 1882
Jane, wife of Saml. Smith/ 31 Jan 1807/ 1 Nov 1879
    Records from Leonard Andrea, Columbia, S.C.]

ROBERT SMITH

Robert Smith b. 20 Feb 1760
Ferguson Smith b. about 1 Nov 1767, on shipboard

    Children of Robert Smith
Hugh Smith b. 27 Nov 1787
Elizabeth Smith b. 4 July 1789
Jane Smith b. 19 May 1792
Robert Wilson Smith b. 10 Mar 1794
Ann Adair Smith b. 15 Aug 1796
Mary Smith b. 14 Dec 1798
David Smith b. 16 Sep 1801
Rosanna Smith b. 4 May 1804
William Smith b. 12 June 1811

[Robert Smith was a Rev. soldier & received land in Butts Co., Ga.
in Lottery of 1827. Robert Wilson Smith was a soldier of the War
of 1812 while living in Charlestown, S.C. Robert Van Smith, son of
Robert Wilson Smith, was a Confederate soldier of 6th Ga. Regiment
& is still living in Butts Co., Ga. Bible records copied from DAR
Magazine, March 1938 by Rosa Thornton Lane (Mrs. John E. Lane)
State Historian, Ga. Soc., DAR, from the Bible, printed by Sir D.
Hunter Blair & J. Bruce, Printers to the King's Most Excellent Maj-
esty, and brought from Ireland by the Smith Family in 1760. The
Bible is now in the possession of S.K. Smith, Cork, Butts Co., Ga.]

ROBERT SMITH

Robert Smith b. 14 Nov 1821, d. 9 May 1870, m. 18 Nov 1846 to Lea-
thy Matlock b. 26 Aug 1814, d. 27 Nov 1895.
    Children
Thompson N. b. 21 Oct 1848
James M. b. 4 Sep 1850
John W. b. 17 Sep 1852
Robert B. b. 8 Aug 1855

Martha Smith, mother of Robert Smith, d. 1 July 1870
Harriet Smith d. 24 May 1887

[This record from Mr. Norman Smith, 1206 Sixth St., Durham, N.C. in
1953.]

WILLIAM HENRY SMITH

Henry Smith d. 18 July 1845, m. Sarah (Adams) Smith d. 22 Apr 1845,
[grandparents of Wm. H. Smith]
James Smith d. 9 Dec 1874, m. Hollon (Little) Smith d. 24 Aug 1849
aged 61 yrs., 3 mos., 18 days [parents of Wm. H. Smith]

Edward Nelson, son of Edward Nelson & Winifred Johnson Nelson, b.
16 Oct 1803, d. 15 Oct 1867, aged 62 yrs., 6 mos., 7 days [signed
"Mary Smith, July 1887"], m. 20 Jan 1825 to Sally Roach, dau. of
Chas. Roach & Polly Summers, his wife, b. 8 Mar 1805

Wm. Henry Smith, son of James & Holland Little Smith, b. 20 Dec
1820, d. 11 Feb 1885, m. 15 Mar 1846 to Mary Nelson, dau. of Edward
& Sarah Roach Nelson, b. 2 Oct 1825, d. 18 Feb 1907.
        Children
Edward Augustus b. 29 Feb 1848
Mary Virginia b. 11 Feb 1850, d. 3 Oct 1852
Emily Evelyn b. 23 Nov 1852
Sarah Roach b. 18 July 1854
Winifred Magdalene b. 11 June 1856
Jas. Henry b. 12 Mar 1858, d. 15 Nov 1893
Claudius Ferdinand b. 21 May 1860, d. 15 Nov 1893
Adelaide b. 16 Feb 1862
Geo. Ferdinand b. 9 Jan 1864
Mary Virginia b. 16 Feb 1866
Holland Little b. 23 Jan 1868

Augustus W. Nelson, son of Edward, Jr., b. 21 Nov 1833
Jennet Nelson, dau. of Edward Nelson, Sr., b. 26 Mar 1790, d. 11
May 1858

[This Bible is owned by Mrs. J. T. Gaylord, Winterville, N.C. 1959]

ROBERT W. SNEAD

Robert W. Snead d. very suddenly, 11 Apr 1854, m. 2 Dec 1828 to
Polly, dau. of Isaac Williams, d. 30 Jan 1849.
        Children
Serena Margaret b. 22 Sep 1829 in Johnston Co., N.C.
Betsy Franklin b. 5 Nov 1830, d. 24 Sep 1812 in Wilmington, N.C.
Thomas D. b. 22 Jan 1832
Charles H. b. 14 May 1833
George Poindexter b. 7 Sep 1835
Edward Dudley b. 20 Jan 1837
Laura b. 22 Oct 1838
Nathan b. 3 Apr 1840
Agnes b. 16 Jan 1842
Catherine b. 21 Aug 1844
Walter Robert b. 7 Jan 1845
Christopher Dudley b. 25 July 1846, d. 21 Apr 1848 of whooping
cough

Franklin Snead d. 24 May 1845 [no relationship given]
Wm. K. Lee d. 25 Feb 1847 of consumption [may be a slave]
Thomas Snead d. 26 Sep 1812 in Wilmington, N.C. [The family has
    proven that he was the father of Robert W. Snead.]

[This Bible was printed in 1832 in Cooperstown, N.Y. by H. & E.
Phinney. A newspaper clipping in this old Bible has this obituary:
"Mrs. Serena Cox was born in Onslow Co., N.C. 4 Sept 1775. She
married Thomas Snead the 10th of Feb. 1791. After hes death she
married William Cox the 26th of Aug. 1817 and died June the 30th,
1856. She was a member of the Methodist Church." This Serena
Snead Cox is obviously the mother of Robert W. Snead. This Bible
is owned by Mrs. Fred O. Bowman, Sr., Chapel Hill, N.C.]

GEORGE SOWERS

Geo. M. Sowers b. 3 May 1821 in Washington Parish, La., m. Margar-
et M. Wallace b. 21 Sep 1818 in Miss.
    Children
Henriette S. b. 27 Dec 1844 in Miss.
Christopher C. b. 24 Jan 1847 in Miss.
John F. b. 27 Sep .... in Miss.
Wm. J. b. 12 Nov 1850 in Miss.
Newton C. b. 8 Jan 1853 in Miss.
Ollif C. b. 21 Oct 1854 in Miss.
Zekiel T. b. 13 Dec 1856 in Miss.
Benj. F. b. 5 Nov 1858 in Miss.
Sarah M. b. 21 May 1862 in Miss.

[This Bible in possession of Wm. Ernest McCarty, Alto, Texas.]

MICHAEL SPAINHOUR

Michael Spainhour b. 15 Apr 1807, d. 26 Feb 1889 at his home in
Burke Co., N.C., m. 16 Mar 1834 to Lettie Estes b. 14 Aug 1814, d.
23 June 1892 in Morganton, N.C.
    Children
James Henry b. 14 Jan 1835, d. 17 Oct 1861 at Fredericksburg, Va.,
    was Chaplain of 1st N.C. troops
Martha Elizabeth b. 2 July 1837, d. 2 Dec 1891, m. 20 May 1858 to
    Lafayette Hemphill
Rufus Atkin b. 5 Oct 1839, d. 23 Mar 1928, aged 88 yrs., 5 mos.,
    18 days, m. 5 Sep 1866 to Mollie Ginnings
John Cornelius b. 18 Jan 1842
William Robert b. 8 Oct 1844, m. 1st on 3 July 1881 to Jennie L.
    Parks d. 10 Aug 1884, m. 2nd on 27 Dec 1892 to Ida Hardin
Julius Noah b. 14 Feb 1847, d. 5 Dec 1848
Joseph Felix b. 7 June 1850, d. 17 Nov 1939, aged 89 yrs., 5 mos.,
    10 days, m. 26 Sep 1883 to Susan Adella Parks d. 3 Feb 1945, aged
    79 yrs., 9 mos., 12 days
Mary Selma b. 2 June 1855
Margaret Ann (Maggie A.) b. 1 June 1858, m. 6 June 1877 to R. L.

Patton

Daughters of Wm. R. Spainhour
Ruby b. 27 Apr 1882, m. Miller
Jessie b. 19 Jan 1884, m. Powell

Children of Joseph Felix Spainhour
Lettie Parks b. 30 June 1884 in Va.
Willie Celia b. 24 July 1888 in Boone, N.C.
Carl Michael b. 22 June 1890
Paul Gordon b. 26 Sep 1893
Annie Elizabeth b. 1 Apr 1895 in Morganton, N.C.
Jos. F., Jr. b. 14 Dec 1898
Ralph Aycock b. 31 Oct 1902
Susan Parks b. 28 Mar 1905
Walter Judson b. 8 July 1908

W. Lee Hemphill b. 13 Feb 1859, d. 13 Apr 1887 in Nebraska
James L. Hemphill b. 17 Apr 1862
Mary S. Spainhour m. 11 May 1873 to John L. Sisk
Peter Spainhour d. 1 Aug 1854, aged 85 yrs.
Catherine Spainhour d. 12 May 1864, aged 87 yrs.
Joseph C. Spainhour d. 9 Aug 1862 near Richmond, Va.
Eliza E. Spainhour d. 1 Sep 1857
Eliza Grayson d. 28 Mar 1926
Mary Jane Parks d. 20 Jan 1855
E. V. Parks d. 18 Jan 1855, both died of scarlet fever
James T. Parkes d. of scarlet fever 25 Jan 1855
Wm. C. Parks d. of scarlet fever 13 Oct 1863

[This Bible is owned by Mrs. Willie C. Spainhour Greer (Mrs. I. G.)
Chapel Hill, N.C. The Spainhours go back to antiquity in Switzerland and had a part in the Reformation. Three brothers came to
America and Peter came to N.C. Mrs. Greer has an ancient Bible
with records going back to the 1500's.]

HENRY A. SPANN

Henry A. Spann b. 28 Jan 1843, d. 29 Sep 1916, m. 25 Oct 1866 to
Lina Cunningham b. 20 Oct 1845, d. 30 Nov 1907.

Lcuile Spann, eldest child of Henry A. & Lina Spann, b. 17 Oct 1868,
    bapt. 1871 by G. W. McCrighton; Lucile Spann Mattison d. 10 Nov
    1902
Joseph Cunningham Spann b. 20 June 1871, bapt. 1871, d. 1 Jan 1874
Virginia Spann b. 21 Jan 1873, bapt. 17 Feb 1874
Lina Bell Spann b. 23 Oct 1874, bapt. 1876
John Cunningham Spann b. 17 May 1876
William Henry Spann b. 11 Mar 1878, bapt. 1879
Emmie Lou Spann b. 23 Sep 1880, bapt. 1881, d. 17 Aug 1904
George Fletcher Spann b. 2 Mar 1882, bapt. 1882
Anna Pearl(e) Spann b. 10 Mar 1886, bapt. 1886, d. 2 Oct 1935, m.

Harry G. Molony b. 30 Mar 1869, d. 13 Mar 1948

Sarah Warnock Molony b. 20 Aug 1910, m. 31 Mar 1927 to Joseph James
Gray, Sr. b. 15 Jan 1907

Joseph James Gray, Jr. b. 7 May 1928
Sarah Frances Gray b. 1 May 1930

[Bible owned by Mrs. James Joseph Gray of Wilmington, N.C., published by H. C. Peck & Theo. Bliss, 1857, Phila. On the fly-leaf:
Presented to Miss Sallie E. Cunningham by her Mother, 15 Mar 1864,
on her 15th birthday.]

PETER STALCOP

Peter Stalcop b. 1712 in Newcastle Co., Dela., d. 19 July 1768, m.
15 Dec 1737 at Holy Trinity (Old Swedes) Church, Wilmington, Dela.
to Susannah Poulson.
    Children
Johan b. 22 Apr 1739
William b. 27 May 1741
Tobias b. 1 Aug 1743
Swithin b. 1745
Rachel b. 1747, m. 31 Aug 1769 to Isaac Bracken
Lady b. 11 June 1750
Susanna b. 10 Aug 1754
Peter b. 21 Jan 1757

[This record was sent to the compiler by Mrs. Ivan L. Nichols of
Salt Lake City, Utah in Mar 1955. She found it in a thesis written
written by Harry G. Stalcop in 1946 for his M.A. degree at the
Univ. of Dela. Isaac Stalcop came with Isaac Bracken & wife Rachel
(Stalcop, sometimes Stalcup) to Orange Co., N.C. & the three names
appear again in the Sumner Co., Tenn. records. The N.C. Brackens
went to Tenn. about 1798 and 1800.]

WILLIAM STALCUP

William Stalcup was the son of William & wife Margaret Anderson who
were married 2 Oct 1762 in Old Swedes Church, Wilmington, Dela. &
both died in Smith Co., Tenn.
    Children of Wm., Jr.
Margaret b. 19 Nov 1797
Nancy b. 29 June 1799
Lydia b. 20 July 1804
Susannah b. 9 Oct 1806
James b. 9 Feb 1809
Mary b. 20 Nov 1810
William b. 10 Feb 1812
George b. 5 Oct 1813
Samuel b. 1 Jan 1815
Elizabeth b. 9 June 1821

Thomas Reed b. 15 Apr 1825

[Bible record from Mrs. Wesley Waldrop, Murray, Ky. who states,
"Margaret is my husband's great grandmother. She married Alex.
Dameron Jackson in 1817 in Smith Co., Tenn. This Alex. D. Jackson
came from Caswell Co., N.C. I think his mother must have been a
Dameron. His father was Isaac T. Jackson & he married in N.C."

JOHN WESLEY STARR

John Wesley Starr b. 7 Aug 1806 near Washington, Wilkes Co., Ga.,
d. 2 Feb 1870 in Bibb Co., Ala., m. 23 Dec 1824 in Washington, Ga.
to Hannah Miller b. 6 Nov 180 , d. 16 Feb 1891 in Camden, Ala.
     Their children
Elizabeth Fenton b. 25 Oct 1826, m. 9 Feb 1848 to Jas. Andrew Day
Joshua F. b. 29 Nov 1828, d. 25 Nov 1856, m. 1852 in Talladega,
     Ala. to Adaline M. Faire
John Wesley (Rev.) b. 22 Oct 1830, d. 20 Sep 1853, unmarried
Sarah Matthews b. 10 Dec 1831, m. 17 Sep 1855 to Jacob S. Hansberg-
     er, Dallas Co., Ala.
Martha Ann b. 16 Sep 1833, d. 19 July 1834
James Wesley b. 10 July 1835, d. 9 Feb 1902, m. 18 Nov 1890 to
     Adele Thalozon Bright, Mobile, Ala.
Emoery Parks b. 15 Feb 1837, d. 1 Apr 1837
Lucius Ernest (Dr.) b. 21 Mar 1838, d. 15 Mar 1913, m. 16 Jan 1879
     to Mary Eloise Tepper
Mary Frances b. 4 Feb 1840, d. 21 Aug 1919, m. 20 Dec in Bibb Co.,
     Ala. to Rev. Wm. Maltbie Winn
Wilbur Fish b. 3 July 1842, d. 20 July 1864 in Civil War
Elbert Soule b. 3 Feb 1845, d. 1908, m. 27 Oct 1868 to Sallie Ann
     Bennett
Wm. Henry Stephen b. 2 Nov 1846, never married
Catharine D. b. 20 Apr 1850, d. 21 July 1866

[This Bible record from Rev. F. S. Moseley of Ala. in 1956. Mrs.
B. W. Gandrud, Tuscaloosa, Ala. notes John Wesley Starr's father
was Joshua Starr and that his wife, Hannah Miller's, parents were
John Paul Miller & Elizabeth Shiptrine (name not clear).]

HISTASPAS STEWART

Histaspas Stewart d. June 1859; Eliza Nunn d. 1884
     Children
Histaspas Stewart b. 16 Feb 1838, d. 23 Feb 1900
Thomas Stewart b. 16 Dec 1827, d. 12 Sep 1886
Joe H. Stewart b. 20 Nov 1833, d. Aug 1893
Mary A. Stewart b. 14 July 1826, d. 9 Feb 1905
Atheldry A. Stewart b. 12 Nov 1846, d. 27 Jan 1908
Jane Stewart b. 1831, d. 6 Dec 1917
Narcissis Stewart Tapscott b. 25 Dec 1842, d. 8 May 1900
Eliza Stewart Key d. 1924
Ann Stewart Long b. 1848 or 1849, d. 1888

Lucy Stewart Woods d. in N.C.
Lizzie Stewart d. aged 5 yrs.

[Information told to Mrs. Lucy Stewart Bennett by Mrs. Lillie Tabscott McCormick, dau. of Narcissis Stewart Tabscott: The first
Histaspas Stewart came to Ala. from Mecklenburg Co., N.C. with a
family of Acocks when he was a young man. He is known to have had
several brothers; we know the names of two of them - Lincoln & Orth-
niel. Their mother was a Miss Hill. Histaspas m. Eliza Nunn whose
mother was a Brown. They belonged to the Presbyterian Church, and
Histaspas gave 20 acres of land for the Fairview Church in Morgan
Co. It is thought that at one time he owned one section of land.
Eliza Stewart died when she was 79 yrs. of age, in 1884. Histaspas
d. in June 1859. One of Histaspas' brothers had twin children,
Martha & Milas Stewart. Martha m. a Coltharp in Charlotte, N.C.
It was reported at one time that an enormous estate of the Col-
tharps was to be divided among relatives.]

LEONARD CROSBY STEWART

Leonard C. Stewart b. 30 Oct 1840, d. 23 May 1899, m. 30 Jan 1867
to Margaret Eliz. Ross b. 7 Jan 1847, d. 9 Mar 1905
    Children
Geo. Bert b. 3 Jan 1868, d. 24 Oct 1893
Cora Catherine b. 21 Mar 1870, d. 19 Mar 1940
Chas. Franklin b. 19 Nov 1871, living in Hamilton, Miss. in 1959

JOHN STINGLEY

John Stingley [of Newberry Co., S.C.] b. 2 Sep 1787, d. 4 ... 182.
[date not wholly legible], m. 30 June 1814 to Sarah Bernhard b. 15
May 1791, d. 21 Oct 1861.
    Children
James David Stingley, son, b. 11 Aug 1815, m. 14 Apr 1853 to Jane
    Campbell Cayce b. 4 June 1828
Louisa Stingley, dau., b. 24 Nov 1817
Mary Ann Stingley, dau., b. 23 Mar 1820, d. 7 July 1855

    Children of James David & Jane Campbell Cayce Stingley
John Jacob Stingley, son, b. 23 June 1854
Robert Cayce Stingley, son, b. 13 Oct 1855
David Bernhard Stingley, son, b. 23 Mar 1857
Bettie Rea Stingley, dau., b. 12 Nov 1857, d. 14 July 1860
Charles Edwin Stingley, son, b. 24 Apr 1860
James Campbell Stingley, son, b. 24 Apr 186-
Bachman Stingley, son, b. 11 Jan 1865
Sarah Wyse Stingley, dau., b. 30 June 1866

William Jane Cayce b. 29 July 1864
Benjamin B. Cayce b. 16 Jan 1867
Daniel Kinsler Cayce b. 15 Mar 1868

[This Bible owned by Ernest DuBard, Sallis, Miss. James David was married in Lexington Co., S.C. & carried the Bible to Attala Co., Miss.]

ROYAL STOKELY

Royal Stokely b. 10 Apr 1784, d. 22 Feb 1842 at Del Rio, Cocke Co., Tenn., son of Jehu & Nancy (Neil/Neal) Stokely, m. in 1804 to Jane Huff, dau. of John Huff & Mary Corder Huff, b. 21 June 1785 in Va., d. 29 Mar 1865 in Del Rio, Cocke Co., Tenn.
        Children
Mary (Polly) b. 10 Oct 1806 in Cocke Co., Tenn., d. 13 July 1868
    [m. Reuben A. Justus]
Joseph b. 22 Oct 1808 [m. a Holland]
John H. b. 1 Dec 1810 [m. Elvira Jones]
Sarah (Sally) b. 11 Apr 1813 [m. Warren Brooks]
Nathan b. 5 Mar 1816 [m. Evalina Jones]
Rhoda b. 5 Mar 1819 [m. Allen McMahan]
Charles b. 19 June 1821 [m. Sally Black]
Stephen H. (?) b. 27 Jan 1824 [m. Elizabeth Farr]
David D. b. 13 Nov 1828 [m. an Allen]

[The marriages given have been found & verified by Mrs. James L. Penland, 375 W. Badillo St., Covina, Calif.]

JEREMIAH STOKES

Jeremiah Stokes b. 19 June 1736, d. 18 Feb 1824, m. 14 Feb 1765 to Elizabeth Hughes b. 15 Feb 1738.
        Children
Jonathan b. 3 Feb 1766
Terry [Teresa] b. 15 Oct 1768, m. Elisha Green
Jeremiah, Jr. b. 2 Nov 1770 [? as to mo. & day], m. Elizabeth Hampton
Eliz. b. 6 Aug 1773, d. 20 Sep 1861, m. twice to Capt. Andrew Paul
    [in her father's will called Payne]
Levi b. 14 Feb 1775 [In a dower his wife is listed as Lucy]
John b. 12 Feb 1777, m. Lucy Wycliffe
Rachel b. 20 Apr 1779, m. Saml. A. Townes
Highes b. 30 May 1781 [? as to mo. & day], m. Mary Thompson

[Comments by L. Andrea, Columbia, S.C., prof. genealogist who says, "Jeremiah Stokes came from Md. to Greenville Co., S.C. after the Rev. War. Settled on the Reedy River & also owned lands just above Jackson Grove Church. His dau. Terry brought with her a rosebush planted in a tub from Md. When I was a boy this rosebush was still alive at the old Hardy Jones Gilreath house which is now owned by Miss Ruth Gilreath. John Stokes, son of Jeremiah, in a letter to his grandson, a son of his dau., Maria Louise Stokes who wed Wm. Goldsmith, stated that "my father Jeremiah Stokes was born in Wales & came to Md. when he was a boy" Mr. Thos. Wier Davis of Columbia, S.C. found the above data in 2 letters to his grandmother & dated

1914 from Greenville, S.C. One from Edna R. Cureton who stated
that Mrs. Kate Townes Corbett owned the Jeremiah Stokes Bible...
Later a letter from Mrs. Kate T. Cauble/Corbett states that her
mother owned the Bible and she was enclosing a partial copy but
said the old Benson Bible that her mother owned had been burned or
lost."]

EGBERT H. STRAYHORN

Egbert H. Strayhorn b. 18 Sep 1832, d. 1 July 1863, m. 18 Dec 1856
to Melinda Borland b. 1 July 1833, d. 30 Aug 1861.
    Children
John A. Strayhorn b. Mar 1859, d. 16 Oct 1859
Susan J. b. 31 May 1861, d. 26 Aug 1878
William G. b. 8 Oct 1863, m. 5 Oct 1892 to Nannie F. b. 15 Apr 1866

[This Bible copied in the home of Winston Strayhorn, just off the
highway between Hillsboro & Chapel Hill, N.C. Mrs. Winston Strayhorn brought out the following small and very old Bible which was
leather bound & with the letter S burned in on both covers and with
a very old metal fastener. She has no idea whose children these
Harts are. One name is missing at the bottom of the page which has
been torn off. This was very hard to decipher because it had been
written over fairly recently and the 8 was almost a guess in 1780,
etc.]

Jane Hart b. 27 Mar 1779
Nancy Hart b. 22 Apr 1780
John Hart b. 20 Nov 1782
Gilbert Hart b. 4 Aug 1784
Sarah Hart b. 10 May 1785

JOHN STRAYHORN

John Strayhorn b. 8 Sep 1791, m. 14 Nov 1822 to Susannah Borland b.
16 June 1799
    Their children
Willie Newton b. 22 Aug 1823
Maletha Ann b. 8 Oct 1825
Quintilian Green b. 27 Sep 1827
Jasper b. 20 Feb 1831, d. 10 May 1832
Egbert Haywood b. 18 Sep 1832
Sidney Gaston b. 15 Feb 1834
James Alexander b. 14 Apr 1836, d. 21 May 1842
John Yancey b. 24 Nov 1837, d. 25 Nov 1838
Susan Elizabeth b. 13 Aug 1839, d. 10 Sep same yr.

John Stryhorn, son of Gilbert, b. 1742, d. 1826, aged 84 yrs., m.
    Elizabeth Johnston, their son: David m. Annie Freeland & they
    were the parents of John who m. Eliza Cole
James, 3rd son of Gilbert Strayhorn, m. Rachel Cabe & their son,
    John m. Susan Borland

[The immigrant, Gilbert, came to N.C. from Dauphin Co., Pa. & was
in the Rev. War in N.C., died in Orange Co., N.C. on 6 Feb 1803.
Family records say he was b. in 1715. His sons John & James were
both in the Rev. War (See N.C. Colonial Records.)]

WILLIAM STRAYHORN

Wm. Strayhorn, Sr. b. 1756, d. 17 May 1834, aged 78 yrs.
Samson Moore b. 25 Apr 1783, d. 16 Feb 1830
Alfred Moore d. 1837, aged 55 yrs.
Thomas C. Moore b. 13 Jan 1821
Emeline Moore b. 18 Aug 1824 [yr. not very clear]
William Craig b. 1741 [was the immigrant], m. the widow of Geo.
Long, nee Logan

[David Craig, son of Wm. Craig, m. Eleanor Johnston. This very old
Bible is owned by Miss Mattie Blackwood, Chapel Hill, N.C., R.F.D.
She doesn't know to whom it belonged originally or how she got it.
She thinks it belonged to Nancy Moore (Strayhorn) Craig.]

MARHARTNEY STRICKLAND

Absalom Strickland b. in England
Joseph Strickland, son of Absalom b. 1778

Wright Strickland, son of Joseph, b. 8 May 1800, m. Lucindy b. 18
Oct 1802.
     Children
Mahartney Strickland b. 11 Feb 1827, m. 6 May 1847 to Catherine
   Bailey b. 8 Feb 1830
Martha Strickland b. 2 Oct 1836
Elizabeth Strickland b. 5 Dec 1838
Mary Strickland b. 22 Apr 1841
Lucinday Strickland b. 21 May 1844

     Children of Mahartney & Catherine Strickland
L. Wiley W. b. 10 Jan 1848 [m. Hattie Hendricks]
Joseph N. b. 20 Oct 1849
Sobedia b. 27 Dec 1851 [m. Henry Webb Hedgepeth]
Nicey Vashti b. 16 Feb 1853 [m. Jackson H. Harper]
Mary b. 16 Dec 1855 [m. Billie Taylor]
Hiram Wright b. 25 Dec 1856
Virginia b. 23 Jan 1858 [m. Charlie Griffin]
Vance [dau., m. Frank Taylor]
Cyrus Mahartney [m. Fannie Taylor]
Turner H.

     Children of Nicey V. & Jackson Harper
Jas. Wm. b. 2 Oct 1885
Mary D. b. 13 May 1887
Jackson H., Jr. b. Oct 1890
John Henry b. 1 Feb 1899

[These Strickland records were sent by Mrs. Clarence A. Griffin, 115 Wildwood Ave., Rockey Mount, N.C. in Aug 1959 to the compiler. The Mahartney Strickland Bible record came from Jas. W. Harper, grandson of Mahartney Strickland, Jefferson Co., Tex. It was notarized by L. R. Blakeman.]

WRIGHT STRICKLAND

Wright Strickland b. 8 May 1800 in Nash Co., N.C., m. [6 Sep 1825 in Wake Co., N.C.] to Lucinda Chamblee b. 18 Oct 1802
    Children
Mahartney b. 12 Feb 1827 [m. 6 May 1847 in Johnston Co., N.C. to Catherine Bailey]
Martha b. 3 Oct 1836 [compare above, m. 1st on 25 Nov 1851 to Joel Evans, m. 2nd on 23 Dec 1856 in Nash Co., N.C. Alex Stallings]
Elizabeth b. 5 Dec 1838 [m. Matthew Strickland]
Mary b. 22 Apr 1841, d. 8 Dec 1863, m. 26 Feb 1863 to James Privett, one child: Geo. Wm. Privett b. 27 Nov 1863
Lucinda b. 12 May 1844, m. 1st on 22 Jan 1862 to Josiah Johnston, m. 2nd on 19 Sep 1867 to Calvin Taylor

    Children of Lucinda Strickland Johnston Taylor
Josiah Johnston, Jr. b. 27 Nov 1862
Martha Ann Temperance Johnston b. 28 July 1866
Sidney Taylor b. 22 June 1868
Lucy A. Taylor b. 11 Jan 1870
Thos. Taylor [b. ca. 1874]

[This Bible was owned in 1955 by Mrs. Mavis Lucinda Griffin Speight who probably lives in Rocky Mount, N.C.]

JAMES SUMMERVILLE

Jas. Summerville b. 18 Mar 1777, m. 19 Feb 1801 to Elizabeth Fletcher b. 3 Jan 1784, d. 10 Sep 1848.
    Children
Mary b. 3 Dec 1801, d. 1864, m. Robt. Cunningham
Martha b. 27 Oct 1803, d. 9 Aug 1852
Ann b. 18 Sep 1805, d. 3 July 1829, m. Archibald Hood
Eliza Jane b. 11 May 1807, m. Saml. Hood
Margaret Lucinda b. 2 Oct 1809, d. 8 Apr 1850 [or 56], m. a Bell
John McWillie b. 1 Aug 1811
Jas. Fletcher b. 8 Jan 1815, d. 11 July 1860, m. Emma Barkley
Geo. Washington b. 11 Sep 1816, d. Apr 1865, m. Ann Mobley
Nancy Amelia b. 10 Mar 1818
David P. b. 7 Mar 1821
Hugh b. 28 Apr 1823, d. 4 May 1862, m. Mrs. Sterling Jones, nee Mary J. Owens, dau. of Wm. Owens & wife Eliz. Hood Owens
John b. 9 Oct 1825
Grace Amanda b. 10 July 183- [not clear]

[Bible now owned by Miss Eddie K. Reed, Aliceville, Ala. The information was sent by Leonard Andrea, Columbia, S.C. who says that Jas. Summerville b. in Beaver Cr. Twp., Kershaw Co., S.C.]

JOHN SUMMERVILLE

John Summerville b. 11 Dec 1780, d. 19 Aug 1857, m. 22 Feb 1810 to Sarah Hood b. 30 Jan 1785, d. 25 Feb 1867.
    Children
James b. 30 Jan 1811, m. 1st on 30 June 1847 to Eleanor Turnipseed,
    m. 2nd on 14 Feb 1856 to Miss L. J. Wilder
William Hood b. 20 June 1812, m. 1st to Mary Ann Turnipseed, m. 2nd
    on 3 Feb 1853 to Hermione Billups
Jane M. b. 5 Apr 1816, m. 10 Jan 1839 to Eli Goings
Margaret A. b. 7 Sep 1817, m. 1st on 17 Nov 184- to J. R. Westley
    Connerly, m. 2nd on 20 May 1856 to James Duncan
Martha Ann b. 9 Jan 1819, m. in 1848 to Henry G. Turner [or Turney]
    She & her little dau. were drowned 1 Mar 1859 on the Steamer
    Eliza Battle which sank on the Tombigbee River [Ala.]
Sarah E. b. 3 Feb 1821, m. 22 Aug 1844 to Wm. V. Stanton
Mary S. b. Aug 1825, d. 30 Jan 1855, m. 10 Jan 1846 to Milton Giles
John, Jr. b. 15 June 1827, m. 20 Oct 185- to Florida Billups

[Bible record from Miss Eddie R. Reed, Aliceville, Ala. who says, "Hugh Summerville was born in 1780. He was a brother of John. Both brothers wed daughters of William Hood of Beaver Creektownship, Kershaw Co., S.C. Hugh married Jane N. Hood and his brother John married Sarah Hood." William Hood left a will in Kershaw Co., S.C. signed 5 Oct 1827. This record and notes sent by Leonard Andrea, Columbia, S.C.]

THOMAS SWIFT

Thomas Swift b. 19 May 1759, m. Peggy b. 26 Aug 1762

Betsy Swift b. 2 Jan 1784
Harvey Swift b. 8 May 1785
Polly Swift b. 22 Oct 1786, d. 25 Mar 1816
Robert Swift b. 23 Oct 1788
Susanna Swift b. 8 Sep 1792
John Swift b. 4 May 1794

[This Bible is owned by Mrs. Pattie Gardner Gwaltney, Reidsville, N.C.]

WILLIAM TADLOCK

William Tadlock, son of Lewis & Elizabeth Tadlock, b. 19 Oct 1813 in Cashie Neck, Bertie Co., N.C., d.1 Jan 1869, aged 56 yrs.; Mary Heckstall, dau. of Wm. H. & Elizabeth Heckstall, b. 8 Feb 1819.

William J. Tadlock d. 9 Aug 1895, aged 52 yrs., m. lst on 31 Oct
1867 to Annie C. Northcutt d. 24 Mar 1888, m. 2nd on 26 Sep 1888 to
Georgia Harding.
    Children
Lela (Lila) Roeng Tadlock, dau., b. 20 Feb 1870, d. 12 Sep 1880,
    aged 11 yrs.
Core Elizabeth, dau., b. 10 Mar 1872
Emma Heckstall, dau., b. 15 Apr 1874, m. 17 Jan 1900 to Joseph
    Northcutt, their dau: Nannie b. 27 Dec 1900 in Edenton, d. 21
    Jan 1901, aged 3 weeks
William Andrew, son, b. 25 Nov 1875

Thos. W. Tadlock m. 30 Nov 1868 to Lue A. Bailey
William Gervis Tadlock d. 24 Oct 1838, aged 14
Elizabeth Mary Tadlock d. 5 Sep 1845, aged 5 yrs., 21 days
Walter R. Tadlock d. 7 June 1885, aged 2 yrs., 11 mos.
Mary Roberta Tadlock d. 24 Nov 1893

[Bible owned by Mrs. Northcutt of Aiken, S.C.]

ELISHA TARVER

Elisha Tarver b. 25 Dec 1787, d. 18 Mar 1860; Maria Sanders Tarver
b. 6 Aug 1793, d. 9 Sep 1851.
    Child
Josephine M. (Tarver) Driver b. 27 Feb 1830, m. lst on 4 Sep 1849
    by Rev. J. Starr to Elbert J. Driver, m. 2nd on 3 Feb 1875 by
    Rev. M. Brittain to Wm. N. Brogaw

    Children of Elbert J. & Josephine Driver
Chas. W. b. 25 June 1850
Geo. E. b. 23 Apr 1852
Louis S. b. 4 Oct 1853
Elbert J., Jr. b. 24 July 1855
Josephine M. b. 23 June 1857
Wm. A. b. 4 July 1859
Martha E. b. 10 Feb 1861
Harriet O. b. 10 Dec 1863
Mary M. b. 18 Aug 1865
Sallie R. b. 22 Feb 1867
Nellie J. b. 13 May 1868
Annie Lula b. 24 July 1870
Minnie E. b. 24 Dec 1871

[Information given by Mrs. Annie Driver Drake (Mrs. J. Hodges) to
her nephew L. F. Driver, Thomasville, Ga. from the Bible she owned.
Her address then was Auburn, Ala.]

ABNER TATOM

Abner Tatom [or Tatum], 5th child of John Tatom, Sr. & his wife Ann
Wright of Norfold, Va., b. 15 Oct 1755, m. 3 May 1780 Mary Currin.

```
           Children
Elizabeth Ann b. 20 Mar 1781
James b. 23 Feb 1783
Absalom b. 7 Aug 1785
Cynthia b. 7 Mar 1788
Barnett b. 14 Feb 1791
John b. 17 Nov 1793
Nancy b. 10 June 1798
William b. 29 Nov 1801, d. 2 Nov 1802
```

[Leonard Andrea of Columbia, S.C. says, "Abner Tatom was the first clerk of the Superior Court of Lincoln Co., Ga. & the above family is found inscribed by him on one page of the Clerk of Court Records." Abner Tatom was from Norfolk, Va. & went to Granville Co., N.C., then to 96 Dist., S.C., to Lincoln Co., Ga. & then to Madison Co., Ala.]

ISAAC TAYLOR

Isaac Taylor b. 4 Sep 1744, d. 29 Oct 1823, m. Henrietta b. 11 July 1762, d. 19 Oct 1843.
```
           Children
```
Isaac, Jr. b. 23 Sep 1786, d. 3 Mar 1829
Stanton b. 8 Sep 1784, d. 30 May 1841
Green b. 24 Apr 1794, d. 22 Apr 1860, m. Penelope Simmons d. 27 Sep 1867

Richard B., son of Green & Penelope Taylor, b. 15 Mar 1821, d. 4 Aug 1899
Lemuel T., son of Green & Penelope Taylor, b. 14 Feb 1823
Amos W., son of Green & Penelope Taylor, b. 26 Dec 1824
Wm. G. b. 11 Dec 1826
Jos. O., son of above, b. 15 Nov 1828, d. 29 Jan 1864
Narcissa Ann, dau. of above, b. 18 Jan 1831, d. 26 Aug 1891
Danl. G., son of above, b. 27 Mar 1833, d. 1 Feb 1908
Jas. LaFayette & John Everett b. 23 Mar 1835
Penelope Susan b. 5 Apr 1837
Isaac Green b. 26 Sep 1830
Nancy Caroline b. 25 Feb 1842, d. 28 Aug 1847
Margaret Ann b. 1 Mar 1844, d. Mar 1848

[This record copied from a newspaper clipping in possession of Mrs. Lucy Midyette, Oriental, N.C., sent by Ida B. Kellam, Wilmington, N.C. A N.C. record.]

JOHN H. TAYLOR

John H. Taylor b. 26 Mar 1797 in Richland Co., S.C., moved to Ala. in 1838, d. 4 Mar 1852, m. 12 Oct 1826 in Richland Co., S.C. to Luvenia Turnipseed b. 6 Oct 1805, d. 28 Nov 1873.
```
           Children
```
Louise Sibyl b. 7 Sep 1827, d. 7 July 1832

Sarah Frances b. 7 June 1829, d. 21 July 1873, m. 5 May 1852 to
Nicks B. Chappell
James Thomas b. 19 Aug 1831, d. 22 Aug 1841
Meredith b. 29 Dec 1833, d. 15 Jan 1836
Eliz. Catherine b. 10 Apr 1836, m. 20 Dec 1855 to Jas. B. Newell
John Wm. b. 2 Nov 1838, d. 2 Mar 1870, m. 20 Oct 1863 to Leila Re-
becca Wilkins
Mary Ellen b. 6 Mar 1841, d. 25 May 1855
Luvenia Ann b. 27 Apr 1843, d. 17 July 1845
Curtis Manley b. 24 Jan 1846, d. 9 July 1862, CSA Army
Eliz. Henrietta b. 29 Oct 1848, m. 3 Jan 1872 to Parks O. Longmire

Jacob Turnipseed b. 25 May 1758, d. 9 Sep 1819 [Another place says
1833], m. Katherine Voight b. 14 Aug 1764, d. 31 Dec 1827
Meredith Taylor, Sr., father, d. 29 Mar 1833, aged 70, m. Anna Duke,
mother, d. 6 Oct 1825, aged 61 yrs.

[Miss Eddie Reed, Aliceville, Ala. copied this Bible. It is owned
by Mrs. Luvenia L. Puckett, Covington, Ala who is past 80 yrs.
Miss Reed has copied many Turnipseed tombstones in Ala., according
to L. Andrea of Columbia, S.C. John H. Taylor went from Richland
Co., S.C. to Covington, Ala. It is supposed that Jacob & Katherine
Turnipseed are the parents of Luvenia Turnipseed but the Bible does
not say.]

JONATHAN TAYLOR

Jonathan Taylor d. 6 Apr 1820 in Edgefield Co., S.C., m. Joanna
Taylor d. 3 May 1839 in Walton Co., Ga.
    Children
Ellyson Taylor, son b. 9 Feb 1788
Pleasant Taylor, son, b. 13 Sep 1789
Wyatt Taylor, son, b. 5 Sep 1791
Cread Taylor, son, b. 3 Nov 1793
Onan Taylor, son, b. 27 Nov 1795
Tackey Taylor, son, b. 1 Mar 1798
Patsey Taylor, dau., b. 6 June 1800 [Shown also as Martha]
Joseph Taylor, son, b. 12 Sep 1803
Betsey Taylor, dau., b. 1806 [Shown also as Elizabeth]

[From page of Bible which was sent to the Pension Office. Rev.
Pension # W.4351, National Archives, Washington, D.C.: Jonathan
Taylor, aged 58 yrs. applied for a Pension from Edgefield Co., S.C.
on 2 Oct 1818 before Jesse Blocker, J.P. The pension was granted
and after his death was paid to his widow. Service: Jonathan Taylor enlisted in service in Cumberland Co., Va. & was discharged at
Cambridge in S.C. 9 June 1781 & was suffering from a severe wound
which he received at the Battle of Herringtown, N.J. ... He was also in the Battles of Brandywine & Monmouth in N.J. ... He served
under Col. Bailee & Col. William Washington. Married in Edgefield
Dist. or 96 Dist. on 9 Feb 1787 to Joanna Morris. The last pay-
ments were made in 1845 for remainder due to Joanna Taylor at her

death in 1839 and to surviving children: Onan E. Taylor of Walton
Co., Ga.; Elizabeth widow of Phillip Johnson of Carroll Co., Ga.;
Pleasant Taylor of Dallas Co., Ala.; Wyatt A. Taylor of Chambers
Co., Ala.; Creed Taylor of Giles Co., Tenn.; Tackey Taylor, where-
abouts not known "He has not been heard from during the past ten
years."]

ELISHA TEER

Elisha Teer b. 15 Sep 1815, m. 23 Dec 1839 tc Dulcena Taylor b. 10
Jan 1823.
    Their children
Amaziah Hughes b. 4 Nov 1841, lost at Missionary Ridge 25 Nov 1863
Albert Iredell b. 2 Sep 1844, m. 17 Nov 1864 to Araminta C. Gray
Theron Sylvester b. 26 Dec 1846, m. 8 Dec 1869 to Parthenia W.
  Freeman
Grant b. 12 Sep 1849, m. 9 Dec 1875 to Maggie P. Jennings
John Ernest b. 6 Dec 1857, d. 28 Oct 1867
Robert Keneda b. 28 Jan 1862, d. 15 July 1867

[Mrs. A. G. Norman, 2220 36th Ave., N., Birmingham, Ala. who owns
the Bible notes, "Elisha Teer was the son of Daniel Teer. Father &
son were b. in N.C., we believe in Orange Co. where the community
of Teer is located. Elisha Teer d. in Oct 1893 in Jefferson Co.,
Ala. Both are buried at Crumley's Chapel Cemetery near Pratt City,
Ala. The W in Parthenia's name stood for Westron. She died 26 Aug
1886 & is buried at Big Creek Baptist Church, Pickens Co., Ala.
Maggie Peninah Jennings was the dau. of Wm. & Margaret Jennings &
was b. in Pickens Co., Ala. in 1853."]

ALEXANDER TELFORD

Alexander Telford b. 1 June 1760, d. 22 May 1844, m. 1st on 6 Sep
1787 to Mary McCampble b. 3 Apr 1762, d. 6 Feb 1796, m. 2nd on 17
Oct 1797 to Elisabeth McClung b. 7 May 1759, d. 20 Nov 1826.
    Children
Mary Ann Telford b. 12 July 1788
Andrew Telford b. 27 Mar 1790, d. 6 Feb 1853
John Gilmore Telford (M.D.) b. 18 Mar 1792, d. 26 June 1863
Nancy Telford b. 20 May 1795; Nancy Hanna d. 7 Feb 1855
James Telford b. 29 Apr 1799, d. 30 Sep 1859
Jenny Telford b. 25 July 1800, d. 6 Nov 1869
Findley Telford b. 1 July 1802

Robert Telford b. 28 Sep 1762, d. 23 Sep 1829, m. 20 Dec 1787 to
Isabella Stirratt b. 27 Oct 1767, d. 13 Feb 1847

James Telford b. 16 May 1789, d. 26 Dec 1857 in S.C., m. 1st on 7
    Jan 1812 in S.C. to Artimisia Brown, dau. of James & Nancy Brown,
    b. 19 Nov 1839, d. 12 Mar 1843 in S.C., m. 2nd in Feb 1845 to Lu-
    cinda Hall b. 25 Feb 1810
Thomas Telford b. 19 July 1791

John Telford b. 8 Dec 1793
Robert Telford b. 23 Dec 1796 [moved to Ill.]
Mary Telford b. 7 [or 17] Apr 1799, m. James Lemon
William Telford b. 2 Dec 1811, d. 13 Feb 1883 [or 1882] [m. Leazy
    Stanton. Children.]
Hugh Telford b. 15 Apr 1804
Elizabeth Telford b. 17 July 1805, m. a Bowman
Eliza Telford b. 31 Jan 1810, m. David Garrison

    Children of James, Artimisia & Lucinda Telford
Amanda b. 28 Oct 1812, d. Jan 1881 in Fla., aged 68 yrs., m. Josiah
    Ballentine
George Brown b. 12 Jan 1815, moved from S.C. to Ga. in 1872, d. 30
    May 1887, aged 72 yrs., 4 mos., 19 days
Mary Louisa b. 10 Jan 1817, went to Tex. 1870, d. 25 May 1873, m.
    W. O. Alexander
William Brazleton b. 28 Oct 1819, preached in Fla., d. 3 Jan 1892
    in Fla., aged 72 yrs.
James Harvey b. 10 Mar 1822, moved to Ga. 1872, d. 8 Nov 1906
Eliza Ann b. 7 Dec 1825, d. 21 June 1868 in Fla., m. James M. Tay-
    lor
Nancy Caroline b. 9 Oct 1828, d. 9 Sep 1866 in Fla.
Robert Carlisle b. 25 May 1832, moved to Miss., d. 2 Apr 1903 in
    Little Rock, Ark.
John Calvin Telford b. 7 Sep 1845, killed at Gaines Mill, Va., 1862
Samuel Stewart Telford b. 30 Jan 1847
Artimesia Telford b. 24 June 1849, died in infancy
Thomas Jefferson Telford b. 29 Sep 1850, d. from accident
David Newton Telford b. 18 Dec 1853, d. 10 Mar 1856

[The above Bible records are copied from the Bible of Mrs. Martha
Jane Telford Burns.]

                        REUBEN THOMAS

Reuben Thomas' father d. 27 Oct 1828
Reuben Thomas' mother d. 24 Mar 1826
Nancy (or Katie) Knight, sister of Reuben Thomas, d. 25 Aug 1855
Gambrell Thomas, brother of Reuben Thomas, d. 19 Apr 1848

Reuben Thomas b. 4 Apr 1798, d. 18 June 1879, m. Lavinia Putnam
Thomas b. 18 Feb 1805, d. 10 Oct 1877.
    Children
Malinda Thomas b. 1 Dec 1823
Leander Thomas b. 18 Nov 1825
Gabriel Thomas b. 8 Sep 1827 [M.D.]
Wm. P. Thomas b. 22 Apr 1829
Nancy E. Thomas b. 20 Mar 1831
Irene Thomas b. 29 Oct 1832
Robt. Y. H. Thomas b. 24 Sep 1834 [M.D.]
Mary Thomas b. 2 Aug 1836
John L. Thomas b. 28 June 1838 [M.D.]; Lieut. John L. Thomas was

killed 8 May 1864 in Spottsylvania, Va. in War between States.]

WILLIAM RUSSELL THOMSON

Wm. Russell Thomson b. 22 Apr 1761 at Belleville, d. 7 Apr 1807, m.
25 Feb 1783 at Bellebroughton to Eliz. Sabb b. 27 June 1761 at
Bellebroughton, d. 8 Nov 1838 at Totness.
    Children
Wliz. Deborah b. 23 Dec 1783, d. 23 Sep 1787 at Smithfield
Wm. Sabb b. 10 Nov 1785 at Richmond Hill, d. 6 Nov 1841 at Totness,
    m. 9 July 1809 at Mt. Thomson to Eugenia Ann Lewis
Mary Eugenia b. 14 Nov 1787 at Smithfield, m. 18 June 1805 at Mid-
    way to Artemas B. Darby
Eliz. Ann b. 1 Jan 1790 at Smithfield, d. 2 Sep 1791
John Linton b. 13 Apr 1792, d. June 1826 at Totness, m. 17 Dec 1816
    to Margaret Ann Sinclair [Sinkler in pencil in margin]
Charles Robert b. 25 Oct 1794, d. 21 July 1855 at Totness, m. 18
    Apr 1820 at Hickory Grove to Eleanor S. Hrabowski
Harriet Deborah b. 20 Feb 1797 at Midway, d. 21 Sep 1826 at Orange-
    burg, m. a Lewis
Charlotte Ann b. 12 Apr 1799, d. 11 Feb 1875 in Columbia, S.C., m.
    1st on 12 Apr 1814 to Derrill Hart, m. 2nd on 4 Jan 1821 at Hart-
    land to Robt. Howell Goodwyn
Caroline Sophia Rebecca b. 28 Aug 1802 at Midway, m. 21 Dec 1819 to
    Thomas S. Smith

[Leonard Andrea of Columbia, S.C. comments, "This Bible was found
in the attic of a Columbia, S.C. house by the physician who owned
the house. The physician gave the Bible to Olga Crossland Huey
(Mrs. Wm. Anderson) of 2803 Gervais St., Columbia, S.C. Mrs. Huey
later discovered a direct desc. of the Thomson-Goodwyn family &
turned the Bible over to her. The Bible is now owned by Mrs. Nell
Peterkin Reid, Oakland Plantation, Fort Motte, S.C." Is this the
Hart family from which Dr. Deryl Hart, President of Duke Univ., is
descended?]

FRANCIS THORNTON, SR.

Francis Thornton, Sr. b. 5 Nov 1651, m. Monday, 13 Apr 1674.
    Children
Elizabeth, 1st born, b. 3 Jan 1676 at 12 o'clock at night, m. in
    1685 to Edwin Conway
Margaret, 2nd child, b. 2 Apr 1678, about 1 o'clock at night [m.
    Wm. Strothers, sheriff of King George Co., Va.]
William & Sarah b. 14 Dec 1680 about 1 o'clock at night of a Monday
    morning
Francis b. 4 Jan 1682, about 2 hrs. before day
Rowland b. 1 Aug 1685 about sunrise
Ann b. 27 Sep 1691

Francis Conway, son of Elizabeth & Edwin Conway, b. 15 Apr 1695, m.
    19 Jan 1719 to Rebecca Catlett

[This record is from Mrs. James Thornton Nuckols, Columbus, Ga. Copied by the compiler in fall of 1957. Francis Thornton was the son of the immigrant William as established by the family of Nuckols et al who descend from the two men. His wife was Alice Savage, dau. of Capt. Anthony Savage. This has also been established by their descendants.]

S. N. TIMMERMAN

S. N. Timmerman b. 21 Aug 1853, m. 22 Dec 1881 in Aiken, S.C. by Rev. Thomas Walker to Mary Frances Berry b. 21 Jan 1856

Walter Timmerman b. 16 Aug 1882
Paris Estell Timmeman b. Nov 1883
Terrell Timmerman b. Nov 1885
Scott Shepard Timmerman b. 14 Aug 1887
Hattie Timmerman b. 4 July 1892
Thomas Timmerman b. 14 Feb 1892 [?]
Percy Timmerman b. 26 Feb 1899

NATHANIEL TINSLEY

Nathaniel Tinsley b. in 1757 in Hanover Co., Va., m. 24 June 1790 to Lucy who d. 20 May 1834
    Children
Thomas Pate b. 15 Jan 1791
Samuel b. 21 Aug 1792
Francis Finch b. 7 Sep 1794
John Ragland b. 21 Mar 1796
Susannah Pate b. 20 Mar 1798
Nathaniel Lewis b. 1 June 1800
Absalom b. 31 July 1802
Minerva b. 8 Sep 1804
William b. 12 Aug 1807
Mary b. 12 Jan 1811
Jeremiah Samuel Beckley b. 27 Aug 1813

ANDERSON HARRISON TITSHAW

Anderson Harrison Titshaw b. 24 Sep 1823, d. 11 Sep 1888, m. 20 Oct 1846 in Walton Co. to Mary Ann Cronick b. 26 Apr 1823, d. 12 Jan 1883.
    Children
Milbrey Elizabeth Titshaw b. 6 Sep 1847, d. 31 Aug 1884, bur. New
   Liberty Methodist Church, Hoschton, Ga., m. 4 Nov 1860 to Elias
   M. Smith
Emmarintha Jane Titshaw b. 29 Jan 1849, d. 16 July 1908, bur.
   Friendship Baptist Church, Hall Co., m. 29 Aug 1869 to Calvin
   Clinton Blankenship
Willis Lumpkin Titshaw b. 27 Dec 1850, d. 12 Feb 1851, bur. New
   Liberty Church
Vandelia Antine Titshaw b. 27 Feb 1852, d. 11 July 1881, bur. Zion

Baptist Church, Hoschton, Ga., m. 5 Nov 1865 to A. N. Smith
Simeon Simpson Titshaw b. 4 Oct 1854, m. Adaline Phillips
Margaret Josephine Titshaw b. 2 Nov 1856, d. 24 Nov 1904, bur. Baptist Church, Chestnut Mt., m. 9 Nov 1876 to James J. Pirkle
John Anderson David Titshaw b. 6 Feb 1862, d. 4 June 1892, bur New Liberty Methodist Church, Hoschton, Ga., m. 3 Oct 1883 to Mattie Elizabeth Johnson who m. 2nd on 16 July 1893 to Harrison Taylor Cronic

    Children of M. Elizabeth Johnson Titshaw Cronic
Ernest Preston Titshaw b. 8 June 1885, m. 29 Dec 1923 in Atlanta to Gertrude Anderson
Homer Scott Titshaw, M.D. b. 13 Jan 1888, m. 28 July 1920 to Nannie Maude Hartley
John Chestia Titshaw b. 1 Nov 1892, m. 15 Sep 1917 to Steve Clay Moon
Jerome Irene Cronic b. 15 June 1894, m. 22 Sep 1928 to Robert Cary McClure
Mayrell Elizabeth Cronic b. 26 Jan 1897
Ruby Ann Cronic b. 10 Oct 1899, d. 8 May 1920, m. 12 Apr 1920 to Fred Arnold
William Harrison Cronic b. 9 Apr 1903, m. 9 Sep 1933 to Ruby Prater

Alexander Johnson b. 17 Feb 1817, d. 25 Feb 1884, m. 4 Jan 1844 to Martha Ann Smith b. 4 May 1828, d. 6 May 1908
Sylvester Johnson b. 11 June 1787, [d.] 17 May 1868, m. 4 Sep 1815 to Elizabeth Cummins b. 3 May 1797, d. 5 Apr 1870
Peter Cronick b. 6 June 1756, d. 16 Mar 1816, m. 24 Dec 1779 to Rachel Funderberg b. 29 Jan 1762, d. 26 July 1836
Simeon Smith b. 1805, m. 24 Apr 1826 to Lucindia Pippin b. 24 Apr 1808, children: Martha Ann, Mary Elizabeth, John W., Sallie, Fannie, Becky, Liza, Thomas B.
Benjamin Franklin Smith, brother of Simeon Smith, m. Harriet Davis, a widow with two children
Alex Cummins b. 1750, d. Sep 1811

[Holy Bible - International Publishing Co., Phila., Pa., owned by John Anderson D. Titshaw, copied in 1920 by Mrs. S.C. Moon, was lost by fire in 1924/25.]

FANNIE MELISSA TITSHAW

James T. m. Fannie Melissa Titshaw, dau. of John Sampson & Lucindia Thompson Titshaw b. 10 May 1868.
    Children
James Omer Titshaw b. 14 Feb 1892
Ara Frances Titshaw b. 28 Sep 1893
Ezra Tyler Titshaw b. 10 May 1896
Eric Sampson Titshaw b. 28 Sep 1899
Grady Wilson Titshaw b. 30 June 1901
Lorena Serena Titshaw b. 6 June 1903, d. 6 Feb 1904
Carl Shaw Titshaw b. 2 Dec 1905

James Tyler Titshaw b. 1 Feb 1908, d. 6 Mar 1908
Maude Myrtle Titshaw b. 2 Oct 1910

[From a recent Bible of James T. & Fannie Melissa Titshaw]

MILBREY TITSHAW

Milbrey Titshaw b. 6 Sep 1847, d. 31 Aug 1884, bur. New Liberty
Church, m. 1st on 4 Nov 1860 to Elias M. Smith b. 19 Aug 1843, en-
listed in war, was never heard from, m. 2nd on 29 Aug 1867 to John
Deaton, son of Bill Deaton b. 6 Feb 1844.

Paddy (Patrick) Smith d. 17 Sep 1879
Drucilla Smith d. 11 Dec 1876
General Marion Smith b. 26 Apr 1862, united with New Liberty Church
   (Methodist) 1879, Rev. D.F. Rutherford, d. 6 Mar 1942, m. 4 July
   1883 to Leila Carolina Bennett (dau. of Thomas Bennett b. 13 June
   1825 & Martha C. Hunter Bennett b. 14 Dec 1835, of Va.) b. 15 Dec
   1866

Antine Titshaw b. 27 Feb 1852, m. 5 Nov 1865 to Abraham Neelin
   Smith, brother of Elias M. Smith [known as Jim] b. 13 Nov 1842
      Children
Anderson Elias Smith b. 1 Dec 1866
John A. Smith b. 30 Sep 1869, was killed, aged 22, bur. in Osteen,
   Volusia Co., Fla.
Mary Josephine Smith b. 31 Jan 1871, m. Wm. B. Cronic, son of Rev.
   John H. Cronic
Simeon Patrick Smith b. 8 Feb 1873, m. 1st to Betty Clarke, m. 2nd
   to Lula Thomas
Margaret Elizabeth Smith b. 6 May 1875, m. a Murphy .
Preston D. Smith b. 8 June 1877, d. 1 July 1878
Winnie Lee Smith b. 16 May 1878, m. Elijah Bell

Simps Pike, Gid Duncan, Sim Cronic, Anderson Titshaw, Seab & John
   Maddox, Eph Matthews, left today to report at Anderson's Bridge
   to join civil war [no date given]
John J. Hunter, brother of Martha C. Hunter, b. 17 Dec 1843, m.
   Eulalia (Bush) Johnson, dau. of William Franklin & Mary Elizabeth
   Smith Johnson
John William Bennett b. 18 Oct 1857
Jefferson Davis Bennett b. 21 Mar 1861

[Testament & Psalms, published by American Bible Soc., 1848. Of
Milbrey Elizabeth Titshaw Smith in possession of her son, General
Marion Smith.]

STEPHEN TITSHAW, JR.

Stephen Titshaw, Jr. b. 15 Sep 1797, d. 26 Sep 1875, [m.] Elizabeth
Titshaw b. 7 Nov 1797, d. 8 [Jan or June, illegible] 1848, m. 2nd
on 23 Oct 1849 to Elizabeth Lacky.

Miles A. Titshaw b. 23 Dec 1821, m. 5 Dec 1852 to Emily I. Clegg
Anderson Harrison Titshaw b. 24 Sep 1823, d. 11 Sep 1888, m. 20 Oct
  1846 to Mary Ann Cronick
John Sampson Titshaw b. 30 Dec 1825, d. 13 Jan 1907, m. 13 Jan 1853
  to Lucindia S. Thompson
Isaac E. Titshaw b. 5 Dec 1829, moved to Ala., m. 24 Sep 1848 to
  Sarah Reed
Lewis Wilson Colubus Titshaw, b. 13 Nov 1833, was Priv. Co. C, 9th
  Regt. Ga. Inf., Col. E. R. Goulding, Walton Co., united, with
  wife, with Methodist Church on 12 Aug 1908, Rev. J.L. Hall, m.
  1st on 19 Nov 1867 to Serena Pirkle Wheeler, m. 2nd on 5 Mar 1904
  by Rev. J. C. Forrester to Fannie M. Lyle. L.W.C. appointed
  guardian of Sheriff Titshaw, orphan (minor) of Stephen Titshaw,
  Jr., deceased 11 Dec 1875
Serena Pirkle Titshaw [b.] 31 Aug 1836, d. 8 Oct 1903
Manley H. Titshaw, son of Elizabeth Lacky Titshaw, m. 26 July 1877
  by Rev. J. W. Davis to Calvina Strange
Sheriff Titshaw, son of Elizabeth Lacky Titshaw, m. 14 Sep 1876 by
  Rev. J. W. Davis to Mary (Moley) Strange d. 25 June 1879, moved
  to Ala.

S. W. & Mary Titshaw, Ch. of Sheriff Titshaw, d. 6 Mar 1879
Wilson Titshaw d. 6 Nov 1915
Mary Titshaw, dau. of Manley Titshaw, b. 12 Jan 1883, d. 12 Jan
  1889
Emma Rintha Titshaw d. 2 Jan 1835
Cornelia A. Titshaw b. 26 June 1837, m. 16 Oct 1859 to John J. Wil-
  kins, son of Samuel M. Wilkins
Rosina Titshaw ... Florida [?]
John Wilson Titshaw b. 27 Aug 1868, m. 13 Jan 1895 by Rev. R. F.
  Sloan to Sarah Jane Tuggle
Lewis Columbus Titshaw b. 30 June 1870, m. 17 Dec 1891 by Rev. J.
  Frank Jackson to Lillie Greeson
James Tyler Titshaw b. 21 Sep 1871, m. 21 Sep 1890 to Fannie Melis-
  sa Titshaw

[Holy Bible - Containing Old and New Testaments, published by Jes-
per Harding, 1842, in possession of Wilson Titshaw & has been destroyed by fire in home of his second wife.]

ROBERT TORRENTINE

Robert Torrentine b. 1785, d. 1862, m. 30 Dec 1806 to Jane Davister
d. 15 Mar 1862, aged 76 yrs., 4 mos.; Elizabeth Torrentine b. 16
July 1787.
        Children
Eliza b. 31 Dec 1807, m. 27 Mar 1834 to Gilbreth T. Kerr
Mary b. 10 June 1810, m. 8 Mar 1830 to James R. Nesbitt

[It isn't clear whether Elizabeth b. 1787 above is a wife or a sister of Robert. This record is taken from a Nesbitt Bible that is
owned by Mrs. David Overcash, Troutman, N.C. It was copied by Mr.

J. M. Houston, Mooresville, N.C. It is not yet determined what re-
lation this Robert Torrentine was to the brothers Alex. & Saml. of
Orange Co. Robert lived in Rowan Co., N.C. He is undoubtedly a
son of Saml., Sr. by his 1st wife, but if so, he was not named in
Saml., Sr.'s will and John, son of a 1st wife, was. However, there
were no Turrentines by any spelling in America early except Saml. &
Alex. Robert is bur. in Perth Cemetery which is in Rowan or some
county cut off from Rowan.]

ELISHA TRAMMELL

Elisha Trammell b. 30 June 1802, d. 4 Aug 1886 in Langdale, Ala.,
m. 1st to Mary Carnes (Dunlap) d. 30 Nov 1851, aged 37 yrs., 11
mos., 18 days, m. 2nd on 1 Oct 1856 in Chipley, Ga. to Anne Knight
b. 23 Apr 1833, d. 9 Jan 1909 in Langdale, Ala.
    Their children
Joseph D. b. 13 Nov 1833, m. Hattie Sapp, no children
Robt. J. b. 23 July 1835, m. 11 Sep 1871 to Nannie Stephens
John Randolph b. 15 Sep 1837, m. Ann Aimes
Wm. H. Harrison b. 29 July 1840, d. Richmond, Va., Confederate Sol.
Mary Ann b. 3 Nov 1842, m. David C. Shutze
Elisha Carnes b. 23 July 1845, d. 29 Nov 1845
Sallie Lee b. 14 Nov 1846, m. Lewis Schuessler
James Dawson b. 5 July 1849, m. Susie Boyd
Daniel W. b. 19 Nov 1851
Antionette E. b. 23 July 1857, d. 9 Apr 1894 in Griffin, Ga.
Elisha Thos. b. 28 May 1859, d. & bur. in Laurel, Del.

Virginia Helen b. 22 May 1844, d. 1 Sep 1853
Susan Antionette b. 26 Sep 1846, bur. in Lee Cemetery, Stonewall
    Co., Tex., never m.
Ellis b. 14 July 1850, d. 13 Sep 1853
Francis Ulysses b. 9 July 1853, went to Tex.
Daniel Trammell, father of Elisha, d. Nov 1815
Sarah Trammell, mother of Elisha, d. June 1808

MASTON TURNER

Maston Turner b. 13 Apr 1800, m. 20 Feb 1822 [or 20?] to Nancy Hargus b. 10 Sep 1803, d. 15 Sep 1863, aged 60 yrs.

Janey Turner b. 15 Nov 1821
John Turner b. 21 Nov 1823, d. 28 Oct 1862, aged 40 yrs.
Wm. Milam Turner b. 4 June 1826
Katherine Turner b. 24 Jan 1828
Mary Turner b. 20 Feb 1830
Permelia Turner b. 11 Feb 1832
Fletcher Turner b. 27 Mar 1834, d. 9 May 1850
Maston G. Turner b. 3 Apr 1836 [29 Sep 1909 in pencil, d. date?]
Elizabeth Turner b. 11 Apr 1838; Marget Elisabeth Cain d. 28 Sep
    1863, aged 25 yrs.
James Turner b. 9 Dec 1840

Martin Luther Turner b. 15 Dec 1842, d. 3 Mar 1894 in Ark.
Thomas Turner b. 1 Dec 1844
Monroe Turner b. 11 July 1847

Lorrict [?] Abbot b. 13 Nov 1817
Majicia [?] b. 31 July 1820
Simpson Abbot b. 14 Aug 1823
Museum Abbot b. 4 Sep 1825, d. 27 June 1841
Amanda Abbot b. 24 June 1827
Brice M. Abbot b. 16 Aug 1830
Willford Abbot b. 20 May 1832
Mancefield Abbot b. 11 Sep 1833
America Abbot b. 24 Sep 1836
Emeranda Abbot b. 24 Sep 1838
Thomas D. Abbot b. 11 Nov 1840
Rebecca Abbot b. 4 Aug 1799

Jane Pounders d. 6 Oct 1864
Maston Greenfield Turner d. 9 June 1865

Wm. Milam Turner b. 4 June 1826 in Lincoln Co., Tenn., m. 13 Oct
1852 to Miss Eliza C. E. Carter. Embraced religion in the fall of
1865 & joined the Methodist Church. In 1874 was elected circuit
steward in which relationship he continued steadfast, zealous &
successful till the close of his excellent life, which occured 4
Apr 1881 at his residence in Colbert Co., Ala. [from back of Bible]

[Bible in possession of Mrs. Alice Williams Turner (Mrs. Chas. F.)
Copied by Mrs. E. S. Gregory, Tuscumbia, Ala.]

                    ALEXANDER TURRENTINE

      Children of Alexander & Deborah Turrentine

Elizabeth b. 29 Jan 1759
Martha b. 6 Apr 1761
Samuel b. 3 Aug 1763
Jean b. 4 Apr 1766
Daniel b. 4 Nov 1769
Alexander b. 12 Sep 1772
James b. 26 July 1774
Mary b. 17 Mar 1777
Saael [?] Moore b. 23 Feb 1783

[Alex. & Deborah whose maiden name is not known were married ca.
1758. Alex was b. in 1725 in Ireland; date of b. from tombstone
in same cemetery as his brother Saml., Sr. Alex. d. in 1784 without a will in Orange Co., N.C. He was in the Rev. War. This old
Bible record was found some years ago in an old trunk owned by the
late Wm. R. Turrentine, Shelbyville, Tenn. & copied by G. Ruford
Turrentine, Russellville, Ark., a desc. of Alex. & Deborah and
Historian of the Turrentine Family Assn. Alex. came to Amer. in

1745 on the Couli Can & landed at Philadelphia. Deborah was on
this ship & was a Hudson. They married in Pa. & came to Orange
Co., N.C. in 1755.]

ARCHELAUS TURRENTINE

Archelaus Turrentine b. 12 Feb 1885, m. in Orange Co., N.C. to Mar-
garet d. 4 Oct 1853.
    Children
Geo. S. b. 1 Sep 1820 [S for Smith?], m. 1st on 9 Sep 1844 to My-
   linda G. Hamilton, m. 2nd on 6 Dec 1846 to Zerelda Bradshaw
Saml. A. b. 2 Mar 1823
Phebe b. 11 Mar 1825, d. 23 Oct 1910 as Phebe Steel
Daniel b. 5 Dec 1827, d. 30 Dec 1827
Sarah J. b. 25 Feb 1829
Mary Elvira b. 3 Nov 1831
Wilson E. b. 29 Mar 1834
Nancy Eliz. b. 15 Oct 1836
Eleanor b. 7 Mar 1839
James F. b. 25 Aug 1842

[Sarah Turrentine d. 6 Sep 1835. She was the mother of Archelaus
& wife of Major Saml. Turrentine who d. 1824 in Bedford Co., Tenn.
Sarah was Sarah Wilson & she m. Major Saml. in Orange Co., N.C. He
was High Sheriff of Orange Co., N.C. for some 20 odd yrs. Bible
owned by F. W. Park, DeQueen, Ark. In the Bible Archelaus says
that he bought the Bible in 1821 from John A. Mars for $8. Sent by
G. Ruford Turrentine, Russellville, Ark., family historian.]

JAMES TURRENTINE

James Turrentine, Sr. b. 9 Jan 1770, d. 17 Sep 1831, aged 61 yrs.,
m. 19 Sep 1793 to Katherine Clower b. 4 Jan 1775.

Danl. Clower Turrentine, son of Jas. & Katherine, m. 3 Dec 1838 to
   Caroline E. Lucy b. 19 Mar 1822
Wm. Turrentine, son of D. C. [must be James] & Katherine, b. 4 June
   1794, m. 8 June 1815 to Priscilla d. 22 Sep 1824 in her 29th yr.
Samuel Turrentine b. 7 Apr 1796 (or 1790), m. Mary Ann Howey [or
   Harvey, page torn]
Geo. Turrentine b. 28 Apr 1798

Eliz. Turrentine b. 22 ... 1812
Nancy Turrentine b. 29 Aug 1815
Thos. Clower Turrentine b. 4 Dec 1817
Joseph T. Turrentine b. 26 Jan 1821
Frances L. Turrentine b. 28 Jan (June) 1805
Morgan C. Turrentine b. 17 Sep 1817

Belinda Turrentine d. 19 Sep 1817
Lucy Jones Turrentine d. 15 Dec 1831

[This Bible is owned by Mrs. Ruth Randall Cross of Turrentine Ave., Gadsden, Ala., granddau. of Daniel C. Turrentine who, with Gen. Gadsden, moved from S.C. to Ala. & founded the town of Gadsden. James Turrentine, Sr. was the oldest child of Samuel Turrentine, Sr., see below. Jas. & Katherine were married in Orange Co., N.C.]

MARTIN J. TURRENTINE

Martin J. Turrentine b. 10 Dec 1810, m. Seany Day b. 29 Mar 1815.
    Their children
Joel W. b. 14 July 1840
Richard J. b. 30 Nov 1841
Frances M. b. 8 Feb 1844
James D. b. 16 Nov 1845
Thos. J. b. 20 Feb 1847
Wm. M. b. 9 Feb 1850
Martin B. [Byrd] b. 8 Oct 1852
Jonathan O. b. 22 Nov 1854
Seany E. b. 23 Apr 1857
Mary A. b. 1 Mar 1861

[Martin J. Turrentine lived in Morgan Co., Ala. From Turrentine Family files of the compiler & Geo. Ruford Turrentine, Russelville, Ark.]

SAMUEL TURRENTINE

Samuel Turrentine m. 2nd to Mary [Bryant]
    Their children
James b. 9 Jan 1770
Sarah b. 1772
Samuel b. 13 Sep 1774, d. 15 Nov 1845
Lydia b. 7 Feb 1776, d. Aug 1824
Susanna b. 24 July 1779
Nancy b. 11 Sep 1782
Absalom b. 15 Nov 1784, d. 13 Aug 1856
Daniel b. 3 Oct 1788, d. 4 Nov 1854

[Samuel Turrentine, Sr. b. in 1717 in Ireland & came to Pa. in the Couli Can in 1745. He & his brother Alexander came to Orange Co., N.C. by 1755 when the first deeds are recorded for them. The date of his birth is from his tombstone on his own plantation near Rougemont, N.C. He died in 1801 in Orange Co., N.C. with will dated 1800. The name of his 1st wife is not yet known. He probably married her in Pa. The name of his 2nd wife is obtained from affidavits made in 1856 in Gadsden, Ala. by his dau.-in-law, Catherine Clower, widow of his oldest son by 2nd wife, James above. He & Mary Bryant were m. probably in 1769. This Bible is owned by a desc., Mrs. Lillian McMannen Fitzgerald, Perry, Fla. The compiler is also a desc. through Saml., Sr.'s oldest son by 1st wife, John.]

SAMUEL TURRENTINE, JR.

Samuel Turrentine m. Nancy [Wilson] Turrentine
        Their children
Mary Ann b. 2 Oct 1830
Nathan b. 5 Sep 1832
William b. 5 Aug 1834
Mariah b. 1 Jan 1837
Henry b. 27 Sep 1838
Rachel b. 2 Oct 1840
Viny b. 7 Sep 1841
        Slaves
Celia b. 2 May 1842
Ester b. 25 Mar 1843
Sarah b. 10 Feb 1845
Sinthy Emmeline b. 26 Apr 1847
Gilbert b. 20 Dec 1849
Martha b. 5 Apr 1851
Augusta b. 29 July 1856

[Bible owned by Mrs. Lillian McMannen Fitzgerald, Perry, Fla.]

ISAAC SIMMONS UTSEY

Isaac Simmons Utsey, son of Isaac & Mary Ann (Clayton) Utsey, named
for the Methodist Minister, Isaac Simmons, b. 16 Feb 1824 in Colle-
ton Co., S.C., d. 17 Apr 1881 in Dorchester Co., S.C., m. 5 Jan
1860 in St. Matthews Parish, S.C. to Mary Elizabeth Carroll, dau.
of Margaret (Gray) & Jacob Fair Carroll, son of Jacob Carroll &
Elizabeth Fair, b. 29 Oct 1840 in St. Mathews Parish, S.C., d. 7
July 1929 in Dorchester Co., S.C.
        Children
Margaret Utsey b. 29 Oct 1860, d. 19 May 1916, m. 18 Dec 1888 to
    Joseph Henry Stokes
Paul Fletcher Utsey b. 5 Dec 1863, d. 1 Nov 1916 in Ariz.
Mary Alice Utsey b. 21 Nov 1866, d. 12 Apr 1893, m. 8 Dec 1885 to
    Isiah Elizabeth Horn d. 19 July 1899
Isaac Olin Utsey b. 17 July 1869, m. 7 Dec 1929 to Alice Sheider
Daisey Gertrude Utsey b. 30 May 1872, d. 1 Apr 1954, m. 16 Mar 1898
    to Lonnie Pierce Conner
Minnie Carroll Utsey b. 14 May 1876, m. 14 July 1914 to Charles
    David Dukes
Walker Scott Utsey b. 2 Oct 1878, m. 14 Aug 1906 in New Canton,
    Va. to Mary C. McKenna
Simmons Fair Utsey b. 4 Sep 1881

Mary Margaret Elizabeth Carroll, child of Robert & Margaret Gray
William Scott Utsey b. 10 May 1822, bro. of Isaac, m. Mary Bowyer
Jemima Utsey b. 22 Feb 1835, sister of Isaac, m. Thomas David
    Johnston
James Olin Horn b. 27 May 1891, m. 26 July 1916 Eliz. Louise Duncan
Thomas Carroll Horn b. 3 June 1888, d. 15 Nov 1888

NATHANIEL VANCE

Nathaniel Vance, Sr. d. 4 Nov 1812, m. 27 Mar 1788 to Mary Dunbar McTier b. 6 Mar 1769.

Samuel Vance, eldest son of above, b. 19 Mar 1789 in Laurens Co., d. 13 July 1868 within 3 miles of his birthplace, in his 70th yr., served a short time on the coast of S.C. in the War of 1812, m. 3 Mar 1818 to Mrs. Eliza Kincaid Armstrong
Frances Vance b. 29 Aug 1790, m. 20 Dec 1814 to William Greer
William M. Vance b. 6 Mar 1792, m. 18 July 1820 to Elizabeth Edrington
David Vance b. 1 Mar 1794, m. 23 Dec 1819 to Sarah Edrington
Nathaniel Carr Vance b. 9 Feb 1798, d. 12 Mar 1846, never married
Elizabeth Vance b. 24 July 1799, d. 13 Apr 1800
Allen Vance b. 2 Jan 1803
John Vance b. 29 Apr 1804, d. 23 Apr 1877, m. 13 Nov 1838 to Nancy Watson (nee Wright)
Larkin Vance b. 20 Oct 1806, d. 8 Mar 1809
James Washington Vance, M.D. b. 12 Feb 1809, d. 26 Oct 1868 in his 59th yr. at the residence of Dr. S. W. Vance, Buck Hall, Bosier Parish, La., never married
Joseph Harrison Vance b. 8 July 1813 [Posthumous], d. Aug 1889 near Cokesbury, never married

Sarah Vance d. 6 Dec 1827, m. Oct 1826 to John Cole
Mary Caroline Vance d. 31 Sep 1820
Robert Milton Vance [son of Robert S. Vance, Sr.] b. 2 Sep 1839, killed 1864 at battle of Spottsylvania, Va.
Henry Young Vance, son of Robert Vance, d. 13 July 1862 in Richmond, Va.
Robert S. Vance m. 10 Jan 1828 to Nancy M. Farrew

Children of Samuel & Eliza Vance
James Kincaid Vance, only son, b. 26 Dec 1818 in Laurens Co., S.C., m. 1 Aug 1844 to Louisa Watson, dau. of Dr. Elijah Watson
Mary Prudence Vance, dau., b. 30 Mar 1816 in Lancaster Co., S.C.

Children of James Kincaid Vance & Laurens Louisa Watson
James Wister Vance b. 16 Sep 1845, m. 2 Dec 1875 in Memphis, Tenn. to Susan Shelby
Samuel Watson Vance b. 6 Nov 1847, m. 21 Nov 1871 to Mary Caroline Young
William Washington Vance b. 25 June 1849, m. 6 Dec 1892 in New Orleans, La. to Sidney Ballard
John Harrison Vance b. 5 June 1851
Nancy Eliza(beth) (Lillie) Vance b. 5 May 1853, m. 24 Nov 1875 to James Walter Gray, children Harry Gray; Lawrence Gray, Walter Gray; Miss. Willie Gray m. Don Linthicum of Atlanta

Bigie Lou Vance b. 28 Mar 1855, m. 23 Apr 1879 to Zachary Taylor
Dobbs
Hearst Vance b. 18 Dec 1856
Norwaood Kincaid Vance b. 16 Sep 1858
Mary Ame(r)lia Vance b. 1 July 1860, m. 1st on 17 Jan 1883 to David
Griffin Dorroh, m. 2nd in 1897 to Arthur Lawrence Ewbank, child-
ren: Griffie Vance Dorroh b. 27 Mar ..., m. 17 Nov ... to Richard
Mims Sullivan of Greenville, S.C.; one Dorroh child d. in infancy;
Amy Vance Ewbank b. 22 Apr 1898, m. John E. Sloan of Greenville,
S.C.; Marie Corinne Ewbank b. 20 Apr 1899, m. 14 Sep 1929 in
Flora, Miss. to Charles Hinton
Elizabeth Perla (Bessie) Vance b. 17 Oct 1861, m. 24 Feb 1886 to
Wiley Smith Killingsworth
Frank Hampton Vance b. 23 May 1863
Susan Laurens (Laurie) Vance b. 29 Oct 1864, m. 30 Apr 1889 to Wil-
liam McIntosh Norwood
Alpha Anna Vance b. 26 June 1868, d. in infancy

Children of Griffie Vance Dorroh & Richard Mims Sullivan
Richard Mims Sullivan, Jr. b. 3 Jan 1910
Mary Vance Sullivan b. 10 Sep 1914
Laurens Norwood Sullivan b. 1 Jan 1919
Griffin Dorroh Sullivan b. 1 Mar 1923

Lucia Marie Sloan, child of John E. & Amy Vance Ewbank Sloan, b.
23 Feb 1919, m. Major Horace Brown of Gaffney, S.C. -- Susan Major Brown b. 12 July 1946 at Washington
Charles Russell Hinton, child of Charles & Marie Corinne
Hinton, b. 18 July 1930

SAMUEL VANCE

Samuel Vance b. 10 May 1766, d. 20 Oct 1846, bur. on Saml. Vance
place, 1 mile west of Lydia Mill, Adj. Robt. C. Davis place, m. to
Elizabeth Gilmore b. 10 Aug 1766, d. 29 Nov 1842, bur. on Saml.
Vance place.
Children
Susannah Vance b. 11 Jan 1785
Ealy Vance b. 25 Mar 1790
Sarah Vance b. 23 Mar 1792
Wm. G. Vance b. 14 Apr 1794
Mary (Polly) Vance b. 7 Apr 1797
Robert S. Vance b. 23 Apr 1799, m. Nancy H.
Joseph Vance b. 1 Jan 1802
Samuel Vance b. 3 May 1804
Elizabeth G. Vance b. 13 Oct 1808

Children of Robt. S. & Nancy H. Vance
Joseph Patillo b. 7 Oct 1828
Saml. Farrow b. 8 Nov 1829
Wm. Thompson b. 3 May 1831
Thos. J. b. 3 Oct 1834, m. Belle Pratte, Mindon, La.

Henry Y. b. 6 May 1830
Robt. Milton b. 27 Sep 1838
Laura (Laughra) b. 20 Feb 1841, m. Dr. W. C. Irby of Laurens

Children of Laura Vance & Dr. Irby
Claudia Irby m. Dr. Durroh Ferguson
Vance Irby m. Mary Todd
Lillian Irby m. Dr. J. Preston Marion, Greenwood, Miss.
Lyde Irby m. Tom D. Darlington

[Mrs. Price R. Reid, a desc. now owns the above Bible & adds that
Susannah Vance m. John D. Boyd who died 1833 (estate) & had 7 ch.;
Wm. G. Vance m. Cicily Davenport; Eliz. G. Vance m. John Simmons,
both bur. Laurens cemetery (Laurens, S.C.)]

EDWARD KING VANN

Edward K. Vann b. 21 Oct 1823, d. 26 May 1883, m. 1st on 23 Sep
1849 to Elizabeth Ramsey b. 5 Nov 1823, d. 11 June 1854, m. 2nd on
24 Feb 1855 to Caroline S. Ramsey (widow) b. 22 Sep 1833, d. 18 Nov
1856, m. 3rd on 6 Jan 1858 to Sarah Caroline Denson b. 31 Jan 1834,
d. 10 Aug 1896.
        Children
Edward Leon b. 15 July 1850, d. 23 Sep 1882
Eliz. Julia b. 8 Nov 1851
Margaret Samantha b. 5 Jan 1854, d. 15 July 1855
Martha Caldonia Mary, dau., b. 22 Sep 1858, d. 16 Nov 1859
Sarah Gertrude, dau., b. 29 May 1860
Hoosey Haywood, son, b. 10 Oct 1862
Frances Lilia Vann, dau., b. 3 Oct 1865
Jas. Thos., son, b. 4 Sep 1868
Wm. Henry, son, b. 13 May 1871, d. 12 Aug 1872
Caroline Leona b. 30 Jan 1874
Bertone Edith b. 11 Apr 1879

WILLIAM VEREEN

William Vereen, son of Jeremiah & Mary Vereen, b. 3 Nov 1729, d.
Sunday, 20 Sep 1789 about noon, m. 20 Nov 1754 to Elizabeth Lewis,
dau. of Charles & Martha Lewis, b. 30 Nov 1734, d. 7 June, aged 45
yrs., 5 mos., 7 days.
        Children
William Vereen, Jr. b. 27 Jan 1756
Charles Vereen b. 29 Oct 1757
Jeremiah Vereen b. 3 June 1760, d. 14 Aug 1813 at 10:00 P.M., aged
    54 yrs., 2 mos., 11 days, m. Elizabeth Vereen
Martha Elizabeth Vereen b. 31 Mar 1762, d. Saturday morning about
    sunrise 1786, aged 22 yrs., 8 mos., 17 days, m. Daniel Morrall
John Vereen b. 12 May 1765
Elizabeth Vereen b. 21 Dec 1767
Mary Vereen b. 10 Dec 1774
Daniel Vereen b. 20 Aug 1777

Joseph Jeremiah Vereen, son of Jeremiah & Elizabeth Vereen, b. 16
  July 1812
Elizabeth L. Vereen, dau. of Eliz. B. Vereen, d. 25 June 1854
Amelia L. Thomas d. 9 Aug ...

[This Bible is owned by Jackson H. Vereen of Mandarin, Fla. The
will of Jeremiah Vereen was dated 10 July 1767; the will of Charles
Lewis was proved 4 Nov 1769. Name also spelled Varin.]

                          JOSEPH VORE

Joseph Vore b. 7 Sep 1810, d. 20 Aug 1898, m. 21 Nov 1832; Bethany
Sheets b. 17 July 1812, d. 26 Feb 1886.
     Children
Harriet Rebecca b. 1 Sep 1833
Wm. Westley b. 15 Oct 1835
David Luther b. 8 Oct 1837
Thos. Perry b. 14 Sep 1839
John Esty b. 31 Jan 1842
Austin Arthur b. 29 June 1844
Joseph Saben b. 15 Aug 1846
Nathan Warren b. 30 Aug 1848
Alen Omar b. 8 Sep 1851
Mary Ellen b. 17 Aug 1857

[From Miss Helen Pemberton, West Milton, Ohio.]

                          WADLINGTON

Wm. Wadlington, son of Thomas & Sarah (Wyatt) Wadlington his wife,
  b. 4 Dec 1736,
Ann Wadlington b. 5 Mar 1738, d. 22 Oct 1794
Thomas Wadlington b. 5 Mar 1740
Sarah Wadlington b. 18 Jan 1742
James Wadlington b. 2 Jan 1745
Edward Wadlington b. 7 Jan 1751, d. 27 Dec 1790
Geo. B. Wadlington b. 10 June 1763
Sarah Wiatt Wadlington b. 16 Aug 1765
Sina Wadlington b. 30 Mar 1768
Wm. Wadlington b. 10 Aug 1770, d. Feb 1793
Mary Wadlington b. 25 Mar 1772
Thomas Wadlington b. 22 Mar 1774, d. 16 Sep 1810 at 4 o'clock P.M.
Elenor Wadlington b. 20 June 1778
Ezekiel Wadlington b. 23 Jan 1778, d. 12 Oct 1790
James Wadlington b. 10 Apr 1782
Eliz. Wadlington, dau. of Thos. & Dorothy Wadlington, b. 14 July
  1801
Dorothy Ann Wadlington, dau. of Thos. & Dorothy Wadlington, b. 7
  Dec 1803
Mary Brooks Wadlington, dau. of Thos. & Dorothy Wadlington, b. 25
  Dec 1807
Sarah [T. S. F.?] same as above b. 16 Dec 1810

Jesse Wadlington b. Aug 1782
Bailey Wadlington b. 16 Sep 1784
Spencer Wadlington b. 26 Sep 1786
Ann Wadlington b. 28 Mar 1788
Thos. Wadlington, son of Wm. Sina (Bounds) Wadlington, b. 22 Mar
    1774, d. 16 Sep 1810
Marcus Littleton, Sr. b. 8 Apr 1761
Sina Littleton b. 30 Mar 1768 [presumably the wife of Marcus]

[The above records were copied in Apr 1951 by the compiler from an
old ledger kept by an ancestor of Mr. Keitt of Newberry, S.C. who
had a store in Winchester, Frederick Co., Va. It had much personal
data in it, but there were not always any relationships listed.]

A. B. WALKER

John Walker b. in Antrim, Ireland, m. a Bo d
    Children
Andrew Walker (Capt.) Irvin's N.C. Regt., Rev. War on his tombstone
    at Walkersville, Union Co., N.C., near Lancaster Co., S.C., b. 5
    Dec 1756, d. 20 Sep 1845, m. 1st to Sarah Cry b. 25 Mar 1757, d.
    11 Sep 1798, m. 2nd to Anne Grant (no issue by 2nd wife)
Jane Walker m. James Huey
Thomas Walker d. in 1847, aged 88 yrs.

    Children of Capt. Andrew & Sarah Cry Walker
John Walker, first child, b. 23 Jan 1781 near the Waxhaws, Union
    Co., N.C., d. 27 July 1858, m. 1st to Sarah J. McCain Walker d.
    6 Jan 1822, aged 38 yrs., 5 mos., 15 days, 7 children, m. 2nd to
    Mary Tirzah Crims, no children, m. 3rd on 16 Nov 1841 to Hannah
    E. McCorkel, four children
Elizabeth Walker Houston
Sallie Walker Matthews
Margaret Walker Porter
Catherine Walker

    Children of John Walker
Andrew Boyd Walker b. 16 July 1805, d. 22 Mar 1890 in his 85th yr.,
    m. 8 Jan 1828 to Mary Doak Matthews b. 18 May 1808, d. 30 Mar
    1884 in her 76th yr.
James Millen Walker b. 16 Oct 1842, killed in Battle 31 Oct 1863
Mary Jane Walker b. 9 Apr 1844, m. 24 Nov 1859 to Col. W. J. McCain
Martha L. Walker b. 6 Oct 1846, m. 2 Oct 1866 to Robert J. Billue
Easter Caroline Walker b. 2 Sep 1849, m. 4 Dec 1866 to Allison
    Simpson

James Matthews, Jr., son of James, Sr., b. 12 Aug 1739 in Co. An-
    trim, Ireland, bur. in Matthews Cemetery, Union Co., N.C.; Mary
    Doak b. 30 June 1749, d. 17 Mar 1833, bur. Matthews Cemetery

    Children of Andrew Boyd Walker & Mary Doak Matthews
Sarah McCain Walker b. 9 Nov 1828, d. 11 Nov 1908, m. 24 June 1847

to Robert M. Scott
Margaret Eleanor Walker b. 5 Nov 1830, d. 18 Dec 1915, m. 11 Nov
  1852 to James C. Moore
William Rose Walker b. 21 Feb 1833, d. 27 Aug 1880, m. 27 July 1859
  to Ann J. Gilmer
John Anderson Walker b. 18 Jan 1835, d. 20 Nov 1833
John Matthews Walker b. 18 Aug 1836, d. 21 Aug 1837
Robert Boyd Walker b. 3 June 1838, d. 14 June 1839
Calvert Ellington Walker b. 11 Feb 1840, d. 8 Sep 1840
Neal Gordon Walker b. 1 Sep 1841, d. in Battle 12 May 1863 in Miss.
Eliza Ann Walker b. 31 Dec 1843, d. 13 Apr 1906, m. 6 Oct 1870 to
  Marian Harlow
Mary Adaline (Adeline) Walker b. 22 Aug 1845, d. 18 Jan 1847
Martha Jane Walker b. 24 July 1847, d. 21 Nov 1848
Andrew Boyd Matthews Walker b. 7 Sep 1849, d. 11 Mar 1921, m. 1st
  on 25 Apr 1872 to Adelia J. Nelson, m. 2nd on 9 Jan 1877 to Susie
  H. Morgan d. 6 July 1928
Agnes Louise Walker b. 9 May 1851, d. 1 Feb 1858

Nellie M. Walker m. John Walker
Sallie Walker m. Huey McCain
Margaret M. Walker m. George Winchester
John J. Walker m. Sallie Matthews [John Mack]
William McCain Walker m. 1st to Kisiah V. Hagan, m. 2nd to Pattie
  Alexander

James McCorkle b. 11 Sep 1774, d. 2 Sep 1854, m. Mary Cousar
    Children
Hannah H. (D.) McCorkle b. 7 Mar 1807
Archibald D. McCorkle b. 10 July 1809
Mary D. McCorkle b. 25 June 1811, m. Andrew Ormand
Sarah H. McCorkle b. 20 May 1813, m. James Clark
James J. McCorkle b. 22 Nov 1815
Martha Caroline McCorkle b. 11 Sep 1818
Agnes McCorkle b. 15 Apr 1821, d. 22 Feb 1822
Jane L. McCorkle b. 21 Feb 1823, d. 23 Sep 1846
Margaret L. McCorkle b. 25 Sep 1824, m. James Price

    Children of James W. & Margaret L. McCorkle Price
Sarah E. Price b. 8 Sep 1856
Infant dau. b. & d. 8 Sep 1858
John C. Price b. 16 July 1859
J. Robert Price b. & d. 16 Nov 1860
J. Mack Price b. 18 July 1863
William J. Price b. 18 Apr 1865
Mary M. Price b. 7 Mar 1867
Ben F. Price b. 16 June 1869

[From the Bible of A.B. Walker, owned by Mrs. Kate Walker Ranson of
Lancaster Co., S.C.]

HENRY AUGUSTINE WASHINGTON

Henry Augustine Washington b. in Va., d. in 1825 in Limestone Co., Ala., bur. on his farm off highway 31, m. 2nd in 1778 to Mildred Pratt, dau. of Thomas Pratt & his wife a Miss Vivian, b. in 1757 in Va., d. Mar 1852 in the home of [her son-in-law] Dr. Wm. T. Minor in Trinity, Ala., aged 95 yrs.

Children

Harry d. in 1818 in Phila., a Med. Student
Thacker
William
Bailey
Fanny b. 1788
Catherine Stark b. 1790, m. in 1805 to Wm. Winter
Jane Elliott b. 1792, m. Wm. Foote
Lucy Margaret b. 1794, m. in 1843 to Capt. John Harris
John Pratt m. Sally Jones of Franklin Co., Tenn.
Augustine Burkett b. 1802, m. Martha Jones, nee Haywood, of Tenn.
Fanny Thacker b. 1804, m. 22 Jan 1825 to Dr. Wm. Tompkins Minor
Thos. Pratt b. 1806, m. in 1835 to Eliz. Harris
Wm., III, d. young
Stark b. 1797, m. Miss Jones

[This record from Mrs. Rayburn Neville, Trinity, Ala. who is a desc. of Henry A. & Mildred Pratt Washington. Henry Augustine Washington was a direct desc. of Geo. Washington's father August-ine, possibly his grandson. Henry A. went first to Ky. & then came down to Ala. when it was only recently opened up. He had not im-proved his fortunes by his moves & though he was born to wealth, he died in rather straightened circumstances. He lies in an unmarked grave on land just across highway #31 from the Luke Pryor Place in Limestone Co., Ala. They had been from Prince Wm. Co., Va.]

SILAS WATKINS

Silas Watkins m. 20 May 1773 to Phebe Watkins.

Children

Joel, Jr. b. 5 July 1776
Elizabeth b. 10 June 1778
Phebe b. 30 Sep 1780
Silas, Jr. b. 30 Sep 1782
Major John Watkins b. 31 July 1784 in Va., d. 16 Apr 1870, m. 18 Sep 1816 in Green Co., Ga. to Elizabeth Atkinson b. 10 Sep 1800 in Burk Co., Ga.
Rhoda b. 22 Apr 1786
Benjamin H. b. 28 June 1788
Mary b. 9 Apr 1791
Samuel b. 6 Apr 1794
Francis b. 2 Sep 1795

Children of John & Elizabeth A. Watkins

Joel Warren b. 22 Oct 1817, d. 9 July 1879, m. 7 May 1842 to M. M.

Randon

Maria Louisa b. 29 Apr 1821, m. 5 Oct 1836 to Seth L. Randall
Lucy Quintina b. 24 Dec 1824, d. 8 Nov 1835
John L. b. 24 Dec 1828, d. 28 Oct 1867, m. 16 Aug 1849 to Susannah
   W. Averiett [Averett?]
Musidora A. b. 4 Oct 1835 in Talladega Co., Ala., m. 8 Oct 1851 in
   Talladega Co. to W. J. R. Jameson b. 26 Feb 182? in Wilcox Co.,
   Ala.
Robert H. b. 17 Jan 1839, m. 1st on 29 Sep 1858 to Sallie J. Carter
   d. 16 Jan 1869, m. 2nd on 2 Oct 1870 to Alice Pane

Robert C. Watkins b. 2 Dec 1859
John C. Watkins b. 5 Jan 1862
Edwin E. Watkins b. 21 Apr 1864
Musa M. Watkins b. 5 Dec 1866

Mary Elizabeth Jameson b. 16 Sep 1852 in Talladega Co., Ala., m. 15
   Jan 1874 in Washington Co., Tex. to James W. Carter b. 21 Dec
   1850 in Talladega Co., Ala.
Willie Etta Jameson b. 11 Nov 1854 in Talladega Co., Ala., m. 25
   Nov 1873 in Washington Co., Tex. to E. R. Young b. 19 Dec 1844
   in Knoxubee Co., Miss.
Lauretta (Laura) Jameson b. 11 Nov 1854 in Talladega Co., Ala., m.
   14 Nov 1883 in Washington Co., Tex. to J. H. Irby
Musadora A. Jameson b. 6 Jan 1859 in Talladega Co., Ala.

[Bible record from Mrs. Lucille Garner, Jacksboro, Tex. who states,
"Silas Watkins was from Prince Edward Co., Va. Phoebe Watkins (nee
Watkins) was from Cumberland Co., Va." Mrs. Garner has Young data.]

WILLIAM WATSON

William Watson b. 8 Jan 1755, m. 1 Jan 1784 to Lucy Griffin b. 8
Jan 1765.
      Children
Edward Watson b. 30 Jan 1785
Richard Watson b. 22 July 1787, m. 4 Nov 1812 to Lavinia Brooks

Sarahan, 1st child of Richard Watson, b. 1 Sep 1813, m. 21 Jan 1830
   to Dr. S. Perryman
James T. [or F.] Watson, nephew of Wm. Watson, m. 6 Jan 1826 to
   Petty Watson, niece of Wm. Watson
Margaret Watson, mother of Wm. Watson, d. 12 Nov 1806

[This book bought by William Watson in 1803. The following may be
in the Bible or may be a comment of the person who sent the record:
"Edward Watson and his wife Margaret and three sons, William, James
and Stephen, moved from Va. to Abbeville, S.C.]

CHARLES WATTERSON

Charles G. Watterson b. 1794, d. 13 Nov 1861, aged 68 yrs., m. 1

Oct 1821 [in Morgan Co., Ala.] to Frances C. Turrentine b. 1806, d. 16 May 1872, aged 66 yrs.

Elizabeth W. Watterson b. 26 July 1822
William M. Watterson b. 24 Aug 1824
James R. Watterson b. 5 Dec 1827, m. 15 Feb 1854 [or 1857] to Caro-
  line Nesmith
John Leander Watterson b. 18 May 1830, m. 3rd on 20 July 1869 to
  Eliza (Nesmith) Jolly
Saml. Watterson b. 18 May 1830
Sarah Nancy Watterson b. 20 Oct 1833
Elenor Jane Watterson b. 1 Sep 1836
Mary Frances W. Watterson b. ? July 1840, m. 26 May 1860 to Malcolm
  Jolly
Martha Henrietta Watterson b. 27 Apr 1843, m. 1st on 9 Jan 1867 to
  Wm. Eli Basinger, m. 2nd on 23 Sep 1897 to J. W. Ganus
Charles Ross Watterson b. 26 May 1846

Margarett Gillespie d. 21 Aug 1823
Johnston Gillespie b. 17 Feb 1798, d. same day
Saml. & Margaret Faulkner m. 24 Dec 1811
Saml. & Nancy Wylie m. 18 Jan 1813
Wm. Watterson d. 15 Jan 1854, aged 60 yrs.
John Watterson d. 27 July 1857, aged 72 yrs.
Wm. Eli Basinger d. 18 Oct 1894, aged 75 yrs.

[This Bible record is owned by Mrs. Ollie Padgett, Trafford, Ala., grand dau. of Martha H. Watterson & Wm. Eli Basinger above. In the front of this Bible is: "John Watterson His Book, born in York Co., S.C." John Watterson was a bachelor as was his brother Wm. John left a will in Chester Co., S.C. in which he names his brother Charles & that a tombstone shall be erected to the grave of his brother Wm. & to himself. Mrs. John Meadows of Decatur, Ala., now decd., told her niece, the compiler, the story of Jas. R. Watterson's going back to S.C. to get his father's share of John's estate. John's father was Chas. G. Watterson, then of Lawrence Co., Ala. The family seems to have been gone from S.C. when John died, and his nephew, Jas. R., took his Bible back to Ala. with him in 1857. The three bros., Wm., Chas. & John were all in the War of 1812 from pension records found by the compiler in the National Archives in Apr 1952. It seems clear that the Margaret Faulkner, later Gilles-pie, and Nancy Wylie, both above, were sisters of Chas. G., Wm. & John. In the court records of York, S.C. is an estate settlement for a John Gillespie and wife Margaret. The father of these older Wattersons is not yet known for sure, but the mother was Sara. In Chester Co., S.C. 1810 census there are 3 boys & 5 girls with Sara Watterson. There is a deed for land she bought in Chester Co., S.C. while she was a resident of York Co., S.C. John Watterson had land grant in Craven Co., S.C. 1772; in Tryon Co., N.C., 1774 He died intestate in Lincoln Co., which has old Tryon records, in 1808. From dates of his children, it would appear that this Sara was probably a sister-in-law and came over with him & other Irish

immigrants. Further research should clear this up. There were
Wattersons in Pa. & the valley of Va. long before the Rev. The
ancestor of the famous "Marse Henry" Watterson of the Louisville
Courier Journal descends from the Va. family & came on into east
Tenn. prior to 1840. A brother Edward came to Pa. & lived & died
there; also was a Rev. War soldier. The compiler has several old
letters from the family in Rogersville, Tenn. written in 1803, 1823,
1827, & 1836 from the grandfather of "Marse Henry" to relatives in
Va. & Pa.]

JOHN LEANDER WATTERSON

John Leander Watterson b. 18 May 1830, d. 7 Apr 1910, m. 1st on 4
Apr 1852 to Harriet Clardy, m. 2nd in Tex. to Amanda Sharp, m. 3rd
on 20 July 1869 to Eliza Nesmith Jolly, widow of Joseph Jolly.
Eliza Nesmith had married 1st on 11 Oct 1859 to Joseph Jolly who d.
27 May 1863, their dau.: Laura b. 8 Sep 1860, m. 4 June 1890 to
John Henderson.
    Children of John & Amanda Watterson
Chas. Philip b. 15 Aug 1867, d. 19 Nov 1931, m. 25 Feb 1890 to Lena
    H. Sheets
James d. as a baby
    Children of John & Eliza Watterson
Frances (Fannie) b. 18 Aug 1870, d. 8 Sep 1926, m. 19 Dec 1886 to
    John Sheets
Nancy (Nannie) b. 18 Aug 1870, m. 12 Mar 1891 to John Albert Mea-
    dows
Mary Elizabeth b. 21 Mar 1873
Martha Malinda Alex. b. 16 Jan 1876, m. 9 Aug 1891 to Franklin La
    Fayette Aldridge

Molly Watterson d. 30 Nov 1921, m. 9 Feb 1890 John Allen Bracken

[Nannie Meadows d. 24 Aug 1953. This Bible owned by the granddau.
of John L. S. Watterson, Mrs. Carl Knapps, Danville, Ky., copied by
the compiler in spring of 1938.]

COL. JAMES WASHINGTON WATTS

Col. James W. Watts, son of James Watts, Jr. & his wife Nancy Clark
Williams, b. 30 Aug 1819, d. 27 June 1906, m. 1st on 16 May 1844 to
Sally Williams Jones b. 10 Nov 1828, d. 15 June 1862, m. 2nd on 8
Aug 1865 to Kittie Griffin (Gary) Martin, dau. of Dr. Chas. F. &
Mary S. Gary, b. 23 Feb 1832, d. 10 Mar 1890, m. 3rd on 22 Feb 1894
to Susan Constance Nance b. 17 Sep 1822, d. 26 Dec 1895.
    Children
Nancy Emily, dau., b. 31 Oct 1845, m. 22 Dec 1868 to John Calhoun
    Davis
Lucy Williams, dau., b. 7 May 1847, m. John T. McGowan
Sally Cornelia, dau., b. 2 Feb 1849; Corry V. Watts m. Laurens Mar-
    tin; Mrs. Corrie Watts Martin d. 12 Mar 1902
Louisa Laurens, 4th dau., b. 9 Apr 1851, d. 1 June 1862

Mary Eliza, 5th dau., b. 25 Jan 1853, d. 7 Oct 1853
Sally Jones, dau., b. 9 Sep 1854, d. Nov 1891, m. 10 Oct 1885
  to Thomas J. Snyder
Julia Washington, 7th dau., b. 30 Jan 1856, d. 1 Feb 1857
Jas. Washington, Jr., 1st son, b. 25 Nov 1857, d. 5 Oct 1916
Thos. Jones, son, b. 5 Mar 1859, d. May 1908
Annie Henry, 8th dau., b. 13 Aug 1860, d. 5 Sep 1861
Mary Griffin b. 20 Dec 1866; Mary Watts Shell d. ...
John Drayton Williams b. 9 July 1868
Kittie Gary b. 28 Feb 1870: Kittie G. Watts Wharton d. ...
Eliz. Anderson b. 1 Mar 1872
Antho Willie [dau.] b. 12 Dec 1873; Antho W. Fuller d. 1 Aug 1901
Jannie Boyd b. 18 Aug 1875
[Bible owned by Mrs. R. E. Jones, Clinton, S.C. Col. Watts & one
wife bur. at Greenville Church, Donalds, S.C.]

ABRAHAM WEAVER

Abraham Weaver, the father, b. 25 Nov 1807, d. 7 Apr 1862; Judith
R. Owen, the mother, b. 3 June 1808, d. 27 Dec 1867.

Francis Marion Weaver b. 22 Sep 1828, d. 28 Aug 1844
David Owen Weaver b. 30 Apr 1832, d. 14 Dec 1861
Abner Hughes Weaver b. 2 July 1836, d. 1897
Susannah Jane Weaver b. 16 Mar 1839
Robert J. Weaver b. 6 July 1841, d. 22 Dec 1898, m. 1st to Sarah
  McIver Poindexter, dau. of Benjamin & Mary Poindexter, b. 17 Oct
  1846, m. 2nd to Emaline Matilda McClinton b. 19 May 1850, d. 4
  Feb 1899
Sarah Levinia Weaver b. 17 Sep 1844, d. 11 Feb 1902, m. 20 Dec 1866
  to Burke Lester
        Children of Robt. J. & Sarah McIver P. Weaver
John Walter Weaver b. 14 Dec 1866, d. 10 Jan 1867
Henry Columbus Weaver b. 29 Sep 1868
Mary Emma Weaver b. 1 Mar 1871
Joseph LaFayette Weaver b. 23 July 1873
Eliza Ann Weaver b. 11 June 1878

[Bible owned by Roy Lester of Columbiana, Ala., copied in June 1951
by the compiler.]

JAMES WEBB

James Webb b. 5 Dec 1705, d. 11 Apr 1771, aged 65 yrs. the 5th Dec,
m. 20 Feb 1731 to Mary Edmondson.
        Their children
William b. 10 Feb 1732, d. March following
James b. 2 July 1734, d. ...ber 1773
Mary b. 4 Oct 1736, d. 2 Sep 1736
John b. 7 Apr 1739, d. following Sep
Mary b. 14 Oct 1740
John b. 2 Apr 1743, d. 7 Aug 1745

William b. 1 May 1745
John b. 18 Jan 1747-48
Thomas b. 27 Feb 1751, d. Oct 1783
Elizabeth b. 30 June 1754

JAMES WEBB

James Webb b. 17 Nov 1779, d. 3 Aug 1827, m. 17 Feb 1803 to Ann
Hunt Smith b. 5 Sep 1784, d. 18 Aug 1840
    Their children
Alexander S. b. 21 Feb 1804, d. 31 Jan 1849
John P. b. 17 Jan 1807, d. 28 May 1846
James L. b. 20 June 1811, d. Feb 1860
William H. b. 23 Feb 1814
Mary Ann Amy b. 13 May 1817, d. fall of 1880
Samuel M. b. 11 Oct 1819, d. July 1873
Robert C. b. 20 Aug 1824
Thomas b. 5 Mar 1828, d. 20 Apr 1828

[This Bible was misplaced in Nashville, Tenn. The above record is
a copy sent by Robert C. Webb to his sister Mary Ann Amy Blackwell
which has been preserved. From Mrs. Mary McIver Stanford, Chapel
Hill, N.C., a descendant.]

JOHN WEBB

John Webb b. 18 Jan 1747, d. 29 Aug 1826, m. 20 Feb 1772 to Amy
Booker [b.] 27 Aug 1752, d. 25 Mar 1835.
    Their children
Elizabeth b. 4 Mar 1773, d. 6 Sep 1829
Thomas b. 26 Dec 1776
James b. 21 Nov 1779, d. 3 Aug 1827
Mary b. 22 June 1782
Ann b. 24 June 1784, d. 29 Jan 1825
John b. 1 Apr 1786
William b. 17 Oct 1787
Lewis b. 15 July 1789
Isaac b. 29 Dec 1790
Amy b. 3 July 1792, d. 7 July 1793
Amy b. 31 Aug 1794
Susanna b. 4 Oct 1796

"Mr. William Webb started West with his family 27 Mar 1834."

JOSEPH WELBORN

Grandmother Bell d. 9 Sep 1820
Step grandfather Wm. Bell d. Oct 1821
Father, John Welborn d. 11 Sep 1825
Mother, Jane Welborn d. 5 Jan 1835
Brother, John Welborn d. 15 Dec 1830
Brother, [no first name] Welborn d. 1 Mar 1816

Sister, Martha Mullen d. 12 Dec 1839

[These records written in the Bible by Jos. Welborn. This Bible
now in the possession of Miss Sophronia Swain, granddau. of Jos.
Welborn, Sophia, N.C. in 1932. The name was sometimes spelled Wilborn in this record.]

JOHN WELLS

John Wells b. 25 Aug 1785, d. 28 June 1845, m. Jane Wells b. 22 Apr
1788, d. 25 May 1864.
    Their children
Elizabeth Wells b. 1 Aug 1810, d. 14 Aug 1901
Nancy Wells b. 15 Mar 1820, d. 3 Sep 1841, m. Dec 1839 by Rev.
  Scruggs to Griffin Hamilton
Harriet Wells b. 11 June 1823, d. 2 July 1911, m. 24 Dec 1840 by
  Rev. S. Drummond to Woodward Allen b. 29 Nov 1820, d. 3 Apr 1880

    Children of Woodward & Harriet Wells Allen
James Henry Allen b. 25 Oct 1841, d. 27 Feb 1862
Elizabeth Frances Allen b. 21 Nov 1843, d. 20 Mar 1867
Amanda Ann Allen b. 19 Aug 1845, d. 9 Apr 1900
Mary Henriatta Allen b. 14 Mar 1847
Sarah Mannering Allen b. 28 Oct 1848, d. 13 Apr 1927
Jehu Wells Allen b. 21 Aug 1850
Eber Caleb Allen b. 6 June 1853

John R. Jeffries m. 1 Nov 1866 by Rev. T. Smith to Ettie M. Allen
Willie Allen Wright, son of Louisa Allen Wright, b. 11 Dec 1864
James Moss, husband of Elizabeth Wells Moss d. 8 May 1835, aged 25
  yrs., 7 mos., 17 days
Mary Allen, dau. of James Allen who was son of John Allen, m. 1
  July 1847 to Samuel Pilgram
Mary Allen b. 27 Jan 1816, d. 7 July 1892 of paralysis
Sallie Pilgram b. 1 Sep 1849
Hannah Pilgram, mother of Samuel Pilgram, b. 27 Nov 1786, d. 6 Sep
  1853
Reuben Daniel m. 12 Dec 1781 to Elizabeth Harrison
Isham Harrison m. 20 June 1783 in Granville Co., N.C. to Amey Gil-
  liam

"John Wells Bible bought in 1827" "I give this Bible to my dau.,
Mrs. Sallie M. Perry, as a keepsake."

[This Wells-Allen Bible is owned by Mrs. J. R. Jester, Columbia,
S.C., dau. of Mrs. Sallie M. Perry, dau. of Sarah Mannering Wells
above. This family resided in Spartanburg Co., S.C. in the Woodruff area.]

HENRY WEST

Henry West b. 1785 in N.C., m. in N.C. to Eliz.

Children
Jesse b. 7 May 1807
Mary b. 23 Dec 1809
Reny [Arena] b. 15 Sep 1811 [m. widower Tom Renfrro]
James b. 21 Apr 1812
Henry Jackson b. 4 May 1822 [note 10 yr. gap]
Michael b. 4 Jan 1824 [m. Nacy Beavers, Chesterfield Co., S.C.]
William b. 5 Apr 1828
Stephen B. b. 12 Sep 1830

"Of these children only Jas. remained in S.C. - Chesterfield Co.
Others going at verious [sic] times to Tuscaloosa, Ala. and other
nearby cos."

[From Mrs. Paul B. Murff, Rt. 2, Floydada, Tex.]

JESSE WEST

Jesse West, oldest son of Henry & Elizabeth West, b. 7 May 1807 in
N.C., d. 25 Apr 1881, bur. in Camp Ground Cemetery, Tuscaloosa,
Ala., m. 2 May 1838 in Tuscaloosa to Frances Ann Gwinn [Gwynn] b.
18 Apr 1818 in N.C., d. 20 Aug 1898, bur. in Camp Ground Cemetery.
    Children
Eliz. b. 30 Apr 1839, d. 23 Feb 1928, m. 6 June 1861 to John Harey,
    a Civil War Soldier who d. June 1865
Benj. Franklin b. 30 July 1840, d. 5 June 1907, m. 31 Oct 1865 to
    Mahala Clarentine Tyner [dau. of Thos. B. Tyner & Sarah R. Cline]
    b. 4 Sep 1847 [or 1849], d. 18 Sep 1900
Nancy Abigail b. 18 Jan 1843, d. 1912, m. Geo. Marion Watkins b.
    20 Feb 1853, d. 1930
Morris lost during Civil War, never married
Rhoda Millise b. 5 Jan 1847, d. 26 Dec 1918, m. 14 Jan 1871 to Geo.
    Washington Camp b. 23 Aug 1849, d. 19 Mar 1934
Lewis Henry b. 12 Sep 1850, d. 29 Aug 1928, m. 1st on 22 Feb 1875
    to Sallie Nuckles [Nuckols] b. 22 Jan 1857, d. 28 Dec 1915, m.
    2nd to Earnestine Winters, no children
Parthenia Mahala b. 14 Mar 1855, d. Sep 1930, m. 15 Sep 1876 to
    Sanford Marion Williamson b. 28 Aug 1854, d. 25 Mar 1934
James Livingston b. 7 Aug 1859, d. 1892 somewhere near Howe, Okla.,
    unmarried
Mattie Ann b. 1861, d. 16 June 1941, m. Jas. Thos. Alexander b. 25
    Sep 1855, d. 7 Dec 1911

MERCER NORTON WEST

Mercer Norton West b. 11 Nov 1807, d. 3 Aug 1889, m. 20 Dec 1827 to
Ann Mercer b. 13 Dec 1808, d. 11 Apr 1863.
    Their children
John N. b. 27 Dec 1828
Canzada b. 4 June 1830
Solomon G. b. 16 Apr 1832
Mary J. b. 7 Feb 1834, d. 14 Apr 1863

Hesther Ann b. 30 Jan 1836
Richard M. b. 13 Mar 1838
Elza M. [Milton] b. 6 May 1840
James H. b. 12 July 1842
Margret E. b. 17 Feb 1846, d. 20 Dec 1848
Lorenzo D. b. 2·Nov 1848, d. 9 Jan 1874

Richard Mercer b. 4 Sep 1785, d. 9 May 1859, m. Mary Mercer b. 30
May 1786, d. Jan 1818.
    Their children
Silas b. 14 Mar 1807
Ann b. 13 Dec 1808 [above]
Lorenzo Dow b. 23 Nov 1810
Canzada b. 23 Nov 1811

[This record was sent by Miss Mildred Dulaney, Waco, Tex. In the
chart that she sent of these allied families, she shows them to
have been in Ky. Mercer Norton West was b. in Ky., son of Solomon
West, Jr. who m. Hetty Norton. Solomon West, Jr. was the son of
Solomon West, Sr. b. ca. 1720 & his wife Isabella Boyd, from S.C.]

ALEXANDER WHITE

Alexander White b. 10 Jan 1803, d. 19 June 1876, m. 1st in 1823 to
Sarah Friend b. 15 Dec 1802, d. 4 Oct 1864, m. 2nd to Mrs. Sarah
Payne.
    Children
Darious b. 9 Dec 1822, d. 17 Dec 1900, m. Hester Ann Broom b. 7 Dec
    1825, d. 13 Dec 1912
Mary b. 2 Apr 1824
Martha b. 9 Feb 1826
Elizabeth b. 16 July 1828
Ellen b. 16 Dec 1830
Eliza b. 15 Aug 1832
Sirapta (Siralta) b. 12 Aug 1834
Samantha b. 29 (21) Jan 1836
Lovenia b. 15 Dec 1838
Rufus A. b. 24 July 1842

[Data from the Bible of Darius White whose family still owns it.
Alex. White lived in Ross Co., Ohio & held office in that state.
This copy was sent to the compiler by the late Mrs. Alfred White,
608 Onondaga, Ann Arbor, Mich. who copied it some years ago.]

JOHN WHITE, JR.

John White, Jr. b. 11 May 1770, m. 1792 to Hester Brantley b. 8 May
1774.
    Their children
Sallie b. 11 May 1793
Zachariah b. 9 Apr 1797
Nancy b. 13 Nov 1798

Elizabeth b. 18 Apr 1800
James b. 5 Aug 1801
John, III b. 13 Jan 1802
William b. 14 Mar 1803
Anna Mariah b. 4 Dec 1805
Patsy b. 2 May 1807
Polly Bradford b. 1 Aug 1808
Sherwood b. 29 Aug 1810
Simeon b. 5 Apr 1812
John Brantley b. 1816

[This record from Mrs. Ida B. Kellam, Wilmington, N.C.]

MONROE ATKINSON WHITTINGTON

Monroe Atkinson Whittington b. 4 Aug 1848, d. 18 May 1902, m. 15
Nov 1871 in Greensboro, N.C. by Rev. J. Henry Smith to Mary Ella
Jones, dau. of Jackson & Mary F. Jones, b. 27 Oct 1853, d. 27 Sep
1887.
    Children
Mary Louise b. 4 Sep 1873
Caroline Monroe of Greensboro b. 29 Sep 1877, m. 10 Dec 1902 to
    Thomas Edwin Lynch of Hillsboro, N.C. who d. 16 Oct 1925, son:
    Edwin Monroe Lynch b. 2 Dec 1904

[Bible owned by Mrs. Thos. Lynch, Hillsboro, N.C.]

BRANCH WILLIAMS

Branch Williams d. 27 Nov 1858, m. Tiercy b. 6 Mar 1798, d. 11 Dec
1884.

Wm. W. Williams d. 23 Jan 1859
Amanda M. Williams d. 1 July 1856
Wm. B. Hatch d. 21 July 1860
Joseph R. Hatch d. 9 Feb 1884
Cullen Blackman Hatch d. 22 Aug 1912
Anne Elizabeth Hatch d. 8 Oct 1922
Malvina T. Hatch d. 6 July 1930

[Sent by Mr. Cullen B. Hatch, Mt. Olive, N.C.]

JAMES WILLIAMS

James Williams b. 30 Mar 1785 in Richmond Co., N.C., d. 8 Feb 1876
in Colbert Co., Ala., m. in 1806 to Tamsey Manship b. Aug 1791 in
Marlborough Dist., S.C.
    Children
William Williams b. 23 Apr 1807 in Marlborough Dist., S.C.
Isabella Williams b. 4 Oct 1809 in Marlborough Dist., S.C.
Aaron Manship Williams b. 5 Sep 1811 in Jackson Co., Tenn.
Thos. Wesley Williams b. 27 Nov 1813 in Jackson Co., Tenn.

Chas. Williams b. 27 Dec 1815 in Jackson Co., Tenn.
Mariah Williams b. 27 Dec 1817 in Jackson Co., Tenn.
Sampson Williams b. 8 May 1820 in Jackson Co., Tenn.
Oliver Hazzard Perry Williams b. 1 Mar 1822 in Jackson Co., Tenn.
James Williams b. 6 May 1824 in Jackson Co., Tenn.
George Washington Williams b. 6 Feb 1829 in Franklin Co., Ala.
Belinda Jane Williams b. 3 Nov 1831 in Franklin Co., Ala.

[Williams Bible owned by Mrs. Chas. Turner & copied by Mrs. E.
Gregory, Tuscumbia, Ala.]

JOHN WILLIAMS

John Williams, son of Daniel & Ursula Clark Williams, b. 4 Nov 1737
d. 1823, m. Syntha Allen, dau. of Charles & Lucy Bacon Allen.
    Children
Charles b. 1 Sep 1788, m. Jennie Cunningham
Lucy b. 6 Dec 1790
Elizabeth b. 12 May 1792, m. Charles Fowler
Lydell b. 28 June 1793, m. Peggy Cunningham
Letty b. 27 Sep 1794
Sarah b. 22 Aug 1795
Peggy b. 7 Apr 1798
Nancy b. 30 Aug 1799, m. James Parks or Barks
Mamina b. 14 Dec 1801 m. Bartlett Brooks
Susan b. 19 Sep 1800 m. Robertson Mosley
Matilda b. 25 Jan 1803, m. James Little
Clarissa b. 9 Oct 1804
David b. 1 Oct 1806

John & Mary, emigrants, grandparents of John Williams, b. 26 Jan
    1679 & 26 Sep 1684

[Information by Sarah I. (?) Williams, Rt. 1, Cambridge City, Ind.]

REV. JOHN WILLIAMS

Rev. John Williams b. 1757, d. 7 Apr 1814, m. Margaret Taylor b.
1758, d. 13 Feb 1833.
    Children
Thomas b. in Md.
Linda b. 3 Jan 1785
William b. 23 Aug 1787, m. to Lucinda Phelps b. 28 Jan 1797
Martha b. 3 Sep 1791
Elizabeth b. 22 Oct 1793
Margaret b. 3 Oct 1795
James b. 1797
Nancy b. 16 Aug 1801
Mary b. 28 Aug 1803

[This record was sent to the compiler in July 1952 by Mr. Oscar
Tipton of Columbus, Ohio, a desc., who states that Rev. John Wil-

liams was a Methodist Minister & was a Chaplain in the Rev. War.
The family lived in Md.]

OLIVER HAZZARD PERRY WILLIAMS

Oliver Hazzard Perry Williams b. 1 Mar 1822, d. 15 Nov 1903, m. Dec
1842 to Mary Garrett b. 24 Feb 1824 in Anderson Dist., S.C.
    Children
Belinda Jane Williams b. 17 Oct 1845 in Lauderdale Co., Ala.
Sampson Henry Williams b. 23 Feb 1847 in Lauderdale Co., Ala.
Chas. Washington Williams b. 11 Sep 1849 in Franklin Co., Ala.
Jas. William Williams b. 30 Nov 1851 in Franklin Co., Ala.
Thomas Wesley Williams b. 7 Sep 1854 in Franklin Co., Ala.
Mary Alice Williams b. 18 Feb 1858 in Franklin Co., Ala.
Martha Ida Williams b. 20 Feb 1861 in Franklin Co., Ala.

[Bible owned by Mrs. Chas. Turner & copied by Mrs. E. Gregory, Tus-
cumbia, Ala. Note by Pauline Jones Gandrud: 1850 census of Frank-
lin Co., Ala., Dist. #5, Family #398 & 399 -
James Williams   age 66   b. N.C.   occ. farmer $600 real estate
Fanny (Tamsy?)   age 60   b. blank
Malinda   age 19   b. blank

James Williams, Jr. age 26 b. Tenn. occ. farmer
Elizabeth   age 25 b. Tenn.
Louisa   age 4 b. Ala.
Fanny   age 1 b. Ala.]

JAMES WILLIAMSON

James Williamson b. in 1754, m. 21 Oct 1784 to Ann Edmunds Edwards
b. 22 Sep 1766.
    Children
Mary b. 28 Sep 1785
William b. 5 Mar 1787, d. 1787
George b. 1 Sep 1788
Martha b. 22 June 1790
Priscilla b. 19 Sep 1792, d. 1792
Sarah Edwards b. 2 Feb 1795
Thomas Edwards b. 19 Aug 1797
James b. 13 Aug 1799
Benjamin E. b. 23 Sep 1801

[This is a Caswell Co., N.C. family. The late Mrs. Elizabeth Dixon
of Gastonia, N.C. sent this record & has worked on this line. The
following record is from a scrap of a Bible found in Caswell Co.
Court House.]

Isham Phelps b. 16 June 1793
Sally Hamblet, wife of James Harrison Hamblet, d. 4 Jan 184-

WILLIAM WILLIAMSON

William Williamson b. 7 Sep 1801, d. 1 Dec 1860, m. 15 Dec 1821 to
Mary G. Williamson b. 8 Feb 1802, d. 11 Dec 1880.
  . Their children
Harriet b. 28 Dec 1822
Iverson b. 15 Dec 1825, d. 7 Jan 1850
Alfred b. 29 Feb 1828, d. 22 July 1864
Nancy b. 23 Apr 1830
Jane Elizabeth b. 30 June 1835, m. 25 Dec 1853 to Geo. Henderson
  McKee d. 31 Mar 1908
William, Jr. b. 18 Apr 1832, d. 21 July 1862
Mary Anne b. 6 Mar 1837; Mary Ann Brinson d. 28 May 1871
James Lonzo Cicero b. 31 May 1839
Helen Mar b. 22 May 1841, m. 12 Jan 1862 to B. T. McKee
Beverly Freeman b. 10 Oct 1844, d. 22 Sep 1862
Alexander Hamilton b. 17 Apr 1846

Linton Dawson McKee b. 21 Jan 1863
Ida Pauline McKee b. 13 Feb 1866
Hattie Joslyn Brinson b. 3 Mar 1867, d. 1 Nov 1933
W. T. McKee m. 18 Jan 1899 to Genie Mae Jenkins
Lillian McKee d. 8 Aug 1888, m. 2 Nov 1875 to O. L. Peacock
Mary Eliz. McKee m. 17 Mar 1891
Sidney G. McKee m. 16 Nov 1887 to Geo. T. Chandler
Stephen McKee m. 30 July 1901 to Elizabeth Council
Hilton M. McKee d. 15 Feb 1878
Jane E. Williamson d. 27 July 1883
W. T. McKee, Jr. d. 22 Aug 1912
Ida Peacock Rainey d. 14 Aug 1920

[This record from Mrs. James Thornton Nuckols, Columbus, Ga., 1957]

JOHN WOOD WILSON

John Wood Wilson b. 8 [3?] Jan 1796, d. 8 Mar 1881, m. 1st on 6 Sep
1821 to Anna Bowles, d. 28 Apr 1844, aged 44 yrs., 11 mos., 9 days,
m. 2nd on 10 Feb 1848 to Abigail Davis.
  Children
Sarah Jane b. 27 Sep 1822, m. 11 Apr 1848 to Lemuel Mitchell
Thomas Anderson b. 25 Feb 1824, d. 17 ... 1829, aged 5 yrs., 6
  days, 25 days
Son b. 26 Sep 1826, d. 26 Oct 1826
Nancy b. 14 Dec 1827, m. Feb 185- to Wm. Taylor
Martha b. 14 Aug 1830; Martha (Wilson) Forrest d. 30 May 1903
John Harrison b. 26 Dec 1837 [?], m. 30 Apr 1857 to Sarah A. Tar-
  pley
Caleb Anderson b. Sep 1834, d. 6 Dec 1856, m. 4 Nov 1856 to Betsy
  Ann Airs
Josiah Linch [Lynch?] b. 27 Jan 1837, m. 30 May 1860 to Mary C.
  Wallace, m. 2nd on 11 Nov 1862 to Betty C. Tarpley
Eliza.(beth) Frances b. 28 Aug 1839, m. 22 Aug 1860 William A. Tar-

335

pley

"My father Thomas Wilson d. in July 1829, aged 72 yrs." [See below]

[Bible record from Mrs. C. T. Buss, Bortland, Oregon.]

THOMAS WILSON

Thomas Wilson b. 11 Jan 1759, d. 11 July 1829; Jane [wife according to will in Hillsboro, Orange Co., N.C.] d. 10 Jan 1851.
    Children
Ann b. 11 Jan 1790
Elizabeth b. 9 Apr 1791
Charles b. 6 Nov 1793
John Wood b. 3 [8?] Jan 1796
Robert b. 21 Apr 1798
Josiah b. 9 May 1800
Fanny b. 8 June 1803 [m. 14 Mar 1834 in Orange Co., N.C. to Absalom
    Turrentine, from Orange Co. marriage bonds.]
Anderson b. 14 Apr 1806
Caleb b. 9 Dec 1809

ABNER WINGFIELD

Abner Wingfield b. 8 June 1797, m. Elizabeth [Dow, according to family records] b. 5 June 1795.
    Their children
Leathy b. 2 Sep 1819; Leathy Stites d. 23 Feb 1908
Louisa b. 14 Apr 1821
Emmelin b. 23 Nov 1824; Emaline Leonard d. 1907
Thomas W. b. 26 Oct 1826
Joseph C. b. 1 Jan 1828, d. 24 June 1900
J. S. b. 5 Dec 1833

J. C. Wingfield m. 22 Sep 1862 to Mary Ann Wingfield b. 29 Nov 1846
    Children
Jas. W. b. 2 Sep 1864
John F. b. 30 Oct 1866
Calvin C. b. 12 Apr 1870, d. 29 Mar 1872
Eliza B. b. 14 Mar 1872
Abner F. b. 6 Mar 1875
Ansvil Dow b. 3 Sep 1877
Annie P. b. 23 Dec 1880
J. Leelya b. 2 July 1887, d. 30 Dec 1946

Lucinda M. Gibbs b. 13 Sep 1822
Samuel Whitsett m. 5 June 1925 to Mary Ann Wingfield d. 14 May 1926
A. F. Wingfield m. 14 Mar 1897 to L. J. Scott
Marcus L. Scott m. 28 Dec 1878 to Ruah Wingfield
Leelya Wingfield m. 22 July 1916
Earl G. Wingfield b. 25 Jan 1898
A. M. Wingfield b. 2 Feb 1903

V. A. Wingfield b. 12 June 1904
Quetia Scott b. 4 Sep 1901
J. C. Wingfield b. 21 Nov 1908
E. F. Wingfield b. 17 June 1910
Joseph Scott Wingfield b. 15 Apr 1912
Overall Clemont Wingfield b. 13 Dec 1915
Elmer Allen Wingfield b. 23 Aug 1920
Samuel Paul Wingfield b. 24 Feb 1922
Elgy Wingfield d. 14 Mar 1892 [One record cannot be deciphered.]
John Wingfield d. 26 Sep 1922

[This record from Mrs. Hale Houts, Kansas City, Mo. who also says
that the 1850 census of Crawford Co., Mo. shows Abner Wingfield &
Eliz. & all children except the youngest were b. in N.C.]

WARREN F. WINN

Warren F. Winn d. 30 Oct 1853, m. 16 Feb 1840 to Miss Frances L.
Seigler

Robert Marshall Winn b. 15 Oct 1842, d. 20 July 1864
William Augustus Winn b. 16 July 1844, d. 11 May 1864
Edger Cecil Winn b. 16 Aug 1846
Margaret Elizabeth Winn b. 18 Dec 1848; Miss Maggie E. Winn m. 16
    Dec 1869 to R. A. Cochran; Robert Amrose Cochran b. 5 May 1843
Warren Putnum Winn b. 9 Jan 1851, d. 17 Apr 1917, m. 22 Dec 1875 to
    Miss Sallie (Sarah) E(mma) Cochran b. 6 Nov 1850, d. 8 Oct 1915

Mary Frances Winn b. 21 Nov 1876
William Robert Edgar Winn b. 19 Mar 1878
Whitfield Augustus Winn b. 6 Apr 1879
Warren Littleberry Winn b. 16 May 1880
Walter Ernest Winn b. 22 Sep 1881
Ralph Marshall Winn b. 29 Jan 1886

F. L. Winn b. 5 Nov 1822; Frances L. Winn d. 5 July 1890
Robert Edger Winn Cochran b. 21 July 1873
Thomas Evan Cochran b. 17 Aug 1876
Jeremiah Seigler d. 18 Nov 1854
Martha Seigler d. 4 July 1869, aged 81
Thomas Calvin Winn m. 19 Dec 1915 to Miss Alta Lou Mayson

CRADDOCK WISDOM

Craddock Wisdom, late of Cumberland Co., Va., b. 25 Dec 1766 in
Caroline Co., Va., d. 12 July 1837 in Cumberland Co., aged 70 yrs.,
6 mos., 15 days., m. in 1783 in Cumberland Co., Va. to Ann Glenn,
dau. of Wm. & Frances Glenn, b. in 1764 in Cumberland Co., Va., d.
in 1812 in Buckingham Co., Va., aged 48. Craddock Wisdom was a
Rev. Soldier & present at the surrender of Cornwallis. He was an
acceptable member of the M.E. Church.

Thos. Glenn Wisdom, son of C. & Ann Wisdom, b. 19 Apr 1797 in Cumberland Co., Va., m. 12 Dec 1816 in Pr. Edward Co., Va. to Judith S. Dabney, dau. of John & Ann Dabney, b. 1 Feb 1799 in Pr. Edward Co., Va.

John Craddock Wisdom, son of Thos. & Judieth Wisdom, b. 28 Oct 1817 in Buckingham Co., Va., m. 14 Jan 1846 in Wadesboro, N.C. to Julina H. Winbourn, dau. of Cornelius & Tabitha Winbourn

Wm. Nathaniel Wisdom, son of Thos. & Judieth Wisdom, b. 16 July 1819, m. 20 Oct 1846 by T. W. Archer in Rockingham Co., N.C. to Mary M. Howard

Francis [es?] A. Wisdom, dau. of Thos. & Judieth Wisdom, b. 7 July 1821 in Buckingham Co., Va., m. 19 Aug 1851 in Madison Co., Ala. by A. F. Lawrence to Henry D. Harless

Thos. G. Wisdom, late of Buckingham Co., Va., b. 27 Feb 1823 in Buck. Co., Va., d. 11 June 1824 in Buck. Co., Va.

Garland D. Wisdom b. 6 Feb 1825 in Buck. Co., Va.

Mary E. Wisdom, dau. of Thos. & Judieth Wisdom, b. 11 Oct 1827 in Rockingham Co., N.C., m. in 1850 in Madison Co., Ala. to Wm. G. Winbourn, son of Cornelius & Tobitha [Tabitha?] Winbourn

Martha E. Wisdom b. 26 Nov 1829 in Rockingham Co., N.C., d. 31 July 1841 in Rockingham Co., N.C., aged 12 yrs., etc.

Virginia G. Wisdom b. 13 Mar 1832 in Rockingham Co., N.C.

Judieth A. Wisdom b. 19 Dec 1834 in Rock. Co., N.C.

Thos. G. Wisdom, late of Jackson Co., Ala., b. 31 May 1836 in Rock. Co., N.C., d. 23 July 1862 in Jackson Co., Ala., aged 26 yrs. etc.

Chestina P. Wisdom b. 19 Dec 1838 in Rock. Co., N.C.

Robert N. Wisdom, late of Jackson Co., Ala., b. 11 Oct 1842, d. in 1864 in Hospital, aged 22 yrs. He was a faithful soldier in the C.S.A. & died from the effects of a wound received at the battle of Jonesboro, Ga. Sep 1864

[Property of Mrs. John Stanley Hunt (Mamie Inez Steger), 605 E. 5th St., Tuscumbia, Ala., copied by Mrs. E. S. Gregory of Tuscumbia 1934.]

DAVID WOOD

David Wood (son of John Wood d. 3 May 1794 & Sibbel Wood d. 13 Aug 1791) b. 6 Nov 1759, d. 26 Oct 1830, m. 23 Dec 1779 to Jane Wood b. 1 June 1760, d. 27 Sep 1826.
    Children
John b. 15 Dec 1780, m. 23 Apr 1801
Sibbel b. 10 July 1782, m. 15 Feb 1798
Ezakiel (Ezekiel) b. 1 May 1784, m. 14 June 1804
Elizabeth b. 28 Jan 1786 m. 20 Mar 1804
Reuben b. 10 Oct 1787, m. 13 Nov 1810
Samuel b. 24 Nov 1789, m. 11 Sep 1810
Susannah b. 16 May 1791, m. 26 Sep 1811
Charity b. 23 June 1793, m. 28 Oct 1813; Charity Matthes d. 27 Nov 1814
Millo b. 23 May 1795, m. 4 Nov 1817

David b. 8 Apr 1797, m. 19 Sep 1816
Zebedee b. 29 Apr 1799, m. 2 Sep 1819
Robt. Brownle b. 10 May 1800, d. 19 Dec 1800
Henarity b. 20 Dec 1802; Henrietta Wood m. 4 Mar 1819; Henrietta
  Hendrix d. 3 Aug 1833
Laban b. 11 May 1805, m. 4 Aug 1822

[Sent by Miss Mary Wood, Woodbury, Tenn. "David Wood his book and
the ages of his children"]

HANNAH WOOD

Henderson Wood b. 4 Sep 1812, d. 25 Jan 1853; Hannah Marier Wood b.
12 Oct 1816, d. 3 Nov 1893.
    Children
Martha Jane b. 5 Sep 1837 d. 26 Jan 1872
Sarah Ann b. 16 July 1840, d. 17 Oct 1855
Alex. S. b. 16 July 1843, d. 19 Sep 1862
Saml. Preston b. 19 Mar 1846, d. 19 Oct 1855
Nancy Virlinda b. 12 June 1848
John C. b. 27 Dec 1850
Mary Hannah b. 2 Apr 1853, d. 15 Oct 1855

[This is a N.C. family.]

JOHN WOOD

John Wood, son of John & Sarah Borden Wood, b. 1716, d. 1794, m.
1st to Sarah Clement, m. 2nd to Sibbel Wilborn.
    Children of Sarah Clement Wood
Clement b. 1740, d. 1833
Sarah b. 1743
Zebedee b. 1745, d. 1824, m. Mary
John b. 1747, d. 1828
    Children of Sibbel Wilborn Wood
Reuben b. 1753 [1752?], d. 1812 in Randolph Co., N.C., m. Charity
  Hane of S.C.
Joseph
Alfred
David b. 1759, d. 1830

    Children of Reuben & Charity Hane Wood
Sally m. 1802 to Augustine Willis
Mary m. Joseph Wilson
Laura m. Jethro Wilson, brother of Joseph
Evalina m. Augustine Willis after Sally's death in 1822
John L.
Joseph
Alfred
Edwin
[Children not listed in order, according to Dr. Louis Round Wilson]

```
      Children of Zebedee & Mary Wood
Clement b. 1766
Zebedee b. 1767
Joseph b. 1770
Mary b. 1772 [m. Col. Isaac Lane]
John b. 1774
Robert b. 1776
Sarah b. 1778 [m. Roger Kirkman]
Nancy b. 1781, m. Joseph Elliott
Samuel b. 1783, d. 1862, m. Valinda Smith b. 1785, d. 1870
Isabel b. 1786, m. William Doak [or Doake]
```

[Dr. Louis Round Wilson, Chapel Hill, N.C. says, "Henry Wood 1594-
1670 m. 28 Sep 1644 Abigail Jenny, dau. of John Jenny & Mary Cary
Jenny. All b. in England. Came to America 1632, settled in Mass.
Name was originally Atwood. Changed to Wood in America. Henry
used both names in his will. John Wood b. 23 Apr 1716, d. 3 Apr
1794 in N.C. Sarah Clement (his wife) b. 2 Apr 1721. John & Sarah
m. in Taunton, Mass. 9 Nov 1737. Had 3 children b. in Mass. Reuben d. Aug 1812 intestate in Randolph Co., N.C. Will Book 4. Henry Wood & Abigail Jenny Wood had 12 children. One son was David b.
1651. David m. Mary Baker in 1684. They had John b. 1687 & mar.
Sarah Borden 1711. He m. 2nd Hannah Childs." This record is very
complete. Dr. Louis Round Wilson is a very well known librarian &
one of the few life members of the American Library Association.
The Library at the University of N.C., Chapel Hill, N.C. is named
for him. Wm. Wilson, son of Wm. & Eunice (Worth) Wilson, b. 21 Mar
1784, m. 12 Mar 1821 Margaret Allred, Randolph Co., N.C.]

ROBERT BARCLAY WOOD

Robert Barclay Wood [b. in 1839 in Nantucket, Mass., lived in Wilmington, N.C. 1840-1882, in Brunswick, Ga. 1882-1920], d. 10 Mar
1920 in Brunswick, Ga., aged 82, m. Susan Joicey Wood, d. Thursday,
25 Oct 1899 in Brunswick, Ga.
      Children
Florence, dau., b. 22 Apr 1866 in Wilmington, N.C.
Robert Barclay, son, b. 18 Dec 1867 in Wilmington, N.C., d. 2 Sep
   1868 in Wilmington, N.C.
Willie Vincent, son, b. 7 Nov 1869 in Wilmington, N.C., d. 2 Nov
   1870 in Wilmington, N.C.
Thomas Fanning, son, b. 26 July 1871 in Wilmington, N.C., d. 4 Dec
   1872 in Wilmington, N.C.
Agnes Fanning, dau., b. 18 July 1873 in Wilmington, N.C.
Alfred Carpenter, son, b. 9 Jan 1875 in Wilmington, N.C.
Mary Ann, dau., b. 23 Dec 1876 in Wilmington, N.C., m. to John D.
   Burkheimer d. 16 Sep 1902 in Wilmington, N.C.
Robert Barclay, son, b. 7 Jan 1879 in Wilmington, N.C.
Arthur Jarvis, son, b. 11 Feb 1881 in Wilmington, N.C.

      Children of Mary Ann & John D. Burkheimer
Miriam Wood Burkheimer, dau., b. 17 Sep 1900 in Brunswick, Ga.

Virginia Joicey Burkheimer, dau., b. 12 Oct 1901 in Brunswick, Ga.

[All items except his own death, are in the handwriting of Robert
B. Wood, Sr. This Bible is now in the possession of Mrs. Mary Wood
Burkheimer of Brunswick, Ga. Photostats in possession of A. J.
Wood of Brunswick, Ga. The Bible is inscribed "To Joicey from Car-
oline F. Wood, 16 Oct 1865."]

WILLIAM WOODBERRY

Wm. Woodberry b. 18 June 1797

Richard Woodberry b. 22 Feb 1816
Wm. Woodberry, Jr. b. 5 Jan 1818
John Brown Woodberry b. 6 Feb 1821
Evander McIver Woodberry b. 24 Apr 1823
Eliz. Ann Woodberry b. 16 Dec 1825
Margaret Frances Woodberry b. 11 Dec 1827, d. 31 May 1905, m. 14
   May 1851 to Hugh R. Johnson b. 7 Dec 1821, d. 19 Aug 1884
Jos. Walter Alston Woodberry b. 18 Feb 1830
Jas. R. Erwin Woodberry b. 30 Apr 1832
Mary Woodberry b. 4 Feb 1834
Martha Gause Woodberry b. 15 Oct 1836
Saml. Hodges Woodberry b. 1838

Richard O. Johnson b. 17 May 1855, d. 19 Nov 1934
Jessie Adlaide Herring b. 14 Nov 1871; Jessie Adlaide Herring John-
   son d. 13 Nov 1929
Miles Herring b. 1842, soldier in Civil War, d. 1887, m. 14 Nov
   1867 by Rev. T. L. Smith to Sarah Jones b. 21 May 1850, d. 18 Aug
   1933
Jas. A. Jones b. 28 Oct 1828, d. in the C.S.A.
Armatha Huggins b. 29 July 1848, d. 1 Apr 1900
John D. Jones b. 10 Aug 1850
J. O. Jones b. 29 Aug 1854, d. 18 Mar 1925
Sallie E. Jones b. 22 Feb 1818, d. 4 Nov 1901

[Bible owned by Mrs. Evander E. Johnson, Nichols, S.C., copied by
Mrs. Margaret T. Thompson, niece of Mrs. Johnson.]

THOMAS WRIGHT

Thos. Wright b. 2 Oct 1800, m. 27 Dec 1818 to Frances (Fanny) Good-
win b. 22 Sep 1800

H. T. Wright b. 17 Dec 1819, m. 19 Nov 1844 to Fanny (Fannie) E.
   Kenney b. 19 Oct 1827 [It looks as though this year was written
   1817 & a 2 typed over the 1 to make it 1827.]
Martin M. Wright b. 7 Nov 1862, m. 1st on 15 Feb 1887 to Mary Yonce
   b. 22 July 1871, m. 2nd on 17 Nov 1896 to Minnie Permelia Broadwater b. 12 Nov 1870
Fletcher Theopolus Wright b. 28 June 1893

REDMOND GRISBY WYATT

Redmond Grisby Wyatt d. 17 Oct 1857, bur. at Pisgah Baptist Church, Anderson Co., S.C., m. 1st on 15 Sep 1829 to Elizabeth Richey [dau. of James, Jr. & Elizabeth Dunn Richey] b. 10 Nov 1810, d. 12 Aug 1842, bur. at Greenville Church, Abbeville Co., S.C., m. 2nd 30 Sep 1842 to Eleanor Ann Seawright b. 22 Apr 1808; Nelle A. Seawright Wyatt d. 28 July 1880, bur. at Pisgah Church, Anderson Co., S.C.
    Children
James E. Wyatt b. 13 Feb 1831, d. 17 Mar 1907, bur. at Fairview Church, Pickens Co., S.C., served as Confed. Sol. 4 yrs., m. 27 Dec 1852 to Mary Wilson
William Franklin Wyatt b. 31 Oct 1832, d. 19 Jan 1913, bur. at Pisgah Church, Anderson Co., S.C., C.S.A., m. 13 Dec 1855 to Dorcas La Boon
Mary Jane Wyatt (Andrea) b. 4 Jan 1835, d. 10 Feb 1920, bur. to Jackson Grove, Greenville Co., m. 28 Apr 1857 to August D'Andrea
Harriet Elizabeth Wyatt b. 4 Dec 1836, d. 28 Aug 1875, bur. at Greenville or Sand Mt., Ala., m. 10 Apr 1857 to Enoch Wiginton
John Newton Wyatt b. 28 Dec 1838, d. 19 Feb 1914, bur. at Easley, S.C., C.S.A., m. to Elizabeth McAlister Smith
Samuel Thompson Wyatt b. 25 Nov 1840, d. 18 June 1911, bur. at Corinth Church, C.S.A., m. 24 Apr 1864 to Mrs. Sara Richey
Margaret Luani Wyatt b. 4 July 1844, d. 20 Dec 1917, bur. at Fairview Church, Pickens Co., S.C., m. 15 Nov 1864 to John Henderson
Eugenia Ann Wyatt b. 5 Sep 1846, d. 18 Mar 1899, bur. at Pisgah Church, m. 13 Jan 1892 to E. S. Pepper, no children
Andrew Grigsby Wyatt b. 30 Mar 1848, d. 3 Mar 1908, bur. at Easley, Pickens Co., S.C., C.S.A., m. 29 Nov 1876 to Eveline Lenhardt
Redmond Culwell (Caldwell) Wyatt b. 3 Sep 1850, d. 29 July 1906, bur. at St. Paul Church, C.S.A., m. 1 Jan 1878 to Fanny Sitton
Rebecca Josephine Wyatt b. 9 Jan 1853, d. 6 Dec 1919, bur. at Pisgah Church, Anderson Co., S.C., m. 11 Dec 1879 to L. G. Hendricks

RICHARD YARBROUGH

Richard Yarbrough b. 16 Jan 1793, d. 2 Dec 1860, m. 23 Dec 1817 to Tabitha Johns b. 20 July 1794.
    Children
Temperance Diansha b. 1 Oct 1819, m. 5 June 1833 to Wm. T. Harrison
Joseph Joel b. 24 June 1821, m. 31 Oct 1848 to R. Emily Chipman
Martha Henrietta b. 19 Apr 1823, m. 23 June 1846 to Dabney Terry
Richard Laurison b. 26 Dec 1824
Thomas Scoot b. 5 June 1827, m. 12 Feb 1850 to Eliz. A. Terry
Sally Bott [or Batt] Holmes b. 10 Nov 1829
Saluda I. b. 30 Oct 1831
George Walton b. 12 Oct 1833

[This record is from Mrs. Banks Satterfield, Milton, N.C., copied Aug 1962 by the compiler.]

HENRY YORK

Henry York b. 6 Aug 1732 in Pipe Creek Settlement, Carroll Co., Md. [now Union Bridge, Carroll Co.], m. 15 Jan 1789 to Margaret Lenderman b. 30 July 1774.
   Children
Eli York b. 9 Dec 1789
Eve Dorothy York b. 15 Oct 1792
Sarah York b. 10 Oct 1794
Henry York b. 2 Jan 1796
Elizabeth York b. 30 Sep 1798
Zilpha York b. 29 Nov 1801
Leonard York b. 28 Jan 1804

[These Yorks moved to Orange Co., N.C. about 1755 & were eventually in Randolph Co. due to the formation of new counties from Orange. They never moved. An old paper in the Bible says that the father of Henry York was Jeremiah York. Henry Lenderman, Jr. was the father of Margaret Lenderman. Eve Dorothy was the wife of Henry Lenderman, Jr. This data & the Bible record was from Mrs. Verna S. Bergmann of Sandy, Utah, sent to the compiler in 1953.]

JAMES YOUNG

James Young "our dear pappa" b. 31 July 1771, d. 1 Oct 1824 at 11 o'clock P.M., m. 3 Nov 1803 to Mrs. Rhoda Cox Walker "Mamma" b. 18 July 1782, d. 16 June 1819.
   Children
Gallatin Young b. 13 Feb 1803
Wm. Augustin Young b. 31 Oct 1896, d. 30 May 1822
Keturah Margaret Young b. 23 Dec 1808 [m. Michael W. Christman]
Phoebe Young b. 20 Mar 1810 [m. John D. Williams]
Susan Clove Young b. 16 Aug 1812 [m. Wm. D. Watts]
Rhoda E. C. Young b. 16 May 1816 [m. Jas. Griffin Williams]
Jas. Cox Young "baby brother" b. 22 Feb 1819, d. 14 Sep 1823
Alfred Walker "our half brother" b. 11 Sep 1799

Wm. Cox "grandpa Cox" d. 16 June 1809
Agnes Young "grandma Young" d. 12 Jan 1810
Wm. Young "grandpa Young" d. 11 Sep 1812
Robt. Young "Uncle Robert" d. 16 Jan 1817
Saml. Young "Uncle Sam" d. 23 Apr 1817
Margaret Cox "grandma Cox" d. 19 Sep 1821

[This Bible data was sent to Rhoda E. C. Williams, wife of Jas. Griffin Williams, by her sister, Keturah wife of Michael W. Christman. The letter was written 16 Jan 1834 from Leon Co., Fla. Mrs. Williams lived in Laurens, S.C. The data in quotation marks were added by Mrs. Christman in her letter. She said that she was sending the copy of the Bible as per Mrs. Williams' request. Michael W. Christman went from Abbeville, S.C. to Leon, Fla. & thence to Rodney, Miss.]

JAMES YOUNG

James Young b. 15 Aug 1750, d. 17 Sep 1802, m. 7 Sep 1773 to Mary
Young b. 15 Feb 1753, d. 12 Oct 1812.
    Their children
Elizabeth Young, dau., b. 8 June 1774, m. 8 (6) May 1791
Nancy Young, dau., b. 19 Aug 1775, m. 6 Apr 1794
Mary Young, dau., b. 1 Sep 1777, d. 4 Nov 1834, m. 7 Jan 1799
Abraham Young, son, b. 9 Aug 1780, m. Jan 1802
Joseph Young, son, b. 28 Jan 1783, d. 1820, m. 12 Aug 1806
James Young b. 1 May 1785, m. 18 July 1811
Esther Young, dau., b. 28 Oct 1787, m. 11 Sep 1806
Hannah Young b. 3 Aug 1790, m. 31 Jan 1811
Thompson Young b. 3 June 1793, m. Martha Young who d. 7 May 1874
Rosannah Young b. 10 Oct 1795, d. 12 Oct 1804
Jane Young b. 17 Nov 1797, m. 26 May 1818
Abigail Young b. 10 Dec 1801

[This Bible is owned by a descendant of James & Mary Young, Mrs.
Thomas Crooks, formerly Sadie Lester, of Newberry, S.C. Mary
Young, wife of James Young, Sr. was b. Mary Thompson according to
all the descendants around Newberry. It is also proven by court
records, they say. In the front of the book is, "Mary Young Her
Book" The Bible was published in 1815.]

ROBERT RUTHERFORD

Robert Rutherford b. 1775 in N.C., d. 1833 in Monroe Co., Ala., m.
18 Sep 1817 to Mary Miller, dau. of Margaret Seawright & William
Miller, b. 1796 in Anderson Co., S.C., d. 1869 in Monroe Co., Ala.
    Children
Isabelle Vashti b. 4 July 1818, d. as a child
Fannie Maria b. 3 May 1821, d. as a child
Wm. Miller b. 24 Dec 1822, m. 22 July 1858 to Mary Frances Fraser
John Johnson b. 15 Nov 1824 in Anderson Co., S.C., m. Jane Priscil-
la Smith
Margaret Jane b. 15 Feb 1827, d. as a child
Mary Melvina b. 10 Oct 1828, d. 1853, single
Martha Permelia b. 22 Oct 1832, d. 1847, single

[For other data on this family see: Tombstones from Rutherford-
Black Cemetery, Monroe, Ala.; 1850 census records; Estate File
#1380 in Probate Court, Anderson, S.C.; Rev. War pension file #W.
21805 National Archives, Washington, D.C. He seems to be a grand
son of the famous Robt. Rutherford who served in the N.C. legislature during the Rev. War & later went to Pendleton Dist., S.C.
Robt. served from Chatham Co., N.C.]

INDEX

The Bibles in this volume are arranged alphabetically. Their location is indicated by
names entered in all capital letters. Persons within those Bibles having the same sur-
names have not been indexed.

Aaron, Thos. N. 47
Aasland, Frace 227
Abbot, Amanda 313
  America 313
  Brice M. 313
  Emeranda 313
  Lorrict 313
  Mancefield 313
  Museum 313
  Rebecca 313
  Simpson 313
  Thomas D. 313
  Willford 313
ABERCROMBIE 1
  Mary 118
Able, John G. 97
Ables, Mary Belle 240
ABNEY 1,2
  Daniel C. 74
  Harriet 281
  John 74
  Patsy 74
Abrams, Robt. Abney 78
Ackerman, Stephen 188
Acock, ___ 296
ACUFF 2,3
  Mr. 231
  E.B. 202,229,230
  Edward Blackburn 22
  Wm. 22
Adair, Abigail 54
  Gov. John 54
  Lydia 54
Adam, John R., Esq. 12
Adams, Hannah 197
  Harriet 241
  James 12
  James Columbus 11
  James J. 181
  Jennie H. 175
  John 234
  Lillie E. 132
  Mack H. 181
  Rachel 22
  Rev. Robert 109
  Sarah 291
  Vera J. 210
Aderhold, Michael 206
Adkins, Ann 167
Agnew, Anna 268
  Eliz. 211
  Mary 268
  Rilla 268
  Wilson 268
Aiken, Mrs. E.C. 120
  Hugh 73
  Nancy 28
Aimes, Ann 312

Airs, Betsy Ann 335
Albertson, Benjamin 18
  Francis 18
Alderman, Jane 156
ALDREDGE 3
ALDRIDGE 4,5
  ___ 8
  Rev. Franklin LaFayette 272
  Franklin LaFayette 326
  Hanna 9
  James 138
  John P. 138
  Mary Ann 122
  Sarah 280
  Wanda 265
  Wm. V. 29
Alexander, Jas. Thos. 330
  Martha 211
  Mollie (Mallie 243
  Pattie 322
  W.O. 306
Alford, Rev. 215
  Ann Douglas 20
ALLDREDGE 6-8
  Hannah 176
  Nathan 176
  Sarah 176
Allen, ___ 297
  Mr. 25
  Amanda Ann 329
  Anne 103
  Anne Allenor 161
  B. 245
  Charles 333
  Eber Caleb 329
  Eliz. 52
  Elizabeth 190,232,233
  Elizabeth Brashear 13
  Elizabeth Frances 329
  Ettie M. 329
  Frances 161
  James 329
  James Henry 329
  Jas. Robt. 66
  Jehu Wells 329
  Jesse 66
  John 13,329
  Lucy Bacon 333
  Mary 329
  Mary Henriatta 329
  Mary Jane 122
  Robert 232
  Russell T. 235
  Sarah Mannering 329
  Susan J. 129
  Syntha 333
  William 13,161

  Woodward 329
Allison, Robert 145
Allgood, S.C. 43
ALLRED 9
  Brantley 5
  Margaret 340
Almand, Lear Ruskin 27
Alsy, Alizannah 3
Alton, Martha 60
Amoson, Mary Ann 157
  Nancy 157
  Thos. 157
Anders, Margaret 219
  Margaret E. 219
  Sarah Elizabeth 217
Andersdatter, Marthe 135
ANDERSON 10
  Eliz. 207
  Emily Henrietta 51
  Fanny J. 129
  George 171
  Gertrude 309
  Mrs. Howell B. 166
  Lavina 61
  Margaret 294
  Maria Virginia 171
  Mary 47
  Maude 181,273
  Sally 93
  Susan M. 278
  Thos. W. 68
Andrea, ___ 114
  Mr. 73
  L. 50,80,90,98,111,115,
    117,124,168,195,209,258,
    259,297,304
  Leonard 15,15,65,75,81,88,
    123,171,200,201,211,245,
    261,267,268,273,290,301,
    303,307
  Leonardo 127,267
  Mary Jane Wyatt 342
Andres, Jannet 156
Andrews, Rev. Nash 14
  Thama 202
Anglin, Mary Ann 274
Anthony, John 19
  Sarah 19
Apple, Lewis 158
Archer, Anna Archer 228
  Chloe Ann 113
  T.W. 338
Arent, ___ 76
Arms, Robert 150
Armstrong, Eliza Kincaid 317
  Nancy 133
Arnery, Barclay 17
Arney, Barclay 17

347

Willie King 219
Bowers, Hannah 133
Bowhannon, Ackerall 91
  Richard 91
Bowie, Luther E. 246
Bowles, Anna 335
Bowman, ___ 306
  Mrs. Fred O. 292
  Fred O., Sr. 280
  George Felton 92
  Julius T. 92
  Sarah Caroline Pirkle 92
Bowyer, Mary 316
BOYD 27,28
  ___ 321
  Angie 272
  Eliz. 145
  Elizabeth 140
  Isabella 331
  James 260
  John D. 319
  John Patterson 272
  Martha Craig 140
  Robert Watson 272
  Susie 312
Boykin, William 191
BRACKEN 29,30
  Edward 265
  Isaac 294
  John Allen 326
  Martha Matilda 8
  Minnie V. 243
  Sarah Rhodes 265
BRACKIN 30
Bradford, Elia. Ann 50
  James 263
  Margaret 166
  Maria 140
  Mary Hodge 263
  Napoleon B. 263
  William 263
Bradley, Jack 270
  Lucy 211
  Nancy K. 139
  Rebecca 259
BRADSHAW 31
  Zerelda 314
BRADSHER 31
Brady, Ida Virginia 93
  Jane 169
  Sarah Elizabeth 169
Brailsford, William Welborn
    192
Branch, Elihu K. 50
Brand, Eliz. 234
Branden, Nancy Gordon 122
BRANDON 32
  Josiah K. 277
Brantley, Rev. 15
  Hester 331
Branyon, Nancy Alcanza 221
Braselton, Lavina 181
Brasfield, Polly 270
BRASHEAR 32

Asa 13
Charity 13
Elizabeth 13
Jane 236,237
Nancy 13
Robert 13
BRASHEARS 34,35
  Nancy 271
  Robert Samuel 272
Brasher. Elizabeth 120
Brassieur, Benoit 33
  Mary 33
Bratton, Isabel 227
Brazen, Elijah 67,72
Brazzleton, Emily 263
  James 263
  Julia 263
  Gen. William 263
BREASHEARS 35
Breckenridge, Adam 108
  Nancy 108
Breeden, Annie A. 84,85
  Annie Powers 85
  Carlisle 84
  Clarence E. 84
  Cook 85
  Edward 85
  Gwendolin 85
  Hennie E. 85
  Henriatta E. 84,85
  Hilda 85
  J. Lindsey 84
  Jessie P. 85
  Joseph L. 85,86
  Josie O. 84,85
  Lindsey J. 85
  Louise 84
  Mattie Cook 84,85
  May Carlisle 85,86
  S. Josephine 85
  Sarah Josephine 84
  W.C. 85
  W. Cook 84
Brewer, Miss 1
  Sarah Simms 258
  Tabitha 245
  William 245
Bridges, Anna 279
  Ava Pierson 227
  Bessie 227
  Eleanor 227
  Elizabeth 227
  Frace Aasland 227
  Mabel Eleanor 227,228
  Parham Blackburn 227
  Pleasant Burton 227
  Robert Walker 227
  Robert Walker, Jr. 227
  Ruth 227
  Talbot Steel 227
  William Parham 227
Bridwell, ___ 117
Bright, Adele Thalozon 295
  Margaret 35

Brinson, Hattie Joslyn 335
  Mary Ann 335
  Nancy 175
Bristow, Anna Hudson 163
Britnell, Ben Frank 238
Britt, Sudie 132
Brittain, Rev. M. 302
BROADFOOT 36
  Frances 13
  Margaret 13
  May Catherine 12
Broadnax, Susan M. Ruffin
    185
Broadus, Rev. Luther 132
Broadwater, Minnie Permelia
    341
Brock, Caroline 207
  Mrs. John 258
Brockman, John 139
Brogaw, Wm. N. 302
Brook, Eliza 122
  Elizabeth 95
BROOKS 36-45
  Bartlett 333
  Betsy 257
  Caroline Williams 187
  Charles 257
  Cully 257
  Eddie Woodson 72
  Eleanor 258,259
  Ida 23
  Jacob 194
  Jacob, Sr. 108
  James 257
  Jesse Michael 257
  John 257
  John, Jr. 257
  John H. 187
  Lavinia 324
  Milly 108
  Nancy 8
  Nancy Cannon Hudgins 259
  Naomi 257
  Priscilla 193
  Rance 123
  Rosanna 194
  Sally 257
  Sara 282
  Sarah A. 187
  Susan Ferguson 123,151
  Thomas 257
  Warren 297
  William 257,282
  Wm. 259
  Wm. Elisha 57
  Zach. Smith 57
Broom, Hester Ann 331
BROWN 45-48
  ___ 285,296
  Mr. 45
  Mrs. 267
  Rev. 138
  Artimisia 305
  Caroline Matilda 142

350

Cheek, Annie 170
  Rev. F.V. 93
Cherry, Eliz. 207
  Margaret 207
  W. 147
Chew, Ann 170
  Hannah Roy 170
  Larkin 170
Childs, Hannah 340
  Laura Jane 238
  Lucy 171
  Rev. S.G. 175
Chilton, Miss 254
  Raleigh 255
Chipman, R. Emily 342
Christhilf, Ellen R. 215
Christian, Juanita 106
  Mary Isabel 28
  Peter 106,107
  Presley F. 28
CHRISTMAN 75
  Michael W. 343
Christopher, Buckner G. 89
Clack, Charity Smith 94
  Mary 95
  Starling 94
  Tommie H. 255
Clardy, Harriet 326
Clark, ___ 97
  Anna Maria 211
  Bro. J.J. 278
  James 322
  Jane 30
  Mrs. John W. 203
  Jonn Wm. 202
  Mary 210,280
  Mary (Polly) 256
  Nancy 326
  Sarah H. McCorkle 322
  Capt. T.H. 118
  T.N. 118
  Ursula 333
Clarke, Betty 310
CLARY 75
Clary, Agrippa 150
  Danl. 1
  Fanny 1
CLAY 75
Clayton, Eleanor 258
  Mary Ann 316
  Nancy 258
CLEGG 76
  Emily I. 311
CLELAND 77
  Elizabeth 220,221
  Jane 220,221
  William 220
Clement, Sarah 339,340
Clements, Woodson 115
Clifton, Annie Farr 266
  Rev. J.A. 256
Cline, Inez 234
  Sarah R. 330
CLINKSCALES 77

John B. 281
Clonch, May 226
Clove, Susan 75
Clower, Catherine 315
  D.M. 236
  Jonathan 119
  Katherine 314
Cluck, John Calvin 216
Coakley, Lucy Ann 31
Coates, Martha C. 59
COBB 78
  ___ 94,220
Cochran 78
  Mrs. 147
  Robert Amrose 337
  Robert Edger Winn 337
  Sallie E. 337
  Sarah Emma 337
  Thomas Evan 337
Coffey, E.S. 248
Coit, Sarah 195
COKER 79,80
  Sarah Margaret 164
Colbert, Letty 52
  Selasty 52
Cole, Betty Eastland 228
  Dealey 142
  Eliza 298
  Eula Noble 228
  Henry Sim(m)s 227,228
  Inez Viola 228
  Izora 142
  James Clifton 228
  John 317
  John Simms 228
  Mary Lillian 228
  Sallie Berta 228
Coleman, Andrew 2
  Nancy 2
Collingsworth, Bro. 278
COLLINS 80
  Amanda J. 217
  Charles L. Mongomery 217
  Charles Losie M. 217
  Eliz. 137
  John 217
  John Jeremiah 217
  John William 217
  Laura 85
  Lewis 217,218
  Lollie S. Moore 85
  Malcolm W. 85
  Mildred Moore 85
  Minnie Moore 85
  Neomie L. 217
  Salie Rutha Eleanor 217
  Sarah 168
  Sarah E. Ruthie 218
  W.A. 157
COLQUHOUN 81
Coltharp, ___ 296
Colton, Caroline M.C. Smith
  143
Comer, Sarah 1

Compton, John 285
Comstort, Lindon 56
Conally, Lavina 235
Conekin, Sophia B. 40
Connally, Ernest Allen 232
  Lavina 235
  Sarah 38
CONNER 82
  Mrs. Dudley Winston 80
  Lonnie Pierce 316
Connerly, J.R. Westley 301
Conning, May 36
Connor, Mrs. Adam 62
  Adam, Jr. 62
  Ann 62
  Dorothy Sutton 62
  Susannah McDonald 62
CONRAD 83
  Bettie A. 183
  John 83
  John J. 183
  Keziah 183
Conway, Edwin 307
  Francis 307
  Rebecca Catlett 307
Conwell, Bailey 281
Conyers, Elizabeth 10
COOK 83
  Benjamin 53,163
  Effey 53
  Eleanor 82
  Elizabeth 53
  Judith Read 188
  Mary 82,188,189,201
  Mary Ann 53
  Narcissa 163
  Thomas 201
  William, Esqr. 52
  Wilson 188
  Wm. T. 53
Cooksey, ___ 254
COOPER 86
  Ansel R. 180
  Eleanor Cook 82
  Mrs. Furman 111
  George 82
  George Washington 82
  Jesse A. 52
  Luvany 82
  Mary Ann Elizabeth 82
  Mary George Fleming 276
  Penelope Luvaney 82
  Sarah 94
  Thomas 233
  Thomas B.C. 82
  Wilson Conner 82
Copeland, Lewis 239
  Sarah 9
Corbett, Kate Townes 298
CORBIN 86
Corder, Mary 297
Core, Rev. S. 165
Cork, Jas. 216
Corley, Ida Sally 118

351

352

355

Richard Stanford 229
Gray, Ann 275
  Araminta C. 305
  Bethia 246
  Eliza 281
  Harry 317
  James Walter 317
  Joseph James 294
  Joseph James, Sr. 294
  Lawrence 317
  Margaret 316
  Robert 316
  Sarah Frances 294
  Walter 317
  Willie 317
  Winona 102
Grayson, Eliza 293
  Jos. Luther 21
Grear, S. Marshall 248
Green, Annice 200,201
  Caroline 16
  Elisha 297
  J.B. 131
  Dr. Jas. B. 78
  Julia Casey 131
  Martin 178
  Rev. Samuel M. 139
Greene, Charlotte Eliz. 212
Greenhill, Pamelia 238
Greer, Cynthia 248
  I.G. 248
  Mrs. I.G. 293
  William 317
  Willie C. Spainhour 248, 293
Greeson, Lillie 311
Gregg, Burrell 70
Gregory, Mrs. E. 333,334
  Mrs. E.C. 56
  Dr. E.S. 212
  Mrs. E.S. 66,313,338
Grey, Fannie 88
Griffen, Elizabeth 82
Griffin, Adelia 236
  Charlie 299
  Mrs. Clarence 151
  Mrs. Clarence A. 300
  David 143
  Henry W. 50
  Ida Henry 237
  James Conner 82
  John 82
  Lucy 324
  Mary H.R. 52
  Mavis Lucinda 300
  P.B. 252
  Samuel C. 83
  Samuel Conner 82
Griffith, Amanda 2
  Andrew 2
  Andrew B. 2
  Anne 2
  Henry 2
  John A. 1

Jos. 2
Jos. Marion 2
Martha 196
Martha Ann 1
Mary 2
Matthew Wills 2
Mattie 166
Nancy 1
Polly 1
Sophia Isabella 2
Wm. 1,2
Grigsby, Miss 57
  Alice 275
Grimes, Miss 1
Griswold, Benj. J. 152
Groble, Martha Precious 252
Groover, Charles 174
  Nelle 175
  Sarah Reissier 175
Groves, Nina Brooks 38
Gruber, Ann Rumph 188
  Nancy 188
Guffey, Mary P. 196
Guffin, Thomas Newton 272
Guggan, Mrs. Sam 62
Guice, Elizabeth C. Dickson 104
  Morgan 131
Gulbrandsdatter, Ida Louise 135
  Karaline 135
  Laura Rosine 135
  Matilda 135
Gulbranson, Alfred 135
  Anners 135
  Bernet Wilhelm 135
  Christofor 135
  Elvin Anton 135
  Gustav Martinus 135
  Oluf 135
  Peder 135
Gulley, Civil Ann 11
Gunter, Candis 23
Gurley, Matilda 236
Guthrie, James 77
Gwaltney, Pattie G. 162
  Pattie Gardner 301
Gwinn, Frances Ann 330
GWYN 145
  James 191
  Richard 191
  Richard Ransom 191
  Sarah Ransome 191
Gwynn, Frances Ann 330

Haddon, Rev. David F. 287
  Mary Ann 289
Hadley, Julia 79
Haefer, Mrs. Johnny Alda 241
Hagan, Kisiah V. 322
Hagood, Elizabeth 141
  George Cleveland 141
  William, Jr. 141,142
Hail, Jos. 119

Mary 119
Mary Eliz. Lindsey 119
Sarah 119
Hale, Eliz. 119
  James 113
  John F. 126
  Lindsey 119
  Mary 119
  Mary D. 220
  Nancy 119,120
  Ophelia Hunt 126
  Sarah 119
Hall, Mrs. Andrew 67
  Mrs. Andrew L. 73
  Mrs. Andrew Lyman 192
  Bolling 1
  Rev. J.L. 311
  John 47
  Lucinda 305
  Mary Cornelia 77
  Rachel 204
  Rev. Robert 260
  William S. 179
Halliday, Dr. Decatur 72
  Francis Leurany 72
  Hampton 71
  Robt. Seymore 72
  S.A. 72
Hallum, Mary 244
HAM 146
Hamblet, James Harrison 334
  Sally 334
Hambrick, Rebecca 226
Hamilton, Eleanor 1,2
  Elise E. 18
  Ettie 39
  James O. 259
  Griffin 329
  Sir John 2
  John 79
  Mary 79
  Mylinda G. 314
  Tabitha Thweatt 79
Hamiter, Adad F. 109
  Barbara 109
  Elizabeth 110,111
Hamlett, Lettie Spainhour 248
  Peter W. 248
Hamlin, Barclay A. 17
  Barclay Arney 17
  Daisy White 17
  F.M. 17
  F.M., Jr. 17
  Francis M. 17
  Francis Mallory 17
  George Vance 17
  J. Larner 17
  James Turner 17
  Martha Reamy 17
  Reamey 17
  Sallie Bell
  Sarah E. 17
Hammer, Mary Louise 139

Hammond, Lizzie 126
Hammonds, Mary Lou 122
Hampton, Elizabeth 297
  Hiram 52
Hanby, Capt. Jonathan 65
HANCOCK 146
  Sarah 258
HANDCOCK 146
Handricks, Ann Campbell
  Johnson 154
  Thomas Alston 154
Hane, Charity 339
Hanes, George Candler 93
  Laura Simpson 93
  Thomas 93
Haney, ___ 119
  Henry 201
  John 330
Hanley, Dr. B.F. 14
Hanna, Nancy 305
Hansberger, Jacob S. 295
HANSELL 147
Hansen, Angie Boyd 272
  Joseph B. 28
Hanson, Alizannah Alsy 3
  Sarah 21
Harber, Mrs. W.Y. 210
Harbin, Edward William, Esq.
  83
Hardee, Thos. 147
Hardeman, Joel 53
Harden, Fern Dodd 204
  Leola Lillian 204
  Linda 204
  Patricia Jean 204
  Ray 204
  Wm. #. 204
  Wm. Eldred 204
Hardin, Ida 292
HARDING 147
  Georgia 302
  Jasper 95
Hardy, Jos. 65
  Lizzie 106
Hargroves, Emma 134
Hargus, Nancy 312
Harless, Henry D. 338
Harley, Wm. 195
Harlow, Marian 322
HARPER 148
  Ada J. 126
  Ada Jane 125,127
  Ansel 125,126
  Asa 235
  George W. 124,125,126
  Georgia Ann 125
  Jackson H. 299
  Jackson H., Jr. 299
  Jas. W. 300
  Jas. Wm. 299
  John 126
  John Foster 125,126
  John Henry 299
  Lucinda Melton 125

Maggie Foster 125
Margaret E. Foster 126
Margaret F. 124
Margaret Foster 125
Martha 212
Mary D. 299
Mary Georgia Ann 125
Ophelia Hunt Hale 126
W.T. 127
Winton F. 127
Winton T. 127
Winton Travis 125,127
Harrington, Jeptha 98
HARRIS 148
  ___ 172
  Ann 147
  Augustin 147
  Billy 201
  Eliz. 323
  Rev. J.S. 133
  Capt. John 323
  Laney 253
  Lucy Margaret Washington
    230
  Nat. H. 194
  Rebecca 233
  Susan Byne 147
  Walton 147
  Capt. Wm. 10
  Wm. E. 137
HARRISON 149
  Amey Gilliam 329
  Amie 274
  Amy 275
  Burr 274
  Charlie Lewis 194
  Elizabeth 329
  Frances 255
  Isham 329
  Julia A.L. 103
  Kathleen 194
  Lois Virginia 127
  Marcus Paul 127
  Narcissus Smith 95
  Ruth Barton 127
  William 95
  William H. 194
  Wm. H. 194
  Wm. T. 342
Harrolson, E.S. 245
HART 149,150
  Charlotte Ann 143
  Derrill 307
  Dr. Deryl 307
  Gilbert 298
  James 197
  Jane 298
  John 298
  Dr. John L. 48
  Nancy 298
  Sarah 298
Hartley, Agnes 189
  Nannie Maude 309
HARVEY 150,151

Eliz. 137
Mary Ann 314
Susan 122,123
Harwell, Elizabeth 163
HATCH 151
  Anne Elizabeth 332
  Benjamin 264
  Charles 264
  Cullen B. 160,252,264
  Cullen Blackman 332
  Edmund 264
  Mrs. Edwin B. 55
  Eliz. Chapin 55
  Elizabeth 264
  Hephzibah 264
  Joseph 264
  Joseph R. 332
  Lemuel 264
  Lucy 264
  Lucy Richard 264
  Malvina T. 332
  Mary Bryan 264
  Sarah 264
  Wm. B. 332
Hatcher, Elizabeth 102
Haughey, Priscilla 87
Hawkins, Joseph Curtis 168
  Lucy H. 249
  Luther P. 273
  M.A. 277
  Martha 32
  Patience 61
Hawthorne, Cornelia 282
  James 155
  L.C. 282
  Polly 268
Hay, Margaret 246
  Sarah 55
Hayes, ___ 285
  George White 79
  James Thweatt 79
  Julia Hadley 79
  Martha Hamilton 79
  Mary Hamilton 79
Haygood, Judson 166
HAYMAN 152
Haynes, Elizabeth 187,188
Haynsworth, Elizabeth 133
Haywood, Martha 323
Head, Dosie 42
  Nancy Johnson 42
  William Henry 42
  Mrs. Wm. G. 195
Heard, ___ 166
  Rev. J.T. 189
Hearn, James 145
  Sue E. 145
Hearne, Albana 236
Heath, James Roger 187
  Rebecca 187
  Samuel 187
  Samuel A. 187
  Sarah 215
Heckstall, Elizabeth 301

370

371

Lettie 248
Mary Jennings 248
Maud Mast 248
Paul Gordon 248
Sue 248
Walter 248
Willie 248
Willie C. 248
Wm. R. 248
Spangler, Electa Julian 178
SPANN 293
Sparkman, Earl 227
  Ruth Bridges 227
Spearman, Ann Herring 156
  David Hagood 141
  David Ralph 141
  Elizabeth Hagood 141
  William Benjamin 141
Speck, Anna 9
Speight, Mavis Lucinda Griffin 300
Spenc-, Nancy 210
Spigner, Lucy E. 85
Spillers, Jane 260
Spivey, Capt. E.A. 92
  Elizabeth Bird 154
Spoon, Susan 288
Spraggins, Nancy (Nannie) 2
Sprague, Miriam 43
Spratlin, HEnnie 149
Spratt, Jane Elizabeth 141
Sprigg, Rev. Mr. 70
  Mary 70
Spring, Eliz. 162
Springs, Laura 23
Spruell, Simeon 266
Squire, Rev. 222
Stacey, John 173
  John L.D.H. 173
Stadler, Elder John 9
  Nancy A. 9
  Nancy Arnold 9
  Wm. B. 5
Stafford, John 177
  Sarah 176,177
Stakely, Louise Carlton 53
STALCUP 294
  ___ 294
STALCOP 294
Staley, Herbert 204
Stallard, John Julian 176
  Joseph 176
Stallings, Ales 300
Stanford, Arianna 229
  Mrs. Chas. 225, 229
  Elijah Graves 229
  Mary McIver 225,229,328
  Hon. Richard 225
Stanley, A.E. 15
  Dr. B.F. 14
  Edda 15
  Elizabeth 15
  Eva B. 15

Lucy 15
Maury 15
R.M. 15
Susan 23
Stanton, Leazy 306
  Wm. V. 301
Stapleton, George 227
  Jas. 162
STARR 295
  Rev. J. 302
  Martha Lee 27
  William Steele 27
  William Stewart 27
Starrett, Benjamin 47
Starritt, Hannah 241
Stearne, Annie 250
  Grace Smith 250
Steddom, Mary 251
Steed, Eliz. Hill 211
  Eleanor Bridges 227
  Martha W. James 168
  Phebe 314
  Talbot 227
Stegall, Hester Ann 78
  Wm. 78
Steger, Mamie Inez 338
Stephens, ___ 232
  Eliz. 81
  Nannie 312
Stepp, Mary Georgia Ann Harper 125
  William A. 125
Sterling, Mary Brassieur 33
  Thos. 33
Stevens, Julia 48
Stevenson, Ermie 246
  Robert 178
STEWART 295,296
  Antionette Adelle Cureton
  Eliz. Howard 148
  Eugenia Abby Johnston 148
  Harriet A. 224
  Jas. H. 148
  Jas. Harber 148
  John O. 148
  John Pinckney 148
  Josephine Lulear 142
  Mary H. 148
  Pauline Withers 148
  Richard P. 148
  Wm. Howard 148
Stillwell, Margaret 9
  Rachel 9
STINGLEY 296
Stirratt, Isabella 305
Stites, Lenthy 336
Stivender, Margaret 86
Stockard, Jane 204
Stockboger, Mary S. 157
Stocker, ___ 166
Stoddard, ___ 285
STOKELY 297
STOKES 297

Joseph Henry 316
Rev. L. 132
William 189
Stone, Eliz. 137
  Jane 268
Storne, Mrs. Benjamin F. 189
Story, Dorothy Jane 22
Stott, Drayton 178
  Harriet Richardson 178
  Martha Jane 178,179
Stout, Susan 247
Stowe, White 141
Stradley, Sarah 273
Strange, Alex. R. 185
  Anne 184
  Calvina 311
  Elizabeth 146
  James 184
  Jane 185
  John K. 185
  Mary (Moley) 311
  Robert 184
  Robt. 185
Stratford, ___ 203
Strayborn, Jas. 23
STRAYHORN 298,299
  Aaron 249
  Mary 58
STRICKLAND 299,300
  Lucretia 253
  Mary 266
  Rubin 253
Stringfield, Mrs. 65
  Alisa Ann 219
  Alista Ann 219
  May Shearer 64
Stroberge, Victorine 166
Strode, Betsy 222
Strong, Lucy J. 91
Strothers, Wm. 307
Strosnider, Dr. Charles F. 219
Stuard, Elizabeth 171
Stuart, Nancy 39
Stuckey, Alice Gertrude 259
  Sally E. 259
Stulting, Grace S. 212
Sullivan, Diana Martha 204
  Griffie Vance Dorroh 318
  Griffin Dorroh 318
  Joe 204
  Laurens Norwood 318
  Leola Lillian Harden 204
  Mary Vance 318
  Richard Mims 318
  Richard Mims, Jr. 318
  Thelma Lucile 204
  Tully Francis, III 19
Sullivant, Mary Ann 82
  Thomas C. 82
Summer, Mary 73
Summerford, Isaac 98
Summers, Polly 291